THE 1986 NEW YORK METS

THERE WAS MORE THAN GAME SIX

Edited by Leslie Heaphy and Bill Nowlin

Associate editors—Greg Erion, James Forr, Len Levin, and Carl Riechers

Society for American Baseball Research, Inc.
Phoenix, AZ

The 1986 New York Mets: There Was More Than Gave Six
Edited by Leslie Heaphy and Bill Nowlin
Associate editors—Greg Erion, James Forr, Len Levin, and Carl Riechers

ISBN 978-1-943816-13-2
ebook ISBN 978-1-943816-12-5

Cover and book design: Gilly Rosenthol
Cover photograph and materials courtesy of Bob Brady

All photographs courtesy of the National Baseball Hall of Fame, with the exception of the following:
Courtesy of Bob Brady: frontispiece, 274, 304.
Courtesy of Alan Cohen: 211
Courtesy of Steve Zabriskie: 270.

Society for American Baseball Research
Cronkite School at ASU
555 N. Central Ave. #416
Phoenix, AZ 85004
Phone: (602) 496-1460
Web: www.sabr.org
Facebook: Society for American Baseball Research
Twitter: @SABR

TABLE OF CONTENTS

Manager

General Manager

Scouting Director

Coaches

Announcers

Seven 1986 Mets Games

Courtesy of Bob Brady.

INTRODUCTION

A LIFELONG METS FAN AND A LIFELONG Red Sox fan were talking at a SABR board meeting. Leslie Heaphy (the Mets fan) mentioned to Bill Nowlin (the Sox fan) the idea of a book on the 1986 Mets. Bill responded that Mark Armour, the head of BioProject, had been pushing him to do a 1986 Red Sox book sometime. "But they lost!" Bill said to Mark. "And that's too recent." "Wait a minute," he said to Leslie. "It's been nearly 30 years. OK, let's do a combined book." Leslie responded, "That could be fun, putting the two teams together again." Thus, the germination of this book.

The goal was to create a book that would draw upon people's memories of that classic World Series but also challenge those recollections. When we think of 1986, Bill Buckner and Mookie Wilson first come to mind but there is so much more to that season than that. How did each respective team find their way into the Series? What were the various ups and downs each team faced to set up that final confrontation?

As with many of the books published by the Society of American Baseball Research, this was a true collaborative effort. We may have set a record with this one—there are 74 different SABR members who contributed to making this book a reality. In fact, we also had so much material that we ran past the page limit for one volume through the Print on Demand service we use – so we decided to print two companion books.

If you're reading the 1986 Mets book, be advised that there is a companion 1986 Red Sox book. If you're reading the 1986 Red Sox book, be advised that there is a companion 1986 Mets book.

Greg Erion, James Forr, and Russ Lake did all the fact-checking. Veteran copy editor Len Levin put the final touches on the more than 100 items which make up these two volumes.

It was quite a Series, with each team losing the first two games at home, first the Mets at Shea and then the Red Sox at Fenway. After four games, it was 2-2 and no team had won at home. Then the Red Sox won Game Five at Fenway, and were one game away from winning their first World Championship in 86 years. It came to the point they were one pitch away from baseball Nirvana.

And then....

Just about everyone knows what happened, but there are takes on it here you might not have read elsewhere. Mostly, this is the story of each of the players, coaches, managers, and broadcasters, their lives in baseball and the way the 1986 season fit into their lives.

As between the teams, things have balanced themselves out since 1986. The Mets returned twice more to the World Series, but came up short both times. The Red Sox have fared better. In baseball, things do sometimes seem to even out. But don't tell that to any Chicago Cubs or Cleveland Indians fan.

RICK AGUILERA

By Alan Cohen

"I'm on the bench with two out. My heart was breaking. Just a terrible feeling I had, as well as we played all game. You sit and try to comprehend what we just did. It's hard to believe. It's something you sit back and say, 'Geez, how did we do it?' I don't (understand). I just really don't."

Rick Aguilera, sometime past midnight October 26, 1986, after giving up two runs in the top of the 10th inning only to see the Mets come back to score three runs and win Game Six of the 1986 World Series.[1]

"Maybe this is the best thing for me. Actually, I don't remember what it feels like to start. But if I keep getting the ball in important situations, fine. I can get as much satisfaction out of a save as I used to get when I won as a starter."

Rick Aguilera of the New York Mets, June, 1989[2]

LARGELY REMEMBERED AS AN ACE RELIEVER for the Minnesota Twins, Rick Aguilera first came to the major leagues as a starter with the New York Mets and was their fifth starter as they cruised to the 1986 National League Eastern Division championship and went on to win the World Series against the Boston Red Sox. Four years later he was in the bullpen in another city in another league.

Richard Warren Aguilera was born on December 31, 1961, in San Gabriel, California. In 1979, after batting .486 for Edgewood High School in West Covina, Aguilera was named to the All-California Interscholastic Federation second team as an infielder.

Originally selected by the St. Louis Cardinals in the 37th round of the 1980 amateur draft after he was MVP as a junior and senior in high school, Aguilera opted to attend Brigham Young University, where, when not on the ballfield, he majored in architectural design. At the collegiate level, his skills as an infielder were impeded by his slowness afoot. He remembered one of his coaches saying he "ran like a tombstone." As a result, "By the end of my freshman year of college, I wasn't getting a lot of playing time at third base, so they started working me off the mound. I'd always thrown the ball pretty hard, so that's what made them think I could pitch."[3] In short order, Aguilera, who had had limited experience as a pitcher in high school and American Legion baseball, became a full-time pitcher, and was tutored by BYU pitching coach Bob Noel. He was noticed by the scouts, who were actually eyeing his teammates Cory Snyder and Wally Joyner.

After his junior year at BYU, where he spent the season coming out of the bullpen,[4] Aguilera was drafted in the third round (58th overall) of the 1983 amateur draft by the Mets and signed by scout Roy Partee.

He was still somewhat raw and had yet to show the composure that would later characterize his presence on the mound. He was described as a tense athlete who, BYU head coach Gary Pullins observed, "was ready to jump out of his skin in some of those close (relief) situations."[5]

Aguiliera began his professional career in 1983 with Little Falls (New York) in the short-season Class-A New York-Penn League, going 5-6 with a 3.72 ERA. The following season, he moved up to Lynchburg in the Class-A Carolina League (8-3/2.34) and in June he was moved up to Jackson (Mississippi) in the Double-A Texas League. His first start for Jackson was not particularly good as he allowed three runs and three hits in his first inning of work against Shreveport. In his next outing, against Arkansas, he allowed only two hits as Jackson won, 8-0.[6] A month later, on July 29, Aguilera struck out 10 and did not allow a hit until the fifth inning as Jackson won 11-2. In his time with Jackson, he went 4-4, and over the course of the season, with Lynchburg and Jackson, struck out 172 batters in 155 innings. In 1985, Aguilera began the season at Triple-A Tidewater, where he recorded a 6-4 record with a 2.51 ERA before being called up to the Mets on June 10.

Aguilera's first big-league appearance was in relief against the Philadelphia Phillies on June 12, 1985. He came into the game in the bottom of the 10th inning and retired all three batters. The Mets exploded for four runs in the top of the 11th, and Aguilera completed the game, striking out the last two batters for his first major-league win.

Aguilera started for the first time on June 16, losing to the Montreal Expos, 7-2. He remained in the starting rotation for the balance of the season. He pitched back-to-back complete-game wins on July 5 and 10, and went 3-1 with a 0.89 ERA in five July starts. He ended the year with a 10-7 record and 3.24 ERA while hitting an impressive .278.

As the Mets and Cardinals fought each other for the pennant, it became apparent that their three-game series in St. Louis in the last week of the season would be do-or-die. The Mets won the first two games to pull within one game of the division-leading Cardinals. Aguilera started the third game. Manager Davey Johnson observed, "I was asking a lot from a rookie pitcher. I was starting him in the most pressure-packed game we've played all year. He was pitching for the pennant in front of fifty thousand [the actual figure was 47,720] unruly Cardinal fans."[7]

New York took the early lead when Keith Hernandez singled in Mookie Wilson in the top of the first inning. The Cardinals tied the game in the bottom of the second and took a 3-1 lead in the fourth. Aguilera left the game for a pinch-hitter in the seventh inning with the score 4-2 in favor of St. Louis. The Mets got within one run but lost the game, putting them two back with three to play. The Cardinals clinched the division two days later.

A year later, there would again be pressure, and the result would be much different, as Aguilera pitched in two games that no Mets fan of the era will ever forget. But to get to that point, the Mets would have to have their best regular season ever.

Things started slowly for Aguilera in 1986. After three disappointing starts, during which he went 0-2 and failed to get past the sixth inning, he was moved to the bullpen, where he spent most of his time through the end of June. His low point came on May 13 against Atlanta in his second appearance in relief. Bruce Berenyi started for the Mets and New York led 3-2 after five innings. Aguilera entered the game to pitch the top of the sixth inning, and the Braves took the lead with three runs in the seventh inning. The turning point of the inning came when he was called for a balk, on a 3-and-2 pitch, by umpire Bob Davidson, and, in an unnerved state, gave up a home run to Claudell Washington on the next pitch.[8] Aguilera stayed in the game until he was removed with one out in the ninth inning. He was charged with the loss and his record stood at 0-3 with an ERA of 8.38. He gave the folks behind home plate a good view of the back of his uniform as he allowed nine home runs in his first 18 innings of 1986.

Nevertheless, manager Johnson was not about to give up on him and, at the beginning of July Aguilera replaced Berenyi in the Mets' starting rotation. He got his second win of the season on July 12, going seven innings as the Mets defeated the Braves 10-1. Johnson said, "That was the outing I was looking for. That was the Aguilera of last year. He was outstanding with everything. He mixed his pitches well ... curve, split-finger fastball, and slider." Aguilera said, "I've been waiting for this for a long time. It couldn't come at a better time, and now I'm ready to make a contribution in the second half."[9]

But there would be a brief and surprising interruption. On July 18, during a series in Houston, Aguilera and three teammates were in the wrong place at the wrong time. On a team known for its rowdiness, four of the more quiet players were Aguilera, Bob Ojeda, Ron Darling, and Tim Teufel. They went to a place called Cooters Executive Games and Burgers to celebrate Teufel's becoming a father for the first time.[10] As they left Cooters, Teufel was holding his unfinished glass of beer and was confronted by local policemen who were providing security for Cooters. A scuffle ensued, and the four players were arrested. In January 1987, misdemeanor charges against Aguilera and Ojeda were dismissed.[11]

In the first game after the Cooters incident, Aguilera struck out a career-high nine batters and pitched eight innings as the Mets defeated Cincinnati 4-2. He reeled off five straight wins between July 12 and August 7. Over this stretch, his ERA was 1.33. Aguilera credited his renewed success to his "slow curve that I could use to keep the hitters off stride."[12]

The Mets were on a roll, and so was Aguilera. But in mid-September, the Mets were having trouble nailing down the Eastern Division championship. They lost six of seven, but on September 16 Aguilera righted the ship with a 4-2 win over the Cardinals, and the following evening, at Shea Stadium, the Mets defeated the Cubs in the clincher. In the delirium that erupted at the end of the game, one of the 47,823 exuberant fans in attendance knocked Aguilera to the ground, and Aguilera suffered a severe bruise to his shoulder that resulted in his missing his next start.[13]

The injury proved not to be serious and over the balance of the season, Aguilera went 2-1, to bring his record to 10-7. In the League Championship series with Houston, Aguilera, the Mets' fifth starter, spent his time in the bullpen and pitched in two games, including the clincher.

That clincher, Game Six at Houston, was one for the ages. The Mets considered it a must-win: Although they were leading three games to two, Houston had Mike Scott waiting to pitch a potential Game Seven and the Mets had not been able to figure out Scott's sinker all season. Houston took an early lead with three first-inning runs against Bob Ojeda, and Aguilera was summoned in the sixth inning. In three innings he allowed only one runner to reach first base and the score was 3-0 going into the top of the ninth inning. Aguilera was scheduled to lead off the top of the ninth for the Mets. As a hitter, he posed a threat. He had homered twice during the season and over the course of his career posted a decent .201 batting average. But there were good bats on the bench and strong arms in the bullpen. Len Dykstra pinch-hit for Aguilera and his leadoff triple propelled the Mets to a three-run inning that tied the game. Seven grueling innings later, the Mets had won, 5-4, and were on their way to the World Series.

Aguilera's World Series performance went from being mildly disappointing in Game Two to a Game Six appearance that in short order changed from despair to delight in a game where viewers still remember what they were doing when the game reached its climactic ending with the Mets on top.

In Game Two, the Mets trailed 6-3 when Aguilera entered the game and pitched a scoreless sixth inning. However, the game was blown open in the seventh inning when he surrendered five consecutive singles to the Red Sox, who went on to win 9-3 and take a Series lead of two games to none.

Aguilera's next appearance was in Game Six. Aguilera entered the game in the ninth with the score tied. He pitched a scoreless ninth inning, but the wheels came off in the 10th and he gave up two runs. In the bottom of the inning, with two outs and a runner on first, Kevin Mitchell pinch-hit for Aguilera, singled to keep the Mets alive and scored the tying run. The game ended shortly when Bill Buckner booted Mookie Wilson's groundball. The win went to Aguilera, who despite a 12.00 Series ERA won arguably the most critical game of the 1986 season.

After successive 10-7 seasons, Aguilera sought to improve his effectiveness in 1987 with a new pitch, the split-finger fastball. Eventually the pitch would turn Aguilera's career in a new direction, but it would take a while.

Aguilera struggled with injuries over the next two seasons, appearing in only 18 games in 1987 and 11 in 1988. His problems in 1987 began on May 26 when he felt a pain in his elbow while warming up. His stint on the disabled list, during which time he spent some time rehabbing at Tidewater, lasted until August. Despite limited duty in 1987, he ran off a streak of seven straight winning starts that lasted from May 20 to September 19, and finished the season with 11 wins. In 1988 elbow problems resurfaced and Aguilera was put on the disabled list on April 19. He was sent to Port St. Lucie and Tidewater in June on rehab assignments, and eventually had arthroscopic surgery on July 13, at which point he had an 0-4 record and an 8.41 ERA. He returned to the Mets during the final weeks of the season and pitched in three games. In the League Championship Series against the Los Angeles Dodgers, he pitched in three games, mostly in mop-up roles, as the Mets lost to the Dodgers in seven games.

The Mets moved Aguilera to the bullpen in 1989, and it was a successful transition. He got his first save on May 10 and eventually displaced Roger McDowell as the Mets' closer. By mid-June Aguilera had a 3-1 record with six saves and a 0.84 ERA, with 51 strikeouts in 43 innings.

However, Aguilera was unhappy with the Mets. During the prior two seasons, when he was missing many games, his teammates were not conciliatory. As Howard Blatt of the *New York Daily News* noted, "He was painfully aware of the derisive whispers of his Mets teammates while he was sidelined with elbow pain in 1987 and 1988. Perhaps he even knew that some of them referred to him as 'The Bearded Lady' because of how they believed he babied his talented right arm."[14]

In a season that saw much disassembling of the 1986 squad, Aguilera was dealt at the July 31 trading deadline, along with Kevin Tapani, David West, and Tom Drummond to the Minnesota Twins for Frank Viola and Jack Savage. At the time the Mets had lost seven games in a row, were looking to Randy Myers as their closer, and were in dire need, due to injuries to key personnel, of top-shelf starting pitching. In the long run, the Twins got the best of the deal as Aguilera and Tapani helped celebrate a world championship in 1991, while Viola, after winning 20 games in 1990, sank to 13-15 in 1991 for the fifth-place Mets, and left for free agency after the season.

On arrival in Minnesota, Aguilera was moved into the Twins' starting rotation and he compiled a 3-5 record with a 3.21 ERA in 11 games. Those 11 starts were his last with the Twins for seven seasons. Before the 1990 season Aguilera got a call from Twins manager Tom Kelly. With the departure of Jeff Reardon to free agency, the Twins needed a closer. With the Mets, Aguilera's bullpen role had been ill-defined. He had been a closer, but had also been used in long relief and as a mop-up man. With the Twins he would be the closer, but he still had some doubts. "Deep down, when I was first told by T.K. (Kelly) that I was going to be in this short role, I wondered if I would be able to handle the pressure of the job," he said.[15]

As the Twins closer Aguilera got off to a spectacular start, saving four games in April and posting a 1.17 ERA. However, the team was not in contention and at the end of May was in sixth place, with a 23-25 record, trailing the first-place Texas Rangers by 5½ games. Then the Twins caught fire. From June 1 through 25, they won 21 of 23 games and took over first place.

Aguilera pitched in 12 of the games and earned 10 saves. By season's end he was third in the league with a career-high and team record 42 saves. He had his career best 2.35 ERA, and the Twins won their division by eight games. Aguilera was named to the first of three consecutive All-Star teams and finished 18th in the MVP balloting.

In the American League Championship Series, Aguilera pitched in three games and saved all three, including the decisive Game Five. In his 3⅓ innings of work he allowed no runs and one hit.

Aguilera pitched in four World Series games against Atlanta. He saved the first two games at the Metrodome in Minneapolis. Game Three was tied 4-4 and went into extra innings. In the top of the 12th inning, the Twins mounted a threat. They loaded the bases with two outs and pitcher Mark Guthrie was scheduled to hit. Aguilera was warming up to take the mound in the bottom of the inning but his warmups were rushed to an unexpected conclusion. Manager Kelly was out of pinch-hitters and needed Aguilera's services as a batter. He had not swung a bat in a game since leaving the Mets. Aguilera recalled the moment. "After I got the phone call, I wondered why they wanted me to hit. Then I realized we didn't have any players left. It was definitely a little surprising but looking back at it now, there were not a whole lot of other alternatives."[16] He got good wood on the ball and it sailed to center field, but disappeared into the glove of Ron Gant. Aguilera then pitched the bottom of the 12th and, with two outs, gave up a game-winning single to Mark Lemke.

The Braves won the remaining two games at Atlanta and the teams returned to the noisy confines of the Metrodome with Atlanta needing one win to gain the championship. Game Six went into extra innings with the score tied 3-3, and Aguilera came on to pitch in the 10th inning. In two innings he allowed no runs and two hits. Both runners were erased, one on a double play and the other (ironically Kevin Mitchell, who had pinch-hit for Aguilera in the 1986 Series) was caught stealing. In the bottom of the 11th, Kirby Puckett's leadoff homer secured the win for the Twins and forced Game Seven. Only one pitcher was needed by the Twins in Game Seven as Jack Morris beat the Braves 1-0, and the Twins were the world champions.

Over the next two seasons Aguilera continued to excel and was named to two more All-Star teams. In his three All-Star games, all won by the American League, he pitched three innings, struck out five, and had a 3.00 ERA. The only blemish was a home run by Will Clark in 1992.

In 1992 for the second-place Twins, Aguilera pitched in 64 games and had 41 saves with an ERA of 2.84. He followed that up with 65 appearances and 34 saves in 1993, but the Twins dropped to fifth place. On June 6 of that season, Aguilera began a stretch that bordered on the unfathomable. He retired all four Cleveland batters he faced for his 16th save of the season. Over his next eight appearances Aguilera faced 23 batters, retired them all, and earned five saves. In the month of June he faced 42 batters in 13 games, and allowed but two hits and one walk. His ERA for the month was 0.00.

In the strike year of 1994, Aguilera pitched in 44 of the Twins' 113 games, saving 23. He said he achieved success as a closer by not trying "to show any emotion at all, whether positive or negative, and that's what works best for me. I don't want to try to put any more importance on the last three outs of the game than the first three outs."[17] Life was good in Minneapolis. Rick and his wife, the former Sherry Snider, who had been his childhood sweetheart, had moved to Minneapolis with their young daughter and Sherry had gotten into the act when she contributed a recipe to a book called *Home Plate Hits, Recipes from the Kitchens of the Minnesota Twins' Wives, Players, and Staff*, that was published early in 1994.[18] And then, things would change. Before the strike in 1994, the Twins had a losing record, and things were not going well in 1995.

A July 6, 1995, trade brought Aguilera to the Boston Red Sox, and at the time of the trade, the Red Sox were playing at Minneapolis. The timing and circumstances of the trade were steep with irony. Aguilera was, at midnight, to become a 10-and-5 man (10 years in the majors and 5 with the Twins), and have the right to veto a trade. As the trade was being finalized he was waiting his turn in the bullpen to go into a game against the Red Sox. Within 24 hours, he made his first appearance with Boston, and it was against his former teammates. The Red Sox took a 5-4 advantage into the top of the ninth inning, and Aguilera retired his former mates in order after surrendering a leadoff single to Chuck Knoblauch. His first save with the Red Sox was his 13th of the season and gave Boston a three-game lead in the AL East. He was 2-2 with 20 saves with the Red Sox in 30 appearances, as Boston won the American League East by seven games.

In the playoffs the Red Sox faced the Indians and were swept in three games. The first game of the series went into extra innings and after the Red Sox took the lead in the top of the 11th inning on a home run by Tim Naehring, Aguilera came in for the save but yielded a tying homer to Albert Belle. Cleveland went on to win the game in the 13th inning on a home run by Tony Pena off the Red Sox' Zane Smith. That was Aguilera's only appearance in the series.

Aguilera returned home to the Twins as a free agent the next year, signing a three-year contract, and was not only put in the rotation but was counted on to lead the staff.[19] But an injury, alleged to have occurred when he picked up a suitcase during spring training, delayed his return and, except for a three-inning stint on April 20, he did not pitch regularly until June. After an 8-6 campaign as a starter, he moved back to the bullpen in 1997. In 1998, he had a subpar season. In May 1999, with his potential free agency looming, he was traded to the Chicago Cubs with pitcher Scott Downs for pitchers Kyle Lohse and Jason Ryan. His 254 saves for the Twins were the franchise record until 2011, when he was passed by Joe Nathan.

With the Cubs Aguilera was reunited with former Mets teammate Ed Lynch, now the general manager of the Cubs. He was also reunited with Kevin Tapani.

Aguilera went 6-3 with eight saves for the Cubs in 1999, and was re-signed after the season, spending one more year in the majors. It was an unhappy and disappointing season for the Cubs and Aguilera. His season highlight came on June 2, when he recorded his 300th career save. But by July, there was frustration in Aguilera's voice when he said, "Coming out of camp this year, or even when I was traded (to Chicago) last year, you think, 'This is a good team.' Then things fall apart. You find yourself shaking your head and saying, 'What happened?'"[20] After the season he retired.

After his playing days, the Aguileras returned to California to raise their family, which included a daughter Rachel Rae, born in 1991, and a son Austin, who was born in 1997. In 2008 Aguilera was elected to the Twins' Hall of Fame. At the time he was the head baseball coach at the Santa Fe Christian School in Solana Beach, California. He held that position while his children attended school there.

When Aguilera retired after the 2000 season, he was eighth on the all-time saves list with 318. In 1998, as he was passing Dan Quisenberry on the list, Quisenberry was battling cancer. Putting things into perspective, Aguilera said, "Are we playing for glorification through numbers, or are we playing the game for the love of the game?"[21]

SOURCES

In addition to the sources cited in the Notes, the author also relied on:

Baseball-Reference.com

Smith, Claire. "Aguilera, a Quick Study in Relief, Is Now at the Head of the Class," *New York Times*, October 20, 1991: S8.

Aguilera's file at the Baseball Hall of Fame Library.

NOTES

1 Malcolm Moran, "Even Mets Are Amazed," *New York Times*, October 26, 1986: S-1.

2 Dan Castellano, "Amazing Transition," *The Sporting News*, June 26, 1989: 14.

3 J.G. Preston, "Fire and Ice," *Twins Magazine*, September 1993: 21.

4 *Omaha World-Herald*, May 13, 1983: 33.

5 Preston, 23.

6 *The Sporting News*, July 16, 1984: 43.

7 Davey Johnson with Peter Golenbock, *Bats* (New York, G.P. Putnam's Sons, 1986), 314.

8 Murray Chass, "Aguilera Falters as Mets Lose," *New York Times*, May 14, 1986: D-29.

9 *Los Angeles Times*, July 13, 1986: 5.

10 Mookie Wilson with Erik Sherman, *Mookie: Life, Baseball, and the '86 Mets*, (New York: Berkley Books, 2014), 137.

11 Joseph Durso, "Darling, Teufel Get Probation; Charges Dismissed for Two Others, *New York Times,* January 27, 1987: A-19.

12 Jack Lang, *The Sporting News*, July 28, 1986: 23.

13 Michal Martinez, "Aguilera Sits Out; Mets Lose," *New York Times,* September 22, 1986: C-4.

14 Howard Blatt, "Aguilera Has Last Minny Ha-Ha," *New York Daily News*, July 15, 1990: 48.

15 Preston, 21.

16 Jayson Stark, "Twins' Aguilera a Pitcher Who Was Caught in a Pinch," *Philadelphia Inquirer*, October 24, 1991.

17 Preston, 25.

18 Ann Burckhardt, *Minneapolis Star Tribune,* April 13, 1994: 4T

19 Jon Souhan, *Minneapolis Star Tribune*, February 19, 1996: 1C.

20 Jon Souhan, *Minneapolis Star Tribune*, July 14, 2000: 9C.

21 La Velle E. Neal III, *Minneapolis Star Tribune*, July 21, 1998: 4C.

RICK ANDERSON

By Joel Rippel

IN THE SPRING OF 1986, AS HE WAS BEGINNING his ninth professional season, Rick Anderson wondered if he would ever get the chance to pitch in the big leagues.

Anderson, who had spent the previous six seasons in the pitching-rich New York Mets' organization at Triple-A Tidewater, was 29 and knew he was running out of time.

"I told my wife (Rhonda) if I don't get the chance this year, I'd be a coach or scout," Anderson said. "I didn't dream I'd get a chance. I just figured it would never come."[1]

But the opportunity to pitch in the major leagues finally presented itself in 1986.

Anderson was born on November 29, 1956, in Everett, Washington, just north of Seattle. His father, Dick, was a lineman for a power company, and his mother, Jane, was a homemaker. The family also included four daughters.

As a youth Anderson played baseball and basketball, but in junior high he decided to focus on baseball. At Everett's Mariner High School, he pitched a no-hitter and earned all-state honors as a senior in 1975. After high school, he spent two years at Everett Community College. A highlight of his two seasons with Everett was a no-hitter against Fort Steilacoom Community College (now Pierce College). After two seasons at Everett, Anderson enrolled at the University of Washington.

As a junior in 1978, Anderson led the Huskies in starts (13) and complete games (10) and was 5-6 with a 4.23 ERA to help the Huskies record their first winning season in 12 years. The Huskies, who won just 114 of 261 games between 1967 and 1977, were 29-16-2 in 1978. On April 14, 1978, at Washington's Graves Field, Anderson pitched 10 no-hit innings in a 0-0 tie with Oregon State. The game was called after 10 innings because of darkness. "I think I walked 10 and struck out 10," Anderson said. "I probably threw around 200 pitches."[2]

In June of 1978, Anderson was selected by the Mets in the 24th round of the amateur draft. At 21, he began his professional career with Little Falls of the New York-Penn League. In 14 appearances with Little Falls, Anderson went 2-3 with two saves and a 2.25 ERA.

Anderson spent the 1979 season with Double-A Jackson (Texas League), going 8-11 with a 3.85 ERA. There were several highlights. On May 1, pitching for just the second time in 25 days because of rains and floods, Anderson scattered four hits and allowed just

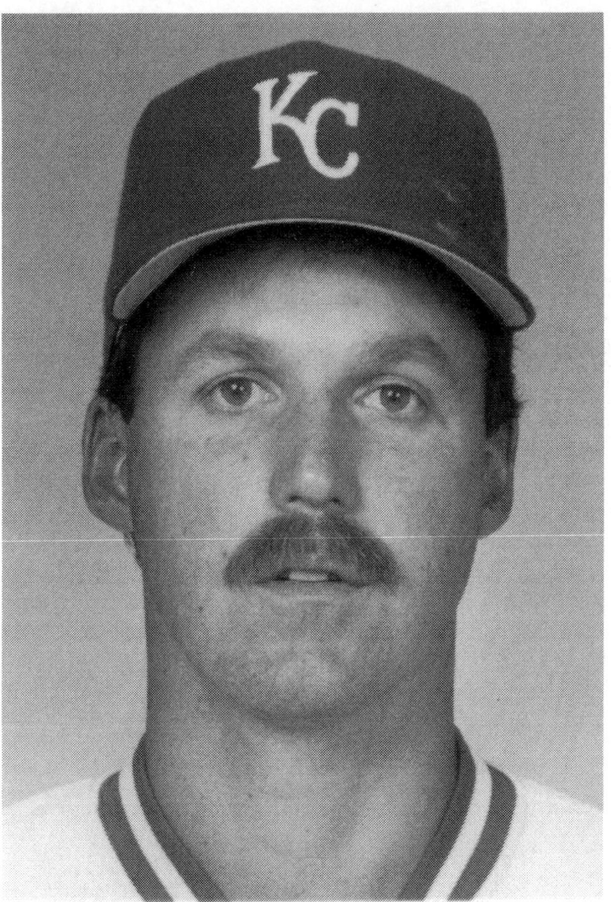

Rick Anderson sporting a KC cap.

a ninth-inning solo home run in a 6-1 victory over Arkansas. He helped his cause by getting three hits.

"It was really a wet spring," Anderson said. "Everything was flooded. The Pearl River flooded. We couldn't get to the ballpark. We had to go to gyms to throw. It was crazy."[3]

Eleven days after the victory over Arkansas, Anderson tossed a no-hitter in Jackson's 8-0 victory over Shreveport in Jackson. Anderson, who walked three (the Mets turned three double plays) and struck out two, credited catcher Jody Davis. "Davis told me before the game that changeups would work with these guys," Anderson said.[4]

Anderson began the 1980 season at Jackson but was promoted to Triple-A Tidewater (International League). With Jackson, he was 3-2 with four saves and with Tidewater he was 1-3 with one save. He spent the 1981 and 1982 seasons at Tidewater. In 1981 he was 3-5 with three saves in 37 relief appearances, and in 1982 he was 4-2 with two saves in 31 appearances.

He split the 1983 season between Tidewater and Jackson. In 15 appearances (14 in relief) for Tidewater, which was managed by Davey Johnson, Anderson was 2-1 with two saves and a 4.05 ERA. At Jackson, he made 12 starts and was 5-1 with a 3.59 ERA. In his only relief appearance he earned a save. Still, the Mets didn't beckon; the 1984 and 1985 seasons were also spent at Tidewater. In 1984, he was 6-9 with three saves and a 3.38 ERA in 26 appearances (17 starts). In 1985, he made a career-high 48 appearances (46 in relief)—going 6-3 with seven saves and a career-best 1.98 ERA.

Anderson returned to Tidewater for the 1986 season, but got a break in early June. Mets starting pitching Bruce Berenyi sprained an ankle while jogging. Anderson, five months shy of his 30th birthday, was called up to replace him.

On June 9 at Shea Stadium, Anderson, after 185 appearances with Tidewater, started against the Philadelphia Phillies. He went seven innings, allowing just four hits and no earned runs, walked two and struck out five. The Mets led 2-1 when Anderson was pinch-hit for in the bottom of the seventh inning. The Phillies eventually won the game, 3-2 in 10 innings.

"It's remarkable what he did," Davey Johnson said. "He's been pitching in relief mostly, and this was only his third start all year. I'll bet we start getting calls from other teams."[5]

Anderson's debut came with his parents in the stands and just two days after his wife had given birth to their second child.

"After all that time in the minor leagues I finally made it to the big leagues and I'm on the mound and Gary Carter is behind the plate," Anderson said. "It was a dream come true. It was fun. My wife had just had a baby. I was at the hospital when they gave me the call that I was being called up."[6]

After the game, Anderson was sent back to Tidewater, but he was called up again in mid-July. His second major-league appearance came July 20 against the Astros in Houston. Anderson pitched three scoreless innings of relief in the Astros' eventual victory in 15 innings. Two days later, in Cincinnati, he pitched 1⅓ innings of scoreless relief in the Mets' 14-inning victory over the Reds.

Anderson finally allowed an earned run in his fourth major-league appearance. In his second inning of relief against the Braves, in the second game of a July 26 doubleheader in Atlanta, Anderson allowed an earned run—the first after 12⅓ innings with no earned runs.

On August 6, Anderson earned his first major-league victory. He started and went five innings in the Mets' 7-6 defeat of the Cubs in Chicago. Anderson allowed five hits and three runs (two on a fourth-inning home run by Jerry Mumphrey) and left the game with the Mets leading 6-3. Four days later, in Montreal, Anderson pitched three perfect innings in relief of starter Sid Fernandez to earn his first major-league save.

On August 14, in the second game of a doubleheader against St. Louis at Shea Stadium, Anderson suffered his first major-league loss. He allowed four runs in six innings in a 5-1 defeat by the Cardinals. On August 30 Anderson was sent back to Tidewater when the Mets recalled shortstop Kevin Elster from Jackson.

Back in Tidewater, Anderson helped the Tides, who finished fourth in the International League regular season, capture the league championship. In the deciding game of the Governors' Cup series, Anderson tossed a four-hit shutout as the Tides defeated the Columbus Clippers, 2-0, in Norfolk to win the best-of-five series, 3-1.

Anderson then rejoined the Mets. On September 18 he pitched five shutout innings in a 5-0 defeat of the Cubs, outpitching future Hall of Famer Greg Maddux for his second victory. Anderson, who was 2-1 with a save and a 2.72 ERA in 15 appearances, was left off the Mets' postseason roster, when the Mets kept just nine pitchers. But he remained with the team during the postseason as an insurance policy in case of injury. "Look at how many guys would die to put on a uniform and sit in the dugout for the playoffs and the World Series," he said. "Ever since I was a kid, I wanted to. It's an honor."[7]

Late in spring training of 1987, Anderson and catcher Ed Hearn were traded to the Kansas City Royals for pitcher David Cone and outfielder Chris Jelic. "Anderson can flat-out pitch, and Hearn was a big help to us last year," Davey Johnson said. "But in both cases we have an abundance of people at their positions."[8]

Anderson spent most of the 1987 season with Triple-A Omaha, where he was 6-5 with a 4.52 ERA in 14 starts. In six appearances with the Royals, he was 0-2. In 1988 he was 7-4 with a 2.62 ERA in 14 starts for Omaha, and 2-1 with a 4.24 ERA in seven appearances with the Royals.

After the 1988 season, Anderson became a free agent and signed a minor-league contract with the Detroit Tigers. "It didn't include an invite to the big-league camp," he said. "I told my wife it might be time to retire. My wife agreed. I got the opportunity to go into coaching. I never looked back."[9]

The opportunity came from a tip from former teammate Ron Gardenhire, whom Anderson had known since 1980 in the Mets organization. Gardenhire, who was beginning his second season as a manager in the Minnesota Twins' minor-league system, called Anderson. "I was set to retire," Anderson said. "Ron said the Twins were looking for a pitching coach for their rookie ball team."[10]

"Our first day in Jackson, we worked out," Anderson said. "And Ron said he and his wife couldn't find an apartment. I said, 'Why don't you come live with my wife and I?'"[11]

At 32, Anderson began his coaching career with the Gulf Coast League Twins (in Sarasota). He then spent three seasons (1990-92) at Kenosha of the Class-A Midwest League before moving up to Double-A Nashville in 1993. After two seasons in Nashville, Anderson moved up to the Twins' Triple-A affiliate in Salt Lake City.

At Salt Lake City the manager was former big-league catcher Phil Roof. "Rick has been with me for two years and he takes the pressure off my shoulders," Roof said. "You can talk to the pitchers he has worked with and they will tell you he is a big part of their success. Rick is a student of the game and he has a lot of patience and just does a great job."[12]

Anderson spent the next seven seasons at Salt Lake City. After the 2001 season, Gardenhire replaced Tom Kelly as the manager of the Minnesota Twins. Gardenhire, who had been a coach under Kelly since 1991, named Anderson his pitching coach.

Anderson and Gardenhire spent the next 13 seasons with the Twins. In their first season (2002), the Twins won the AL Central title to reach the postseason for the first time since 1991. The Twins reached the postseason six times in the first nine seasons under Gardenhire. But in 2014, after the Twins' fourth consecutive 90-loss season, Gardenhire and Anderson were let go. In 2015 Anderson was living in Florida, taking time off from baseball.

Nearly 30 years after his major-league debut, Anderson said he still had fond memories of the 1986 Mets. "Being around those guys was great," Anderson said. "To this day, I'm still friends with a lot of those guys. The reunions have been great."[13]

NOTES

1 *The Sporting News*, June 2, 1979.

2 Author's telephone interview with Rick Anderson, May 15, 2015 (Hereafter Telephone interview).

3 Telephone interview.

4 *The Sporting News*, June 2, 1979.

5 *New York Times*, June 10, 1986.

6 Telephone interview.

7 *New York Times*, October 9, 1986.

8 *New York Times*, March 28, 1987.

9 Telephone interview.

10 Telephone interview.

11 Telephone interview.

12 *Deseret News* (Salt Lake City), April 5, 1995.

13 Telephone interview.

WALLY BACKMAN

By Nick Waddell

WALLY BACKMAN WAS PERHAPS THE first major-league manager fired before his team played a game. His fiery personality may have cost him another chance at managing in the majors. Three times he spent short stints in jail. He declared bankruptcy. From this sordid interval in life, he emerged to become a successful minor-league manager.

Walter Wayne Backman was born on September 22, 1959, in Hillsboro, Oregon, to Sam and Ida Backman. Sam was a railroad switchman who had spent a few years in the Pittsburgh Pirates system. Wally was the third of six children.[1] Sam taught his son the game, while both parents instilled the desire to win. "I was raised to win. I credit my parents for that," Backman said.[2]

Backman was drafted 16th overall in the 1977 June amateur draft out of Aloha (Oregon) High School. He was assigned to the Little Falls Mets of the New York-Penn League. There, Backman played in all but two of Little Falls' games in 1977, mostly at shortstop. The 17-year-old led the team in most offensive categories, including at-bats (255), runs (44), hits (83), stolen bases (20), and batting average (.325)

Backman continued his ascention in 1978, playing for the Lynchburg Mets of the Class-A Carolina League, where he helped lead the team to the league championship. He played the entire season at shortstop, and again showed off his offensive skills. Backman led the team in at-bats (494) and runs (86), and was second on the team with a .302 batting average. His speed was on display as well; he led the team in stolen bases (42) and triples (9), but his 99 strikeouts were the third most in the league. Bakcman's fielding, however, was of concern. He had a .947 fielding average at shortstop and led the team with 30 errors. Despite the shaky fielding, the Mets promoted Backman to Jackson of the Double-A Texas League, most likely due to his offense and ability to get on base at a nearly .400 clip.

Backman's 1979 season was his first facing some challenges. His offensive numbers dipped, but he was still second on the team in runs (63) and led the team with five triples. Once again, his defensive skills were subpar: 30 errors with a .933 fielding percentage.

The Mets still liked what they saw offensively from Backman, enough to promote him to Triple-A Tidewater for 1980. The organization had a plan. Backman was switched to second base. In his limited action at shortstop that season, his fielding percentage was .931 but in games at second, it jumped to .965. His skills on offense became sharper. He was among the

team leaders for most offensive categories. When the Mets made their September call-ups, Backman was on the list, and was immediately thrown into the fire. Mets second baseman Doug Flynn had fractured his right wrist on August 20, paving the way for Backman to play.[3] Backman played in 27 of the Mets' remaining 32 games, primarily at second. His fielding was stellar—only one error—and he batted .323 with a.396 on-base percentage, better than any of the Mets regular starters.

Backman's 1980 call-up and 1981 spring training earned him a spot on the 1981 Mets as a reserve infielder.[4] He played in 26 games, mostly as a pinch-hitter, before the Mets sent him back to Tidewater on June 8, just days before the players elected to strike. Backman was upset by the demotion and the lack of steady playing time.[5] He played in only 21 games for Tidewater before tearing his rotator cuff. Backman missed the rest of the 1981 season while rehabbing the injury.

After the 1981 season the Mets decided to retool their middle infield. They traded their starting shortstop, Frank Taveras, and their starting second baseman, Doug Flynn, with the idea of giving Backman a chance to take over second base, and Ron Gardenhire to take over at shortstop.[6] New manager George Bamberger worked out the infielders at all positions during spring training in an effort to create a well-rounded infield.[7] Backman batted.272 and his on-base percentage (.387, best among starters on team) was again his calling card, but he gained a reputation for bad defense, which he attributed to his rotator cuff injury. "I got labeled that year for a bad glove and it really bothered me," he said a couple of years later. "The season before I tore my rotator cuff, and in 1982 it still bothered me."[8] Like 1981, Backman's 1982 season ended early when he fell off a bicycle and broke his collarbone.[9]

Backman was on the trading block during the offseason but again found himself in the mix for a starting role on the 1983 Mets.[10] He impressed the coaches with his offense during the spring. Bobby Valentine, the Mets' infield coach, called Backman the best hitter[11] but fans and writers still regarded him as a poor defender.[12] He made the team, but played sparingly until he was sent down to Tidewater on May 17. The demotion upset Backman, and he requested a trade. "I'll go and play hard, but at the end of the season I hope the Mets trade me or release me," he said. "I really need to get away from this organization. There is no place in it for me."[13] Tidewater (and future Mets) manager Davey Johnson helped Backman get back on track. Backman praised Johnson. "The best thing that happened to me was having Dave Johnson as a manager last year," he said in 1984. "Dave put me leadoff to begin the season. He saw what I could do and had confidence in me. That took a lot of the pressure off. I could relax and play my game."[14] Backman's typical good offense became better, with a .316 batting average, but it was his defense that was the story. He made only 10 errors at second. Backman credited former second baseman Johnson with this turnaround too, saying, "In the field he showed me how to anticipate situations, and showed me what I'd been doing wrong on the double play."[15] Johnson's work paid off, as Backman was the favorite for a Mets starting position entering 1984 spring training. Johnson had also been named the Mets manager.[16]

In 1984 Backman started 108 games at second for the Mets, batted .280 and made only 10 errors at second base. For the first four months of the season, Backman platooned with Kelvin Chapman. When Chapman was sent down to the minors, Backman was given the job full-time job and he performed well offensively and defensively.[17] The 98-win Mets finished in second, three games behind pennant winner St. Louis in the NL East.

Still, Backman's splits against left-handers and right-handers (.122 and .324 respectively) were cause for concern, so before the 1986 season the Mets traded for Minnesota second baseman Tim Teufel.[18] Backman initially took the trade in stride, saying, "They're looking for anything to strengthen the team."[19] Meanwhile, he lost his arbitration case against the Mets. He asked for a salary of $425,000 but was awarded $325,000.[20]

Spring training did nothing to clear up the competition at second. Backman entered the season platooning with Teufel, playing against right-handed pitchers.[21]

He rose to the challenge, batting .320 as the Mets took first place on April 23 and never gave up the position. Backman played in 12 of the 13 Mets postseason games, batting.238 in the NLCS against Houston, and.333 in the World Series.

Before the 1987 season Backman signed a three-year, $2 million contract to continue to platoon at second for the Mets.[22] Backman was outspoken about his teammates and their willingness to play hard. He and teammate Lee Mazzilli accused star outfielder Darryl Strawberry of faking an injury for two games. Strawberry responded, "I ought to bust that little redneck (Backman)."[23]

Backman had two solid seasons platooning for the Mets. However, the team wanted to give one of its top prospects, Gregg Jefferies, a chance at second so Backman was put on the trading block again, and in December 1988 he was traded to the Minnesota Twins for three minor-league pitchers.

After a 100-win 1988 season, the Mets were expected to compete for the league lead, but a slow start to 1989 had people questioning many of the offseason moves, including the trade of Backman. One columnist called the trade of "feisty Wally Backman" a move more questionable with every lethargic game the Mets play."[24] But Backman was having his worst year ever in Minnesota, hitting .231 for the fifth-place Twins, and was released after the season. (The Mets finished in second place in the NL East and Jefferies was third in Rookie of the Year voting.)

Backman bounced around once he left the Twins. He spent 1990 with Pittsburgh, and 1991 and 1992 with Philadelphia, and was released by both teams. Before the 1993 season, he signed a minor-league deal with Atlanta, but was cut before the season began.[25] He caught on with Seattle for 10 games, but was released on May 17. Backman retired to Oregon to live with his wife, Sandi, and his four children, but found himself wanting to get into managing.[26]

Backman spent his first three managerial years with independent teams. In 1997 he managed the Catskill (New York) Cougars of the Northeast League, but could muster only a 3-23 record. In 1998 Backman managed the Bend (Oregon) Bandits of the Western Baseball League. Just before spring training, he was bitten on the forehead by a poisonous spider. While recovering, he was hit by a foul tip while standing next to the batting cage, causing more swelling. Despite his travails, his team finished the season in second place at 43-46. He then spent two years with a Bend rival, the Tri-City (Washington) Posse. Backman finished that stint with an overall 88-92 record.[27] The Chicago White Sox hired him to manage their Winston-Salem team in the Carolina League. He then spent two successful years with Double-A Birmingham, going 152-125 with the Barons. Backman's outspoken personality got him fired, though, for openly campaigning for the job of White Sox manager Jerry Manuel.[28]

After the 2004 season the Mets fired manager Art Howe. Backman was mentioned as a potential replacement after he led the Lancaster JetHawks of the California League, an Arizona Diamondbacks farm team, to an 86-54 record and being named the Minor League Manager of the Year by *The Sporting News.* (His fiery personality continued to shine through; he was ejected six times and suspended for bumping an umpire.)[29] Backman withdrew his name from Mets consideration when the Diamondbacks decided to interview him for their managerial opening.[30]

Backman was hired as the Diamondbacks' manager on November 1, 2004, but was fired four days later after the *New York Times* ran a story about legal issues in his past that he had not disclosed to the Diamondbacks during his interview. His first wife, Maggie, had filed for a restraining order against him. (A judge later vacated the order.[31]) Backman had also been convicted of drunk driving in January 2001. He was sentenced to a year in jail, but served only one day, and the remainder of the sentence was suspended unless Backman committed another crime within five years. On October 7, 2001, Backman was charged with five misdemeanors stemming from an incident involving his second wife, Sandi. He again served one day in jail, and was placed on an alcohol-free one year probationary period.

(Sandi later said the incident was overblown and "[t]he idea of Wally hitting me is comical."[32]) In February 2003 Backman filed for Chapter 7 bankruptcy. The Diamondbacks said they were unaware of any of the issues surrounding Backman.[33] Backman later served 10 days in jail for violating the conditions of the 2001 suspended sentence.[34]

Backman remained out of baseball until 2007, when he took over the South Georgia Peanuts of the South Coast League. "[If] this is what I need to get another shot in Organized Baseball, I'll do it," he said.[35] He shared his $40,000 salary with three of his coaches.[36] While with the Peanuts, Backman unleashed a memorable on-field tantrum. One of his players was ejected for arguing balls and strikes. Backman emerged from the dugout to protect his player, and was thrown out of the game. He then littered the field with 22 bats and a bucket of baseballs.[37] The incident was caught on tape for a TV show documenting the South Coast League, *Playing for Peanuts.* Even with this incident, Backman's tenure with the Peanuts was successful. His team won the league championship and five Peanuts were signed to major-league contracts.[38]

Backman stayed in the independent leagues for 2008, managing the Joliet JackHammers of the Northern League. He lasted through mid-2009, when a 24-42 record got him fired. Backman acknowledged his failure to lead the team, saying, "The fans in Joliet deserve a winner. I'm disappointed that we could not get the job done."[39]

Before the 2010 season, the Mets brought Backman back into the fold to manage the Brooklyn Cyclones of the New York-Penn League. He had not been affiliated with Organized Baseball since the Arizona firing, and quickly addressed that issue. "I take full responsibility for the things that I did wrong," Backman said at his introductory press conference. "But I want to move forward again and to start here, I think, is a good start for me."[40] The Mets inserted a zero-tolerance clause in his contract.[41]

Backman responded by guiding the team to a league-best 51-24 record. Brooklyn lost in the playoff finals to Tri-City, but Backman made an impact on the Mets organization. When Jerry Manuel was fired as the Mets' manager after a fourth-place finish, Backman was interviewed and considered a finalist, but lost out to Terry Collins.[42] Instead, Backman was promoted to Binghamton (Double-A Eastern League) for the 2011 season. For 2012 he was promoted to manage Triple-A Buffalo. The team finished 67-76, and Backman was his typical outspoken self. He described one of his pitchers as a "4-A guy" and opined "[f]or the major leagues, he has no real swing-and-miss pitch."[43]

In 2013 the Mets switched their Triple-A affiliation to the Las Vegas 51s of the Pacific Coast League. Backman led the team (81-63) to a first-place finish, but lost in the playoffs to Salt Lake. In 2014 they finished first again with the same 81-63 record. Despite losing in the playoff semifinals again (this time to Reno), Backman was named PCL Manager of the Year. In 2015 the 51s missed the playoffs.

Backman also had a hand in the Mets' success in 2015. Three pitchers who played important roles in the team's march to the World Series, Matt Harvey, Steven Matz, and Noah Syndergaard, as well as infielder Wilmer Flores, all played for Backman in the minors. Through the 2015 season, Backman had a 422-369 record while managing in the Mets organization.

NOTES

1 Jeff Pearlman, "Three Years Later, Backman Still Trying to Get to the Bigs," ESPN, sports.espn.go.com/espn/page2/story?page=pearlman/071022 (accessed December 1, 2015).

2 Ibid.

3 Joseph Durso,"Mets Lose 7th in Row; Flynn Idled 2-6 Weeks," *New York Times*, August 21, 1980.

4 Joseph Durso, "Leary Earns a Place on Mets Roster and Will Face Cubs Sunday," *New York* Times, April 6, 1981.

5 Thomas Rogers, "Baseball Notebook: Mets' Backman Expands Strike," *New York Times*, June 16, 1981.

6 Murray Chass, "Mets Trade Flynn; Expos Get Taveras," *New York Times*, December 12, 1981.

7 Jane Gross, "Met Plan: Versatile Infield," *New York Times*, February 24, 1982.

8 William C. Rhoden, "Backman Fills Gap for Mets," *New York Times*, July 12, 1984.

9 Ibid.

10 Joseph Durso, "Stearns on Disabled List, Seaver Ailing," *New York Times,* March 28, 1983.

11 Gerald Eskenazi, "Mets Try 5 Players in Double-Play Role," *New York Times*, March 21, 1983.

12 Joseph Durso, "Second Base Is Puzzling Mets," *New York Times,* March 3, 1983

13 Joseph Durso, "Strawberry's 3-Run Homer Paces Mets," *New York Times,* May 18, 1983

14 Rhoden.

15 Ibid.

16 Lawrie Mifflin, "Backman Stays In Mets' Plans," *New York Times,* December 21, 1983.

17 "Backman Responds to Full-Time Duty," *Chicago Tribune*, August 1, 1985.

18 Joseph Durso, "Backman Facing Challenge At Second Base," *New York Times,* February 25, 1986.

19 Ibid.

20 Murray Chass, "Backman Loses Case to Mets," *New York Times,* February 20, 1986.

21 Michael Martinez, "Backman is Facing Another Battle," *New York Times,* March 30, 1986.

22 Murray Chass, "Mets Give Backman a $2 Million Pact," *New York Times,* January 22, 1987.

23 Johnette Howard, "Strawberry's Latest Strikeout May Be Last," *Washington Post*, April 14, 1994.

24 George Vecsey, "Baseball, Everybody, Baseball," *New York Times,* June 2, 1989.

25 "Braves Jettison Backman for Cabrera," *New York Times,* April 2, 1993.

26 Filip Bondy, "Arachnophobia: Spider Bite Adds to Backman's Web of Miserable Luck," *New York Daily News,* May 24, 1998.

27 Ibid.

28 Jack Curry, "Backman Named Arizona's Manager," *New York Times*, November 2, 2004.

29 Lee Jenkins, "As Mets Look Ahead, They Look Back," *New York Times*, September 23, 2004.

30 David Waldstein, "Mets Will Hire Backman to Manage In Brooklyn," *New York Times*, November 14, 2009.

31 Pearlman.

32 Ibid.

33 Jack Curry, "The Past Costs Backman His Job, Four Days After He Received It," *New York Times*, November 6, 2004.

34 "Sports Briefing," *New York Times*, December 4, 2004.

35 Pearlman.

36 Jack Curry, "Backman Ready for His Show of Shows," *New York Times*, June 17, 2007.

37 Pearlman.

38 Ibid.

39 oursportscentral.com/services/releases/?id=3875509.

40 Ben Shpigel, "After 5 Years, Backman Gets a Second Chance," *New York Times*, November 18, 2009.

41 Ibid.

42 David Waldstein, "Mets Choose the Intense Collins as Their Manager," *New York Times*, November 22, 2010.

43 Hunter Atkins, "A Long Road Home, With Further Still to Go," *New York Times*, June 17, 2012.

BRUCE BERENYI

By David E. Skelton

IN THE WINTER OF 1981-1982 THE CINCINNATI Reds began dismantling remnants of the powerful Big Red Machine. Outfielder George Foster's contract was scheduled to run out after the 1982 season and the slugger was rumored to be seeking a $20 million renewal. On the heels of the departures of Ken Griffey and Ray Knight, Foster was traded in February. But general manager Dick Wagner drew the line on three untouchable pitchers: future Hall of Famer Tom Seaver and two promising youngsters Mario Soto and Bruce Berenyi. The lofty company Berenyi shared was not undeserved. The third overall pick in the 1976 June draft (secondary phase) had shown great promise through the minors and in 27 appearances with the Reds. Wagner looked to the righty as one of the cornerstones to the rebuilding of the team.

Instead hard luck and injury derailed Berenyi's future. In 1982 he was saddled with a National League-leading 18 losses for the last-place Reds despite a respectable 3.36 ERA (league average: 3.60). Little success followed as Cincinnati, last in the league in runs scored in 1982, continued its offensive malaise. As losses mounted, the frustrated youngster petitioned for a trade. The appeal was granted and Berenyi found success with the young, emerging New York Mets. But shoulder problems developed and Berenyi was soon out of baseball. He concluded a seven-year major-league career with a pedestrian record of 44-55, 4.03—a far cry from what was once projected.

Bruce Michael Berenyi was born on August 21, 1954, one of four children of Frank and Madeline F. (Sims) Berenyi, in Bryan, Ohio, in the state's northwest corner. At 15 Frank had emigrated with his family from Hungary in 1938. He found early employment alongside his father in a sugar-beet refinery but, as the industry began dying out in Ohio, he settled into a long career in the motor-vehicle industry. On January 10, 1948, he married Ohio native Madeline Sims.[1] They remained in Bryan until their passing in 1991 and 2008, respectively.

Their children attended Fairview High School in Sherwood, Ohio. Bruce, their second son, excelled at baseball and eventually—as an admittedly late bloomer—basketball. In the early 1970s Berenyi entered Glen Oaks Community College in Centreville, Michigan. He soon attracted attention from major-league scouts. In 1975 the Detroit Tigers selected Berenyi in the 19th round of the June amateur draft. The first Glen Oaks player ever drafted—and through 2014 the only Viking to advance to the majors—Berenyi spurned the Tigers and transferred to Truman State University in northern Missouri. The next year he rewrote the record books for the TSU Bulldogs with the most strikeouts in a single game (21), most consecutive shutout innings (30), and most innings pitched in a season (65). He was named to the 1976 Mid-America Intercollegiate Athletic Association's All-Conference

team and the NCAA Division II All-District team. These achievements earned Berenyi a first-round selection by Cincinnati in June 1976.

Berenyi spent a short time in the Northwest League followed by promotion to the Shelby (North Carolina) Reds in 1977. A pedestrian start to the season unfolded into a brilliant second half campaign (7-4, 1.80 ERA in his final 13 appearances), placing Berenyi among the league leaders in wins (10), ERA (2.30), and strikeouts (120). Success followed him into the Double-A Southern League with the Nashville Sounds in 1978. Berenyi won his first five decisions, and seven of his first eight. On May 23 he twirled a one-hitter and struck out nine in a 4-2 victory over the slugging Columbus Astros (though he did exhibit a streak of wildness with seven walks and four wild pitches). A record of 8-2, 1.99 in his first 10 appearances[2] captured considerable attention. A slight second-half sag did not detour Berenyi's steady climb in the Reds' farm system.

At Cincinnati's 1979 spring-training camp the Reds' new pitching coach, Bill Fischer, enthused over his first glance at Berenyi: "[N]ow that I've had a chance to see [him] throw, I'm even more impressed."[3] Berenyi was assigned to Triple-A Indianapolis, where he got his first peek at what lay in store for him in Cincinnati. For the first of two consecutive years the Indians were last in the league in runs scored. The futility became blatantly clear on May 16 when Berenyi tossed a one-hitter against the Omaha Royals only to suffer a 1-0 loss. In his first nine appearances he possessed a league-leading ERA of 1.43 yet was saddled with four losses. Berenyi took matters into his own hands on June 1 in a scoreless duel against the Denver Bears, delivering the Indian's first run with an RBI single in the eighth inning in a 2-0 win. Berenyi struck out 12 while also adding to his string of 38⅔ innings without surrendering an earned run. Even more remarkable was his dominance over the Bears that evoked comparisons to the four-man softball squad The King and His Court as the Indians' catcher, first baseman, and second baseman accounted for nine of 12 assists, 24 of 27 putouts.

But the losses proceeded as the Indians scored more than two runs in only three of Berenyi's first 15 starts. On June 30 he endured another heartbreaking loss, yielding just six hits and one earned run in a 2-0 loss to the Iowa Oaks. Berenyi finished with a pedestrian record of 9-9 despite a league leading 2.82 ERA. He paced the league in shutouts (3) and strikeouts (136) while disconcertingly leading in wild pitches (13) and placing second in walks (98). In a postseason poll of American Association managers Berenyi was voted runner-up to righty Dewey Robinson for the Allie Reynolds Award as the circuit's best pitcher. Indianapolis skipper Roy Majtyka said, "[Berenyi] could be the nucleus of Cincinnati's pitching staff in a couple of years."[4] This sentiment was echoed the following spring when pitching coach Bill Fischer predicted Berenyi as the Reds' "sleeper" to enter the rotation.

But on the eve of the 1980 season the Reds, possessing few left-handed hurlers, chose southpaw rookie Charlie Leibrandt to proceed north while Berenyi was reassigned. The dejected Berenyi's performance suffered considerably. On April 16 he surrendered his first home run in two years (a string of 168 innings). Over his first 48⅔ innings Berenyi yielded 38 walks and 9 wild pitches and had a 6.10 ERA. He grabbed a Houdini-like 3-1 win over the Evansville Triplets on May 28 by escaping numerous scoring opportunities after yielding 11 walks in six-plus innings. The three runs came from his first professional home run. Asked to assess the bizarre outing, Berenyi said, "I'm kinda happy. ... I'm kinda embarrassed."[5]

Soon Berenyi began exhibiting the type of performances to which the organization was accustomed. On June 9 he struck out six consecutive Denver batters and appeared on track to break the league record of eight before being lifted after a 67-minute rain delay. Indians manager Jim Beauchamp explained, "Very few pitchers will return with the same stuff and there is always the chance they can get stiff. I would take a loss every day of the week instead of hurting an arm like Berenyi's."[6] As for Berenyi's abrupt turnaround: "I convinced him that [his despondency over the spring demotion] was only hurting himself. Since then his pitching has been awesome."[7] As it turned out, Berenyi's surge could not have been more propitious.

Since the spring Reds ace Tom Seaver had been struggling with shoulder problems that helped push his ERA over an uncharacteristic 4.00. In San Francisco on June 30 he did not make it past the fourth inning. The next day Seaver was placed on the 21-day disabled list and Berenyi was called up. On July 5 the 25-year-old made a forgettable major-league debut in Cincinnati against the Houston Astros, who jumped on him for six runs in the first inning. A more promising start occurred seven days later when Berenyi was locked in a tie against the Giants' John Montefusco. Berenyi yielded two walks to start the sixth — nine walks total — and was lifted from the game.

Berenyi curbed his wildness on July 18, yielding just six hits and three walks in seven innings to earn his first major-league win, an 8-3 victory over the New York Mets. A similar outing on July 23 resulted in a 7-3 win over the Philadelphia Phillies. His record on the year with the Reds was 2-2 and a 7.81 ERA with 23 walks in 27⅔ innings. When Seaver came off the disabled list on August 4, Berenyi was returned to Indianapolis. Control problems continued to plague him when he surrendered a bases-loaded walk in a 1-0 loss to Evansville. He concluded his last season in the Reds farm system with league-leading marks in walks (100) and, for the second consecutive year, strikeouts (121).

Significantly, throughout Berenyi's five years in the farm system, the organization largely ignored his periodic complaints about arm soreness. Their skepticism stemmed from Berenyi's ability to continually deliver the ball at 90-plus miles per hour. On the few occasions when the Reds acknowledged that there was a problem they tried to work with Berenyi on his mechanics in hopes of ameliorating the soreness, while going so far as to label him a hypochondriac. Their actions would eventually exact a heavy price.

After a strong start to the 1980 campaign, lefty Charlie Leibrandt struggled in the second half. The following spring the Reds felt he needed further development in the minors, thus opening the door for Berenyi to make the team. On April 14 the confidence shown the young righty was immediately rewarded with a two-hit shutout of the San Diego Padres. Four days later Berenyi labored against the St. Louis Cardinals, then delivered a strong performance against the Astros (despite six walks) to capture his second victory. His season continued to seesaw back and forth. On May 24 he complained about the umpire "squeezing the plate"[8] as he threw 15 balls in succession for five walks in a 10-3 loss to the Los Angeles Dodgers. (As he left the field after having been removed from the game, a comment directed to umpire Randy Marsh earned Berenyi an ejection.) Two weeks later, in his last appearance before the 1981 players' strike, Berenyi twirled his second major-league shutout, a one-hit, 10-strikeout outing against the Montreal Expos, a performance that catcher Joe Nolan described as a "once-in-a-lifetime"[9] gem.[10]

Berenyi spent the two-month strike at his parents' home in Sherwood, Ohio. He joked that he had no problem staying in shape during the layoff because in the 1,400-population village, "there aren't many distractions for me."[11] His conditioning paid off when the season resumed in August. In 10 appearances after the strike, Berenyi compiled a 2.64 ERA (team ERA over the same period: 3.67) in 61⅓ innings with 68 strikeouts. This stretch included two career-high 12-strikeout performances, a shutout of the Mets and a 4-2 win over the Astros in which Houston manager Bill Virdon claimed Berenyi "show[ed] us the best stuff we've seen all season."[12] Berenyi's record of 9-6, 3.50 in 126 innings earned him a tie for fourth in the balloting for the National League Rookie of the Year. He was named to the NL Topps All-Rookie team. The success prompted the aforementioned "untouchable" label assigned by the Reds' general manager.

Over the winter Berenyi often commuted 340 miles round-trip to Cincinnati for special tutoring under Coach Fischer, his fierce advocate. Fischer sought to adjust Berenyi's release point in order to improve his control. The strategy appears to have failed as Berenyi, for the second consecutive year, placed among the league leaders in wild pitches and walks. Starting 1982 soundly (4-1, 2.93) through the end of April, he followed on May 8 in a game against the Pittsburgh Pirates abuot which *The Sporting News* stated that Berenyi "never was more overpowering."[13] He surrendered one "tainted"[14] hit through eight innings but wound up with a no-decision when the game went into extra innings. Thereafter Berenyi struggled to get into the win column, usually had a hard time getting a win after having gone 4-1.

Despite a respectable 3.36 ERA (league average: 3.60) Berenyi was victimized by many heartbreaking losses. In two consecutive August starts he did not surrender an earned run but could not capture a win. In his final 12 appearances he was saddled with a record of 1-8 despite a solid 3.16 ERA over 79⅔ innings. (The victory was a shutout, seemingly the only way he could win a game). As the losses mounted so did Berenyi's frustration. Through his agent, the 27-year-old requested a trade but the Reds were reluctant to part with the righty whom Philadelphia Phillies' first baseman Pete Rose described among the league's "fine crop of young pitchers."[15] Berenyi had the lowest home-run yield among National League starters but his run support was nonexistent. He lost four games by one run, six games by two and finished the year with a league-leading 18 losses.

He fared just slightly better in 1983. In 12 starts Berenyi had a superb 2.41 ERA that, for the offensively challenged Reds (next to last in the league in runs scored), got him a record of 0-7. He was injured in May and, perhaps unwisely, chose to pitch through it—he was 1-5, 6.11 in his next nine appearances. A respectable season-ending 3.86 ERA unduly merited a dismal 9-14 and once again Berenyi's agent sought greener pastures for his client. This time the Reds tried to accommodate their disgruntled hurler. A trade to the New York Yankees for catcher Rick Cerone during the season was allegedly vetoed by the veteran backstop, whose contract contained trade restrictions. In October the Detroit Tigers aggressively pursued Berenyi for outfielder Glenn Wilson but the pursuit dried up when the Tigers successfully re-signed free-agent righty Milt Wilcox in November.

A glimmer of hope surfaced for the Reds in general—and Berenyi in particular—in the spring of 1984. Improved offense was expected with the signing of free-agent slugger Dave Parker, while Berenyi produced perhaps his finest Grapefruit League campaign: a 1.29 ERA. Though the Reds offense improved slightly over preceding seasons, it was largely nonexistent in Berenyi's first four appearances. Burdened with an record of 0-3 (it easily could have been 2-2 with run support), he complained "I'm not a loser. I've never been a loser."[16] But a different picture emerged in May. In two of three starts Berenyi could not get a single out as his ERA shot above 6. Two promising starts in June were followed by a disastrous outing against the Astros on June 12. Three days later Berenyi was traded to the Mets for three minor-league prospects.

Since the notorious "Midnight Massacre" seven years earlier (when the Mets dumped 11 players via four trades in one day), the team had suffered through hard times. But in 1984, under the guidance of their new manager, Davey Johnson, the league's youngest team was competitive again. When Berenyi joined the Mets he became the most senior member of the staff despite just four years of major-league service under his belt. Johnson, who'd been in awe of Berenyi's slider in an April 4 match against the Mets, was elated with the addition: "He's going to fit right in here. … I liked what I saw from him the first time. He's going to do just fine with us."[17] Berenyi's season immediately turned for the better. With the Mets he went 9-6 with a 3.76 ERA and won five of his final six decisions. When Walt Terrell was traded to Detroit on December 7, Berenyi was projected as the Mets' third starter in 1985.

But fate had something else in store as Berenyi struggled with a tender shoulder the following spring. He pitched only 13 Grapefruit League innings. These worries appeared to be for naught on April 12 when Berenyi came out of the gate with a spectacular seven-inning one-hit performance against his former teammates. The win was his only decision of the 1985 season. Berenyi pitched only 6⅔ more innings in two appearances before a tear in his rotator cuff was discovered. Surgery in May placed him on the shelf the rest of the season.

After the season Berenyi reported to St. Petersburg, Florida, to pitch in the winter Instructional League. But the shoulder did not respond. He instead rehabbed with Mets trainer Tom McKenna. Having to wait until spring to ascertain Berenyi's status, the Mets traded with the Boston Red Sox for lefty Bob Ojeda. Even Berenyi sounded conflicted about a rapid return, stating, "It's hard to keep from having second thoughts. Every now and then when you throw, your arm might feel funny. But then the next time, it doesn't. You try to push it out of your mind but it's difficult. Right now I feel great, and the doctor says there is no reason I can't be ready for next season."[18]

Berenyi reported to spring training early and began pitching throwing every other day under the supervision of pitching coach Greg Pavlick. When he experienced no pain, Davey Johnson predicted that "he will throw as hard as he used to, maybe even harder."[19] The manager confidently announced Berenyi's return to the staff. But the righty did not begin the 1986 season in the rotation. In a cautionary approach, he was initially assigned to the bullpen and did not receive a starting nod until May 13. He started six more games but never worked beyond the sixth inning. Despite Johnson's earlier optimism, Berenyi's velocity was lacking. He proved hittable. Having generated a 6.35 ERA in July, Berenyi agreed to be assigned to the Tidewater Tides in the International League, where he showed little improvement. Shortly after the Mets secured a World Series win over the Red Sox, Berenyi was released. On January 23, 1987, he signed with the Montreal Expos and went to spring training as a nonroster invitee. It was not long before the shoulder problems resurfaced and he was released on March 11. Berenyi had a second surgery, whose success provided him the confidence to re-sign with the Expos in 1988. This stint also proved short-lived. In late February he signed a minor-league contract with the Pittsburgh Pirates, but was released before the start of the season. With a major-league ledger of just 142 appearances, Berenyi retired from baseball.

Berenyi returned to the Sherwood, Ohio, home he had built on a 25-acre tract he purchased in 1984. With a second residence in Florida, he worked for a resort/golf course in North Miami in the winters. Berenyi retained the winter home while forsaking his native state for New Hampshire. In 1993 his collegiate exploits were recognized with his induction into the Truman State University Athletic Hall of Fame.

Unfulfilled were the grand expectations surrounding Berenyi when he made his way through the professional ranks. His complaints of arm soreness were ignored—even ridiculed—as the hard throwing righty advanced. Those problems were unmistakable when two shoulder surgeries were unable to resurrect Berenyi's once-promising path. Unknown is the career that might have developed had the Reds been more attentive when the aches and pains initially surfaced.

SOURCES

The author wishes to thank SABR members Bruce Slutsky, Randy Rice, and Anne Surman for their assistance.

Baseball-reference.com

Ancestry.com

technicians.truman.edu/csweb07/hallOfFame3/myXML.xml

NOTES

1 Madeline's younger sister, Dorothy Louise, married pitcher Ned Garver, whose major-league career spanned 14 years.

2 "Southern Averages," *The Sporting News*, July 1, 1978: 48.

3 "McNamara Checks Band, Finds All on Key," *The Sporting News*, April 7, 1979: 11.

4 "American Association," *The Sporting News*, August 4, 1979: 39.

5 "American Association," *The Sporting News*, June 21, 1980: 37.

6 "Rain Stops Berenyi Streak," *The Sporting News*, July 5, 1980: 39.

7 "End of Trail Looming for Seaver," *The Sporting News*, July 19, 1980: 21.

8 "Berenyi Runs Wild," *The Sporting News*, June 6, 1981: 26.

9 "Soto's Spurt Spurs Reds," *The Sporting News*, June 27, 1981: 33.

10 The victory was the last of four consecutive complete games for the rotation, a string that had not been reached by a Reds staff since five straight complete games in 1962.

11 "Reds: Pastore In Dark," *The Sporting News,* August 8, 1981: 32.

12 "'Bullets' Berenyi Finds the Range," *The Sporting News,* October 3, 1981: 37.

13 "Reds Attack Dulled By Power Shortage," *The Sporting News,* May 24, 1982: 34.

14 Ibid.

15 "Pete on Winning Side of Another Record," *The Sporting News,* April 4, 1983: 6.

16 "Is Berenyi Trapped In Twilight Zone?" *The Sporting News,* April 16, 1984: 21.

17 "Young Hurlers Leading Mets," *The Sporting News,* July 2, 1984: 21.

18 "N.L. East—Mets," *The Sporting News,* January 6, 1986: 50.

19 "Pleasant Complications For Pitching-Rich Mets," *The Sporting News,* March 31, 1986: 38.

GARY CARTER

By Rory Costello

IT SIMPLY SHOULD NOT HAVE TAKEN SIX YEARS for Gary Carter to get into the Hall of Fame. He was one of the best catchers of his era, and many observers put him in the top 10 in major-league history. He was an outstanding defender with a strong arm who did all the other things expected of a receiver. He combined that with a powerful bat—Carter's 298 homers as a catcher were seventh-most at that position as of 2015—and a gung-ho competitive spirit. A broad grin and pumping fist were The Kid's visual trademarks.

Carter's best years came with the Montreal Expos in the late 1970s and early '80s, but he was still in his late prime when he joined the New York Mets in 1985. Carter was the final ingredient that helped a promising young club become a World Series champion in 1986. He became the team's cleanup hitter and handled its excellent pitching staff. One of those hurlers, Ron Darling, called Carter the moral compass of the hard-living squad.[1]

Knee injuries ground Carter down—in part because he always wanted to stay in the lineup. His last season as a full-time regular came at age 34 in 1988, though he hung on for four more years. Subsequently, he stayed involved in baseball as a broadcaster with the Florida Marlins and the Expos. He then coached and managed in the minors, independent ball, and college, but his hopes of returning to the majors went unfulfilled. Alas, Carter also died in 2012 at the too-young age of 57.

For the definitive account of this man's youth and family background, one must turn to *Before the Glory* (2007), by Billy Staples and Rich Herschlag. All the details one could want are in Carter's chapter, as told by The Kid himself. Of necessity, this story offers only a tiny selection.

Gary Edmund Carter was born on April 8, 1954, in Culver City, California, near Los Angeles. He was the second of two boys born to James H. Carter and his wife, Inge. Jim Carter, a mechanically minded man from Kentucky, moved to California after World War II to work in technical jobs in Hollywood. When Gary was born, he was working as an aviation-parts inspector for Hughes Aircraft Company.[2] (The aerospace industry was a big employer in Southern California.)

Inge Charlotte Keller was born in Chicago in 1929. Her parents were German immigrants who came to the United States in the 1920s. Gary later attributed his athletic ability to Inge, a champion swimmer, although Gary himself said, "Funnily enough, I'm a terrible swimmer."[3] His older brother, Gordon, was also good enough to be a second-round draft pick of the California Angels in 1968 and the San Francisco

Giants in 1971. Gordy played two years of Class-A ball (1972-73) in the Giants organization.

Gary Carter started playing Little League at age 6, but he also loved and was talented at football. In 1961 the National Football League sponsored the first Punt, Pass & Kick contest. At the Los Angeles Coliseum, 7-year-old Gary became the national champion in his age group. He was a finalist again two years later, but lost in subzero conditions in Chicago.

When Carter was 12 years old, his mother died at age 37 after a battle with leukemia. This crushing loss at a young age was at the root of Carter's later charitable work, raising funds for leukemia research and on behalf of children with other disorders. Jim Carter took on the role of both parents, making great sacrifices for his boys. In addition to his job in procurement for McDonnell Douglas, another aerospace/defense company, he coached Gary at various levels of youth baseball and supported him in all his sporting endeavors.[4] Brother Gordy was also a mentor and role model for Gary.

Carter followed Gordy to Sunny Hills High School in Fullerton, California (the family had moved there when he was 5). There he was a three-sport star, becoming captain of the football, basketball, and baseball teams. He was also a member of the National Honor Society. In football, he was a high-school All-America quarterback and received nearly 100 scholarship offers. He signed a letter of intent with UCLA. (If he had played for the Bruins, he would have competed with and/or backed up Mark Harmon, who went on to become a well-known actor.) Carter suffered torn knee ligaments in his senior year in high school, however, and had to sit out the football season. Noted sports surgeon Dr. Robert Kerlan warned him that one more bad hit could end his athletic career.[5]

That prompted Carter to turn pro in baseball instead. The Expos had selected him in the third round of the 1972 amateur draft. He had played shortstop, third base, and pitcher for Sunny Hills—and only six games as a catcher.[6] But Expos scout Bob Zuk, special-assignment scout Bobby Mattick, and farm director Mel Didier looked at the ruggedly built teenager (6-feet-2, 205 pounds) and envisaged him behind the plate. Zuk also craftily downplayed his interest in Carter, which enabled Montreal to draft him earlier than other teams expected.[7]

Although Carter was totally raw as a receiver, his ascent through the minors was rapid. He played in rookie league and Class A in 1972 and jumped to Double A for 1973. He got his first promotion to Triple A at the end of '73 and needed just one more year at that level in 1974, when he became the Topps Triple-A All-Star catcher. He never returned to the minors except for a brief injury-rehab stint in 1989.

According to Carter, he got his enduring nickname—"The Kid"—during his first spring-training camp with the Expos in 1973. "Tim Foli, Ken Singleton, and Mike Jorgensen started calling me Kid because I was trying to win every sprint. I was trying to hit every pitch out of the park."[8] One history of the 1986 Mets, Jeff Pearlman's *The Bad Guys Won*, wrote that pitcher Don Carrithers (an Expo from 1974 to 1976) sarcastically hyped "The Kid" as a way to get the goat of incumbent catcher Barry Foote. Pearlman then went on at length to describe how Carter's naïve enthusiasm rubbed a lot of his teammates the wrong way. Another nickname—"Camera Carter"—later came from his love of doing interviews. "Lights" and "Teeths" were two more labels that captured the behind-the-back sniping in Montreal.[9]

Yet there wasn't anything phony about Carter—his chatty, cheery exterior truly reflected what was in his heart. As Ira Berkow of the *New York Times* wrote upon Carter's induction to Cooperstown, "He delighted in relationships."[10]

In that first camp in 1973, Montreal assigned Carter to room with John Boccabella, a veteran catcher. "Boc" was traded for Carrithers toward the end of March 1974, and after the deal, Boccabella said of Carter, "He impressed me both as a player and a person. He learns fast and I think he has the stuff to become a superstar."[11]

Boccabella's personal influence on Carter was even stronger. The veteran was a man of deep religious faith who attended Mass daily and had led Sunday services for the Expos. Carter, who had lost his faith after his mother died, found it again. As his daughter Christy recalled in 2013, "John Boccabella led Dad to Christ and he accepted Jesus in his heart."[12]

Carter told Montreal sportswriter Ian MacDonald about this himself in 1977. He called Boccabella "a beautiful guy. Always enthusiastic. Always up. Always reading from the Scriptures or [basketball coach John] Wooden's book [*They Call Me Coach*, 1972]. I had met Wooden two or three times when I was being recruited by UCLA but I hadn't read the book until Boccabella gave me a copy. It was overwhelming. It reinforced everything that I believed in and gave me the physical strength to practice my beliefs—to be happy to be alive, to be enthusiastic, to not fill your life with hate over the stupid things. ... I learned a lot from 'Boc' and I'll always be grateful to him."[13]

Playing winter ball in Puerto Rico also aided Carter's development. He played for the Caguas Criollos in the 1973-74 season. Montreal sent a number of its prospects to Caguas, which was loaded with future big leaguers. One of them, Otto Vélez, called that club the best Puerto Rican team he ever played on—they became league champions and went on to win the Caribbean Series. Vélez told author Thomas Van Hyning, "There was no envy on that team, though there were many who could really play. Gary Carter wanted to become a better player, [Mike] Schmidt had to overcome a season with a lot of strikeouts."[14]

Carter started that winter in the Instructional League, but a month into the Puerto Rican season, Caguas needed a backup catcher. Montreal's general manager, Jim Fanning, recommended the 19-year-old, who became the youngest member of the Criollos. He got a chance to play when the regular catcher, Jim Essian, got hurt. As was true everywhere Carter played, the fans loved him for his enthusiasm and desire to win.[15] In the Caribbean Series, Carter hit a homer off Pedro Borbón of the Dominican Republic and was named the catcher on the series all-star team.

The Expos called Carter up to the majors for the first time in September 1974. He made his debut at Montreal's old Jarry Park on September 16, going 0-for-4 as he caught all nine innings. On September 28, also at Jarry (and playing right field), he hit his first of 324 regular-season homers in the majors. It came against a great pitcher, Philadelphia's Steve Carlton. In 27 at-bats, Carter got 11 hits for a .407 average.

Carter wore uniform number 57 in that brief appearance. The following season, Carter was assigned the number 8, and considered it fate. "I was born on April 8. I got married on February 8. We moved into our first home in California on November 8. And look at all the great players who wore No. 8. Carl Yastrzemski. Willie Stargell. Yogi Berra. Bill Dickey. Joe Morgan. Cal Ripken, Jr. All Hall of Famers. So when I was assigned No. 8, I remembered all those things and figured it would be a lucky number for me, and it was," Carter wrote in 2008.[16] He wore it for the rest of his career.

Carter played with Caguas again in the winter of 1974-75. He hit .261 with 5 homers and 32 RBIs; of interest was that he alternated between catcher and third base. Though the Criollos wanted him behind the plate, Jim Fanning sought to get him action at third and in right field. The experiment at the hot corner was curious, since one of Montreal's other prize prospects was third baseman Larry Parrish.[17]

The Criollos made it to the league finals once more, and had they repeated as champions, the resulting trip to the Caribbean Series would have endangered Carter's wedding date. The Bayamón Vaqueros won in seven games, though—and so, on February 8, 1975, Carter married his high-school sweetheart, Sandra "Sandy" Lahm.[18] At the time, Sandy was training to be a flight attendant. The couple spent their honeymoon in the Expos' training camp at Daytona Beach![19] They later had three children: Christina (Christy), Kimberly (Kimmy), and Douglas James (D.J.).

In March 1975 sportswriter Brad Willson of the *Daytona Beach News-Journal* wrote a spring-training feature about Carter and his enormous promise. He quoted Karl Kuehl, who had managed Carter in the minors and in Instructional League, as well as Jean-Pierre Roy, the Montreal native and former Brooklyn Dodger who later went into broadcasting with the Expos. They both gave glowing assessments—but what mattered even more were the opinions of Fanning and manager Gene Mauch.

Fanning said that Carter's tools were as good as those of any player they had, but added, "He also has the intangibles not all the others possess—desire, determination, and hustle. He's a superkid." After much deliberation, Mauch said, "Gary Carter is a highly gifted, intelligent young man. In every league in which he's played, he's adjusted to the caliber of play. In Double A, Triple A and winter ball he had some difficulty at first. But he adjusted; that's where the intelligence comes in. I've seen players who can run better and who can hit better but I've never seen a better package. I've never seen someone who loves to play the game more."[20]

Carter finished second in the voting for National League Rookie of the Year in 1975 behind San Francisco Giants pitcher John "The Count" Montefusco. He was also named to his first of 11 All-Star teams. That year, however, he started 80 games in right field and only 56 behind the plate. Carter and Barry Foote continued to share the catching duties for Montreal in 1976, though Carter missed most of June and July after breaking his thumb in a "spectacularly ugly" outfield collision with Pepe Mangual.[21] It was his worst season in Montreal.

The Expos had a rising young star in right field: Ellis Valentine, who had power and a cannon arm. Carter seized the catching job from Foote in 1977. From then through 1984, he started 89 percent of the games that Montreal played and posted an OPS of .823 (simple averages of seasonal statistics are distorted by the strike of 1981). He won three Gold Gloves in succession from 1980 through 1982 and was runner-up to Mike Schmidt for the NL's Most Valuable Player award in 1980. His Wins Above Replacement (WAR) numbers were consistently high.

At the plate, Carter was an imposing figure. Players were not nearly as bulked up in that era, and Carter had one of the burlier upper bodies in the game then. He gave the impression of using his upper half and especially his forearms when he swung—it was a chopping horizontal stroke, like a lumberjack attacking a tree. He stood up almost straight at the plate, with just a slight knee bend; he held his bat high and nearly vertical.

As a receiver, Carter cited his own hard work and natural progression with experience, especially once he could focus on catching full-time. He also seconded the opinion that Norm Sherry, whom Expos manager Dick Williams had hired as catching coach after the 1977 season, had been a very helpful tutor.[22]

Carter remained one of the best in the game at stopping enemy runners. From 1974 through 1976, he threw out 49 percent of would-be base stealers (49 of 99). That ratio remained at 40 percent from 1977 through 1984 (481 of 1189). Larry Bowa, who stole more than 300 bases in the majors, offered extra insight in 2003. "This guy put a little fear in you when you were on first base even if you got a good jump. ... A lot of catchers were on ego trips, they didn't want you to steal, so they would call just fastballs. ... I respect Gary Carter because he would call breaking balls. He was not intimidated by any base stealer. He would call his game."[23]

The Expos became one of the better teams in the National League in the late 1970s, thanks to Carter, Parrish, Valentine, André Dawson, pitcher Steve Rogers, and other members of a homegrown core. In 1981 they made it to the postseason for the only time in the franchise's history. Carter was 8-for-19 with two homers as Montreal beat the Phillies in five games in the NL Division Series. He was 7-for-16 in the NL Championship series against the Dodgers, and drew a walk in the bottom of the ninth after Rick Monday's homer had put LA ahead. The Expos could not get the tying run in, though, and their chance for a pennant was gone. They fell back to third place in 1982, despite another strong year from their catcher.

Ahead of the 1983 season, *Sports Illustrated* put Carter on its cover, proclaiming him "The Best in the Business." In the accompanying feature article, Ron Fimrite covered Carter's game and personality in depth. Among the notable points, in summary:

Batting: It wasn't just about slugging for Carter—he had worked to cut down on his strikeouts. "I've learned to be more disciplined," he said. "If you want a sacrifice, I'll do it. If you need someone to go to right field on the hit-and-run, I'll do that."

Fielding: Aside from his strong arm and quick release, Carter excelled at all the other valuable catching skills—framing pitches, blocking the plate, and calling the game. Fimrite also observed, "Carter's nonstop commentary behind the plate has been known to drive even the most single-minded and level-headed hitters to distraction."

Character: Beyond the ceaseless boyish enthusiasm (which caused cynics to doubt his sincerity), the genial Carter could also get angry on the field. He once shattered Bill Buckner's bat and the two came to blows. Johnny Bench called Carter "a fiery, forceful, aggressive player."[24]

In February 1982, Carter had signed a seven-year contract for roughly $14 million plus incentives—then the sport's richest deal, or close to it. "He's a franchise-type player," said Expos president and general manager John McHale. "If you can ever justify paying that kind of money, he's one who earns it."[25] The Expos could not make it back to the playoffs, though, and owner Charles Bronfman was disappointed because he was also losing money on the club. In September 1983, Bronfman said, "Two months before Carter signed the contract, we were perfectly aware we were making a mistake. The next day and a month later we still knew we were wrong. I'll know it until my dying day. And I'm not just saying that because Carter had a bad year."[26]

Indeed, Carter had fallen off with the bat while battling assorted injuries. He bounced back in 1984, leading the NL in RBIs, but Montreal still finished fifth in the NL East. The club decided it was time to reload and get value for their star. (John McHale also said that Carter wanted out, though Carter denied that he had broached the idea.[27]) That December, after lengthy talks, the Expos traded the catcher to the Mets. They got four players in return: infielder Hubie Brooks, catcher Mike Fitzgerald, outfielder Herm Winningham, and pitcher Floyd Youmans. Brooks moved to shortstop and gave the Expos some solid (if not huge) years. Fitzgerald was a good defender, though not a big hitter, whose career was spoiled by a badly broken finger in 1986. Perhaps the biggest setback for Montreal was the talented Youmans, who developed arm and substance-abuse problems.

Meanwhile, Carter fit in immediately with the Mets. On Opening Day 1985, he hit a game-winning homer in the 10th inning at Shea Stadium, smacking former Met Neil Allen's 1-and-0 curveball over left fielder Lonnie Smith's head and the fence. The delighted Met fans roared and Carter got his first-ever curtain call. "I learned right away that New York was going to be different," Carter wrote later. "I was now playing for a special breed of fans. If hitting a walk-off home run in your first game with a new team is not special, I don't know what is."[28]

He set a career high with 32 homers that year while making less visible yet invaluable contributions. Manager Davey Johnson later called Carter "a one-man scouting system." Both Johnson and Ron Darling observed how important the catcher's detailed knowledge of hitters was to working with the talented but young staff.[29]

Carter was back on a home field with natural grass at New York's Shea Stadium, which helped ease his main physical concern. In a 2010 interview, he referred to "that god-awful Olympic Stadium [in Montreal] that tore our knees up, 'cause I've had 12 knee surgeries and both my knees replaced."[30] Torn cartilage was a concern in mid-1985, but he gutted it out with a brace and waited until the season was over before getting arthroscopic surgery.

The Mets could not overtake the St. Louis Cardinals in 1985, but ran away with the NL East in 1986. Carter had his last truly big year, remaining a near-constant in the lineup except for a two-week stretch on the sidelines in August. (He hurt his thumb diving for a ball during one of his occasional starts at first base.) He finished third in the MVP voting.

During the National League Championship Series, against the Houston Astros, Carter got just one hit in his first 21 at-bats. But in the bottom of the 12th inning of Game Five, with the count full, he hit a game-winning single. It was a grounder up the middle, past Astros reliever Charlie Kerfeld (who, according to some viewers, had taunted Carter by showing him the ball after making a behind-the-back play in Game Three). Carter said after the game, "I kept telling myself, 'I'm going to come through here.' I knew it was just a matter of time." At that point—he had no idea of the drama to come—he also said, "It's at the top of all the games I've ever played in."[31]

After the Mets finally overcame the Astros—the concluding Game Six was an excruciating 16-inning battle—they faced the Boston Red Sox in the World Series. Carter was 8-for-29 (.276) with 9 RBIs. He cracked two homers in Game Four at Fenway Park as the Mets tied the Series. Yet his most crucial hit came three days later, in Game Six. Carter's single in the bottom of the 10th sparked the most improbable two-out, three-run rally that snatched the championship away from Boston.

In 2012 teammate Bob Ojeda said, "If you watch the video with Gary walking to the plate, you see that sense of determination ... in his step, in his swing. ... (H)e was not going to make that out. You can see [it] in his face."[32] Carter told reporters exactly the same thing after the game. According to first-base coach Bill Robinson, when Carter reached base, he let loose a rare expletive –"No f***ing way"—to intensify the statement.[33] (Carter is credited with coining the euphemism "f-bomb" in 1988.[34]) It's also noteworthy that he had donned his catcher's gear, ready to play another extra inning, when the winning run scored on the ball that got by Bill Buckner.

In April 1987 Carter published the first of his three books, *A Dream Season*. That year, the physical pounding of his position became harder to endure. Ahead of the 1988 season, the *Palm Beach Sun-Sentinel* wrote, "It took six cortisone shots [for Carter] to get through last season—to sustain a troublesome ankle, knee, shoulder, back and elbow. No wonder his offensive production slipped (.235, 20 HR, 83 RBIs)." Carter said, "I was hurting every day last year. I should have been put on the disabled list several times, but they weren't disabling injuries. In my early- to mid-20s, a lot of the type of injuries I have today were easier to shake off. You learn to appreciate the good days in which you feel like a human being."[35]

That spring, Davey Johnson also made Carter a co-captain of the Mets. In 2012 Johnson said, "I had a captain of the team—Keith Hernandez, he ran the infield—before Gary got there, but after seeing what he did, he was so special, I made him a co-captain. It was an honor he deserved."[36] The dropoff continued, however: even though Carter still started 116 games behind the plate, his basic batting line fell off to .242-11-46. His caught-stealing percentage also hit a career low of 19 percent. He was 6-for-27 in his final postseason activity, as the Mets lost the NLCS to the Los Angeles Dodgers.

The decline was even more severe in 1989—Carter played in a career-low 50 games after knee problems forced another arthroscopy, costing him nearly three months from early May through late July. He hit just .183-2-15 in 153 plate appearances. The Mets released him (and Hernandez) after the season. In typical form, Carter said, "I know I can still play this game. I know there will be an opportunity out there."[37]

In January 1990 Carter signed with the San Francisco Giants. He platooned with another veteran, Terry Kennedy, who had been with the Giants during their pennant-winning season in 1989. Nonetheless, he still had the desire to play every day and didn't want to hang on if he wasn't contributing.[38] Indeed, he made a respectable comeback (.254-9-27 in 92 games).

Even so, Carter became a free agent again, and did not sign with another team until March 1991. This time it was the Dodgers, the team he had followed as a boy. He made good on a nonroster invitation from manager Tommy Lasorda and backed up Mike Scioscia. When Scioscia was sidelined by a broken hand, Carter played every game for two straight weeks, including both ends of a doubleheader against the Braves. He did another creditable job (.246-6-26, while throwing out 32 percent of basestealers).

Carter did not file for free agency, and the Dodgers placed him on waivers. As a result, he returned to Montreal in 1992 for his final big-league season. He said it was something he'd always had in the back of his mind.[39] At age 38, his teammates still called him "The Kid." As it developed, he played more than any other catcher for the Expos that year, and though he didn't hit much (.218-5-29 in 95 games), he still helped the team rebound from sixth place to second in the NL East. Carter went over the 2,000 mark in games caught and the 1,200 mark in RBIs in 1992, both milestones he wanted to achieve.

Carter's career ended on an upbeat note. At Olympic Stadium on September 27, 1992, he drove in the game's only run with a double. As he told it in 2004, "I had announced my retirement, and [manager] Felipe Alou said, 'You will catch that game.' In the seventh inning, in my last at-bat, I got the opportunity. Felipe Alou was going to pull me out of the game. He said, 'Go on up there. Whatever happens, happens, but this is your last at-bat.' It turned out to be a game-winner in front of that fan appreciation crowd. Nice way to finish."[40]

After retirement, Carter became a color commentator on television for the Florida Marlins. He held that job for four years, but his contract was not renewed after the 1996 season.[41] Shortly thereafter, he returned once more to the Expos, working in their TV broadcast booth from 1997 through 1999. His main focus in 2000 was golf with the Celebrity Players Tour. Carter felt a desire to get back on the field, though—as early as 1998, he had expressed managerial ambitions.[42] In 2001 and 2002, he was a part-time roving catching instructor in the Mets minor-league system.[43] He took on that role full-time in 2003 and became minor-league catching coordinator in 2004.[44]

Off the field, Carter's strong character manifested itself again in 1995, when the Internal Revenue Service began investigating active and retired ballplayers for failing to report income earned from appearances and autograph signings at baseball card shows. Under the microscope were Met stars Darryl Strawberry, Lenny Dykstra, Hernandez, Darling, and Carter. But when the IRS subpoenaed Carter to appear before a grand jury, they found that he was as honest about his taxes as everything else in his life. Carter spent $25,000 in accountants' fees to produce his invoices and receipts. When he left the witness stand and the courtroom, he said, "There was nothing the US Attorney's office was ever going to be able to question me about."[45] Carter was swiftly dropped from the probe.

On another front, the Gary Carter Foundation began operations in 2000. Its mission, through its own donations and funds raised externally, is to better the physical, mental, and spiritual well-being of children in addition to supporting faith-based initiatives. Among the endeavors it supports is the Autism Project of Palm Beach County, Florida. The Carter family made its home there for many years.

Carter was elected to the Hall of Fame in 2003, his sixth year of eligibility. The vagaries of the process are well known, but his pattern was still unusual. In his case, "first-ballot" bias may have reflected his lack of milestone career numbers, yet Carter suffered an odd dip in his second year before gaining momentum.[46] The voting disparities between him and two other top catchers of his day—Carlton Fisk and Lance Parrish—were also peculiar.[47]

Carter's Hall of Fame plaque shows him in an Expos cap. He suggested that "it would be nice to have a split hat" that also featured the Mets, but the decision rested with the Hall, and he abided by it.[48] During his induction speech, Carter grew very emotional as he honored his parents' memory—Jim Carter had died that January, less than a month after his son was voted in—and thanked his brother, Gordy.[49]

In 2004 the press bandied Carter's name about as a future manager of the Mets after some grooming in the minors.[50] He drew some flak for lobbying for the job with the big club that September, while Art Howe was still the incumbent.[51] Carter got his first opportunity as a skipper in 2005 and led their rookie-ball club in the Gulf Coast League to a 37-16 record. He then had another winning season with the St. Lucie Mets of the Florida State League (high Class A). In both 2005 and 2006, Carter was named Manager of the Year in his league. The Mets offered him a job with their Double-A affiliate, Binghamton, for the 2007 season. He turned down that promotion, however, citing the rigors of the long Eastern League bus rides.[52]

Carter was also disappointed not to have landed a coaching job with the Mets' major-league squad—he wanted to bring his experience and inspiration. He hinted that it might have helped as the club folded down the stretch in 2007.[53] As it developed, Carter took all of 2007 off. In 2008, though, he returned to managing with the Orange County Flyers (based in Fullerton) of the Golden Baseball League. That March Carter again voiced his desire to manage the Mets, while Willie Randolph still held the job.[54] He stayed in Orange County and again was named Manager of the Year.

For the 2009 season, Carter was skipper of another independent team, the Long Island Ducks of the Atlantic League. After his year with the Ducks, he became head baseball coach at Palm Beach Atlantic University in Florida. That was near his home in Palm Beach Gardens. Carter joined his daughter, Kimmy, who had been a star catcher in softball at Florida State University from 1999 through 2002. She was named head softball coach at the university in 2007.

In May 2011, Carter began to experience headaches and forgetfulness. He was diagnosed with glioblastoma, an aggressive form of brain cancer. His case was inoperable, but he fought it with a course of radiation and chemotherapy, displaying the same positive outlook and competitive fire as always. Kimmy chronicled the grueling battle in an extensive journal on the website CaringBridge.org. The account was filled with hope and faith, which continued even after a magnetic resonance imaging scan showed the presence of several new spots on Carter's brain in January 2012.

Carter's assistants had taken over his coaching duties at Palm Beach Atlantic, but he visited his team on February 2, 2012, when it opened its season in Jupiter, Florida, against Lynn University. It was his last public appearance—two weeks later, he died in hospice care. He was survived by his wife, three children, and three grandchildren.

The Expos retired Carter's uniform No. 8 in 1993, and it retains that status with the Washington Nationals (which the Expos became after the 2004 season). There have been frequent calls for the Mets to do likewise. In May 2013 the city of Montreal renamed a section of a street—adjacent to Jarry Park—Rue Gary-Carter. The following month, it inaugurated Gary Carter Stadium in Ahuntsic Park. A crowd of old Expos diehards greeted Gary's widow, Sandy, and daughter, Christy, who emphasized how much Montreal meant to the Carter family.

Gary Carter captured essential parts of himself in the titles of his two other books, *The Gamer* (1993) and *Still a Kid at Heart* (2008). Yet to round out the picture, one may choose from among the many tributes this man received from his teammates after his passing. Perhaps the most fitting came from Darryl Strawberry: "I wish I could have lived my life like Gary Carter. … He was a true man."

Thanks to Christy Carter Kearce for her input. Continued thanks to David H. Lippman for his input during peer review.

SOURCES

In addition to the sources in the notes, the author relied on:

garycarter.org

NOTES

1 Tim Kurkjian, "This 'Kid' had a passion for the game," ESPN.com, February 16, 2012.

2 Laurence Arnold, "Gary Carter, 'Kid' Who Helped Mets Win 1986 World Series Title, Dies at 57," Bloomberg.com, February 17, 2012.

3 Jim Murray, "He's Hunkered Down and Worthy of Being the MVP," *Los Angeles Times*, September 12, 1985.

4 Barry M. Bloom, "Carter dedicates speech to parents," MLB.com, July 27, 2003. Murray, "He's Hunkered Down and Worthy of Being the MVP."

5 Ron Fimrite, "His Enthusiasm Is Catching," *Sports Illustrated*, April 4, 1983. Ian MacDonald, "Gary Carter finding his niche," *Montreal Gazette*, October 7, 1977: 17.

6 Ian MacDonald, "Carter Winning Universal Acclaim for Canadian Progress Program," *The Sporting News*, June 9, 1979: 3.

7 Andy O'Brien, "The Bubble Gum Kid," *Windsor* (Ontario) *Star*, May 3, 1975.

8 "Montreal's 'The Kid' tabbed baseball's best," Associated Press, May 9, 1981. Richard Goldstein, "Gary Carter, Star Catcher Who Helped Mets to Series Title, Dies at 57," *New York Times*, February 16, 2012.

9 Jeff Pearlman, *The Bad Guys Won* (New York: HarperCollins Publishers, 2004), 89, 91.

10 Ira Berkow, "Two Different Stars Find Same Reward," *New York Times*, July 28, 2003.

11 Tim Burke, "'Boc' gets what he hoped for with trade to San Francisco," *Montreal Gazette*, March 28, 1974: 35.

12 Email from Christy Carter Kearce to Rory Costello, October 15, 2013.

13 MacDonald, "Gary Carter finding his niche."

14 Thomas E. Van Hyning, *Puerto Rico's Winter League* (Jefferson, North Carolina: McFarland & Co., 1995), 133.

15 Héctor Barea, "Gary Carter," *El Nuevo Periódico* (Caguas, Puerto Rico), February 29, 2012.

16 Gary Carter and Phil Pepe, *Still a Kid at Heart* (Chicago: Triumph Books, 2008), 22.

17 Bob Dunn, "Expos Place Carter, Parrish Under Lock and Key," *The Sporting News*, November 30, 1974. Bob Dunn, Expos Searching for Spot to Play Prospect Carter," *The Sporting News*, March 15, 1975: 47.

18 Billy Staples and Rich Herschlag, *Before the Glory* (Deerfield Beach, Florida: Health Communications, Inc., 2007), 164.

19 O'Brien, "The Bubble Gum Kid."

20 Brad Willson, "Press Box," *Daytona Beach News-Journal*, March 23, 1975: 1B, 7B.

21 Bob Dunn, "Docs Work Overtime Repairing Expo Cripples," *The Sporting News*, June 26, 1976: 25. Mangual suffered a concussion.

22 MacDonald, "Carter Winning Universal Acclaim for Canadian Progress Program."

23 Tim Kurkjian, "Congrats to The Kid," *ESPN The Magazine*, January 7, 2003.

24 Fimrite, "His Enthusiasm Is Catching."

25 Ibid.

26 "Expos' Chairman Claims Club's Signing of Carter a Mistake," United Press International, September 27, 1983.

27 Terry Scott, "Carter cleans out his Expos locker, sheds a few goodbye tears," *Ottawa Citizen*, December 20, 1984.

28 Carter and Pepe, *Still a Kid at Heart*, 39.

29 Arnold, "Gary Carter, 'Kid' Who Helped Mets Win 1986 World Series Title, Dies at 57." Kurkjian, "This 'Kid' had a passion for the game."

30 Patrick Reddington, "Hall of Fame Catcher Gary Carter on the Washington Nationals, Montreal Expos and Tim Raines," federalbaseball.com, August 11, 2010.

31 Dave Anderson, "'I'm Not an .050 Hitter,'" *New York Times*, October 15, 1986.

32 Steven Marcus, "Gary Carter sparked Game 6 rally in 1986," *Newsday*, February 16, 2012.

33 Kurkjian, "This 'Kid' had a passion for the game."

34 *Merriam-Webster's Collegiate Dictionary* (2012 edition) gave this article as the earliest known usage: Steve Marcus, "Carter Thrives as Pinch-Hitter," *Newsday*, August 11, 1988. See also David Haglund, "Did Gary Carter Invent the 'F-Bomb'?," slate.com, August 14, 2012.

35 Craig Davis, "Men Behind the Masks," *Palm Beach Sun-Sentinel*, March 3, 1988.

36 Kurkjian, "This 'Kid' had a passion for the game."

37 Ronald Blum, "Carter, Hernandez Released by Mets," Associated Press, October 4, 1989.

38 Erik K. Lief, "Gary Carter Adjusts to New Role," United Press International, May 12, 1990.

39 Joe Gromelski, "For Gary Carter, there's no place like Montreal," *Lewiston* (Maine) *Sun-Journal*, May 11, 1992, 25.

40 Steve Rosenbloom, "Gary Carter: Our guy catches up to 'The Kid,'" *Chicago Tribune*, August 31, 2004: Sports-8.

41 Scott Tolley, "Marlins Let Randolph, Carter Go," *Palm Beach Post*, October 2, 1996.

42 "Carter has managerial ambitions," *Kitchener* (Ontario) *Record*, March 21, 1998: E4.

43 "Kid Glad to Be back," *New York Daily News*, March 3, 2001.

44 "Carter back as roving minor league catching instructor," MLB.com, December 13, 2002. "Gary Carter to manage St. Lucie Mets," MLB.com, January 9, 2006.

45 Bob Klapisch, *High and Tight* (New York: Villard Books, 1996), 140-141.

46 Carter's vote percentage started with 42 percent in 1998, dipped to 33 percent, and was still just 49 percent in 2000. He then gained momentum, rising to 65 percent and 73 percent before finally breaking through with 78 percent.

47 One voter, Jack O'Connell of the *Hartford Courant*, wrote about this—"Fisk, Carter: Why Not Kid in Hall?"—on December 29, 1999.

48 Kevin T. Czerwinski, "Kid catches Cooperstown spotlight," MLB.com, January 16, 2003. As of 2013, André Dawson is the only other member of the Hall whose plaque shows an Expos cap (though he would have preferred to show the Chicago Cubs). Tim Raines was the only other reasonable possibility, though he fell short again in the 2015 voting, at 55 percent.

49 Bloom, "Carter dedicates speech to parents."

50 Kevin Kernan, "Kid Stays in the Picture—Carter Could Be Next Met Manager," *New York Post*, July 4, 2004.

51 Michael Morrissey, "The Kid Makes His Pitch," *New York Post*, September 11, 2004.

52 Eric Pfahler, "Gary Carter currently has no job offer from Mets organization," TCPalm.com, December 14, 2006.

53 Adam Rubin and Nicholas Hirshon, "Gary Carter thinks he was missing piece for Mets in 2007 collapse," *New York Daily News*, February 20, 2008.

54 Adam Rubin, "Gary Carter would love to take Shea reins as Mets manager," *New York Daily News*, May 23, 2008.

TIMOTHY CORCORAN

By Leslie Heaphy

TIM CORCORAN SHOWED PROMISE WITH THE bat but never seemed to be in the right place to catch on as a regular, full-time player. His hitting never seemed to be quite enough to convince his managers that he could handle playing day-to-day. Corcoran spent parts of the first month and a half of the 1986 season as a reserve first baseman with the 1986 New York Mets, appearing in six games before being released on June 9 so he was not a part of the championship team later that season. Corcoran came to bat seven times for the Mets and scored one run on two walks. The Mets needed a lefty bat but more importantly they needed a backup in case Keith Hernandez received a suspension due to a pending drug case. Once the Mets realized Hernandez was in the clear they released Corcoran.

Born Timothy Michael Corcoran on March 19, 1953, in Glendale, California, he grew up playing sports. He attended both Mount San Antonio College in Walnut, California, and California State University Los Angeles before being signed as an amateur free agent by Detroit in 1974. Corcoran is one of 18 players from Mount San Antonio who have played in the major leagues (132 drafted). He played for Tigers' Rookie League and Class A teams in his first year and worked his way up, playing at Double-A Montgomery in 1975 and 1976 and then 39 games for Triple-A Evansville in 1977 (hit .346) before earning a promotion to the major leagues in mid-May after a spring in which he hit .378. In an exhibition game against the Pirates, Corcoran helped the Tigers by hitting a home run in the bottom of the 13th inning for a 5-4 win. He followed that with a two-run homer in the 11th inning of a 3-1 win over the Phillies. Manager Ralph Houk stated, "The kid is opening a few eyes, isn't he? He's hot right now."[1]

Corcoran played in 55 games with the Tigers in 1977, playing every outfield position and even as the DH in a couple of games. He hit .282 with 29 hits in 103 at-bats. His first big-league hit was a two-run homer in a 7-4 win over the Chicago White Sox on May 20. Corcoran's play helped earn him a spot on the roster in 1978, when he played in 109 games in the outfield, 116 games overall, and batted .265. (When not on the field, he served double duty as the Tigers' bullpen catcher.) Corcoran's average was respectable but he hit only one home run in 363 plate appearances. He was a contact hitter with a good eye at the plate but was not a large man (5-feet-11, 175 pounds) and never generated the power that most teams demanded from their first basemen and corner outfielders. In 1979 Corcoran split his time between the Tigers and their Triple-A affiliate in Evansville and in 1980 played another 84 games with the Tigers, enjoying one of the most productive seasons of his major-league career. Performing mostly as a pinch-hitter and as a platoon first baseman against right-handed starters, Corcoran

batted .288 with a .379 on-base percentage in 177 plate appearances.

For three winters starting in 1977, Corcoran played in Venezuela for Leones del Caracas and Tigres de Aragua. He played in a total of 104 games, hitting .341 while knocking in 50 runs and scoring 54.

Despite that solid performance, Corcoran could not find a regular spot in Detroit—he had become typecast as a Triple-A player. He spent most of the 1981 season at Evansville, where he hit .298 with a .400 OBP before the Tigers traded him to the Minnesota Twins late in the year. On his ups and downs with Detroit, Corcoran explained, "I got 300 at-bats that year, but I was platooned in right field. It was the first time in Organized Ball that I'd ever been platooned, and I didn't know how to handle it. It was a learning experience. Up and Down." He appeared in 22 games with the Twins that September, batting just .176, and drew his release near the end of spring training in 1982.

The 29-year-old Corcoran signed with Philadelphia, where he spent the next two seasons in the minors, posting his usual solid averages and on-base percentages, but minimal power. Corcoran hit .289 for last-place Oklahoma City in 1982. In 1983 he played for the Phillies' Triple-A affiliate in Portland and hit .311 to help his club win the Pacific Coast League crown. His manager, John Felske, said, "If you look at him play once or twice, he might not do anything to excite you. But you watch him every day, and you find out that though he doesn't have a great arm, he always throws accurately and quickly while also being an excellent defensive first baseman."[2] Corcoran's performance earned him a brief call-up when the rosters expanded in September, and he appeared in three games for the pennant-winning Phillies.

As the aging Phillies dipped to .500 in 1984, Corcoran spent the entire season in the major leagues and turned in a career year. Manager Paul Owens used him almost exclusively as a pinch-hitter through mid-June and he responded with an average of .409. When starting first baseman Len Matuszek went down with a broken finger, Corcoran finally received a chance to play every day. From June 10 until Matuszek returned to the starting lineup on July 27, Corcoran started 30 games and remained hot, posting a slash line of .366/.459/.554 with 5 home runs. He returned to his bench role in August and received a cluster of additional starts in September, finishing the year with an average of .341 to go with an OBP of .440. When asked about how the Tigers could have let him go Corcoran's attitude was one of practicality. He stated, "No complaints. Detroit wanted a guy who could play every day in right field. They'd been trying to fill that position for a long time, and Kirk Gibson is doing the job pretty well now. But at that time, Gibson was in center, and they wanted a right fielder with power, whereas I can just hit a homer every now and then."[3] Corcoran also said the Tigers never lied to him about the role they wanted him to play as a platoon player. When they traded him to the Twins, he thought his chances would be better, but he was hurt when he arrived and never really got a good chance to show what he could do.

When the Twins released him, Corcoran joined the Phillies because he had played in the Pacific Coast League before. His real break came with Portland and Corcoran credited manager John Felske for his return to the big leagues. "Thank God for John Felske," he said. "I think he had a lot to do with me making the big club this year. He gave me a chance to play every day in Portland and he helped me this year in spring training. He gave me confidence. When I made the club, I knew exactly what my role was: I'd be a pinch hitter and fill in if somebody got hurt. Unfortunately, Lenny (Matuszek) got hurt, but I'm glad I was able to do the job when Paul (Owens) called on me."[4]

The magic wore off in 1985, though, as Corcoran's average tumbled to .217. Philadelphia cut him loose in December, and he signed a free-agent contract with the Mets in March 1986, near the start of their championship season. Corcoran was surprised by the release, saying, "'It was a heck of a Christmas present. They told me they needed a roster spot. And I'd just gone out and bought a new truck and a house. It was a shock."[5]

The Mets had high hopes for Corcoran when they signed him because of his versatility. New York newspapers described him as a "crisp fielder and line-drive hitter with some long-ball power."[6] Due to his earlier catching duties, Corcoran told the Mets when he arrived that he had a catcher's mitt if they needed him behind the plate. After he made a couple of appearances in April, New York assigned him to its Triple-A Tidewater club, and recalled him in June. His six games in 1986 were the last he played in the majors. He drew his release on June 9. He played in parts of the 1987 and '88 seasons with Philadelphia's Triple-A affiliate, the Maine Guides, before he called it quits at age 35. For Corcoran it always seemed he was in the wrong place at the wrong time, being traded to make room for younger players or filling in until a stronger player came back from injuries. Then there was no permanent place for him on any roster, though he played parts of nine seasons in the majors.

In 2000 the Anaheim Angels named Corcoran a scout. Since 2002 he has worked as a coach for the Angels Elite program, whose goal is to give the top 30 incoming high-school seniors in Southern California a chance to perform each summer for colleges, universities and the Angels. The coaches work one-on-one with the players, and the work yields results. Since the program began, 180 graduates of the Angels Elite squad have been drafted, including pitcher/shortstop Tyler Chatwood, a second-round pick for the Angels in 2008, who made his big-league debut for the club in 2011.[7]

Tim and his wife, Tina, have two children, Travis and Tara. Tara played soccer and volleyball in high school and went on to play soccer for Long Beach State.

NOTES

1 "Tim Corcoran Has Night to Celebrate on St. Pat's Day," *Gettysburg* (Pennsylvania) *Times*, March 17, 1977.

2 Jack Lang, "Corcoran Finally Getting His Chance," in Player File, National Baseball Hall of Fame, Cooperstown, New York.

3 Ted Meixell, "Tim Corcoran 'Just Happy to Be on a Club with Chance to Win A Division' Baseball," articles.mcall.com/1984-08-02/sports/2433686_1_tigers-and-twins-minor-tim-corcoran.

4 Ibid.

5 "Mets' Handyman Reports Equipped," *New York Times*, March 2, 1986.

6 Joseph Durso, "Mets Get Corcoran, a Versatile Player," *New York Times*, February 27, 1986.

7 angelselitebaseball.com/; Lyle Spencer, "Waiting Is the Hardest Part for Halos," MLB.com, June 5, 2008.

All statistics come from baseball-reference.com/players/c/corcoti01.shtml. and purapelota.com/lvbp/mostrar.php?id=corctimo001.

RON DARLING

By Audrey Apfel

IF YOU WERE LUCKY ENOUGH TO BRING RON Darling to a party, how would you introduce him? Especially if the party was outside the New York City area, it's possible you would have to do just that. While he has numerous accomplishments on and off the baseball field, he hasn't grabbed the headlines (for all sorts of reasons good and bad) like other members of the 1986 Mets, Dwight Gooden, Daryl Strawberry, etc. So, what would you say? All-Star? Gold Glove recipient? World Series ring holder? Ivy League All American with the longest no-hitter in NCAA history? Emmy award winner? All would be true and might leave your friends wondering why they wouldn't have known all of this before.

At every point along the way, there seemed to be just a few things burning brighter in Ron Darling's vicinity, something that stole some of the spotlight. Perhaps in '86 (and after) it was all the attention paid to the other members of that famous (or sometimes infamous) team. Or that though he started the seventh game in the '86 World Series, more people remember the Bill Buckner blunder in Game Six. Or that the longest college no-hitter actually ended up in a loss for the Yale Bulldogs, Darling's team. Or perhaps it is just that there is little in the way of "negative press" that might have made even bigger headlines.

In total though, it all adds up to the solid, successful multifaceted career of someone who left a positive mark wherever he went. His life before and after baseball has had highs and lows but his achievement continued with a level of consistency most pitchers would love when standing on the mound. The best introduction might just be, "This is Ron Darling. Have a chat with him. He's smart, accomplished, and has some great stories to tell."

Ronald Maurice Darling Jr. was born on August 19, 1960, in Honolulu but grew up in Red Sox country—Millbury, Massachusetts. His mother was Hawaiian-Chinese, while his father was French Canadian, leading Darling to be fluent in Chinese and French as well as his native English.[1] When asked what the best 10 years of his life were, he said, "Right now I think from 10 to 20 were my favorite years. I had an idyllic family life, great parents, three younger brothers who adored me, thought I was the cat's meow. Went to an amazing high school. Went to Yale between those years. Played in the Cape Cod League, which was the last time I had fun. Now we use that term loosely. The last time I had fun playing the sport, you know, because it was before I was a professional. Yeah, 10 to 20 was amazing, because it got real serious after that."[2]

While Darling called his stretch in the Cape Cod League the last time he had fun in baseball, the league is serious business for major-league prospects. Part of the fun may have been due to the many roles he got

to play. His major-league career as a starting pitcher overshadows the versatility he displayed throughout his years in the Cape Cod League. As an example, in the league's all-star game at Yankee Stadium, he played left field but jumped in to pitch and retire the final two batters in a one-run game. It is also worth mentioning that he came close to hitting for the cycle in this game, missing only a triple.[3] In 2002 Darling was inducted into the Cape Cod Baseball League Hall of Fame along with 11 others, including Nomar Garciaparra, Jason Varitek, and Buck Showalter. At the time, he was considered "one of the best-all around players in Cape league history." His league statistics include a .336 batting average, six home runs, and a 4-3 pitching record.[4]

Darling attended Yale University from 1979 to 1981, leaving after his junior year for professional baseball. He majored in French and Southeast Asian history. Upon entering Yale, his plan was to play both football and baseball. Once there, though, he focused on baseball, not for lack of love of the sport. A Yale sports department publication quoted him as saying, "If there were five or six regrets in my life, one is that I didn't continue to play football at Yale. I would've loved to play for Carm [referring to legendary Yale football coach Carmen Cozza].[5]

At Yale Darling was a strong hitter (usually hitting second or third in the lineup) and a top pitcher. He was the Yale pitcher on the mound for an NCAA regional tournament game against St. John's in 1981, called by some the "greatest college baseball game ever played." Darling was up against opposing pitcher Frank Viola, who later became a fellow Met and a very good friend. For 12 innings the two teams fought until St. John's eked out a 1-0 victory. In a powerful display of pitching prowess, Darling pitched a no-hitter for 11 of those innings and struck out 16. The game ended on a double steal by St. John's.[6]

In 1981, after his junior year at Yale, Darling was drafted by the Texas Rangers in the first round of the amateur draft. That year he pitched for the Rangers' Double-A affiliate, the Tulsa Drillers of the Texas League, where he ended with a 4-2 record as a starting pitcher. Before the 1982 season he was traded to the Mets along with pitcher Walt Terrell for infielder-outfielder Lee Mazzilli, and pitched in 1982 and '83 for the Tidewater Tides. Called up to the Mets in September 1983, he made his major-league debut on September 6, starting and losing to the Philadelphia Phillies, 2-0. Darling gave up one run in 6⅓ innings with six strikeouts and one walk. He started five games for the Mets in September, ending up with a 1-3 record and a 2.80 ERA.

In 1984 Darling won a spot in the starting rotation, but had a mediocre start to the season. In April and May he had a 3-3 record and a 4.61 ERA. But in June and July he won seven straight and finished the season 12-9 and with a 3.81 ERA. He finished fifth in the voting for the Rookie of the Year Award; teammate Dwight Gooden was the winner.

In 1985 Darling shaved almost a run off his earned-run average (2.90) and had a 16-6 record despite giving up a league-leading 114 walks. He was the number-two starter behind Gooden and made the All-Star team that year. He made his first major-league relief appearance in a celebrated 19-inning game against the Atlanta Braves, which the Mets won 16-13. Although the Mets (98-64) did not make the postseason, the strong season and Darling's continuing improvement left them positioned well for the future.

The next year the Mets won the World Series over the Boston Red Sox with Darling as a key contributor. After posting a 15-6 record and a 2.81 ERA, he started World Series Games One, Four, and Seven, losing Game One, winning Game Four, and getting a no-decision in Game Seven. He posted a 1.53 ERA.

The years after the 1986 World Series were tough ones for the Mets and for Darling, described as "the dynasty that never happened." While the team remained competitive for a few more years, the decline was clear. Darling continued to pitch solidly in 1987 with a 12-8 record but a 4.29 ERA. His highest career win total came in 1988 when he recorded a 17-9 record with a 3.25 ERA in 240 innings, another career high.

Darling followed up in 1989 with a .500 record (14-14) and 3.52 ERA.

The 1990 season saw the Mets in transition, coming off a lackluster 1989 and management uncertainty. Darling found himself split between starting and a new role as a relief pitcher. The bullpen did not serve him well, and 1990 went down as Darling's first losing season (7-9) with a bloated 4.50 ERA.

In 1991 Darling was again a starting pitcher; in fact, he started games for three teams. On July 15 he was traded along with pitcher Mike Thomas to the Montreal Expos for pitcher Tim Burke. Two weeks later, at the trading deadline, the Expos sent him to the Oakland Athletics for minor-league for pitchers Matt Grott and Russ Cormier. With all the moving, Darling was 5-8 in the NL and 3-7 in the American league.

Darling had some success as a starter in Oakland, particularly in 1992, going 15-10. With his best stuff behind him, he made the adjustments that all major-league pitchers with long careers need to make. The A's led the AL West Division that season. (Darling lost his only start in the ALCS as the Athletics fell to Toronto.)

Darling found the A's welcoming and family-friendly.[7] The good times in Oakland may have just added to the somewhat disheartening way that his playing career ended. On August 19, 1995, which also happened to be his 35th birthday, he was released; he chose to be released rather than be placed on the disabled list, which would have allowed him to remain with the team for the rest of the season. (He later admitted that he wasn't prepared for the ending when it finally came, still believing he could fight his way back to a semblance of his prior performance. However that was not to be.[8])

Darling won 136 major-league games and lost 116. His career ERA was 3.87. His performance on the mound could never be called flawless. There were times when he struggled with control (leading the National League in walks in 1985 was an example) but his "stuff" could be counted on to keep enough batters from putting together enough hits that runs would generally still be hard to come by. He also contributed through effective fielding, which earned him a Gold Glove in 1989. Darling was always a game-smart pitcher who was always ready to take the ball, and said he as proud of having a career that never included a trip to the disabled list.

For Darling, the 1986 Mets season and World Series win were important moments, but were just one stop in his multifaceted career of highs, lows, and reinvention. "I'm not always great at things, but I'm smart," he told the *New York Daily News*.[9]

His post-baseball life has been active and never too far from the sport. He moved into broadcasting and was involved with various sportscasts and shows for several years. In 2005 Darling was the color commentator for the first Washington Nationals season. In 2006 he joined Gary Cohen and Keith Hernandez in the broadcast booth for Mets games on the SNY network, and has won an Emmy award. As of 2015 he continued in the role of commentator/analyst.

In between the baseball, there was family, philanthropy, and writing a book. Darling and Antoinette Reilly, a model, were married in January 1986. They had two sons, Jordan and Tyler. They later divorced and in 2004 Darling married Joanna Last, a TV makeup artist.

In 2009 he founded the Ron Darling Foundation to help fund diabetes research (which his son Jordan contracted as an 11-year-old). The foundation later expanded its work to include collaborating with and donating to several organizations including Habitat for Humanity, the NYPD Foundation and Hurricane Sandy Relief.[10]

In 2009 Darling published a book, *The Complete Game: Reflections on Baseball and the Art of Pitching*, in which he gave a detailed view of what is going on inside the head of a major-league pitcher—inning by inning, pitch by pitch. He combined moments from his own games with the Mets and the Athletics as well as key innings he witnessed as a broadcaster.

With his current days full as a New York Mets broadcaster, active philanthropist, father, and husband it seems his spectacular baseball career is certainly not Ron Darling's whole story, but just an important chapter among many.

SOURCES

In addition to the sources cited in the Notes, the author consulted the following:

Darling, Ron. *The Complete Game: Reflections on Baseball and the Art of Pitching* (New York: Random House, 2009).

newyork.mets.mlb.com/team/broadcasters.jsp?c_id=nym.

"The Web of the Game," *The New Yorker*, July 20, 1981.

All stats come from: baseball-reference.com.

NOTES

1 diabetesresearch.org/Ron-Darling-bio.

2 blogs.villagevoice.com/runninscared/2010/06/ron_darling_on.php?page=2.

3 capecodbaseball.org/about/welcome/#sthash.DPgtxjXY.dpuf.

4 capecodbaseball.org/news/league/?article_id=241.

5 yalebulldogs.com/sports/m-basebl/2014-15/releases/20150227l81ndr).

6 nytimes.com/2012/06/09/sports/baseball/darling-viola-pitchers-duel-lives-on-in-st-johns-baseball-lore.html?_r=1.

7 nytimes.com/1992/10/10/sports/sports-of-the-times-darling-s-chess-comeback.html).

8 deadspin.com/5912078/how-a-career-ends-ron-darling-celebrated-his-35th-birthday-by-getting-cut-and-being-left-alone-at-home.

9 nydailynews.com/blogs/bitterbill/ron-darling-talks-mets-sny-blog-entry-1.2168993.

10 ondarlingfoundation.org/.

LENNY DYKSTRA

by Andy Sturgill

"(For Dykstra) no dare was too bold, no drink too strong, no car too fast, no poker hand too big."

— Jeff Pearlman, author of *The Bad Guys Won!*[1]

"The Dude would be an experience even if it had nothing to do with baseball. You could meet the Dude away from the field and come away dazed and confused as to what had just happened."

— Phillies teammate Terry Mulholland[2]

"I wouldn't call the Dude over to help me put a jigsaw puzzle together, but the guy was born to play baseball."

— Phillies teammate Mitch Williams[3]

THE HOUSTON ASTROS LED GAME THREE OF the 1986 National League Championship Series, 5-4, over the Mets with a runner on and one out in the bottom of the ninth inning. The Mets' skinny, 160-pound center fielder Lenny Dykstra stepped up to the plate and cranked Houston closer Dave Smith's 0-and-1 fastball over the wall in right field to give the Mets an improbable 6-5 victory. Dykstra leapt onto home plate amidst a sea of ecstatic teammates.

Seven years later, the Philadelphia Phillies and Atlanta Braves were knotted at 3-3 in Game Five of the 1993 NLCS. In the top of the 10th inning, Philadelphia's bulky, muscular, 200-pound center fielder Lenny Dykstra stepped to the plate and crushed Atlanta closer Mark Wohlers' 3-and-2 pitch over the wall in right center to give the Phillies a 4-3 lead that proved to be the final score. As Dykstra rounded third and slapped hands with third-base coach Larry Bowa, he yelled "DIDN'T I???" as if he had called his own shot.

In March of 2012, Dykstra stood in a different arena — a Southern California courtroom. The graying, middle-aged Dykstra was there to receive a sentence of three years in a California state prison for grand theft auto and providing a false financial statement. It was hardly his first encounter with the court system.

Lenny Dykstra always lived for the action. He went a million miles an hour, whatever the venue. He played hard, on and off the field, before, during, and after his major-league career. The attitude and tenacity that allowed him to become an all-star outfielder and build financial success in his post-playing days also likely shortened his playing days, ruined his finances, sent him to prison, and nearly cost him his life. Dykstra is many things, but boring has never been one of them.

Leonard Kyle Dykstra was born on February 10, 1963, in Santa Ana, California, to Jerry and Marilyn Leswick.

He was the middle of three sons born to the couple, joining older brother Brian and younger brother Kevin. Three of his Leswick uncles played in the National Hockey League in the Original Six era. Jerry Leswick left his family when Lenny was a toddler. At about the same time, Marilyn met a man named Dennis Dykstra while both worked for the Pacific Telephone Company. Dennis was recently divorced and had three young daughters. The couple married and became a Brady Bunch-type family, with the boys taking the Dykstra surname when formally adopted by Dennis.

Given what the world would come to know of him, it is unsurprising that Dykstra was mischievous as a youth. One of his favorite stunts was stealing a fire extinguisher and spraying people outside Disneyland from the passenger seat of a car.[4] The mischief also included getting busted sneaking into Angels Stadium on Christmas Day and playing around on the field.

Dykstra wasn't much for books or studying, but he did find time in school to play football and baseball. During his freshman year at Garden Grove High School, Lenny became the first and only freshman to play on the varsity squad. Before the major-league draft in his senior year, 1981, he went to a Mets tryout camp. Asked by a Mets employee if he was the batboy, Dykstra retorted some version of "I'm Lenny Dykstra and I'm the best player you're going to see today."[5] The Mets liked what they saw enough to draft Dykstra, but waited until the 13th round because they were convinced other teams were not very interested in him. (The Mets' 12th-round pick was a pitcher from Texas named Roger Clemens. ... He did not sign with the team.)

Dykstra had committed to play baseball at Arizona State and was not happy about being drafted so low. He eventually did sign with the Mets, but insisted that he was too good for rookie ball and should be sent directly to Class A. He won this battle with the Mets, and spent the rest of 1981 and all of 1982 with the Shelby Mets of the Class-A South Atlantic League.

In 1983 Dykstra really began to assert himself as a prospect. Playing for Lynchburg of the Class-A Carolina League, he hit .358 with a .472 on-base percentage and stole 105 bases on his way to league MVP honors. The next year, 1984, Dykstra put up another productive season, becoming the first player in the history of the Double-A Jackson franchise to score more than 100 runs in a season. For good measure, he met his future wife, Terri, while playing in Jackson. The couple married in 1985.

Dykstra spent the first month of the 1985 season with Triple-A Tidewater, but was called up to the Mets in early May and made his major-league debut on May 3. He led off and played center field against the Reds in Cincinnati. Dykstra got Lenny notched his first-major league hit in his second at-bat, a home run off Reds starter Mario Soto.

For the year, Dykstra played in 83 games, platooning in center with Mookie Wilson. About three-quarters of his plate appearances came against right-handed pitching, and his first big-league hit turned out to be his only home run of the season. The Mets won 98 games in 1985, but finished three games behind the St. Louis Cardinals in the National League East, New York's second consecutive season of 90 or more wins that ended with a second-place finish and no playoffs.

Perhaps stung by coming up empty with good teams two seasons in a row, the Mets blew the doors off the NL East in 1986. They reached first place in the division 10 games in and never trailed again, posting a 108-54 record and winning the East by 21½ games.

The Mets were not just legendary on the field. They were notorious for their raucous, partying ways off the field as well. With a few exceptions, the squad ferociously attacked alcohol, drugs, chasing women, and every other activity young men with disposable income are susceptible to. The 23-year-old Dykstra was an important cog on and off the field. He remained a platoon player in center field with Mookie Wilson, but saw his playing time increase as Wilson missed significant time to injury. Dykstra hit .295 with a .377 on-base percentage and swiped 31 bases. He combined with second baseman Wally Backman to form a gritty 1-2 punch atop the Mets lineup and routinely wreaked havoc on opposing pitchers and defenses while setting the stage for the likes of Darryl Strawberry, Keith Hernandez, and Gary Carter. Away from the field, Dykstra was one of the boys, with a particular affinity for gambling until the sun came up.

While the Mets were never seriously challenged in the regular season, the playoffs were a different matter. In the National League Championship Series, New York took on the NL West champion Houston Astros. But perhaps more than the Astros, the Mets took on one Astro in particular: pitcher Mike Scott. The former Met had had a relatively pedestrian career until he learned to throw a split-fingered fastball. The movement on the pitch left many around the league convinced that Scott was illegally scuffing the baseball. The Mets were among the believers.

Scott started Game One of the NLCS and was untouchable, pitching a shutout with 14 strikeouts. The performance only further established Scott's place deep inside the Mets collective psyche.

The Mets won Game Two and then in Game Three trailed 6-5 going to the bottom of the ninth when Dykstra's two-run shot off Astros closer Dave Smith rescued the game and put them up in the series. In Game Four Scott again shut down the Mets, this time allowing one run in another complete game. Game Five went to the Mets, sending the series back to Houston for an epic Game Six. The Mets had the chance to close out the series, but the specter of Mike Scott pitching a decisive Game Seven hung over the entire affair.

The Mets trailed 3-0 going in to the ninth inning when Dykstra led off as a pinch-hitter. He tripled to center and scored the first Mets run in a rally that tied the game. The teams traded single runs in the 14th, and then the Mets pushed three across in the 16th inning, punctuated by Dykstra's RBI single. With the Mets up 7-4, the Astros scored twice before Mets reliever Jesse Orosco struck out Kevin Bass to end it. The Mets were headed to the World Series.

For the NLCS, Dykstra led the Mets in batting, on-base, and slugging averages, and was the only Met to homer aside from Strawberry. While he may have been the Mets' best player in the series, MVP honors went to Mike Scott.

The Mets went on to defeat the Boston Red Sox in an equally epic seven-game affair. Dykstra again was central to the action, leading off Game Three in Boston with a home run off Oil Can Boyd to set the stage for a four-run first inning and a 7-1 win. He added another homer the next day, this time a two-run shot off Red Sox reliever Steve Crawford. Dykstra was one of six Mets to play in all seven games, hitting .296 with the two home runs, three RBIs, and four runs scored.

The 1987 and '88 seasons went about the same as 1986 for Dykstra. He was a valuable, productive, and popular player for the Mets, but he was never able to shake the platoon label or usage by his manager Davey Johnson. He never exceeded 500 plate appearances in a season with the Mets, despite his consistent production and no time lost on the disabled list. The 1988 Mets again won 100 games, but were shocked in a seven-game NLCS loss to the Los Angeles Dodgers.

Increasingly unhappy with his role as a part-time player for the Mets, Dykstra was traded on June 18, 1989, with relief pitcher Roger McDowell to the Philadelphia Phillies for infielder Juan Samuel. Free of the limitations placed on him in New York, Dykstra started 85 games the rest of the season and struggled as he never had in the majors. He hit only .222 with the Phillies and scuffled to a sub-.300 on-base percentage, both marks well below anything he had posted in his time with the Mets.

Coming into the 1990 season, Dykstra knew he would have his first real chance to be an everyday major-league center fielder. He responded to the opportunity by putting together his finest season to date, leading the National League in hits and on-base percentage, and making his first All-Star Game appearance as the starting center fielder for the NL team. He flirted with .400 for a while in early summer, but dismissed his chances, saying, "If I hit .400 this year, the world will end. It can't be done, not with forkballs and relief pitchers and the schedule. I saw a lot of Rod Carew while I was growing up in Anaheim, and if he couldn't do it, I sure as hell can't. It's hard enough just hitting four out of 10 balls, much less hitting them to where people ain't even standing."[6] Dykstra finished the season at .325 with 9 home runs and career highs in RBIs (60) and stolen bases (33).

He also entered the 1990 season having added about 30 pounds of muscle in the offseason. He attributed the gains to "special vitamins," even at the time seen as a smirking, winking nod to steroid use.

As the 1991 season began, Dykstra was coming off an All-Star season in his first full year as an every-day player. The 1991 season was, however, a disaster. Dykstra's enjoyment of high-stakes poker games led to a spring-training meeting with Commissioner Fay Vincent that resulted in a stern warning to keep away from such activities. After never having been on the disabled list before, Dykstra missed two large segments of the season. In early May he nearly killed himself and Phillies catcher Darren Daulton when he drunkenly wrecked his sports car after teammate John Kruk's bachelor party. Dykstra escaped with broken ribs, a broken collarbone, and a broken cheekbone, and Daulton suffered similar injuries. Dykstra missed nearly two months. Then in late August his season ended after he broke his collarbone again running into the outfield wall in Cincinnati. When he did play in 1991, Dykstra a productive, finishing the season with a .297 batting average and 24 stolen bases in 63 games played.

The 1992 season did not start much better. Leading off the Phillies' season at home on Opening Day, Dykstra was hit on the wrist by a pitch from the Cubs' Greg Maddux, breaking a bone and missing the next two weeks. A broken bone in his finger in August again ended his season prematurely. He played in 85 games and hit .301. For the 1991 and 1992 seasons, the Philadelphia Phillies were 76-72 with Dykstra playing and 72-104 without him. If he could ever stay healthy atop the Phillies' lineup, which finished second in the NL in runs scored in 1992, the team could realistically compete for a playoff spot.

In 1993 everything came together for the Phillies. They got out of the gate with a 17-5 record and never looked back, winning their first NL East title and playoff berth since 1983. They never trailed after April 9, and led by as many as 11½ games with a final margin of three.

For his part, Dykstra had a career year. He played in 161 games, missing only the game after the Phillies wrapped up the division. He hit .305 with 19 home runs, 66 RBIs, and 37 stolen bases, all career highs. His 143 runs, 194 hits, and 129 walks all led the NL. If not for an otherworldly season by the Giants new star, Barry Bonds, Dykstra would have been the Most Valuable Player in the league. One sour note: Dykstra was left off the National League All-Star team.

The Phillies' run to the playoffs was surprising to most observers. The team gained attention for its scraggly beards and shaggy hair, with more than one or two mullets prominent throughout the season. The colorful cast of characters included grown men known by nicknames such as Dutch, Wild Thing, Inky, Schil, and the doubly-dubbed Dykstra, known as either Dude or Nails.

"Dude" was a fairly straightforward moniker, ostensibly attached because of Dykstra's inability to complete a sentence without using the term. "Nails" was more descriptive, as in "tough as." Nails is a statement to the entire world that the bearer of the name was not one to be taken lightly or underestimated. Nails is tough, rugged. Nails would run into the wall to make a play. Nails would never stand for leaving the game with a clean uniform, but would scrap and fight for every pitch, every play of every game. Nails is hard-nosed and hard-working, and has the scrappy, underdog attitude needed to become a fan favorite in two of the most demanding sports cities in the world. Nails played hard all the time, on and off the field.

As the 1993 major-league playoffs dawned, Dykstra was known to the baseball world, but he was about to loudly announce his presence on the game's biggest stage. The Phillies entered the National League Championship Series as decided underdogs against the two-time defending NL champion Atlanta Braves.

The teams traded blows through the first four games, leaving the series tied for game five in Atlanta. The Phillies led 3-0 entering the bottom of the ninth, when the Braves stormed back to tie it. Batting second in the top of the 10th, Dykstra hit a homer off Mark Wohlers, providing the winning run for the Phillies in the pivotal Game Five. The Phillies clinched the series in the next game. For the series Dykstra hit .280 with five walks, two home runs, and five runs scored.

The 1993 World Series is best remembered for Joe Carter's series-ending home run off Mitch Williams in Game Six, but the Phillies' loss could not be pegged at all on Dykstra. He hit .348 with a .500 on-base percentage, scored 9 runs, hit 4 home runs, and stole 4 bases. In the wild 15-14 Game Four Toronto victory, Dykstra went 3-for-4, scored four runs, hit a double and two home runs, stole a base, and drove in four runs. After the season Dykstra was rewarded with a four-year, $25 million contract extension. How did Dykstra view his 1993 performance? "I basically went from star to superstar," he said. "I basically proved I'm more than the best leadoff hitter in the game. It's nice to have that recognition, but I'm more than a leadoff hitter. I proved I'm the impact player I've always considered myself to be, a situation hitter capable of getting the home run, double, walk, whatever the situation requires. I've worked hard and made myself into one of the top five players in the game. Do they pay leadoff hitters what they're paying me?"[7]

"He was a red-light player," said former Phillies coach John Vukovich. "But he was a horrible 10-2 player. What I mean is, he hated to play in a 10-2 game, whether we were ahead or behind. He'd lose focus. He only wanted to play with the game on the line all the time."[8]

Dykstra gained a reputation as a money player. In the modern era of sabermetrics, the idea of a player being "clutch"—to rise up and play his best when it matters most—is generally dismissed. But the numbers with Dykstra tell a different story. In his 1,278 regular-season games, Dykstra hit a home run every 56 at-bats, and posted a slash line of .285/.375/.419, with a .793 on-base plus slugging (OPS). In his 32 playoff games, he hit a home run every 11 at-bats, with a slash line of .321/.433/.661 and a 1.094 OPS. The merits of clutch will remain debatable, but if any player has ever been clutch, it is Lenny Dykstra.

After the World Series whispers began to surround Dykstra, his bulked-up physique in particular. The formerly lithe and sinewy Dykstra was by now a beefy fireplug with a thick neck and rippling biceps. Anyone who had seen him over the course of a few seasons saw an obvious change in his physical appearance. Media outlets speculated on the cause of Dykstra's transformation.[9]

In 1994 and '95 Dykstra made the All-Star teams, but his production and health never again matched the lofty heights seen in the magical season of '93. He missed a month of the strike-shortened 1994 season with appendicitis, and missed more than half of '95 with a variety of ailments.

In 1996, at age 33, Dykstra left a May game against the Dodgers in the fifth inning and never appeared in a major-league game again. He was diagnosed with spinal stenosis, a narrowing of the spinal canal, and missed the rest of 1996 and all of '97 before a short-lived comeback attempt in spring training in 1998 put the final end to his baseball career. MLB's 2007 report on steroids in baseball, led by former Senator George Mitchell, identified Dykstra as having admitted to the commissioner's office in 2000 that he used steroids during his career.[10]

After his playing days, Dykstra ran a chain of car washes in California, and seemed to be adjusting well to life after professional baseball. In the mid-2000s, in an odd twist, Dykstra began to emerge as a respected voice in the world of Wall Street stock picking. He was given a column by Jim Cramer of *Mad Money* TV fame.

By 2009, after a series of poor business deals and financial decisions turned sour, Dykstra had filed for bankruptcy protection. The sprawling map of plans turned bad included the purchase of a Southern California estate once owned by hockey great Wayne Gretzky, a high-end magazine aimed at professional athletes, and more spurned friends, associates, and even family members than anyone should have in a lifetime.

The number of cases and the litany of charges and countercharges are too long and complicated to enumerate. In 2012 Dykstra was sentenced to prison for what amounted to selling property that was to remain under the control of his bankruptcy trustee. He was released in the summer of 2013, after which he completed his court-mandated 500 hours of community service and resided with his ex-wife Terri, who had no plans to remarry him.[11]

Two of his three sons, Cutter and Luke Dykstra, played in the minor league systems of the Washington Nationals and Atlanta Braves, respectively.

The next chapters in Lenny Dykstra's life are anyone's guess. But if those already written tell us anything, they are likely to be anything but boring.

SOURCES

In addition to the sources cited in the text, the author consulted Baseball-Reference.com.

NOTES

1 Jeff Pearlman, *The Bad Guys Won!* (New York: Harper Collins, 2004), 151.

2 Robert Gordon and Tom Burgoyne, *More Than Beards, Bellies, and Biceps* (New York: Sports Publishing, 2002), 207.

3 Gordon and Burgoyne, 208.

4 Christopher Frankie, *Nailed!* (Philadelphia: Running Press, 2013), 16.

5 Frankie and Pearlman give variations of the same quote. Pearlman's was the adult version. The spirit of the quote is identical in both sources.

6 Steve Wulf, "Off and Running," *Sports Illustrated*, June 4, 1990.

7 Ross Newhan, "In Your Face, If Not Your Hair," *Los Angeles Times, March 20, 1994.*

8 Gordon and Burgoyne, 208.

9 George Mitchell, "Report to the Commissioner of Baseball of an Independent Investigation Into the Illegal Use of Steroids and Other Performance Enhancing Substances by Players in Major League Baseball." (files.mlb.com/mitchrpt.pdf).

10 Mitchell, 150.

11 Richard Sandomir, "Lenny Dykstra: Out of Prison and Still Headstrong," *New York Times*, August 3, 2014.

KEVIN ELSTER

By Joel Rippel

AFTER 13 YEARS IN THE MAJOR LEAGUES and at the age of 37, Kevin Elster's defensive skills still got noticed.

In 2002, after sitting out the 2001 season, Elster went to spring training with the New York Yankees. A pair of players who each knew what it took to play shortstop in the major leagues noticed Elster.

"Elster's hands are as good as anyone I've ever seen," Derek Jeter said.[1]

Former infielder Clete Boyer said Elster's release was so quick and effortless, "it's like he puts on a clinic" during infield practice.[2]

Early in Elster's major-league career, Mets coach Bud Harrelson, who spent 16 years in the big leagues and won a Gold Glove at shortstop in 1971, said, "Defensively? I don't mess with him. He's got it all."[3]

But it took a while for Elster's skills to develop. Born on August 3, 1964, in San Pedro, California, Elster was encouraged to play baseball by his father, Don, who was one of his youth baseball coaches. After graduating from Huntington Beach Marina High School in 1982, Elster began his college baseball career at nearby Golden West College, a two-year college.

"Kevin told us we were the only one that recruited him," said Golden West coach Fred Hoover. "We recruited him for his athletic ability. We couldn't project then that he would be in the big leagues (as a regular) by 1988, but by the middle of his first season, we knew he had something special."[4] Before his second season at Golden West, the 6-foot-2, 180-pound Elster was selected by the New York Mets in the second round of the January 1984 draft, and signed with the Mets after the college season. Elster, who had been offered a scholarship by Arizona State, received a reported signing bonus of $44,000.

The Mets assigned Elster, who wouldn't turn 20 until August, to Little Falls of the New York-Penn League, where he began his quick ascent through the Mets' minor-league system. In 71 games with Little Falls, Elster batted .257.

He opened the 1985 season with Lynchburg of the Class A Carolina League. In 59 games with Lynchburg he batted .295 with 7 home runs and 26 RBIs to earn a midseason promotion to Jackson of the Double-A Texas League. In 59 games with Jackson, he batted .257. Defensively, his range at shortstop was considered outstanding.

Elster returned to Jackson in 1986. In 127 games, he batted .269 with 52 RBIs. In late August, as the Mets

were cruising to the NL East Division title, manager Davey Johnson was considering his postseason roster.

"You look at your ballclub and see where you have a weakness," Johnson said. "I experimented with shortstop in the year, but I quit experimenting. As good as Rafael (Santana) has played, what if I have a bases-loaded situation and I'm down in a game? I would need another shortstop if I hit for him."[5]

With a trade not considered realistic, Johnson said, "So, you go to your system. What's the closest you've got at shortstop?"[6]

The closest was in Jackson, Mississippi, where manager Mike Cubbage informed the 22-year-old Elster that he was being called up by the Mets.

Elster's major-league debut came on September 2, 1986, against the San Francisco Giants as an eighth-inning defensive replacement. The next day, Elster singled off Giants reliever Frank Williams in his first major-league at-bat (in the eighth inning of the Mets' 4-2 victory).

Over the final month of the season, Elster played in 19 games and was 5-for-30. Given a spot on the postseason roster, he played in four games in the National League Championship Series against the Houston Astros and in one game in the World Series as a defensive replacement.

Elster blossomed offensively in 1987. He opened the season at Triple-A Tidewater. In 134 games with the Tides, he batted a career-high .310 with 170 hits, 33 doubles, 8 home runs and 74 RBIs. In September, he was recalled by the Mets and he went 4-for-10 in five games.

After four seasons in the minor leagues, the Mets were so confident that Elster was ready to be their starting shortstop in 1988 that they traded Rafael Santana, their starting shortstop for the previous three seasons, to the New York Yankees in December 1987. And in spring training the Mets returned 20-year-old Gregg Jefferies, the minor-league player of the year the previous two seasons, to the minors with the plan of moving him from shortstop to third base or the outfield.

"Sure it puts pressure on me," Elster said of the moves, "but all baseball players deal with pressure every game. You just have to learn to deal with it—how to turn it into good nervous energy."[7]

For most of the next four seasons, Elster was the Mets' regular shortstop.

As a rookie in 1988, Elster batted just .214 but made only 13 errors, none after July 19. (His errorless streak of 88 consecutive games at shortstop—then a major-league record—ended on May 9, 1989.) In the NLCS against the Los Angeles Dodgers, Elster started three of the seven games (Howard Johnson started the others) and was 2-for-8..

In 1989 Elster showed some offensive improvement, hitting .231 with 10 home runs and 55 RBIs. Defensively, he was solid, making just 15 errors while compiling a .976 fielding percentage in 150 games. He led NL shortstops with 235 putouts.

Elster got off to a slow start in 1990, hitting just .207 in 92 games and committing a career-high 17 errors. In August he was placed on the disabled list because of shoulder pain. Later in the month Elster had surgery and missed the rest of the season.

Elster wasn't expected to be ready for the start of the 1991 season, but he was on the Mets Opening Day roster. Howard Johnson, the Opening Day shortstop, started the first six games before manager Bud Harrelson gave him a day off on April 14. Elster, making his first start, got three hits, including a double and home run, in the Mets' 7-1 victory over the Montreal Expos. Elster made four starts in the next week and won back the starting job, as Harrelson shuffled his infield—moving Johnson to third and Gregg Jefferies to second.

On May 6 Elster was placed on the disabled list with a groin injury. After returning to the lineup, he struggled, hitting.194 in June and .176 in July. But he hit .297 in

August and .260 in September to finish the season with a .241 batting average in 115 games.

In 1992 Elster's shoulder problems returned in spring training. He opened the season with the Mets but played in just six games before returning to the disabled list on April 13. On May 7 Elster had surgery again and he missed the rest of the season.

The Mets didn't offer Elster a contract after the 1992 season, and he became a free agent. In January of 1993, he signed a minor-league contract with the Los Angeles Dodgers. He opened the 1993 season with the Dodgers' San Antonio farm team in the Double-A Texas League. He batted .282 in 10 games before being released on May 17. On May 22, he signed a minor-league contract with the Florida Marlins but was released two weeks later.

In December of 1993, Elster signed with the San Diego Padres, but was released near the end of spring training. On May 1, 1994, he signed with the New York Yankees. He hit .240 in 44 minor-league games (three with Class-A Tampa and 41 with Double-A Albany-Colonie). In late June the Yankees called him up and he played in seven games, going hitless, before returning to the disabled list with shoulder inflammation.

Off the field in 1994, Elster appeared in the Hollywood movie *Little Big League*.

Elster opened the 1995 season with the Yankees. In 10 games, he hit .118 and was released on June 8. He signed with Kansas City in late June and played in 11 games with Triple-A Omaha before being released. Elster quickly signed with the Philadelphia Phillies. After five games with Triple-A Scranton/Wilkes-Barre, he was called up by the Phillies (joining former Mets Sid Fernandez, Lenny Dykstra, and Gregg Jefferies). In 26 games with the Phillies, managed by former Met Jim Fregosi, Elster hit .208. He was released after the season and signed with the Texas Rangers for the 1996 season.

Completely healthy in 1996, Elster had a career year. He set career highs in games (157), at-bats (515), hits (130), doubles (32), home runs (24), RBIs (99) and batting average (.252) to earn AL Comeback Player of the Year honors from *The Sporting News*. He had a .981 fielding percentage and led AL shortstops with 285 putouts while committing just 14 errors.

After the season, Elster signed a one-year contract with the Pittsburgh Pirates. He broke his left wrist in a collision at first base with Kurt Abbott of the Florida Marlins and missed all but 39 games of the season. Released after the season, Elster returned to the Rangers for 1998. After hitting just .232 in 84 games, he was released by the Rangers on July 31.

Elster sat out the 1999 season, retiring to live in Las Vegas where he planned to open a bar, but in December of 1999 he got a phone call from former Mets manager Davey Johnson, now managing the Dodgers.

"Davey called out of the blue," Elster said. "...He said that he needed a shortstop and invited me to come to the Dodgers spring training camp. I won the starting job."[8]

Elster got off to a good start in 2000—hitting three home runs and driving in four runs in the Dodgers' 6-5 victory over the Giants on April 11 in the first game played in San Francisco's Pacific Bell Park.

In 80 games with the Dodgers, Elster slugged 14 home runs (second-most of his career) and hit .227. After the season he retired. But in early 2002, the Yankees invited the 35-year-old Elster to spring training. "I figured, why not give this one more shot? I've got nothing to lose and it just might work out," Elster said.[9]

But Elster did not make the Yankees' regular-season roster as a backup infielder, despite his hands that were, according to Yankees scout Gene Michael still "the best in the world."[10]

SOURCES

In addition to the sources in the Notes, the author also consulted:

baseball-almanac.com.

imdb.com.

NOTES

1 *Bergen County Record* (Hackensack, New Jersey), February 23, 2002.

2 Ibid.

3 *New York Times,* July 31, 1988.

4 *Orange County Register* (Anaheim, California), March 30, 1988.

5 *New York Times*, September 2, 1986.

6 Ibid.

7 *Orange County Register*, March 30, 1988.

8 *Utica* (New York) *Observer-Dispatch*, September 7, 2013

9 *Bergen County Record*, February 23, 2002.

10 Ibid.

SID FERNANDEZ

By Rory Costello

NO PITCHER BORN AND RAISED IN HAWAII has had more wins in the majors than Sid Fernandez, who notched 114 (against 96 losses) from 1983 through 1997. Charlie Hough (216) grew up in Hialeah, Florida. Ron Darling (136) looked the part of a Hawaiian, thanks to his Chinese-Hawaiian mother, but he called Massachusetts home from before the age of 2.[1] Milt Wilcox (119) had a father with deep Hawaiian roots, but the Wilcoxes moved to Oklahoma when little Milt was also just 2.[2] But Fernandez—who attended Kaiser High School in Honolulu, was quiet and laid back, and loved surfing—never stayed away from the Pacific for too long. As he said in 1987, "Hawaii is my home. I go there whenever I can. I grew up in the water; I love to be on the ocean."[3]

The hefty southpaw had a live arm and knew how to use it. When "El Sid" was on top of his game, which was often, he baffled hitters. Fernandez was most often described as "sneaky-fast." His delivery was deceptive—he hid the ball behind his body and slung it in after a long drive step. The pitches seemed to come out of his uniform. "His release point is so low, it is almost impossible to pick up," said Ben Wade, who was director of scouting for the Los Angeles Dodgers in 1982.[4] But Sid was particularly tough with his beautiful sweeping slow curve—righty batters would be simply locked up as they watched it drop in over the outside corner for a called strike three. He was an important member of the New York Mets as they rose to become World Series winners in 1986.

Charles Sidney Fernandez IV[5] was a fourth-generation Hawaiian. His father, Charles, worked as a civilian foreman at the Pearl Harbor Shipyards; mother Sheila was a teller in the credit union on the Marine base.[6] Sid had one older brother, Roger. The family's heritage is mostly Portuguese, with little bits of Irish and Maori.

Baseball was a part of Sid's life from the age of 6, when he began playing tee-ball. He was never interested in any other competitive sport. As a 9-year-old, he represented Hawaii in the Pitch, Hit, and Run contest in San Diego—the lad's first trip away from the islands.[7] There were a handful of Hawaiians in the majors to root for when he was young—the most notable being Mike Lum—but Sid was a fan of the San Francisco Giants. "They had the Dodger and Giant games on the radio every day in Hawaii, so most of the people are either Dodger fans or Giant fans," he remembered in 1994. "I listened to the Giants every day on the radio. Willie McCovey, Jim Ray Hart."[8]

Fernandez was a champion at all levels throughout his career. Kailua, the town on the windward coast of Oahu where he grew up, won the state Little League championship in 1975.[9] His Colt League and American Legion teams both won national titles. For Moiliili manager Clyde Hayashida's 1980 Legion club, Sid won the Bob Feller Award (most strikeouts in regional and national competition). He threw a no-hitter in his first start at Kaiser High in '80, as coach Stu McDonald helped him develop the three-quarter delivery that would make him a star. As a senior in '81, Sid posted another 5-1 record and led Kaiser to the state championship.[10]

In the June 1981 draft, the Los Angeles Dodgers selected Sid in the third round. Local scout Ichiro "Iron" Maehara made the initial recommendation, and Gail Henley confirmed the opinion. One special local factor, according to Sid: "The high school season isn't long enough to attract too much attention. . . . I think Iron saw me do most of my pitching in one of the other island leagues, like maybe in the American-Japanese Association."[11]

The Dodgers assigned Fernandez to Lethbridge (Alberta) of the Pioneer Rookie League, where he averaged an eye-popping 15.2 strikeouts per nine innings in 11 starts. At Class-A Vero Beach in '82, Fernandez was again devastating. He blew away batters at the rate of 14.6 per nine innings, including a 21-strikeout tour de force. It was then that Sid first wore uniform number 50, in honor of his home state and favorite TV show, *Hawaii Five-O*. Dodgers manager Tommy Lasorda came up with the idea.[12] When Fernandez pitched for the Mets, the show's well-known theme music always played before his starts at Shea Stadium.

Sid jumped to Triple-A in midseason 1982, cause for relief among batters throughout the Florida State League—he had thrown two no-hitters in 12 starts.[13] Wildness was a problem at Albuquerque, though, and so he stepped back to Double-A the next year. Though still issuing a lot of walks, Sid was again dominant with San Antonio, winning Texas League Pitcher of the Year. The big club called him up in September 1983.

Over in New York, meanwhile, a remarkably talented young pitching staff had begun to take shape. J. Frank Cashen had become general manager of the Mets in February 1980, less than a month after Nelson Doubleday and Fred Wilpon bought the club. Cashen was the president or GM of the top-notch Baltimore teams from 1966 to 1975, and he set about replicating the Orioles formula: rebuilding the farm system and stockpiling young arms. The acquisitions of both Ron Darling and Fernandez rank among his greatest coups.

The trade with LA in December 1983—Sid and infielder Ross Jones for handyman Bob Bailor and fellow Hawaiian lefty Carlos Diaz—appeared logical. The Dodgers had an excellent rotation, blending youth and experience in Fernando Valenzuela (23), Bob Welch (27), Alejandro Peña (24), Jerry Reuss (34), Burt Hooton (33), and yet another lefty in Rick Honeycutt (29). With that kind of depth, and Orel Hershiser in the pipeline too, they could afford to deal even such a promising prospect to bring in needed bullpen help. (Steve Howe was battling his drug problem.)

In addition, "the Dodgers started a whispering campaign that Fernandez had quit playing winter ball in the Dominican Republic because of arm trouble." The real reason he left, however, was homesickness for Hawaii.[14] Sid was disappointed because he had expected to be a Dodger, and he wasn't overly enthusiastic about coming to New York either. "Let's face it, I come from paradise and I've come to a concrete city," the avid bodysurfer remarked.[15] Looking back in 1994, though, he said, "I liked New York. You hear some people say the people are nasty, but I didn't find it to be that way. I found everyone to be pretty friendly. It took a little getting used to at first, but I liked it."[16]

A couple of months before the trade (October 1983), Frank Cashen had named Davey Johnson Mets manager. Earl Weaver's old second baseman was also steeped in the Orioles pitching-oriented philosophy. During spring training in 1984, he insisted that the spectacular 19-year-old Dwight Gooden was ready for the majors. Johnson, who had managed the Mets' Triple-A Tidewater club in '83, installed Darling in the rotation too. However, Fernandez required some more seasoning with the Tides. In fact, Johnson wasn't crazy about the deal at first. In his book *Bats*, Johnson said, "[Cashen] traded two guys I could have used ... for a pitcher who wasn't ready to play regularly in the spring. In the end it turned out for the best, but in the short run, it handicapped me."[17]

Fernandez came up at midyear 1984 and made 15 starts, posting a respectable record of 6-6, 3.50. That summer, though, the Mets did not have enough weapons to stay with the Chicago Cubs, who won the NL East behind unanimous Cy Young Award winner Rick Sutcliffe. In 1985 New York added star catcher Gary Carter to the mix, and Doc Gooden burst out with a solar flare of a season. Although Sid had to begin the season at Tidewater once more after a poor spring, he was called up after five polished starts (including an 18-strikeout performance) when veteran Bruce Berenyi went down with chronic shoulder miseries. Though his won-lost record was again even at 9-9, he struck out more than a batter an inning and had a clean 2.80 ERA.

Whitey Herzog's Cardinals, a speedy gap-hitting team tailored to the pool-table turf at Busch Stadium, outfenced Davey's Mets in the gripping 1985 race. However, New York blew everybody's doors off during the regular season in '86, going 108-54. Though no starter won more than Bob Ojeda's 18 games, it was a potent, balanced staff. Sid went 16-6 (which turned out to be his career high in wins) with a 3.52 ERA. He also tossed a scoreless eighth inning in the All-Star Game, striking out the side after walking the first two batters.

Baseball fans remember the 1986 postseason as perhaps the most excitingly tense ever. In the NL Championship Series against Houston, Sid started Game Four. He pitched respectably but yielded homers to Alan Ashby and Dickie Thon in a 3-1 loss to sandpaper-scuffing suspect Mike Scott, who was on a lethal roll.

After the Mets finally dispatched the Astros in the draining 16-inning Game Six—which many observers place among the greatest games ever played—Davey Johnson decided to go with three starters against the Boston Red Sox in the World Series. Fernandez was odd man out for the rotation, but he played a pivotal role. When Ron Darling was knocked out of the box in Game Seven, Sid (making his third relief appearance of the Series) entered in the fourth inning. He walked his first man but then mowed down seven straight, including four strikeouts. He stabilized the situation and enabled the Mets to stage their final triumphant comeback.

"We just had a great team," Fernandez told journalist Patrick Hickey Jr. in a 2006 interview, when he was honored at the Hawaiian Night held by the Mets' Class-A affiliate, the Brooklyn Cyclones. "People thought we were cocky because we just beat everyone. We just played well as a team. I wish that whole team could have stayed together just a little bit longer. That would have been nice."[18]

Fernandez was an All-Star again in 1987, picking up the save for Lee Smith as the NL won 2-0 in 13 innings. He finished with only 12 wins, however, and his 3.81 ERA was unusually high for him. Again the White Rat's Cardinals came out ahead in September. In 1988 the Mets won the NL East; Fernandez was a hard-luck 12-10 with a 3.03 ERA. In the playoffs against the Dodgers, he gave up six runs in four-plus innings in Game Five, and the Mets lost the series. That year also featured work with sports hypnotherapist Peter Siegel, who incorporated heavy-metal music—which Sid loved—to get him in "The Zone."[19]

Another pair of frustrating second-place finishes for New York followed in 1989 and 1990, though in '89 Sid put up one of his best years. He went 14-5, 2.83, and on July 14 he pitched what might have been the most brilliant game of his career. Against the Braves in Atlanta, he struck out 16 (five of them looking) as his big curve was just deadly. It turned out to be a flawed gem, though, as Lonnie Smith hit a game-winning homer in the ninth.

In 1989 the division belonged to the Cubs, with Greg Maddux, Ryne Sandberg, and Rookie of the Year

Jerome Walton. The 1990 season was another disappointment for Sid (9-14, 3.46). Better years from him and Darling might have enabled the Mets to catch the Pirates and Cy Young winner Doug Drabek. The 1991 campaign was a washout; a hot smash broke Sid's wrist in spring training, and he injured his knee after he came back. That offseason Fernandez attended the Duke University clinic and slimmed down markedly.[20] He regained his form in '92, leading "The Worst Team That Money Can Buy" with a record of 14-11, 2.73. With a different team, that could have been his long-awaited 20-win season.

After that, though, the injuries started to catch up with Sid—he never started more than 19 games in a year again. After the 1993 season, when he again hurt his knee covering first base, he signed a three-year, $9 million contract with the Orioles. It was clear, though, that his physical problems weren't allowing him to get anything on the ball. Sid had always been a pronounced fly-ball pitcher—indeed, he once had a complete game (September 12, 1993) in which the infield did not record a single assist—but now the ball wasn't staying in the park. He allowed a frightening 27 homers in 115 innings in '94 and nine more in just 28 innings in '95. In July Baltimore bought Fernandez out for $2 million after a year and a half.

Yet there was still a last charge left in the battery. The Phillies picked Sid up three days later, and he responded with a 6-1 record in 11 starts, even capturing Pitcher of the Month honors in August as he won five straight. Manager Jim Fregosi also named him Philadelphia's Opening Day starter in '96, a career first. Although Sid went just 3-6 in 11 starts, he struck out well over a batter an inning, as he had the year before, and he remained difficult to hit.

Big 5-0 made his 300th and final start for the Astros in 1997. Houston GM Gerry Hunsicker, who knew Sid well from his years in the Mets front office, decided to take a flyer. On April 5 Fernandez got the W as he allowed two runs in five innings against St. Louis. However, elbow woes finally proved to be too much to battle through. Sid submitted to a final operation in May, went on a rehab assignment to Triple-A New Orleans, and decided to retire on August 1. His announcement came before a game at the Astrodome against the Mets.

After retirement, among other things, Fernandez served as Honolulu sports development coordinator. In 1998 he went with Mayor Jeremy Harris to Japan to speak with baseball executives there about using the proposed sports complex in Kapolei. This facility was a pet project of State Senate President Norman Mizuguchi and his old friend, Maui native Wally Yonamine, a member of the Japanese Baseball Hall of Fame.[21]

In July 2000 Fernandez returned to Shea Stadium as part of the celebration of the "Ten Greatest Moments in Mets History." He told the New York media that he was enjoying extensive time on the beach and golf course at home, and who could begrudge this agreeable fellow the lifestyle of a gentleman of leisure? Yet there was still another postscript to Sid's baseball career. He worked out hard over that winter and threw in front of big-league scouts in Arizona in February 2001. The Yankees were impressed enough to invite him to spring training, with the idea that he could be a lefty bullpen specialist.

"I went to a Mets reunion in January and a lot of people said, 'You look great, why don't you try and pitch again?'... I went home and thought about a comeback. I had thought about it in '99 and let it go. I guess I didn't want to be sitting around two or 20 years from now and regret not doing it."[22]

Fernandez noted that eminent orthopedist James Andrews had found nothing wrong with his elbow in 1998. He believed that a chiropractor had solved his problems by diagnosing and treating nerve damage in his neck. Although the big curveball still had bite, the longshot bid for a job in the Bronx did not come through. Fernandez went to Triple-A Columbus to get in some more work. After two innings in one start, though, he finally did hang it up for good. Yankees manager Joe Torre observed that Sid's knee was "just too bad, bone on bone."[23]

Fernandez resumed his easygoing life in Hawaii. He continued to enjoy golf, joining the Celebrity Players Tour in 2004.[24] He and his wife, Noelani Gillis Fernandez, were married in 1991. They had two children.[25] They run the Sid Fernandez Foundation, which for many years has awarded college scholarships to seniors from their alma mater, Kaiser High.

This man endured a lot of criticism during his career. When he arrived in the majors, he was shy and timid, to use his own words.[26] He was also naïve and unworldly, as depicted in Jeff Pearlman's book about the 1986 Mets, *The Bad Guys Won*.[27] That book and John Harper and Bob Klapisch's *The Worst Team Money Could Buy* portrayed him as "The Big Pineapple," who believed that professional wrestling was real. In particular, he drew flak about his weight, which did indeed fluctuate, contributing to his knee problems. On occasion Sid also puffed himself out running the bases, but he was one of the NL's better-hitting pitchers, batting .190 as a Met. All in all, if Sid had not been so strongly built, especially in the legs, it is doubtful that his elbow could have endured such a stressful motion as long as it did.

In addition, some observers felt that Fernandez did not sustain the concentration necessary to be a really big winner. On the contrary, others—particularly outside New York—believed that his competitive toughness was not properly appreciated. A rep as a six-inning pitcher was to a great extent unjustified in comparison with other starters around the league. And those who regard the Mets of the late '80s and early '90s as underachievers should think about Herzog's Cardinals and Tony La Russa's Oakland A's. Arguably both of those clubs should have won more championships too.

In the final analysis of Sid Fernandez, there are some eye-catching statistics:

* As of 2011, his strikeout ratio of 8.40 per 9 innings ranked 21st on the all-time list among pitchers with more than 1,000 innings pitched.

* Three times (1985, 1988, and 1990) he led the NL in lowest opponents' batting average.

* In both lifetime lowest opponent's batting average (.209) and fewest hits per nine innings (6.85), he ranks third behind Nolan Ryan and Sandy Koufax–exalted company indeed.

NOTES

1 Peter Gammons, "More Than a Media Darling," *Sports Illustrated*, April 6, 1987.

2 E-mail from Milt Wilcox to Rory Costello, July 20, 2011.

3 Tim Layden, "For Hawaii's 'El Sid,' The Surf's Always Up," *Albany Times Union*, March 27, 1987.

4 Ralph Wiley, "This Duke's a Real Hazard," *Sports Illustrated*, June 28, 1982.

5 Dan Cisco, *Hawai'i Sport*. (Honolulu: University of Hawai'i Press, 1999), 36.

6 Dave Nightingale, "Sidney Smoke: Super Prospect Fernandez May Have Climbed Too Fast." *The Sporting News*, August 2, 1982: 41.

7 Ibid.

8 Tom Keegan, "Wary Fernandez issues surfing an intentional pass." *Baltimore Sun*, April 20, 1994.

9 Cisco.

10 Nightingale.

11 Ibid.

12 Bill Kwon. "Sid quits." *Honolulu Star-Bulletin*, August 1, 1997. During spring training 1987, Fernandez briefly wore number 10.

13 Wiley; Dave Nightingale, "A Collective Sigh of relief in FSL." *The Sporting News*, June 21, 1982: 42.

14 Jack Lang and Peter Simon, *The New York Mets: Twenty-Five Years of Baseball Magic* (New York: Henry Holt and Company, 1986), 195.

15 George Vecsey, "Fernandez's State of Mind," *New York Times*, August 26, 1984. Fernandez gave up bodysurfing after a scary accident in 1987, though (Keegan).

16 Keegan.

17 Davey Johnson and Peter Golenbock. *Bats* (New York: G.P. Putnam, 1986), 37.

18 Patrick Hickey Jr., "Fernandez Still Remembers '86." (patrickhickeyjr.tripod.com/sid_fernandez_interview.html).

19 Jessica Bendinger, "Mental Metal," *SPIN*, September 1988: 14.

20 Marty Noble, "From El Sid to El Slim," *Newsday*, February 12, 1992.

21 Bruce Dunford, "Hawaii Complex Gets Wake-Up Call," Associated Press, July 16, 1999.

22 Tom Keegan, "A Return to Slender," *New York Post*, February 21, 2001: 70.

23 George King, "Torre Says Family Comes First for Bernie, Bombers," *New York Post*, April 15, 2001.

24 Bill Kwon, "Fernandez Looking to Make Mark on Celebrity Golf Tour," *Honolulu Advertiser*, April 22, 2004.

25 Erika Engle, "He Built It, but Now He's Leaving." *Honolulu Star-Bulletin*, February 5, 2002.

26 Steve Wilder, "The Best Is Yet to Come for the Mets' Sid Fernandez," *Baseball Digest*, June 1986: 28. Originally published in the *New York Post*.

27 Jeff Pearlman, *The Bad Guys Won* (New York: HarperCollins Publishers, 2004), 78-79.

GEORGE FOSTER

By Cindy Thomson

A RIGHT-HANDED POWER-HITTING OUTfielder, George Foster was a feared presence at bat and in the outfield for most of his 11-year run with the Cincinnati Reds. Once he mastered the mental aspect of his game, Foster became a key ingredient in manager Sparky Anderson's Big Red Machine of the 1970s. But as powerful as he was on the field, Foster led a very quiet life off it. A columnist once summed up Foster's discipline in his mind and on the field by writing, "It is against George Foster's convictions to smoke, drink, chew, curse or leave men on base."[1]

Born in Tuscaloosa, Alabama, on December 1, 1948, to George and Regina (Beale) Foster, George Arthur Foster spent his early life picking cotton and hoping, despite his small size, to be chosen for neighborhood ballgames. When he was 8 his parents separated, and he moved to Hawthorne, California, near Los Angeles, with his mother, his older brother, John, and his older sister, Mamie.

In Hawthorne, Foster played in the same Little League as future major-leaguer Dave Kingman. He played several sports at Leuzinger High School in Lawndale, California, but broke his leg playing basketball in his senior year and did not play baseball that spring. Instead, he established a workout routine, gained weight, and got stronger. After high school, while playing in a fall league, he was spotted by San Francisco Giants scout Jack French, and in late 1968, after playing baseball at El Camino Junior College in Torrance, California, Foster was drafted in the third round of the amateur draft by the Giants, the team of his boyhood hero, Willie Mays.

The Giants sent the 19-year-old Foster to their low-level Class-A team in Medford, Oregon. The next season he advanced to Single-A Fresno, made the 1969 California League All-Star team, and led his team with 14 home runs and 85 runs batted in. The 6-foot-1, 185-pound powerhouse was drawing attention, and the Giants called him up after the California League season.

Foster's first major-league hit was an infield single to third base off the Dodgers' Claude Osteen on September 27. The Giants and Foster repeated the process in 1970: He spent the season at Triple-A Phoenix, where he hit .308 but with less power and fewer RBIs than the season before. Again he got a late-season call-up and on September 25, he hit his first major-league home run as a pinch hitter off San Diego's Pat Dobson. In 1971 Foster made the Giants' roster as a reserve outfielder, backing up Bobby Bonds, Willie Mays, and Ken Henderson. The reclusive Foster roomed with Bonds, who became his mentor and helped him adjust. Foster avoided the media and rarely engaged in small talk with his teammates, afraid of

bothering anyone. His time on the bench, after playing every day in the minors, sent him into a batting slump as he lost 54 points off his batting average during May.

On May 29, the Giants traded Foster to the Reds for shortstop Frank Duffy and pitcher Vern Geishert. The trade turned out to be vastly one-sided in favor of Cincinnati. Duffy was traded to the Cleveland Indians after the season and Geishert never pitched again in the majors. But Foster was sorely disappointed. The day he was dealt the Giants were in first place in the National League West Division and the Reds were near the bottom. He was discouraged, but the trade proved to be a blessing for Foster, and for the Reds. Foster became the Reds' regular center fielder (in part because his predecessor, Bobby Tolan, sat out the entire season with an Achilles tendon injury). Foster hit .241 with 13 home runs for the season, including .234 with 10 homers for the Reds. On September 16 in San Francisco he avenged himself against his old team by hitting a grand slam off Don McMahon in the eighth inning that assured the Reds victory. Still, despite flashes of excellence, Foster earned only a backup role in the Reds' outfield in 1972 after Tolan returned to the lineup. Foster played in 59 games and hit just .200 with two home runs. His most memorable moment of the season undoubtedly was the deciding Game Five of the NLCS against the Pittsburgh Pirates when, as a pinch-runner, he scored the winning run from third base on a wild pitch by Bob Moose in the bottom of the ninth inning.

The dramatic finish to the 1972 NLCS brought Foster attention from the press but he made just two brief appearances as the Reds lost the World Series to the Oakland Athletics in seven games. And the next season he was sent back down to Triple-A Indianapolis. Sparky Anderson said, "What George needs to learn is to make contact. When he does, the ball really jumps off his bat."[2]

At Indianapolis in 1973, Foster roomed with Ken Griffey, who became a friend and later a teammate on the Reds. Griffey said of Foster, "At first we had a hard time communicating because he was so upset about being sent down, but after a while we'd just have such a good time on the field just laughing that he forgot his situation and started to play ball."[3] That season was a turning point for Foster. He soon accepted the reasoning that more playing time would only help. Anderson and his staff had hoped the stint in the minors would help Foster to mature. He had the skills but needed to develop and improve his mental attitude. Foster's friendship with Griffey and others helped him to relax, and his hitting improved. This was also a time of spiritual renewal for Foster, who came to profess a strong Christian faith. He worked to stay in shape, began to eat healthy foods and shunned alcohol and tobacco. In September the Reds brought him up to the majors, and he played in 17 games, hitting .282 with four home runs. Anderson confirmed his previous assessment of Foster's ability, saying, "When George gets into a pitch, no one hits a ball harder than he does—not Willie Stargell, Willie McCovey, or Lee May."[4]

As his hitting improved, Foster began to admire another player's hickory stained bat and ordered one for himself. Foster's big, black, 35-ounce, 35-inch bat was well known. Foster joked about having integrated the bat rack.

The Reds won the NL West again in 1973 but Foster had been called up too late to be eligible to play in the postseason. Even so he had impressed the Reds enough that he stuck with the team the next season. Anderson declared, "He'll never be a loudmouth, but his new attitude will make him a better ballplayer."[5]

In 1974 the Reds had outfielders Griffey, Cesar Geronimo, and Pete Rose, and Foster was still a part-time player, but this time he was mentally prepared for the role. The hitting coach, former Reds power hitter Ted Kluszewski, worked with Foster on his batting stance, focusing on the inside pitches that Foster had been avoiding. Foster hit .264 with seven homers that season, and broke through in 1975, when he became the regular left fielder after Anderson moved Rose to third base. Foster's batting average rose to .300 and he hit 23 home runs, helping propel the Reds to a World Series victory over the Boston Red Sox, their first Series championship since 1940. In the bottom of the ninth inning during the dramatic Game Six, Foster threw out the potential winning run at the plate to keep the game going. In the 12th, Foster actually caught and kept the Fisk home run ball after it ricocheted off the foul pole. The ball was sold at auction in 1999 for over $100,000. Foster hit .364 in the NLCS and .276 in the World Series. Anderson said, "Having George in left field made the difference in our ballclub winning the World Series."[6]

The 1976 season was even better for Foster. He hit 29 home runs, had a league-leading 121 RBIs, and was voted to the National League's starting lineup for the All Star Game in Philadelphia. He hit a two-run home run off Catfish Hunter, drove in three runs, and was named the game's Most Valuable Player. He was named the National League's Player of the Month in May and July, and the Player of the Year by *The Sporting News*. He had been in contention for the Triple Crown (home runs, RBIs, and batting average), and finished second to teammate Joe Morgan in the voting for the Most Valuable Player. After Morgan was announced as the MVP, Foster declared that he should have won the award, something he immediately regretted saying.[7] The Reds swept the Philadelphia Phillies in the NLCS and the Yankees in the World Series. Foster hit .429 in the Series (6-for-14) with four RBIs.

During the season Foster smashed the seventh home run ever to be hit into Riverfront Stadium's upper deck since the ballpark opened in 1970. In the ballpark's 33-season existence only 35 home runs were hit there and Foster hit the most, six.

Deprived (in his mind) of the MVP in 1976, Foster responded with a better season the next year and copped the award on the strength of a .320 batting average, and being the league leader in home runs (52), RBIs (149), and runs scored (124). Once again Foster was voted to the All-Star Team (he was 1-for-3 with one RBI as the National League won). On July 14, just before the All-Star break, Foster hit three home runs in a game against Atlanta, and he wound up with 12 that month. Of his home run total that season, Foster said, "I saw the ball so well. It seemed almost any pitch would do."[8] Foster's home run total in 1977 was the most since Willie Mays hit 52 in 1965. The 50-home run milestone not reached again until Detroit's Cecil Fielder hit 51 in 1990.

After the 1977 season Foster combined an exhibition tour to Japan (he was voted the MVP for the tour) with a honeymoon. He married Sheila Roberts on November 3. They later had two daughters, Starrine and Shawna.

In 1978, his batting average slipped to .281, but he again led the National League in home runs (40) and RBIs (120). But over the next two seasons his production fell as he battled injuries and missed playing time. He rallied in 1981 and drove in 90 runs in 108 games in the strike-shortened season. Before the next season, on February 10, 1982, Foster was traded to the New York Mets for catcher Alex Trevino and pitchers Jim Kern and Greg Harris. His nearly 11-year run with the Big Red Machine was over.

Foster, 33 years old by this time, signed a five-year, $10 million contract with the Mets—the largest in the National League at the time—but struggled from the start. After seven straight seasons of hitting at least 20 home runs, he managed only 13 in New York, and his batting average plummeted to .247. Mets fans took to booing him.

Foster improved his home-run numbers in the next three years as the Mets vaulted into contention in 1984 after years of ineptitude. But by 1986, as the Mets were having one of their greatest seasons, the 37-year-old Foster was struggling in part-time play. A comment Foster made in August to a sportswriter appeared to accuse Mets manager Davey Johnson of favoring white players. "I'm not saying it's a racial thing. But that seems to be the case in sports these days," Foster was quoted as saying. "When a ballclub can, they replace a George Foster or a Mookie Wilson with a more popular white player. I think the Mets would rather promote a Gary Carter or a Keith Hernandez to the fans so parents who want to can point to them as role models for their children, rather than a Darryl Strawberry or a Dwight Gooden or a George Foster."[9] Foster told Johnson and his teammates that his comments had been taken out of context, and some of the teammates supported him, but he was released the day the article appeared.[10] With a huge contract and a lackluster performance, Foster was destined to be released anyway. The Chicago White Sox picked him up and he hit a home run (the 348th and last of his career) in his first game with the team, but he was released after three weeks.

Foster was a minor-league hitting instructor for the Reds in the late 1990s and later a special instructor with the team. He has also coached in high school and college. He has spent time as a corporate speaker, and with a baseball training organization called the George Foster Baseball Clinic. In 2003, Foster was inducted into the Cincinnati Reds Hall of Fame.

During Foster's playing days he spent time with young baseball players, giving them equipment and instructing them on batting. Dayton, Ohio, sportswriter Hal McCoy who covered Foster when he was with the Reds, called him "the greatest person in baseball," adding, "I mean as a person, not just as a player. He never raises his voice, no matter how harassed he may be by fans. I asked him once if he'd let me use his name for Building Bridges, an organization for underprivileged kids. He said, 'No, you'll have more than my name. I'll be there too.' "[11] Foster seeks to teach future ballplayers to work hard and believe in their abilities.

NOTES

1 Thomas Boswell, *Washington Post*, August 18, 1976.

2 *Cincinnati Reds Yearbook*, 1973, 34.

3 Malka Drucker with George Foster, *The George Foster Story* (New York: Holiday House, 1979), 55-56.

4 Drucker and Foster, 58.

5 Drucker and Foster, 61.

6 Drucker and Foster, 75.

7 Drucker and Foster, 87-88.

8 Drucker and Foster, 94.

9 Gannett Westchester-Rockland Newspapers, August 7, 1986.

10 Joseph Durso, "Mets to Drop Foster Amid Racial Controversy," *New York Times*, August 7, 1986.

11 Drucker and Foster, 72-73.

JOHN GIBBONS

By Nick Waddell

JOHN GIBBONS HAS SEEN A LOT OF UPS AND down in his career. A highly-touted prospect for the Mets, he was expected to be their future catcher, but a lack of production and the acquisition of Gary Carter stood in the way. Gibbons became a major-league manager for the Toronto Blue Jays, but mediocre success and publicized fights with his players led to his dismissal. He was rehired as the manager of the Blue Jays and finally broke through in 2015, when he managed the Blue Jays to the American League Championship Series. Throughout his career, Gibbons determined to succeed while staying true to his roots.

Gibbons based his philosophy on the game on simplicity. "Baseball's not rocket science. ... It's really pretty much a simple game."[1] His colleagues said this simple philosophy and his easygoing demeanor made Gibbons a successful manager. "I think one of the things he brings, other than great baseball knowledge, is a great way with people," said former Blue Jays coach Brian Butterfield. "He's always got his players' backs, he always has his coaches' backs."[2]

Gibbons' high-school baseball coach, Syl Perez, said, "John has never been full of himself. Just the fact that we still have a relationship 33 years later indicates he's never forgotten where he came from."[3] His best friend said: "Look at John, major-league status, manager, still the same guy."[4] Describing himself as "a normal guy," Gibbons said, "I'm not too fascinated by myself."[5] The simple approach to the game and to himself made Gibbons the second-winningest manager in Blue Jays history.

John Michael Gibbons was born on June 8, 1962, in Great Falls, Montana. His father, William, was a US Air Force colonel[6] and his mother was a dental hygienist.[7]

Gibbons spent his high-school years in San Antonio, Texas, where he was drafted 24th overall in 1980 after playing at Douglas A. MacArthur High School. He turned down a scholarship from the University of Texas to begin his pro career.[8]

Gibbons was assigned to Kingsport of the rookie-level Appalachian League, along with fellow Mets first-round selection Darryl Strawberry. Gibbons caught in 34 games, the most of any catcher on the team, and batted.276. For the 1981 season, he was promoted to Shelby of the Class-A South Atlantic League., where his batting average plunged to .189.

Gibbons stayed with Shelby to start the 1982 season, and was the team's primary catcher. He raised his batting average to .265 and late in the season was

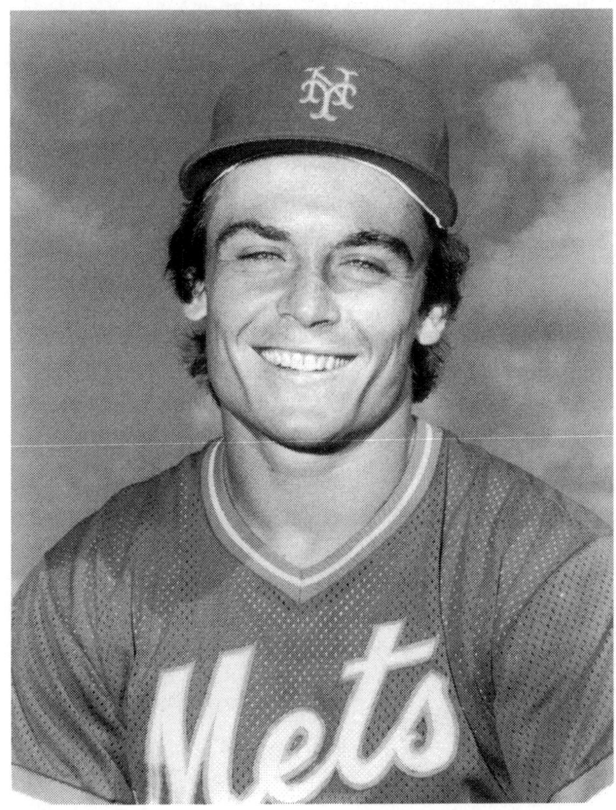

promoted to Jackson of the Double-A Texas League, playing in six games.

Gibbons stayed with Jackson as the starting catcher in 1983, and posted career bests in offense and defense up to that point. He batted .298 and posted solid defense, with a.982 fielding average. This was enough to promote him to Triple-A Tidewater for the International League playoffs. He went 3-for-5 (including two doubles) during Tidewater's march to the league title.[9] His 1983 production earned Gibbons a spot on the Mets' 40-man roster.[10] Manager Davey Johnson thought Gibbons needed a full year at Triple A, but a "desperate"[11] catching situation forced Gibbons onto the 1984 Mets. By mid-March Johnson seemed to change his mind on Gibbons, saying, "He's mentally mature, with a lot of heart and a lot of drive."[12] Gibbons' offense, his ability to call a game, and his past performances earned him the chance. Fellow rookie Dwight Gooden was a supporter as well, saying of Gibbons after a spring-training game, "He calls a good game. I didn't have to shake him off much, maybe once."[13]

Gibbons was hitting .280[14] and had seemingly convinced the Mets that he was the number-one catcher, until a collision with the Philadelphia Phillies' Joe Lefebvre landed him on the 15-day disabled list to start the season.[15] After his activation on April 9, he started six straight games at catcher, seven for the month. His offense was anemic (.040), but his defense was error-free. Another injury, this time a sore arm, landed Gibbons on the disabled list again at the end of April.[16] Fellow rookie Mike Fitzgerald stepped in and took the starting job away. Gibbons was sent back to Tidewater when he was reactivated. He was recalled in September, but played in only two games.

Gibbons was still considered to be the catcher of the future when the Mets acquired All-Star Gary Carter from the Montreal Expos in December 1984 in a package deal that sent Mike Fitzgerald to Montreal.[17] Gibbons went into spring training in 1985 hoping to be Carter's backup,[18] but the Mets brass decided that he would benefit from being the everyday starter in Tidewater.[19] Davey Johnson said, "I like John Gibbons, but he may be too young to sit around (backing up Gary Carter)."[20] Gibbons took the news of the Carter acquisition in stride. "I was frustrated when I heard we got Carter, but you can't get ticked off when it's the best catcher in baseball. I've got something to prove, coming off a tough year. I want to be here, but I know I need the work."[21] Once again, the "catcher of the future" showed his potential, his solid defense, and decent hitting. This time, though, the Mets would not call him up in September.

Gibbons' offense slipped a bit in 1986 at Tidewater, but his solid defense (.993 fielding percentage) once again earned him a late-season call-up. He played in eight games and in the last one, he hit his only major-league home run, against Phillies pitcher Michael Jackson.[22] Gibbons was left off the postseason roster inasmuch as the Mets already had two solid catchers, Gary Carter and Ed Hearn. Although he earned a World Series ring as a bullpen catcher, he never played in the major leagues again.[23] He spent 1987 at Tidewater before being traded to the Los Angeles Dodgers for utility man Craig Shipley, and played in 1988 for Triple-A Albuquerque before being released. Gibbons spent 1989 with the Texas Rangers' Triple-A team at Oklahoma City, and 1990 with Scranton /Wilkes-Barre, the Phillies' Triple-A team.

After the 1990 season Gibbons decided to retire as a player and venture into coaching. He spent four years in the Mets organization as an instructor and coach with Capital City (Columbia South Carolina) of the South Atlantic League. This earned him the job as manager of Kingsport, his first minor-league team, in 1995. The lack of experience as a manager did not hurt him; Kingsport went 48-18 en route to the Appalachian League championship. Gibbons was named Appalachian League Manager of the Year, and subsequently promoted to manage St. Lucie of the Class-A Florida State League, and won another league championship in 1996. After a 54-81 performance in 1997, Gibbons was promoted to Double-A Binghamton, where he earned another Manager of the Year award, going 82-60. The Mets organization took notice, and gave him the Casey Stengel Award as the Mets organizational Manager of the Year. Along with the award came a promotion to manage Triple-A Norfolk. Gibbons's three-year record at Norfolk was 227-199, and his team had a first-place finish in 2001.

In 2002 Gibbons returned to the major leagues as the bullpen catcher for the Toronto Blue Jays. When manager Buck Martinez was fired in June and replaced by third-base coach Carlos Tosca, Gibbons was promoted to first-base coach. He held that positon through 2003 and until August 8, 2004, when Tosca was fired and Gibbons was named interim manager. (This was not the first time Gibbons had managed the Blue Jays. He filled in for Tosca in two games in May 2003 when Tosca's daughter was graduating, and for a game in September 2003 when Tosca was suspended for his actions toward an umpire. The Blue Jays won all three games.) Gibbons went 20-30 for the rest of the 2004 season. On October 4, 2004, Toronto general manager J.P Ricciardi (a teammate of Gibbons at Class-A Shelby in 1981) named the 42-year-old Gibbons the permanent manager.[24]

The 2005 Blue Jays (80-82) finished in third place in the AL East. Expectations were high for 2006. Toronto brought in closer B.J. Ryan, starting pitcher A.J. Burnett, and third basemen Troy Glaus. The Blue Jays (87-75) finished second, 10 games behind the New York Yankees. The season was marked by two confrontations between Gibbons and one of his players, Shea Hillenbrand. Hillenbrand, upset over his lack of playing time, wrote negative comments about the team on a whiteboard in the clubhouse, including the comment that the "ship was sinking."[25] Gibbons and Hillenbrand got into a heated argument and the manager challenged Hillenbrand to a fight. Hillenbrand was later designated for assignment,[26] then traded to the San Francisco Giants. Later, in August 21, Gibbons and pitcher Ted Lilly got into a shoving match in the tunnel leading to the dugout after Gibbons removed Lilly from a game, with Gibbons getting a bloody nose.[27] Lilly left Toronto as a free agent during the offseason.

For 2007 Toronto obtained free-agent slugger Frank Thomas and called up young outfielder Adam Lind from Syracuse. These changes produced little change as the Jays (83-79) finished in third place in the AL East.

The 2008 campaign started off rocky for Gibbons. He benched DH Frank Thomas after a slow start. Later released, Thomas accused the Blue Jays of preventing him from reaching an option clause in his contract. (If Thomas reached 364 at-bats, his 2009 option would be guaranteed for $10 million.) The club played mediocre ball through late June, when Gibbons was fired with Toronto mired in last place in the division. He was replaced by Cito Gaston, who had led Toronto to World Series championships in 1992 and 1993.

In 2009 the Kansas City Royals hired Gibbons as the bench coach under manager Trey Hillman. When the Royals dropped Hillman, Gibbons was not rehired. After a couple of seasons, he managed Double-A San Antonio for the San Diego Padres in 2012. Toronto came calling again in the offseason. Gibbons was named manager for 2013, taking over for John Farrell, who had left to manage the Boston Red Sox. The Blue Jays went 74-88 in his first season, and improved to 83-79 in 2014.

In 2015 the Blue Jays improved dramatically. Bolstered by midseason trades for shortstop Troy Tulowitzki and pitcher David Price, along with a November 2014 trade for All-Star third baseman Josh Donaldson, the team finished first in the AL East at 93-69, their best record since the World Series-winning 1993 Blue Jays won 95 games. The 2015 team advanced to the American League Championship Series before falling in six games to the eventual World Series champion Kansas City Royals. Gibbons was disappointed by the loss but remained hopeful for the future. "The good outweighed the bad," he said. "We have a lot to look forward to next season."[28]

As of 2015 John and Julie Gibbons reside in San Antonio, Texas.[29] They are the parents of three children.

NOTES

1 Robert Macleod, "Jays' Gibbons: A Keen Mind Behind a Good-ol'-boy Exterior," *Toronto Globe and Mail*, theglobeandmail.com/sports/baseball/manager-john-gibbons-knows-job-is-on-

the-line-if-blue-jays-dont-improve/article20087549/?page=all, accessed December 1, 2015.

2 Ibid.

3 "John Gibbons, Lucky or What?" *Waterloo* (Ontario) *Region Record*, therecord.com/sports-story/2621866-john-gibbons-lucky-or-what-/,February 8, 2013, accessed January 8, 2016.

4 Ibid.

5 Macleod.

6 Bob Elliott, "Toronto Blue Jays to Name John Gibbons Manager," *Toronto Sun*, torontosun.com/2012/11/20/toronto-blue-jays-to-name-john-gibbons-manager, accessed December 1, 2015.

7 Brendan Kennedy, "Blue Jays Manager John Gibbons Opens up about Quitting Tobacco," *Toronto Star,* thestar.com/sports/bluejays/2015/06/07/blue-jays-manager-john-gibbons-opens-up-about-quitting-tobacco.html, accessed December 1, 2015.

8 "Mets Pick Outfielder Strawberry; Bosox Take Vienna's Brown," *Washington Post*, June 4, 1980.

9 Jane Gross, "Gibbons, a Rookie, May Catch for Mets," *New York Times*, March 19, 1984.

10 "Scoreboard," *Chicago Tribune*, November 11, 1983.

11 Gordon Edes, "NL notebook," *Los Angeles Times*, March 25, 1984.

12 Gross.

13 Ibid.

14 "Orioles Trade Landrum to Cardinals," *Philadelphia Inquirer*, March 26, 1984.

15 "Transactions," *New York Times*, March 29, 1984.

16 Peter Gammons, "Equal Dollars Make Sense," *Boston Globe*, May 6, 1984.

17 Joseph Durso, "Mets get Expos' Carter for Brooks and 3 Others," *New York Times*, December 11, 1984.

18 Joseph Durso, "Met Pitching Vulnerable," *New York Times*, February 18, 1985.

19 Joseph Durso, "Carter Connects in Catching Debut," *New York Times*, March 12, 1985.

20 Joseph Durso, "For Mets, the Sweet Smell of Success," *New York Times*, February 21, 1985.

21 Durso, "Carter Connects."

22 youtube.com/watch?v=H436iRMu40w.

23 Macleod, "Jays' Gibbons."

24 "Blue Jays Name John Gibbons as Manager," *Canada News Wire*, October 4, 2004.

25 Rob Gilles, "Jays' Gibbons, Lilly Get Into Argument," ABC Sports, abcnews.go.com/Sports/wireStory?id=2340295 (accessed December 1, 2015 through web.archive.org/web/20070309224524/http://abcnews.go.com/Sports/wireStory?id=2340295).

26 Ibid.

27 ESPN.com news services, "Lilly-Gibbons Confrontation Leads to 'Mayhem' in Tunnel," ESPN.com, sports.espn.go.com/mlb/news/story?id=2556925, accessed December 1, 2015.

28 Hal Bodley, "Sting of Blue Jays' Loss Fading for Gibbons," MLB.com, m.mlb.com/news/article/157153560/alcs-loss-still-stings-for-blue-jays-gibbons,accessed January 8, 2016.

29 Macleod, "Jays' Gibbons."

DWIGHT "DOC" GOODEN

By Lee Kluck

THERE IS NO DOUBT THAT DWIGHT "DOC" Gooden should be considered one of baseball's biggest stars of the 1980s. There is also no doubt that he should be thought of as one of the game's largest cautionary figures of the same period.

Dwight Gooden was the youngest of three children born to Dan and Ella Gooden on November 16, 1964, in Tampa, Florida, where Dan—who had only a third-grade education—worked for the Cargill Corporation and coached youth baseball while Ella, his second wife, worked in a nursing home and a pool hall. According to Gooden, baseball was one of his father's great passions and it permeated the relationship between the father and the son from the beginning. Often this meant that Dan and Dwight would spend countless hours talking, practicing, or watching the game in order to make Dwight the best player possible. This treatment paid off quickly as the lanky Gooden aged. At 7, he learned the overhand curveball that would help him dominate hitters during his big-league career. At 9, he was an integral part of a 10-14-year-old Little League team that qualified for the Little League World Series (though Dwight couldn't play in the tournament because he was too young), and also playing softball against adults who played semipro baseball for his father.[1]

Despite this early success and what Gooden considered a fairly idyllic, nurturing, childhood, his home life was also full of turmoil that would foreshadow many of the pitcher's struggles later in life. Most importantly, Gooden was exposed to a heavy dose of substance abuse (his father was a heavy drinker), adultery, and violence. This included being present the day his sister was shot five times by her husband while 5-year-old Dwight played with his cousin Derrick.[2]

Still, Gooden continued to excel on the baseball diamond, eventually becoming a standout pitcher for Hillsborough High School in Tampa. He was scouted by teams including the New York Mets, Cincinnati Reds, and the Chicago Cubs. He also received college scholarship offers. The Mets took Gooden with the fifth overall pick in the 1982 amateur draft and he signed a deal worth $40,000 with an $85,000 signing bonus.[3]

Like most prospects, Gooden started out in the low minors, in this case, the 17-year-old Gooden was assigned to Kingsport in the Rookie-level Appalachian League and after just two starts (18 strikeouts in 13 innings) was promoted to Little Falls in the Class-A New York-Penn League. Overall, he went 5-5 with a 2.75 ERA in 11 starts, and was promoted to Lynchburg in the high Class-A Carolina League for 1983.

At Lynchburg it looked as if Gooden's progress may have stalled. Like most young pitchers, he tried to survive purely on his fastball and was beaten around by the more advanced hitters. At that point, Gooden said, it took the tutoring of his pitching coach, John Cumberland, to get him back on track by teaching him to set up hitters by throwing inside. From that point on, Gooden was dominant on the mound. Off the field a number of incidents foreshadowed the problems he would face later in his career. At Lynchburg Gooden became a frequent drinker. At the time, he thought this was a normal part of being a young professional. However, when he missed a bus after partying with teammate Darryl Strawberry, the Mets brass became concerned for the young righty.[4]

Despite these problems, the future was bright for Gooden. At Lynchburg he finished the season 19-4 and struck out 300 hitters in 191innings. This earned him a promotion to Triple-A Tidewater in time for the International League playoffs. Gooden got two starts for manager Davey Johnson's team. The first was a loss to Columbus in the semifinals. Gooden then started the decisive game of the playoff finals and defeated the Richmond Braves 6-1 to win the International League title.[5] Gooden finished his season by pitching a complete-game win against Denver as Tidewater won the Triple-A World Series, a round-robin event.[6]

The biggest event that propelled Gooden's career coming into 1984 occurred off the field. The 1983 Mets (68-94) went through two managers (George Bamberger and Frank Howard) and finished sixth in the NL East. General manager Frank Cashen embarked on a rebuilding. At the heart of the rebuild was the core of the 1983 Tidewater team, including manager Davey Johnson and playoff call-up Dwight Gooden.

As for whether he felt he belonged at the big-league level, Gooden was up and down on the idea. He made his major-league debut on April 7 at the Houston Astrodome, and won, surrendering one run in five innings and striking out five. After the game Gooden told his father he felt he would "win a lot of games" at the big-league level if he continued to pitch the way he did that day.[7] However, Gooden was a little unsure of his impending success after a rough outing in his next start, against the Chicago Cubs at Wrigley Field. He pitched 3⅓ innings and gave up six runs. This time he told his father that he "may not be ready yet" for life in the big leagues. Luckily for the Mets, Gooden was wrong.

During the rest of 1984, the young right-hander dominated the National League on his way to a 17-9 record with a 2.60 ERA. His weapon of choice? The strikeout. During his rookie season Gooden averaged 11.4 strikeouts per nine innings and struck out a total of 276. Fans and the media took to calling him "Doctor K" or "Doc." His performance earned him Rookie of the Year honors in the National League.

In 1985 Gooden was even better. He continued to rack up wins and strikeouts. He would go 18-1 during one stretch of the season and ended the season 24-4, mowing down hitters with an overpowering fastball and a devastating curveball. He struck out 268 hitters in 276⅔ innings and finished with an ERA of 1.53. All of this would earn him the 1985 National League Cy Young Award. His dominance on the field helped the Mets begin to look like contenders, and made Gooden a proven commodity for advertisers. By the start of the 1986 season, Gooden was a spokesman for Polaroid, Kellogg's, Spalding, and Toys R Us. Nike put up his likeness in Times Square. It seemed as if the sky was the limit for Gooden. But this was about the time his off-the-field demons began to overshadow his baseball prowess.

By Gooden's admission, during the 1985 season he began to sample the nightlife of major-league baseball with the help of some of his Mets teammates. For Gooden, who was 20 at the time, this meant a continuation of his heavy drinking. Then, while in Tampa after the season, Gooden experimented with cocaine. Cocaine use in the majors was no huge shock at this time. It permeated clubhouses throughout the league much as performance-enhancing drugs would a generation later. Gooden became a seasoned user during the 1986 season. All the while he continued to dominate on the field. In 1986 he went 17-6, struck out 200 hitters and led the Mets to the National league pennant all while falling deeper into drug addiction amid the party atmosphere that was the 1986 Mets.[8]

In the World Series, Gooden was less successful. In his first start, in Game Two, Gooden earned the loss as he struggled and was chased after giving up six runs (five earned) in five innings to the Boston Red Sox. Then, in Game Five, Gooden lost again. This time, he gave up four runs (three earned) in four innings. Still, four nights later the Mets won the World Series and Gooden celebrated by doing cocaine until the sun came up. He missed the Mets victory parade.

Gooden's drug use continued in the offseason. He began to have troubles at home despite fathering his first child, Dwight Gooden Jr. Rumors of his drug use spread like wildfire throughout baseball and his hometown of Tampa. All of this led Gooden to suggest that he would submit to a drug test to quell the talk. Gooden was arrested later in the offseason in Tampa. Then, early in 1987 spring training, he failed a test for cocaine. At the Mets' urging, he entered the Smithers Alcoholism and Rehabilitation Center in New York City.

This first stint in rehab cost Gooden the first two months of the 1987 season and did not cure him of his addiction. Off the field, by his own admission, he continued to drink throughout the 1987 season though he did stop using cocaine for a prolonged period. On the field, Gooden was still the dominant pitcher the Mets had counted on since 1984. In 25 starts he went 15-7 with an ERA of 3.21 while striking out 148.

Gooden was also on form through the end of the 1980s, though there were signs that all the innings and possibly the hard living were catching up with him. In 1988, with a still strong Mets squad, Gooden stayed clean and was 18-9 with a 3.19 ERA as the Mets won the National League East. He was still off cocaine in 1989, though he missed two months with a shoulder injury made only 17 starts (9-4).

As the 1990s opened, there was a changing of the guard with the Mets. Gone, or about to be so, were many of the key players from the playoff runs of 1986-1989. Gooden however, was in great shape and pitched like it. In 1990 he went 19-7 while striking out 223 in 232 innings. His numbers fell off the next three seasons though he remained somewhat sober. That changed in 1994.

That season, Gooden became a historical footnote when he gave up three home runs to journeyman outfielder Tuffy Rhodes on Opening Day at Wrigley Field. He kicked a bat rack and broke his toe. The injury required a rehab assignment and during that time Gooden began using cocaine again. He was suspended by Major League Baseball and entered the rehabilitation program at the Betty Ford Center. Once again, this program did not help Gooden and two days after his release from the center he was using cocaine again.

Gooden's second relapse coincided with the beginning of the players strike in 1994. While at home he continued to use cocaine in his room while his wife and children were in the house. Gooden failed another drug test, and was suspended for all of the 1995 season. Gooden entered Narcotics Anonymous with the help of Ray Negron, a consultant with the Yankees, and he began working toward a comeback.

Gooden's comeback began in the winter of 1996. In February he signed a free-agent contract with the Yankees. During his early starts that season he was largely ineffective and it seemed that the comeback would be a short one. Still, Gooden rallied to pitch a no-hitter against the Seattle Mariners at Yankee Stadium on May 14. He finished 11-7 with the Yankees and was firmly back in the majors, albeit as a journeyman.

Gooden was back with the Yankees in 1997 and even made a start in the American League Division Series. (He got a no-decision as Cleveland defeated the Yankees, 3-2.) After the season he signed a free-agent contract with the Indians and went 11-10 over two seasons. Gooden pitched for Houston, Tampa Bay, and the Yankees in 2000. After a tough spring in 2001 he chose to retire before the Yankees released him. "It has been a joyous ride," Gooden said.[9]

Gooden worked as a front-office assistant for the New York Yankees but began using cocaine again. This led to his third attempt at rehab, in 2004. Drugs were not Gooden's only problem during this period. In March 2005 he was arrested for hitting his girlfriend, at which point he left the Yankees. In August Gooden led police on a high-speed chase in Tampa that quickly became a citywide manhunt after he was pulled over during a routine traffic stop. He missed a court-ordered domestic abuse prevention class which triggered a 10-day incarceration in the Hillsborough County Jail. Gooden was sentenced to three years' probation and community service stemming from the traffic stop and fugitive arrest. As part of this, he underwent rehab for a fourth time in 2006.

After three months of sobriety, Gooden relapsed in the spring of 2006. This relapse was a parole violation and Gooden was sentenced to a year and a day at a maximum-security state prison in Lake Butler, Florida.

After the prison stint Gooden tried once again to establish a firm footing in his personal life. This included reconciling with the Mets during the final year of play at Shea Stadium in 2008 and the first year of play at Citi Field in 2009. He was inducted into the Mets Hall of Fame in 2010 along with Davey Johnson and Darryl Strawberry.

Despite this Gooden relapsed again that year. A string of erratic behavior followed and Gooden was arrested on a litany of charges including child endangerment in New Jersey when he operated his vehicle under the influence of cocaine and Ambien with his son, Dylan, in the car. That arrest led to more spiraling behavior and Gooden was a recluse for much of the summer of 2010 while living in a hotel in New Jersey. Then, with the help of his Narcotics Anonymous sponsor, Gooden attempted to reclaim his life. He appeared on TV's *Celebrity Rehab.* Gooden continued treatment in Bergen County, New Jersey, and in 2011 he was placed on five years' special probation in 2011 on charges stemming from his last arrest.

As of 2015 Gooden has been sober since March 11, 2012. Living in New York, he is the spokesman for Pinktie.org, a sports charity that helps in the fight against cancer. (Two of his aunts died from the disease.) In 2015 he said he still loved baseball and especially the Mets. "I appreciate what the Yankees did for me, but I'll always be a Met at heart," Gooden said.[10]

SOURCES

In addition to the sources cited in the Notes, the author referred to baseball-reference.com and retrosheet.org. Insights into Gooden's addiction timeline come from *Doc: A Memoir,* cited in Note 1.

NOTES

1 Recollections of Gooden's early life in Tampa appear in Dwight Gooden and Ellis Henican, *Doc: A Memoir* (Las Vegas: Amazon Publishing, 2013).

2 Ibid.

3 Ibid.

4 Ibid.

5 Associated Press, "Tidewater Wins IL Flag," *Lewiston* (Maine) *Journal*, September 12, 1983.

6 George Rorrer, "Tides Rule Triple A, Sitting in the Stands," *The Sporting News*, October 3, 1983, 28.

7 Gooden and Henican.

8 The best recap of the 1986 Mets can be found in Jeff Pearlman, *The Bad Guys Won: A Season of Brawling, Boozing, Bimbo-chasing, and Championship Baseball with Straw, Doc, Mookie, Nails, The Kid, and the Rest of the 1986 Mets, the Rowdiest Team to Ever Put on a New York Uniform—and Maybe the Best* (New York: HarperCollins, 2004).

9 Buster Olney, "Baseball: Gooden Concludes his Memorable Career," *New York Times*, March 31, 2001.

10 Jim Baumbach, "Dwight Gooden Rooting for Mets, Says He'll Attend World Series games at Citi Field," *Newsday* (Long Island, New York, October 27, 2015; Kevin Kernan, "Doc Gooden's Life of Alcohol, Drugs and Ks: 'Never Thought I'd Make It to 50,'" *New York Post,* November 16, 2014.

ED HEARN

By Alan Cohen

> "What I was meant to do was impact people's lives."
>
> Ed Hearn (2015)

> "You never know what you are truly capable of until situations or circumstances force you to strive beyond what you ever thought possible. When we come face to face with our own mortality, often we begin to see life in a whole new perspective. We begin to see the value of little things. Money can buy a house, a bed, a companion, and a good time. But it cannot buy a home, a good night's sleep, friends, and memories."
>
> Ed Hearn (1999)[1]

BACKUP CATCHER ED HEARN PLAYED IN 49 games for the New York Mets in 1986. He would never play in that many games again in his three-season career in the major leagues. Nevertheless he was a presence on a New York Mets team that won it all in 1986. In 10 of his appearances he had multiple-hit games, and the Mets won 34 of his 49 games. Before the next season he was traded for David Cone. But in actuality, baseball, for Ed Hearn was just a prelude.

Born on August 23, 1960, in Stuart, Florida, Hearn grew up in nearby Fort Pierce, the first of Bill and Jeanne Hearn's two sons. There was also an adopted daughter, Debbie. The parents operated a print shop. In 1973 Ed, Debbie, and younger brother Tommy all won awards in local golf competition. Tommy joined the PGA tour in 1995, and went on to work as a rules official for the PGA. Debbie worked with IBM before raising a family.

For six years, starting at age 8, Ed won the local punt, pass, and kick competition. As a 10-year-old he won the regional competition at the Orange Bowl in Miami and went on to represent Florida at the Punt, Pass, and Kick finals during the AFC championship game in San Diego, finishing fourth in a field of 13 contestants. He was the high scorer for his Lakers team in the YMCA basketball league in 1973. Excelling as well in the classroom, he won St. Anastasia Elementary School's science fair competition in 1971, and finished third in his class at Fort Pierce Central High School.

On the baseball field, Ed was coached for many years by his father, Bill, and combined with a teammate to pitch a no-hitter in Little League. When not pitching, he was behind the plate and an offensive force, leading his league in batting. He was a standout catcher for the Fort Pierce Central High School Cobras.

In his senior year Hearn was the football quarterback, but suffered a shoulder injury in midseason, an injury that would come back to haunt him several years later.

In his last season of high-school baseball, Hearn got off to a slow start at the plate, and began wearing eyeglasses after a trip to the eye doctor. His hitting improved, and his average for the season climbed to .342. On June 6, 1978, he, on the recommendation of former Phillie Andy Seminick, was drafted by Philadelphia in the fourth round of the amateur draft. (He had an opportunity to go to West Point, but elected to play baseball.)

Hearn toiled in the Phillies' farm system for four years, putting up some good numbers. In 1978 with Helena, Montana, in the Pioneer League (Rookie), he was chosen as the team MVP by the fans on a team that included Ryne Sandberg. After Helena, he played with the Phillies team in the Florida Instructional League, but the pain from his football injury required surgery and he was forced to sit out the 1979 season. Before the 1980 season he injured his ankle while working out at home in Florida, went under the knife again, and missed spring training.

Hearn was able to play first base and DH with Spartanburg in the Class A Sally League in 1980. He batted .300 in 66 games, but it looked as though his catching days were over. In 1981 he again split his time between first base and DH, and had a solid season at Peninsula (Hampton, Virginia) in the High-A Carolina League, batting .303 with 10 homers in 101 games, and hitting a home run in the Carolina League All-Star Game.[2]

Hearn was reassigned to Peninsula in 1982, but was promoted to Double-A Reading (Eastern League) after 21 games in which he batted .329. He did little catching, getting into only five games behind the plate with Peninsula and five with Reading in 1982. He hoped to be released by the Phillies so he could take his chances elsewhere.

Hearn got his wish. Released after the 1982 season, he signed with the New York Mets. He spent most of the 1983 season back in the Carolina League, with Lynchburg. He got off to a poor start, but got hot late in the season, batting .272 and earning a late-season call-up to Double-A Jackson (Texas League). With Lynchburg, he won the first of four consecutive championships in his years in the Mets organization, as the team went 96-43.

After the season Hearn spent time in the Florida Instructional League and played winter ball in Colombia. It was, as he recounted in his book *Conquering Life's Curves*, "absolutely one of the most horrifying experiences of (my) life. The place was just wall-to-wall poverty. Everywhere you looked was a negative picture. There were no phones in the apartment. You had to go to the hotel, and getting calls through (to the people back home) was a nightmare. Just getting out of that place was a challenge."[3]

The following season with Jackson, Hearn shared catching duties with Greg Olsen and in 86 games, had 11 homers and 51 RBIs, batting a team-leading .312, as the team finished 83-53 to lead its division and won the Texas League championship in the playoffs.

In the spring of 1985, Hearn went to spring training with the Mets and was one of the last players cut when the team headed north. He spent the season at Triple-A Tidewater in the International League. He batted .263 for the Tides and became one of the team's top pranksters. Everyone was fair game, but he had particular fun with Kevin Mitchell and pitching coach John Cumberland. The only downer that season came when Hearn suffered a knee injury that forced him to miss the end of the season as Tidewater won the International league title. During that season, he shared an apartment with Calvin Schiraldi and Billy Beane, who called him "Ward" for Ward Cleaver of the *Leave It to Beaver* TV show.

Hearn's resourcefulness as a prankster reached a climax of sorts in the offseason. Schiraldi, who was traded to Boston later that offseason, was getting married. Before the wedding Hearn sneaked into the groom's apartment and found his wedding shoes. On the heel of the left shoe, he painted the letters H and E. On the heel of the right shoe, he painted the letters L and P. During the ceremony, as Calvin and his bride knelt before the altar, backs to the onlookers, everyone could see HELP.[4] Schiraldi would pay back the "favor" when Hearn got married two years later.

After spring training in 1986, the Mets went with Barry Lyons as their backup catcher behind Gary Carter, and once again Hearn was sent to Tidewater. Through 22 games, he was batting .265, and on May 8 Hearn, almost eight years after signing his first professional contract, was called up to the Mets.

Hearn saw his first action on May 17, starting behind the plate and going 2-for-3 in a 6-2 loss to the Dodgers at Los Angeles. In his first two major-league at-bats, with his parents in the crowd applauding him, he singled to right and doubled to left field off Bob Welch.

In his second game, a 7-3 loss to the Giants at Shea Stadium, after making a couple of errors and allowing four stolen bases, Hearn made no excuses. "I've been through a lot to get to this point in my career, a lot of adversity," he said after the game. "I know that if I face difficult times and get something out of it, I know I'm going to be a lot better for it."[5]

On June 15 Hearn had what he would go on to remember as his career highlight. He smacked his first major-league homer, a three-run shot off Pittsburgh's Cecilio Guante in the bottom of the sixth inning that stretched the Mets' 4-3 lead to 7-3. His teammates pushed him up the dugout steps to take a curtain call. His parents were there, and Hearn presented the ball to his father as a Father's Day gift.

On July 3 Hearn once again provided some power. His second-inning homer cut an early Houston lead to 2-1 and the Mets went on to win 6-5 in 10 innings.

Stories abound about the 1986 Mets, but amid a gang of boozers, Hearn was an abstainer. Nevertheless there is an interesting story about his off-the-field activities during that wondrous season. On a summer evening he found himself stranded on a fishing boat in Long Island Sound, out of gas. He radioed for help, and a couple of people in Connecticut, who intercepted the mayday call, would not at first believe him. They questioned him about his batting average, home runs, and even the identity of the Mets' third-base coach. He answered the questions and a call was placed to the Coast Guard. Hearn signed autographs for his rescuers.[6]

The Mets were also brawlers and their most celebrated on-field brawl resulted in Hearn's entering a game against Cincinnati on July 22. The Mets had a comfortable lead in the standings. The game was tied at 3-3 in the bottom of the 10th. Eric Davis of the Reds singled and stole second base. He then stole third. sliding hard into Ray Knight of the Mets. Punches were exchanged, the dugouts emptied and a brawl ensued. Knight and Kevin Mitchell were ejected from the game. Hearn took over behind the plate and Gary Carter was moved to third base. Hearn led off the top of the 14th with a double and scored on a three-run-homer by Howard Johnson as the Mets won 6-3.

In August Hearn saw quite a bit of action as Gary Carter suffered a partial ligament tear in his left thumb that kept him on the disabled list for a couple of weeks. Hearn said, "I think John (Gibbons) and I can handle it for two weeks. We've got a good lead. Nobody's going to fill Gary's shoes but I think two weeks (off) will be good for him. It will give him a rest and let him come back in September."[7] During Carter's absence, Hearn started 11 games, and the Mets went 8-3 as Hearn batted .275 and played errorless ball. In the last of those games, on August 31, at Shea Stadium, Fernando Valenzuela was pitching for the Los Angeles Dodgers and took a 7-3 lead into the bottom of the ninth inning. With one out, Hearn stepped to the plate. Hearn had singled and scored in the third inning, but had struck out in the fifth and popped out to the catcher in the sixth. Hearn was determined to "bust him" if he threw an inside pitch. The first pitch was, indeed, inside and Hearn slammed it over the left-field wall. There was no further scoring and the Mets lost, 7-4. Hearn didn't realize it at the time, but his fourth major-league homer was to be his last.[8]

Actually, the highlight of Hearn's time with the Mets came in early September and it was off the field.

Teammate Randy Niemann had been trying to fix Hearn up with a young nurse Niemann and his wife knew. Hearn turned down the offer. On September 9 Hearn attended a luncheon given by the local chapter of the cystic fibrosis society. The mother of a 5-year-old girl who had cystic fibrosis asked Hearn to sign a ticket stub for a nurse friend of hers. As it turned out, the nurse was Tricia Trienens, Randy Niemann's friend. Ed gave Tricia a call and the two were married on November 28, 1987.[9]

In the World Series, after the Mets lost the first two games, they traveled to Boston and won two of three and returned the series to New York for the historic Game Six. Rain postponed Game Seven to Monday night and the Mets once again came from behind to win the World Series. It was Hearn's fourth championship in as many years.

"Sometimes you think slumps are the worst thing that can happen to you, but this has slumps beat to death," Hearn said as April 1987 came to a close.[10] On March 27, 1987, Joe McIlvane had informed Hearn that the Mets had traded him to the Kansas City Royals as part of a package that brought David Cone to the Mets. Shortly thereafter, the Royals traded catcher Jim Sundberg, and Hearn became the first-string catcher. He was batting .294 in his first six games with the Royals. However, in his haste to impress his new mates, he had overworked his shoulder and was experiencing pain.

On April 18 Hearn had the highest of highs followed by the lowest of lows. The Royals were in New York to play the Yankees. Early in the day, Steve Schryver, the Mets' former farm director, presented Hearn with his World Series ring. In that day's game, with Yankees on second and third in the third inning, Gary Ward singled to right field. Don Mattingly scored from third and Dave Winfield came in behind him to find Hearn guarding home plate. In the ensuing collision, Winfield scored. Hearn finished the game, but the pain in his shoulder, which had already caused him to miss three of his team's first nine games, was unbearable. It would be his last game played for close to two years. Hearn was sidelined by what was thought to be bursitis in his right shoulder. It was later diagnosed as a partial rotator-cuff tear. He missed the rest of the season, undergoing surgery by Dr. Frank Jobe on June 30. Hearn was in rehabilitation for the balance of 1987 and the bulk of the 1988 season before being activated at the beginning of September 1988. Playing for Baseball City in the Class-A Florida State League, he batted.304 in 17 games. On September 2 Hearn was recalled by the Royals and played in seven games at the end of the season, going 4-for-18. In his first major-league at-bat in almost 17 months, he doubled down the left-field line against Chuck Finley of the Angels. On September 29 his pinch-hit single in the 10th inning was the decisive hit in the Royals' 7-6 win over the Chicago White Sox. Afterward, Hearn said, "It's been so long. ... To win the game is just super. Contribution is just the biggest word I can say. That means the most to me, just to say I contributed."[11] Three days later, on October 2, 1988, Hearn played his last major-league game.

Sent to Triple-A Omaha in 1989, Hearn batted .281 in 67 games, and was selected to play in the Triple-A all-star game. However, he did not get near the playing time he needed to show that he was ready to play in the major leagues. Despite a good spring training, the Royals released Hearn before the 1990 season and he signed with the Double-A Canton-Akron Indians He got off to a good start, but an expected call-up, at least to Triple-A, was not immediately in the offing. Hearn was batting .270 through 29 games and after one excruciatingly long 11½-hour minor-league bus ride, he was ready to call it quits. He went home to Kansas City and, in mid-July, he got word of a promotion to Triple-A Colorado Springs, where he batted .288 in 17 games. But he was injured shortly before the end of the season, and was not called up to the Indians.

When there were no major-league offers in 1991, Hearn retired from baseball and took a job selling insurance with New York Life. He did not want to take a job as a minor-league coach or manager.

Ed and his wife, Tricia, faced far more serious challenges in the years ahead. In a high-school physical, he had been told that he had abnormal creatinine levels in his blood and urine. This eventually led to kidney problems, which surfaced in July 1991. He was diagnosed with Focal Segmental Glomerulusclerosis (FSGS), and dialysis and a kidney transplant were on the horizon. It was not his only problem. He also suffered from hypoglammaglobulinemia. His gamma globulin levels were not normal and he had difficulty fighting off infection.

Hearn kept working at his new job, but was feeling weaker and weaker. And as if his kidney and gamma globulin problems weren't enough, he was diagnosed with sleep apnea, a condition where, during the night, the body gasps for oxygen, depriving victims of sleep. Victims spend their nights in bed hooked up to a machine with a mask over their face. In early 1992 Hearn had begun dialysis, was hooked up to his C-pap machine at night, and getting monthly injections of gamma globulin.

Shortly after beginning dialysis in April 1992, Hearn received a kidney transplant from a young man who had died in an accident. It was the first of what would ultimately be three kidney transplants. Four weeks after the first surgery, his body began to reject the kidney, and he had to take more than 30 pills a day and go through dialysis to prevent the rejection and save his failing kidney. The anti-rejection medicines he was taking had the side effect of attacking his immune system, making him susceptible to viruses. Ed was not well and he grew despondent.

As he said, "One day, I'm sitting on top of the world—and then before I really know what is happening, it's all over. It seemed so fast, and it seemed like such a long fall, like a sad movie."[12] From the depths of despair in early 1993, when he even contemplated suicide, he began a physical and emotional rally that propelled him to a new career.

A man of faith, he reached deep inside and found the strength to continue. "When everything else around me was crumbling, I sensed the Hand of God reaching out to comfort me."[13] And then came a life-changing moment. In the fall of 1993, he was asked to give a talk at a Rotary Club. He told his story, recounting his highs and lows. The Rotary Club president, Brad Plumb, encouraged Hearn to share his message with corporate groups. The vibes were positive for the first time in a long time, and even better news came when Tricia told him that they were going to be parents. Cody Carter Hearn was born on August 29, 1994. (The baby's middle name was for Gary Carter.)

In 1994 Hearn committed to telling his story through motivational talks, and came "to the realization that I actually looked forward to speaking more than I used to look forward to playing in a major league game."[14] He sought to instill in others the values that not only helped him cope with adversity and illness, but also enabled him to grow and make the best of the worst circumstances. He has been awarded the Certified Speaking Professional designation, and he was inducted into the St. Lucie County Sports Hall of Fame in 1997.

Hearn works with the NephCure Foundation, which funds research into the causes of FSGS and Nephrotic Syndrome, diseases of the kidney for which there is no cure. He also has had bouts with skin, head, and neck cancer. He had his second kidney transplant in 2000, and his third transplant, in 2002, came from a childhood friend, Chuck Satterwhite. That transplant has proved successful.

Hearn has had more than 20 surgeries to remove growths from his head, but has kept his sense of humor about it. After a surgery in early 2015, he posted a picture showing before and after results and blamed it on being hit by a ping-pong ball by his son Cody.

He has sought to help others through his Bottom of the Ninth Foundation. The foundation's website quotes him: "The bottom of the ninth in baseball doesn't happen unless the home team, the good guys are tied or behind. I believe in our country today that we're losing the battle and losing the game. I say that very loosely but we're losing in the character and moral value department. That is the essence of what made our country strong. I say that it's the bottom of the ninth and we have to step up, swing and make a comeback or else we're going to lose."[15]

In November 2011 Cody Hearn was diagnosed with Burkitt's lymphoma, a rare form of aggressive non-Hodgkin's lymphoma. Cody went through chemotherapy and the following summer traveled with his parents to his grandparents' home in Fort Pierce, where he showed himself to be a great fisherman just like his dad and role model—Ed Hearn.

SOURCES

Baseball-Reference.com.

Hearn's file at the National Baseball Hall of Fame library.

Smith, Curt, ed. *What Baseball Means to Me: A Celebration of Our National Pastime* (New York: Warner Books, 2002)

Associated Press. "Former Royal Ed Hearn Makes Comeback Despite Mistake Label," *Iola* (Kansas) *Register*, July 22, 2000: 4.

McEntire, Gwen. "Former Major League Catcher, Ed Hearn, to Speak on Handling Life's Curves," *Frederick* (Maryland) *News Post*, June 4, 1999: B-13, 14.

Mazenko, Mary Ann. "Ex-Catcher Catching on to a New Life," *Alton* (Illinois) *Telegraph*, July 31, 1995: A-6.

Del Rio (Texas) *News Herald.*

Fort Pierce (Florida) *News Tribune.*

Email correspondence with Ed Hearn and telephone interview with Ed Hearn, July 10, 2015.

NOTES

1. Gwen McEntire, *Frederick News Post*, June 4, 1999: B-14.
2. *Washington Star*, July 8, 1981: E-4.
3. Ed Hearn with Gene Frenette, *Conquering Life's Curves: Baseball, Battles, and Beyond* (Indianapolis: Masters Press, 1996), 113-115.
4. Hearn and Frenette, 125.
5. Helene Elliot, *Newsday*, June 3, 1986.
6. Jeff Pearlman, *The Bad Guys Won* (New York: Harper Collins, 2004), 110.
7. George Vecsey, "It's My Team Now," *New York Times*, August 18, 1986: C3.
8. Hearn and Frenette, 139.
9. Hearn and Frenette, 140.
10. *Salina* (Kansas) *Journal*, April 30, 1987: 13.
11. *Salina* (Kansas) *Journal*, September 30, 1987: 15.
12. Associated Press, *Iola Register*, July 22, 2000: 4.
13. Hearn and Frenette, 225.
14. Hearn and Frenette, 226.
15. Bottom of the Ninth Foundation website.

DANNY HEEP

By Mark Simon

DANNY HEEP WAS A RESPECTABLE MAJOR leaguer who made a career not out of being a star, but of being a highly useful role player who fit in well on championship-caliber teams. He was born on July 3, 1957, in San Antonio, Texas, where he grew up and went to college. His father, Jacob, was a semipro baseball player who worked in logistics at Kelly Air Force Base.

Heep's uncle, Matt Batts, had a 10-year major-league career, mostly as a backup catcher. He spent half of it with the Boston Red Sox and as a result, most of the Heep family rooted for Boston. But Heep picked his own path and rooted for the Pirates teams that were led by Roberto Clemente and Willie Stargell.

Jacob Heep got his son involved in baseball at a young age and Danny established himself as being pretty good, good enough pitch and play the outfield locally at St. Mary's University, an NAIA school. This was not an ordinary NAIA program.

Heep was more of a star as a pitcher than as a hitter. As of 2015 he ranked second in St. Mary's history in career ERA (2.33). In 1978 he posted an 0.69 ERA and 11 saves. Heep earned All-Conference honors for three years and was Big State Conference Player of the Year in 1978. He was selected by the Houston Astros with the 37th overall pick in the 1978 major-league draft.

The minor leagues would pose a bit of a challenge. Heep was used to playing 40 games a year, not 140. "It took me a little while to get used to that," he said.[1]

Heep hit .340 in 66 games for Daytona Beach in the Florida State League, then the next year for Columbus (Georgia) in the Double-A Southern League, the power came. He hit .327 with 21 home runs and was named the league MVP.

Said his manager, Jim Johnson: "I've never seen anyone who can swing the bat like Heep can. He has good arm extension on the inside pitch or the outside. It's his stroke that separates Heep from the rest."[2]

Heep earned a call to the big leagues at the end of the 1979 season, and went 2-for-14 for the Astros. Johnson and Heep moved up to Triple A in 1980 and both thrived in Tucson of the Pacific Coast League. The team went 87-59 and Heep led the Toros with a .343 batting average, while hitting 17 home runs in 96 games. "He's the best hitter in the organization," Johnson said. "He's very serious, very dedicated."[3]

This time the Astros brought Heep up in mid-July for a longer look and he made the playoff roster as the Astros won the NL West and faced the Philadelphia Phillies. They lost in an epic five-game series that ranks among the best in postseason history. Heep, who hit .276 in 87 regular-season at-bats, had one at-bat in the series, flying out in the 10th inning of Game Five. The Astros made the playoffs again the next season and

lost to the Dodgers in the Divisional Round. Heep, again a late-season call-up from Tucson, did not play in that series.

The Astros outfield had Jose Cruz in one corner and Terry Puhl in the other, and since Heep's best fit was as a corner outfielder, it was hard for him to crack the lineup. On December 10, 1982, a month after Heep married his wife, Jane, the Astros traded him to the Mets for pitcher Mike Scott. (The move happened the same day the Mets agreed to a deal with the Reds to bring back Tom Seaver.)

Though Heep didn't match Scott's Houston stardom, the Mets got good value from him as a pinch-hitter and backup outfielder. Heep wanted to play more often than he did and made that known publicly in August, venting to a reporter from the *New York Post* that "they can get anyone to do what I'm doing for them."[4] But with time, Heep adjusted to his role. He hit four pinch-hit home runs in 1983. And he found a fan in new manager Davey Johnson, who took over in 1984 and got Heep into the lineup.

"(Pinch-hitting) was brutal," Heep said. "I was never really very good at it. No one is really good at pinch-hitting. To face other team's closers, that's not the best situation. The key to me having a decent couple of years as a pinch-hitter was that Davey Johnson gave us all one or two starts per week. Everybody got some playing time. I learned a lot from Rusty Staub — how to prepare and how to watch pitchers."[5]

In 1985 Heep found himself a part of a baseball milestone when his former Houston teammate, Nolan Ryan, made him his 4,000th strikeout victim. "I remember they called a pitch six inches outside for strike two, so I was pretty much toast," Heep said.[6]

Heep was also a part of one of baseball's most unusual highlights. On July 4, 1985, the Mets and Atlanta Braves played a bizarre 19-inning game in Atlanta. Heep watched the game-tying 18th-inning home run hit by Braves pitcher Rick Camp sail over the left-field fence and put his hands on his head in disgust. The Mets won the game, 16-13 in 19 innings. It ended at close to 4 A.M.

"The one thing I do remember (from that game) is that we were on the way back from the hotel, we were trying to cross an intersection, we're crossing a low-water area and we said. 'This bus feels like it's floating,'" Heep said with a laugh. "This would be the last thing we need."[7]

The Mets did more than stay afloat. The 1985 team won 98 games, finished second to the Cardinals and was in the race for the NL East title until the season's final days. After finishing second in each of the previous two seasons, the Mets came into 1986 with the intent of dominating.

Heep had his best season to that point, hitting .282 with a .379 on-base percentage and 5 home runs in 195 at-bats. He was solid as a pinch-hitter, with nine hits, eight RBIs and a .300 batting average off the bench.

"Danny Heep is a reflection of the depth of the 1986 Mets," said Greg Prince, a Mets historian and the author of *Faith and Fear in Flushing*. "To have carried a player who was capable of starting for most teams almost as an afterthought shows just how loaded the 24-man roster was.[8] He was the embodiment of usefulness, in the best sense of the word, providing insurance in left, right and first and was a proven bat off the bench."[9]

When the Mets made the World Series, Heep got a chance to play. The Mets lost the first two games, with Heep coming off the bench in both, but he got a chance to start at DH in Game Three. After the Red Sox botched a first-inning rundown to keep a Mets rally going, Heep singled in two runs against Red Sox starter Oil Can Boyd. That extended a 2-0 lead to 4-0 and the Mets were on their way to a 7-1 romp. It cut Boston's lead in the series to two games to one.

"There wasn't any panicking," Heep said of the Mets' early deficit in the Series. "We just came back in, prepared the same way and had confidence that we were good enough that we could (win at least two games). We didn't want to put any more pressure on ourselves than we really had."[10]

The Mets got even in the series by winning Game Four, 6-2 (Heep went 0-for-4) but lost Game Five (with Heep on the bench) to trail three games to two. Heep played a peripheral role in the Mets' comeback in Game Six. With the team down 2-1 and men on first and third with nobody out in the fifth inning, Johnson had Heep pinch-hit for Rafael Santana. Though Heep hit into a double play, the tying run scored.

The Red Sox took a 5-3 lead into the bottom of the 10th inning of Game Six. As the first two outs were made, Heep was among those players watching with Keith Hernandez in Davey Johnson's office, where players would often hang out during games. He saw the groundball go through Bill Buckner's legs there.

Heep was one who wanted to go watch from the dugout, but once the rally started, Hernandez would not let anyone leave. "Keith said no, no, no, no, no," Heep said with a laugh. "Nobody wanted to move."[11]

With Heep and his friends watching on TV, the Mets won that game. Heep knew they wouldn't lose Game Seven. "After we won (Game Six), we thought this has to be destiny," he said.[12]

It was. The Mets won Game Seven to win the World Series. Heep got to be a participant in a championship parade.

Among the things he remembered most about his playing time was the camaraderie of the 1986 Mets. Though Heep was a member of the "Scum Bunch" (the nickname for a group that drank and goofed off on plane trips), he stayed out of trouble.

"We were all 28, 29, 30 years old," Heep said. "Everybody on that team got along. I don't know if you'll ever see a team that close-knit. We were like a college team, a bunch of friends doing what they like to do."[13]

Heep was a free agent that offseason and ran into the same issue that other free agents had that offseason. Teams did not make any free-agent signings. (An arbitrator later found owners guilty of collusion and they were forced to pay a penalty.) As a result, Heep, who wanted to return to the Mets, agreed to a deal with the Los Angeles Dodgers.

Heep spent two years with the Dodgers, where his role was as a backup outfielder and pinch-hitter, similar to that which he had with the Mets. He was a member of the 1988 Dodgers team that stunned the Mets in the NLCS and the Athletics in the World Series. When injured pinch-hitter Kirk Gibson hit his game-winning home run off Athletics reliever Dennis Eckersley, Heep got a view from the dugout, rather than the clubhouse.

In February 1989 Heep signed with the Red Sox and, at age 31, got the most playing time he'd ever gotten in his career as the Red Sox had injury issues in their outfield. He hit .300 in 320 at-bats with more walks (29) than strikeouts (26).

In 1990 Heep had back problems and needed surgery. When he tried to come back, near the end of the season, he was not effective, though the Red Sox still thought enough of him to put him on their postseason roster. He went 0-for-2 in the ALCS as the Red Sox were swept by the Athletics. That offseason Heep became a free agent and was invited to spring training with the Chicago White Sox. The Atlanta Braves gave him a chance but after a month on their roster in May/June, he was asked to accept a demotion.

Heep's wife was eight months pregnant with their daughter, Joanna, at the time and Heep realized it was time to end his playing career. He declined the demotion and retired.

Not long after that, an assistant-coach position opened up at the University of the Incarnate Word, a private Catholic college in San Antonio. Heep applied and was hired. He became the program's head coach in 1998 and had 18 seasons on the job as of 2015. He steered it through promotions from NAIA to NCAA Division II in 2000 and Division I in 2014. Through 2014 Heep's team had won more than 500 games and he was a three-time conference coach of the year.

"I'm teaching the way I was taught," Heep said. "The fundamental parts of the game and hitting are very basic. It wasn't really changed since 1985. Coaches like Walt Hriniak and Bill Robinson taught the same fundamental swing that is taught today. I never made a lot of money playing, but I'm comfortable and I like what I'm doing."[14]

A handful of Heep's players have been drafted, but he has preached caution with regard to considering a pro career. He took a similar approach with his son, Robert, who was a Dean's List student studying business at Texas A&M. (His daughter planned a career as a lawyer.)

"I'm more proud of his making the Dean's List than any home run he hit or game he played," Heep said. "The proudest thing for me as a coach is the academic side. I tell our guys let's make a 3.5 or better in the classroom. That's what's going to make you money."[15]

Heep was a player respected by his peers and became a coach respected by his players. His playing days remained an important part of his persona. "I'd like to be remembered as a good team player who got along with everybody," Heep said. "You want to be the best player, but you want to be *remembered* as a teammate."[16]

NOTES

1 Phone interview with Danny Heep, July 16, 2015 (hereafter Heep interview).

2 Cecil Darby, "Heep Hitting a Heap at Columbus," *Columbus Ledger*, September 1979. Undated clipping in Heep's player file at the National Baseball Hall of Fame.

3 *The Sporting News*, August 9, 1980.

4 Mike McAlary, "Heep fuming over part-time role," *New York Post*, August 16, 1983.

5 Heep interview.

6 Heep interview.

7 Danny Heep radio interview with Mike Silva, *Blogtalk Radio*, July 9, 2008.

8 Rosters were 24 players instead of 25 that season and three others, as noted at baseball-reference.com/bullpen/Roster.

9 Email interview with Greg Prince, July 28, 2015.

10 Heep interview.

11 Heep interview.

12 Heep interview with Mike Silva.

13 Heep interview.

14 Heep interview.

15 Heep interview.

16 Heep interview.

KEITH HERNANDEZ

By Michael Martell

KEITH HERNANDEZ, ONE OF THE MAJOR leagues' all-time best fielding first basemen, played a key role in the New York Mets' late 1980s successes. Hernandez, who was originally a St. Louis Cardinal standout, found himself in a predicament when he was traded in mid-season to the struggling 1983 Mets. His trade was due to conflicting interests between him and Cardinals manager Whitey Herzog. However, Hernandez would not be denied the thrill of victory for long, as he and his Mets teammates quickly became one of the National League's most dominant teams.

Keith Hernandez was born on October 20, 1953, in San Francisco and grew up in nearby San Bruno. He and his brother, Gary, spent hours honing their baseball skills with the help of their father, John Hernandez, who had been a baseball prospect for the Brooklyn Dodgers.[1] Keith was a standout athlete at Capuchino High School, but because of disagreement with his coach over playing time, opted to sit out his senior season. After high school, Hernandez attended the College of San Mateo, where he played baseball in 1971 before being drafted in the 42nd round of the amateur draft by the St. Louis Cardinals.

Hernandez began his professional career in 1972 with the St. Petersburg Cardinals of the Class-A Florida State League. He batted .256 with a .388 slugging percentage and 41 RBIs. Late in the season the Cardinals advanced him to the Triple-A Tulsa Oilers (American Association), for whom he played in 11 games. Hernandez showed the Cardinals that his game was developing and he still had much to prove.

In 1973 the Cardinals placed Hernandez with the Double-A Arkansas Travelers (Texas League), where his batting figures were pedestrian but notably he posted a .991 fielding percentage for the second straight season, and was among the top-fielding minor-league first basemen. Late in the season the Cardinals again promoted him to Triple-A Tulsa, where in 31 games his offensive production increased dramatically (.333 batting average,.468 slugging percentage), and his fielding percentage rose to a sensational.997.

It was becoming clear that Hernandez was almost major-league ready and he earned a spot at Triple-A to start the '74 season. Playing in 102 games for Tulsa, he batted .351 with a .555 slugging percentage and 14 home runs. Hernandez got the call to the Cardinals near the end of August and made his big-league debut on August 30, 1974, against the San Francisco Giants. That night he went 1-for-2 at the plate with two walks and an RBI. In 14 late-season games with St. Louis, he batted.294 with a .441 slugging percentage.

Hernandez spent April and May of 1975 with the Cardinals but his production on offense was woeful.

Batting .203, he was sent back to Tulsa in early June. He returned to the Cardinals as a September call-up and by the end of the season he had lifted his batting average to .250. And he was in the big leagues to stay.

While Hernandez made his presence known as a batter, he also quickly gained a reputation as one of the slickest fielders in the game, as evidenced by his 11 consecutive Gold Glove Awards (1978-1988).

In 1979, his fourth full season with the Cardinals, the 25-year-old Hernandez had a breakout campaign, capturing the National League batting title with a .344 batting average, leading the league in doubles (48), and runs scored (116) for the third-place Cardinals (86-76), playing in his first All-Star Game, and sharing the National League MVP Award with Pittsburgh's Willie Stargell.

In the Cardinals' 1982 world championship season, Hernandez batted .299 and drove in 94 runs. He helped push the Cardinals past the Atlanta Braves in a three-game sweep of the National League Championship Series, and during the seven-game World Series triumph over Milwaukee, he drove in eight runs.

Hernandez was performing well on the field but his attitude and off-field troubles marked him as trouble in the eyes of Cardinals manager Whitey Herzog. The root of the problem was cocaine. A 2010 article on the Bleacher Report website said, "Hernandez stated that he had used massive amounts of the substance starting in 1980 after he and his wife separated. He developed what he described as an 'insatiable desire for more' and admitted that he played under the influence of cocaine in his career."[2] The Cardinals decided that Hernandez was causing more problems than what he was worth to them, and on June 15, 1983, traded him to the Mets for pitchers Neil Allen and Rick Ownbey. Amid the controversy, Hernandez's play stayed sharp; he batted .306 in 95 games for a dismal Mets team and won his sixth consecutive NL Gold Glove.

The Mets were a team struggling to stay relevant in their division, winning only 41 games in 1981 and winning fewer than 70 per season from 1977 to 1983. Hernandez believed that was why he was traded to the Mets. "Whitey thought he was going to bury my ass in New York when he traded me here," Hernandez said. "He had no idea what the minor-league system was like. He thought he was going to stick me here to suffer for two years. Didn't happen. There was such a wealth of talent. And it was just amazing to see it all come together in '84. It revitalized my career."[3]

Upon Hernandez's arrival in the Big Apple, he was bound and determined, along with manager Davey Johnson, to make the Mets a legitimate contender for a championship. In 1984, Hernandez's first full season with the Mets, he made an impact, batting .311 with 15 home runs and earning a spot on the National League All-Star team for the first time since 1980. He won another Gold Glove and a Silver Slugger Award and finished second to Ryne Sandberg in the National League MVP voting. That season the Mets won 90 games, 22 more than they had won the previous season. They finished second in the NL East, the first time they had finished higher than fifth since 1976. Hernandez's efforts (combined with the maturing of Darryl Strawberry and the arrivals of rookie pitchers Dwight Gooden, Ron Darling, and Sid Fernandez) proved to be the spark that the Mets were looking for.

In 1985 the Mets proved to the rest of the baseball world that they were for real. They won 98 games and finished second to the Cardinals in their division. In 158 games Hernandez batted.309 with 91 RBIs, and had a .997 fielding percentage.

Though the Mets had finally turned the page on their misfortunes, there was some uncertainty at the beginning of the 1986 season. Hernandez was a target in a massive investigation of drug use by major-league players. On March 1, Commissioner Peter Ueberroth suspended Hernandez and seven other players for a year, but offered to lift the suspensions if the players agreed to take a number of steps, including contributing 10 percent of their salaries to antidrug programs and undergoing drug tests for the rest of their careers. Hernandez at first said he would appeal, but then changed his mind so he could play the 1986 season. "I feel strongly that I have an obligation to my team, the fans and to baseball to play this year," he said. "… I hope this finally puts this issue to rest."[4] Hernandez proceeded to bat.310 (fifth in the league) with 83 RBIs. His 94 walks led the National League, he won his ninth consecutive Gold Glove, and he was voted a starter in the All-Star Game for the first time. Hernandez's performance helped propel the Mets (108-54) to a first-place East Division finish. Assessing his role on the team, Hernandez said, "'I've played 12 years, and if you don't know pitchers by then, and where to play against different hitters, then you haven't learned anything. I don't have the raw talent of other guys. I have to be prepared."[5]

The 1986 postseason was Hernandez's second career playoff appearance, and he looked to duplicate what he and the Cardinals had done during the 1982 post-season. The Mets' first challenge would be to defeat the West Division champion Houston Astros, no easy task. Their offense was led by MVP runner-up Glenn Davis, while the anchors of the pitching staff were two former Mets—future Hall of Famer Nolan Ryan and Cy Young Award winner Mike Scott. But the Mets vanquished the Astros in six games, the clincher a 16-inning classic, and advanced to the World Series against the Boston Red Sox. Hernandez had seven hits and three RBIs in the six NLCS games.

Hernandez started the World Series slowly at the plate, with just one hit in the first two games as the Mets lost both games. In their 7-1 victory in Game Three, he collected two hits and a walk, and scored a run. As the Mets forced a deciding Game Seven with their improbable extra-inning victory in Game Six, Hernandez had a hit and a walk.

The Mets fell behind, 3-0, in Game Seven, but Hernandez drove in two runs with a single in the sixth, and the Mets got another run to tie the game, 3-3. In the seventh, the Mets scored three more runs, the third one on a sacrifice fly by Hernandez. The Red Sox rallied, but the Mets hung on for an 8-5 victory and the world championship.

Hernandez was 33 years old at the 1987 season began. He played four more seasons, three with the Mets and a final season with the Cleveland Indians. He made his final All-Star team in 1987. During the 1989 season Hernandez's skills began to fade dramatically; he hit just .233 with four home runs, due partly to a broken kneecap, suffered in a collision with Dave Anderson of the Los Angeles Dodgers, that sidelined him for eight weeks from mid-May through mid-July.[6] After the season the Mets let Hernandez go in free agency and he signed with the Cleveland Indians for $3.5 million over two years. "This is a new league, a new city, a new stadium and a new challenge," Hernandez said. "The Indians pursued me more than anyone else. It's important to me to be wanted."[7] But his time in Cleveland was a bust; he played in only 43 games in an injury-plagued 1990 season. He announced his retirement before the season's end. He then had back surgery in 1991.

Hernandez began to seek out ventures that would help promote his celebrity. Most notably he guest-starred in several episodes of the TV comedy *Seinfeld.* While Hernandez did not say much, his presence alone was enough to make the episodes instant classics. He told the *New York Post*, "Saying 'I'm Keith Hernandez' is still worth a lot of money." (As of 2015 he was still receiving royalty checks for the *Seinfeld* appearances.[8]) Hernandez starred in *The Boyfriend: Part 1* and *The Boyfriend: Part 2*, then came back for the series finale in 1998. The royalties for that continued, too. He also made commercials for the Just for Men hair dye product line, including a series of laugh-inducing ads with former New York Knicks star legend Walt Frazier.[9]

In 2000 Hernandez began tutoring Mets first basemen in spring training. In 2006 he started a second career, doing color and commentary on Mets game telecasts on the SNY cable channel. Hernandez said he was a reluctant recruit to the announcing booth but felt he had to do something productive. He became known for being direct and opinionated about the "young men" on the diamond.[10]

Hernandez also took part in Mets community events. In 2012 he arranged to shave off his trademark mustache at an event for charity. It attracted 300 fans and raised $10,000 for a Brooklyn day care center for Alzheimer patients. Hernandez chose this charity because his mother, Jacquelyn, died of Alzheimer's disease in 1989.[11]

Hernandez has been married twice and has three children from his first marriage. As of 2015 he lived in Sag Harbor, New York. Of his post-baseball career, he said, "I mean, how bad is this? I am paid handsomely, with six months off, and it's baseball. Not bad, right?"[12]

SOURCES

Besides the sources cited in the Notes, the author consulted baseball-reference.com and Hernandez's file at the National Baseball Hall of Fame.

NOTES

1 William Berlind, "Keith Hernandez, Hero of '86 Mets, Navigates His Life after Baseball," observer.com/1999/07/keith-hernandez-hero-of-86-mets-navigates-his-life-after-baseball/, July 19, 1999.

2 Harold Friend, "Keith Hernandez Used Cocaine and Was Forced to Name Others," Bleacher Report, February 17, 2010. bleacherreport.com/articles/1070283-keith-hernandez-used-cocaine-and-was-forced-to-name-others.

3 Berlind.

4 Joseph Durso, "Hernandez Won't Challenge Ueberroth," *New York Times*, March 9, 1986.

5 Craig Wolff, "Hernandez Blends Instinct and Savvy," *New York Times*, October 8, 1986.

6 Joseph Durso, "Hernandez Fractures Kneecap; Out 8 weeks," *New York Times*, May 19, 1989.

7 Joseph Durso, "Hernandez Is Signed by Indians for Two Years," *New York Times*, December 8, 1989.

8 Zach Braziller, "Keith Hernandez Still Lining His Pockets with *Seinfeld* Money," *New York Post,* June 16, 2015; Ron Dicker, "Keith Hernandez Says He Gets $3,000 in Royalties for *Seinfeld*," Huffington Post, June 16, 2015.

9 Richard Sandomir, "Just for Men Just Right for Former Stars," *New York Times*, January 6, 2008.

10 Michael Powell, "Driving to Work with Keith Hernandez, the Real Mr. Met," *New York Times*, September 28, 2015.

11 Joseph Berger, "Farewell to a Mustache Forever Linked to the Mets," *New York Times*, September 27, 2012.

12 Powell.

STAN JEFFERSON

By Armand Peterson

IT WAS A DREAM COME TRUE FOR 23-YEAR-OLD Stan Jefferson when he led off against San Diego lefty Dave LaPoint in the first game of a doubleheader at Shea Stadium on Sunday, September 7, 1986. He grew up in the Bronx, had been the Mets' first-round choice in the 1983 amateur draft, and had just been called up from Tidewater, the Mets' Triple-A International League farm team. Jefferson struck out in his first major-league appearance, but he reached base and scored after he was hit by a pitch in the bottom of the second, and got his first big-league hit when he singled to left in the fourth.

Jefferson was the focus of more media attention than your usual September call-up. Some of the attention came from his status as a highly touted draft choice, but at least as much came from the fact that he was a native of New York City. When rowdy elements of the 47,823 fans in attendance stormed onto the field after the Mets clinched the NL East pennant on September 17 and tore up the field in a riot reminiscent of those in 1969 and 1973, scribes naturally interviewed general manager Frank Cashen. When they turned their attention to players, though, many approached Jefferson first, not one of the team's stars—even though the pennant-clinching game was only his fifth in the majors, and he had entered the game as a pinch-runner in the seventh inning. He was too young to remember the 1969 riots, but said he remembered 1973. "That was the way to show your emotions," Jefferson said. "In the past, that's what you did, but it's not cute anymore."[1] He started in center field the next three nights and got firsthand experience navigating in the patched-up outfield turf.

When Jefferson stepped to the plate in the bottom of the sixth against the Phillies on September 20, he was only 2-for-16 for the month. He later admitted that he had been suffering under the desire to perform well for his family and hometown friends. "I put the pressure on myself," he said, "because I know my ability and I wanted to do well in front of my folks. I mean, I was playing against Mike Schmidt."[2]

With Danny Heep on second base and two outs, Phillies reliever Tom Hume intentionally walked Mets leadoff hitter Mookie Wilson. Jefferson looked toward manager Davey Johnson in the dugout, expecting to be removed for a pinch-hitter. "He looked back at me," Johnson recalled, "but I just gave him a wink and said, 'Let's go.' It gave him confidence."[3] Jefferson responded with a three-run homer, and was pushed from the dugout to doff his cap for the 39,000-plus

Stan Jefferson sporting a Padres Cap

fans still celebrating the team's clinching of the NL East pennant the previous week.

Jefferson finished with a .208 batting average (5-for-24) in 14 games, five of them as a starter. Not great, but a promising start to what appeared to be a long major-league career.

Stan Jefferson was born on December 4, 1962, in New York City. His father, Everod, a subway conductor and immigrant from Panama, later moved his family from a tough South Bronx neighborhood to the quieter Co-op City cooperative housing development in the Baychester section of northeast Bronx. The huge development, claimed to be the largest single residential development in the United States, was completed in 1973, and has more than 15,000 residential units in 35 high-rise buildings and seven townhouse sites. "Co-op was a great place to grow up," Jefferson recalled in a 2015 interview. "Co-op was very sports-conscious and very supportive. There was no shortage of people to play with. We had teams for every sport and lots of room and places to play. I played all day long — baseball, basketball, football on the greenway, stickball against a wall, everything."[4]

Jefferson graduated from Little League — coached by his father — to the Bronx Federation League, where he developed his skills and earned a reputation as one of the best and fastest sandlot players in the city. But he did not go out for baseball at Harry S. Truman High School until he was a junior. "I was just a little guy, maybe 5-foot-6 and about 130 pounds," he said. "It would have been uncool to be cut from the team, and I didn't want to take that chance."[5] (He later grew to a well-muscled 5-foot-11 and 175 pounds.) He also wrestled at Truman, and ran track one year. He loved football, but the school did not have a team until his senior year.

Jefferson's baseball exploits attracted the attention of Earl Battey, the four-time All-Star catcher with the Minnesota Twins in the 1960s. Battey was also a resident of Co-op City and since 1968 had been running the Con Ed Answer Man community relations program for Consolidated Edison of New York. The company purchased bleacher seats from the Yankees and gave them free to inner-city kids. Battey chaperoned the kids at the games and answered baseball questions. He also conducted clinics that included advice on school and general behavior in addition to teaching baseball. Jefferson was a volunteer mentor two summers for the program while in high school.

In 1980 Battey decided to attend Bethune-Cookman College in Daytona Beach to earn his college degree. Battey had accepted an offer to become an assistant baseball coach there, and recruited Jefferson to play for head coach Don Dungee's team. Jefferson was also attracted by the strong academic reputation of the historically black college. He was a standout performer at Bethune. In 1983, his junior year, he attracted major-league scouts by hitting .408 in 52 games, with a .591 slugging average and a .512 on-base percentage.[6] His 67 stolen bases — in 68 attempts! — led the NCAA.

Willie Daniels, a friend from Co-op City who played with Jefferson in Little League, at Truman High, and at Bethune, claimed Jefferson was caught that one time only because his spikes slipped on a wet track. "I played with Devon White, Shawon Dunston, Walt Weiss, a lot of guys," said Daniels in an interview years later. "Stanley is one of the best pure athletes I've ever seen."[7]

Coaches Dungee and Battey told Jefferson that a couple of major-league scouts had been asking about him, and wanted to know if he would sign a contract if picked early in the June 1983 free-agent draft. Jefferson had not actually thought about entering the draft early until then. He had seen a couple of scouts in the stands, but had not talked to any of them. "At Bethune our field was at the Rec Center in a black neighborhood in Daytona," he said. "The only white people at our games were scouts or families from the other teams. One day I saw a very tall, gangly white guy standing behind me in center field, carrying a small baby. Eventually he went to the bleachers. I saw him a couple more times during the season, but didn't know who he was."[8] (Later he learned that the gangly scout was Joe McIlvaine, the Mets scouting director.)

Jefferson gave it some thought and decided to sign if drafted in the first two rounds. "It was a no-brainer, actually," he said. "I didn't see my stock go any higher by staying [in college] one more year."[9] Dungee and Battey were supportive.

The Mets drafted Jefferson in the first round, 20th overall, and in July he was voted to *The Sporting News* College All-American Team. His professional career got off to a great start at the Mets' short-season Single-A Little Falls team in the New York-Pennsylvania League. He hit .320, compiled a .402 OBP, led the league with 35 steals, and was voted to the league's all-star team. The Mets had the right-handed Jefferson convert to switch-hitting in 1984, figuring he could take advantage of his speed from the left side to leg out more infield hits. (Some news stories claimed he began switch-hitting in 1983, and baseball-reference.com lists him as a switch-hitter in 1983, but Jefferson said he hit right-handed at Little Falls.) He had a solid year in 1984 with the Mets' Lynchburg team in the Single-A Carolina League, hitting .288 in his first year as a switch-hitter, leading the league with 113 runs scored, and stealing 45 bases. He was also selected to the league's all-star team.

The Mets were optimistic about 1985 and the team's future. They had gone from 68-94 and last place in the six-team NL East in 1983 to 90-72 and second place in 1984. Their farm system was stacked—the overall winning percentage was .574 (400-297), and three of their six teams were pennant winners. General manager Frank Cashen was enthusiastic as he ran down the list of up-and-coming minor-league outfielders during spring training. "In A-ball," he said, "we have Stanley Jefferson, who may have the most potential of all."[10]

Jefferson struggled a bit at the plate in 1985 at Jackson of the Double-A Texas League. He hit .277, led the league with 39 steals, and finished third in runs scored with 97. The Mets sent him to the Florida Instructional League after the season, and were impressed with his continuing progress as a left-handed hitter in his second year as a switch-hitter. Mets beat writer Jack Lang wrote, "He suffered a letdown from the left side in midseason, but made a late recovery and continued to improve in Florida."[11] The team placed Jefferson on its 40-man roster in November, protecting him from the December Rule 5 draft.

Jefferson married Carmelita Jenkins on November 5, 1985. They had met when he was playing in Lynchburg. He was settling down, the future looked bright, and he could not wait to report to the Mets' 1986 spring-training camp. Jefferson turned heads with his early performances in camp. Veteran slugger George Foster was among many who were impressed. "You don't find too many batters who can drive the ball from both sides as well as Stanley can," said Foster. "He's going to win a batting crown."[12]

Unfortunately for Jefferson, the Mets were favored to win the NL East and likely to go for it with experience. They seemed set in the outfield with veteran Foster (37 years old), Mookie Wilson (30), and youngsters Darryl Strawberry (24) and Len Dykstra (23). Utilityman Kevin Mitchell (24) could fill in for the fifth outfield spot. Despite the fact that Mookie Wilson was going to start the season on the disabled list, and despite hitting .500 (13-for-26) in 11 "A" games, with two doubles, a triple, and a home run, Jefferson was optioned to Tidewater on March 26. He took it philosophically. "They want me to play every day," he said, "so I'll go down and do what I can. They said if they need help they'll give me a ring."[13]

Jefferson hit .290 at Tidewater in 1986, but was sidelined for several weeks because of injuries and played in only 95 games. He led the team with 25 stolen bases, which managed to rank fourth in the league. In hindsight, the injuries probably foreshadowed the physical problems he would contend with the rest of his career. He had also been briefly sidelined in spring training by a slight Achilles tendon strain in his right foot and a back strain.

As a September call-up Jefferson was not eligible for the postseason roster, and was not around to watch the Mets win the NL playoffs and the World Series. Instead, the Mets sent him off to get more experience by playing for Mayaguez in the Puerto Rico Winter League. He was surprised, but not that disappointed, when the Mets announced a December 11 eight-player trade with San Diego—Jefferson was traded to the Padres, along with Kevin Mitchell, Shawn Abner (the Mets' number one draft choice in 1984), Kevin Armstrong, and Kevin Brown in exchange for Kevin McReynolds, Gene Walter, and Adam Ging. McReynolds was the key for the Mets. They felt they needed more right-handed power in the outfield to complement their young left-handed-hitting right fielder, Darryl Strawberry—the Mets already had two speedy singles-hitting outfielders, Lenny Dykstra and Mookie Wilson. Realistically, Jefferson was expendable.

Even though he had just 14 games of experience in the majors, San Diego was counting on Jefferson to lead off and play center field. Larry Bowa, the new Padres manager, traveled to Puerto Rico to watch a couple of his young players and came back impressed with Jefferson. So were his new teammates, especially with his speed and outfield range. "Put it this way: fly ball to center with two outs in the ninth?" said Amos Otis, a former Gold Glove outfielder with Kansas City and now a Padres outfield coach. "Start the car 'cause he's got it. Pop fly to short center? Send the kids for hot dogs because he's got it."[14]

On March 30 Jefferson suffered an injury that threatened to derail his season. The Padres were playing the California Angels in Palm Springs, in the last exhibition series before starting the season in San Francisco. Jefferson was looking forward to playing against his old pal, Devon White, now a rookie outfielder for the Angels. Their families were friends, and Jefferson's father had often picked up Devon on weekends when the two youngsters played against each other back in the Bronx Federation. Jefferson's father had traveled to Palm Springs for the series, and got together with Stan and Devon on the night before the March 30 game.

Jefferson led off with a hit to left center off Don Sutton. "I knew Devon was going to get to the ball," he recalled years later. "My mentality was that if Devon was a little lazy or nonchalant getting to the ball I was going to go for second base. What happened was that the ground was a little wet and I slipped and twisted my left ankle really bad. One of those basketball-type ankle injuries. I was down on the ground and couldn't move."[15]

Manager Bowa did not think the injury was as serious as Jefferson did, and was angry when Jefferson said he couldn't play on Opening Day, April 6. Jefferson consented to play on April 7 to stop the bickering. "I couldn't stop, turn, or anything," he claimed in a 2015 interview. "My ankle, from then on has never been the same."[16] He played five games, but was placed on the disabled list and missed 23 games.

The Padres were having a miserable time. On May 7, when Jefferson was reactivated, the team's 7-23 record was the worst in the majors, and the volatile Bowa had reacted with several clubhouse tirades. On April 26 in Los Angeles "he took the team behind closed doors for a 'discussion' that one player rated a 9.5 on a 10 scale. Bowa not only kicked, threw, and screamed, but pointed out specific players who he felt weren't pulling their weight."[17]

Players coped in different ways. When Tony Gwynn, the team's best player, was asked how life was in the clubhouse, he said, "I don't know. I just stand in the clubhouse, back into my locker stall and watch the manager scream."[18]

Future Hall of Fame reliever Goose Gossage was happy to be traded to the Cubs in 1988. "Every day with him is a crisis," Gossage said. "The man's insecure. It's like getting out of prison, getting away from Bowa."[19]

Jefferson was the victim of another Bowa clubhouse tirade during a series in Pittsburgh on May 12-14, just a few games after he came off the DL. The manager did not know what to think about his rookie center fielder, who was hampered by a sore wrist and a sore shoulder as well as the ankle. Bowa still thought he was not trying hard enough to play through his injuries, and could not figure out the player's personality. In spring training Bowa and the other coaches had been on Jefferson because of his perceived lackadaisical attitude. They did not understand that it was just Jefferson's New York City streetwise "cool," not a lack of effort. He had always had a heads-down, laid-back attitude. "I'm always looking down, I guess," Jefferson said. "I've always had this relaxed attitude, and people get the wrong impression. I do the same thing, whether I'm going good or bad."[20]

Pittsburgh swept the series, and Bowa was yelling and screaming in the clubhouse after the 9-5 loss on May 13. He dialed it up a notch when he came upon Jefferson sitting in front of his locker, staring at the floor. "I didn't even notice that Bowa was having a fit," Jefferson remembered. "I was just shaking my head back and forth, lost in my own thoughts, not believing we'd lost another one. Then I heard Bowa shout, 'What the [bleep] are you smiling about, Jefferson?' I tried to ignore him, but he kept shouting at me. Then I lost my cool and shouted back at him, 'What is wrong with you? Every day you are yelling at me.'"[21]

Bowa grabbed Jefferson by the collar, and Jefferson shoved back. It took several players to separate the two. "Jefferson was carried out of the locker room, kicking and screaming, by five of his teammates," wrote the *San Diego Union-Tribune's* Barry Bloom.[22] Years later Jefferson realized it was a youthful error, and figured he should have just sat there and taken his punishment.

Bowa apologized a little later, claiming he had been fired up about Jefferson skipping an extra batting-practice session, but learned that no one had told Jefferson about it. He kept Jefferson in the lineup despite the dustup. Jefferson played in the next 14 games, starting all but one, but continued to have problems with shoulder tendinitis in his throwing arm, and was placed on the 15-day DL after the May 29 game in San Diego. When he came back he went into a slump, dropping his batting average from .250 when he went on the DL to .216 on July 11. For the next month he went on a 34-for-95 hitting spree, bringing his average up to .267. That corresponded with a modest surge by the team, and it appeared that Jefferson was starting to live up to expectations that he would be a leadoff hitter who could ignite the offense. The Padres, 30-58 at the All-Star break, had a 15-10 record during Jefferson's spree, and 35-39 for the second half.

But from August 10 to the end of the season Jefferson hit only .169 (27-for-160), and finished with a .230 batting average. He could not wait to get back home with his wife Carmelita and two daughters, 2-year-old Tiffany and newborn Brittany. "I was in a sour state toward the end of last year," he said. "I wasn't happy with the way I was playing or how I was feeling physically. I was just glad when the season was over."[23]

After a short time at home Jefferson decided to put the last season behind him and started spending long hours in the batting cage. He reported early to spring training in Yuma, Arizona, with a positive attitude. Teammates and coaches immediately noticed the changes. He seemed to be having fun again, and it showed on the field. He was more patient at the plate and hitting well over .300 in exhibition games.

The Padres got off to a slow start again in 1988, and so did Jefferson—he went hitless in his first 16 at-bats. Manager Bowa stuck with him as his everyday center fielder for a while, but eventually lost patience. Jefferson, hitting just .105 (4-for-38), was sent down to Las Vegas in the Triple-A Pacific Coast League on April 20. He responded well to the demotion, hitting .317 in 74 games with the Stars, with some power—24 of his 88 hits were for extra bases and his .453 slugging average was a career best. And even better, his .396 on-base percentage was what the parent team was looking for in their presumed leadoff hitter.

The Padres called Jefferson back up in late July. While he was gone, Larry Bowa had been fired and general manager Jack McKeon stepped in to manage. The team, 16-30 under Bowa, responded well to their new manager, and were 67-48 for the rest of the season. Jefferson went hitless in his first game back on July 29 but then went on a seven-game hitting streak. After the streak ended he went into another slump and was relegated to spot duty by mid-August. He had only four hits in his last 44 at bats, finishing the season with a .144 batting average, 16-for-111 in 49 games. San Diego batting coach Amos Otis placed the blame for Jefferson's hitting woes on his refusal to listen to his coaches. "I can understand wanting to do something your way," Otis said. "But when your way doesn't work, you've got to change."[24]

Jefferson claimed the problem was all the conflicting advice the team was giving him. "I was left alone [in Las Vegas] and found my hitting stroke all by myself," he said. "But I wasn't back in San Diego three hours before I was getting advice. Everyone is telling me what to do and how to do it. I didn't get this much advice in elementary school."[25]

The Padres also were not pleased that Jefferson refused to play winter ball. He said he had already done that once, in Puerto Rico, and did not see how that helped him. "The thing is," he argued, "I've done it everywhere, at every level, except here. The only way I am going to improve here is to do it here."[26]

On October 24 San Diego traded Jefferson, along with pitchers Jimmy Jones and Lance McCullers, to the New York Yankees in exchange for slugger Jack Clark and pitcher Pat Clements. New Yankees manager Dallas Green said Jefferson would compete with Roberto Kelly and Bob Brower for the starting center field job.

Kelly won the starting job in spring training, and Jefferson was optioned to Triple-A Columbus on April 16 after starting only one of the Yankees' first 10 games. He was called up again on April 26 when outfielder Mel Hall was placed on the disabled list. Three days later Jefferson blew up in Green's office when the manager told him he was being sent down to Columbus again. "I busted my [bleep] every day and all you do is ridicule me," Jefferson shouted as he stormed out of Green's office. "Every [bleeping] day. I gave you 150 percent. The only guy that was in my corner was Hondo (hitting instructor Frank Howard)."[27] Green stepped out of his office and shouted back, "Look in the [bleeping] mirror, big boy."[28] Pitching coach Billy Conners stepped in front of Jefferson to prevent a physical altercation.

The Yankees traded Jefferson to Baltimore on July 20 for Triple-A pitcher John Habyan. Jefferson was called up by the Orioles on August 8 after playing at Rochester for two weeks. At that time, Baltimore had led the AL East all year, but had a 10-16 record since the All-Star break, and were fighting to hold off the Toronto Blue Jays. Jefferson got off to a slow start at the plate, but got hot down the stretch, hitting .319 (23-for-72) in his last 21 games. For the season at Baltimore, he batted.260 in 35 games.

Jefferson started the season with Baltimore in 1990, but did not figure in the Orioles' long-term plans. He was hitless in 19 at bats in the team's first 19 games, and then was released. Cleveland claimed him off waivers on May 7. The Indians played Jefferson in about half of their next 66 games (27-for-66) and then sent him down to Triple-A Colorado Springs. He hit .345 in 33 games for the Sky Sox, and was called back up by the Indians in September. He put on a good show for them. He hit .317 (20-for-63) while playing in 22 of the team's final 27 games.

Despite his September surge, Jefferson did not think he got a fair shot with Cleveland in spring training, believing the team was concerned about his physical condition. "I was never really healthy," he admitted. "They probably saw me in the training room a lot, trying to get myself together."[29] He started the season back in Colorado Springs, and although he had hit a respectable .284 in 28 games, was released by Cleveland on July 5. Cincinnati signed him as a free agent on July 18, and assigned him to Triple-A Nashville. The Reds called him up on August 30, but he sat on the bench. He played in 13 of the team's remaining 35 games (only three as a starter) and hit 1-for-19.

The Reds granted Jefferson free agency on October 15. He went to play winter ball with Ponce in Puerto Rico at the suggestion of Cincinnati manager Lou Piniella, who told him to get some at-bats and come to spring training to battle for a job. Two other young Cincinnati outfielders, Chris Jones and Reggie Sanders, would be playing with San Juan.

In just his third game for Ponce, Jefferson fell awkwardly on a muddy field while chasing down a fly ball in center field, and ruptured his left Achilles tendon. It was effectively the end of his career, at age 28. The ankle and lower Achilles were a mess. Yankees surgeon Stuart Hershon performed surgery to reattach the tendon. Jefferson said the doctor told him that there was little healthy tendon left, and that the surgery might not work well enough for him to return to baseball. Jefferson figured he was running on scar tissue for years after his 1987 injury.

Jefferson was on crutches for months, and went into depression. The Reds refused to pay any of his medical bills because he was not under contract with them, and other bills mounted. He owed $4,000 to Dr. Hershon, and bill collectors were calling constantly. His wife, Carmelita, could not take the stress and left for Virginia with their two daughters. (They eventually were divorced.) Just barely off crutches, Jefferson tried out with Kansas City's Omaha Triple-A team, but it was too soon after the surgery. He also tried out for the Monterrey Industriales in the Mexican League in 1994, but his ankle did not hold up. "The ankle just blew up like a balloon after a game," he said. "That was my last hurrah."[30]

The Mets called Jefferson in early 1995, asking if he would go to spring training as a replacement player. (The Players Association had been on strike since August 12, 1994, and the MLB Executive Council voted on January 13, 1995, to use replacement players for spring training and the regular season.) Jefferson told the team he did not think he could play every day. He made a deal to go to camp in return for a job as a coach in the organization. He had not been able to find a regular 9-to-5 job since 1991, and felt he needed a baseball job to help get out of debt. He was a little uncomfortable about joining the strikebreakers. "If any of those ballplayers out there on strike want to call me, I'll explain," said Jefferson. "I'm pulling for the union. I want those guys to get everything they are asking for. But this is about life."[31]

Jefferson was released on March 30, but the Mets gave him a job as bench/outfield coach with short-season Single-A Pittsfield. That was his last job in baseball. He found a regular job as a warehouse manager for a lighting company, and went back to school at Mercy College to finish his degree. He had dreamed about becoming a detective while growing up, and passed the New York Police Department civil-service exam and interviews in 1994. He was accepted into the Police Academy on December 8, 1997, graduated in the spring of 1998, and was assigned to the Midtown South Precinct.

Police work was everything Jefferson hoped it would be. "You got to live your dream twice [baseball and NYPD]," his old friend Willie Daniels told him. "Most people don't even get to live their dream once."[32]

Jefferson was on duty on Tuesday morning, September 11, 2001, when he and his partner were directed to proceed to Union Square to help direct and comfort people fleeing from the explosions and collapse of the World Trade Center towers. He saw the second plane crash into the second tower, and worked at the site until 9 P.M. the 11th and worked 12 hours on September 12. Then he worked 12-hour shifts on the "pile" on September 13 and 14, and many other shifts at Ground Zero in the following weeks. By the end of the year he was severely depressed and having coughing spells and nightmares. In the spring of 2002 Jefferson was experiencing panic attacks and had difficulty sleeping. He took 41 sick days in the first few months of 2003 as his panic attacks worsened. In March, days after he underwent angioplasty to correct a coronary artery blockage, his mother died suddenly, and his depression and agoraphobia got worse. He was a regular visitor to the emergency room at Our Lady of Mercy Hospital in Queens.

In July 2004 the New York police commissioner's office submitted an application to place Jefferson on ordinary disability retirement, and on November 8, 2004, the department Medical Board approved the request, finding that he suffered from a major depressive disorder. On May 5, 2005, Jefferson, now represented by an attorney, applied for accident disability retirement, claiming he was suffering from post-traumatic stress disorder. By definition, an ordinary disability retirement finding means that the individual is mentally or physically incapacitated for the performance of his duties and ought to be retired, while an accident disability finding means that the disability was caused by an injury sustained in the line of duty. There are significant differences in pension benefits—25 percent of base salary for ordinary disability, 75 percent for accident disability.

On October 17, 2006, the New York County Supreme Court ruled in favor of the police commissioner. The court agreed with the police department's contention that Jefferson's disability was not caused by his work at Ground Zero, ruling that "There were numerous references in the materials reviewed linking petitioner's anxiety and panic, as well as the depression that came with them, to the death of his mother and his incipient cardiac disease."[33] On May 20, 2008, the New York Supreme Court, Appellate Division, denied Jefferson's appeal of the ruling.

More tough times were to come. Jefferson's father died in August 2010, and his second wife, Christie, died in December 2010. (They were married in Las Vegas in August 2004.) But in 2011 Jefferson was finally granted an accident disability disorder, thanks to the 2005 World Trade Center Disability Law that established a presumption that certain disabilities were caused by work at Ground Zero unless evidence proved otherwise. In the first few years after the law was enacted, the police Pension Fund was still forcing officers to prove that their disabilities were directly related to work at Ground Zero. However, appeals courts gradually forced the Pension Fund to reverse its logic to conform to the law—that an accident disability was granted unless it was proved that the disability was not caused by work at Ground Zero.

As of December 2015, Jefferson lived in a high rise in Co-op City. He did not go out much. "I'm just trying to stay healthy, trying to fight PTSD," he said. "I don't like to be around crowds. I am boxed in, and it's kind of hard. But I have my good days."[34]

Special thanks to Brian Williams at Harry S. Truman High School in the Bronx for helping me find Stanley Jefferson and speaking to him on my behalf. Also thanks to Dan Ryan for finding some of Jefferson's old statistics at Bethune-Cookman College. And, especially, thanks to Stanley for graciously responding to all my questions in two lengthy telephone interviews.

SOURCES

In addition to the sources listed in the notes, the author also consulted:

Johnson, Lloyd, and Miles Wolff, eds. *The Encyclopedia of Minor League Baseball* (Durham, North Carolina: Baseball America, 1997).

Baseball-reference.com.

FindLaw.com.

Hennepin County (Minnesota) Library online sources: Ancestry Library Edition; ProQuest Historical Newspapers, the *New York Times*; and ProQuest Newsstand.

Law360.com.

NCAA.org, "Division I Baseball Records."

NYC.gov, "Workers' Compensation and Pension Benefits."

Paper of Record, for *The Sporting News*, accessed via sabr.org.

Retrosheet.org.

Baseball Hall of Fame Library, player file for Stanley Jefferson.

NOTES

1 George Vecsey, "The Mark of the Fans," *New York Times*, September 19, 1986: D17.

2 Michael Martinez, "Met Rookies Get Into the Act," *New York Times*, September 21, 1986: S7.

3 Ibid.

4 Stan Jefferson, telephone interviews with author, December 11 and 17, 2015.

5 Jefferson, telephone interview.

6 "Final 1983 Men's Baseball Statistics Report, Bethune-Cookman," provided by Dan Ryan, Bethune Cookman Sports Information Staff, December 17, 2015.

7 Wayne Coffey, "Forgotten Hero," *New York Daily News*, March 4, 2007: 76.

8 Jefferson, telephone interview.

9 Jefferson, telephone interview.

10 Joseph Durso, "Mets' Architects Looking for Room at the Top," *New York Times*, February 11, 1985: C1.

11 Jack Lang, "Middle Infield of Future Reshuffled," *The Sporting News*, November 18, 1985: 51.

12 Steve Wilder, "Foster 'pupils' earn high grades," *New York Post*, March 13, 1986.

13 Michael Martinez, "Wilson to Go on Disabled List: Met to Miss Opening Trip," *New York Times*, March 27, 1986: B15.

14 Tom Friend, "Padres' New Center Fielder Says He's Ready for the Big Time: Cool on the Outside but Hot to Play," *Los Angeles Times*, March 2, 1987: S3.

15 Jefferson, telephone interview.

16 Jefferson, telephone interview.

17 "N.L. West," *The Sporting News*, May 11, 1987: 26.

18 Peter Pascarelli, "N.L. Beat: Raines Is a Thorn in Owners' Credibility," *The Sporting News*, May 18, 1987: 22.

19 Peter Pascarelli, "N.L. Beat: Will 1988 Be 'The Year of the Balk' in N.L.?," *The Sporting News*, March 21, 1988: 35.

20 Friend.

21 Jefferson, telephone interview.

22 Barry Bloom, "Jefferson, Padres Get It in Gear," *San Diego Union-Tribune*, August 10, 1987.

23 Curt Holbreich, "Losing His New York State of Mind: Stanley Jefferson Is Learning to Leave Last Season, Last Team Behind," *Los Angeles Times*, March 24, 1988.

24 Bill Plaschke, "Jefferson's Way Just Not Working," *The Sporting News*, September 26, 1988: 22.

25 Ibid.

26 Ibid.

27 Steve Serby, "Green, Stanley in Blowup," *New York Post*, April 30, 1989.

28 Ibid.

29 Jefferson, telephone interview.

30 Ibid.

31 Jennifer Frey, "Met Camp Attractive to Players in Need," *New York Times*, February 18, 1995: 31.

32 Coffey.

33 "Matter of Jefferson v. Kelly," 2006 NY Slip Op 26417 [14 Misc 3d 191], October 17, 2006, Published by New York State Law Reporting Bureau, courts.state.ny.us/Reporter/3dseries/2006/2006_26417.htm (accessed November 20, 2015).

34 Jefferson, telephone interview.

HOWARD JOHNSON

By Dave Raglin

HOWARD JOHNSON WAS A SOLID MAJOR-league player for several years. He was probably best known for a combination of power and speed that made him the darling of fantasy baseball owners as that variant of the national pastime took off in the 1980s. He was a member of two World Series championship teams, the 1984 Detroit Tigers and the 1986 New York Mets.

Howard Michael Johnson was born on November 29, 1960, in Clearwater, Florida. He was named for his grandfather, Raymond Howard Johnson, who was known by his middle name. Howard said there were advantages to his name. "Every Sunday after church, my mother would take my brother and me to the Howard Johnson's restaurant for ice cream and lunch. The restaurant people knew me, and never charged for my lunch."[1] His parents, Bill and Sue Johnson, were active in the community. "My father and mother worked with abused children when I was growing up, so I heard about those things," Johnson said in 1989 after he donated money from a prize he won to a home for abused children.[2]

Johnson played several positions while growing up. He was a natural left-hander, but his father taught him how to throw righty so that he could have more positions to play; it was a skill that served Johnson well not only on the sandlots but throughout his pro career. A graduate of Clearwater High, he was drafted by the New York Yankees in the June 1978 draft in the 23rd round as a pitcher, but he did not sign. He was drafted by the Detroit Tigers with the 12th pick of the first round of the January 1979 secondary draft as a relief pitcher, but the Tigers moved him to shortstop.

Johnson played for the Lakeland Tigers of the Class-A Florida State League in 1979. After a few games at short, the Tigers moved him to third. His main offensive statistics in his rookie season were not great (.235 average and only 18 extra-base hits), but he showed fine strike-zone judgment playing in a good pitchers' league, with 69 walks in 132 games. He also made 36 errors at shortstop and third base, which led to a move to the hot corner in 1980.

Johnson spent a second season in Lakeland in 1980 and did much better, slamming a league-leading 28 doubles, hitting .285 with 39 extra-base hits, stealing 31 bases, walking just about as often as he stuck out (73 walks and 75 strikeouts), and slicing his errors to 13. He was named the third baseman on the Florida State League's postseason Northern Division All-Star Team. Johnson followed that up with a strong showing in the Florida Instructional League, cementing his status as a big-league prospect.

The 1981 season was a breakthrough year for Johnson. Playing for the Birmingham Barons of the Double-A Southern League, he hit 22 home runs and drove in 83

runs, with his 75 walks helping him to a .360 on-base percentage. He received notice for a two-homer game on May 25—one of them a broken-bat homer, a rare event in those days. After the season Johnson returned to the Florida Instructional League and hit .331. That fall the Tigers added him to their 40-player major-league roster.

Johnson was assigned to the Evansville Triplets of the Triple-A American Association to start the 1982 season, but he did not stay there long. On April 13 the Tigers called up Johnson and outfielder Glenn Wilson when first baseman-outfielder Rick Leach and outfielder Eddie Miller were put on the disabled list, and Johnson made his big-league debut the next day. He hit leadoff and started the game in right field before moving to third later in the game. Johnson got his first hit to lead off the ninth against Toronto starter Jim Clancy, a hit that started a four-run rally that almost tied the game. (Toronto won, 5-4.) Johnson hit .188 in 12 games before being returned to Evansville on May 6. He starred for the Triplets with 23 home runs and 35 steals in 98 games before being recalled by the Tigers on August 13. He hit .347 for the Tigers the rest of the season, with a 12-game hitting streak in September, part of a 32-game stretch during which he hit .367. Johnson wore number 5 for the Tigers, the last player to wear it before it was retired in 1983 in honor of Hank Greenberg. As Tigers equipment manager Jim Schmakel told him, "Look at it this way, Howard, you're the first rookie to have his number retired."

Johnson went to spring training in 1983 fighting with Tom Brookens for the regular third baseman's job. Manager Sparky Anderson liked Johnson's bat but was concerned that his glove needed more work, after he fielded .901 at third base for the Tigers in 1982. (Part of the problem was that, amazingly, he was using an outfielder's glove at third base.) When the season started, the plan was to platoon Johnson and Brookens, but soon the right-handed-hitting Brookens was given all of the starts against lefties while they split the starts against right-handers. Johnson was also thought to be so tense that it affected his play, a charge that would dog him during his years with the Tigers. Johnson was hitting .212 in 27 games when he was sent back down to Evansville on May 27. (Ironically, his best game of the season with the Tigers was his last, a 2-for-4 game with a home run, two RBIs, and two runs scored.) He played only three games with the Triplets before he suffered a broken finger on June 1 and then a refracture on June 24 that eventually led to season-ending surgery. After the season the Tigers signed third baseman-first baseman Darrell Evans, the club's first big free-agent deal ever, so Johnson was sent to the instructional league to work on his outfield play.

The 1984 season started with another competitor for the third-base job, outfielder Glenn Wilson, whose poor fielding ended that experiment, helping lead to one of the biggest spring-training trades in Tigers history: Wilson and catcher John Wockenfuss to the Philadelphia Phillies for reliever Willie Hernandez and first baseman Dave Bergman. That did not give Johnson the third-base job permanently, as Anderson was still enamored of Brookens' glove, and at times both Barbaro Garbey and Marty Castillo were front-runners as well. Johnson started at third on Opening Day in Minnesota, and for a while he and Brookens platooned until players like Castillo and Garbey started to get some playing time near the end of the Tigers' 35-5 start. Johnson played in 20 of those 40 games, and while he hit only .265, his 10 walks led to a .383 on-base percentage.

Though the Tigers were able to cruise to the pennant, Johnson struggled. In early June he won the everyday third-base job, starting 72 games in an 80-game stretch, but hit only .234 and started only nine of the final 35 games. There were whispers that Anderson still did not have confidence that Johnson could play under pressure. There was a story told of a late-season game in which Anderson, picking a pinch-hitter, looked down the bench, and when his eyes met Johnson's eyes, Johnson looked away. Johnson played in only one of the Tigers' eight postseason games, coming in for defense in the final game of the World Series, getting one hitless at-bat. It was clear that he was on the outs in Detroit.

However, one club was hot after the 24-year-old, and that club could help fill a hole for the Tigers. The New York Mets had been asking about Johnson for a couple of years, and their interest intensified when they were working on a deal with the Expos for Gary Carter. Part of the price in that trade would be Hubie Brooks, so they felt they needed to get a replacement infielder. The Tigers needed starting pitcher Walt Terrell after it was clear that Milt Wilcox's arm was shot, so Johnson was traded to the Mets for Terrell in December.

Unfortunately for Johnson, he was moving from one crowded third-base situation to another, as the Mets also had Ray Knight to man the hot corner. In his book *Bats*, Mets manager Davey Johnson (no relation) talked a lot about how to get both third basemen playing time without harming either player's confidence. It did not help that HoJo got off to a terrible start, his average bottoming out at .127 on May 5, or that Terrell began his Tigers career by going 5-0. Johnson started hitting a little better, but did not get his average above .200 until an epic 19-inning victory over the Atlanta Braves that started on Independence Day and ended close to 4 A.M. on July 5. Johnson did not even start that game; he entered in the ninth inning as a pinch-hitter for shortstop Rafael Santana, got a single, and scored the tying run. He blasted a two-run homer in the top of the 13th and hit a single and scored the lead run in the 18th, but both times the Braves battled back to tie the score. In the Mets' five-run 19th that finally finished off Atlanta, Johnson was intentionally walked and later scored. That game and an injury to Knight got Johnson the starting job in July, but he did not hit and Knight recovered, so the platoon arrangement returned. The Mets and the Cardinals battled all season, trading the lead back and forth, but the Cards eventually pulled in front for good, and despite a 98-64 record, the Mets were on the outside looking in when the playoffs began. During the winter, Johnson moved to the New York area, got his broker's license, and took a job on Wall Street.

The plan for 1986 was the same as for 1985—a third-base platoon for the Mets—but Knight hit six home runs in his first nine games to win the job full time. Johnson was shifted to shortstop, the first time he had played the position regularly since his first year in pro ball. He hit a pivotal pinch-hit two-run homer on April 24 off the Cardinals' Todd Worrell to tie the game in the ninth inning in the first game of a big four-game set between the Mets and St. Louis. The Mets scored a go-ahead run in the top of the 10th, and Johnson's error at short put on the tying run with nobody out, but Roger McDowell held the Cards at bay.

Johnson was hurt on June 1 when he and Lenny Dykstra collided on a fly ball; he suffered a hairline fracture of the right forearm that kept him out of action for 21 games. In his first game back he hit two home runs, and even though the Mets lost, they were 46-20 and in first place by 9½ games. Johnson did not return to short after he came off the disabled list and played in only 56 of the final 97 games, with just 29 of them starts. He hit nine home runs in 135 at-bats during that stretch but his average was only .237 (even though his frequent walks led to a respectable .331 on-base percentage).

The Mets won 108 games, finishing in first by 21½ games, and beat the Houston Astros and Boston Red Sox in two of the most exciting postseason series in baseball history. Johnson pinch-hit in two games against Houston and in the ninth inning of Game Six of the World Series. He played the entire second game of the Series, going 0-for-4. (He was also hitless in his other games.) Johnson was involved in a controversial situation in the Houston series when he and Mets catcher Ed Hearn produced balls they claimed had been scuffed by Houston starter Mike Scott, who had a reputation for helping himself in such ways. The winter brought rumors of Johnson going to San Diego as part of a trade for slugger Kevin McReynolds, but Kevin Mitchell ended up being the biggest hitter who went west in the deal.

Knight left the Mets for the Baltimore Orioles as a free agent after winning the 1986 World Series MVP award, but that did not mean Johnson had inherited the third-base job. Rookie Dave Magadan was the new competition in 1987, but Magadan needed surgery late in spring training for swollen lymph nodes, leaving the job to Johnson. He was hitting only .220 with two home runs in 18 games when Magadan returned and was given the third-base job, but Rafael Santana was the odd man out as Johnson moved to shortstop briefly. Johnson soon moved back to third, and for the first time since his rookie season in 1982, he had a really hot streak—five home runs in 17 games in May. So even though he went homerless in the next 15 games and hit .178, he stayed in the lineup. It was the first time in Johnson's career that he was able to go through a rough stretch without being yanked from the lineup, and he took advantage of the situation.

Johnson hit three home runs in April, five in May, seven in June, and a whopping 10 in July, giving him 25 home runs with two months to go in the season, which attracted a lot of attention. He wasn't the only one; home runs in the majors were up 17 percent in 1987. It was the story of the summer, and Howard Johnson was the poster boy for the home-run surge. On July 28 he became the third Met to reach the 20/20 (home runs/stolen bases) plateau. It happened in the first game of a three-game series against the Cardinals that vaulted Johnson onto the national stage, a surprise to many people in that he had stolen only 31 bases in his five previous major-league seasons.

The Mets had been playing a little over .500 ball all season and entered the series in St. Louis 7½ games back, but the Mets swept the Cards to pull within 4½ games of their nemesis. In the second game of the set, HoJo went 4-for-5 with a home run, and his two-run homer in the eighth inning off Bill Dawley the following day led the Mets to the sweep.

After that home run, St. Louis manager Whitey Herzog asked umpire Joe West to inspect Johnson's bat. West found nothing wrong and later said he felt the bat was OK, but he had the groundskeeper keep the bat to avoid an incident with the volatile Herzog. Later, Houston manager Hal Lanier also accused Johnson of corking his bat. HoJo denied the charges, declaring that the rival managers were "insulting my talent with those charges. I'm not the first guy accused of using cork in my bat, but it's like they think I'm not capable of doing what I'm doing. But I'm doing it, and I'm doing it fair and square."[3]

The controversy continued. Johnson's bat was confiscated by umpire Dutch Rennert when Giants manager Roger Craig accused Johnson of using a corked bat to hit his 30th home run of the season on August 19. Craig said, "When a man hits a ball 480 feet, I have to take a precaution. I knew HoJo well when I was with Detroit. He really hit that ball, and I don't recall him hitting them that far in Detroit."[4] The bat was X-rayed and Johnson was exonerated. Later, Montreal manager Buck Rodgers added his name to the list of skippers accusing Johnson of cheating. The allegations were never proved.

Did Johnson cork his bats? After his career was over, Johnson said, "All I've ever said is that when they X-rayed my bats, they came up clean" and "I know a few good carpenters, yeah." Davey Johnson chimed in, "If it was corked, he had a carpenter who could do just about anything with wood. Did I see the cork? No. Did he probably cork his bat? Yes."[5]

Johnson and Mets general manager Joe McIlvaine attributed Johnson's newfound power to his opportunity to play every day. When Knight left the Mets, Johnson said, he spent hours in the batting cage hitting right-handed to prepare himself for the full-time job. It also might have helped Johnson to know that he was secure as the team's third baseman; there was no Tom Brookens, Glenn Wilson, or Ray Knight available if he had a bad week. After all, he started taking off in May after a slump that in the past might have put him on the bench.

The sweep of the Cardinals helped jump-start the Mets and they closed to within 1½ games in early September, but they ran out of gas and ended up in second place, three games back, with a 92-70 record. It ended up being a red-letter season for Johnson, who hit 36 home runs, stole 32 bases, and drove in 99 runs. He became the eighth player in major-league history to post a 30/30 season. He broke the record for home runs by a National League switch-hitter, formerly held by Rip Collins, who hit 34 home runs for the 1934 Cardinals.

Johnson headed to camp in 1988 with a regular job sewed up for the first time, but he started off slow in spring training, with a .115 average, until some pointed comments from manager Davey Johnson woke him up. "I haven't reached my peak yet," HoJo said. This is another proving year for me. A lot of people don't think I can do it again, so I'm out to end the skepticism."[6] Johnson got off to a slow start, not crossing the .200 mark for good until May 11, but the Mets were off to a great start, finishing the quarter-mark of the season with a 30-11 record and a 5½-game lead in the National League East.

On April 30 Johnson had played a peripheral role in one of the big stories of the season, scoring from second on an infield single by Mookie Wilson in the top of the ninth to put the Mets in the lead for good, 6-5. The play at first was close and umpire Dave Pallone called Wilson safe. In the ensuing argument, Reds manager Pete Rose shoved Pallone, earning him a 30-game suspension. On June 2 Johnson's 13th-inning home run off Frank DiPino of the Cubs led the Mets to a thrilling 2-1 victory, one of three extra-inning game-winning home runs by the Mets in a five-game span.

By the end of July the Cardinals had almost caught up to the Mets, getting to within 1½ games, but the Mets kicked it into gear, quickly lengthening the lead back to six games. In early September their lead hit double digits, and on September 8, Johnson had the first five-hit game of his career in a 13-6 win against Chicago. The Mets finished first with a 100-60 record, and Johnson had a chance to be a regular in the postseason for the first time.

However, he would be playing shortstop. In late August the Mets brought up uber-prospect Gregg Jefferies. Initially, Jefferies was installed at second base, but he later saw substantial time at third base, with HoJo moving to short in place of Santana. It was a move typical of the Mets at the time to try to squeeze as much offense into the lineup at the expense of defense. In the playoffs Wally Backman was the second baseman, Jefferies the third baseman, and Johnson the shortstop.

It didn't work; the heavily favored Mets fell in seven games to the Los Angeles Dodgers in the NLCS. Jefferies hit .333 but between them, Backman and Jefferies drove in only three runs. It was a terrible series for Johnson, who went hitless in the first three games, leading to a benching for Game Four. (He later appeared as a pinch-hitter.) Johnson started Game Five and got his only hit of the series before watching Game Six from the bench. The Mets staved off elimination that day but fell 6-0 in a Game Seven that saw Johnson come off the bench to pinch-hit in the ninth and strike out. It turned out to be the last postseason appearance of his career.

It was a disappointing season for Johnson. He hit only 24 home runs, drove in only 68 runs, and hit a full-season career-low .230. That was followed by the playoff problems. He revealed after the season that part of the problem was a sore right shoulder he'd kept quiet about, and he subsequently underwent arthroscopic surgery on October 29.

There was also lots of trade talk involving Johnson over the winter, as the Mets tried to clear up the infield logjam caused by the emergence of Jefferies. A deal to send Johnson and others to Seattle for pitcher Mark Langston and others fell through when concerns about how Johnson's shoulder might heal scared off the Mariners. The Mets also talked with Atlanta about sending Johnson to the Braves.

Meanwhile, Johnson worked to put the problems of 1988 behind him, reporting a month early to Port St. Lucie in 1989 to work out with several teammates. Manager Davey Johnson announced that HoJo would be the third baseman and Jefferies would have to learn how to play second. Johnson, though, was still having trouble with the shoulder and did not hit well in Florida that spring. He almost did not leave the Sunshine State a Met; a blockbuster deal fell through at the last moment that would have sent Johnson and Sid Fernandez to Seattle, Mark Langston to Boston, Wade Boggs to Kansas City, and Danny Tartabull to the Mets to give them the right-handed power hitter they craved.

It turned out to be the best deal the Mets never made, as Howard Johnson had the finest season of his career in 1989. His 36 home runs and 101 runs batted were not his career best, but his 104 runs scored led the National League and his .287 batting average, .369 on-base percentage, and .559 slugging percentage were all career highs.

The season started with the only really good April of Johnson's career. He had previously hit .203 in April, but in 1989 he hit .333 with four home runs. Unfortunately for the Mets, they continued their pattern of not playing well when Johnson did and vice versa, finishing April with a 12-10 record. That pattern continued all season. At the All-Star break Johnson had 22 home runs, his first All-Star selection, and the first long-term contract of his career (three years for $6.1 million), but the Mets were treading water in third place with a 45-39 record. Johnson celebrated his new contract by hitting two home runs in the All-Star home run contest to help the National League win the competition.

As the season progressed, Johnson's numbers kept piling up. On August 20 he hit home run number 30, making him only the third player to have more than one 30/30 season to that point. (Willie Mays and Bobby Bonds were the others.)

Johnson's 1989 season brought him many awards: the National League Player of the Week for June 19-25, the National League Player of the Month for June (a .340 batting average with 11 home runs), the third-base spot on *The Sporting News'* National League All-Star team, the Silver Slugger award at third base for the National League, and the Sport Channel/Leukemia New York Athlete of the Year award. Johnson said upon receiving the latter honor, "It's amazing. A year ago, I couldn't have been elected dog catcher in New York." After the season, he went to Tokyo to conduct hitting clinics.

However, Johnson kept his "odd season on/even season off" pattern going in 1990, hitting .244 with 23 home runs and 90 runs batted in. The season also saw him move to shortstop in early August for the rest of the season after regular shortstop Kevin Elster injured his shoulder. The Mets rebounded a bit from their 87-75 1989 campaign, but their 91-71 record in '90 left them four games behind the Pittsburgh Pirates. Manager Davey Johnson was not around to see them climb back into the race. He was fired early in the season with the club 20-22, replaced by former Met Bud Harrelson, and HoJo lost his most fervent supporter in the Mets hierarchy.

But true to the pattern, Johnson had a great season in 1991. He had career highs in home runs (38), runs batted in (117), and runs scored (108). He started the season as the regular shortstop, but was back at third by the end of April. The 1991 season was also the year that Johnson professed his Christianity publicly. He said his wife was already a strong Christian and "a lot had been eating at me. There was the sense of emptiness, that I was missing out on something. I had come up as a baseball player wanting to make a lot of money and enjoy success. I'd done it, but was bothered about where it would go from there." He vowed that he "certainly [was] not going to forsake my love of the game or my competitiveness in it." He also switched his uniform number from 20 to 44 before switching back after five games, saying that he was uncomfortable with the new number.

Johnson was part of a bigger switch in September when the Mets, still trying to unclog their infield, asked him to play right field. It did not seem to hurt his bat; he got two hits in each of his first three games in right. Johnson welcomed the switch: "This year, for the first time, I felt old at third base. I'm 30 now, and it's taken a toll on my legs and knees."[7] Even though he played short and right, he was named the third baseman on the National League Silver Slugger team. It was not a good season for the Mets; their 77-84 record was their first losing season since 1983, and Harrelson was fired in late September.

The Mets were in disarray, and nothing showed it more than their treatment of HoJo. After playing him at short, third, and right in 1991, new manager Jeff Torborg moved Johnson to a position in 1992 where he'd never played before: center field. Johnson did the best he could, but he did not play well in center, and it affected his bat; in 83 games in center, he hit .224 with only seven home runs. After Johnson misplayed a game-winning triple off the bat of the Dodgers' Mitch Webster, Torborg moved him to yet another position, left field.

Soon after the move, in the last week of July, Johnson hurt his wrist (probably on a slide in Philadelphia), and doctors found a hairline fracture. With the wrist keeping him from playing, he underwent season-ending surgery in late August on his left shoulder and both knees (he had a cartilage tear in the right knee, and a degenerated piece of tendon in his left knee was removed.)

The Mets learned from their mistakes with Johnson in 1992 and moved him back to third base in 1993, the last year of his contract. Johnson was concerned about third base wearing him out, but he vowed to work out over the winter to prepare his body for the challenge. At the age of 32, his body was beginning to betray him, however, and word was getting around the league that pitchers could sneak a fastball by him. He was clearly becoming frustrated, as he was ejected from a game for the first time and suspended for three games for bumping umpire Jerry Layne and spinning him around.

As it turned out, Johnson was sick with an "acute viral syndrome." He went on the disabled list to recover, but even after returning three weeks later, in early July, his bat was still not responding. For the second straight year his season ended with an injury to his hand/wrist area when on July 22 he slid thumb-first into second, chipping his right thumb and ending his season—and his playing career with the Mets.

With his contract completed, Johnson was a free agent, and two injury-filled unproductive seasons greatly hurt his marketability. After overtures from the Reds, he signed a one-year contract with the Colorado Rockies with a club option for 1995. The Rockies saw Johnson as a player who could give the second-year expansion club power from both sides of the plate and offer defensive versatility. But Johnson got off to his typical slow start, hitting only .133 in April, and by mid-June most of his appearances were coming as a pinch-hitter. His season ended early for the third straight year, but this time it was not because of an injury; in early August of 1994 the players walked out, and the season was over.

The Rockies did not pick up Johnson's option, and after baseball resumed, he was one of many players who was out of work. Johnson joined the group of unemployed players at a camp in Homestead, Florida, organized by the Major League Baseball Players Association. The Cubs signed him, but he did not hit well (in 169 at-bats, he managed just a .195 average), and his big-league playing career was over. At least Johnson went out with a bang, going 3-for-4 in his final game, with a single off Todd Jones in his last major-league at-bat. He went to play in Venezuela that winter, but nobody picked him up for the 1996 season, and he took a minor-league coaching job with the Butte Copper Kings, a rookie-league club of the Tampa Bay Devil Rays, who would begin play in the major leagues in 1998.

Johnson tried to come back with the Mets in spring training in 1997. While he did not make the team, the comeback helped heal some old wounds. The fans were really behind their former hero, and it meant a lot to Johnson: "This is something I won't ever forget," he said. "I wasn't expecting it. When I was here, I was just a player everybody just liked, and being gone for a while and out of the game, I think people can relate to that. They can relate to someone taking on a challenge and trying to meet that challenge."[8]

One overarching aspect of Johnson's career was his seeming need to be appreciated, and when that happened he performed well. Sparky Anderson clearly had little respect for Johnson, and it seemed to affect his play. Davey Johnson treated him with a lot of respect, but for his first two years in New York, the manager could not play HoJo full time because he also had Ray Knight. Once Knight was gone and Johnson won the job in spring training of 1987, and kept the job even when he got off to a slow start, he could relax, and he became a star player. As his performance deteriorated and his career with the Mets ended in the early 1990s, Johnson lamented that the people who had known him during the glory years with the Mets were gone and the new people did not have confidence in him.

Johnson was hired by the Mets as a scout in October 1997, a position he held until he was named hitting coach of the brand-new Brooklyn Cyclones of the short-season A-ball New York-Penn League in late 2000. He was promoted to manager of the Cyclones for the 2002 season and managed the Mets' Florida Instructional League team that season. He progressed through the Mets' system as a hitting coach, working for the Port St. Lucie Class-A club in 2003, the Double-A Binghamton Mets in 2004, and the Triple-A Norfolk Tides in 2005 and 2006. He was promoted to first-base coach for the Mets for the 2007 season, and on July 12, 2007, he was named the hitting coach for the Mets, a post he held through the 2010 season. Johnson left the Mets following the firing of Jerry Manuel, the Mets manager. He was offered a couple of minor-league posts but he declined. Johnson returned to coaching in 2013 as hitting coach for the Tacoma Rainiers, the Seattle Mariners' Triple-A farm club. In 2014 he was promoted to the Mariners staff as hitting coach. Midway through the 2015 season Johnson was reassigned to the Mariners farm system.

NOTES

1 Joseph Durso, "Scouting; New Met Asks What's in a Name," *New York Times*, January 18, 1985.

2 "The Notebook," *The Sporting News*, November 13, 1989: 50.

3 "Corked-Bat Charges 'Insulting My Talents,' Says Mets Johnson," *The Sporting News*, August 17, 1987: 16.

4 Joseph Durso, "Mets are Beaten by Giants in 10th," *New York Times*, August 20, 1987.

5 "A Corked Bat? Well, Maybe," *New York Times*, March 27, 1997.

6 Dan Castellano, "Manager Lights a Fire Under Hojo," *The Sporting News*, April 4, 1988: 40.

7 "Gwynn Spins Refreshing Tale in Final Month," *The Sporting News*, September 16, 1991: 14.

8 Buster Olney, "Johnson Returns to Cheers of Fans," *New York Times*, March 26, 1997.

RAY KNIGHT

By Ralph Carhart

BY THE TIME RAY KNIGHT LEAPT DOWN THE third-base line on the night of October 25, 1986, landing on home plate and forever cementing his legacy in New York baseball history, he was already an 11-year veteran. He had seen much in his professional career, including a trip to the postseason in 1979, but he had never seen anything like the events that led to his scoring the winning run in one of the most dramatic games in baseball history. Few had. But there was even more magic to come two nights later. A completely unexpected turn of events, orchestrated in a New York minute by a country boy from Albany, Georgia, sealed the fate of the Boston Red Sox and allowed the New York Mets to hoist the second world championship banner in their history.

Knight's beginnings were the humble stuff of a typical baseball rags-to-riches tale. He was born on December 28, 1952, in Albany, Georgia. His father worked for the city parks department.[1] Ray attended Dougherty High School (also the alma mater of one other major leaguer, Gene Martin, who played in nine games with the Washington Senators in 1968). Ray made a name for himself in high school as a ballplayer and boxer. A fighter at heart, he became a Golden Gloves boxer in addition to World Series hero.

Knight's high-school performance on the diamond was impressive enough for the Cincinnati Reds to select him in the 10th round of the 1970 draft. The next summer, after graduation, Knight was in Sioux Falls, playing for the Reds' affiliate in the Class-A Northern League. Uncertain where to play the versatile athlete, the Packers had Knight play every position except catcher, even pitching in three games. His primary positions were in the outfield and at shortstop. Batting .285 with six home runs in 64 games, the promising youth was promoted to Double-A Trois-Rivieres (Eastern League) for 1972.

That was a more challenging year for Knight; his average dipped to a weak .212 and he hit only two home runs. Knight would never be known as a power threat, but his .265 slugging percentage, 20 points lower than his previous season's batting average, was troubling. The Reds kept him in Trois Rivieres for the start of the 1973 season, and he rebounded enough (.280 in 57 games) to earn his way to the Triple-A Indianapolis Indians in midseason.

Knight struggled again, and was hitting a poor .227 in 1974 when he got an unexpected September call-up. Knight's major-league debut came on September 10, when he was inserted at third base in the sixth inning of a game against the San Diego Padres. He struck out in his lone at-bat, and fared little better throughout the month, going 2-for-11 in 14 games. He got his first

major-league hit, a two-run double, in a September 28 blowout of the San Francisco Giants.

It took two more full seasons before Knight returned to the majors. He spent 1975 and 1976 in Indianapolis, becoming a more reliable hitter and watching from afar as the Reds won the World Series in those two seasons.

Promoted to the Reds in 1977, Knight would never play in another minor-league contest. He played in half of the team's games in '77, mostly as a pinch-hitter, and batted.261 in 103 plate appearances as the Reds finished 10 games behind the eventual National League champion Los Angeles Dodgers.

The next season was a disappointment for Knight. His batting average fell to .200. The Reds finished just 2½ games behind the Dodgers, but the future of the team and Knight's role were in doubt by season's end. Knight was firmly ensconced as a backup third baseman, the realm of Reds superstar Pete Rose.

Rose, however, moved to the Philadelphia Phillies as a free agent for the 1979 season, and the Reds' third-base job fell the still unreliable Knight. But Ray surprised by batting .318 and slugging .454, both career highs. He finished fifth in MVP voting and his emergence played no small part in the Reds' return to the postseason, though they did not go far, being swept in three games by Pittsburgh in the National League Championship Series. Knight batted .286 in what was his lone postseason appearance with Cincinnati.

Knight continued to shine at the start of 1980, making his first appearance in the All-Star Game. He went 1-for-1 in the game, with a walk and an unlikely stolen base (Knight had only 14 for his career). He entered the game in the sixth inning and scored the tying run, helping the National League go on to win 4-2. But from that point Knight's season began to slip downhill. Entering the All-Star Game he was batting a respectable .289, but after the break his average slipped to .264 by season's end, and he led the league in grounding into double plays.

Knight's statistics in the strike-shortened season of 1981 were similar to 1980's, with a slightly higher on-base percentage and a slightly lower slugging percentage. It was another disappointing season for the Reds. Afterward they lost outfielders Ken Griffey to a trade with the Yankees and Dave Collins to free agency. In an attempt to shore up their outfield, the fan favorite Knight was traded to Houston for Cesar Cedeno.[2] In a strange twist of baseball fate, Knight (who was known as a fighter throughout his playing career) and Cedeno had participated in an on-field brawl on the Fourth of July in 1979 after Knight challenged the entire Astros bench to fisticuffs.[3]

The same year Knight was traded, he divorced his first wife, Terri Schmidt. The trade to Houston put him in closer contact with future Hall of Fame professional golfer Nancy Lopez, whom he had met and previously befriended in 1978 when they were both playing in Japan. Recently divorced herself, Lopez and Knight grew even closer and ultimately became lovers. In 1982 they married, becoming one of sport's higher profile couples.[4]

Perhaps it was the rejuvenation of his love life, or perhaps it was inspiration born of a Southern boy returning below the Mason-Dixon line, but Knight's first season in Houston was a rebirth. In 1982 he batted .294, leading all other regulars by over 15 points on a weak Astros squad that finished in fifth place, ahead of only the truly woeful Reds in the NL West. Knight made his second All-Star Game appearance, and once again figured in MVP voting. Knight and the Astros seemed to be a match made in heaven.

The happy marriage continued in 1983 when Knight hit over .300 for the second and final time in his career. Knight, who had begun to transition to first base with the trade to Houston, played the entire 1983 season at that position.

Knight split time between the two corners in 1984. Plagued by persistent pain in his right shoulder, he saw his numbers fall sharply. By late August he was batting only .223 in 88 games. That was when the Mets, who had been looking for a consistent third baseman seemingly since their inception in 1962, came calling. Knight was dealt to the Mets for three players.

When Knight arrived in New York on August 28, 1984, it was the beginning of a period of transition for the historically woeful Mets, whose last postseason appearance had been a World Series loss to the Oakland A's in 1973. They had acquired first baseman Keith Hernandez the year before, slugger Darryl Strawberry was proving that he was not a one-year fluke and phenom Dwight Gooden was en route to the Rookie of the Year award. With the addition of future Hall of Fame catcher Gary Carter during the offseason, Knight had become a part of a team with tremendous promise.

During the offseason Knight underwent orthoscopic surgery on his nagging shoulder and the Mets, concerned that he would not be 100 percent for 1985, traded Walt Terrell to the Detroit Tigers for Howard Johnson in December.[5] The Mets' concerns seemed justified in 1986 as Knight hit a paltry .218, the lowest full-season average in his career to that point. Johnson fared only a little better, batting .242. Entering the 1986 season, the hot corner in Flushing still seemed to be a question mark.

That question did little to deter the Mets however, as they started winning right out of the gate. They were 13-3 and five games up at the end of April, including an 11-game winning streak. Knight was batting .306 with six home runs in the first month of the season and Johnson found himself relegated to a part-time role.

Knight was a perfect fit for the rowdy Mets, known for their wild (some say arrogant) antics on and off the field. Of his many on-field altercations, perhaps the most famous was a brawl on July 22 with the Reds' Eric Davis. After Davis came in hard on a slide into third, Knight started barking at the athletic outfielder. Davis gave Knight a shove, and that was when the Golden Gloves boxer slugged the Reds outfielder in the jaw. The benches cleared and, by the time it was over, so many players were either injured or ejected that Gary Carter was playing third and relievers Jesse Orosco and Roger McDowell alternated between pitching duties and playing the outfield.

The Mets dominated the NL East throughout the season and finished with a record of 108-54, leading the second-place Phillies by 21½ games. Knight had an opportunity to exact a measure of vengeance on his former employers, the Houston Astros, in the Championship Series, but mostly failed to live up to the chance. With Knight batting only .167 in 26 plate appearances, it was Strawberry who provided the offensive heroics throughout the series. Knight did have the final say, however, in the 16-inning war that was the deciding Game Six. He knocked in two runs, including the go-ahead run, in the 16th.

It was be the World Series, against the snake-bitten Red Sox, in which Knight put on an offensive show previously unseen in his career. He batted .391, knocking in five runs and scoring four, including the iconic winning run in Game Six as Mookie Wilson's slow grounder dribbled through the legs of the hobbled Bill Buckner.

That moment has become so famous in Mets lore that it is often forgotten that Knight's best game of the Series may have been the final one. With the game knotted at 3-3 in the seventh, Knight led off the inning against Calvin Schiraldi with a home run that put the Mets ahead for good. After a base hit in the eighth, making him 3-for-4, Knight scored the Mets' final run of 1986 when pitcher Jesse Orosco knocked a single to center field, making the score 8-5, the score of the game that secured the Mets their second world championship. Knight was named the World Series MVP as well as the National League Comeback Player of the Year by *The Sporting News.*

It was with some surprise, then, that on November 12, just two weeks after Knight was the toast of the city, that the Mets granted him free agency after Knight refused the team's $800,000 salary offer.[6] The market showed little interest in the recent hero and he ultimately signed for $600,000 with the Baltimore Orioles in February 1987. Although the contract was for two years, Knight's lackluster 1987, in which he batted only .256, resulted in his being traded to the Detroit Tigers in February 1988. Now slowed by age (he was 35) and lingering injuries, Knight managed only a .217 average for the Tigers in '88 and saw a brief power surge from the previous year dissipate. By the final months he was a part-time player, missing huge chunks of playing time throughout August and September. At season's end, he was waived by the Tigers, and retired as a player.

Upon retirement, the energetic Knight briefly became the caddy for his still successful wife. It was an experiment that didn't last long, as the two competitors would find themselves fighting on the golf course.[7] Knight simultaneously shouldered the blame for the failed experiment, but also pointed the finger at Lopez. "I'm too intense. Nancy and I have always had this relationship where when we feel something, we express it. As a husband, I can do that. It doesn't make any difference—I can tell her she looks heavy, or the clothes she wears are not good or her hair doesn't look good, and she accepts it. But on the golf course, I could not say anything—right, wrong or indifferent."[8]

Unable to leave the game that meant so much to him, Knight became an ESPN analyst until 1993, when he joined the Reds coaching staff, serving under his old Mets manager Davey Johnson. The Reds finished first in the strike-shortened seasons of 1994 and 1995. Because the postseason was canceled in '94, Knight would have to wait until 1995 to once again participate in October baseball. The Reds swept the Dodgers in three games in the Division Series, but were then swept themselves by the Atlanta Braves in the Championship Series.

Despite Johnson's success as the skipper of the Reds, his relationship with the team owner, the volatile Marge Schott, was precarious.[9] After the 1995 season Johnson was fired and Knight was promoted to succeed him. Although he had been a coach for Johnson for three years, Knight had never managed before. His foray was less than successful. Leading a squad that included future Hall of Famer Barry Larkin, Hal Morris, and, ironically, Eric Davis, the team managed only a .500 record (81-81). The brawler side of Knight survived past his playing days, and made a memorable appearance in his short managing tenure. He was suspended for three games in May of 1997 for an altercation with umpire Jerry Layne. In the heat of the argument, he spit on Layne. After the infamous episode between Roberto Alomar and John Hirschbeck the previous September, the league was cracking down on spitting. In discussing the suspension, Knight's made clear his passion for staying connected to the game: "I don't mind paying a $10,000 fine, but let me stay with my ballclub. The worst thing in the world is to suspend me and get me away from my team. It hurts me; it crushes me."[10] He lasted only 99 games into the 1997 season before he suffered Johnson's fate. Of the experience, and of working for Schott, Knight said, "That probably took years off my life. I was in the worst possible situation you could possibly be in."[11]

Knight returned to ESPN and then, in 2002, again rejoined the Reds as bench coach after the team was purchased by Carl Lindner. Knight managed the squad for one final game, a victory, after manager Bob Boone was fired in the middle of the 2003 season. The next night he handed the reins over to Dave Miley. He left the Reds again after that season.

In 2007 Knight joined MASN, the television home of the Washington Nationals. He became the host of "NatsXtra," the pregame and postgame show, and still filled that role as of 2016. In honor of his philanthropic work, Knight had a road named after him in 2013 on the campus of Phoebe Putney Memorial Hospital in his hometown of Albany. Ray Knight Way intersects with Nancy Lopez Lane, a poignant symbol considering that the couple divorced after 28 years of marriage. Despite the split, there was still an obvious affection between the two. According to Knight, Lopez's contributions to the hospital far outweighed his own. "The only thing wrong (with the street sign at the intersection of Nancy Lopez Lane and Ray Knight Way) is that I am on the top. She should be on the top."[12]

If there is someone who understands what it means to be on top, it's Ray Knight. From a career that began at the completion of the dynastic Big Red Machine, saw the ultimate reward of World Series victory in the City That Never Sleeps, and continued as a part of the Washington Nationals, Knight was never been far from success. And for a brawler like Ray Knight, he wouldn't have it any other way.

NOTES

1 Richard Lemon, "On the Beach No More, Nancy Lopez and Ray Knight Score a Tie for Golf and Baseball," *People,* April 25, 1983.

2 "Reds Trade Knight for Cedeno," *New York Times,* December 19, 1981.

3 John Royal, "Cesar Cedeno and the Astros Career That Could Have Been," *Houston Press,* July 9, 2012.

4 Lemon.

5 Joseph Durso and Thomas Rogers, "Scouting; More Speculation on Ray Knight," *New York Times,* December 11, 1984.

6 "Orioles Sign Reluctant Knight," *Los Angeles Times,* February 11, 1987.

7 Mal Florence, "Lopez Minus Part-Time Caddy Today: Husband Ray Knight Goes Home After Having Problems at Rancho Mirage," *Los Angeles Times,* April 14, 1989.

8 Mike Penner, "Secret of Their Success Is Look but Don't Help: Lopez and Knight Love Each Other, but He Couldn't Cut It as Her Caddie," *Los Angeles Times,* September 21, 1990.

9 Frank Ahrens, "The Johnsons: Not Your Traditional Couple," *Washington Post,* November 17, 1997.

10 "Reds' Knight Is Suspended," *New York Times,* May 21, 1997.

11 Rick Maese, "Why's Ray Knight So Excited?," *Washington Post,* September 26, 2014.

12 Jennifer Maddox-Parks, "Meredyth Streets Dedicated to Nancy Lopez, Ray Knight," *Albany* (Georgia) *Herald.* March 7, 2013.

TERRY LEACH

By Jon Springer

TERRY LEACH HAD AN UNUSUAL DELIVERY, took an abnormally long and circuitous route to the major leagues, eventually found uncommon success, and recounted it all in a book entitled *Things Happen for a Reason.*

There were in fact lots of reasons for the things that happened during Leach's unique baseball career, which spanned 18 professional seasons—one in independent ball—among seven organizations including two that employed him twice. Leach was traded three times, released four times, spent at least part of all but six years in the minor leagues, and didn't make an Opening Day roster until he was 33 years old. Along the way he authored one of the most stunning single-game pitching performances in the history of the New York Mets; shocked the baseball world while racing to a 10-0 start in 1987; and served a key role in the bullpen for the 1991 World Series champion Minnesota Twins.

Terry Hester Leach was born on March 13, 1954 in Selma, Alabama, the youngest of Alma and Cecil Leach's three boys. Cecil, a cotton buyer, was a one-time football player at Auburn University and his boys—Billy, 14 years older than Terry, and Alan, seven years Terry's senior—were each good athletes, so young Terry had to work hard to keep up with his siblings. "Being younger pushed me to being a little bit better," Terry wrote in his book. "Being at a disadvantage can work for you if you take your failures and learn from them."[1]

Leach played baseball for Selma High and for a Dixie Senior League team that finished as the runner-up in the 1969 Dixie World Series and was its champion in 1971. After high school graduation in 1972 he was offered a partial baseball scholarship to Auburn, where he began as a third baseman before being converted to a pitcher.

Listed as 6-feet and 215 pounds, Leach was a stocky, hard-throwing right-handed pitcher whose success at Auburn earned him a draft pick by the Boston Red Sox in the January 1976 supplemental draft, but the pick was voided when Leach was ruled ineligible due to his age. His shot at getting drafted a second time vanished when he injured his elbow pitching for Auburn that spring.

Leach said the injury—which he later surmised was a torn collateral ligament—forced him to abandon a previous focus on mid-90s fastballs, expand his repertoire, and learn to retire batters with finesse rather than fire. Undrafted and still overcoming the injury, Leach latched on briefly with the Baton Rouge Cougars of the independent Gulf States League in 1976, and impressed Atlanta Braves scouts enough at an open tryout the following spring to get an assignment

with their Greenwood team in the Class-A Western Carolinas League.

Leach credited his pitching coach in Greenwood, Kenny Rowe, a middle reliever with the Dodgers and Orioles in the 1960s, with suggesting that he try throwing side-arm in attempt to get more movement on his pitches, and Leach said the change brought immediate and dramatic results. "With my new way of coming at hitters from down under, pitching for me suddenly stopped being a matter of blowing people out with my power and became a matter of finessing with my movement," Leach wrote. "When I'd thrown overhand and hard I'd had to beat people up, overpower them. Now I adopted a completely different approach. … I was a whole new pitcher."[2]

Leach in coming years would refine the style, developing a distinctive delivery that featured a full side-arm whip released close to the ground, his right knee trailing behind in the dirt. The action provided good sink to his two-seam fastball and a rising effect to his slider, even as his velocity rarely exceeded the low 80s. When he was going well, Leach got his share of strikeouts, but he excelled at keeping hitters from making hard contact, often inducing groundballs and rarely allowing home runs—just 38 in 700 innings pitched in the big leagues.

Buoyed by the new approach, Leach, 23, struck out 67 batters in 67 innings for Greenwood in 1977, and was on his way up in the Braves organization.

Leach split 1978 between Kinston of the Class-A Carolina League and Savannah of the Double-A Southern League, going a combined 6-4, with a 3.76 ERA in 43 games including two starts. Pitching to a 1.96 ERA in 40 relief appearances for Savannah in 1979, he earned a promotion to Triple-A Richmond where he posted a 1.93 ERA in seven games including two starts.

Leach was pitching well in Savannah again in 1980 (5-1, 3.21, mostly in relief) when he was released in midseason, saying in his book that his advanced age for that level (26) and status as an undrafted player made him expendable in the eyes of the Atlanta organization. Days later he was picked up by the Mets, who had a vacancy for a starting pitcher with their Jackson club of the Double-A Texas League, and Leach finished the year there with a 5-1 record and a 1.50 ERA, ranking second in the league.

Beginning a lengthy turnaround, and hungry for talent at the top level, the Mets proved to be a good place for a determined minor leaguer to land. Leach within a year would make his major-league debut after going a combined 10-3 in stops with Jackson and Tidewater of the Triple-A International League. He made his major-league debut on August 12, 1981. Pitching in relief of Ed Lynch at Wrigley Field, Leach had a rough inning, surrendering three hits including a two-run home run by the Chicago Cubs' Mike Lum over the ivy in right field. The outing cost Lynch a win, but the Mets rallied to win the game.

Leach got a no-decision in his next appearance, a start against the Philadelphia Phillies at Shea Stadium, and finished the season with a 1-1 record and a respectable 2.55 ERA in 21 appearances.

Leach split 1982 between Tidewater and the Mets, exclusively in relief except for one spot start, but that was a memorable one. Called on when scheduled starter Rick Ownbey was sidelined with a blister on the season's final weekend, Leach fired a 10-inning, complete-game, 1-0 victory in Philadelphia, surrendering five walks and a single hit—a fifth-inning triple by Luis Aguayo, becoming the first Mets player to throw a one-hitter since Tom Seaver in 1977. Leach described having an unusually active slider that night—including one that broke between the legs of Philadelphia's Ozzie Virgil. Pete Rose, who went 0-for-4 with a strikeout in the game, in an 1984 interview listed Leach among the toughest pitching opponents he faced.[3] Rose was 2-for-9 in his career against Leach.

Leach's performance—which bettered nine innings of scoreless, one-hit ball by his counterpart, John Denny of the Phillies—wasn't the only unusual aspect of that memorable game: Due to a luggage mixup at the airport, the umpiring crew dressed in spare Phillies uniforms and groundskeepers' gear.

As spectacular as the one-hitter was, it was more than two years—and two trades—before Leach resurfaced in the big leagues. He spent all of 1983 in Tidewater, going 5-7 in a swingman role and helping the club to victory in the Triple-A World Series. Leach said his performance in that event attracted the attention of the Chicago Cubs, who shortly afterward traded prospects Jim Adamczak and Mitch Cook to the Mets for him.

A subsequent Cubs managerial change, to Jim Frey for the 1984 campaign, made for a short stay in Chicago. Concerned that Leach's style made him vulnerable to left-handed hitters—borne out in career splits showing lefties hit .294 off Leach with a .409 slugging percentage, while right-handers combined for a respective .233 and .323—Frey insisted that Leach change his pitching style, but Leach was uncomfortable with the switch, fell out of favor, and was swapped to Atlanta for pitcher Ron Meredith in early April.

The second stint with the Braves ended just how the first one did, with a midseason release from Triple-A Richmond and subsequent re-signing by the Mets. Assigned again to Tidewater, Leach went 11-3, with a 3.34 ERA in 43 relief appearances for the Tides.

Spending 1985 in Tidewater, Leach was dominant in relief, posting a 1.59 ERA and a 0.90 WHIP before being recalled to the Mets in June. In 22 games he posted a 2.91 ERA, and was even better in four spot starts, going 3-1 with a 2.70 ERA. Davey Johnson, who had managed Leach in Tidewater in 1983 and now managed the Mets, liked his versatility, desire to pitch, and what he considered a "rubber arm." Teammates took to calling Leach "Jack" as in "Jack of all trades."[4]

"He just wants the ball," Johnson said of Leach. "He doesn't want to give it up when he's on the hill, and if he's not on the hill he can't wait to get there. Fact is, if you tell him to get warm, he may call down and tell you he's ready after three pitches, he wants to be in the game so bad."[5]

The Mets, who won 98 games in 1985 but finished just short of St. Louis for the National League East crown that year, fielded a dominant, 108-win team in 1986 that had no room for the 32-year-old Leach, who was invited to camp as a nonroster player and spent all but five weeks of the year in Tidewater. Although expecting a call-up when rosters expanded in September, Leach missed his chance after dislocating his shoulder in a home-plate collision in a late-season Tidewater game. Leach, as it turned out, would be one of four members of that World Series-winning Mets team not to be awarded a ring—although the Mets relented years later when, under pressure from Randy Myers, co-owner Fred Wilpon agreed to split the cost with Myers.

Leach was again assigned to minor-league camp late in spring training in 1987, and the normally easygoing Southerner made a show of his disappointment with the news, slamming the door on his way out of Johnson's office. But fate intervened, when Dwight Gooden checked into drug rehab and reliever Roger McDowell went to the disabled list just before Opening Day, providing the 33-year-old Leach with his first Opening Day major-league assignment. "I hated to get a job this way, but that's why they keep me around," Leach surmised at the time. "I'm an insurance policy in case someone gets hurt."[6]

Although the Mets failed to defend their title in 1987—with all five of their vaunted starting pitchers missing at least part of the year due to injury—the disarray proved to be just the opportunity Leach needed.

After 18 games in relief, Leach was tabbed to start for the first time on June 1 when Rick Aguilera went down with an injury. Leach that day bested Fernando Valenzuela, 5-2, at Dodger Stadium. He got a no-decision against the Cubs eight days later then started a remarkable run of six wins and two no-decisions in eight consecutive starts, allowing two earned runs or less in six of them, and running his record to 10-0 by August 11—still the Mets record for an unbeaten start to a season.

Fans that summer campaigned to get Leach named to the National League All-Star team—however, Johnson, as the NL manager, declined. But Leach's sizzling streak helped the battered Mets, struggling at .500 in June, to roar back into the National League East race. Leach's streak ended with a loss to Chicago on August 15, and when David Cone returned from the disabled list later that month, Leach returned to the bullpen. His 11th win that year came in relief over the Phillies on September 8. Leach finished 11-1 with a 3.22 ERA.

Lynch had knee surgery after the 1987 season, but for the first time in 1988 had a role all but assured. Spending the entire season in New York, Leach went 7-2 with a 2.54 ERA in 52 games and 92 innings pitched for the National League East champions. He appeared three times in the NLCS against Los Angeles, pitching five scoreless innings, as the Mets lost the series in seven games.

Leach began the 1989 season in New York but was traded to Kansas City in June, to make room for 24-year-old prospect David West, promoted from Tidewater and inserted into middle relief. The trade—bringing back prospect Aguedo Vasquez after the season—was the first of several that eventually disassembled the once-mighty Mets. McDowell, Aguilera, Mookie Wilson, and Lenny Dykstra were all gone before the 1989 season was complete.

Leach, who went 5-6 with a 4.15 ERA in Kansas City in 1989, returned to the club the following spring only to suffer a familiar disappointment — a release just before Opening Day. He quickly caught on with the Minnesota Twins, however, and spent two productive years in the Twins bullpen, pitching in 55 games in 1990 (3-5 with a 3.20 ERA) and 51 in 1991 (1-2, 3.61), when the Twins surprised baseball with a World Series championship. Leach pitched twice during the World Series, surrendering one run in 2⅓ innings. He secured a key out in Game Three in Atlanta, striking out left-handed-hitting Mark Lemke with the bases loaded. "I was tempted to ask T.K. [Twins manager Tom Kelley], 'Do you know what you are doing here, Tom? You're bringing in a side-armer against a left-hander. You never do that,'" Leach recounted.[7]

The Twins gave Leach a ring, but did not elect to offer him a new contract. Leach subsequently signed a deal with Montreal for 1992, only to see the Expos release him just prior to Opening Day.

Undaunted, the 38-year-old Leach resurfaced with the Chicago White Sox and, thanks to adding a new wrinkle to his slider and mixing in a changeup, turned in a fine year in relief, going 6-5 with a 1.95 ERA over 73⅔ innings—the best ERA of his career. He returned in 1993 only to encounter elbow trouble, and got into just 14 games between lengthy rehab stints in the minors. He eventually saw elbow surgeon James Andrews, who discovered extensive damage to his elbow. Leach attended training camp with the White Sox in 1993 and the Tigers in 1994 and 1995 but didn't make any of those clubs, and reluctantly retired to Florida, where among other things, he penned his memoirs.

Co-written with Tom Clark, the American poet who also wrote several books on baseball, *Things Happen for a Reason: The True Story of an Itinerant Life in Baseball* was published by Frog Ltd. in 2000 and highlighted Leach's folksy Southern charm and skill as a storyteller. In it he cheerfully and at times wistfully recounts a hard life on the road as a minor-league survivor, the pursuit of cheap food and cold beer with teammates, how his met his wife, the former Chris McCowan, in Savannah, and later named their daughter after the city, all while gently whipping a few hard sliders past a myopic baseball world that so often failed him.

"The fact that *Things Happen for a Reason* is a classic baseball book shouldn't obscure that fact that it is also a gorgeous piece of pure writing, of human language got onto the page," author Jonathan Lethem wrote in a blurb published on the back cover.

Leach finished his career with a 38-27 lifetime record, with 10 saves, pitching 700 innings in 376 games.

"Baseball's a frustrating game at times, other times it's exciting, and then again strange, even kind of deep," he wrote. "Spending your life in it, you'll find insecurity, confusion, joy, boredom, friendship, mistrust, surprise, despair, hope and pain. So much happens—you just have to be conscious of the fact that you're not in control of any of it, and from that point it does make sense, in a funny kind of way."[8]

SOURCES

In addition to the works cited in the Notes, the author consulted the following:

Ultimatemets.com.

Baseballreference.com.

scouts.baseballhall.org.

studiousmetsimus.blogspot.com.

uni-watch.com.

NOTES

1 Terry Leach with Tom Clark, *Things Happen for a Reason: The True Story of an Itinerant Life in Baseball* (Berkeley, California: Frog, Ltd., 2000).

2 Leach with Clark.

3 Richard Grossinger, *The New York Mets: Ethnography, Myth, and Subtext* (Berkeley, California: Frog Ltd., 2007).

4 Leach with Clark.

5 Davey Johnson and Peter Golenbock, *Bats* (New York: G.P. Putnam's Sons, 1986).

6 Jack Lang, "Mets' Terry Leach (5-0) Just Don't Get No Respect," *The Sporting News*, June 29, 1987.

7 Leach with Clark.

8 Leach with Clark.

ED LYNCH

By Jon Springer

NEVER POSSESSED OF AN OVERPOWERING fastball or a devastating curve, Ed Lynch relied instead on his command, and his wits. The latter, it was said, were among the sharpest of their time, and led to a second act as a baseball executive.

"I'm a competitive person and I have confidence in my abilities," Lynch told the *New York Times.* "I wouldn't have pitched seven years in the big leagues throwing 81 miles per hour if I couldn't get the most out of my abilities."[1]

The above remark—made as Lynch assumed the job of general manager of the Cubs in 1994—may have been an exaggeration but it was not a big one. And it was typical of the witty quips and one-liners that made for lively newspaper copy during Lynch's big-league playing career, which spanned 1980 to 1987 for the New York Mets and Chicago Cubs. A small sampling of his way with words:

On the Mets' pitching staff losing Tom Seaver to a surprise compensation draft pick by the Chicago White Sox: "The day he left the Mets it was like the president being assassinated. We all moved up a notch in our jobs but we'd rather it not happened."[2]

On the wave of young talent that lifted the Mets into sudden contention in 1984: "They have no idea the Mets have been brutal for eight years. While we've been stinking up the league the Mets have built the best farm system in the majors. These kids are winners. They don't care if we're playing the Montreal Expos or the Bad News Bears."[3]

On fan reaction to his pitching as compared to that afforded to his teammate, strikeout phenomenon Dwight Gooden: "What are they going to do for me? Put cards on the wall that say '4-3'?"[4]

When Mets teammate Ray Knight named his daughter Erin Shea: "It's a good thing you didn't play for the Giants."[5]

Edward Francis Lynch was born on Feb. 25, 1956, in Brooklyn. He grew up in Westchester County, New York, and in Miami. He attended Christopher Columbus High School, a Catholic school in Miami where he was named All-City in basketball and baseball. It was the former sport in which he excelled. Lynch was not the best baseball player in the school, or even his family: That honor belonged to his brother Chris.

A year older than Ed, Chris Lynch, also a right-handed pitcher, impressed scouts enough to be drafted three times. The Cardinals selected him in the 13th round out of Christopher Columbus in 1972, but he elected

to go to college at Miami-Dade instead. The Mets made him a third-round selection in the January 1973 draft, and the Dodgers picked him in the 20th round in 1974, but he didn't sign, choosing instead to complete his college degree, then go on to law school.

Ed in the meantime rode his basketball skill to a scholarship at the University of South Carolina, only to wind up as a key member of the Gamecocks' baseball squad. In 1977 South Carolina, under first-year coach June Raines, advanced to the finals of the College World Series, only to lose twice to champion Arizona State. Lynch started and lost the first of those games, a 6-2 complete-game decision.

Lynch, a 1977 business-management graduate, was one of four future major leaguers on that South Carolina squad. Ace starting pitcher Randy Martz was selected by the Cubs 12th overall in the 1977 June amateur draft and went on to a four-year big-league career with the Cubs and White Sox. Outfielder Mookie Wilson, a second-round draftee of the Mets that year, played in the big leagues for 12 years, while reliever Jim Lewis, signed as an undrafted free agent by Seattle, made appearances for the Mariners, Twins, and Yankees.

As for Lynch, he was selected by the Rangers in the 22nd round that year and assigned to their Gulf Coast League affiliate, where he went 1-4 with a 3.70 ERA. Lynch made rapid progress up the organizational ladder for Texas, getting an all-star bid with Asheville of the Class-A Western Carolinas League and a promotion to Double-A Tulsa during 1978. He won 10 games for the Triple-A Tucson Toros in 1979, including a complete-game, 6-1 victory over Spokane on August 8 notable for the fact that Lynch needed just 78 pitches to complete the effort.

Texas, on the outskirts of the AL West pennant race that summer, less than two weeks later traded with the reeling Mets for veteran first baseman-outfielder Willie Montanez. The deal called for the Mets to receive two players to be named: veteran utilityman Mike Jorgensen was one; Lynch was the other, assigned to the Mets after the end of Tucson's season.

Lynch arrived in the Mets organization only months before new ownership and a new management team commenced a thorough and lengthy rebuilding. Lynch became a mainstay of the team as it rebuilt, enduring several grim seasons only to be traded months before it culminated in a 1986 World Series championship. As he succinctly put it, "It was like living with a family all year, then getting kicked out on Christmas Eve."[6]

Lynch spent most of the 1980 season pitching for the Tidewater Tides, the Mets' Triple-A team in Norfolk, Virginia, but was summoned to the big leagues in late August when Mets pitcher Craig Swan went down with shoulder trouble. Lynch made his major-league debut on August 31, 1980, in Candlestick Park, entering a game in which the Mets were trailing 6-4 in the seventh inning, and was hit hard — the first batter he faced, Mike Ivie, ripped a double to center field and by the time Lynch departed in the eighth he'd be charged with four runs in an inning and a third on four hits including a run-scoring triple by the opposing pitcher, Al Holland.

Lynch redeemed himself in his next appearance, a start at Shea Stadium on September 18, earning his first major-league win in a 4-2 victory over the Chicago Cubs. Lynch overall made five appearances in 1980 (four starts), with 1-1 record and a 5.14 ERA.

Lynch began the 1981 season with Tidewater but was summoned to New York in April, again after an injury to Swan, this time a broken rib suffered when he was struck by a ball thrown by catcher Ron Hodges, who was attempting to throw out Tim Raines stealing second. Lynch remained with the Mets until Swan returned in June, just two days before a strike interrupted the season. Lynch returned to the Mets in August, finishing the year with a 4-5 record and a respectable 2.91 ERA in 17 games including 13 starts.

The Mets fired manager Joe Torre after the 1981 season and replaced him with George Bamberger, best known as Earl Weaver's trusted pitching coach with the Orioles teams of the 1960s and '70s. Bamberger had a special admiration for the 26-year-old Lynch, who in his first full season at the big-league level provided reliable middle relief and 12 starts, finishing 4-8, 3.55 for a team that struggled through a 97-loss campaign.

"Eddie did everything you had to do to win," recalled Marty Noble, a former beat writer for *Newsday* who covered that team. "He fielded his position properly. He always covered first base. He was one of the first guys I remember using the slide step, and he held runners very well. He could bunt and help himself. All those little things they talk about to help yourself, he did. And George Bamberger just loved him for that."[7]

Although Lynch possessed the frame of a power pitcher (6-feet-6, 230 pounds), he was anything but. Lynch's fastball rarely traveled faster than 84 miles per hour, but it had good sink, and he commanded it well, backing that up with a slider and changeup. He pitched to contact, striking out just 396 batters in 940⅓ innings pitched in his big-league career, and walking even fewer (229).

Batters combined to hit .284 off Lynch during his career, but some felt they could do better. Some opposing players referred to Lynch as "Ed Lunch," feeling they could "fatten up" on his pitching,[8] but Lynch could also be a frustrating opponent, as revealed in a nationally televised game from Dodger Stadium in September of 1985.

In that contest, hard-swinging Dodgers Mariano Duncan and Pedro Guerrero, each evidently fed up with Lynch's slow-and-slower repertoire, told him as much. "I told him he didn't have (bleep)," Guerrero told the *Los Angeles Times*. "I told him to stop throwing all that junk."[9] When Lynch struck out Duncan with a fastball in the sixth and punctuated it with a "take that," Duncan instead of returning to the home dugout at Lynch's invitation raced toward the pitcher's mound, only to be intercepted by Mets enforcer Ray Knight.

"It's no secret," Keith Hernandez wrote in his book on the 1985 season, *If at First*.... "Eddie is sensitive to the charge that for being such a big guy, he doesn't throw very hard. He would have fought Duncan gladly, if Knight hadn't intervened."[10]

The addition of veteran starters Tom Seaver and Mike Torrez to the 1983 Mets squad initially cost Lynch starting assignments, but he joined the regular rotation in May when back-end starters Scott Holman and Rick Ownbey faltered. Lynch won 10 and lost 10 in 30 games (27 starts) that year, while his earned-run average ticked up to 4.28. Under managers Bamberger (who resigned in May) and Frank Howard, the 1983 Mets finished in the National League East basement for the second straight year, although the midseason addition of All-Star Keith Hernandez and the promotion of rookies including Darryl Strawberry and Ron Darling during that year signaled the turnaround effort that would begin to bear fruit.

Under new manager Davey Johnson, who brought along sensational rookie Dwight Gooden, the Mets made a sudden surge into contention in 1984. Lynch, who became the senior member of the pitching staff when Mike Torrez was released in June, got off to a 7-1 start as the Mets mounted a surprise challenge to division-leading Chicago. Lynch served a "swingman" role for the team, making 40 appearances overall, including 13 starts.

"He's the most consistent pitcher on the staff," Johnson said of Lynch in June. "I know no matter what way I use him he'll get the job done."[11]

Lynch became a focal point of the burgeoning Mets-Cubs rivalry during an August 7 doubleheader at Wrigley Field, when after a five-run Chicago outburst in the fourth inning, he hit Cubs slugger Keith Moreland in the back with a pitch, inciting Moreland to charge the mound and take down Lynch with a flying body block. The Cubs got the better of the scrum, and the National League race, taking both games of the twin bill and all four games in the series as they pulled away en route to a division title. The Mets finished with 90 wins, 6½ games behind Chicago, and a fatigued Lynch faltered down the stretch, finishing with a 9-8 record and a 4.50 ERA.

Lynch found himself back in the Mets' starting rotation in 1985 and turned in what was probably his best overall year, going 10-8 with a 3.44 ERA and setting career highs in innings pitched, complete games, games started, and strikeouts. His walks-per-nine-innings rate of 1.272 ranked third in the National League that year and his WHIP (walks and hits per inning pitched) of 1.126 was 10th. The Mets finished 98-64 that season, fighting the St. Louis Cardinals until the season's final week, but falling just short of a division title.

Lynch by then had become familiar to New Yorkers for his humorous quotes, often highlighting the lighter side of baseball. Noting Lynch's mastery of clubhouse slang, Noble of *Newsday* asked the pitcher to put together a "story" using such phrases. Decades before social media, it "went viral." Baseball fans can buy toilet paper printed with the following quote today, Noble noted.

"The bases were drunk, and I painted the black with my best yakker. But blue squeezed me, and I went full. I came back with my heater, but the stick flares one the other way and chalk flies for two bases. Three earnies! Next thing I know, skipper hooks me and I'm sipping suds with the clubby."[12]

Slowed by nagging injuries in spring training, Lynch made only one appearance for the 1986 Mets before going on the disabled list with a balky knee that eventually required surgery. When he regained his health, the steamrolling Mets—fortified over the offseason with the addition of Bob Ojeda—packaged Lynch in a deal with the Cubs, receiving two prospects, pitcher Dave Lenderman and catcher Dave Liddell. Liddell eventually made it to the Mets in 1990 and singled in his first—and as it turned out, his only—major-league at-bat.

There was some press speculation that Lynch's departure was precipitated by an arbitration win over the offseason that provided him a $530,000 salary for 1986, a bump of $200,000 or 60.6 percent from 1985, while the Mets had proposed $400,000. When asked if he felt his salary was a factor, the normally loquacious pitcher responded with just two words: "No comment."[13]

In any case, Lynch was crestfallen upon being traded to the Cubs, who would struggle to 90 losses while his former club was on its way to winning 108 games and a World Series. But he pitched adequately in a familiar swingman role in Chicago, going 7-5 with a 3.79 ERA. And the Mets made sure he wasn't forgotten: While four members of the 1986 squad who made small contributions to that team—Terry Leach, Randy Myers, Tim Corcoran, and John Mitchell—were not awarded World Series rings, Mets general manager Frank Cashen made certain that Lynch received one.

A second season with the Cubs in 1987 was not as successful, as Lynch dropped to 2-9, with a 5.38 earned-run average in 58 appearances for a last-place team.

The 1987 season was the 31-year-old Lynch's last in the big leagues. Although invited to camp by the Red Sox in 1988, he was cut shortly before the season began.

Putting his playing career behind him, Lynch, like his brother Chris, enrolled at the University of Miami in pursuit of a law degree. Shortly after obtaining it in 1990, he was hired as director of player development for the Padres by Joe McIlvaine, who then was San Diego's general manager. McIlvaine and Lynch had first crossed paths in the Mets organization, where McIlvaine worked in the front office during much of Lynch's tenure.

McIlvaine returned to New York to succeed Al Harazin as Mets GM in 1993, and shortly thereafter named Lynch his special assistant. The combination of McIlvaine's tutelage, and Lynch's personal charm, in October of 1994 earned Lynch an offer from new Cubs CEO Andy MacPhail to become general manager of the Cubs. At 38, he was then the game's youngest GM.

"I was looking for a general manager who was young, bright, and enthusiastic, and Ed possesses all of those attributes, and has the added dimension of having pitched in the major leagues," MacPhail said upon appointing Lynch to succeed Larry Himes.[14]

Lynch proposed founding a team behind speed, defense, and pitching, with mixed results. Inheriting a team that finished last in the National League Central in 1994, the Cubs improved to a winning record (73-71) and a third-place finish in 1995, and fell to fourth place (76-86) in 1996 and fifth place (68-94) in 1997, before a 90-win season in 1998 secured the team's first postseason berth in nine years. (The Cubs advanced to the Division Series by defeating San Francisco in a one-game playoff, then were swept by Atlanta in three games in the NLDS.)

The 1998 club, fueled by Sammy Sosa's phenomenal 66-home run season, included a number of veteran contributors acquired by Lynch in trades and through free agency, including Lance Johnson, Mark Clark, and Manny Alexander (all acquired in a 1997 trade with the Mets), Mickey Morandini, Henry Rodriguez, and Kevin Tapani. These players bolstered an inherited base of Sosa, Mark Grace, and Steve Trachsel, along with Lynch's first draft pick, fireballer Kerry Wood, who was on his way to winning Rookie of the Year honors. The club was managed by Jim Riggleman, whom Lynch selected to succeed Tom Trebelhorn shortly after taking the reins.

Lynch had a special admiration for Wood, notably speaking out when the freshly drafted high schooler threw 177 pitches during a school playoff tournament. "It's just unbelievable that a so-called coach would jeopardize this kid's future," Lynch said. "This kind of behavior is borderline negligence."[15] Critics point out that Lynch, however, was at times too careless with other Cubs prospects. He traded 1997's top draft pick, Jon Garland, then a minor leaguer, to the White Sox for ineffective reliever Matt Karchner. Garland went on to have a 13-year big-league career. Kyle Lohse was a throw-in when Lynch traded for his former Mets teammate, Rick Aguilera, in 1999: Lohse's big-league career was still going 15 years later.

While much of the same cast returned for the 1999 season, the Cubs nosedived in June, and the 95-loss, last-place finish cost Riggleman his job. When new manager Don Baylor and a host of newly acquired players — Eric Young, Damon Buford, Ismael Valdes, and Joe Girardi among them — got the Cubs off to a slow start in 2000, Lynch offered to resign, but MacPhail elected to give the team more time to coalesce. But things only got worse amid weeks of speculation over a potential trade of Sammy Sosa, and MacPhail accepted Lynch's resignation in late July.

Lynch, succeeded by MacPhail on an interim basis, remained in the Cubs organization for another decade as a special assistant to the GM before joining the Toronto Blue Jays as a professional scout in 2010. Lynch married the former Kristin Ann Kacer in 1986 and raised two children in Scottsdale, Arizona. Their son James, an outfielder, was drafted by the Blue Jays out of Pima (Arizona) Community College in 2014.

SOURCES

In addition to the sources cited in the Notes, the author consulted the following:

Ultimatemets.com.

Baseball-reference.com.

scouts.baseballhall.org.

NOTES

1 Jennifer Frey. "Lynch 'Flattered' to Become Cubs' GM," *New York Times,* October 11, 1994. Lynch actually pitched eight seasons in the major leagues.

2 Joe Goddard, "White Sox '84 Rotation: The Best Ever?" *The Sporting News,* April 2, 1984.

3 Joe Gergen, "Darryl Strawberry," *The Sporting News,* May 21, 1984.

4 Author interview with Marty Noble, September 23, 2015.

5 Noble interview.

6 Frey.

7 Noble interview.

8 Noble interview.

9 Gordon Edes, "Dodgers Fight Off Mets for 7-6 Win: Duncan Starts Melee in 6th," *Los Angeles Times,* September 8, 1985.

10 Keith Hernandez and Mike Bryan, *If At First...* (New York: McGraw-Hill, 1986).

11 Jack Lang, "Dependable Lynch a Steal for Mets," *The Sporting News,* June 25, 1984.

12 Noble interview.

13 Malcolm Moran, "View from Top Elusive for Lynch," *New York Times,* July 24, 1986.

14 Joseph A. Reaves, "MacPhail Names Lynch Cubs' GM," *Chicago Tribune,* October 11, 1994.

15 Dwain Price, "Cubs upset with coach after overthrowing top pick," *Fort Worth Star Telegram,* June 8, 1995.

BARRY LYONS

By Leslie Heaphy

A CATCHER WHO ALWAYS SEEMED TO BE trying to win a starting spot, Barry Lyons showed occasional signs of power and a solid presence behind the plate. Described once by reporters as "quiet, conservative and even contemplative in appearance," Lyons often found himself overlooked but still had a major-league career that spanned seven years between 1986 and 1995.

Born on June 3, 1960, in Biloxi, Mississippi, Lyons was the youngest of four brothers. He played baseball and football at Notre Dame High School before transferring in his junior year to Biloxi High School. After sitting out his junior year because of the transfer, he played well enough to earn scholarship offers in football and baseball. Lyons played college ball at Delta State University in Cleveland, Mississippi, staying close to his parents, Kenneth and Margaret, as well as his three brothers. He earned a bachelor's degree in business administration while also playing baseball. Lyons earned All American honors and was named Mississippi College Baseball Player of the Year in 1982.

Lyons was drafted by the Detroit Tigers in the 25th round of the June 1981 amateur draft but did not sign because he was only a junior in college and wanted to not only complete his degree but go out on a high note in his baseball career.

Drafted by the Mets in the 15th round in 1982, Lyons signed and got his professional start with Shelby of the Class-A Sally League. Playing in 45 games, he hit .280 with 4 homers and 46 runs batted in. Lyons remembered what a shock it was to play low-level minor-league ball. The Shelby team played at the local high-school field as there was no minor-league ball park for them.[1]

In 1983 Lyons split his time between Columbia and Lynchburg at the Class-A level. He hit .297 in 92 games for Columbia, and earned a full season with Lynchburg in 1984 and a promotion to Double-A Jackson in 1985. "I thought that I'd be in the majors in '84. I remember being at a friend's house watching *Monday Night Football,* and I see on a crawl at the bottom of the screen that the Mets traded for Gary (Carter)," he said. "In my prime years I was stuck as a backup for three-plus seasons."[2] At Lynchburg Lyons was the team captain and was named Carolina League MVP. With Jackson he hit .307 with 11 home runs and 108 RBIs. Unfortunately he also struck out 67 times while walking only 25 times. His accomplishments earned him runner-up honors for the Texas League MVP as Jackson won the league championship. Lyons' solid play earned him a move to Triple-A Tidewater in 1986. He spent part of the season with the Mets, and made his major-league debut on April 19, 1986, against the Philadelphia Phillies. In three at-bats he had no hits but knocked in a run with an infield grounder.

He had made his childhood dream come true. When Lyons was in the sixth grade he wrote an essay about his summer activities and ended it by stating his career goal was to be a major-league ballplayer.[3]

During the Mets championship run in 1986 Lyons played in only six games with nine at-bats. This did not include any postseason play. He played 61 games for Tidewater that season as well, and hit .295. For the following two seasons with the Mets, Lyons played in 50 and 53 games respectively, backing up Gary Carter. One of the biggest highlights of his career came during the 1988 season when he caught David Cone's two-hit shutout on June 19. Cone actually had a no-hitter through 7⅔ innings. Lyons got the start while Carter played first base. He had another big game in a 3-1 win on August 2 over the Chicago Cubs that helped keep the Mets four games ahead of the Pirates. Lyons had a two-run triple in the sixth inning after throwing out Shawon Dunston in the previous inning. Lyons showed his understanding of his situation when he remarked, "I've come to accept what transpired this year. I pretty much realize my role here. The chances have been few and far between. But when I do get a chance I'm going to give it my best. Tonight was very special for me."[4] His lack of playing time earned Lyons a short stint back at Tidewater to start the 1989 season but injuries brought him back for 79 games, his highest season total in the majors.[5]

The 1990 season started as a bright one after Lyons got more playing time in 1989. He hit .533 in the spring, hoping as he said, "I thought things out and decided to come to camp and open some eyes that might have been blinking at me."[6] He was hoping to get the starting job as Gary Carter's career was winding down. Leg and back issues, however, put Lyons on the disabled list for 15 days in late May. This led to his demotion to the minors and his release before the end of the season. He found a home with the Los Angeles Dodgers, playing three games before the end of the season. He thought he was going to be the backup to Mike Scioscia but the Dodgers signed—guess who?—Gary Carter. As a result, Lyons split the following season between the Dodgers and the California Angels.[7] After playing only 11 games in the Majors during the 1991 season and 47 games at Edmonton, Lyons found himself in the minors for the next three seasons. He played in Tucson, Louisville, Indianapolis, and Nashville before getting one last shot at the majors in 1995 with the Chicago White Sox. Lyons played in 27 games, hitting .266 with five home runs before calling it quits at the end of the season. Those five home runs in just 64 at-bats were more than he had hit in any previous major-league season. Lyons played 14 seasons of professional baseball, which included seven in the majors. He was a career .239 hitter with 15 home runs and 89 RBIs. He also played on championship teams at every level of the game, from Class A to the majors.

After retiring as a player, Lyons remained in the game as a minor-league manager with Nashville and the Charleston (West Virginia) Alley Cats. Then he worked for three years in the broadcast booth for the Nashville Sounds before moving back to his hometown of Biloxi in 2002. Lyons operated the Barry Lyons Baseball Academy, providing training, camps, clinics, and private lessons, for over 25 years.

In 2005 Lyons and his family suffered through Hurricane Katrina. Though he lost all his possessions and his baseball academy, his family survived, only to begin to unravel in the aftermath. His parents went into a nursing home and his wife, Marsha, left him over to his drinking and drugs. After going through a Christian rehab program for drugs and alcohol in 2012, Lyons remained in Biloxi with his second wife, Julie, whom he married in 2012, and his daughter, Danielle. He helped bring minor-league baseball to Biloxi with the Double-A Biloxi Shuckers, part of the Milwaukee Brewers system. The team's new ballpark opened in June 2015 and honored Lyons with his own day on July 21, 2015. The city and team wanted to recognize Lyons for his longtime efforts to bring minor-league baseball to his hometown.[8] "Finally, the stadium is going to be completed," Lyons proclaimed. "It has been a long and tedious procedure." As of 2016 he also coached the Bristol Blues in the collegiate summer league. "Where this leads, I'm not certain. But I'm back in the game, and guiding players' dreams," Lyons said. He said he had no regrets about what happened or where he was at that point in his life. "Nothing was ever given to me, nor expected," Lyons said. "There are challenges every step of the way; it's the nature of the game."[9]

SOURCES

Besides the sources cited in the Notes, the author consulted baseball-reference.com and Lyons' file at the National Baseball Hall of Fame.

NOTES

1 youtube.com/watch?v=TAVaSceuS_o&feature=youtu.be.

2 Don Laible, "Former Mets' Catcher Lyons Back in the Game." uticaod.com/article/20150516/BLOGS/305169993, May 15, 2015.

3 Ibid.

4 Steve Marus, "Mets' Lyons Roars on Big Night," *Pittsburgh Press,* August 3, 1988.

5 Howie Karpin, *162-0: Imagine a Mets Perfect Season* (Chicago: Triumph Books, 2011).

6 Joseph Durso, "Lyons Could Be Tiger for Mets," *Gainesville* (Florida) *Sun*, March 14, 1989.

7 "The Rise and Fall of Mets' Lyons," *Pittsburgh-Post Gazette*, September 10, 1990.

8 barrylyonsfoundation.org/; clipsyndicate.com/video/playlist/30835/5879726?title=headline_news; Owen Renick, "Biloxi Baseball Blues," Unpub. Paper in Hall of Fame file.

9 Don Laible.

DAVE MAGADAN

By Rory Costello

DAVE MAGADAN WAS AN ARTIST WITH THE bat. He lacked power. He lacked speed. He wasn't known for his glove at either first or third base. But his deft spray hitting and patience at the plate—.390 lifetime on-base percentage—kept him in the majors from September 1986 through 2001. This skill also led Magadan to an ongoing career as a batting coach, starting in 2002.

David Joseph Magadan was born on September 30, 1962, in Tampa, Florida. His father, Joe Magadan, was also born in Tampa but spent part of his childhood in Spain.[1] That was the birthplace of Dave's grandparents, Marcelino and Benigna Magadán.[2] (In Spanish, the accent is on the last syllable of the family name, but in America it came to be pronounced MAG-a-dən). His mother was Alice (née Alicia Samalea), whose father came from Spain and whose mother was from Cuba. Dave was the youngest of three children. He followed a sister named Diana and a brother, Joe Jr.

Spanish was his parents' mother tongue, and so it's not surprising that Dave learned it as a child. "Our family spoke mostly Spanish in the household," he said in 2014.[3] He understands "everything" in Spanish and can speak "about 90 percent" of it. However, both of his parents worked full time, so he also spent much of his time with English-speaking neighbors in Tampa. Being bilingual helped him in coaching Latino players.[4]

Magadan's first cousin—and godfather—is Lou Piniella, another Tampa native. Piniella, whose mother was Joe Magadan's sister Margaret, played in all or part of 18 major-league seasons and managed for another 23. As a boy, Magadan traveled with his parents in the summers to see Piniella play in various cities. "I wouldn't say we're close," he remarked in 1993, "Close enough, I guess."[5]

Joe Magadan Sr. was a fine athlete who played both football and baseball. He went to Loyola University in New Orleans on a football scholarship, but lost his chance at a possible professional career when a defensive player's knee broke a rib and punctured a kidney. Joe was given last rites and dropped from 230 pounds to 145. After recovering, he got a tryout with the New York Yankees, but he was not the same player he had been before. After Joe died at the age of 92 in 2010, Dave said, "One of the big frustrations of his life was that the injury prevented what could have been."[6]

Joe worked for Corral Wodiska, which was one of many cigar companies in Tampa's historic Ybor City area. The family moved to Venezuela, then back to Tampa after three years (that was before Dave was born).[7] Joe continued to play baseball in Tampa's Intersocial League, a high-quality recreational league

founded in 1938. His teammates included his brother Mac and Louis Piniella Sr.[8]

After returning to Tampa, Joe took a job as an accountant at a produce plant but made sure that his shift ended by early afternoon, so he could coach Joe Jr. and Dave.[9] "My dad's the one who really taught me how to play," said Dave in 1981. "He also worked with Lou and really helped him."[10] Dave first had thoughts of making pro baseball a career at age 6. He practiced with the same team as his brother Joe, who was five years older.[11] Starting when he was 7 years old, Magadan was part of a thriving Little League scene in West Tampa—there were so many kids playing that they could be on the field for just two out of four practice days, and the stands weren't big enough to hold all the noisy fans. His parents were devoted to their children, sports, and the Little League.[12]

Magadan attended Jesuit High School in Tampa, as did his father and Piniella. Though he threw right-handed, he batted left. He played third base and "was an accomplished pitcher who beat arch-rival Tampa Catholic three times. ... (H)e won the Tony Saladino Award as the top prep baseball player in Hillsborough County."[13] Several other winners of this award went on to the majors, the most notable being Tino Martinez and Gary Sheffield.

The Boston Red Sox selected Magadan in the 12th round of the June 1980 amateur draft, but he did not sign. Instead, he went to the University of Alabama. "I wanted to go to a four-year school," he said in 1983. "I wasn't heavily recruited. I got some letters from some schools that said they were interested, but not anything like Alabama. I decided that playing away from home at Alabama was the best chance for me to improve as a player, a student, and a person." He succeeded on all counts, with the help of the woman who became his wife, Kelly Ann Horton from Tuscaloosa.[14]

Magadan had a fine college career. In 2015 he still held many of Alabama's individual batting records. He was named to the Southeast Conference's All-SEC team in each of the three years he played. He was an All-America for two years. In 1983 *Baseball America* named him its College Player of the Year. Magadan entered the College Baseball Hall of Fame in 2010, becoming the second University of Alabama player to do so, after Hall of Famer Joe Sewell.

As a freshman in 1981, Magadan set a school record with a hitting streak in his first 27 games. To keep the pressure off, his teammates tricked him into believing that the record was 22 when it was actually 18. "If I had known I was near it, I probably would have gone 0-for-7," Magadan said.[15]

In September 1981, Magadan was also named American Legion Player of the Year after his team (Post 248, West Tampa) won the national championship. As part of the honor, he attended the 1981 World Series.[16] He also got to visit Cooperstown. He viewed the latter as the greatest experience of his life to that point.[17]

After his sophomore year ended, Magadan went to play ball in Alaska. His team was the Peninsula Oilers.[18] "I gained a lot of confidence playing in the Alaska League that summer," he recalled. "I faced a lot of guys from other parts of the country. It was such a great experience facing guys I had read about and had a lot of respect for."[19]

As a junior in 1983, Magadan shifted from third base to first base. The reason was the emergence of sophomore shortstop Craig Shipley, the first player trained in Australia to reach the majors (the incumbent shortstop moved to third). Magadan batted .535 with 114 hits and 95 RBIs; his slugging percentage was .829. "I was locked in the whole year," he said.[20]

The Crimson Tide went to the College World Series that spring, fulfilling one of the team's major goals. Alabama made the final game, but lost to the University of Texas, which featured Roger Clemens and Calvin Schiraldi. Magadan hit safely in his first eight at-bats, including 5-for-5 in one game, and wound up hitting .550 in the CWS.[21]

The New York Mets made Magadan their second-round pick in the June 1983 draft. He gave up his final year of eligibility at Alabama, signed with the Mets, and reported to Columbia in the South Atlantic

League (Class A). He hit .336 with 3 homers and 32 RBIs in 64 games. That fall, he observed that switching from an aluminum bat to wood was a challenge at first. "The wooden bat was a little bit heavier and I tried to overcompensate," he said. "The first two weeks I struck out a lot more than I usually do. But I got used to it and got a little bit stronger, and then it didn't bother me at all."[22]

After the season ended, Dave and Kelly were married on September 17.[23] The honeymoon was brief, though, because the Mets wanted Magadan to go to Instructional League.[24] The couple had two sons, Jordan (born 1988) and Christian (born 1991). They were divorced in 1997.

In November 1983 Magadan was the winner—by unanimous vote—of the Golden Spikes Award as the nation's best amateur baseball player. Presenting the award was cousin Lou Piniella. "I'd like to move up one league a year," said Magadan after winning, "but if I don't I can live without it."[25]

That turned out to be a pretty accurate timetable—he spent just three more seasons in the minors. At Lynchburg (Class A) in 1984, although he missed the last month of the season with a broken wrist, he lifted his average to a league-leading.350.[26] His on-base percentage was a tremendous .494, thanks to 104 walks. Moving up to Double-A Jackson in 1985, he hit .309 with an OBP of .441. He shifted back from first base to third base that year. (There had been talk of converting him to catcher after the 1983 season but that did not take place.[27])

Despite his size (6-feet-3 and 190 pounds), Magadan hit no homers in either 1984 or 1985. *The Sporting News* remarked, "A lack of power could restrict his progress."[28] That was not the case; he advanced to Triple-A Tidewater in 1986. His average was .311 and his OBP was .411. He hit just one homer, and that was late in the season. In early September *The Sporting News* again speculated, "Can a player without power make it in the majors as a third baseman?"[29] Nonetheless, the International League's managers still regarded Magadan as one of the league's top 10 prospects.[30]

And when the big-league rosters expanded that month, the Mets called Magadan up for the first time. He made his debut at Shea Stadium on September 7. Pinch-hitting for Kevin Elster in the fifth inning, he singled off Ed Wojna of San Diego. Magadan appeared in 10 games for the team that became world champions, starting four of them at first base. He was 8-for-18 (.444)—including a 3-for-4 outing with two RBIs at Shea on September 17, when the Mets clinched the National League East title by defeating the Chicago Cubs. Keith Hernandez was out sick that night; Magadan said, "I was just concentrating so much on not screwing up. You never know how you'll react in that situation."[31]

Magadan said of himself and the other call-ups, "What we did was give [the veterans] some opportunities to take some days off and rest up for the postseason. It was a strange feeling, something I'd never experienced before. You get your call-up like that and I had a lot of success right away, but at the same time, you feel like it was someone else's party and you were just hanging out."[32] He was not eligible for the postseason—he watched the games from home—and he did not get a World Series ring until 1995, when "Randy Myers just made so much noise about it that they finally released the jeweler to make the rings for like four or five of us that didn't receive them then, and [Myers] paid for them.[33]

After the 1986 season, Ray Knight and Kevin Mitchell were both gone from the Mets' roster. Howard Johnson and Magadan were the only legitimate third basemen remaining on the team. Magadan missed most of spring training 1987, however, with a lump that developed in his right armpit. There was some concern that it might be lymphatic cancer, but Magadan's belief was that it was cat scratch fever caused by his wife's pet.[34]

Johnson seized the third-base job and entered the prime of his career. Magadan was left with spot duty, starting 35 times at third and 7 times at first. In 216 plate appearances across 85 games, he hit .318 with 3 homers and 24 RBIs. He was most pleased, though, with the strides he had made as a defensive player. He cited the help of coach Bud Harrelson.[35]

Magadan's first of 42 major-league homers came at Pittsburgh's Three Rivers Stadium on April 20. It was notable for two reasons. First, it was off a lefty, John Smiley. He hit just three more off southpaws during the remainder of his career while hitting .263 against them, vs. .296 against righties. Second, it was as a pinch-hitter. Magadan finished his career with 92 pinch hits, and he hit a capable .265 in that demanding role. In 1987 he talked about how he typically liked to use his first at-bat to feel out a pitcher and see what he liked to throw.[36] Looking back in 2014, he offered this insight:

"My approach as a pinch-hitter was similar to my approach as a starter later in the game. I did my homework on how I was going to get pitched as a pinch-hitter, and remained patient to get my pitch. I had confidence hitting with two strikes so I was not afraid to go deep in the count to get my pitch." Indeed, even Magadan's email address contains the phrase "3n2."[37]

In 1988 Magadan got a chance to play more first base after Keith Hernandez pulled his hamstring on June 6 and reinjured it on June 23. He later said, "When I came in for Keith, I really didn't take advantage of it. I think I put too much pressure on myself. When I was in there we weren't playing well and the whispers were it was because Keith wasn't there. When you start making this a job and a grind, and think about all the negative things instead of the positive things, then it's no fun."[38] He hit .277-1-35 in 380 plate appearances. He continued to draw walks, but his slugging percentage was a mild .334.

Although the Mets won the NL East in 1988, Magadan said, "I really didn't feel like I was part of it."[39] He went to the postseason for the only time in his career and was 0-for-3 as a pinch-hitter as the Los Angeles Dodgers won the pennant. Several years later, Magadan—a normally placid and quiet man—admitted, "I was really bad when I was younger. I would sulk and pout and be very angry all the time." It carried over off the field, but that changed after the birth of his first son that fall—he was able to forget about the bad days.[40]

In May 1989 Hernandez got hurt again—he fractured his kneecap and was out of action for nearly two months. Magadan became part of a platoon at first base with Tim Teufel. Manager Davey Johnson commented, "I don't expect to see him hit home runs, but I'd like to see a bunch of doubles."[41] Magadan got 22 two-baggers while hitting .286-4-41 in 429 plate appearances. His slugging percentage rose to .393.

After the 1989 season, the Mets parted ways with Hernandez. To start with in 1990, the first-base job went to Mike Marshall, but he was a bust. Magadan took over in early June and had his best season in the majors. He reached career highs in batting average (.328, third-best in the NL), homers (6), RBIs (72), and slugging percentage (.457).

Magadan's strength as a hitter was grounded in his knowledge of the strike zone—he took a lot of pitches, close ones as well as bad balls. He most often batted second in the lineup. When he swung, he went with the pitch. For example, if he was facing a lefty, and got a late-breaking ball low and away, he could serve it over the third baseman's head with a neat little flick of the wrists. STATS Inc.'s *Scouting Report* for 1991 observed, "He can hit doubles down the line and into the gaps, but when he hits a home run, it's not by design."

That book also offered a fair assessment of his defensive ability. "Magadan is short on range, but his glove is soft enough, and his arm is as strong as you would expect from a former third baseman."[42] He worked hard to improve in the field and overcome frustrating negative perceptions, especially by comparison with Hernandez, one of the finest fielders ever at first base.[43]

Troubled by torn cartilage in both shoulders, Magadan fell off to .258-4-51 in 1991. That November the Mets signed veteran star Eddie Murray to be their new first baseman. The durable Murray started 152 games at first in 1992, and Magadan appeared just twice there all season long, for a mere 10 innings. He shifted back to third base, sharing time with Bill Pecota. In 99 games for "The Worst Team Money Could Buy," he hit .283-3-28. His season ended on August 8, upon suffering a broken wrist when he was hit by a relay throw while sliding in the middle of a potential double play at Chicago's Wrigley Field. He later likened the sound to eggshells cracking.[44]

Magadan became a free agent that fall, but New York never even called him. "I never did have the success with the Mets I imagined I would," he said. "I always thought I'd have a longer, better career in New York than that."[45] He signed with the Florida Marlins, an expansion club, in December 1992. He later said, with a laugh, "I figured it was finally the time in my career when I was going to be stable. I was always the subject of trade rumors in New York. I really thought, for the first time, that I'd be able to settle down."[46]

Instead, in late June 1993, the Marlins traded Magadan to the Seattle Mariners for outfielder Henry Cotto and pitcher Jeff Darwin. A few days before, Florida had acquired third baseman Gary Sheffield from the San Diego Padres. Magadan said, "I understand why they did it. Gary Sheffield is one of the best players in the game and they had a chance to get him. But I was still disappointed. I thought they were going to commit to me for a couple of years and it was my understanding that they didn't have the money to go get somebody like that. I guess you live and learn, though."[47]

Seattle's manager at the time was none other than Lou Piniella, who said, "We haven't been in contact, but I've followed his career very closely." Third baseman Edgar Martínez was out with a pulled hamstring, and Piniella said, "We needed another left-handed bat in the lineup and somebody who is professional like Dave is." Magadan responded, "[Piniella] is something different with that fiery temper, but I look forward to playing for him. He's also a great hitting instructor on top of that."[48]

As it turned out, Magadan spent just the remainder of that season in Seattle. That November, the Mariners dealt him back to Florida—oddly enough, Jeff Darwin was part of the trade again, along with cash. Florida had decided to put Gary Sheffield in right field, and general manager Dave Dombrowski said, "We liked what Dave did for us; there was never a dissatisfaction with his play. It was just a matter of circumstances at the time." A delighted Magadan said, "You never know what will happen."[49]

STATS Inc.'s *Scouting Report* for 1994 offered further insight on Magadan in the field, saying, "[He] outperforms his reputation. … His range at third is adequate, and he makes few errors thanks to his soft hands and accurate arm. As a first baseman, he digs out throws pretty well, and starts the 3-6-3 double play with the best."[50]

Magadan hit .275-1-17 in 74 games for the Marlins in 1994, while plagued by assorted injuries. He started the season on the disabled list with a sprained wrist; he then suffered a bruised knee and a broken toe. The strike didn't end his season that year—a broken foot did, suffered on July 20 when Cincinnati's Hector Carrasco hit him with a pitch.[51]

After the strike ended, Magadan signed a one-year free-agent deal with the Houston Astros. "He's amenable to being a support player," said general manager Bob Watson. "He will back up [Jeff] Bagwell at first and also be in that mix over at third and be a left-handed pinch-hitter."[52] Magadan wound up playing more third base than anybody else for Houston that year, and he hit .313-2-51 in 422 plate appearances. The team's other main third baseman that year was old college teammate Craig Shipley.

Magadan then moved on to the Chicago Cubs for the 1996 season. The Cubs had lost Todd Zeile to Philadelphia via free agency and needed to fortify third base. Magadan had surgery for a bone spur in his hand in March, and the soreness took time to subside. He then went to the minors for the first time since 1986 to serve a rehab assignment. Upon returning to Chicago in late May, he backed up Leo Gómez at third and Mark Grace at first. He hit .254-3-17 in 201 plate appearances.

In early 1997 Magadan pulled up stakes again as a free agent. This time he went to the Oakland A's. He hit .303-4-30 in 328 plate appearances his first year there, but his second season in Oakland was cut short by a sprained hand on May 15. At the time, he was hitting .321, and he was excited because he had won the starting third-base job. The injury was strange—Magadan's stickum-laden batting glove stuck to the bat on his follow-through while swinging at a pitch, and just before he was ready to go on another rehab assignment, he aggravated the hand on a practice swing.[53]

In December 1998 Magadan signed with the San Diego Padres to provide a lefty bat off the bench and infield depth. He did so for the next three seasons, even playing second base and shortstop for the first time on a few brief occasions. He backed up George Arias (until Arias was demoted) and Phil Nevin at third base, while spelling Wally Joyner and then Ryan Klesko at first base. He also was frequently used as a pinch-hitter. His plate appearances diminished from 300 to 166 to 142. His batting average was .268 as a Padre, with 5 homers and 63 RBIs. In August 2000, *The Sporting News* observed, "He's a valuable hitting mentor."[54]

On May 4, 2000, Magadan got married for the second time, to Monique Dumouchel. They originally met in spring training 1997, while Monique was on vacation in Arizona.[55] "We had a church wedding after the season on November 4, 2000, in Boston, Massachusetts."[56] They eventually had two daughters, Peyton and Avery.

Aged 39, Magadan retired after the 2001 season. That November he was named roving minor-league hitting instructor for the Padres; he served in that position during 2002. He became San Diego's major-league batting coach in November 2002 and spent 3½ seasons at that level. But in the middle of June 2006, the Padres—playing in pitcher-friendly Petco Park—had the NL's worst batting average and the fewest homers in the majors. Magadan was fired. "I was shocked when I was let go," he later said. "I didn't see it coming at all."[57] General manager Kevin Towers said, "As much of a professional as Mags is—dedicated, passionate—we just weren't getting the results we were looking for. A lot of it could be the ballpark, a lot could be the product."[58]

That October, though, Magadan landed with the Boston Red Sox. Theo Epstein—who knew Magadan from his years with the Padres' front office in the late 1990s and early 2000s—had become Boston's GM. Red Sox manager Terry Francona was a friend too. Upon his hiring, Magadan said that his coaching philosophy was to keep it simple. He noted, "Every hitter has got his own personal quirks at the plate," and added, "I believe in looking at a lot of video. David Ortiz isn't going to get pitched the same way as an Alex Cora."[59]

Magadan remained with Boston for six seasons. The Red Sox won the World Series in his first year there, 2007. Although they lost in the playoffs during the following two seasons, and missed the postseason altogether for three years after that, their offense remained productive.

In October 2012, the Texas Rangers hired Magadan, who'd been allowed to speak to other teams about jobs although he had an option remaining on his contract.[60] Upon joining Texas, he gave further insight into his school of hitting. "To be a hitter at the big-league level, you have to have the attitude that you're swinging at every pitch until it's a ball," he said. "That little bit of passiveness or delay on being ready to hit, once you decide, it's too late, you hit it foul late. That's something you look for in all hitters. Even your very patient hitters, their attitude is they are swinging at every pitch and your eyes will tell you whether to swing." General manager Jon Daniels emphasized, "He's got an individual plan for each guy."[61]

After Ron Washington stepped down as manager of the Rangers in September 2014, the front office gave the team's coaches permission to discuss opportunities with other clubs. Magadan interviewed with the New York Yankees for their vacant position as batting coach, but they went in another direction. He was also mentioned as a candidate for spots with the Mets and A's, but in October 2014, he decided to stay with Texas.

Aged just 52 at the beginning of the 2015 season, Magadan still had many years ahead of him in baseball if he chose. His interpersonal skills helped him there.

"In today's game, you've got to reach everybody," he said in late 2014. "You have to be able to bounce from a 10-year guy to a five-year guy to a rookie to be an effective hitting coach."[62]

"As far as how long I want to stay in the game? The travel at this point in my career is pretty grueling, especially with a new family and young kids. It gets tougher and tougher every year. I take it a year at a time and when it starts to get too tough to get on that plane for spring training, then it'll be time to hang it up. I'm not quite there yet."[63]

SOURCES

Grateful acknowledgment to Dave Magadan for his input (via email, December 16, 2014).

Internet resources

baseball-reference.com

retrosheet.org

rolltide.com

ancestry.com

tonysaladinobaseballtournament.com

NOTES

1 Andrew Meacham, "Joe Magadan lost a sports career to injury, but helped relatives reach the majors," *Tampa Bay Times*, August 7, 2010.

2 "Horton-Magadan," *Tuscaloosa News*, August 14, 1983. Melissa Isaacson, "Lou Piniella was born into baseball," ESPN.com, August 30, 2010.

3 E-mail, Dave Magadan to Rory Costello, December 16, 2014.

4 Gordon Edes, "No speaking ill of Magadan: Bilingual coach hit with players," *Boston Globe*, April 26, 2007.

5 Jim Cour, "Trade reunites cousins Magadan and Piniella," Associated Press, July 6, 1993.

6 Meacham, "Joe Magadan lost a sports career to injury, but helped relatives reach the majors."

7 "Joe Magadan lost a sports career." E-mail, Dave Magadan to Rory Costello, December 16, 2014.

8 Wes Singletary, "The Inter-Social League: 1943 Season," *Sunland Tribune*, vol. XVIII (Tampa:

Tampa Historical Society, November 1992), 82. Melissa Isaacson, "Lou Piniella was born into baseball," ESPN.com, August 30, 2010.

9 Mary Jo Melone and Art Keeble, "Baseball Was My Life: The Stories of West Tampa," in *Tampa Bay History*, Volume 23, 2009, 62-64.

10 Chris Welch, "Magadan sets Alabama record," *Tuscaloosa News*, March 24, 1981: 9.

11 Andrew Carroll, "Will he go pro? David Magadan will wait and see," *Tuscaloosa News*, April 29, 1983: 15.

12 Melone and Keeble, "Baseball Was My Life."

13 "Will he go pro?"

14 "Will he go pro?"

15 Chris Welch, "Magadan sets Alabama record," *Tuscaloosa News*, March 24, 1981: 11.

16 "First Magadan, now Snyder in baseball HOF," *Tuscaloosa News*, September 22, 1982: 20.

17 Carroll, "Will he go pro?"

18 Lew Freedman, *Diamonds in the Rough: Baseball Stories from Alaska* (Kenmore, Washington: Epicenter Press, 2000), 241.

19 Jonathan Mayo, *Facing Clemens* (Guilford, Connecticut: Globe Pequot Press, 2008), 9.

20 Mayo, *Facing Clemens*, 5.

21 "Alabama's Magadan wins baseball award," Associated Press, November 10, 1983.

22 "Alabama's Magadan wins baseball award."

23 "Horton-Magadan."

24 Cecil Hurt, "Magadan getting hitched, then off to Instructional League," *Tuscaloosa News*, September 16, 1983: 14.

25 "Alabama's Magadan wins baseball award."

26 Howard Blatt, "Magadan, Dykstra prepared for duel," *New York Daily News*, August 10, 1990.

27 "Sports People: Piniella's Cousin," *New York Times*, November 10, 1983

28 "Minor League Notes: Mets," *The Sporting News*, September 9, 1985: 31.

29 "Around the Minors: Mets," *The Sporting News*, September 8, 1986: 32.

30 "Around the Minors: Mets," *The Sporting News*, September 15, 1986: 36.

31 Dick Brinster, "Gooden survives rowdy fans as Mets clinch it," Associated Press, September 18, 1986.

32 Mayo, *Facing Clemens*, 12-13.

33 Maureen Mullen, "His new home is a hit with Magadan," *Boston Globe*, January 3, 2008. The other two recipients were Terry Leach and Barry Lyons. "'86 Series Rings Arrive at Last," *New York Times*, December 25, 1995.

34 Andrew Carroll, "'Mags': Toughest adjustment in majors is wondering when he'll play," *Tuscaloosa News*, July 5, 1987: 1B.

35 Carroll, "'Mags'"

36 Carroll, "'Mags'"

37 Email, Dave Magadan to Rory Costello, December 16, 2014.

38 "Sub Magadan leads Hernandez-less Mets," Associated Press, May 19, 1989.

39 "Mets' Hernandez out two months," Associated Press, May 19, 1989.

40 Amy Niedzielka, "Marlins' Magadan mad again? Not anymore," *Calhoun Times and Gordon County News* (Calhoun, Georgia), June 4, 1994: 2B.

41 "Sub Magadan leads Hernandez-less Mets."

42 John Dewan, ed., *The Scouting Report, 1991* (New York: HarperCollins, 1991), 528.

43 Joe Sexton, "Defensive Effort," *New York Times*, March 19, 1991.

44 Bob Klapisch and John Harper, *The Worst Team Money Could Buy* (New York: Random House, 1993), 235.

45 Klapisch and Harper, 237.

46 Cour, "Trade reunites cousins Magadan and Piniella."

47 Cour, "Trade reunites cousins Magadan and Piniella."

48 "Seattle gets Magadan," wire service reports, June 28, 1993.

49 "Seattle trades Magadan back to Marlins," Associated Press, November 10, 1993.

50 *The Scouting Report, 1994*, 291.

51 "Magadan may be lost for year," *Sarasota Herald-Tribune*, July 23, 1994: 4C.

52 "Magadan, Astros agree to deal," wire service reports, April 14, 1995.

53 Mark Fainaru-Wada, "Hands-off year for Magadan," *San Francisco Examiner*, August 18, 1998.

54 Tom Krasovic, "See a Different game," *The Sporting News*, August 7, 2000: 34.

55 Alan Siegel, "'What a feeling': Sox hitting coach reflects on championship run," *The Eagle-Tribune* (North Andover, Massachusetts), November 27, 2007.

56 Email, Dave Magadan to Rory Costello, December 16, 2014.

57 "Red Sox hire ex-Padres hitting coach Magadan," *Associated Press*, October 21, 2006.

58 Brian Hiro, "Padres' poor hitting cost Magadan a job," *San Diego Union-Tribune*, June 16, 2006.

59 "Red Sox hire ex-Padres hitting coach Magadan."

60 Richard Durrett, "Dave Magadan leaves Red Sox," ESPN.com, October 19, 2012.

61 Richard Durrett, "Dave Magadan wants aggressive, smart bats," ESPN.com, October 19, 2012.

62 Anthony McCarron, "Dave Magadan could be hit as Yankee coach," *New York Daily News*, October 17, 2014.

63 Email, Dave Magadan to Rory Costello, December 16, 2014.

LEE MAZZILLI

By Jon Springer

HE WAS A HANDSOME, STYLISH ITALIAN-American from the streets of Brooklyn who strutted into prominence at the same moment John Travolta's Tony Manero did the same on the silver screen. But there was more to Lee Mazzilli than a pair of tight-fitting pants. He was a graceful athlete with a good eye who could hit—and throw—either left-handed or right-handed. He was a seven-time national youth speedskating champion. And after a 14-year playing career, he found success as an actor, a businessman, a big-league manager, and a broadcaster.

Lee Louis Mazzilli was born on March 25, 1955, in Brooklyn, the youngest of Libero and June Mazzilli's three children. Libero, whose family had immigrated to America from Bari, Italy, worked the family trade as a piano tuner and was also a professional welterweight boxer. The family lived in a second-floor apartment on East 12th Street between Avenue Y and Avenue Z in the Sheepshead Bay section of Brooklyn, minutes from Coney Island. Neighborhood kids played stickball, punch-ball, and other baseball variations on the street and organized games in the Gil Hodges Little League, but young Lee grew up with a second sporting passion.

Introduced to ice skating by his father, Lee became the standout among of a group of young speedskaters in his family including his sister, Joanne, and his cousins Raymond and Arthur Mazzilli. Skating at area rinks including Prospect Park in Brooklyn, Flushing Meadows Park across from his future working address in Queens, and Wollman Rink in New York's Central Park, Lee was soon winning local and regional tournaments. Between the ages of 12 and 16, he won or shared national age-group Long Track national championships three times and won a Short Track national title four times. Records from the National Speedskating Hall of Fame show Mazzilli winning a long-track title in 1970 as a 15-year-old while Olympian Eric Heiden, then 13, took the same title in his age group.

"Lee was very fast, and had very good agility and balance," recalled Bob Fenn, who skated with Lee as a youth and became a top skating coach. "Skating short track, you've got to be a bit of a daredevil, and Lee was very confident in himself, very determined."[1]

While Heiden a decade later would post what's considered to be the most dominating performance in speedskating history in the 1980 Olympics, Mazzilli's skating career came to a crossroads in 1971 when a qualifying event conflicted with playoff games for his club baseball team. Mazzilli chose to stay with baseball. "It was a no-brainer," Mazzilli told the *Baltimore Sun* in 2003. "I had a passion for speedskating, did it with all my heart. But I don't know that I would have made the [1972] Olympic team. And it was a different era back then; there weren't all these other sports. Baseball was the No. 1 sport by far, and it was always my first love."[2]

In baseball Mazzilli had made a name for himself with blazing speed he flashed on the bases and in the outfield. His game was further distinguished by the fact that he could bat, throw, and catch with equal ease with either hand. Mazzilli owned two gloves and didn't seem to care which he used. An admirer of Willie Mays, Mazzilli perfected his own version of Mays' "basket catch," catching fly balls in an upturned glove just as they reached his waist, exhibiting a cool economy of movement. On the bases, he preferred dramatic head-first slides, adapting the aggressive style of Pete Rose. At Lincoln High School he hit .386 over three seasons.

When the Mets selected Mazzilli with 14th overall pick in the first round of the June 1973 draft, Joe McDonald, then the Mets' director of scouting, announced it this way: "Bats right-left. Throws right-left."[3] After negotiating through the summer, the kid from Brooklyn signed with the Mets for a $50,000 bonus and an audience with his idol, who was then finishing his career in New York. "I signed the contract at Shea [Stadium]," Mazzilli recalled in a 2008 interview. "Joe McDonald asked me if there was anything I wanted to see, and I told him, 'Yeah, Willie Mays. I'd like to meet Willie Mays.' So they took me down to the clubhouse, the trainer's room. I walk in, and Willie Mays is on the trainer's table."[4]

Before Mazzilli made his professional debut the following spring, he and the Mets came to a fateful decision. Eschewing what might have been his more natural throwing arm, the Mets encouraged Mazzilli to throw exclusively right-handed, figuring it would afford him greater defensive flexibility.

Mazzilli spent all of the 1974 season at Anderson of the Western Carolinas League, hitting .269 but already exhibiting an exceptional batting eye, drawing a team-best 76 walks and stealing 46 bases, second-most in the six-team circuit. As a 20-year-old at Visalia of the Class-A California League in 1975, Mazzilli upped his batting average to .281 and his on-base percentage to .409, and stole 49 bases—seven during a single seven-inning game at San Jose, tying a record set twice before in nine-inning games. Mazzilli accomplished the feat by walking twice and singling in his first three at-bats, and stealing second and third each time. In a fourth turn at the plate, he walked, went to second on a single, then stole third.

An even stronger season at Jackson of the Double-A Texas League in 1976—Mazzilli batted .292 with a slugging average of .456 and an on-base percentage of .439, and led the league with 111 walks—earned him a September call to the Mets. He made his major-league debut on September 7 as a late-inning defensive replacement for outfielder John Milner at Wrigley Field and, batting left-handed, bounced out to Cubs pitcher Joe Coleman. The next afternoon he entered as a pinch-hitter in the ninth inning and lined a first-pitch fastball from lefty Darold Knowles over the fence in left for a three-run home run.

Mazzilli's signature arrival came a few weeks later at Shea Stadium, when he pinch-hit a two-out, two-run home run off Pirates relief ace Kent Tekulve to spark a 5-4 walk-off win for the Mets. The loss devastated the Pirates, who in the month prior made up more than 11 games chasing down faltering Philadelphia for the National League East pennant, but they never got any closer after Mazzilli struck. PIRATES BURIED BY UNKNOWN SLUGGER, lamented the *Pittsburgh Press*.

These moments of high drama helped to raise Mazzilli's profile as a candidate to take over center field on a full-time basis in 1977, although there were detractors. Veteran Tom Seaver, for one, arrived at spring training in 1977 loudly complaining about the team's lack of a center fielder. His tirade was more a criticism of the front office's decision to eschew the inaugural free-agent class of 1976—Gary Matthews in particular—than a specific swipe at Mazzilli, but it set the tone for a dysfunctional and chaotic few months that resulted in the shocking trade of Seaver to Cincinnati and an environment that ensured that young players like Mazzilli, ready or not, would absorb the spotlight. Despite remarks in the press suggesting that Mazzilli would need more seasoning, Mets officials offered little resistance to his ascendancy. Pepe Mangual, foolishly acquired in a trade for veteran center fielder Del Unser in the summer of '76, flopped in his late-season audition and would spend most of 1977 in the minors. Fellow youngster Bruce Boisclair was viewed more as a reserve corner outfielder and, as Seaver reminded everyone, they failed to get a center fielder over the offseason. The 22-year-old Mazzilli played in 159 games in 1977.

He was fortunate to have a veteran mentor in teammate Joe Torre, who like Mazzilli was an Italian-American from Brooklyn and took the youngster under his wing. Weeks before the Seaver trade, Torre was named Mets manager, and the two New Yorkers would remain with the Mets for the next five years.

Mazzilli hit .250 in his rookie year and improved to .273 in 1978, mainly as a result of big strides in his performance as a right-handed hitter, boosting his batting average against left-handers from .228 in 1977 to .286 in '78; and his slugging percentage from a paltry .289 to a robust .446.

By 1979 Mazzilli was one of the National League's brightest young stars, hitting better than .300 from both sides of the plate (.302 righty, .306 lefty) with 15 home runs, 34 steals, and a .395 on-base percentage, fourth in the National League. The Mets in the meantime had deteriorated around him. They lost 98 games in 1977, 96 in 1978, and 99 in 1979, finishing comfortably in last place each year. With attendance plummeting to historic lows, Mazzilli became a focus of the Mets' marketing pitch. It was a role he was ideally suited for but uncomfortable fulfilling.

There was no doubt Mazzilli oozed fan appeal. Listed at 6-feet-1 and 180 pounds with the prominent thighs of a speedskater, Mazzilli could fill a uniform like few others—though it was often suggested he had it cut extra tight. Dark-haired, dark-eyed, and olive-skinned, he had a look that recalled stars in popular culture of the time including John Travolta—whose *Saturday Night Fever* captured the phenomenon of the disco era—and Sylvester Stallone, whose Rocky Balboa character shared the "Italian Stallion" nickname with Mazzilli. Young fans, particularly females, mobbed him wherever he went. He fielded offers from Hollywood, including a role on TV's *Laverne & Shirley* and a part in Martin Scorcese's film *Raging Bull,* but he'd put acting off until after his baseball career.

Pizzazz on the field played into Mazzilli's appeal as well. Fans cheered his basket catches and head-first slides. But even Mazzilli's habit of stretching his chest as he approached the plate before at-bats broke thousands of hearts. Keenly conscious of his image, and of his statistics, Mazzilli clearly liked earning the adulation of fans, including members of his extended family who became a constant presence at Shea Stadium. But he also tried to keep a low profile off the field. The first Mets player to be featured in a beefcake poster giveaway day often described himself as quiet, shy, and low-key, and preferred pinball arcades to discotheques.

Style notwithstanding, Mazzilli aspired to make an impression with substance. "I just want to be known as a guy who works hard and does things right," he said in a 1980 interview. "I want to be known as a ballplayer's ballplayer."[5]

Mazzilli put on a show in the 1979 All-Star Game in Seattle. Entering as a pinch-hitter for Gary Matthews with the National League trailing 6-5 in the eighth, Mazzilli tied the game with an opposite-field home run off Texas relief ace Jim Kern. In the ninth inning, Mazzilli worked a two-out, bases-loaded walk from Ron Guidry of the Yankees, driving in what would hold up as the winning run in a 7-6 National League win. For Mets fans Mazzilli's performance in what turned out to be the only All-Star Game appearance of his career ranked as one of the rare highlights of a black era in the team's history.

There was some irony in the fact that the Most Valuable Player Award in the game went not to Mazzilli but to Dave Parker, whose powerful arm in right field gunned down AL rivals at third base and home during the contest. It underscored the one major flaw in Mazzilli's game.

The joke with Mazzilli—one repeated by the Mets' former chairman M. Donald Grant in a 1979 *Sports*

Illustrated article—was that he could throw with either arm but neither one was strong enough for the major leagues. Although Mazzilli worked hard to overcome this weakness—he eschewed the basket catch with men on base, and took to charging fly balls to get in good throwing position—opponents were never afraid to take an extra base and test his arm. After Keith Hernandez tagged up to score the winning run on a shallow fly ball to Mazzilli in center field in a 1983 game, the slow-footed Cardinals player remarked that Mazzilli was "the only guy I would attempt to score against [on such a play] in the big leagues."[6]

Mazzilli paid a price for his swashbuckling play in the outfield when he was hospitalized after a frightening collision with teammate Dan Norman at Dodger Stadium in July 1979. Mazzilli, playing center field, and Norman, in right, were each racing toward a line drive hit by Davey Lopes. Mazzilli appeared to have caught the ball just as Norman arrived, knocking the ball—and Mazzilli—to the turf. Lopes, who would make an inside-the-park home run on the play, said Mazzilli looked as though "a tank hit him."

"I'd never seen such a violent collision," Lopes said. "Danny's a big kid and very strong. It was like a big train hitting a small train."[7]

Mazzilli was held overnight for observation and had a large bruise on his cheek, but was back in the Mets lineup after missing just three games. There was some speculation that a grand mal seizure suffered by Mazzilli long after his playing career might have been related to the incident.

Mazzilli's throwing woes, along with a trade of Willie Montanez to Texas, had the Mets begin experimenting with playing Mazzilli at first base late in the 1979 season—the one place where throwing left-handed would have been an advantage. The organization also knew the day was coming when it would have to make room for a young center fielder then at Triple-A Tidewater, Mookie Wilson. Mazzilli, who once said he was "born to play center field," framed his willingness to make the move as a sign of his respect for Torre.

"If Torre stays as manager, I'm willing to make the change," he said. "If he wants it and he's here, I'll go to [Instructional League in] Florida and work out there for as long as he wants me to."[8]

Appreciative of Mazzilli's work ethic and his ability as a drawing card, the Mets late in the 1979 season gave him a five-year, $2.1 million contract that made him the highest-paid player in team history. At a signing event, Mazzilli arrived with two boxes of long-stem roses, presenting one to his mother, June, and the other to Mets chairwoman Lorinda de Roulet. Both ladies were moved to tears.

Mazzilli opened the 1980 season as the Mets' regular first baseman—veteran acquisition Jerry Morales was in center—but with neither player hitting well by June, Morales was benched and Mazzilli went back to center field. It was only then that Mazzilli hit like a first baseman—including a sizzling stretch in early July when he hit home runs in four straight games. He finished the year at .280 with a .370 on-base percentage and a .431 slugging average, matching a career best with 16 home runs, and stealing a career-high 41 bases. Wilson arrived as expected in September and Mazzilli was moved back to first base.

He was neither place in 1981, moved to left field to accommodate Wilson while the reacquired Dave Kingman took over at first base. But Mazzilli had a rough year, battling elbow and back problems, and finished the strike-interrupted season batting .228, and seeing his mentor Torre fired by the Mets on the season's final day. Then, in an offseason move that ultimately sealed Mazzilli's fate, the Mets acquired superstar left fielder George Foster of Cincinnati. General manager Frank Cashen, acknowledging that the 27-year-old Mazzilli would not likely settle for a reserve role he was to be offered in New York, swapped him to the Texas Rangers during spring training of 1982.

The trade appeared to have wounded Mazzilli's pride, particularly when he learned he was dealt not for a front-line starting pitcher, as had been rumored through the winter, but for two minor leaguers he'd never heard of. But the deal turned out quite well for the Mets. One was Ron Darling, who became a stalwart of the Mets' starting rotation (and incidentally inherited Mazzilli's standing as the team's designated matinee idol); the other was Walt Terrell, who was later flipped in a trade for Howard Johnson, one of the Mets' all-time-best offensive players.

Mazzilli was back in New York before long. Battling wrist and shoulder woes in Texas, he was moved by the Rangers to the Yankees in a trade for Bucky Dent in August. He filled in for the Yankees in 37 games at left field, designated hitter, and first base, but was on the move again that winter, traded to Pittsburgh for four minor leaguers.

The Pirates saw Mazzilli as a successor to departed center fielder Omar Moreno, but his skills were decidedly underappreciated in Pittsburgh. Despite leading the National League in on-base percentage and walks, Mazzilli was benched in June of '83 when the Pirates traded for Mets Triple-A center fielder Marvell Wynne and installed Wynne immediately into the starting lineup. Pirates manager Chuck Tanner suggested that concern over Mazzilli's throwing arm prompted the move. Mazzilli spent most of the rest of the year on the bench.

In 1984 Mazzilli started 71 games for Pittsburgh, almost all in left field, but hit just .237. It turned out to be the 29-year-old Mazzilli's last sustained stretch as a starting player. Over the coming five years, he would become known for pinch-hitting, leading the National League with 72 pinch-hitting appearances and a .437 on-base percentage as a pinch-hitter in 1985. He was one of several Pirates who testified before a grand jury as part of the drug trials but was not among those disciplined by Commissioner Peter Ueberroth. He was released by the rebuilding Pirates in 1986 and was signed to a minor-league deal by the Mets, who'd become a powerhouse since trading him in 1982. Mazzilli spent a week at Triple-A Tidewater while the Mets made room for him on the roster—ironically, by releasing George Foster, whose arrival cost Mazzilli his job back in '82 but whose attitude and production soured with the Mets.

At last comfortable in a reserve role, Mazzilli proved a valuable fit with the streamrolling '86 Mets. In Game Six of the World Series, he singled off Boston's Calvin Schiraldi and later scored the tying run as the Mets rallied to tie the game in the eighth inning. In the decisive Game Seven, Mazzilli's one-out pinch single in the sixth inning sparked the Mets' rally from a 3-0 deficit. As the Mets celebrated their first world championship since 1969—and the only one in Mazzilli's playing career—few players could better appreciate how far they'd come.

Mazzilli remained with the Mets as a reserve outfielder and pinch-hitting specialist through 1989, providing leadership on a team with strong personalities. When moody Darryl Strawberry asked out of a game against first-place St. Louis in 1987 claiming illness despite having attended a recording session for a record he was making that morning, Mazzilli made a point to criticize the decision to writers, saying, "I feel he let his manager down, his coaches down, and he let his teammates down."[9] More blue-collar than macho, the stance earned Mazzilli the threat of a fistfight from Strawberry, but also earned the respect of teammates who might not have had the courage to speak up themselves. "His teammates thought a lot of him for that," said Dan Castellano, a reporter who covered that team.[10]

The Toronto Blue Jays were loading up for a pennant race when they acquired Mazzilli from the Mets on a waiver claim in 1989. Mazzilli was 4-for-7 as a pinch-hitter, including his sixth career pinch-hit home run, as the Jays prevailed to win the American League East, but he went 0-for-8 as the Jays lost the ALCS to Oakland in five games.

Mazzilli retired from baseball after the 1989 season. He and his wife, the television host Danielle Folquet, had a young daughter, Jenna, born in 1988; and twins, Lacey and L.J., were on their way. For a time his flirtation with show business got serious. He appeared as a guest star on the television series *Big Brother Jake*, did commentary for the *Game of the Week* on CBS Radio, and co-hosted *Sports Extra,* a weekly television sports talk show with Bill Mazer, airing on New York's Channel

5. In 1992 Mazzilli landed the starring role of Tony Nunzio in the Off-Broadway interactive comedy *Tony 'n' Tina's Wedding* opposite Sharon Angela. Mazzilli credited the actor Dan Lauria, whom he befriended while auditioning for roles during his playing days, with helping him make the transition.

Mazzilli pursued other avenues as well. He was a partner in a 10,000-square-foot sports bar, Lee Mazzilli's Sports Café, that opened on Manhattan's Upper West Side in 1994. But with a players strike looming, it turned out to be a bad time for a baseball-themed restaurant. He moved on to a position with a mortgage bank and in 1995 became commissioner of the independent Northeast League. In 1997, at the request of his friend Joe Torre, Mazzilli put on a uniform again, managing the Tampa Yankees (Class A) for two years and the Norwich Navigators of the Double-A Eastern League in 1999, helping to usher players including Nick Johnson, Alfonso Soriano, and Marcus Thames to the majors. In 2000 Mazzilli joined Torre's staff as the Yankees' first-base coach, helping guide them to a World Series victory over the Mets.

Along with Don Mattingly, Willie Randolph, and Joe Girardi, Mazzilli was one of several graduates of Torre's Yankees coaching staff to go onto a managing career. The Baltimore Orioles hired him in 2004 to replace Mike Hargrove. The Orioles went 78-84 and finished in third place in his first season, the Orioles' best finish since 1997. The 2005 team jumped out to a 42-28 start then faltered badly, falling all the way to 52-56 when Mazzilli was fired on August 4 and replaced by Sam Perlozzo.

Some writers covering the Orioles suggested that Mazzilli had an especially difficult job in Baltimore, answering to co-general managers (Mike Flanagan and Jim Beattie) and a demanding owner (Peter Angelos), and was forced to work with an existing coaching staff that included candidates he beat out for the managerial job in the first place. Steroid scandals following Orioles veteran stars Sammy Sosa and Rafael Palmeiro that summer were also a likely factor in the decision, some have suggested. These explanations have not come from Mazzilli, who in interviews maintains that the Orioles treated him fairly and recounts a positive experience in Baltimore.

Although another managerial job had not surfaced, Mazzilli remained in demand in New York, serving as Torre's bench coach with the 2006 Yankees and spending two years as a studio analyst for SNY, the Mets' television network. Most recently he was working in the Yankees' front office, and closely following the games of his son, L.J., a second baseman at the University of Connecticut who was drafted by the Minnesota Twins in 2012. L.J. bats and throws right-handed exclusively.

SOURCES

Author interviews with Bob Fenn, Dan Castellano, and Michael Scotti, June-July, 2012.

Arangure, Jorge Jr. "No Bad Feelings for Mazzilli," *Washington Post*, April 22, 2006.

Ellison, Jack. "Mazzilli Shows His Speed With Mets," *The Sporting News*, November 6, 1976.

Feeney, Charley. "Bucs Give Wynne Center Field Post," *The Sporting News*, June 27, 1983.

Groves, Seli. "Lee Mazzilli: Diamonds Guy's Best Friend Too," King Features Syndicate, *Spokane Spokesman-Review*, December 22, 1992.

Lang, Jack. "Mets Smacking Their Chops Over Frilly Mazzilli," *The Sporting News*, September 25, 1976.

——— "Mets All Steamed Up Over Hot Mitt Prospect Stearns," *The Sporting News*, October 9, 1976.

——— "Dissension? It's Name of the Game on Sinking Mets," *The Sporting News*, June 11, 1977.

——— "Mazzilli's Pact Raises Met Question," *The Sporting News*, September 8, 1979.

——— "Torre Circles Wagons and Mets Dig In," *The Sporting News*, June 21, 1980.

Noble, Marty. "Trade to Texas Angers Mazzilli," *Newsday*, April 2, 1982.

——— "Injury to Byrd Forces Cameron to Reflect," MLB.com, May 23, 2011.

Reeves, Jim. " 'Hope I Can Help,' Dent Tells Rangers," *The Sporting News*, August 23, 1982.

Rudel, Neil. "Marvell Wynne in, Mazzilli Out," *Beaver County* (Pennsylvania) *Times*, June 15, 1983.

Reimer, Susan. "The Home Team," *Baltimore Sun*, May 16, 2004.

Shalin, Mike. "Mets Ready to Deal Maz or Youngblood," *New York Post*, February 5, 1982.

Sheinin, Dave. "Slumping Orioles Fire Mazzilli as Manager," *Washington Post,* August 5, 2005.

Smizik, Bob. "Pirates Buried by Unknown Slugger, 5-4," *Pittsburgh Press,* September 21, 1976.

Swift, E.M. "Hometown Kid Makes Good," *Sports Illustrated,* July 23, 1979.

Zeigel, Vic. "Urban Centerfielder," *New York,* August 18, 1980.

"A grand theft effort by Visalia's Mazzilli," *The Sporting News,* July 5, 1975.

"Inside Pitch,"Sports Illustrated, April 25, 1983.

Baseball-Reference.com.

Ultimatemets.com.

NOTES

1 Author interview with Bob Fenn, July 12, 2012.

2 John Eisenberg, "Mazzilli Does It All—And Does it Well," *Baltimore Sun,* November 16, 2003.

3 Hal Bock, "Mets Draft Outfielder," Associated Press, *Newburgh* (New York) *Evening News,* June 6, 1973.

4 Marty Noble, "For Mazzilli, Nothing Like Meeting Mays," MLB.com, September 8, 2008.

5 Pat Calabria, "Just the Kid Next Door," *The Sporting News,* August 16, 1980.

6 "Inside Pitch," *Sports Illustrated,* April 25, 1983.

7 John Nadel (Associated Press), "Lee Mazzilli Kayoed in Collision," *Newburgh (*New York) *Evening News,* July 24, 1979.

8 Jack Lang, "Hebner's Silence Handicaps Mets," *The Sporting News,* September 1, 1979.

9 Associated Press, "Mazzilli Berates Strawberry," *Albany* (Georgia) *Herald,* July 2, 1987.

10 Author interview with Dan Castellano, July 5, 2012.

ROGER MCDOWELL

By Jon Springer

ROGER MCDOWELL KEPT HIS LOCKER stocked with comedy props, costumes, and fireworks, blew bubbles while he pitched, played the notorious "Second Spitter" on *Seinfeld* and was known to set teammates' shoes on fire. But he knew a little about pitching too.

McDowell racked up 70 wins and 159 saves pitching almost exclusively in relief over a 12-year big-league career, highlighted by a win in the decisive Game Seven of the 1986 World Series. After his playing career he rapidly ascended as a pitching coach, and as of 2015 had held that role with the Atlanta Braves for 10 years and counting.

Roger Alan McDowell was born on December 21, 1960, in Cincinnati, the youngest of Herb and Ada McDowell's three children. He graduated from Cincinnati's Colerain High School in 1979 and attended Bowling Green State University on a baseball scholarship, arriving on campus shortly after Orel Hershiser, a 17th-round pick of the Dodgers in the 1979 June draft, departed. Both pitchers were recruited to Bowling Green by coach Don Purvis, a one-time pitcher in the Yankees' system.

McDowell, who studied commercial art in college, selected Bowling Green over a rival offer from Virginia Military Institute. He led the Falcons with a 5-4 record during his junior year, earning All-Mid-American Conference honors, and was selected by the Mets in the third round of the 1982 draft.

A slender right-hander listed at 6-foot-1 and 175 pounds, McDowell made his living on essentially one pitch—a sinking fastball that he could throw at various speeds, almost always for strikes. He said in 1985 that he'd developed the pitch in high school. "I just throw it down the middle knee-high, and it drops late," he told the *New York Times*.[1] McDowell also threw a hard slider and an occasional changeup, but his sinker, augmented by his good control, was his featured delivery. "He never shakes me off," Gary Carter, his catcher with the Mets, remarked. "There's nothing to shake off, actually. He just throws the one pitch."[2]

McDowell made his professional debut at age 21 for the Shelby (North Carolina) Mets of the South Atlantic League in 1982, going 6-4 in 12 games (11 starts) before getting a promotion to Lynchburg (Virginia) of the Carolina League, where he was 2-0 with a 2.15 ERA in four starts. In 100⅔ innings for both teams, he allowed just one home run.

A year later, in 1983, McDowell's career was nearly over. An 11-12, 4.86 season for Jackson of the Double-A Texas League was cut short when he began to suffer elbow pain. When months of rest failed to cure him, McDowell underwent surgery in February of 1984.

Mets doctor James C. Parkes removed bone chips and spurs.

Recovery limited McDowell to just 7⅓ innings for Jackson in 1984 plus another 14 in the playoffs, but during a postseason stint in the Instructional League, McDowell rediscovered his signature sinker and a little something extra. Augmented by a slight adjustment in arm angle, giving him a three-quarters delivery, McDowell found that his sinker broke even more sharply than the one he threw before the injury.[3]

McDowell's work in the Instructional League caught the eye of Mets manager Davey Johnson, who invited him to spring training in 1985 and surprised many by selecting him to go north with the team when camp broke. McDowell, who had a 2.28 ERA that spring, got the nod over incumbent sinkerballer Doug Sisk, who had struggled with injuries and control problems and began the year in Triple-A Tidewater.

McDowell made his major-league debut on April 11, 1985, pitching a hitless, scoreless top of the 11th inning against the St. Louis Cardinals at Shea Stadium, preserving a 1-1 tie. The Mets scored in the bottom of the inning, and he got the win. McDowell made two ineffective spot starts in late April and early May—they would be the only two starts among his 723 big-league appearances—but by midseason he'd established himself as a late-inning weapon in New York's bullpen, and his sinker was the talk of the league.

"He's got a wicked sinkerball. I know it, and so do other hitters," Keith Hernandez said. "They come down to first and talk to me about the kid's nasty sinker. He is awesome."[4]

Ken Landreaux of the Los Angeles Dodgers described facing McDowell's sinker: "The ball is right here," Landreaux insisted, holding his hand chest-high. "You see it so clearly you think you'll get it on the fat of the bat. Then, all of a sudden, poof! It's gone. Goodbye."[5]

McDowell went 6-5 with 17 saves and a 2.83 ERA in 1985, and finished sixth in the Rookie of the Year voting.

Though a 1985 *New York Times* article described him as "a mild-mannered, laid-back, inoffensive and polite young man,"[6] as McDowell's success continued, his confidence grew and a colorful personality emerged. McDowell wore a spiky haircut, often covered by a cap worn backward, and was generally spotted working a thick wad of pink bubble gum, which he took up chewing as an alternative to tobacco. There was a hint of innocent mischief in his countenance.

In 1986 McDowell's reputation as a fun-loving prankster became legendary. On a team with no shortage of style and swagger, McDowell stood out as the class clown. His specialty was in giving unsuspecting teammates a "hotfoot"—McDowell would use bubblegum to wrap a book of matches around a cigarette, secure it to the heel of his victim's baseball shoes with tape, then light the cigarette. When the cigarette ash reached the matches, the pack would ignite, sending flames up the pant leg of the victim.

McDowell performed the stunt dozens of times in his career and despite the elaborate nature of the trick—securing and igniting the device often meant crawling beneath a dugout bench undetected—he was never caught in the act. His favorite victim was Bill Robinson, the team's hitting coach.

McDowell was also known for boyish stunts providing unexpected laughs or commentary on the game:

When the Mets honored retired star Rusty Staub in 1986 in a pregame ceremony, a contingent of teammates led by McDowell emerged from the dugout to present Staub a plaque—each wearing a garish red wig that McDowell had supplied.

Before a game in Los Angeles in 1987, McDowell appeared on the field wearing his uniform upside-down, pants stretched over his head and shoes on his hand.

Also in 1987, he made light of an administrative crackdown on ball doctoring by conspicuously wearing a carpenter's belt in the bullpen, complete with lubricant, sandpaper, a file, and a chisel.[7]

If there was a slumping hitter in the lineup, McDowell could be counted on to toss a lit pack of firecrackers into that player's slot in the bat rack.

He once got the attention of fans seated around the visiting bullpen at Dodger Stadium, then threw open a door to reveal teammate Jesse Orosco seated on the toilet.[8]

McDowell took pride in his assertion that he could eat more than any of his teammates. When presented with 3,500 pieces of bubble gum in April of 1988 as a thank-you for a charity donation, he quipped, "This should last me till June."[9]

When Tommy Greene threw a no-hitter against the Expos in 1991, McDowell fooled his Phillies teammate with a fake congratulatory phone call from Brian Mulroney, the prime minister of Canada. "It was a tossup who was fooled more that day, the Expos batter or Greene, who carried on a lengthy conversation with the phony Mulrooney," writer Paul Hagen observed.[10]

Despite the reputation for goofiness on the sidelines, McDowell was "all business on the mound," in the words of teammate Gary Carter.[11] In 1986 he was 14-9 with 22 saves. His victory total that year still stood in 2015 as a record for a Mets reliever, and his 75 appearances that year set a since-broken club record. His 22 saves were one more than left-hander Jesse Orosco for the club lead in '86.

Though they split saves and save opportunities nearly down the middle, McDowell and Orosco tended to be employed differently by Johnson in 1986. While the manager used Orosco primarily as a short reliever (58 appearances), he called on McDowell for all kinds of assignments, citing his ability to throw strikes and his durability. McDowell averaged more than five outs per appearance in 1986. "I'm aware of how much I use him but you can abuse a sinkerball pitcher like Roger," Johnson said. "The more he's used, the more his ball sinks."[12]

The '86 Mets were a swaggering, powerhouse club with a tremendous will to win. McDowell embodied that spirit in a 14-inning affair on July 22 in Cincinnati, a game in which both clubs emptied their benches, in part due to ejections after a 10th-inning brawl between the Mets' Ray Knight and the Reds' Eric Davis. The shortage of players forced Johnson to swap Orosco and McDowell between outfield positions and the pitcher's mound for four innings, with McDowell eventually recording the win.

In the postseason the Mets' dual closers teamed for another white-knuckle win, eliminating the Houston Astros in Game Six of the National League Championship Series. In that game, a 4 hour 42 minute, 16-inning affair at the Astrodome, McDowell contributed five innings of scoreless relief after the Mets tied the game 3-3 with a two-run ninth-inning rally before turning the game over to Orosco, who blew a 4-3 lead in the 14th but held on despite a two-run Houston rally in the 16th to preserve a 7-6 win.

McDowell appeared in five of the seven games of the Mets' triumphant 1986 World Series, including Game Seven, when he was the beneficiary of the Mets' tiebreaking three-run rally in the seventh inning, earning the victory despite giving two of those runs back in the eighth.

The heavy workload of 1986 may have come at a price; McDowell missed the first six weeks of the 1987 season after surgery for a hernia. He returned in time to again lead the Mets with 25 saves that year, although his ERA climbed more than a full run, to 4.16 from 3.02 in 1986, accompanied by an increase in home runs per inning and a decrease in strikeouts per inning. Facing a barrage of injuries that year, the Mets failed to defend their Eastern Division title, finishing three games behind the St. Louis Cardinals.

The Mets regained that crown in 1988 with a 100-win season helped in part by a return to form by McDowell, who went 5-5 with 16 saves despite surrendering the role of primary closer to young fireballer Randy Myers. In 89 regular-season innings, McDowell allowed just one home run, but in the NLCS, a resounding blast to right-center by the Dodgers' Kirk Gibson off him in the 12th inning of Game Four was a key moment in the Dodgers' seven-game series win. McDowell hardly ever gave up home runs. (As a witness, the author was shocked. "Stunning" if you prefer?)

The 1989 Mets got off to a poor start, losing seven of their first 10 games. Struggling to stay above .500 on June 18, they traded McDowell, outfielder Lenny Dykstra and a player to be named (reliever Tom Edens) to Philadelphia for infielder-outfielder Juan Samuel. The trade was announced shortly after the two teams completed a game that afternoon.

The deal turned out poorly for the Mets — they traded the disappointing Samuel after the season — while in Dykstra, Philadelphia acquired a key figure in their 1993 pennant-winning squad. (Philadelphia the same day acquired pitcher Terry Mulholland, a key starting pitcher for the 1993 squad, in a separate trade with the Giants.) McDowell had a brief renaissance with the Phillies, allowing just one unearned run in his first 20 appearances and finishing with a 1.11 ERA and 19 saves. One of those saves came against the Mets at Shea Stadium on September 27 and ended with a brawl between McDowell and Mets infielder Gregg Jefferies. The fight appeared to have been sparked by words exchanged between McDowell and Jefferies as Jefferies ran out a game-ending grounder to second base. "Gregg's been through some tough times this season. There's been a lot of pressure on him and maybe it all got to him," McDowell remarked afterward. "I never disliked him, but I don't think we'll be exchanging Christmas cards this year."[13]

McDowell signed a three-year contract with the Phillies after the season and in 1990 he led the National League with 60 games finished while recording a team-leading 22 saves.

McDowell lost the closer role to newly acquired Mitch Williams in 1991 and was traded to the contending Dodgers for outfielder Braulio Castillo and reliever Mike Harkey on July 31. McDowell he had a 2.55 ERA in 33 appearances down the stretch but the Dodgers finished one game short of Atlanta for NL West crown.

McDowell stayed with the Dodgers through 1994, enduring lean years for the team, including a last-place finish in 1992 when he led the club with 14 saves and posted a 4.09 ERA, his highest mark since 1987's 4.16.

In 1995 the 34-year-old McDowell signed with Texas for $500,000. "Let's face it — it's not like they signed Christy Mathewson," he remarked — and went 7-4, 4.02 in 64 appearances in middle relief.

McDowell signed with the Orioles in 1996. He was reunited with former manager Davey Johnson, who used him as set-up man for his former teammate Randy Myers as closer. As he had done a decade earlier, Johnson relied heavily on McDowell — he was among the league leaders in appearances before soreness in his 35-year-old shoulder sidelined him in July. He returned briefly in August before again going to the disabled list, ending his season and proving to be his last appearances in the majors.

McDowell signed with the White Sox in 1997 but two shoulder surgeries prevented him from making any appearances that year. He attended spring training again with Chicago in 1998 but announced his retirement after pitching a single inning in spring training. He accepted an offer to tutor some young prospects for the organization.

He retired with a career record of 70-70, with 159 saves and an earned-run average of 3.30. His groundball to fly ball ratio of 1.69 was about twice the league average during his career. (Baseball-reference does not include data on that stat prior to 1988.)

McDowell, who parlayed his prankster reputation into appearances on MTV's "Rock n' Jock" softball games in the early 1990s, gained still more notoriety for an appearance on an episode of the TV comedy *Seinfeld.* Airing for the first time in February of 1992, "The Boyfriend" also starred McDowell's one-time teammate Keith Hernandez in a send-up of conspiracies around the Kennedy assassination. (McDowell told an Atlanta radio station that he continued to get a royalty check for $13.52 each time the episode aired.)

McDowell resumed his career as a pitching coach in 2002 and 2003 with the South Georgia Waves, a Class-A South Atlantic League affiliate of the

Dodgers, who promoted him to oversee pitchers at Triple-A Las Vegas in 2004 and 2005.

Calling McDowell "one of the true up-and-coming teachers of the game," Atlanta Braves manager Bobby Cox chose McDowell to succeed longtime pitching coach Leo Mazzone in Atlanta beginning in 2006.[14]

The Braves ranked fifth or better in the majors in ERA for six straight seasons (2009-2014) under McDowell, whose pupils included Craig Kimbrel, Jair Jurrjens, Javier Vasquez, Jonny Venters, Julio Teheran, Kris Medlen, and Brandon Beachy. McDowell kept a low profile, particularly after getting a two-week suspension in 2011 for what league officials called "inappropriate comments and gestures" while responding to hecklers in San Francisco.

As of 2015 McDowell lived in Marietta, Georgia, near Atlanta, with his wife, Gloria, and their two daughters. He has a son, Logan, from a prior marriage.

SOURCES

In addition to the works cited in the Notes, the author consulted the following sources:

Ultimatemets.com.

Baseball-reference.com.

scouts.baseballhall.org.

mgrittani.wordpress.com.

New York Mets 2015 Media Guide, mlb.com.

Atlanta Braves 2015 Media Guide, mlb.com.

Youtube.com.

NOTES

1 Joseph Durso, "McDowell's Success a Tribute to Faith," *New York Times*, June 2, 1985.

2 Ibid.

3 Jeff Pearlman, *The Bad Guys Won!* (New York: HarperCollins, 2004).

4 Jack Lang, "McDowell Is Mets' Latest Rookie Find," *The Sporting News*, June 10, 1985.

5 Mike Geffner (Associated Press), "Roger McDowell Has Filled a Void on Mets' Roster," *Newburgh* (New York) Evening *Journal*, June 30, 1985.

6 Durso.

7 Joe Gergen, "Airport Metal Detectors in On-Deck Circles?" *The Sporting News,* August 24, 1987.

8 John Eisenberg, "McDowell, Myers to Give Dull O's Fire Next Year," *Baltimore Sun*, December 20, 1995.

9 Stan Isle, "Mr. Efficiency Uses a First-Pitch Plan," *The Sporting News*, May 9, 1988.

10 Paul Hagen, "The Best and Worst of Phillies (So Far)," *Baltimore Sun*, July 12, 1991.

11 Gary Carter and John Hough Jr., *A Dream Season* (New York: Harcourt Brace Jovanovich, 1987).

12 Jack Lang, "Mets Closer With Closer," *The Sporting News*, September 8, 1986.

13 "NL East Beat," *The Sporting News*, October 9, 1989.

14 "Braves Name McDowell Pitching Coach," Yahoo Sports, October 29, 2005.

JOHN MITCHELL

By Skip Nipper

JOHN KYLE MITCHELL'S BIG-LEAGUE PITCHING debut took place exactly where he had hoped it would, in Fenway Park. It was an exhibition game played there between the Boston Red Sox and New York Mets on September 4, 1986, to support Boston's Jimmy Fund and New York amateur baseball.[1]

But he was not with the Red Sox. Mitchell was originally drafted by Boston in the seventh round of the 1983 amateur draft out of Nashville's John Overton High School. The club had signed his brother Charlie the year before, a pitcher for Columbia State Junior College, also by scout George Digby. Roger Clemens was also a member of the 1983 Boston draft class and Mitchell and Clemens were two of only six Boston draftees that year who made it to the majors.

Sent to Elmira in the short-season New York-Pennsylvania League, Mitchell finished with a 5-6 record and 4.90 ERA. It was there where Mitchell's faith journey had its beginning when he began to attend baseball chapel while at Elmira.

"I wasn't as mature in those early days, so my influence on others would not have been very strong other than my personality and the way I conducted myself," Mitchell said.[2]

Dave Magadan agreed, saying, "When John faced tragedy, his faith certainly had an effect on him after the accident, and he lived his life accordingly throughout his career and beyond."[3]

The tragedy Magadan referred to took place in 1983 after Mitchell's season at Elmira. In a deep-sea fishing accident off the coast of Florida on October 30, 1983, a boat carrying Mitchell and two fellow Red Sox farmhands, Scott Skripko and Anthony Latham, capsized. The owner of the boat, Mark Zastrowmy, and Latham drowned. Clinging to a cooler for 20 hours, Skripko was able to survive and Mitchell held on to a bucket for 22 hours.[4]

"Some day," Mitchell told the *Boston Globe* days after the accident, "this is going to be very, very difficult to live with. But right now, we're just glad to be alive."[5]

He reeled off two good seasons: a 16-9 record at Winter Haven (Class-A Florida State League) in 1984 and a 12-8 record at New Britain (Double-A Eastern League) in 1985.

On November 15, 1985, Mitchell was part of a deal that also sent Bob Ojeda, Tom McCarthy, and Chris Bayer to the Mets for Calvin Schiraldi, John Christensen, Wes Gardner, and LaSchelle Tarver. Mitchell was not ready for the trade. "I didn't expect the trade at all," he said. "I was upset; it was like going from one

John Mitchell sporting the cap of the Baltimore Orioles after his trade.

high school to another and you wouldn't be playing with players you'd played with for two years. Standing on the mound at Fenway Park was something I had dreamed of, only in a Boston uniform."

Spring training with New York took place then in St. Petersburg, Florida, where the club shared the grounds with the St. Louis Cardinals. Mitchell's roommate was Barry Lyons. "John was quiet, smart, and had a dry humor," said Lyons. "We roomed together in spring training and John didn't say much. He was not a partyer, but a gentleman in every sense of the word. As a pitcher, he had a good overhand curveball, a two-seam fastball, and showed really good control. I mean he was almost always in control of his pitches."[6]

Mitchell said he just threw a heavy fastball or sinker, and did not try to turn it over. "At times I could throw a changeup," he told the author. "Mr. Digby always wanted me to throw a changeup but I never really did learn to throw it."

Mitchell was assigned to Triple-A Tidewater by the Mets. One of his Tides teammates was first baseman Dave Magadan. "We were roommates and became fast friends," said Magadan. "John was an awesome roommate. Number one, he had manners. We passed the time telling stories and kept it light. John had a great outlook on life."[7]

With a 12-9 record and 3.39 ERA, Mitchell earned a call-up to New York in September 1986. Mitchell related his first pitching experience for the Mets in the game at Boston:

I had not pitched in a big-league game yet, and we go to Fenway, and it's like a playoff, I mean it is packed, there are Mets fans, it's crazy. They told me before the game that (Rick) Aguilera was going to start and I was going to follow him and (Randy) Myers was going to follow me. That game was nerve-racking for me. I was warming up. ... I had so much adrenaline flowing I think the first pitch I threw went about 50 feet. We had a bullpen catcher who didn't have on gear, it hit him right on the knee and bounced away and the fans gave him heck for my wild pitch.

When he began taking his warm-up tosses, the 6-foot-2, 165-pound Mitchell was given a Southern welcome to the game from another Tennessean. "I was really nervous when I was warming up, but once I got in, I still had plenty of adrenaline. Dale Ford was umpiring, and he knew I was from Tennessee."

"You a hillbilly?" Ford asked.

"Yeah, I guess," said Mitchell.

"I tell you what," said the umpire. "Just keep it close and we'll get outa here."

One of the batters Mitchell remembered facing was Dave Sax. "He fouled off a couple and I threw him one about six inches off the ground and Ford rung him up. Sax just shook his head," Mitchell said. The Mets won the game, 7-3.

Mitchell lived in Queens during his tenure in New York, staying with an auto mechanic whose brother had been a teammate in Winter Haven. He remembered how inexpensive his rent was: "I received four tickets to each game, and I traded game tickets in lieu of paying rent."

As the regular-season schedule resumed, Mitchell pitched in four games for the Mets. The first was three days after his Boston debut, on September 8, a night game against the Montreal Expos at Shea Stadium. New York had won four straight and stood at 92-44. Relieving for Rick Anderson in the ninth, Mitchell got his first strikeout when he set down Dann Bilardello with two outs. The Mets lost 9-1.

Six days later, an afternoon game at Veterans Stadium against the Phillies was Mitchell's second appearance, again in relief of Anderson. The first hit he gave up as a major leaguer was a single by Gary Redus, but with two out Mitchell struck out future Hall of Famer Mike Schmidt to end the seventh inning. The Mets lost to Philadelphia 6-0.

Having clinched the National League East championship the previous day, on September 18 the Mets hosted the Chicago Cubs at Shea Stadium. In the sixth inning, with the Mets holding a 4-0 lead, Mitchell relieved Rick Anderson for the third time.

Holding the Cubs scoreless, Mitchell made his first batting appearance in the bottom of the inning. With two out and two on, he grounded out to second to end the inning. In the seventh and eighth innings Mitchell allowed two hits and no runs before giving way to a pinch-hitter in the eighth. New York won, 5-0.

On September 21 at Shea Stadium, Mitchell was called on for his first starting assignment. "I wasn't supposed to start the game. I found out when I got to the park that morning that I was starting," he recalled.

Facing the Phillies in front of a home crowd of 42,631, Mitchell held Philadelphia without a run for three innings before they scored four runs in the fourth on two singles, two doubles, and a home run by Gary Redus, giving the Phillies a 4-1 lead. He was relieved in the sixth as the Mets lost, 7-1.

The season ended on October 5, and neither Mitchell nor Magadan was named to the postseason roster. Magadan related the disappointment they both felt in not receiving a decent share of playoff money after the season was over.

"After we clinched on September 17, and we knew about playoff shares, we'd sit there and think about our share. One-sixth could end up being 20 to 30 grand. We were thinking that's how they did the shares. We just knew we could use that for down payment on a house, or buy a car. When an envelope arrives at the end of the season with a check of about $360.00, I couldn't believe it. Guess who called me first thing? John Mitchell. He told me he was going down to the 7-Eleven to spend his share."[8]

Mitchell remembered that moment well. "I cashed my check and bought an Icee, a snowball, a sleeve of Hostess cakes, and a *Sports Illustrated.* We were at the bottom of the list. The batboys got more than we did."

His assessment of Mets manager Davey Johnson included a word of encouragement Johnson passed along before the club broke spring training in Florida. "The first time he saw me throw in St. Petersburg, I was pitching against a squad of St. Louis Cardinals players. Johnson told me a year of Triple-A ball and with the pitches I have I could win 15 games in the big leagues. You talk about pumping somebody up. That was really the only time he spoke to me much."

"I thought Davey Johnson was a good game manager, but he only talked to Gary Carter and Keith Hernandez. He had a tough group of guys to manage, though," Mitchell said.

Carter and Hernandez stood out in his mind, too. "I liked Gary Carter, he was a regular guy, and very welcoming to younger players. He was often outspoken and sometimes rubbed people the wrong way, but he didn't "big-league" you. Keith Hernandez was like Carter, just not as big a personality. Keith had a great baseball mind."

Mitchell began the 1987 season at Tidewater staff again, but the Mets recalled him in May after putting Bob Ojeda on the disabled list. General Manager Frank Cashen made the decision, and Davey Johnson disagreed with it, saying he would have rather seen Roger McDowell activated off the disabled list.[9]

On May 14 against Houston, Mitchell pitched for six innings and allowed four earned runs with no decision in a 5-4 loss to the Astros at the Astrodome. Three starts later in San Diego, he was charged with the loss as the Padres won 1-0. Mitchell made two errors in the game but neither led to the run.

While lamenting the loss of not only Ojeda but also Doc Gooden, who was battling cocaine use, manager Johnson seemed hopeful in his assessment of Mitchell's potential.

"We will have to live with what we've got," he said. "We lose Dwight Gooden, and it's a great loss. But it's also an opportunity for David Cone to become a big-league pitcher. We lose Bob Ojeda and it's a great loss. But it's an opportunity for John Mitchell to become a big-league pitcher."[10] On June 19 Mitchell earned his first major-league win, 8-1 against Philadelphia, pitching a five-hitter.

By season's end the Mets were in second place in the NL East, three games behind St. Louis. Mitchell pitched in 20 games and was 3-6 with a 4.11 ERA with New York; his record at Tidewater was 3-2 with a 3.33 ERA in eight games.

Assigned to Tidewater for 1988, Mitchell stayed with the club most of the season. He regained the form he had shown in his first few years in the minors, tossing a seven-inning perfect game against Indianapolis on June 27 and completing the season 10-9 with a 2.84 ERA in 27 games. He was recalled by the Mets in September and pitched one inning on the 9th against the Montreal Expos.

Mitchell pitched in two games for the Mets in 1989 but was a mainstay in the pitching rotation with Tidewater once again with an 11-11 record and 3.03 ERA. After the season he was traded to the Baltimore Orioles along with minor-league outfielder Joaquin Contreras for outfielder Keith Hughes and minor-league pitcher Cesar Mejia.

After a 6-6 record in 24 games with Baltimore in 1990 and a 5-0 record at Triple-A Rochester, Mitchell never returned to the major leagues. In five major-league seasons he was 9-14 with a 4.35 ERA.

From 1993 to 1998 Mitchell pitched in Triple A, Double A, and independent leagues.

Mitchell was born in Dickson, Tennessee, on August 11, 1965, one of four children of Bob and Reba Mitchell. One of his two brothers, Charlie, pitched in 1984 and '85 for the Red Sox and had a 10-year minor-league career. "Nat Satterfield [a family friend] and my dad built ball fields in the Tusculum area of Nashville where we learned how to play," Mitchell said. "Nat was the baseball guy. Dad never played, but he loved baseball and they coached together."

When Mitchell was 14, his Nashville Nationals Babe Ruth team was the runner-up in the Southeast Region playoffs. The next year the team placed third in the Babe Ruth League World Series in Mobile, Alabama. His coach during those years was Billy Griggs, who remembered young Mitchell's big, long fingers. "He could throw a curveball like no other I had ever seen. John was a heck of a pitcher," Griggs said.[11]

Bill Tucker was Mitchell's baseball coach at John Overton High School. (Besides John and Charlie, the school has produced major-league players Sam Ewing, Mookie Betts, and others.)

A resident of Murfreesboro, Tennessee, Mitchell as of 2015 worked works for a municipal casting business in Nashville. He and his wife, Leeanne, met in junior high school. Their four boys are Hank, Bobby, adopted son Hyunwoo, and Johnny Latham Mitchell, who is named in memory of his father's deceased friend.

Mitchell was inducted into the Metro Nashville Public Schools Sports Hall of Fame in 2008.

SOURCES

Besides the sources cited in the Notes, the author consulted Baseball-Reference.com, Retrosheet.org, and the *Tennessean* (Nashville).

NOTES

1 Joseph Durso, "Mets Beat Red Sox, 7-3, Just for the Fun of It All," *New York Times,* September 5, 1986.

2 Author interviews with John Mitchell on June 22, October 15, and November 22, 2015. All otherwise unattributed quotations from Mitchell come from these interviews.

3 Dave Magadan, telephone interview with author, October 22, 2015.

4 Dan Whittle, "Mitchell survived sea tragedy before pitching for Mets, Orioles," *Murfreesboro Post,* February 1, 2015.

5 Ibid.

6 Barry Lyons, telephone interview with author, October 27, 2015.

7 Magadan.

8 Magadan.

9 Craig Wolff, "Mets Continue Nose Dive with 12-2 Loss to Reds," *New York Times,* May 11, 1987.

10 Joseph Durso, "Mets Mission: Try to Survive," *New York Times,* May 22, 1987.

11 Billy Griggs, telephone interview with author, January 3, 2016.

KEVIN MITCHELL

By Joseph Wancho

GAME SIX OF THE 1986 WORLD SERIES between the Boston Red Sox and the New York Mets will forever be a part of baseball lore. Many fans will say that no matter how many games you may attend there is always something bound to happen that you may have never seen before. This was certainly true on October 25, 1986, at Shea Stadium.

Boston led the series, three games to two, as Game Six was played to a 3-3 tie through nine innings. Boston's Roger Clemens struck out eight and gave up two runs, one earned, through seven innings. Although "The Rocket" was not in line for the win, things looked mighty bright for the Red Sox as Dave Henderson hit a leadoff homer in the top of the 10th inning to give Boston a 4-3 advantage. A second run scored on a double by Wade Boggs and a single by Marty Barrett. It had been 68 years since Boston celebrated a world championship in baseball. And with the Mets down to their final out in the bottom of the inning, the waiting might finally be over.

But Gary Carter singled, and rookie Kevin Mitchell stepped to the plate. "I was just telling myself that I can't make the last out of the World Series," said Mitchell.[1] And he didn't; he singled to center field, sending Carter to second base. "My grandparents at home must have been doing a lot of praying," Mitchell said later.[2] Red Sox pitcher Calvin Schiraldi, who had relieved Clemens in the eighth inning, wished he could have the pitch back that he threw to Mitchell. "That one was a mistake," said Schiraldi. "I hung a slider."[3]

Ray Knight followed with a single to center field, Carter scored, and Mitchell checked in at third base. Bob Stanley relieved Schiraldi for Boston. "Buddy"—third-base coach Bud Harrelson—"was telling me he was gonna throw a wild pitch—and he did," Mitchell said. Boston catcher Rich Gedman "blocked it where I couldn't see the ball. Nobody told me nothing—or I couldn't hear it because of the crowd. I just saw the ball squeeze past him. I didn't think I was gonna make it at first. I was getting ready to go into a head-first slide three or four steps from the plate, when I saw the ball slow down."[4]

Mitchell's run tied the game, 5-5. Knight went to second base on the wild pitch, setting the stage for Mookie Wilson's dramatic groundball that got past Boston first baseman Bill Buckner. Knight scored the winning run to force a Game Seven, which the Mets won.

"The key to the game was Mitch's baserunning," said Keith Hernandez. "He went to third base on that soft hit and scored on the passed ball. Mitch set up the inning."[5] Mitchell reached back in his memory bank to get the hit off Schiraldi. "I looked at him and we smiled," said Mitchell. "When we were teammates in '83 (Jackson, Texas League), he told me if he ever

pitched to me, he'd try to bust me in, then throw a slider away. And that's what he did."[6]

Kevin Darnell Mitchell, the co-hero of Game Six, was born to Mr. and Mrs. Earl Mitchell on January 13, 1962, in San Diego, California. When he was 2, his parents separated and he was raised by his grandmother, Josie Whitfield. He grew up in a rough neighborhood in San Diego, often running with the wrong crowd, and he was involved with gangs. Kevin attended Clairemont High School, and although he favored football and boxing, Grandma Josie steered him to baseball. She took him to Little League games, and even when he established himself as a major leaguer, she offered him batting tips. "My grandmother convinced me to go with the safest sport, just to get away from San Diego," Mitchell once told a sportswriter.[7]

A friend took Mitchell to a New York Mets-sponsored baseball tryout in San Diego in 1980. He hit two home runs off Bud Black, then a left-hander pitching in the Kansas City farm system. Mitchell's hitting ability impressed the scouts, and the Mets signed him to a $600-a-month contract as an undrafted free agent.

Mitchell ascended through the Mets' minor-league chain, starting with Kingsport of the Appalachian (Rookie) League in 1981 and Lynchburg of the Class-A Carolina League. He hit well, .335 and .318 respectively, while playing mostly at third base but also in the outfield. Mitchell was promoted to Jackson of the Double-A Texas League in 1983. On the field he performed well (.299, 15 home runs, 85 RBIs). Off the field, Mitchell had his troubles. He got into a fight in a Shreveport restaurant. He complained of being singled out because he was black. "Once we were playing the Cardinals farm team in Arkansas, and people in the stands were throwing watermelon at me from the stands," Mitchell said. "They'd talk on how the Klan would be coming to get me that night in my hotel room. I have to admit it got to me. It upset my game. I had never been in a situation like that before. I was never scared because I was always ready to fight."[8]

Fighting was a part of Mitchell's surroundings in San Diego. It was synonymous with gangs and the violence of the neighborhood. The reality hit hard for him in 1984. While he was across the country playing for Triple-A Tidewater, his stepbrother Donald was shot to death in a section of San Diego known as Little Africa. Mitchell's instinct was to leave the club and return home, but teammates Herm Willingham and Clint Hurdle talked him out of it. The distractions may have caused his falloff in offensive numbers, but still he was called up to the Mets at roster-expansion time and made his major-league debut on September 4, 1984, as a pinch-hitter in a home game against St. Louis. He batted against Bob Forsch and flied out.

Mitchell returned to Tidewater for the 1985 campaign. Although his hitting improved from the previous season, he did not get a call-up. However, Mitchell broke camp with the Mets in 1986. Manager Davey Johnson played the rookie at six positions in the field, all but pitcher, catcher, and second base. Even in a part-time role and being moved all over the diamond, the right-handed-batting Mitchell hit .277 and belted 12 home runs. His defense, especially at shortstop, was a bit shaky. Veteran shortstop Bud Harrelson offered no advice to the youngster. "The best thing to do is leave him alone and give encouragement," said Harrelson. "It's a humanistic to worry about errors. He'll get over it. He'll be okay."[9]

After finishing in second place of the National League East Division in 1984 and 1985, New York claimed the division title in 1986. It was the Mets' first return to the postseason since 1973. In a tightly played League Championship Series, the Mets won in six games. Mitchell started three of the games in the outfield and went 2-for-8. He started two games in the World Series against the Red Sox and also was 2-for-8.

After the season Mitchell was traded to his hometown San Diego team as part of an eight-player deal. What could have been a nice homecoming was instead a struggle for Mitchell. He was installed as the starting third baseman for the Padres, replacing Graig Nettles. But Mitchell felt the pressures of playing at home. Nor did he favor playing for Padres manager Larry Bowa, who drove his players hard, was a perfectionist, and could be quite manic at times. On July 5, 1987,

Mitchell was on the move again, this time to division rival San Francisco in a seven-player deal. "It was good for me to get traded again," said Mitchell. "I had a lot of pressure on me to hit home runs in San Diego because they'd lost (Kevin) McReynolds (in the trade with the Mets). And under Bowa, you couldn't make a mistake without him hollering at you. He put a lot of pressure on a lot of younger players."[10] Right off the bat, Mitchell made a contribution to his new team, stroking a pair of two-run home runs against the Cubs at Wrigley Field in a 7-5 Giants victory.

Mitchell settled in at third base and batted .306, clubbed 15 home runs and had 44 RBIs for the Giants, who captured the NL West crown, but lost to St. Louis in seven games in the NLCS. Mitchell was 8-for-30 with a homer and two RBIs.

In 1988 the Giants added center fielder Brett Butler to inject some speed into their lineup, and Matt Williams came up from Triple-A to play third base, moving Mitchell to the outfield. With Will Clark at first base, the Giants had a solid nucleus for a good offensive club.

Early in the 1989 season, Mitchell made a defensive play that has drawn huzzahs over the years. In a late April game at Busch Stadium, the Cardinals' Ozzie Smith sent a fly ball to left field. Mitchell gave chase as the ball headed to foul territory. Just as he crossed the foul line, Mitchell realized that he had overrun the baseball, and reached up with his bare right hand to make the catch on the dead run. It was an extraordinary play, but accurately displayed his athletic ability. Both Mitchell and the Giants had a banner season. Mitchell was voted the NL Most Valuable Player by both the Baseball Writers Association of America and *The Sporting News* after leading the league in home runs (47), RBIs (125), and slugging percentage (.635). He was the National League's starting left fielder in the All-Star Game.

The Sporting News also named Mitchell to its Major League and NL All-Star Teams, and to the NL Silver Slugger Team. "I've never seen a power hitter stay in a groove so long," said Will Clark. "Mitch just crushed the ball from the start and made it a lot easier for all of us. He was outstanding."[11] "It never hit me what I was doing," said Mitchell. "The ball looked as big as a grapefruit and I was going to the plate with a lot of confidence. I really didn't think the pitchers could get me out."[12]

The Giants edged out San Diego by three games to win the division again. Mitchell stayed hot, batting .353 with two home runs and seven RBIs in the League Championship Series, in which the Giants toppled the Cubs in five games. The Giants met up with their neighbors from across the Bay, the Oakland Athletics, in the World Series, and were swept in the earthquake-interrupted Series by rather lopsided scores.

Mitchell avoided salary arbitration, and was rewarded handsomely when he signed a contract for $2,083,000 for the 1990 season. It was a raise of $1,423,000, the largest in major-league history at the time for a one-year contract. Mitchell delivered, smacking 35 home runs, driving in 93 runs, and batting .290, all outstanding figures considering that Mitchell was dealing with bone chips in his right wrist. He was named to the All-Star team again. Before the season was over, Mitchell signed his second contract of the calendar year, a four-year, $15 million pact. He became one of the four highest-paid major-league players.[13]

But Mitchell, hampered by wrist and knee injuries, played in only 113 games in 1991. He still hit 27 homers, and from 1989 to 1991, no player hit as many home runs as he did (109). However, problems were arising off the field during these banner seasons. In 1989 Mitchell missed a flight to Chicago during the LCS and missed a World Series workout. He was constantly late for workouts on game days during the regular season. In 1991 Mitchell left tickets to a game for a friend from San Diego. But the man didn't make the game because he was arrested in connection with the slaying of a San Diego police officer. (After the 1991 season Mitchell was accused of raping an old girlfriend, but the charges were dropped when the woman failed to cooperate with the prosecution.)

Shortly after the rape accusation was made, Mitchell was again traded, to Seattle in a five-player deal.

Giants general manager Al Rosen had had enough of Mitchell. Asked why he was not more patient with Mitchell, Rosen replied: "I saw production going down. I saw age (30) and weight going up."[14] Rosen was frank: "He reminds me of Richie Allen, in a way, or Bobby Bonds. There are certain guys who just aren't cornerstone players to a franchise. They move around constantly, getting traded for players with considerably less talent. Seattle is the fourth club that has had Mitchell, and I'm sure he'll see more before his career is over."[15]

The Mariners were adding Mitchell to a lineup that included Jay Buhner, Tino Martinez, Edgar Martinez, Harold Reynolds, and Ken Griffey Jr. General manager Woody Woodward and manager Bill Plummer were enthusiastic about Mitchell. Said Woodward: "We know this man comes to play. He wants to play. He's a gamer."[16] Plummer said, "This is an opportunity to fill that four spot with a quality hitter. There are not many opportunities to get a guy like Kevin Mitchell."[17]

But a season of promise and predictions of a 50-home-run season in the Kingdome for Mitchell quickly turned sour. In the first two months of the season he hit two home runs and had 20 RBIs. He continued to battle a right wrist injury, was 25 to 30 pounds overweight and was placed on the disabled list when he injured a muscle in his stomach while vomiting. The Mariners finished in last place in the American League West Division. In what was becoming an annual event, after the season Mitchell was dealt straight up to Cincinnati for relief pitcher Norm Charlton.

"One of our prime goals in the offseason was to acquire a batter we thought could hit fourth in our lineup, with the potential to hit 30 homers and drive in 100 runs," said Cincinnati GM Jim Bowden. "It doesn't bother me that Kevin was traded a lot. The important thing is that he's a first-class individual. We did a lot of research into his makeup, and we were satisfied."[18]

The Reds were hoping that being back in the National League would be good karma for Mitchell. And Mitchell played well. In June he had his longest hitting streak (20 games), batting .421 with 5 homers 16 RBIs. But a sore left shoulder and a broken bone in his left foot shut Mitchell down from late August to the end of the season. He bounced back in 1994 to lead the team with 30 home runs and drove in 77 runs. But the season ended prematurely on August 12 when the players went on strike.

The strike wiped out the playoffs and the World Series. Unsure of the future, Mitchell signed to play for the Fukuoka Daiei Hawks in Japan in 1995. But after only 130 at-bats, he left the team over a disagreement about a knee injury. The team doctors advised that he should still be able to play with minor ligament tears in his right knee, but Mitchell left Japan to seek a second opinion without asking permission from the ballclub, which suspended him. Back in the United States, it was discovered that Mitchell had cartilage damage and he had surgery in August.

Mitchell signed with Boston for 1996, but was traded to Cincinnati in midseason. He signed with Cleveland in 1997 and was released. He signed with Oakland in 1998 and was released as well. The most games he played in any of those seasons was 64. After the release by Oakland, Mitchell, 36 years old, retired from major-league baseball. He had hit 234 home runs, driven in 760 runs and batted .284.

In retirement, trouble seemed to find Mitchell. In August 1999 he was arrested for assaulting his father, Earl, whom he was evicting from a rental home he owned. Earl had been a cocaine addict and dealer. He pawned Mitchell's 1986 World Championship ring for drug money. Eventually Mitchell was instrumental in getting Earl into rehab.

In 2000, while managing the Sonoma County Crushers of the independent Western League, Mitchell was suspended nine games for assaulting the owner of an opposing team. In 2002 he was suspended seven games for punching that team's third base coach for allegedly stealing signs.

Shortly after his retirement as a player, Mitchell had been diagnosed with diabetes. He lost almost 40 pounds in three weeks, and as of 2015 had the disease under control. Living in his native San Diego, he worked with children, mentoring and offering advice to them, under the auspices of Athletes for Education, a nonprofit organization.

Most people would agree that Kevin Mitchell was a solid offensive baseball player and fundamentally sound defensively. It was often said that with his natural ability, he might not take batting practice or stretch or read a scouting report. The first pitch he saw at bat in a game was the first one he saw all day. "It's all up here," Mitchell would say, tapping the side of his head.[19] "I miss one day and feel like I don't have any timing or rhythm," said Reds teammate Hal Morris. "He misses a bunch of days and loses nothing. It's amazing to see a guy do that."[20] On July 22, 1994, at Wrigley Field, Mitchell demonstrated his ability. As he sat at his locker, there was a scouting report on Chicago's starting pitcher, Mike Morgan. "Get this out of here," said Mitchell. "I know how Morgan pitches me."[21] With two men on in the first inning, Mitchell sent a ball deep into the bleachers. "The only question was whether it was going to go into Lake Michigan," quipped Morgan.[22]

NOTES

1 *Boston Herald*, October 26, 1986: 71.

2 *New York Times*, October 26, 1986: 2.

3 *Boston Herald*, October 26, 1986: 71.

4 Ibid.

5 Ibid.

6 *Boston Globe*, August 20, 1987.

7 *New York Daily News*, May 11, 1986.

8 National Baseball Hall of Fame, player file.

9 *Albany Times Union*, June 28, 1986.

10 *Boston Globe*, August 20, 1987.

11 *The Sporting News*, December 11, 1989: 45.

12 Ibid.

13 *USA Today*, August 31, 1990.

14 *Inside Sports*, August 1992: 78.

15 *San Francisco Chronicle*, December 18, 1991: D-7.

16 *Seattle Times*, December 12, 1991.

17 Ibid.

18 *Cincinnati Post*, November 18, 1992.

19 *Sports Illustrated*, June 16, 1997: 79

20 Ibid.

21 Ibid.

22 Ibid.

RANDY MYERS

By Richard J. Puerzer

ALTHOUGH RANDY MYERS HAD BEEN JUST promoted from the minors and was but a bit player on the 1986 Mets, his subsequent baseball career was filled with numerous stellar achievements. He was a dominant closer for several teams, was selected for four All-Star teams, was a key contributor to a World Series champion team, and for a time held the National League record for saves in a season. A quirky and sometimes eccentric lefty, Myers pitched for and greatly contributed to six franchises over the course of a fine 14-year major-league career.

Randall Kirk Myers was born on September 19, 1962, in Vancouver, Washington. Myers' father was an auto mechanic, and Myers credited his blue-collar upbringing and the work ethic he learned from his parents for some of his success.[1] Myers grew up in Vancouver, and graduated from Evergreen High School. While at Clark College in Vancouver, he was selected by the Cincinnati Reds in the third round of the 1982 January Draft (Regular Phase). Myers did not sign with the Reds, and proceeded to go to Eastern Illinois University in Charleston, Illinois. As a pitcher at Eastern Illinois, he was drafted by the New York Mets in the first round (ninth pick overall) of the 1982 June Draft (Secondary Phase). Myers signed with the Mets and, at age 19, began his professional career as a starting pitcher for the Kingsport Mets in the Appalachian (Rookie) League. In 13 starts at Kingsport, he struck out more than a batter an inning, but also walked nearly a batter an inning, and threw a dozen wild pitches.

Myers progressed through the Mets' minor-league system, all the while a starting pitcher. In 1983 he started 28 games for the Columbia Mets of the Class A South Atlantic League, where he made great strides in improving his control. In 1984 he split time between the Class-A Lynchburg Mets and the Double-A Jackson Mets, and emerged as a strong prospect. In 27 starts for the two teams, Myers posted a record of 15-6, an ERA of 2.06, and more than a strikeout per inning. He began 1985 in Jackson, and was promoted to the Triple-A Tidewater Tides later in the season. With Tidewater, Myers started seven games, pitching 44 innings and posting an ERA of 1.84. He earned a late-season call-up to the majors, for a cup of coffee with the Mets. Myers made his major-league debut on October 6, 1985, the last game of the Mets' season. He pitched the final two innings of the game against the Montreal Expos, allowing no hits and one walk while striking out two batters. The Mets lost 2-1, in what was Rusty Staub's last major-league game.

In 1986 Myers made the transition from starting pitcher to relief specialist. The Mets of course had an excellent starting rotation with Dwight Gooden, Ron Darling, Sid Fernandez, Bobby Ojeda, and Rick Aguilera. Myers' chances of making the big-league team in the near future would be greatly enhanced if he were to come out of the bullpen. He began the season with Tidewater, and established himself as

Myers pitching later in career for the Padres

the team's closer. He pitched in 45 games, all in relief, finished 35 of them, and earned 12 saves. He allowed only 44 hits in 65 innings, although he also walked 44 batters. Myers was overpowering with his fastball and hard slider, striking out 79 batters, or 10.9 batters per nine innings.[2] Myers was called up to the Mets in mid-July, and pitched primarily as a lefty matchup specialist, making eight appearances until mid-August. He pitched 8⅔ innings, allowing only two earned runs while striking out 10 batters. Myers was sent back to Tidewater in mid-August. In mid-September he was called back up and made two more regular-season appearances for the Mets, but was not included on the postseason roster.

Myers began the 1987 season again with Tidewater, but after only five appearances he was called back up to the Mets to stay. Pitching as a middle reliever and set-up man for the Mets' two closers, Roger McDowell and Jesse Orosco, Myers had mixed success. In his first outing of the season with the Mets, he gave up four earned runs without recording an out against the Atlanta Braves. By the end of April, his ERA stood at 13.50. But by the end of the season he demonstrated that he was as effective as any other option out of the Mets' bullpen. From August 5 to September 25, Myers made 22 appearances and gave up just three earned runs. By season's end, he had three wins and six losses along with six saves. Impressively, Myers struck out 92 batters in 75 innings. His emergence as a reliable pitcher allowed for the Mets to trade Jesse Orosco to the Dodgers, and left Myers to join right-hander Roger McDowell as the closing platoon. He also earned the distinction of Mets announcer Tim McCarver referring to him by the more formal moniker Randall K. Myers.

In 1988, Randy Myers, 25, had his first great season. He picked up the save on Opening Day, the first of 26 saves he would earn that year. For the season, Myers finished with a record of 7-3, struck out 69 in 68 innings, recorded a WHIP (walks plus hits per inning pitched) of 0.912, had an ERA of 1.72, and emerged as the leader of the Mets' bullpen. The Mets had a great season, winning 100 games and finishing first in the National League East. In the National League Championship Series Myers got the win over the Los Angeles Dodgers in Games One and Three. However, Mets manager Davey Johnson's use, or lack thereof, of Myers in Game Four puzzled Mets fans. The Mets led the series two games to one going into that game. Starter Dwight Gooden held a 4-2 lead going into the ninth inning. Gooden walked leadoff batter John Shelby. With left-handed-batting Mike Scioscia coming up and Gooden having thrown more than 120 pitches, it seemed a good time to call Myers from the bullpen. However, Johnson had Gooden stay in the game. Scioscia hit a home run to tie the score. Myers eventually relieved Gooden in the ninth and finished up the inning without giving up a run. He remained in the game until the 11th inning, when he was relieved by Roger McDowell, who would eventually lose the game on a home run by Kirk Gibson. The Mets went on to lose the series in seven games, and Myers did not appear again in the series. Scioscia's homer was the turning point in the series, as it allowed the Dodgers to tie the series instead of being down three games to one.[3]

Myers had another fine season in 1989. The Mets traded former platoon-mate Roger McDowell to the Phillies in mid-June, making Myers the sole closer for the team. He responded well, finishing the season with a record of 7-4 and 24 saves. He again averaged more than a strikeout per inning, appeared in a team-leading 65 games, and had an ERA of 2.35. The Mets finished second, six games behind the Cubs, despite a supremely talented staff of starting pitchers.

After the 1989 season, despite his successes, the Mets decided to trade Myers away. They dealt him and pitcher Kip Gross to the Cincinnati Reds for pitcher John Franco and minor leaguer Don Brown. The motivations behind the trade for both teams were somewhat questionable. The trade was essentially 28-year-old left-handed closer Franco for 26-year-old left handed closer Myers. Franco's contract was far more pricey than that of Myers, nearly $1.1 million per year, to $300,000 a year for Myers. So in making the trade, the Reds were acquiring a less expensive player.

For the Mets, Franco hailed from New York City, making him a potential fan favorite. There were also stories that Myers was pursuing the then unorthodox training method, at least for pitchers, of lifting weights. He was also quirky and known for his interest in weapons and for reading *Soldier of Fortune* magazine in the locker room. Regardless of both teams' motivations, Myers did end up in an excellent situation and would prosper in Cincinnati.

The 1990 Cincinnati Reds were a good team with a great bullpen, led by Myers. He was the de-facto closer, finishing the season with 31 saves, an ERA of 2.08, a WHIP of 1.119, and 10.2 strikeouts per nine innings, and was selected to his first All-Star team. The reliever triumvirate of Myers, Norm Charlton, and Rob Dibble, who became known as the Nasty Boys, had great success in helping the Reds to win the National League West. Charlton, who moved from the bullpen and into the starting rotation midway through the season, starting 16 games, was back in the bullpen with great success in the postseason. Dibble, who was probably the most dominant pitcher of the three, saved 11 games while striking out 12.5 per nine innings. The Reds won the division by five games, and defeated the Pittsburgh Pirates in six games in the National League Championship Series, with Myers pitching in each of the four victories. He and Rob Dibble shared the series Most Valuable Player honors. The Reds went on to face the Oakland A's in the World Series and surprisingly swept the A's in four games. Myers pitched in three of the games, allowed only two baserunners and struck out three in three innings of work. He earned the save in the fourth game and final game, and was on the mound when the Series came to an end. To cap the season for Myers, he placed fifth in the voting for the National League Cy Young Award, and 17th in the MVP vote.

Although the 1991 Reds entered the season with great promise, over the course of the season they repeatedly faltered and ended up in fifth place in their division. The Nasty Boys bullpen of 1990 was intact, and Myers and Dibble began the season as a closer platoon. Dibble continued the dominance he demonstrated the previous year, but Myers did not. His strikeout rate was down and he allowed baserunners at a far higher rate than in recent years. He had a particularly difficult streak of appearances from July 11 to the 20th, allowing 11 runs in 8⅓ innings pitched. Hoping a change of responsibility would do him well, the Reds moved Myers to the starting rotation, as Dibble and Charlton had the bullpen well under control. Myers struggled mightily as a starter, with the Reds losing 9 of the 12 games he started. By the end of the season, he was back in the bullpen.

After the 1991 season the Reds traded Myers to the San Diego Padres for outfielder Bip Roberts. Myers was made the closer of the Padres, and had something of a return to form. He led the pitching staff in appearances with 66, and saved 38 games. However, his strikeout rate was still lower than earlier in his career, and he blew eight saves, leading to a relatively high 4.29 ERA. The Padres ended the season third in their division, 16 games behind the Atlanta Braves. After the season Myers became a free agent, and was among the best relief pitchers on the market. The Chicago Cubs signed him to a three-year contract worth $10.7 million. Myers responded with an excellent season in 1993. He pitched in a team-high 73 games (60 of which were save situations), posted an ERA of 3.11, and struck out 86 batters in 75⅓ innings. But what was most notable about his season was his 53 saves, shattering the National League record for saves in a season, 47, set by Lee Smith. Myers finished eighth in Cy Young Award voting.

Myers began the 1994 season well, but as a team the Cubs were dreadful. He recorded 21 saves and was named to the All-Star team, but the Cubs were in last place, 16½ games behind the NL Central-leading Reds, when the players strike forced the end of the season after the games played on August 11. When baseball came back in 1995, the Cubs were modestly better, and Myers soldiered on, leading the team, and the National League, with 38 saves, and again appearing on the All-Star team. After theseason, Myers, now 33 years old, went back on the free-agent market and was signed by the Baltimore Orioles to a two-year, $6.3 million contract. The move to Baltimore reunited Myers with Davey Johnson, his manager when he came up with the Mets, as well as with Jesse Orosco and Roger McDowell, his former bullpen mates with the Mets.

In 1996 Myers saved 31 games for the Orioles, helped by a much higher strikeout rate (11.4 per nine innings), than in recent seasons. The Orioles finished second in the American League East, good enough for the wild card in the American League. In the Division Series against the Cleveland Indians, the Orioles won, three games to one, with Myers pitching in all three wins and picking up the save in Games Two and Four. In the American League Championship Series against the New York Yankees, Myers was in the thick of the action. In Game One, he was brought into the game in the bottom of the ninth with the score tied 4-4, one out and two runners on base. He was able to get out of the inning on a line-drive double play. Myers pitched a 1-2-3 10th, but gave up a walk-off home run to Bernie Williams in the 11th. He pitched again in Games Two and Five, and did not allow any runs, but the Yankees won the series four games to one.

Myers came back strong for the 1997 season with the Orioles. He led the American League in saves with 45, with only one blown save for the season. His ERA of 1.51 was a career low. He was selected to his fourth All-Star team. The Orioles won 98 games and finished first in the division. They defeated the Seattle Mariners in the Division Series, with Myers finishing two of the three Orioles wins. In the Championship Series, Myers got the save against the Cleveland Indians in Game One, but that was his last solid outing in the series. He took the loss in Game Three, giving up a run in the 11th inning on a steal of home by Marquis Grissom. Myers entered Game Five in the ninth inning to protect a 4-0 Orioles lead. His performance was shaky and he gave up two runs before finishing off the inning and the game. In Game Six, with the Indians leading the series three games to two, Myers relieved starter Mike Mussina in the ninth inning of a scoreless game and pitched two scoreless innings before handing the game over to Armando Benitez, who took the loss when he gave up a home run to Tony Fernandez in the 11th inning. After the season, Myers' contributions to the Orioles' success were well recognized. He finished fourth in the voting for the Cy Young Award and, perhaps more impressively, finished fourth in the Most Valuable Player voting. His time with the Orioles came to an end, however. Myers became a free agent after the season and although the Orioles offered him a substantial two-year contract, he accepted a better offer from the Toronto Blue Jays, a three-year, $18 million contract.[4]

The 35-year-old Myers pitched effectively for the Blue Jays in 1998, earning 28 saves by August 2. However, he did not exhibit the impressive form of his previous few seasons. By August 2 he had blown five saves and his ERA stood at 4.46. The Blue Jays were also out of contention. At the end of July, the Blue Jays trailed the New York Yankees, who would go on to win 114 games, by 25½ games and also lagged behind the eventual wild-card winner Boston Red Sox by 10½ games. As a result, the Blue Jays were willing to part ways with Myers and put him on waivers. The San Diego Padres, apparently afraid that the Atlanta Braves would claim Myers, put in a claim. The Blue Jays traded Myers to the Padres on August 6 for minor-league catching prospect Brian Lloyd, a trade that would go down as disastrous for the Padres.[5] The trade took Myers to a team with more immediate promise—at the time of the trade the Padres held a 12-game lead in their division. However, Myers' role as a reliever was clearly diminished, as the Padres already had a well-established closer, Trevor Hoffman. Myers settled into a role as a middle reliever and left-handed specialist. He made 21 appearances for the Padres to complete the season. While his ERA for the Padres was 6.28, he was charged with earned runs in only six of his appearances. In the postseason, Myers did not appear in the Division Series against the Houston Astros, which the Padres won in four games. He did pitch in four of the games in the National League Championship Series against the Braves, which the Padres won in six games. Myers pitched in three of the four games of the World Series against the juggernaut Yankees, who swept the Series. He struck out both baserunners he faced in Game One and walked the only batter he faced, Paul O'Neil, in Game Three. In Game Four Myers got O'Neil to line out to end the top of the ninth inning. It was Myers' last appearance in a major-league game.

Although Myers was under contract for the 1999 and 2000 seasons, he did not pitch again for the Padres. A shoulder injury and eventual rotator-cuff surgery in 1999 essentially brought about the end to his playing career. Myers was only in the first year of his contract when he was traded to the Padres, who ended up paying him $13 million to complete the three-year contract. Myers attempted a comeback in 2001 with the Triple-A Tacoma Rainiers, but the comeback was short-lived; he pitched in only one game and gave up three hits and a walk without recording an out. After the game he retired as a player. He started a nonprofit foundation, T.O.D.A.Y., to promote youth athletics. He became an assistant women's basketball coach at his alma mater, Clark College. Myers also became a benefactor to the Clark College baseball program, where he got his start, by donating funds to revive what had become a dormant varsity program. As of 2015 he lived in Brush Prairie, in central Washington.

NOTES

1 Larry Stone, "Terminator—Enigmatic Oriole Closer Randy Myers Is Tough for Hitters—and Teammates—to Figure Out," *Seattle Times*, September 29, 1997.

2 Bill James and Rob Neyer, *The Neyer/James Guide to Pitchers* (New York: Simon and Schuster, 2004), 320.

3 Jon Springer and Matthew Silverman, *Mets by the Numbers: A Complete Team History of the Amazin' Mets by Uniform Number* (New York: Skyhorse Publishing, 2008), 234.

4 Murray Chass, "Moving Quickly, Blue Jays Snatch Myers From Orioles," *New York Times*, November 27, 1997.

5 Henry Shulman, "Waiver Claim Backfired on Padres / Despite Big Contract They Grabbed Myers So Atlanta Wouldn't," *SFGATE*, August 11, 1998.

RANDY NIEMANN

By David E. Skelton

THESE WERE HEADY DAYS FOR THE HOUSTON Astros. In 1979 the franchise had mastered just two winning campaigns in its 17-year existence yet found itself in first place through a majority of the season. Manager Bill Virdon accurately predicted this success in a preseason interview with columnist Harry Shattuck. Emphasizing a needed reliance on its veteran mound presence—in 1979 the team would hit the National League's fewest homers (49) and score the fewest runs (583)—Virdon expressed confidence that, should one of his experienced hurlers falter, "[I w]on't fret. If the veterans fail or wear out, the Arm Farm continues to prosper. Randy Niemann—remember [that] name."[1]

When right-handed hurler Vern Ruhle was placed on the disabled list in May 1979, the Astros recalled Niemann. The 23-year-old pitched a career high 67 innings in 1979, and his 100 innings through 1980 accounted for exactly half of Niemann's major-league total. He was cast as a top prospect in the Astros system, but elbow surgery in 1981 limited Niemann throughout the remainder of his career, relegating him to a mere shadow of what was once projected for the prized southpaw.

Born on November 15, 1955, in Scotia, California (a town 300 miles north of San Francisco owned at the time by the Pacific Lumber Co.), Randal Harold "Randy" Niemann was the third child—and only son—born to Robert Niemann and Joy Maxine Denney. Joy's seven-times great-grandfather came to New York from Woodford, England, in 1679. The family migrated west over many generations—Joy's father, LaVern Edwin Denney, was an Idaho native and she was born in California in 1927. Seeking employment during the Depression, Joy's family traveled frequently throughout the West. Her father, a bulldozer operator, worked on the construction of the Grand Coulee Dam in Washington and the Boulder (now Hoover) Dam in Arizona. LaVern eventually settled in coastal Humboldt County, California, where during World War II she worked in the dry docks as a painter. On July 28, 1948, she married Robert Niemann. The couple raised three children.

Niemann attended Fortuna (California) High School and then the College of the Redwoods in nearby Eureka, where his baseball prowess attracted major-league scouts.[2] In 1974 Niemann spurned the Montreal Expos after the team selected him in the fifth round of the January draft. He rebuffed the Minnesota Twins a year later when he was selected in the third round. Chosen by the New York Yankees as the 30th overall pick in the June 1975 draft (secondary phase), Niemann signed and was sent to Oneonta, New York, to play for the Yankees' affiliate in the short-season Class-A New York-Pennsylvania League. His manager, former major-league third baseman Mike Ferraro,[3] inserted

Niemann into eight starting assignments through the rest of the 1975 season. In 55 innings the 19-year-old posted a 2.45 ERA (league average: 3.49) that, due to the team's anemic offense, got him a mere 3-3 record. His strong performance earned Niemann a promotion to Fort Lauderdale of the Class-A Florida State League in 1976. Weeks before his report date—on January 17, 1976—Niemann married Joy Simmons. Though the union would not last, it produced a daughter and two sons.

Hard luck followed Niemann to Fort Lauderdale. Despite a 2.84 ERA (league average: 3.15) in 1976, Niemann placed among the league leaders in losses (10) and hit batters (14). On June 25 he earned his first shutout of the season in yeoman-like style by stranding 14 opposing players in a 2-0 win over the West Palm Beach Expos. Niemann's 190 innings placed second to Cincinnati prospect Mario Soto. This campaign was followed by a stint in the Florida Instructional League where Niemann shared the league lead with five wins. His success in the Sunshine State earned Niemann an invitation to the Yankees spring camp in 1977.

Though his chances of jumping from Class A to the staff of the defending American League champions were slim, Niemann's spring performance earned him a promotion to the West Haven (Connecticut) Yankees of the Double-A Eastern League and also attracted attention from other major-league teams. Niemann was the youngest pitcher on the West Haven squad. His first start was an 11-1 rout of the Holyoke Millers. Though other outings were less successful,[4] Niemann's growing reputation as a "highly touted young prospect"[5] was a factor in his inclusion in a June 15, 1977, four-player trade with the Astros. Assigned to Columbus in the Double-A Southern League and used primarily in relief, Niemann struggled. But he was one of the few left-handers in the Astros system, high hopes were attached to Niemann.

These hopes were largely realized in 1978. Used as both a starter and reliever for the Columbus Astros, Niemann had seven consecutive wins to start the season. An ensuing 1-4 mark was attributed to hard luck losses, each by one run. Niemann carried a Bob Gibson-like 1.65 ERA by the season's three-quarter mark and finished with a 9-5, 2.05 posting. A poll of league managers and media consultants selected Niemann to the Southern League All Star team. This success was followed by a 9-3, 2.06 stint in the Mexican Winter League. Citing Niemann's achievements, *The Sporting News* heralded the "young left-handed pitcher considered a big part of Houston's future plans."[6]

Those future plans were put on hold in the Astros' 1979 spring camp. A respectable exhibition campaign—including a three-inning, one-hit performance against the hard-hitting Cincinnati Reds—was not enough for him to crack Houston's deep mound corps. Niemann was promoted to Triple-A Charleston, and after six weeks he was called up when Astros starter Vern Ruhle was injured. On May 20, 1979, Niemann made his major-league debut in a starting assignment against the San Diego Padres. He held the Padres hitless into the fourth inning and carried a shutout into the sixth. Niemann completed seven innings of five-hit ball with no decision, and his outing earned another start nine days later, when he handcuffed the Reds in a 2-1 complete-game victory.

Niemann made a third appearance on June 4 against the reigning National League East Division champion Philadelphia Phillies. He lowered his ERA to a minuscule 0.72 after blanking the Phillies on six hits, winning praise from all but Phillies manager Danny Ozark: "How long can we lose to Niemann?" the Philadelphia skipper groused. "Our [Double-A] Reading farm club could beat Niemann."[7] Three weeks later, after the 23-year-old's second shutout—another six-hit gem, this time versus the Reds—Niemann cracked, "Not bad for a Double-A pitcher."[8]

Not all of Niemann's appearances went as swimmingly. Only July 7 he carried a record of 3-0, a 1.62 ERA, and one save into a contest against the Chicago Cubs in Wrigley Field and was hammered. On July 22 he did not survive the first inning. As the Astros tried to hold on to their tenuous first-place berth, manager Virdon turned increasingly to his veteran hurlers. Niemann pitched just 12 innings after July 30 and finished his debut season with a 3-2, 3.76 record in 67 innings.

No one expected those marks to represent the apex of Niemann's major-league career.

Challenged to break into the Astros' starting rotation in 1979, Niemann was further tested in 1980 with the team's free-agent signing of future Hall of Famer Nolan Ryan. Relegated to long relief, Niemann saw little mound time on a staff that placed among the National League leaders with 31 complete games. Through the Astros' first 39 contests he pitched just five innings, with a 7.20 ERA speaking to his rustiness. A strong seven innings of work in June yielded to a difficult July and resulted in Niemann's demotion to the Tucson Toros in the Pacific Coast League. Given the opportunity to pitch regularly, Niemann drew accolades from opposing Hawaii pitching coach Chuck Hartenstein as "the best left-hander in the league"[9] following a four-hit, 3-0 win over the Islanders. Called up in the midst of Houston's pennant pursuit, Niemann made eight appearances, losing a starting assignment and earning a save in the waning weeks of the season. A one-inning stint against the Reds on September 28 was his last major-league appearance until May 21, 1982—and that for a different team.

Another season in winter ball proved disastrous when Niemann pulled a muscle below his left elbow. Competing for a bullpen spot in spring training, he reinjured the arm in March and was assigned to Tucson to rehabilitate. He made his Toros debut on May 11, 1981, with an 8-2 win over the Phoenix Giants. He lasted nine additional appearances before surgery on his ailing arm shut down the remainder of his season. On September 9 the Astros sent Niemann and minor-league lefty Kevin Houston to the Pittsburgh Pirates to complete an earlier deal for infielder Phil Garner.

From 1982 to 1984 Niemann bounced between the big leagues and the minors with Pittsburgh and—after a September 7, 1983, swap—the Chicago White Sox. On September 23, 1982, he earned his last big-league save. Eight months later he made his first major-league start in three years, replacing an ineffective Jim Bibby in the rotation. In this May 21, 1983, start Niemann did not survive the second inning as the Astros scored five runs on six hits. The lefty was returned to the bullpen. He made just 33 appearances—54⅓ innings—in the majors over the three-year period, struggling with a combined 5.80 ERA.

In the winter of 1984-1985 Niemann pitched for the Arecibo Lobos in the Puerto Rican Winter League under the guidance of manager (and White Sox pitching coach) Dave Duncan. The experience helped rejuvenate his career. After Chicago traded him to the New York Mets on March 30, 1985, Niemann rebounded with the Mets Tidewater (Virginia) affiliate in the International League, posting a 2.76 ERA while placing among the league leaders in wins (11) and innings pitched (159⅔). That plus a strong September call-up and an equally strong spring camp in 1986, earned Niemann a bullpen spot on the Mets staff.

Due to a clerical error—"a quirk in the formality of the rules," said general manager Frank Cashen—Niemann was pushed off the Opening Day roster. After this hiccup he made his Mets debut in taxing fashion with losses in his first two appearances (April 12 and 14). The inauspicious start was followed by 13⅓ consecutive scoreless innings that included Niemann's first major-league win in four years. Demoted to Tidewater in July, Niemann was recalled as a spot starter in the second game of an August 17 doubleheader versus the St. Louis Cardinals. In what became his last big-league start he surrendered five hits and one earned run in six innings to capture the win in a 9-2 romp. Niemann made eight more appearances in relief as the Mets won the National League East Division crown. He did not appear in either the nail-biting six-game League Championship Series against the Astros the dramatic seven-game World Series versus the Boston Red Sox. Niemann enjoyed the raucous, destructive merrymaking on the return flight from Houston after the NLCS clincher, and the celebration after the World Series victory. "It wasn't just guys destroying a plane," he said. "It was guys destroying a plane after an emotional roller coaster. There's a difference."[10]

Niemann became a free agent after the World Series and signed with the Minnesota Twins. Though most of his 1987 season was spent with Triple-A Portland, in June Niemann was briefly promoted to the Twins.

On June 8 he captured his final major-league victory, against the Kansas City Royals. In 1988 the Royals invited Niemann to spring training as a nonroster invitee but he did not make the cut. He retired as a player after a short return to the Mets Tidewater affiliate.

In 1989 Niemann became a pitching coach in the Mets organization. He started with the Kingsport (Tennessee) rookie affiliate in the Appalachian League and in 1990 moved to the short-season Pittsfield Mets in the New York-Pennsylvania League. In 1996 Mets manager Bobby Valentine selected Niemann as his bullpen coach. Niemann worked in this capacity until June 5, 1999, when he and two other coaches were fired, on the heels of an eight-game losing streak, the final two versus the crosstown rival Yankees. The Mets had posted a May ERA of 5.71, the highest 30-day mark in team history since the dreadful expansion club in April 1962. Reluctant to fire the popular Valentine, general manager Steve Phillips went after the coaches. Retained by the organization, Niemann alternated between minor-league instructor, rehabilitation pitching coordinator, and Mets bullpen coach through 2011.[11]

In 2012 Niemann accompanied Valentine to Boston to serve as an assistant to pitching coach Bob McClure. The Red Sox posted a near league-worst 4.70 ERA as the team plummeted to a last-place finish. On August 20 Niemann was appointed the interim pitching coach after McClure was fired. He was not retained by Valentine's successor, John Farrell, in 2013. In 2015—Niemann's 40th year in Organized Baseball—he was the pitching coach for the Palm Beach Cardinals of the Florida State League. (50 miles south of his home in Port Saint Lucie, Florida). The Cardinals finished second in the league's South Division, and under Niemann's guidance the pitching staff led the league in earned-run average (2.65).

Possessing an ordinary fastball but good control—"The big plus about Niemann is that he can throw strikes," manager Chuck Tanner exclaimed[12]– Niemann drew favorable comparisons to four-time All Star lefty Tommy John. But elbow surgery in 1981 derailed any such resemblance. During an eight-year major-league career Niemann posted a 7-8 record and 4.64 ERA in just 200 innings pitched. Those numbers are a far cry from what was expected of a once "highly touted young prospect."[13] One wonders how Niemann's career might have developed if he hadn't hurt his arm.

The author wishes to thank Julia Skrinde Otto, whose Niemann family research proved invaluable.

SOURCES

Ancestry.com

legacy.com/obituaries/times-standard/obituary.aspx?n=joy-m-niemann&pid=143433480

overthemonster.com/2012/8/21/3256112/randy-niemann-red-sox-pitching-coach

redbirdrants.com/2014/12/11/st-louis-cardinals-announce-2015-minor-league-staffs/

milb.com/milb/stats/stats.jsp?t=l_tpi&lid=123&sid=t279

NOTES

1 "Astros Once-Fertile Arm Farm Now Dust Bowl," *The Sporting News*, January 6, 1979: 33.

2 Through 2014 Niemann is the only major-league player to emerge from either school.

3 Ferraro was the manager at every stop in Niemann's advance through the Yankees minor-league system.

4 Niemann struggled with a 5.52 ERA in 13 appearances.

5 "Astros Play Santa Claus to Johnson, Crawford," *The Sporting News*, July 2, 1977: 16.

6 "Astros Will Rise, Virdon Predicts," *The Sporting News*, February 10, 1979: 37.

7 "Astros Shrug Off Insults, Rack Up Victories," *The Sporting News*, July 7, 1979: 25.

8 "Pinch-Hitter Walling Is Astros' Mr. Clutch," *The Sporting News*, July 14, 1979: 17.

9 "Niemann Impresses Coach," *The Sporting News*, September 6, 1980: 59.

10 "Come fly the rowdy skies," ESPN Page 2, June 3, 2004.

11 After the 2003 season the Mets reassigned pitching coach Vern Ruhle. Niemann was identified as a potential replacement, setting up a scenario where he would have replaced Ruhle for the second time in his career.

12 "Niemann Attracts Pirates' Attention," *The Sporting News*, February 7, 1983: 40.

13 "Astros Play Santa Claus."

BOB OJEDA

By Alan Cohen

"WE DIDN'T JUST WANT TO WIN. WE wanted to step on the opponent's neck," Mookie Wilson said.[1] "What you saw was what you got, like it or hate it,"[2] said Bobby Ojeda of the cantankerous New York Mets of 1986. Any championship team is pieced together over time, although it can appear that the success took place overnight. One of the last pieces of the puzzle known as the 1986 Mets was Bobby Ojeda. When the 1985 Mets fell short of a division championship, general manager Frank Cashen went shopping for another left-handed pitcher. He obtained Ojeda and three minor leaguers from the Red Sox for Calvin Schiraldi, Wes Gardner, John Christensen, and La Schelle Tarver.

What did the Mets get out of the deal? The short end of the stick, or so it seemed; Schiraldi and Gardner were two of the brightest pitching prospects in the Mets organization. Ojeda had pitched to a 9-11 record for the Red Sox in 1985, and had done little to distinguish himself in six seasons with Boston. He was brash and opinionated and out of place in the Red Sox clubhouse. "Let's just say I wasn't their type," he said years later. "I didn't fit the mold."[3] The hope was that Ojeda would win 10 games for the Mets.

With the Mets, Ojeda was in his element and not to be absent from a good prank. Early in the 1986 season, he targeted Kevin Mitchell. After a game in San Diego, Mitchell returned to the clubhouse to find that Ojeda and Ron Darling had cut the sleeves and pants legs off his suit.[4]

But in the season of his life Ojeda injected a sense of calm around the Mets, going 18-5 with a career-best 2.57 ERA. His team-leading 18 wins were also a career high as were his 148 strikeouts. His .783 won-lost percentage topped the league's hurlers and he finished fourth in the voting for the Cy Young Award.

At 24 Ojeda was optimistic for his baseball future. "When I'm 47 sitting in my rocking chair, I'll look back and know I got the most I could have out of myself. I mean the most!" he said in 1981. "So many guys I know are saying now, 'Man, I should have stayed home more. I should have done my running harder.' They're full of should haves and could haves, and now they're digging ditches. I'll tell you though, I'd be happy digging that ditch if I knew I had done the best I could."[5]

For Bobby Ojeda, the story began in Los Angeles, where he was born on December 17, 1957. His father was a furniture upholsterer and his mother worked for the school system as an interpreter for Mexican migrants.

By 1972, he was 15 years old and pitching for his Babe Ruth League team in Visalia, California. Ojeda was

blessed with a live arm and a good fastball but sometimes, like the time he hit five batters in a game, his control was suspect. The scouts did not take notice of him in his days in high school and at the College of the Sequoias in Visalia. He married Tamara Ann Gan in 1977 and became a father in 1978. They had two daughters and a son before the marriage ended in divorce in 1986. In early 1978 Ojeda was working as a landscaper for his brother-in-law, and it looked as though he would not be playing professional baseball. But Larry Flynn, a Red Sox scout who remembered Ojeda from his Babe Ruth days, advised the Red Sox to sign the lefty, who was an undrafted free agent. The Red Sox did so on May 20, 1978.

Ojeda's first stop was Elmira in the short-season New York-Penn League, where his "blazing" speed took him to a 1-6 record and a 4.81 ERA. But during a postseason instructional league Red Sox pitching coach Johnny Podres taught him how to effectively throw a changeup, and Bobby was on his way.

In 1979 Ojeda went 15-7 with a 2.43 ERA for Class-A Winter Haven of the Florida State League, earning a two-level promotion to the Triple-A Pawtucket Red Sox in the International League. He earned his first win at Pawtucket on May 2, 1980, 8-2 over Rochester.

Ojeda's temper got the better of him in a game on June 27. The umpire banished the batboy for being a bit tardy in replacing his supply of baseballs. The enraged Ojeda, who was not pitching in the game, hurled four baseballs from the dugout in the general direction of the umpire and then dropkicked the ball bag halfway down the third-base line to earn the rest of the night off.[6]

Ojeda was 4-5 with a 3.39 ERA when, on July 11, he was called up to the Red Sox and put into the starting rotation. He saw his first action on July 13 against Detroit, pitching into the sixth inning. He was taken out in the sixth inning after surrendering a four-run lead. (Boston went on to win the game 8-4.) Manager Don Zimmer was impressed with what he saw. "Of all the guys we've brought up here in my seven years, he's the coolest we've had, Zimmer said after the game. "You'd think he's been here 10 years. He says it's just a game and all you can do is your best—which is the truth."[7]

Ojeda's first win came against Texas on August 2. Through six innings he shut out the Rangers on five hits and Bob Stanley came on for the save as the Red Sox won 1-0. His record in seven games with the Red Sox in 1980 was 1-1 with an ERA of 6.92. In his last start, on August 11 in Detroit, he allowed a walk, a homer, and a single to the first three batters and Zimmer pulled him from the game, saying he "felt he would be maimed."[8] Ojeda was returned to Pawtucket for the balance of the 1980 season. He was 2-2 with a 2.70 ERA during his late-season stint at Pawtucket, bringing his International League record for 1980 to 6-7 with a 3.22 ERA.

Ojeda worked hard over the winter, using a Nautilus program, and began the 1981 season throwing flames for Pawtucket. "In the big leagues, you have to do the job right away," he said early in the season. "That adjustment had to be speeded up (for me). Either you do it or you don't. I didn't." He impressed Pawtucket manager Joe Morgan, who said, "When he was up there (in Boston), he found that he couldn't be a one-pitch (in Ojeda's case the changeup) pitcher. When some guys learn that, they're finished. But he knew what he had to do and did it. He worked all winter and has improved. He's faster than he was last year."[9]

In that season, Ojeda was involved—in an unusual way—in one of baseball's most historic games, the record 33-inning marathon between Pawtucket and Rochester that began on the evening of Saturday, April 18. Ojeda was scheduled to pitch the next game, and watched as night became late night, very late night, and early morning. As the clock passed midnight and the game entered its 20th inning, Ojeda went home and went to bed. Virtually everybody else (including seven Pawtucket pitchers) saw action as the teams played on and on, completing 32 innings before play was suspended on Sunday at 4:07 A.M. with the score 2-2. When the game resumed on June 23, Ojeda took to the mound for Pawtucket to pitch the 33rd inning. He retired Rochester without allowing a run. Pawtucket won the game in the bottom of the inning and Ojeda was the winning pitcher. Asked to sum up his feelings, he said, "I don't know how to feel." How does anybody feel who played in a 33-inning game? Nobody knows because it has never happened before. This is terrific. I feel like I am at the Mardi Gras. I was home sleeping by 3:30 A.M. the first time they played. I took a lot of heat from the other pitchers who worked their butts off in that game. I come in, pitch one inning, and get the win. I hope they can take a joke."[10]

Ojeda was pitching well, but his stay in the International League was prolonged by the ongoing strike of the major-league players, which began on June 12. Ojeda was called up when play resumed on August 9, by which time his record was 12-9 with an ERA of 2.13. At season's end he was named the International League's Pitcher of the Year.

Rejoining the Red Sox, he said, "I'm mentally ready this time. After what happened last summer, you either get shell-shocked or you get tough. I got tough. I built up my upper body on a Nautilus machine and I've worked hard on my slider."[11] In his first start after his return, he pitched a complete game victory, downing the Chicago White Sox on seven hits. Former Red Sox catcher Carlton Fisk, then with the White Sox, said, "He added at least five feet to his heater."[12] Ojeda was the best pitcher on the Red Sox staff after the strike, posting a 6-2 record with a 3.12 ERA.

His best effort of 1981 came against the Yankees in New York on September 12. After a first-inning walk to Lou Piniella, Ojeda retired the next 22 batters and took a no-hitter into the bottom of the ninth inning, when Rick Cerone of the Yankees doubled and scored on a double by Dave Winfield that cut the Red Sox lead to 2-1. Leaving the game to a standing ovation, Ojeda was relieved by Mark Clear, who saved the win for him.

As the season neared a close, Ojeda was having headaches and feeling tired. He was found to have a blood ailment similar to mononucleosis. He did not pitch after September 27, although the Red Sox were still in contention for the second-half championship. They wound up finishing 1½ games behind the Milwaukee Brewers. Ojeda finished with a 6-2 record for the Red Sox and finished third in the balloting for Rookie of the Year.

Ojeda started 1982 with the Red Sox and, in an injury-plagued season, went 4-6 with an ERA of 5.63. In three of his starts he was unable to get past the first inning. His first win of the season came on April 20 after two losses. He was knocked out, literally, in the first inning of a game against Kansas City on May 16 when he was hit on the shin by a line drive off the bat of John Wathan. His woes were compounded when he pulled his left hamstring muscle on June 11, and after returning to action two weeks later he was sent to the bullpen. His work out of the pen earned praise from manager Ralph Houk, and he was returned to the rotation. But on August 18 he took a fall in the bathtub in his hotel room in Anaheim and injured his shoulder. He did not pitch again in 1982.

Throughout the season Ojeda maintained his confidence and sense of humor. In late June, he said, "There have been moments I have been real, real down. But they don't last for more than four or five weeks. No, just a few minutes. But twice, it probably just hit me. I mean, everything's hurting me. But that goes away pretty quick. I mean, I don't like it. I'm not happy with it. But I'm not a me-guy. As long as the team is winning, it's not tough."[13]

After the season Ojeda pitched in Puerto Rico and came to spring training in 1983 poised to win back his job in the rotation. He was the team's fifth starter, which meant that he would not see much action early on. He didn't get his first win until May 15, defeating Milwaukee 6-1. In his next start, on May 21, he got his first complete-game win in a long time when the Red Sox defeated Minnesota 11-4.

But Ojeda was erratic in his performances, and on one occasion manager Houk paid an unexpected visit to the mound and urged him, not so subtly, to throw strikes. As August came to a close, Ojeda's record was a disappointing 6-7. But Ojeda had become a different pitcher, showing the aggressiveness he had late in the 1981 season. He won seven of his last eight starts and never allowed more than two runs in a game. He brought his final record to 12-7. His 1.83 ERA in his last eight starts fell from 5.18 on August 17 to 4.04 at the end of the season.

In 1984 Ojeda pitched 216⅔ innings and went 12-12 with a 3.99 ERA. The Red Sox finished fourth in the AL East. His first win of the season, on April 23 in a rain-shortened 2-0 shutout of the California Angels, was his first major-league shutout. He pitched four more shutouts in 1984, and his five blankings were the most by an American League pitcher that season.

But inconsistency, inaccuracy, and injuries stood in the way of Ojeda emerging as a top-flight pitcher in 1984. He had five shutouts and a 9-7 record through July 27. Soreness in his left elbow put him on the disabled list in mid-August and he went 3-5 with a 4.34 ERA over the last two months of the season. In that stretch he walked 27 batters in 66⅓ innings, bringing his walks per nine innings to 3.99, his worst in four years.

In 1985 new manager John McNamara moved Ojeda to the bullpen, not as a punishment, but to groom him as a closer. The experiment was short-lived as the starting pitchers were failing and Ojeda was returned to the rotation. For the season, he went 9-11 with an ERA of 4.00.

Toward the end of his time in Boston, player militancy was brewing again. During a players-only team meeting, the Red Sox discussed the merits of a potential strike. Ojeda dispelled any notions that he went along with the prevailing pro-ownership mood when he said, "I don't care what you say. They (the owners) are going to try and pay us as little as they can. Yes, if you are older, you don't want to miss a paycheck being out on strike. But I'm young!" Three months later, he was gone, traded to the Mets.[14]

Ojeda joined a staff headed by Dwight Gooden, Ron Darling, and Sid Fernandez and to the surprise of some, became the pitching staff's stopper. By early July he had the 10 wins that were expected of him for the entire season. Win number 10 was especially important. The Mets had lost three games in a row, and although their division lead was at 10½ games, a win was needed. Ojeda held the Atlanta Braves in check, scattering seven hits as the Mets won 5-1. He was 10-2 at that point. His record included two shutouts and five complete games. His ERA stood at 2.24.

By July 18 the Mets were well in command of the NL East and had a 12-game lead. After a loss at Houston that night, Ojeda and teammates Ron Darling, Tim Teufel, and Rick Aguilera went to a place called Cooters Executive Games and Burgers to celebrate Teufel's becoming a father for the first time.[15] As they left Cooters, there was a scuffle between the players and local policemen who were providing security for Cooters. The four players were arrested. As Mets coach Bud Harrelson summed things up, "Things got a little rambunctious and four of our upstanding examples of athletic prowess ended up spending the night in one of that fair city's finest holding establishments."[16] In January 1987, misdemeanor charges against Ojeda were dismissed.[17]

Toward the end of the 1986 season, Ojeda began to experience stiffness in his left shoulder. But on September 23 he pitched six innings against the Cardinals and got his 17th win. "It felt good and it took a load off my mind," said Ojeda after the 9-1 win in which he allowed only three hits. He added, however, that "until you do it again, there's always a worry."[18]

In the playoffs Ojeda cemented his role as stopper. In Game One against Houston, the Astros' Mike Scott had been dominant, defeating Dwight Gooden 1-0. Ojeda pitched the second game, against 39-year-old fireballer Nolan Ryan. The Mets were not intimidated by Ryan and staked Ojeda to a 5-0 lead. The lefty went the distance, scattering 10 hits as the Mets won 5-1 to even the NLCS at a game apiece. The game was the essential Ojeda.

The Mets advanced to the World Series, only to lose the first two games at Shea Stadium to Ojeda's former team, the Red Sox. Game Three was at Fenway Park and Ojeda was handed the ball. He went up against another outspoken player, Boston's Dennis "Oil Can"

Boyd. Did the game have any extra meaning to Ojeda? Of course it did, although he said it was "just another game. That's how I'm approaching it. Nothing personal."[19] Ojeda rose to the occasion, allowing only five hits in seven innings as the Mets won 7-1. As Roger Angell noted, Ojeda "nibbled the corners authoritatively."[20] "That game was the most proud I'd ever been on a baseball field," Ojeda said later. "Because I didn't like the Red Sox. I had new friends, real friends. I had teammates who would fight and bleed for me. To do something important for my guys was awesome."[21] He would, in subsequent years, state that it was his greatest triumph on the baseball diamond.[22] Ojeda's win was the first by a left-handed pitcher in a postseason game at Fenway Park since 1918.[23]

After Ojeda's win, the teams split the next two games, and the Red Sox were on the verge of winning the World Series. Nevertheless, at least one observer felt that the Series was lacking something in the way of excitement.

Indeed, a *San Francisco Chronicle* reporter, Bruce Jenkins, was suffering from an extreme case of boredom after the first five games.

"In terms of aesthetics, the World Series has been a stimulating experience this year," Jenkins wrote "The Eastern fall weather has been magnificent, the cities are first-rate, and there's the usual charge one gets from walking into Fenway Park or Shea Stadium on a high-stakes evening.

"There's been only one problem: the games. This is shaping up as the most lifeless, uneventful World Series in 81 years.

"Where's the drama? Where are the comebacks? Where are the clutch hits in the late innings? Until further notice, the Series' official theme song is 'Everything's Coming Up Teufel.'

"Maybe things will change tonight, when Roger Clemens faces Bob Ojeda in Game 6 at Shea Stadium ... with the proud and arrogant Mets one game from elimination."[24]

Well?!

It was a must-win for the Mets. Ojeda gave up two runs and five hits in the first two innings. By the time he left the game after six innings, the Mets had tied the score, 2-2. Ojeda's work was done and it would be up to his teammates to keep the dream alive—they did. Two days later, the Mets had their second World Series championship.

What was the essence of Ojeda's success in 1986? He told Roger Angell: "A run is a run and you try to prevent those. There's so much strategy that goes into that. Each day is different. Each day you're a different pitcher. Consistency is the thing, even if it's one of those scuffle days. When I've started, I've been very consistent, and that's something I'm proud of. I led the league in quality starts last year—you know, pitching into the seventh inning while giving up three runs or less. That means something to me."[25]

Coming off his 18-5 performance in 1986, great things were expected of Ojeda in 1987 but it became a season of frustration. Ojeda's first start was on Opening Day, when he took on the assignment after Dwight Gooden was placed on the disabled list after testing positive for cocaine. Ojeda was up to the task, allowing one run in his seven innings of work as the Mets defeated the Pirates 3-2. Not only was it his first win of the season, it was also to be his best outing of the season—by far.

On April 21 Ojeda began to experience pain in his left elbow. He missed 10 days, and upon returning lost two games. In a game against Atlanta on May 9, he left after one inning, was charged with the loss, and his record stood at 2-4. Surgery to reposition the ulnar nerve in Ojeda's elbow was performed on May 23, and it was expected that he would miss the balance of the season. But he was able to return to action earlier than expected. As August turned into September and the Mets were still in the chase, Ojeda returned. On September 8 he pitched two scoreless innings in relief as the Mets defeated the Phillies to remain within 2½ games of the division lead.

Time was running out on the Mets when on September 20, in a slugfest with the Pirates, Ojeda entered the game in the 10th inning with the score 7-7. His first two innings were virtually flawless—no runs, no hits, one walk. The Mets scored a run in the top of the 12th, but the Pirates got one in their half of the inning. In the bottom of the14th inning, Barry Bonds tripled and scored on a sacrifice fly to end the 4:59 marathon. Ojeda was tagged with the loss, but deserved a better fate—and the Mets were still 2½ games behind. They finished three games behind the Cardinals.

In 1988, after elbow surgery, Ojeda went 10-13, but was more effective than the record would indicate. His ERA was 2.88, he equaled his career high in shutouts, and his strikeout-to-walk ratio was a league-leading 4.03. In 10 of his losses, the Mets scored two runs or less. But the most telling blow of all came when Ojeda was not pitching. On September 21, as the Mets were poised to win their second division championship in three years, he partially severed part of his left middle finger while using clippers to do some hedge trimming. Surgery by Dr. Richard Eaton to repair the finger was successful and Ojeda was able to look forward to 1989.

While recuperating from the surgery, Ojeda became involved with the Tole Indian reservation near his hometown of Visalia, California. He sought to raise funds to build a home for displaced children on the reservation. He also married for the second time in 1988. He and his wife, Ellen, have two children.

Not only did Ojeda return in 1989, but he had one of his better seasons, finishing with a 13-11 record and a 3.47 ERA. He lost his first start of the season to the Cardinals, 3-1, but pitched into the seventh inning, scattering six hits and allowing only two earned runs. He received a standing ovation when he left the game. After the game, Ojeda said, "In my dreams, I pitched to a different scenario. I wish we had won, but I'm very grateful to be here. Spring training is great, but this is the real McCoy."[26] Although feeling no pain, Ojeda was unsuccessful in his first four starts. On May 2 he unleashed his fastball to complement his ever-present "dead fish" changeup and defeated the Braves 7-1. He spun a three hit 1-0 shutout against the Phillies on June 17 for the Mets' first complete-game shutout of the season, but his record stood at a disappointing 5-9 on July 16. His ERA had ballooned to 4.19. And then Ojeda turned his season around, going 8-2 in his last 13 starts with an ERA of 2.60. But in his final appearance of the season, he lost 2-1 to the Phillies in a game that eliminated the Mets from the race for the division championship. The Mets finished in second place, six games behind the Chicago Cubs.

In 1990, after acquiring Frank Viola, the Mets had an abundance of starting pitchers and Ojeda did not have a regular turn in the rotation. Before May 22 he had started only one game and was 0-2. He was inserted into the rotation on that day and responded with his first win of the season, 8-3 over the Los Angeles Dodgers. But the team, despite the wealth of pitching, got off to a poor start, and on May 27 were 20-22 and in fourth place. Manager Davey Johnson was replaced by Bud Harrelson and Ojeda remained in the starting rotation. In June he went 3-0 in five starts and the Mets moved into a one-day tie for first place. However, inconsistency set in during July, and Ojeda spent most of the balance of the season back in the bullpen. For the season, he appeared in 38 games, starting 12. His record was 7-6 with an ERA of 3.66 as the Mets finished second to the Pittsburgh Pirates.

At the end of the season, Ojeda was traded to the Dodgers along with pitcher Greg Hansel for infielder Hubie Brooks, a one-time Met. In his two years with the Dodgers he was used exclusively as a starter. In 1991 he went 12-9 with a 3.18 ERA. In 1991 he was reunited with two teammates from the 1986 Mets, Darryl Strawberry and Gary Carter. On May 31, it was just like the good old days as the Dodgers defeated Cincinnati 7-4. Strawberry doubled and homered, Carter doubled and threw out two baserunners, and Ojeda pitched the first six innings to get his fourth win of the season—and the Dodgers were in first place! The Dodgers were in the race the entire season, finishing second to the Braves by one game.

In his second year with the Dodgers, Ojeda was less successful. He went 6-9 with a 3.63 ERA. There were flashes of brilliance like his 6-0 shutout of

Cincinnati on April 20, but for the season he had only two complete games. The Dodgers went 63-99 and finished in last place in their division. After the season, Ojeda became a free agent and signed with the Cleveland Indians.

Ojeda was in spring training with the Cleveland Indians when tragedy struck on March 22, 1993. A fishing and boating enthusiast, he went fishing on a scheduled day off from practice with teammates Tim Crews and Steve Olin. As they returned in the early evening darkness, their boat crashed into the dock. Crews and Olin were killed and Ojeda was badly injured. He suffered severe head lacerations and lost nearly four pints of blood. He went away for a bit after getting out of the hospital to grieve and decide what he wanted to do. He did return to the playing field, first with Cleveland at the end of the 1993 season and then as a free-agent pickup with the Yankees, who released him early in the 1994 season. In his 15-year career, Ojeda had a 115-98 record with an ERA of 3.65.

After the Yankees, Ojeda's life took a different path. He stayed away from baseball until 2001, when he became the pitching coach fort the Mets' Brooklyn affiliate in the Class-A New York-Penn League. In 2003 he moved to Double-A Binghamton in 2003 but was unhappy and went back home to New Jersey at the end of the season. In 2009 Ojeda was lured back to baseball, this time as a postgame commentator on the Mets' Network SNY, a position he held through the 2014 season.

SOURCES

In addition to the sources cited in the endnotes, the author also consulted Baseball-Reference.com, the Bob Ojeda file at the National Baseball Hall of Fame.

NOTES

1 Mookie Wilson with Erik Sherman, *Mookie: Life, Baseball, and the '86 Mets* (New York: Berkley Books, 2014), 134.

2 Jeff Pearlman, *The Bad Guys Won!* (New York: Harper Collins, 2004), 5.

3 Pearlman, 44.

4 Pearlman, 156.

5 Steve Harris, "Ojeda Proves the Scouts Wrong on Potential," *Boston Herald-American*, October 6, 1981: 55.

6 *The Sporting News*, July 19, 1980: 53.

7 Mike Scandura, "Inches as Good as a Mile for Ojeda in Boston Debut," *Pawtucket Evening Times*, July 14, 1980.

8 Joe Giuliotti, "Red Sox: Ojeda Arrives," *The Sporting News*, September 12, 1981: 55.

9 Steven Krasner, "Stock Rises for Beefier Ojeda," *The Sporting News*, May 30, 1981: 46.

10 Steven Krasner, "Curtain Falls on 33 Inning Drama," *The Sporting News*, July 11, 1981: 45.

11 Tim Horgan, *Boston Herald-American*, August 10, 1981: B-1.

12 Joe Giuliotti, "Red Sox: Ojeda Arrives," *The Sporting News*, September 12, 1981: 55.

13 Steve Harris, "Frustrated Ojeda Maintains a Positive Pitching Attitude," *Boston Herald-American*, June 29, 1982: 42.

14 Pearlman, 223.

15 Wilson, 137.

16 Bud Harrelson, *Turning Two: My Journey to the Top of the World and Back With the New York Mets* (New York: Thomas Dunne Books, St. Martin's Press, 2012), 194.

17 Joseph Durso, "Darling, Teufel Get Probation; Charges Dismissed for Two Others, *New York Times*, January 27, 1987: A-19.

18 *The Sporting News*, October 6, 1986: 13.

19 Pearlman, 225.

20 Roger Angell, *Once More Around the Park: A Baseball Reader* (New York: Ballantine Books, 1991), 254.

21 Pearlman, 227.

22 Wilson, 189.

23 Angell, 254.

24 Bruce Jenkins, "The Most Boring Series Ever?—Boston Can End it Tonight," *San Francisco Chronicle*, October 25, 1986.

25 Angell, 303.

26 Joseph Durso, "Ojeda's Comeback Provides Met With a Gain in Defeat," *New York Times*, April 6, 1989: D27.

JESSE OROSCO

By Rory Costello

JESSE OROSCO APPEARED IN 1,252 REGULAR-season games during his career, the most of any major-league pitcher. As of Opening Day 2015, the active hurler with the most appearances was LaTroy Hawkins with an even 1,000, so Orosco's record endured for at least some time. The lefty spent most of his 24 seasons in the majors as a specialist. From 1988 until 2003 (when he was 46), Orosco averaged 0.8 innings per game.

His finest moments, however, came during his years as a closer with the New York Mets in the 1980s. When the Mets won the National League pennant in 1986, Orosco won three games in the Championship Series against Houston. He leapt for joy after finishing the grueling 16-inning Game Six that clinched the series. He was also on the mound when Game Seven of the World Series against Boston ended, once again hurling his glove skyward. "If you ever get a chance to throw the last pitch, that's a dream come true," said Orosco in 1987.[1]

Jesse Russell Orosco was born on April 21, 1957, in Santa Barbara, California. His father, Raymond Orosco, was a native of Austin, Texas. Ray's parents, who were of Mexican origin, moved their family from Texas to Michigan before settling in the town of Goleta, right next to Santa Barbara, in the 1940s.[2] Ray worked in construction, including at the University of California, Santa Barbara. He had a chance to play professional baseball but chose family life instead.[3]

Ray's wife, Tomasa Mata, was born in Mexico and came to California when she was young. Jesse was the fifth of her seven children.[4] He had an older brother named Raymond Jr. and five sisters.[5]

Tomasa Orosco tried for a while to make a right-hander out of little Jesse when he was first sitting up to eat. "We would give him his plate," she said, "and he would reach for the spoon with his left hand. I took it away and put it in his right hand. But he immediately switched back to the left hand. Finally we just let him go. We realized we had a left-hander."[6]

The southpaw showed talent at a young age. "Ever since I was a little tot, my plan was to play in the majors," he said in 1999.[7] Previously, his mother had said, "Jesse started at 6 years old on a baseball team with the Boys' Club in Santa Barbara. He was supposed to be 7 years old. But my husband and the manager of the Boys' Club got him in. He was a good pitcher then."[8]

As *Sports Illustrated* wrote in 1983, "Raymond Orosco Sr. had a powerful influence on his son's life. He had founded and funded, pitched and played first base for a semipro team called the Santa Barbara Jets. 'He bought the bats and balls and uniforms,' says Tomasa, who kept score at the Jets' games. 'I sewed on all the words.' Jesse and Raymond Jr. were batboys, while the five Orosco daughters sold sno-cones and tickets to

raise money for the churches and charities the team supported."[9]

Ray Orosco also managed the Jets. In addition, he sponsored and played for a team called the Goleta Merchants. Furthermore, he maintained Laguna Park Stadium in Santa Barbara.[10] When Jesse was a boy, the Santa Barbara Rancheros (a Mets farm club) played there from 1961 through 1963; then the Santa Barbara Dodgers were there from 1964 through 1967.[11]

Orosco, who grew to a height of 6-feet-2, went to Santa Barbara High School and went on to Santa Barbara City College. In 2000 the city's Athletic Round Table made him a member of its Hall of Fame.

In 1977 the St. Louis Cardinals made Orosco their seventh-round pick in the January phase of the amateur draft. He did not sign, but he did the following January, when the Minnesota Twins took him in the second round. Orosco played rookie ball in the Appalachian League in 1978. He was impressive in 20 relief outings, posting a 1.12 ERA and striking out 48 batters in 40 innings. He then put up a 0.26 ERA in the Instructional League and earned the label of top southpaw prospect in Minnesota's farm system.[12]

Orosco became a Met in February 1979. He was the player to be named later in the deal that sent Jerry Koosman, one of the heroes of the Mets' 1969 World Series champions and 1973 NL pennant winners, to the Twins. Despite his lack of experience, Orosco went to spring training with the big club as a nonroster invitee. Mets beat writer Jack Lang said, "He is a couple of years away."[13]

Nonetheless, Orosco made it all the way to New York. It did not hurt that two veteran lefties, Kevin Kobel and Bob Myrick, were on the disabled list—but later that summer, Jack Lang wrote that the franchise's parsimony at the time was also a factor. "[General manager Joe] McDonald and the people at the Mets who count pennies shoved Neil Allen, Mike Scott and Jesse Orosco down [Joe] Torre's throat. ... They just weren't ready this year."[14] Torre, who was then the Mets' manager, allegedly vowed that he would never again rush a young pitcher the same way.[15]

The rookie pitched well in limited opportunities during April and early May, but he then hit a rocky patch. The Mets gave Orosco two starts in June but sent him down to Triple-A Tidewater after obtaining veteran lefty Andy Hassler. Orosco started in 15 out of his 16 appearances for the Tides. He stepped down to Double A for all of 1980, but was back in the bullpen, starting just once in 37 outings. Returning to Tidewater in 1981, he was a part-time starter (10 starts in 47 appearances). New York recalled Orosco in September 1981, and he did not appear again in the minors until 2000, when he served an injury-rehab assignment.

During this period, Orosco also gained experience in winter ball. For three seasons (1980-81 through 1982-83), he played in Venezuela for Tiburones de La Guaira. In 69 total games, he was 6-6 with a 1.92 ERA and five saves. He also pitched in the playoffs each year; the Sharks became league champions in 1982-83.

In 1982 the Mets focused Orosco on the bullpen for good—his two starts that summer were his last in the majors. George Vecsey of the *New York Times* quoted Bill Monbouquette, who was New York's pitching coach in 1982: "He'd go four innings and his ball would drop into the 70s. We thought Jesse should be a relief pitcher, and we could see Jesse was pitching defensively. It wasn't exactly fear of the bat, but he was nibbling. You're not going to get the calls from the umpire that way and you're not going to finish off the batter that way." Monbouquette added, "We dug into him. It wasn't exactly an ultimatum, but we told him he could be a good relief pitcher if he learned to attack the hitters."[16]

The key part of "we" was George Bamberger, a former pitcher and pitching coach, who managed the Mets from 1982 until June 1983. As Vecsey wrote that month, "Orosco believes Bamberger turned him around, kept him in the majors, taught him a slider, taught him tenacity." Technical teaching from "Bambi," including a higher arm angle on the slider, was certainly important—but the confidence he instilled was something for which Orosco was even more thankful.[17]

On August 16, 1982, Raymond Orosco Sr. died of a heart attack on his construction job.[18] He was just 55. Tomasa recalled, "At the funeral Jesse told me, 'Mom, Dad got me this far, and I'm going to work harder for him and you.' But I didn't know he was going to work this hard."[19] The southpaw continued to develop with the Mets that summer. His won-lost record was 4-10, but he posted a 2.72 ERA in 54 games, striking out 89 men in 109⅓ innings.

Orosco viewed the game of September 10, 1982, as a key juncture in his career. At St. Louis, with two outs in the seventh inning, he relieved Craig Swan with runners on first and second and the Mets leading 1-0. He got the third out, and the Mets added an insurance run. In the ninth inning, Keith Hernandez—who came to New York the following summer—hit a home run. Two outs later, Gene Tenace walked. "Any other manager might have taken me out," Orosco said. But Bamberger told him that it was his game to save, and Jesse retired Ozzie Smith to finish it.[20]

Other teams again wanted Orosco in trade, but the Mets did not want to deal him. It was a wise choice. Orosco's work paid off even more handsomely in 1983, when he had his best overall season and perhaps the best of any reliever in Mets history. "Strikes, confidence, concentration—I've got it all right now," he said that May. "I'm sky-high!"[21] He pitched a career-high 110 innings in 62 games, posting a remarkable 1.47 ERA. His 13 wins—which included both ends of a doubleheader on July 31—were also a single-season best, and he lost just seven while posting 17 saves. Orosco was named to the NL All-Star team and struck out the only batter he faced, Ben Oglivie. He finished third in the voting for the NL Cy Young Award.

Orosco was an NL All-Star again in 1984, though he did not get into the game. His 31 saves were by far his best one-season total, and he was 10-6 with a 2.59 ERA.

In December 1984, Orosco married Leticia Banda, a native of East Los Angeles. He met her one day while he was in the bullpen at Dodger Stadium. "It was the first game I ever went to," Leticia remembered in 1988. "My girlfriend dragged me there. I was just a spectator and we met by chance."[22] The Oroscos had three children: Jesse Jr., Natalie, and Alyssa. Jesse Jr. became a 38th-round draft pick of the Arizona Diamondbacks in 2008. He pitched in the low minors in 2008 and 2009, and continued in independent leagues as late as 2011.

Orosco's save total dipped to 17 in 1985. Early that year, he had some elbow problems and struggled before righting himself (he finished the season at 8-6, 2.73). That August, manager Davey Johnson said, "I might have babied him a little too much earlier. He had a time, earlier on in the season, when he was successful only about half the time on his save situations. He wasn't winning the matchups he would normally win."[23]

That remark showed how bullpen management was continuing to evolve in the 1980s. At that point, bullpens were smaller and not as specialized as they became over time. The distinction between setup men, situational relievers, and the closer had not yet developed fully. Doug Sisk, a righty, got 11 saves in 1983 and 15 in 1984. Then in 1985, rookie Roger McDowell, also a righty, emerged. McDowell equaled Orosco's 17 saves. In his book about the 1985 season, *Bats*, Davey Johnson referred to how McDowell replaced Sisk as his number one right-handed short man. It was not uncommon then to see co-closers.

At that time, top relievers were also still often deployed as "firemen" rather than coming in with bases empty at the start of the ninth. Against Philadelphia at Shea Stadium on August 13, the Mets were up 4-1 in the eighth inning, but the Phillies loaded the bases with three singles off Rick Aguilera. Orosco came in with nobody out. He retired Ozzie Virgil on a harmless sacrifice fly, got Hall of Famer Mike Schmidt to pop out, and struck out Von Hayes. A scoreless ninth inning followed.

Orosco was unflappable on the mound. Looking back in 2014, he said, "I had nerves a lot of the time, but I embraced the pressure and loved it."[24] The calm that Orosco projected influenced perceptions. Davey

Johnson later said, "I don't think he looks at every situation as life and death, and that's what a reliever has to do."[25]

The McDowell-Orosco tandem remained very effective in 1986. McDowell had 22 saves and Orosco had 21—marking the third of six times as of 2015 that a big-league team has had two pitchers with 20 or more saves in a season.[26]

A unique instance of how Johnson juggled the two—and an indication of Orosco's athleticism—came on July 22 in an extra-inning game at Cincinnati's Riverfront Stadium. Orosco was on the mound in the 10th inning when Eric Davis of the Reds slid hard into Ray Knight while stealing third base. A fight broke out between them and it erupted into a 15-minute bench-clearing brawl. Knight and Kevin Mitchell were ejected, so Gary Carter had to fill in at third base. Darryl Strawberry had previously been ejected too. Thus, one out later, Orosco went to right field and McDowell relieved him. With two out in the 11th, Orosco returned to the hill to face lefty Max Venable, prompting a protest from Reds manager Pete Rose, who contended that Orosco should not have been allowed to warm up. Jesse finished out that inning and threw a scoreless 12th. He then went back to right field for the 13th inning—cleanly handling a liner from Tony Pérez—and the 14th, when McDowell (who had earlier played both right and left field) got three outs to end the game.

"I hoped the game would last 20 innings," Orosco said. "We were having a lot of fun."[27] Though born of necessity, Johnson's maneuvering would have made Paul Richards proud.[28] Orosco never got another chance to play a different position, but he often helped himself with his fielding on the mound—his reflexes were excellent.

Only twice during the 1986 regular season did Orosco pitch as many as three innings in a game. His third three-inning effort that year came in Game Six of the NL Championship Series against Houston, the 16-inning battle royal. Ideally, it would have been a straightforward one-inning save, but Billy Hatcher's home run extended the game. "Orosco watched the ball sail into the left-field foul pole, fighting his anger. 'I told myself, 'It's not over. Not yet.'"[29]

By the time that outing was done, Orosco was running on fumes, having faced 14 batters and thrown 54 pitches. When the last batter, Kevin Bass, came to the plate, Doug Sisk (a.k.a. "Doug Risk") was warming up. The only other available option was Randy Niemann, who didn't appear at all that postseason. As coach Bud Harrelson wrote, "This was going to be Orosco's game, win or lose."[30]

"I was tired," Orosco confirmed when interviewed for an episode of the MLB Network show *MLB's 20 Greatest Games*. "I was just trying to make those pitches. In that time of the moment, you just have to reach back and get everything you have inside you and go for it."[31] Of course, the situation imposed mental as well as physical demands. "Was Orosco nervous? Could any human not be? 'Sure I was,' he said. 'But I told myself, 'You have the ball. You have the power. Don't let these guys down."[32]

Orosco was the first reliever to win three games in a postseason series, and he remains the only one to do so. He had no decisions in the 1986 World Series, but he did get two saves. In Game Seven he entered with the tying run on second and nobody out in the eighth inning. He later admitted to being nervous again. "I wasn't thinking about baseball. I was looking for the bathroom. … I just told myself, 'Stay within yourself, this is no time to fold.'"[33] The image of him after recording the last out—on his knees with arms and face thrust to the heavens—is one of the most memorable in Mets history.

Less well remembered, though, is how Orosco drove in the final run of the Series. In a rare plate appearance—just his eighth of the year—he came up with runners on first and second. On NBC-TV, Joe Garagiola said, "I'd almost bet the house that he's gonna bunt." Orosco did show bunt on the first pitch, a ball. He had squared on the second pitch too—but drew back his bat and chopped a single, prompting Vin Scully to say, "Joe, you just lost your house!"[34]

"We didn't have anything going on in the early '80s, took our licks the first few years," Orosco said upon his retirement. "That was great, that was very memorable, to go from the worst to the best." Only Mookie Wilson and Wally Backman had longer consecutive service in the Mets organization, and they both first reached the majors in 1980.[35]

Whether Orosco's glove ever came down after he threw it up to celebrate the end of the Series was the subject of jokes. What really happened, though, was that he donated it as part of a drive to support New York City policeman Steven McDonald, an avid Mets fan who'd been paralyzed by a gunshot while on duty.[36] Orosco also became known for buying and donating hundreds of tickets so that children from broken homes could enjoy a day at a big-league ballpark.[37]

The 1987 season was not a happy one for Orosco. He had 16 saves (the last time he reached double digits in this category) but was 3-9 with a 4.44 ERA. His performance brought him into disfavor with Davey Johnson—his agent, Alan Meersand, described it as "a real cold war"—and with the New York fans, who went so far as to subject him to death threats.[38] Orosco asked for a trade, and that December he went to the Los Angeles Dodgers as part of a three-way deal that also involved the Oakland A's.

On March 3, 1988, during spring training, an Orosco prank became memorable. He daubed eye black inside the cap of another new Dodger, ultra-intense outfielder Kirk Gibson, who wiped his forehead and smudged the stuff all over his arm. As their teammates laughed, Gibson left angrily. But when he returned to camp the next day, he said, "I'm the best teammate you'll ever have, you just don't realize it yet." As Gibson further recalled in 2010, "From that point on, we went out there and got after it. We were world champions and nobody picked us to do so."[39]

On the way to winning the other World Series ring of his career, Orosco was 3-2, 2.72 in 55 games. He picked up nine saves, third on the team behind Jay Howell and Alejandro Peña. Howell, who had come to Los Angeles in the same three-way deal, was originally viewed as Orosco's righty co-closer.[40] As it developed, though, Dodgers manager Tom Lasorda reduced Jesse's role. In the playoffs, Orosco faced his old team, the Mets. He allowed two earned runs in 2⅓ innings across four games, getting no decisions. He did not appear in the five-game upset of the Oakland A's.

After the 1988 season, the Dodgers let Orosco—"widely perceived to be over the hill," according to Peter Gammons in *Sports Illustrated*—walk into free agency.[41] He signed with the Cleveland Indians and spent three seasons there. He was most effective in 1989, striking out 79 men in 78 innings with a 2.08 ERA. His second year with the Tribe, 1990, was the last time in his career that his innings pitched total exceeded his number of appearances. However, "everything seemed to hit the wall for me in my second year in Cleveland," Orosco recalled in 1994. "One day I almost quit and didn't go to the park. My wife talked me into hanging with it."[42]

As the *Toledo Blade* wrote in 1996, those were "lean times for the franchise. Eventually, the veteran reliever got his wish and was traded to Milwaukee after the 1991 season."[43] To illustrate Orosco's discontent, after the deal Alan Meersand quipped, "Terry Anderson [the American journalist who'd been held captive in Lebanon for nearly seven years] wasn't the last hostage freed—it was Jesse Orosco, from the bondage of the Cleveland Indians."[44]

Orosco spent three seasons with the Brewers too. He loved it in Milwaukee—how he was treated and how manager Phil Garner told him what his role would be. "I felt like part of the team again," he said. He revived his career in 1992 as a setup man and re-emerged as a closer in the second half of 1993, getting eight saves after Doug Henry lost the job.[45]

General manager Sal Bando viewed Orosco as an interim solution, though, saying, "It's unrealistic to ask Jesse to be that guy all year."[46] Thus the veteran was back in his situational role in 1994. It was a down year for him—his ERA was 5.08 in 40 appearances, and he blew all four of his save chances. Even in August, a few days after the historic players' strike had begun, the Milwaukee press wrote that he was not expected back.[47] He became a free agent that October.

Five years with the Baltimore Orioles then followed. Orosco signed in April 1995, not long after the crippling strike had ended. He led the American League with 65 appearances that year, a figure that is quite low by today's standards.[48] Two years later, he reached a personal single-season high with 71. The Orioles reached the postseason in both 1996 and 1997, managed by Davey Johnson. In both years Orosco pitched in the AL Division Series and AL Championship Series.

By that time, the tension between Johnson and Orosco was a thing of the past. When Baltimore hired Johnson, Orosco noted how the skipper was central to the Mets' turnaround in the mid-1980s.[49] During the 1996 playoffs, both men expressed their faith in each other.[50]

Approaching his 40s, rigorous offseason conditioning and his knowledge of hitters kept Orosco in the game. Ray Miller, Baltimore's pitching coach in 1997, said, "He's got a great body and excellent agility." Miller added, "He's very relaxed under pressure and very confident. No matter how old a guy is, that's what you want to see out there."[51]

On August 17, 1999, Orosco broke the record for games pitched in the major leagues, then held by Dennis Eckersley. Appearance number 1,072 came at Baltimore's Camden Yards. In the stands was Tomasa Orosco, along with Leticia, Natalie, and Alyssa. Twelve-year-old Jesse Jr. served as batboy and sat beside Ray Miller, who had become manager. Orosco retired lefty swinger Todd Walker on two pitches and his work was done for the night. Jesse Jr. ran out to greet his father, who noted the anniversary of Ray Orosco Sr.'s death the previous day.[52]

In December 1999 the Orioles traded Orosco to the Mets for Chuck McElroy. The veteran waived his 10-and-5 rights, in part because Baltimore's new manager was Mike Hargrove, and they had not seen eye to eye in Cleveland. Orosco never got a chance to pitch for New York again—although he was excited about the opportunity—because the Mets sent him on to the St. Louis Cardinals for Joe McEwing the following March.[53] He got into just six games that year for St. Louis, three in April and three in June. A sore elbow landed him on the disabled list twice; the torn flexor muscle wound up requiring surgery. It was the only serious injury of his career.

In the spring of 2001, Orosco returned to Los Angeles. Teammate Mike Fetters, whom Orosco had mentored with the Brewers, said, "As soon as I heard his arm was fine, I knew he was going to make this team because nothing about Jesse has changed from his first day in the big leagues until now, he's just more polished."[54]

As it turned out, the Dodgers released Orosco at the end of March 2001—but in late April, they re-signed him to a minor-league contract. He pitched in 10 games for Triple-A Las Vegas and was back with LA by late May. He appeared 35 times for the Dodgers over the remainder of 2001 and 56 more in 2002, after he signed another one-year deal. That April, he said, "They're joking about me still being in the big leagues, and I'm glad I'm still around so they can joke about it. I've probably heard them all by now. … It doesn't bother me at all because it's all in good fun."[55]

Orosco and the Dodgers parted ways after the 2002 season. That November he signed with the San Diego Padres, an attractive team because they were close to his home. In spring training 2003, Jeff Pearlman—author of the '86 Mets chronicle *The Bad Guys Won*—described for *Sports Illustrated* how Orosco had adapted as a pitcher over the years. "When his velocity dropped off, he depended more on his slider, and when his slider began to flatten, he picked up a split-finger changeup that has become his out pitch."[56] A little later that season, another article noted Orosco's "wicked changeup" while also observing that he used a cutter more often and knew how to spot his "still decent" fastball. "You always need to make adjustments in this game," he said.[57]

Orosco got into 42 games as a Padre in 2003, recording the last two of his 144 major-league saves. That July the New York Yankees obtained the 46-year-old. Jesse was reunited with his first big-league skipper, Joe

Torre, and his pitching coach with the Mets in the mid-1980s, Mel Stottlemyre. "He continues to pitch and he continues to have a passion for it," said Torre.[58]

Orosco pitched 4⅓ innings in 15 games for the Yankees before they traded him to his original organization, Minnesota. He made his last eight appearances in the majors with the Twins that September. They included his last of 87 big-league wins (against 80 losses) on September 24.

In November 2003, Orosco signed a minor-league deal with the Arizona Diamondbacks. That winter, though, he found that he'd lost the excitement to get going. He told Leticia, "I just don't think I have it in me to get prepared this year." In January 2004 he retired.[59]

For most of the following decade, Orosco enjoyed a life of leisure, watching his children grow up and playing lots of golf. In 2011, however, he wanted to get back in baseball. He didn't seek a coaching job in the minors or indie ball, so he took a position with the San Diego branch of the Frozen Ropes baseball and softball training centers, close to his home in Carmel Valley.[60] Daughter Natalie later joined the clinic as a softball instructor. As of 2015, though Jesse was no longer with Frozen Ropes, he remained active in teaching kids how to pitch.[61]

Jesse Orosco frequently said that he would have been happy playing just several years in the majors. He didn't make it to age 50, as was often speculated, or to 47, his longstanding uniform number. But only five men have pitched in more seasons as a major leaguer.[62] His arm was a great natural gift, but he worked very hard to stay in shape. Affordability was also a factor; the most Orosco ever made in one season was $1.215 million. A strong mental approach—with a boost from his supportive family—helped a lot too.

The bottom line, though, was effectiveness. During his career, batters hit just .223 against Orosco, with an on-base percentage of .309, a slugging percentage of .335—and not that marked a difference between lefties and righties.[63] He summed it up nicely in 1999: "What I'm most happy about is the fact that I've been able to be out there every day. The manager knows I'll be there. There have been some ups and downs but I've been pretty consistent over the course of more than 1,000 games."[64]

SOURCES

purapelota.com (Venezuelan statistics).

frozenropes.com.

ancestry.com.

NOTES

1 George Vecsey, "Sports of the Times: Jesse Orosco and the Law of Gravity," *New York Times*, February 23, 1987.

2 Obituary of Jesse Orosco's aunt, Simona Orosco Manriquez, *Santa Barbara News-Press*, November 19, 2014.

3 Richard A. Santillán, *Mexican American Baseball in the Central Coast* (Charleston, South Carolina: Arcadia Press, 2013), 66.

4 Gordon S. White Jr., "Orosco, a Golden Arm in Met Bullpen," *New York Times*, August 10, 1983.

5 E.M. Swift, "Oh, what a relief he is," *Sports Illustrated*, September 5, 1983.

6 White, "Orosco, a Golden Arm in Met Bullpen."

7 David Ginsburg, "Baltimore's Orosco just keeps throwing strikes," Associated Press, June 29, 1999.

8 White, "Orosco, A Golden Arm in Met Bullpen."

9 White, "Orosco, A Golden Arm in Met Bullpen."

10 Santillán, *Mexican American Baseball in the Central Coast*, 66.

11 Barney Brantingham, "The Short, Happy Life of Laguna Ball Park," *Santa Barbara Independent*, May 5, 2011.

12 Jack Lang, "Mets' Farm Crop Fails to Yield Bat Prospects," *The Sporting News*, February 24, 1979: 36. Bob Fowler, "Fast-Dealing Twins' Target: Ivie," *The Sporting News*, February 24, 1979: 43.

13 Lang, "Mets' Farm Crop Fails to Yield Bat Prospects."

14 Jack Lang, "Mets Get Two Vets to Replace Kid Hurlers," *The Sporting News*, June 30, 1979: 27.

15 Swift, "Oh, what a relief he is."

16 George Vecsey, "Orosco Says Thank You," *New York Times*, June 15, 1983.

17 Vecsey, "Orosco Says Thank You."

18 Vecsey, "Orosco Says Thank You."

19 Swift, "Oh, what a relief he is."

20 Vecsey, "Orosco Says Thank You." Jack Lang, "All-Star Orosco Credits Bamberger," *The Sporting News*, July 11, 1983: 15.

21 Bruce Lowitt, "Mets rally past Cincy," Associated Press, May 9, 1983.

22 Dick Young, "Vegas bookie picks Washington," *New York Post*, January 4, 1985. Sam McManis, "They Wanted Out to Escape Doubts," *Los Angeles Times*, February 23, 1988.

23 "Mets trip Phils for 9th in row," Associated Press, August 14, 1985.

24 Facebook Q&A with Jesse Orosco, organized by the New York Mets, August 15, 2014.

25 Josh Robbins, "Orosco Still Has Something Left," *Orlando Sentinel*, May 13, 2002.

26 The other pairs: Eddie Fisher and Hoyt Wilhelm (1965 Chicago White Sox); Greg Minton and Gary Lavelle (1983 San Francisco Giants); Tom Henke and Duane Ward (1991 Toronto Blue Jays); Norm Charlton and Rob Dibble (1992 Cincinnati Reds); Matt Lindstrom and Brandon Lyon (2010 Houston Astros).

27 "Tuesday night fights," Associated Press, July 24, 1986.

28 Indeed, "the proviso prohibiting pitchers from assuming a position other than pitcher more than once in the same inning was added to Rule 3.03 largely to thwart managers like Paul Richards." David Nemec, *The Official Rules of Baseball Illustrated* (Guilford, Connecticut: The Lyons Press, 2006), 39.

29 Bob Klapisch, "Clincher Is One for the Books," in *The Amazin's* (Chicago: Triumph Books, 2011), 111.

30 Bud Harrelson with Phil Pepe, *Turning Two* (New York: St. Martin's Press, 2012), 203.

31 Episode 16, MLB's 20 Greatest Games, originally aired April 17, 2011.

32 *The Amazin's*, 111.

33 "Orosco Admits Nervousness," Knight News Service, October 28, 1986.

34 The broadcast is preserved in various ways, one being *The New York Mets 1986 World Series Collector's Edition* DVD.

35 It's also noteworthy that Lee Mazzilli was the Mets' first-round draft pick in 1973 and returned in August 1986 after being traded away in 1982.

36 Robert McG. Thomas Jr. and Gerald Eskenazi, "This Mitt Calls for a Big Hand," *New York Times*, February 25, 1987.

37 "Jesse Orosco," Santa Barbara Athletic Roundtable web page (sbroundtable.org/hall-of-fame/inductees/athletes/jesse-orosco/).

38 Sam McManis, "They Wanted Out to Escape Doubts," *Los Angeles Times*, February 23, 1988.

39 Dylan Hernandez, "Arizona's Kirk Gibson pulls no punches," *Los Angeles Times*, July 3, 2010.

40 McManis, "They Wanted Out to Escape Doubts."

41 Peter Gammons, "And Here We Go Again," *Sports Illustrated*, December 19, 1988. Ben Walker, "Trade talks remain the highlights," Associated Press, December 4, 1988.

42 Tom Haudricourt, "Team Player: Orosco thankful for opportunity to help Brewers," *Milwaukee Sentinel*, April 1, 1994: 1B.

43 "Ex-Indian Orosco struggles," *Toledo Blade*, October 5, 1996: 26.

44 Tom FitzGerald, "Some memorable quotes from 1991," *San Francisco Chronicle*, January 3, 1992.

45 Haudricourt, "Team Player: Orosco thankful for opportunity to help Brewers."

46 Tom Haudricourt, "Construction ahead: Bando says bullpen will get overhaul," *Milwaukee Sentinel*, October 1, 1993: 1B.

47 Tom Haudricourt, "Brewers' roster includes others with shaky futures," *Milwaukee Sentinel*, August 15, 1994.

48 No one has led either the American or National League with fewer than 75 appearances since 1995.

49 Brad Snyder, "O's players won over by Johnson's success," *Baltimore Sun*, October 31, 1995.

50 Elliott Teaford, "Johnson Shows Faith in Orosco," *Los Angeles Times*, October 6, 1996.

51 David Ginsburg, "Orosco: Still going strong...," Associated Press, March 5, 1997.

52 Joe Strauss, "Orosco pitches in for record," *Baltimore Sun*, August 18, 1999.

53 Ben Walker, "Newly arrived Met traded again," Associated Press, March 19, 2000.

54 Jason Reid, "Colborn Likes What He Sees From Orosco," *Los Angeles Times*, March 16, 2001.

55 Jason Reid, "Old Faithful," *Los Angeles Times*, April 21, 2002.

56 Jeff Pearlman, "Old Reliable," *Sports Illustrated*, March 10, 2003.

57 Tom Haudricourt, "Lasting Relief," *Milwaukee Sentinel*, May 21, 2003: 1C.

58 Mark Hale, "Seems Like Old Times—Newest Yankee Orosco Reunited with Mel, Torre," *New York Post*, July 24, 2003.

59 "Lefty's record: 1,252 pitching appearances," Associated Press, January 21, 2004.

60 Brian Hiro, "Shooting the Breeze: A Q&A with former major league pitcher Jesse Orosco," *San Diego Union-Tribune*, September 23, 2012.

61 Facebook Q&A with Jesse Orosco, August 15, 2014.

62 Nolan Ryan (27), Tommy John (26), Jim Kaat, Charlie Hough, and Jamie Moyer (25).

63 Lefty slash line: .210/.287/.301. Righty slash line: .229/.320/.353.

64 Ginsburg, "Baltimore's Orosco just keeps throwing strikes."

RAFAEL SANTANA

By Leslie Heaphy

STANDING AT 6-FEET-1 AND WEIGHING ONLY 165 pounds during his playing days, Rafael Santana may not have been a big man but he played big for the New York Mets when they needed him to. Santana did not carry a big bat but he fielded his shortstop position with flair at times. Some of Santana's best numbers came in the Mets' 1986 championship season when he said, "We had the best chemistry."[1]

Born on January 31, 1958, in La Romana, Dominican Republic, Rafael Francisco Santana played in the majors for seven seasons. He spent the majority of his career with the Mets but also spent time with the Yankees, Cardinals, and Indians. Little is recorded about his life before he came to the United States to play baseball. He got his chance in professional baseball after being scouted in winter ball by scout Eddy Toledo.[2]

Santana was originally signed by the New York Yankees as an amateur free agent in 1976 at the age of 18. He played for Oneonta, Fort Lauderdale, and Nashville in the Yankees' minor-league system from 1977 to 1980. His best year as a Yankee farmhand came in 1979 when he hit .263 in 133 games at Class-A Fort Lauderdale. He was traded by the Yankees to the Cardinals in February 1981 for a player to be named later, who turned out to be pitcher George Frazier. Santana played for 2 ½ years for Cardinals' Double-A and Triple-A teams. His best season while in the St. Louis system came in 1982 with Louisville. He played in 121 games and hit .286, scored 65 runs and knocked in 53. He made only 11 errors in the field while splitting time at second base, shortstop, and third base.

Santana made his major-league debut with the Cardinals on Opening Day 1983 against the Pittsburgh Pirates, going 0-for-1 in the game after entering as a late-inning defensive replacement in a 7-1 loss. He did not get much of a chance to play in St. Louis because Ozzie Smith was the Cardinals' shortstop. After playing in just 30 of the Cardinals' first 72 games, with only 17 plate appearances to show for his time, Santana was sent back to Triple-A Louisville, where he spent the balance of the season.

The Cardinals released Santana on January 17, 1984, and the Mets picked him up as a free agent that same day. He remained with the club through the 1987 season. When he learned that the slick young shortstop was available, Mets manager Davey Johnson reportedly exclaimed, "Hell, yes, I like him. Sign him."[3]

In Santana's first full season with the Mets, 1984, he backed up starting shortstop Jose Oquendo and hit .271 in 51 games. During one 1984 game against the Pirates, manager Chuck Tanner raved about a play Santana made, saying it was an impossible catch but somehow Santana made the grab. Santana missed two weeks late in the season when he went on the

disabled list with a lacerated right thumb. He proved to be durable in the long run, though; this was his only stint on the DL until he hurt his elbow toward the end of 1988 and had to have Tommy John surgery in 1989.[4] The Mets traded Oquendo away after the 1984 season, entrusting the shortstop position to Santana. The 27-year-old Santana had his best season at the plate in 1985. He hit a career-high .257 in a career-high 154 games. He also showed that he would not provide much power at the plate, though he did hit one home run that season. When the Mets beat the Phillies 10-6 Santana provided some of the pop. "I hit a home run a year, but when I hit it, I hit it good," he said.[5]

As the starter in 1986, Santana hit only .218 but he had some worth to the club as he batted in the eighth spot in the lineup. Hitting right in front of the Mets pitchers, Santana had 12 intentional walks, tying him for 10th in the NL. One of his highlights came on August 26 when the Mets pounded the Padres, 11-6. Santana's contribution was his first home run of the season and only the third in his career. He almost hit a second homer in the same game but a catch by Kevin McReynolds on the warning track ended that brief power surge. Santana's best fielding percentage was .973 in both 1986 and 1987. He made just 16 and 17 errors respectively those seasons. With these numbers and his range, Santana was considered a solid defensive player. More importantly, Santana proved a steadying influence on a team known for its fire and its antics. Santana simply wanted to play and win. One reporter described him as "a quiet and pivotal piece of the '86 Mets." In the National League Championship Series against Houston, Santana set an NL record for most putouts (13) and assists (18) in a six-game series as a shortstop. During the World Series win over Boston, Santana hit .250 with five hits in 20 at-bats and three runs scored.[6] He thought the overall 1986 year was a bit boring compared with previous seasons because of the Mets' large lead in the pennant race. He said, "It's nice to have a big lead. But I missed that. I liked the pressure. Last year I'd wake up and the first thing I'd think about was, how are we going to win tonight? This year the first thing I think of is breakfast."[7] Santana's most productive hitting came in 1987 when he hit .255 with 5 home runs and knocked in 44 runs in 139 games. The Mets needed his glove in the lineup every day and got a little boost with his bat. The Mets, however, traded Santana in the offseason.

The 1988 season found Santana across town playing for the Yankees after being traded for prospects Steve Frey, Phil Lombardi, and Darren Reed. The trade to the Yankees came because the Mets wanted to give Kevin Elster a chance to be the everyday shortstop. For Santana that meant no more everyday playing, so he was excited for the trade. Yankees manager Billy Martin wanted Santana because Wayne Tolleson was recovering from shoulder surgery. Santana was happy to be back with the Yankees organization as he had fond memories of his opportunity with the club. Recalling his days in the Yankees farm system, he said, "My locker was there, in that corner. I was just a kid, and it felt strange because it was my first time in a big-league camp. But I was happy to be here; to join all the guys and meet someone like Reggie Jackson."[8] Santana had one claim to fame that season as the Yankees made their playoff run. He was lifted for a pinch-hitter more times (40) than anyone else in the majors. Santana did prove durable for the Yankees, however, playing much of the season with bone chips in his elbow. In fact George Steinbrenner said, "I'd love to have Santana on my football team."[9] Unfortunately for Santana, he missed the entire 1989 season after having elbow surgery.

After the Yankees released Santana at the end of the 1989 season, he signed a free-agent contract with the Cleveland Indians, the final stop in his major-league career. With the Indians he had a chance to reunite with three of his teammates from the 1986 championship Mets,Keith Hernandez, Stan Jefferson, and Jesse Orosco. Santana played only seven games with the Indians, who had the youngster Felix Fermin as their everyday shortstop. Santana had a tough time holding on to a starting spot in his career as teams were always looking to someone younger who they hoped would provide more offense.[10]

After his playing career ended, Santana went into scouting and managing. His managing stints include the Azucareros del Este in the Dominican Republic (1992-93), the Single-A Winston-Salem Warthogs (2006), and the Double-A Birmingham Barons (2007). Santana's managerial stint with the Warthogs was his first in the United States. His two years managing in the United States resulted in a .460 winning percentage in 278 games. Santana also spent four seasons coaching in the Kansas City Royals' minor-league system. He joined the Boston Red Sox organization in 1996 and spent parts of three years overseeing their Dominican program and working as an infield instructor for their Class-A team in Lowell.

Santana joined the White Sox in 1999 and as of 2015 was the Dominican Republic scouting and player-development supervisor for the club, after working as an infield instructor and first-base coach. One of the players he kept an eye on was his son Alex who was drafted by the Los Angeles Dodgers in the second round in 2011.[11] While working with the Dominican program, Santana became aware of some irregularities. He learned about the financial exploitation of young Latin players in 2008. Santana reported to White Sox owner Jerry Reinsdorf that the senior director of player personnel, David Wilder, was involved in kickbacks from signing bonuses and contract buyouts. Wilder was Santana's direct boss. In addition to launching an internal investigation, Reinsdorf informed the league and it began an investigation as well. Wilder was fired along with two Yankee scouts and one Red Sox scout for their roles.[12]

Santana and his wife, Gloria, have two other children, Audry and Dhayan. Audry was drafted in the 38th round by the White Sox and played 18 games at the Rookie League level in 2013 and 2014. Santana often returned to New York for Mets events and said fans still recognize him. He told a New York sportswriter he loved playing in the city and felt appreciated by the fans. Santana said he got the most out of his playing career, which is all anyone can ask for. He did not want to look back with any regrets and said he had none. Seven years in the majors and a World Series ring is not a bad career.[13]

NOTES

1 Anthony McCarron, "Where Are They Now: Rafael Santana," *New York Daily News*, June 17, 2015.

2 Santana Player File, National Baseball Hall of Fame, Cooperstown, New York.

3 *The Sporting News*, February 25, 1985.

4 Craig Barnes, "Santana Mad About Surgery Prospects," *Sun-Sentinel* (Fort Lauderdale, Florida), March 23, 1989.

5 "Santana Gives Mets Big Boost," *Ocala* (Florida) *Star Banner*, April 18, 1985.

6 Tom Friend, "Padres Can't Get Anybody Out," *Los Angeles Times*, August 27, 1986; Santana Player File, National Baseball Hall of Fame.

7 Howard Burman, *Season of Ghosts: The '86 Mets and the Red Sox* (Jefferson, North Carolina: McFarland Publishing, 2012), 260.

8 "Santana Still Loves New York," *The Day* (New London, Connecticut), February 28, 1988.

9 "Stats Entertainment," *The Sporting Life*, March 27, 1989; Ira Berkow, *Summers at Shea* (Chicago: Triumph Books, 2013).

10 "Met Shortstop Santana Traded to the Yankees," *Los Angeles Times*, December 12, 1987; Craig Barnes, "Santana, Old City, New Home," *Sun-Sentinel* (Fort Lauderdale, Florida), February 26, 1988.

11 "Barons Manager Not Returning," *Birmingham* (Alabama) *News*, October 3, 2007; "Santana to Make Managerial Debut with the Warthogs," oursportscentral.com/services/releases/?id=3259455, January 16, 2006.

12 James Warren, "Whistle-Blower Shows Courage at Center of White Sox Kickback Scheme," *New York Times*, December 4, 2014.

13 Mitch Abramson, "Shortstop Rafael Santana a Quiet and Pivotal Piece of 1986 Mets," *New York Daily News*, October 3, 2009; McCarron.; milb.com/player/index.jsp?player_id=643519#/career/R/hitting/2014/ALL.

All statistics from baseball-reference.com.

DOUG SISK

By Alan Cohen

"The people in New York are the most sports-oriented people I've ever been around. I mean they are geared into it. The game on the field carries over. They hate you so bad and they don't even know who you are."[1]

—Doug Sisk, 1989

ON A TEAM OF PRANKSTERS AND CUT-UPS Doug Sisk, who hailed from Tacoma, Washington, would fit right in in 1986, even if the fans were not always in his corner. The unusual started early for Sisk. During his freshman year of college Sisk suffered the first of a number of arm injuries that would define his career. "I threw a Wiffle ball at the paperboy. He was teasing my dog. I nailed him, hit him in the head." But in so doing, Sisk ripped the tendons in his elbow. "The doctors called me into the office, showed me the x-ray, and told me to forget about a career in baseball. They told me not even to pick up a ball for a year, and I didn't."[2]

Douglas Randall Sisk was born in Renton, Washington, on September 26, 1957. His father was a lieutenant in the Sheriff's Department. During his years at Lincoln High School in Tacoma, Sisk not only was hurling baseballs, but he was also proficient at shooting a .22-caliber rifle. He even was asked to try out for the 1976 Olympics but passed on the opportunity due to his baseball commitments.[3] Sisk excelled in the Senior Babe Ruth League tournament in 1976. The 18-year-old pitched a complete-game (seven innings) 1-0 shutout, allowing only four hits.[4] After graduating from high school, Sisk played at Green River Community College in Auburn, Washington. He came back from the Wiffle-ball injury to pitch in his sophomore year and then transferred to Washington State University in Pullman, Washington, pitching for the Cougars in 1980, and winning his first four outings[5] before graduating that spring with a degree in criminal justice. During his college years, he spent his summers playing in the Southwest Semi-Pro League in Tacoma.

Because of that early arm injury, Sisk was not drafted. He signed as a free agent with the New York Mets on June 10, 1980. His first stop was Rookie League ball at Kingsport, Tennessee, in the Appalachian League. In his first outing as a professional, he defeated Paintsville, 6-3.[6] He pitched in 15 games, each as a starter, and went 8-5 with a 2.66 ERA.

Sisk made three moves in 1981. The first was to Lynchburg, Virginia, in the Carolina League and the second was to the bullpen. He went 3-2 with seven saves in 36 games at Lynchburg before the third move, a promotion to Jackson, Mississippi, in the Double-A

Texas League. At Jackson, he pitched in 14 games for manager Davey Johnson, went 3-0, and added another four saves to his résumé.

In 1982, still at Jackson, Sisk had an 11-7 record with a 2.67 ERA and five saves. Of his 44 appearances, 35 were in relief, and his performance earned him a late season call-up to the Mets.

Sisk made his major-league debut on September 6, 1982, against the Pittsburgh Pirates in Pittsburgh. After he retired the first two batters, he faced perennial Met nemesis Willie Stargell, who was in his last season. Before the game the slugger had been showered with gifts. Against Sisk he came off the bench as a pinch-hitter and capped his night with a single to right field. He left the field to a standing ovation, and Sisk retired the next batter to record a scoreless inning in his first appearance.

Sisk's appearance on September 15, 1982 provided the only blemish on his initial season with the Mets. New York was playing at Montreal and the game went into extra innings. The Expos were very much in contention and the last-place Mets were playing out the schedule. Mets manager George Bamberger used 21 players. The 21st was Doug Sisk, who entered the game to pitch the bottom of the 11th inning. The only batter he faced was Andre Dawson whose home run, on a 3-and-1 pitch, ended the contest and saddled Sisk with his first major-league loss.

Dawson's home run was the only run allowed by Sisk in 1982. He recorded his first major-league save on September 22 when he got the last four outs, all on groundballs, as the Mets defeated the Cubs, 5-2, at Wrigley Field. During his first go-around in the big leagues, Sisk pitched in eight games and had a 1.04 ERA in 8⅔ innings.

In 1983 Sisk enjoyed a good spring and was prepared to head north with the Mets when he received a shock. He was summoned to manager George Bamberger's office at the team's spring-training facility. "I thought, 'Oh God! Did they change their mind? What did I do?' George said, 'Sorry Doug, I can't keep you. You've got to report to Tidewater.' He was looking down at me and he says, 'Do you have anything to say,' and I said, 'No, George.' And he said, 'That's good because that's a crock.'" At that point, his teammates, who had been in on the gag, and were listening in, were howling.[7]

Sisk saw his first 1983 action on Opening Day. It was an electric atmosphere fueled by Tom Seaver's return to the Mets after almost six seasons with the Reds. When Seaver, whose left thigh was beginning to tighten, left the scoreless game for a pinch-hitter in the bottom of the sixth inning, Sisk took over on the mound. The Mets gave him a 2-0 lead in the bottom of the seventh inning, and Doug pitched scoreless ball over the final three innings. There were a couple of anxious moments in the final stanza when the Phillies put runners on first and second with one out. But Sisk was up to the task, retiring Mike Schmidt on a fly ball and striking out Tony Perez with a slider for his first major-league win.

"I must be dreaming. I can't believe it. Tom Seaver's return, Steve Carlton pitching for the other guys, and I win the game. And I have to get Mike Schmidt and Tony Perez for the last two outs of the game. Naw, talk to me tomorrow when I wake up."[8]

"I thought about taking him out in the ninth inning," said Mets manager and pitching coach George Bamberger. "And if it had been the middle of the season, I might have. But these kids are never going to learn how to pitch out of a tough situation if you're going to take them out all the time." Said Sisk, "There was no way they were going to beat me. I wanted to win it for George. I wanted to show him that he made the right decision by leaving me in."[9]

The 1983 Mets, despite the presence on the roster of some of the players who would take them over the top in 1986, were still losing more games than they won and finished last in their division. Sisk was an asset nonetheless, posting a 5-4 record with 11 saves. He was the top right-handed reliever on the team and appeared in a team-high 67 games with a 2.24 ERA. By June 23, Frank Howard had replaced Bamberger as manager. On that day, the Mets were playing the

St. Louis Cardinals at Shea Stadium, and Sisk had his best outing of the season. Howard called on him in the top of the fifth inning after the Mets had taken a 7-4 lead. Sisk pitched the last five innings, allowing only one unearned run and five hits. Of the 15 outs Sisk recorded, 12, including the last nine, were via the groundball.

There were some new faces on the Mets in 1984 as they made the jump from mediocrity to contention. In the second game of the season, the Mets were playing in Cincinnati. One of the new faces, Ron Darling pitched the first six innings before being removed for a pinch-hitter in the top of the seventh. Sisk relieved and pitched three scoreless innings for his first save of the season. He went on to pitch in 50 games. Although his won-lost record was only 1-3, he saved a career-high 15 games. His ERA, which was under 2.00 as late as September 7, was a career-best 2.09 for the season. In one 23-game stretch, from April 29 through July 1, Sisk saved nine games and allowed only one earned run in 39⅓ innings. He teamed with lefty Jesse Orosco to form the best relief tandem in the National League. They were also a team off the field, sharing a house in Queens during the season.

Mets pitching coach Mel Stottlemyre was high on his relievers, particularly Sisk. In July he said, "We used to use Sisk to get to Orosco. Now, they're both game-enders." Sisk relied on his sinker, which Stottlemyre said "is better than mine ever was. Doug's sinker explodes. If I didn't know better, I'd suspect him of throwing a spitter."[10]

The tandem was the talk of the league as Davey Johnson's squad vaulted to first place in late July. Johnson said, "Our best scenario is for the starter to carry us six or seven innings. Then I can go to my bullpen and one of those guys will finish up." Orosco noted, "It's not that we're so close buddies. We just get along. We're actually different types. He's an outdoorsman. He hunts and fishes. I like to paint and draw, maybe go bowling. The main thing is, there's no rivalry. When Doug gets the call, I tell him, 'Close the door.' We go home and replay the game. But we don't care who gets the save."[11]

It was during the 1984 season that Sisk began to hear the booing that would become louder and louder during his remaining time with the Mets. In a game at Houston on July 17, he was brought in to save a game for Darling. He walked Terry Puhl and gave up a home run (his first and only homer of the season) on a 3-and-2 pitch to Mark Bailey to lose the game. On July 21, in the Mets' 91st game of the season, Sisk got his 14th save. He would not have another until September.

The booing really began to rain down in late July. The Mets were playing the Cubs at Shea Stadium on July 28. Sisk entered the game in the eighth inning with the score tied 3-3. By the time he left the field, he had given up the lead and the bases were loaded. He faced four men and failed to get an out. He walked his first batter, threw a wild pitch, allowed two singles and then misplayed a bunt. The Cubs went on to score eight runs in the inning, won the game 11-4, and pulled to within 3½ games of the first-place Mets in the NL East. (The Cubs overtook the Mets on August 1 and pulled away over the final two months of the season.)

"All I know is I screwed it up. I walked the first guy. I almost hit the second guy in the head. And (Leon) Durham [who singled] well, I got behind again. You know, that's the first time I've ever been booed. Oh well, I guess you've got to get booed once in a while."[12] The Cubs cemented their lead when they swept the Mets in a four-game series in early August. In less than two weeks, the Mets went from 4½ games ahead of Chicago to 4½ games behind them.

It was also during this season that Sisk began to experience pain in his shoulder that caused him to lose control of his sinker. The strike zone and Sisk had never been on the friendliest of terms, causing manager Johnson to rely on Rolaids to the point where he got a commercial endorsement. But this was different. Sisk recalled that the pain began in a game against the Cardinals on July 24. In that game, "I didn't even feel like I had any leverage on the ball anymore. It started doing different things on me."[13] It was the beginning of a rough patch for Sisk that limited his availability down the stretch. He appeared in only six games with one save during the final two months of the season. The pain was diagnosed as tendinitis and, on August 9, Sisk was placed on the disabled list. He began to question his future. "Yeah, you think about all kinds of things when you're on the bench. You wonder, 'Is my arm going to be all right when I start airing it out, or is it going to keep hurting? Then if it's okay, how are (the Mets) going to use three short men in the bullpen, now that Wes (Gardner) is here'?"[14] He was reactivated on August 30. During Sisk's stay on the DL, the Mets lost ground on the Cubs and were 5½ games behind when he returned.

The Mets finished in second place at 90-72, 6½ games behind Chicago. Injuries were to plague Sisk for the balance of his career. In 1995 he reflected, "For me, it's always been some sort of physical problem, not a question of talent."[15]

In 1985 the Mets once again fell short. Sisk had only two saves. Roger McDowell emerged as the Mets' top right-handed reliever while Sisk continued to struggle with injury. He pitched the entire season with loose bone chips in his right elbow,[16] and his ERA skyrocketed to 5.30. The Shea faithful grew more impatient with him; the Mets were only 14-28 in games he pitched. In one seven-game stretch between April 17 and May 4, he allowed 17 runs, including two homers, with an ERA of 13.11. After a disastrous performance on May 4, when his ERA rose to 8.53, the Mets sent Sisk briefly to Tidewater.

When Sisk returned to the Mets on May 24, he was pitching exclusively out of the stretch. "I got in trouble before because I was throwing the ball, just trying to get it over, and not even bothering picking my spots. With a stretch, you basically have less time to screw up and you can spot the pitch more effectively."[17] But he was still inconsistent.

The Mets were in first place on June 7 when they faced the fourth-place Cardinals at Shea Stadium. The game went into extra innings tied at 1-1, and Sisk relieved in the 13th inning. Disaster ensued. As Keith Hernandez wrote, "[Shortstop Rafael] Santana starts things with an error. Sisk gets a groundball out, then everything collapses. Five hits, six runs, and a second error later, we're finished; it's our worst inning of the year. It's all or nothing with Doug these days. I understand why Davey (Johnson) continues to use him—we'll need Sisk later on, in the stretch—but I don't know of another manager who would stick with him this long. Add in the fact that Doug is pitching in some bad luck, too. The team may start thinking negatively when he comes in: 'How will things go wrong this time?'"[18]

Sisk was on the wrong end of hate mail. One letter urged him to "Take one Tylenol and one cyanide capsule—per day."[19]

But occasionally things went right in Sisk's enigmatic season. On June 21 the Mets took a 4-3 lead in the bottom of the sixth inning and handed Sisk the ball. He pitched a perfect three innings. His reward was his second win of the season, and the Mets were tied with the Cardinals for the division lead. Sisk's view of his season was philosophical. "I've been terrible. I gave up walks, home runs, grand slams. You name it, I've done it. I've even been getting letters recommending I take cyanide. When you're going bad, you don't know what to do to get better. Fortunately, I stayed within myself and didn't go nuts. But you feel like a weight on the team."[20]

The Mets game on July 4 showed the best of Sisk and the worst of Sisk. The Mets were in Atlanta to play the Braves and it was fireworks night. Although it was raining, the Braves were not about to postpone the game and send the big crowd home. Finally the game began at 9:04 P.M. In the bottom of the eighth inning Sisk was summoned to relieve Orosco and protect a 7-5 lead. There were two outs, but Orosco had walked in a run and the bases were loaded. Davey Johnson ordered Sisk to throw strikes and the first batter, Dale Murphy sent one of those strikes to the outfield wall for a double that cleared the bases. Sisk stayed in the game and retired the Braves. The Mets tied the contest at 8-8, and Sisk pitched scoreless ball through the 12th. The game was interrupted by rain and did not end until 4:00 A.M., with the Mets winning 16-13. The Braves then exploded the fireworks, much to the consternation of the neighborhood.

By August Sisk had become the forgotten man in the bullpen, and when the stretch drive came, he was on the disabled list. His last win of the season came on September 8. The Dodgers and Mets played a 14-inning marathon in Los Angeles that took almost five hours to complete. Sisk entered the game in the bottom of the 13th inning and was the Sisk of old, retiring the side in order with two groundouts and a strikeout. Mookie Wilson led off the top of the 14th inning with a home run. Then Sisk retired the Dodgers on three groundouts to secure the win and move the Mets to within a half-game of the division lead.

But Sisk did not pitch after September 13 and had elbow surgery just before the end of the season. He was a question mark for 1986, and the love affair between Met fandom and Sisk was definitely over.

Sisk did find love away from the ballpark and in December of 1985, he married Lisa Michaelson.

In 2011 Sisk remembered those days. "You're supposed to ignore the negativity and pitch well. But it's much, much, much easier said than done. When you know that your home fans are going to kill you every time you take the field, well, that isn't helpful. I don't care what people say about mind over matter—always getting booed takes a toll. It has to."[21]

Sisk started the 1986 season with Tidewater in the International League. To strengthen his arm, he started and relieved, and after nine appearances and 30 innings he was recalled by the Mets on May 20. He quickly established his place in a quartet of relievers (Sisk, Orosco, McDowell, and Randy Niemann) who would complement the team's outstanding starting rotation. The Mets started the season by winning 44 of their first 60 games. The bullpen quartet won 11 of those games and saved 16. Sisk pitched in seven of the games and was the winner on June 16 as the Mets established a division lead of 11½ games.

For the season, in 41 appearances, Sisk's record was 4-2 with a 3.06 ERA. He had one save; there were not many save opportunities for Sisk as McDowell was now the right-handed closer. Down the stretch, however, Sisk won two games as the Mets cruised to their first division championship since 1973.

On August 27 the Mets were wrapping up a successful road trip in San Diego. They had taken a 5-0 lead and were sailing toward their eighth victory of the nine-game trip. Then the Padres tied the game in the eighth as McDowell and Orosco faltered. Sisk relieved in the bottom of the 10th inning and retired the side on three straight groundballs. The Mets pushed across a run in the top of the 11th inning to take the lead, and Sisk was looking to finish things up as the Padres came to bat.

Garry Templeton led off with a double and Davey Johnson's already depleted inventory of Rolaids took another hit. With the Padres' bench depleted, Sisk struck out pitcher Craig Lefferts, who was pinch-hitting for Goose Gossage. Then Tim Flannery singled to center field. As Templeton raced home with the tying run, Len Dykstra charged the ball and unleashed a perfect throw to catcher John Gibbons. Gibbons absorbed a collision with Templeton and held on to the ball after tagging the Padres shortstop. Flannery had not stopped running on the play and, seeing Gibbons sprawled on the ground, dashed toward third base. Sisk called for Gibbons to throw the ball to third base, where Howard Johnson put the tag on Flannery to end the game.[22] The Mets had extended their first place lead to 20 games. The magic number was 16, and it was still August.

August turned into September and the Mets just kept on rolling. Sisk came into a 3-3 game against San Diego on September 7 at Shea in the top of the sixth inning. Things did not go well in his first inning of work. He allowed a run on a single and three walks. The Mets scored three runs in their half of the inning to take Sisk off the hook and Roger McDowell held the lead over the final three innings. Sisk had his fourth win of the season, the Mets had won another four in a row, and the magic number was whittled to six.

By the time Sisk registered his only save of the season, on September 27, the Mets had clinched the division title. In the postseason, Johnson used him sparingly. He pitched a scoreless inning in the League Championship Series, and a scoreless two-thirds of an inning in Game Two of the World Series.

Sisk enhanced his reputation for keeping the ball in the ballpark; he was the only pitcher in the league to face 200 or more batters without giving up a home run. During his first 334 innings with the Mets, over five seasons and 208 appearances, Sisk allowed only six home runs. He went into the 1987 season not having allowed a homer in 122⅓ innings. His streak started on May 31, 1985, and included 70 appearances.

The homerless streak ended in 1987 but Sisk had a good season, posting a 3-1 record with three saves. His 55 appearances were the most since 1983 and he posted a 3.46 ERA. His best outing came on June 14 in Pittsburgh. He entered the game with one out in the fourth inning, the Mets leading 4-2 and runners on first and second. He allowed one of the inherited runners to score and then pitched effectively through the eighth inning. In 4⅔ innings, he allowed three hits and got his second win of the season.

But throughout the 1986 and 1987 seasons, Sisk was the target of irate fans and it was not just the booing. One time, as he waited to bat, fans threw ice at him. Another time, fans trashed his car in the parking lot at Shea Stadium. Toward the end of the 1987 season, he requested a trade.

After the season, New York traded Sisk to Baltimore for two minor leaguers. He essentially went from the penthouse to the poorhouse, as the Orioles finished the 1988 season with a 54-107 record, the worst in the American League. Sisk went 3-3 with an ERA of 3.72. Although he had no saves, there weren't many save opportunities that season. It was a year of lost causes as the Orioles lost 44 of the 52 games in which Sisk pitched. He suffered tendinitis in his shoulder during the season, and spent most of July at Triple-A Rochester on rehab. After the season, the Orioles released him.

In 1989 Sisk found his way to spring training with the Oakland A's but before the season began, he had reconstructive surgery on both knees and missed the entire season.[23] He signed as a free agent with the Cleveland Indians before the 1990 season, and was released after pitching briefly with Colorado Springs. He then signed with the Mets and pitched effectively at Tidewater, where he posted a mark of 5-1. The Mets traded Sisk to Atlanta and he returned to the big leagues with the Braves in July, appearing in three games without a decision. Sisk by then was 32 years old with not much in the way of a future in baseball. When the Braves placed him on release waivers, there were no takers.

Sisk earned a spot on the Braves roster again in 1991, and pitched in 14 games in the first two months of the season, going 2-1 with a 5.02 ERA. In his last major-league appearance, on May 23 against San Diego, he pitched an ineffective two-thirds of an inning, yielding three hits and four unearned runs. Atlanta placed him on the disabled list with tendinitis in his shoulder and released him after the season.

Four years later Sisk had his last hurrah. The strike that had brought the 1994 season to a screeching halt continued into spring training in 1995, and Sisk went to the Mets camp as a replacement player. The then 37-year-old started a spring-training game against the Yankees on March 4. He pitched two innings, allowed a run, and was tagged with the 2-1 loss. He knew that "Whenever I fly back home, I know that this thing [his beleaguered arm] will not throw another baseball."[24]

After his brief re-emergence, Sisk returned to Tacoma, where he did some scouting for the Mets, worked for a beer and wine distributor, worked at the local Boys and Girls Club, and announced for the Triple-A Tacoma Rainiers. He and his wife, Lisa, have three children.

SOURCES

Barnes, Craig. "Sisk Relieved to Escape Mets' Fans (and Manager)," *Sun Sentinel* (West Palm Beach, Florida), March 7, 1988.

Moran, Malcolm. "For Sisk, Darkness is Beginning to Lift," *New York Times*, September 12, 1985: D33.

"Sisk on Disabled List, Says He Fears a Trade," *New York Times*, August 14, 1984: B9.

Sisk's file at the Baseball Hall of Fame library.

NOTES

1 Wayne Coffey, "At Shea, Sisk Was at Risk: Road Was Relief for Doug," *New York Daily News*, June 27, 1989: C30.

2 James Tuite, "Sisk Accepts Mets Relief Role," *New York Times*, April 7, 1983: B18.

3 "Missed Opportunity," *New York Times*, May 30, 1983: 26.

4 *The Daily Chronicle* (Centralia, Washington), July 30, 1976: 10.

5 "Cougars Whip Up on Gonzaga," *Walla Walla* (Washington) *Union-Bulletin*, April 2, 1980: 8.

6 *Lexington* (Kentucky) *Herald*, June 20, 1980: D-3.

7 Malcolm Moran, "Another Step Up for Sisk," *New York Times*, June 18, 1983: 15.

8 Emery Filmer, "Pitcher Perfect," *Stamford* (Connecticut) *Advocate*, April 6, 1983: C-1.

9 United Press International, April 5, 1983.

10 Jack Lang, "Orosco, Sisk Form No. 1 Bullpen Duo," *The Sporting News*, July 16, 1984: 20.

11 Joseph Durso, "The Odd Couple," *The Sporting News*, August 6, 1984: 29.

12 Kevin Dupont, "Sisk Is Dismayed After His Collapse Against the Cubs," *New York Times*, July 29, 1984: S-4.

13 Bob Klapisch, "Shoulder Aching, Sisk Put on 15-day DL," *New York Post*, August 10, 1984.

14 Klapisch, "Sisk Watches as Gardner's Value Grows," *New York Post*, August 17, 1984: 91.

15 David O'Brien, "Sisk Is Willing—if Able," *Sun-Sentinel* (West Palm Beach, Florida), March 7, 1995.

16 Jeff Pearlman, "The One Met Their Fans Most Loved to Hate," *Wall Street Journal*, March 21, 2011.

17 Filip Bondy, "Sisk Hopes to Turn Jeers into Cheers," *New York Daily News*, May 22, 1985: C30.

18 Keith Hernandez (with Mike Bryan), *If at First ... A Season with the Mets*, (New York: McGraw-Hill, 1986): 124.

19 Craig Carter, "Negative Prescription," *The Sporting News*, July 16, 1985

20 Joseph Durso, "Surging Mets Are First Again," *New York Times*, June 22, 1985: 47.

21 Pearlman, "The One Met."

22 Matthew Silverman, *Mets Essential*, (Chicago: Triumph Books, 2007): 93.

23 *Pharos Tribune* (Logansport, Indiana), April 1, 1990: C-10.

24 Jack O'Connell, "An Unsure Sign of Spring: Sisk," *Hartford Courant*, March 5, 1995.

DARRYL STRAWBERRY

By Shawn Morris

FOR MANY AFRICAN AMERICAN MALES growing up in poverty-stricken households throughout Los Angeles, sports offered a chance to break away from the cultural and economic restraints imposed on them by their surroundings. This was no different for a young Darryl Eugene Strawberry (born March 12, 1962, in Los Angeles). Darryl was the third boy born to Henry and Ruby Strawberry, and would be followed by two sisters. By 1970 the family was residing in a small house in the Crenshaw neighborhood of South Central Los Angeles. Strawberry recalled his father as being a negative influence early in his life. Henry Strawberry held down a steady job as a postal clerk, but suffered from many of the same vices that would plague Darryl's life. He would often come home in drunken rages and physically assault Ruby, as well as Darryl and his older brother Ronnie. Much of Darryl's younger years were spent in fear of their father until one night when he was about 10 years old. On that night Henry came home intoxicated, and began to verbally and physically assault Ruby. The police showed up and just like that, Henry was gone from his children's lives,[1] only to reappear when it was evident Darryl was a remarkable talent on the baseball field and would be a top pick in the major-league draft.

"It's sad. I never had a real relationship with him. He never sat me down and talked to me kindly, never gave me a word of fatherly advice or counsel, never taught me to tie my shoe or hit a baseball. None of those things a father and son are supposed to do, he either ignored me or beat me, period," Strawberry said in 2009.[2] What Henry did give his youngest son was a love for sports and athletic abilities. Like many of the other children in the Crenshaw neighborhood, Darryl went to the local park to watch his father play on one of the many softball teams in the area. His father could "whip the ball across the plate so fast you wouldn't know where to start your swing. … He'd hit the long ball over and over again, every time he came to bat."[3] After his father disappeared from his life, Darryl felt an absence and turned to sports as a refuge and escape from everything bothering him. "I was very good at every sport I tried," he said. "I'm not bragging. It was just in me. I loved it. It was pure joy for me to play baseball, basketball, and football. While I was playing I could almost forget my anger and my troubles. Almost."[4] Ruby was devoted to her family, held a full-time job at a local telephone company, and supported Darryl playing baseball. She knew how happy it made him, and she was shocked to see that on the field he was not the same, lazy Darryl she knew at home.

After attending numerous junior high schools, Strawberry attended the predominantly African-American Crenshaw High School. Crenshaw was

an athletic powerhouse. Scouts came to Crenshaw games; it was Darryl's chance to get noticed, to gain the fame and notoriety so many young athletes from similar circumstances were searching for. Basketball was his first love and his gangly frame gave him an advantage on the court, but baseball came the most natural to him. "Right from the start I could pitch, I could hit home runs, I could steal bases, I could field. I didn't think much about it, I didn't study the game, I just went out there and did it."[5] By the time he reached Crenshaw, Strawberry had earned a reputation throughout the Los Angeles Little League, but none of that mattered to Crenshaw baseball coach Brooks Hurst.

When Darryl entered Crenshaw High for the 10th grade, he was already 6-feet-3. He was long and lean and covered with sinewy muscle, not the type created by hours in a weight room or supplements, but the real thing. "He had the body of a basketball forward and the natural baseball swing, a powerful, looping uppercut, of a historic homerun hitter," a writer said of him.[6] To Brooks Hurst, Darryl was just like many of the young black men he had coached, full of talent and lacking discipline. At Crenshaw, Hurst did his best to instill the qualities his players were lacking to help them succeed on and off the field. Any backtalk or mouthing off to him and he would make them run till they dropped from exhaustion.[7]

For many of his players, Hurst was the only stable male figure in their lives. He was familiar with Darryl and his situation; both older brothers had played for him at Crenshaw. Hurst did his best to watch over Darryl and guide him to make the right choices during his three years at Crenshaw. Strawberry struggled his first year in high school; although there was no denying his talent, he was given no special treatment under Hurst. He tried to drill into Darryl to "beat the ball to the spot" when playing the outfield and to run hard for balls that fell in for base hits, not just glide to them and let singles turn into extra bases. Coach Hurst often found himself annoyed with Darryl and his approach of only giving a half-effort. "I had to sit him down and talk to him a lot. I had him run laps. I would tell him: The scouts come in here with assumptions about inner-city ballplayers. You have to counteract that. Don't give them the ammunition. But finally, I just ran out of patience."[8] Finally, Darryl's first high-school season ended early when he was kicked off the team. "I just said to him, 'This isn't working out. I hope you want to come back next year,'" Hurst recalled. "Darryl took it pretty well. He still came to games. He helped lug the equipment."[9]

Despite his talent, when Strawberry came back for the 1979 season there were some who thought he was not the best talent on the team. He also had to contend with Corrie Dillard and another player who would go on to the major leagues, Chris Brown. Besides those three, the rest of the Crenshaw team was also talented, so much so that many of the second-stringers would end up with professional contracts. On the playing field the 1979 Crenshaw team was in the midst of a spectacular season. Strawberry was having an outstanding year at the plate, in the outfield, and when he took the mound. The team easily defeated many of its inner-city opponents. Early in the season, the *Los Angeles Times* reported, "(A)fter a 15-5 mugging of Hamilton, Crenshaw has now scored 31 runs in its last two games."[10] Many of Darryl's relatives who had been largely absent from his life began to appear at his games as well, including his father. Coach Hurst did his best to shield his players from the circus enveloping them, and keeping their focus on the game itself. Throughout the season the team kept playing at a high level and by the time the regular season was drawing to a close Crenshaw had lost only a handful of games—and in each of those cases Hurst had benched one of his star players for disciplinary reasons.

When the regular season finished, the Crenshaw High Cougars entered the Los Angeles Unified School District baseball playoffs. Anchored by senior Chris Brown and junior Darryl Strawberry, it was the first inner-city school in many years that had the talent to compete against those in the San Fernando Valley that benefited from manicured fields, booster clubs, and year-round instruction.[11] Playing the way they had many times during the regular season, the Cougars cruised their way through the first two rounds of the playoffs by a combined score of 23-4. Nothing, it seemed could keep Crenshaw from hitting. In the semifinal round they powered their way over Monroe High by a score of 10-7.[12] In the three playoff games Strawberry hit three triples in addition to a home run, and was the winning pitcher in two of the contests.[13] Next stop for Crenshaw was the championship game at Dodger Stadium.

On June 6, 1979, the Cougars boarded the bus for the short trip to Dodger Stadium. Their opponent was Granada Hills, a team that played with few mistakes and relied on the "small ball" approach, lots of bunting, and good defense. Their third baseman was a high-school football standout, Stanford-bound John Elway. The Crenshaw players had their work cut out for them, and when Granada Hills jumped out to an early 2-0 lead; their task became much more difficult. A strong third inning put Crenshaw back on top by a run and the Granada Hills coach pulled Elway from third base and put him in as pitcher. After his eight warmup pitches, Elway struck out the next batter to end the inning. On the mound Strawberry began to crumble. Unnerved by the Little League tactics of fake bunts, he began to become erratic and after walking several batters he was pulled and sent to the outfield. By the end of the fifth inning, Granada had scored another six runs on three hits because of Crenshaw's bad pitching and sloppy fielding, and the Crenshaw hopes were in rapid decline.[14] Elway shut the Cougars down. "The team that scout George Genovese considered from top to bottom, the most talented assemblage of high-school talent ever, could not win the LA city championship."[15]

When Strawberry returned to Crenshaw for his senior year all of the attention was lavished upon him. Without Brown to share the spotlight, it became the season of Strawberry. Coach Hurst was continuously chasing agents off the baseball field and out of the Crenshaw hallways. Strawberry often found himself surrounded by an entourage and those looking for any piece of stardom that association with him brought. As his ego grew, his attitude only seemed to worsen, according to some teammates. George Cook recalled, "Darryl Strawberry didn't listen to [Coach Hurst]."[16] The press buildup surrounding Strawberry and the coming baseball draft overshadowed anything else he accomplished his senior year. *Sports Illustrated* published a feature on Strawberry late in his senior season, with a picture caption that said, "Darryl, 18, is likened to Ted Williams."[17] "He's got a Williams-type physical makeup—tall, rangy, good leverage," scout Phil Pote told *Sports Illustrated*. "He's got bat quickness, he can drive the ball. The ball just jumps off his bat."[18]

Strawberry had dreamed about being the first overall pick in the draft, and in June of 1980, the New York Mets made that happen. The Mets were hoping he would help turn the franchise around. Not only did he have the potential to help on the field, he could provide them with much-needed box-office revenue as well. The team provided him with a $200,000 signing bonus to forgo college and flew him to New York to show him off to the press. But before Strawberry was able to play in Shea Stadium he had to first prove himself in the minor leagues.

A few days later, Strawberry found himself in a landscape vastly different than that of Manhattan or Los Angeles. Kingsport, Tennessee, was home to the Mets' team in the rookie-level Appalachian League and Strawberry's first step in the Mets farm system. During that 1980 season, in 180 plate appearances he batted .268 with five home runs. His work ethic was still sloppy, according to some and he was often late arriving to the stadium, onetime even missing a game.[19] A player not of Strawberry's status would have had harsh repercussions for missing a game, but not Strawberry; his absence was largely ignored by those in the organization.

The following season Strawberry was assigned to the High-A Lynchburg Mets. He continued to struggle and failed to live up to all the hype that was heaped upon him before the draft. Off the field, the 19-year-old Strawberry was homesick and called his mother every day. On the field he was struggling against many of the pitchers he faced. They easily fooled him with hard fastballs inside and breaking balls. Strawberry possessed the power to put the ball into play, but he struggled to make the contact that had made him a legend at Crenshaw. In 123 games with Lynchburg in 1981, Strawberry managed to hit 13 home runs and bat .255 for the season.

The next spring Strawberry continued to climb the farm-system ladder, and started the season with the Double-A Jackson Mets. It was in Jackson, Mississippi, where he became locked-in at the plate and began to flash the talent the Mets saw in him when they drafted him. He began to see the ball better and figure out opposing pitchers. Although he struck out 145 times, by the end of the season he had driven in 97 runs and hit 34 home runs. Rather than take the winter off, the Mets had Strawberry extend his year by playing winter ball for a team in Caracas, Venezuela. He credited the experience with speeding up his development and better preparing him for the coming season. Strawberry remarked, "I felt confident after my season in South America because I'd been able to hit some of their best pitchers."[20]

To start the 1983 season, the Mets sent Strawberry to their top affiliate, the Triple-A Tidewater Tides. The organization wanted to keep him in the minors for one more season before bringing him up to New York, but many believed he would see the Big Apple before the year was over. Under manager Davey Johnson, Strawberry got off to a great start at Triple A. "My first ten or so games at Tidewater were spectacular. Whether I had improved to the point where I could hit anything any Triple-A pitcher could throw, or whether Triple-A pitching wasn't as good as it was supposed to be, I don't know," he said.[21] At the same time, the Mets were off to a dreadful start and the New York newspaper headlines began to call for Strawberry. In early May Darryl was summoned from Tidewater. Mets general manager Frank Cashen regretted having to call him up ahead of schedule, but Strawberry had the potential to help fill the empty seats and on May 6, 1983, he made his major-league debut.[22]

Strawberry stood an imposing 6-feet-6 with a playing weight of 190 pounds; he batted and threw left, and was a right fielder for most of his career. His debut, against the Cincinnati Reds was less than spectacular, with three strikeouts and a foul popup during six plate appearances in an extra-inning win by the Mets. Strawberry also worked a couple of walks and stole a base late in the game. The Mets' manager, George Bamberger, encouraged the rookie to go out onto the field and have fun. However, Bamberger resigned on June 2 and was replaced by Frank Howard, one of his coaches. Howard began to demand more out of Strawberry and assigned hitting coach Jim Frey to help. Under Frey's tutelage, Strawberry began to blossom and adjust to major-league pitching. His struggles at the plate began to disappear and in September Strawberry found his groove. It was also at this time that Strawberry began to succumb to the New York lifestyle and started experimenting with cocaine. His immaturity and desire to be liked left him vulnerable to negative influences. "Darryl was someone who always wanted to be liked," said his mother, Ruby.[23] During his rookie campaign Strawberry was introduced to cocaine by two Mets veterans who told him, "It was the thing to do in the big leagues."[24] Despite his off-field habits, Strawberry continued to produce quality numbers. His 108 hits, 26 home runs, 74 RBIs, and 19 stolen bases were enough for him to be voted the National League Rookie of the Year. After the season Howard was replaced as manager by Davey Johnson. Under Johnson, Strawberry and the Mets became a powerhouse franchise for the rest of the decade.

Once Johnson was at the helm, the Mets began to turn things around on the field and produce wins with regularity. The attendance at Shea Stadium began to increase, and it was becoming clear throughout the city that the Yankees were not the only show in town anymore. Rookie Dwight Gooden was a stud on the mound, and Strawberry was continuing to rise to stardom in the outfield, being named to the All-Star team in July. He also began to use amphetamines with regularity during the 1984 season.[25] Most members of the hard-partying Mets team already were, as amphetamines allowed the players to go drink and abuse drugs all night, and play the next day with no hangover or ill feelings. By the end of the season, Johnson had guided the Mets from a team that came in last place the previous year to a second-place finish in the NL East.

The 1985 season again saw an increase in the number of Mets victories; the team that won only 68 games in 1983 rang up 98 victories in 1995. Strawberry continued to produce at the plate and help put fans in the seats. Attendance at Shea Stadium was now more than double that of his rookie year: 2.7 million vs. 1.1 million. Strawberry was also married that year to Lisa Andrews, a tumultuous relationship that resulted in court appearances and ultimately divorce. Although he appeared in 37 fewer games than he did in 1984 due to minor health issues and slight injuries, Strawberry still scored 79 runs and hit 29 home runs, both more than his previous year's total. While it was enough to earn Strawberry a trip to his consecutive All-Star Game, his performance was not enough to help power the Mets into the postseason. But that would change the next season.

"We had a sense of destiny in 1986, a belief that it would all come together for us in a great, historic display of baseball power," said Strawberry.[26] The expectations were high for the Mets as early as spring training; they had won 98 games the season before and were in almost every aspect more skilled, more intense, and more arrogant than the Cardinals, Cubs, and the rest of the NL East.[27] After an indifferent start to the season, things began to turn around for the Mets. They went on one of the greatest runs in franchise history, reeling off 11 wins in a row before losing a game, then winning another seven in a row. The Mets were on fire through May. Although he was having a great year on the field, off it Strawberry continued to alienate himself from teammates as his ego grew. His head was as large as the Goodyear Blimp, and with each new magazine cover story and autograph request it only got bigger. His teammates felt he was vicious and selfish, taking a great deal of pride in making others feel inferior.[28] By now Strawberry was routinely abusing drugs and drinking heavily in the clubhouse. Under the MLB drug policy in place in the 1980s, no team could compel a player to take a drug test, and with the Mets winning in amazing fashion on a regular basis, no one was willing to rein in Strawberry and get him under control.

For most of the 1986 season the Mets were the first-place team and the others in the division futilely chased them. The 108-win Mets were heavy favorites to capture the World Series. The National League Championship Series, went six games and included two thrilling extra-inning contests before the Mets emerged victorious over Houston. Strawberry hit a crucial home run in Game Three to help propel the Mets to victory, and finished the NLCS with two home runs and five RBIs. The 1986 World Series, pitting the Mets against the Boston Red Sox, opened at Shea Stadium on October 18. After six games the teams were tied with three victories apiece, and Strawberry was a nonfactor at the plate. But in Game Seven, when it came time to deliver, Strawberry stepped up. Boston had mounted a mini-rally in the top of the eighth inning to pull within one run of the Mets, but when Strawberry led off the bottom of the inning with a solo home run, there was no doubt it was New York's night. The miracle season of 1986, highlighted by so many late-game heroics and the team's never-say-die attitude concluded with the Mets as the world champions.

The Mets' descent from the World Series heights started before the 1987 campaign when ace pitcher Dwight Gooden was admitted into a drug-treatment center a week before the start of the season. Strawberry was able to hide his demons throughout the season and produced at the plate. He had career highs with 108 runs scored, 104 RBIs, 36 stolen bases, and 39 home runs. Despite his increased offensive output, the Mets finished second in the division and missed the playoffs. In 1988 Strawberry again reached the century mark in runs scored and RBIs, smashed a league-leading 39 home runs, and led the National League in slugging and OPS. He was named to his fifth straight All-Star Game and was runner-up to Kirk Gibson for the MVP. The Mets finished in first place in the NL East, winning 100 games. However, they failed to recapture the magic of 1986 and fell to the Los Angeles Dodgers in seven games in the NLCS. In 1989 Strawberry was unable to repeat the success of the two previous seasons. Across the board his numbers fell off dramatically and the turmoil in the Mets clubhouse spilled out in front of the media when Strawberry and teammate Keith Hernandez got into a scuffle during team picture day with the cameras rolling.[29] As Strawberry suffered through his worst year with the Mets statistically (.225 batting average), the team began to falter and failed to make the postseason.

When Davey Johnson was fired early in the 1990 season, Strawberry declared he would leave the Mets at the end of the season as a free agent. He performed well and earned a seventh consecutive All-Star appearance. His last season as a Met concluded with 37 home runs and a career-best 108 runs batted in. That offseason Strawberry was true to his word and left the Mets to return home to Los Angeles, signing a five-year contract for $20.25 million with the Dodgers.

Strawberry's first year in LA, 1991, was his best in Dodger blue, but even though he was named to his eighth All-Star contest in July, he batted just .265 and his other numbers were down. In 1992 Strawberry played in only 43 games before injuring his back. He had back surgery in September. He tried to return far too soon and was off and on the disabled list of much of 1993, getting just 100 at-bats as his batting average tumbled to a disappointing .140.[30] As he fell apart on the baseball field, his personal life was no better. He was going through a messy and public divorce from Lisa, and the ever-present drug- and alcohol-abuse rumors swirled around him despite his claims of sobriety. Eventually Strawberry came clean to the Dodgers about his addiction and they placed him on the disabled list, and sent him off to the Betty Ford Clinic. When he was finally released from treatment, the Dodgers cut ties with the once-hailed hometown hero.

After being away from the game for a little over a year, Strawberry found a team willing to take another chance on him and signed with the San Francisco Giants on June 19, 1994. Strawberry was now 32 and promised the team he was ready to live a drug-free lifestyle. The Giants felt his guarantee of sobriety was genuine and took a chance on the slugger. With Strawberry in the lineup, the Giants flourished and won nine straight to come within 4½ games of the division-leading Dodgers. Despite his less than overwhelming numbers—4 home runs, 17 RBIs, and a .239 average in 92 at-bats—the Giants were impressed. The players' strike of 1994 interrupted the team's plans to capture the division from the Dodgers, but the Giants were left with a positive impression of Strawberry and his recovery.[31] He had a job waiting for him in 1995 in San Francisco.

But Strawberry would not get the chance to go back to the Bay Area. Troubles with the IRS arose over unreported income from card-show appearances, and, facing the prospect of jail time, Strawberry relapsed into using hard drugs and began to fail drug tests and display erratic behavior. While he was prepared to go to jail for the income-tax charges, Strawberry was let off with probation, community service, and a hefty bill for back taxes. But once again he would get another chance to turn his baseball career around, this time with the New York Yankees.

Yankees owner George Steinbrenner believed he could rehabilitate Strawberry and that the 296-foot porch in right field was no match for his uppercut swing. From 1995 through the 1999 season Strawberry was a member of the Yankees, but the dreams of Strawberry home runs landing in Yankee Stadium's right-field porch with consistent regularity were never realized. He was never able to recapture the glory he had experienced across town at Shea Stadium.

The 1995 season was full of setbacks for Strawberry. His legal troubles resulted in court-ordered restrictions that dictated where he could reside and the hours he was able to be away from his residence. Steinbrenner's determination to help Darryl turn his life around resulted in the Yankees appointing a full-time "guardian" to shadow Strawberry at all times, as well as regular drug testing to ensure that he would not slip up again. After rehabbing at the Yankees' facilities in Tampa, Strawberry was ready to hit the field. In 1995 he played in 31 minor-league games for the Tampa Yankees, Gulf Coast League Yankees, and the Columbus Clippers before rejoining the big-league club for 32 games toward the end of the season.

Strawberry spent 63 games in 1996 with the big-league club and hit 11 home runs. He helped the Yankees defeat the Orioles in the ALCS, hitting three home runs and collecting five RBIs, then went on to win another World Series, over the Atlanta Braves, alongside former Mets teammates David Cone and Dwight Gooden. In 1997 injuries derailed Strawberry and he played in only 16 minor-league games and 11 for the Yankees. For the first time in his career he failed to hit a home run that season. Then 1998 was a bounce-back season for Darryl at the plate, as he played in over 100 games for the first time since the 1991 season. In a part-time role he belted 24 home runs and had 57 RBIs to go along with a.247 average. For the third time in his career he became a World Series winner, but that accomplishment was overshadowed by a diagnosis of colon cancer that kept him from playing in the World Series.

In 1999 after cancer treatments after a 140-day MLB-mandated suspension for possessing cocaine and soliciting an undercover police officer for sex, the 37-year-old Strawberry returned to the Yankees. In limited playing time he managed only three home runs. However he was able to recapture postseason glory once again when he hit a decisive three-run home run that played a critical role in helping the Yankees sweep the Texas Rangers in the Division Series, then hit another homer as then the Yankees knocked off Boston in the ALCS before moving on to another World Series championship, over Atlanta. When the season concluded Strawberry retired from baseball as an eight-time All Star with four World Series rings—not a bad accomplishment for an inner-city kid from an impoverished neighborhood.

After baseball Strawberry continued to struggle with addiction and run-ins with the law. In 2000 his cancer returned and he started chemotherapy. However, this setback was not enough to quench his desire for drugs and he spent much of the next three years in and out of treatment centers and prison on drug-related charges. As of 2015, Strawberry was married to his wife, Tracy, and was an ordained minister. He devoted a great deal of his time to his family, church, and his charity work for those affected by autism. He said he remained remorseful for his past actions and was fully aware of the impact they had on his career. With his natural talent Strawberry could have been one of baseball's greatest hitters if it were not for his naïve nature, immaturity, and ultimately his substance abuse. In a book published in 2009 he admitted, "I made some good choices, and I made some really bad ones."[32]

NOTES

1 Darryl Strawberry with Arthur Rust Jr., *Darryl* (New York: Bantam Books, 1992), 82-88.

2 Darryl Strawberry, *Straw: Finding My Way* (New York: Ecco, 2009), 9.

3 Strawberry, *Darryl*, 76-77.

4 Strawberry, *Straw*, 21.

5 Strawberry, *Straw*, 21-22.

6 Michael Sokolove, *The Ticket Out: Darryl Strawberry & the Boys of Crenshaw* (New York: Simon & Schuster Paperbacks, 2004), 51.

7 Sokolove, 35.

8 Ibid.

9 Sokolove, 54.

10 Sokolove, 75.

11 Sokolove, 80.

12 Sokolove, 82-84.

13 Sokolove, 87.

14 Sokolove, 87-89.

15 Sokolove, 90.

16 Sokolove, 59.

17 Sokolove, 96.

18 Cited in Sokolove, 96.

19 Sokolove, 100.

20 Strawberry, *Darryl*, 128-129.

21 Ibid.

22 Sokolove, 101.

23 Bob Klapisch, *High and Tight: The Rise and Fall of Dwight Gooden and Darryl Strawberry*. (New York: Villard Books, 1996), 26.

24 Ibid.

25 Klapisch, 23-26.

26 Strawberry, *Darryl*, 188.

27 Jeff Pearlman, *The Bad Guys Won* (New York: Harper Collins, 2004), 43.

28 Pearlman, 137-138.

29 Klapisch, 71.

30 Klapisch, 77.

31 Klapisch, 135-138.

32 Strawberry, *Straw: Finding My Way*, 199.

TIM TEUFEL

By Rory Costello

TIM TEUFEL, WHO PLAYED MOSTLY AT SECOND base but filled in at all three other infield positions, had good line-drive power, with 86 home runs in the majors. After breaking in with the Minnesota Twins in September 1983, he went on to play 10 full seasons. He spent a little over half that time with the New York Mets, platooning with Wally Backman on the 1986 world champions. Mets fans remember him as a mild-mannered member of that hard-partying crew. Yet Tim had a scrappy side too, as he showed when he got the better of hulking reliever Rob Dibble after the flamethrower drilled him with a pitch in 1989. The lasting visual image of Teufel as a player is the "Teufel Shuffle" hip movement as he settled into the batter's box.

Timothy Shawn Teufel was born on July 7, 1958, in Greenwich, Connecticut. Fairfield County is known for affluence, but the Teufel family was working class. Tim's father, William Teufel Jr., was a carpenter. His mother, Marjorie McKenzie Teufel, had two other boys before Tim.[1]

In his youth Tim was a Yankees fan. He played Little League and then Babe Ruth ball, with the Knights of Columbus team in Greenwich. It helped that his father, who had played baseball in the Army, was a local youth coach. So was his uncle Robert, for whom a field in Greenwich is named.[2] Teufel attended the Catholic Middle School and St. Mary's High School. At that time, he was a third baseman.[3] In 1990 his middle-school coach in baseball and basketball, Peter Borchetta, remembered the youngster as intelligent and hard-working: "He used to like to come to practice early and leave late and have me throw to him for hours on end. I always felt he had the potential because he had the stick-to-itiveness."[4]

Teufel's coach at St. Mary's, Bill Bergeron, said he was a fine high-school ballplayer, but that he developed into a pro player in college. "He was a later bloomer," Bergeron said.[5] Tim himself pointed to the short schedule in Connecticut—"we only played 15-16 games a season"—as another factor. He went south to St. Petersburg Junior College to attract more attention from scouts.[6] However, he was a walk-on with the baseball team in 1977, and "He garnered playing time only after injuries shelved the two third basemen in front of him."[7]

The Milwaukee Brewers drafted Teufel in the 16th round of the 1978 amateur draft, but he did not sign. Instead, he transferred to Clemson University in South Carolina; a friend named Steve Gordon recalled, "He was discovered by the Clemson coach at a summer league game at Cubeta Stadium" in nearby Stamford. Teufel was playing for the Greenwich Collegiate baseball team.[8]

In the 1979 draft, the Chicago White Sox wanted Teufel — by then a second baseman —in the third round of the draft's secondary phase (since he had gone unsigned the previous year). Again, however, he chose to stay in school. That summer, he played in the Cape Cod League for the Cotuit Kettleers. He set league records (all since broken) with 16 home runs, 52 runs batted in, and 48 runs scored. His stock continued to rise. Teufel was Clemson's MVP in 1980; in 46 games he hit 11 homers (tied for the lead in the Atlantic Coast Conference) and had 66 RBIs (sole leader). He made the NCAA's Division I All-America team. The Tigers—also featuring freshman lefty Jimmy Key, who won 186 games in the majors—went to the College World Series, though they were knocked out early.

Shortly thereafter, the Twins selected Teufel in the second round of the regular phase of the draft (for which he was again eligible). Having graduated, this time he decided to sign. The new pro was placed in Double-A ball but was not out of his depth, batting .265 with 11 homers and 47 RBIs in 86 games with Orlando of the Southern League. Back in Orlando for 1981, his batting was not as strong (.248-17-60 in 128 games), and so the Twins started him off in the same place in 1982. After a solid 100 games, making the first-half All-Star team in the Southern League, Teufel earned promotion to Triple-A Toledo in late July. He batted .282 in both places and finished with combined totals of 15 home runs and 76 RBIs. Minnesota added him to its 40-man roster.

With Toledo in 1983, Teufel reached a new level, becoming International League MVP. He hit .323 for the Mud Hens, with 27 homers and 100 RBIs in 136 games, and his batting eye went from good to superior. He drew 102 walks, lifting his on-base percentage to .437. The Twins called him up in September, and he would never play another game in the minors.

On September 16, at the Metrodome in Minneapolis, Teufel had his first of two five-hit games in the majors, which included his first two big-league homers. Number one came off Jim Gott, then with the Toronto Blue Jays. That matchup tickled many broadcasters over the years. Teufel's surname means devil in German, while Gott's means God. It was hardly a biblical struggle, but over their careers, Tim came to the plate 10 more times against Gott. Overall, he was 2-for-9 with two walks.

John Castino had been the Twins' regular second baseman in 1983, but he graciously recognized that Tim was going to be taking his place.[9] Plagued by a bad back, Castino played his final eight games in the majors in 1984. Meanwhile, coming off a season of winter ball in Colombia, Teufel finished fourth in the voting for American League Rookie of the Year with a batting line of .262-14-61.

Tim's 1985 season was generally similar (.260-10-50), but while he was hitting over .300 in May, he cooled off after that. Toward the end of the season, manager Ray Miller wanted to look at another young second baseman, Steve Lombardozzi, whom he considered better defensively. The Associated Press wrote, "Teufel, knowing Miller's leaning toward Lombardozzi, asked to be traded during the offseason. And when the Twins were unable to deal him during the winter meetings ... he repeated his request."[10]

On January 16, 1986, Minnesota obliged, trading Teufel and minor leaguer Pat Crosby to the Mets. In return, they received Billy Beane—the former top draft pick who attained fame as the general manager of the Oakland A's—plus Joe Klink and Bill Latham. The deal worked out well for the Mets. Beane hit .213 in 80 games for Minnesota in 1986 and played only 55 more games in the majors after that. Tony La Russa got the best out of Klink as a situational lefty reliever for Oakland in 1990 and 1991. Latham pitched in seven games for the Twins in '86 and that was all for his big-league career.

At the time Teufel said, "I think the Twins were looking for more speed ... and I didn't give them that. I've got a positive attitude. The main thing is to play on a team that has reasons for you being there."[11] That was certainly the case in New York. Marty Noble in *Newsday* wrote, "The Mets achieved what manager Dave Johnson identified as 'my No. 1 priority' when they obtained Teufel. ... 'We made a great deal today,'

Johnson said."[12] The Mets' incumbent second baseman, Wally Backman, was a speedy, gritty sparkplug—but the switch-hitter never did hit lefties well. The 1985 season was the only time Backman got to face southpaws frequently, and he hit just .122 against them. He even temporarily abandoned batting righty.

Teufel became a contributor to the Mets—but it took time. As author Jeff Pearlman portrayed it in his book about the '86 champs, *The Bad Guys Won*, it didn't help Teufel that he "was taking away at-bats from the beloved Wally Backman." According to pitcher Ron Darling, being the new guy and having a quiet, humble nature also made Tim "the foil for a lot of jokes."[13]

The teammate who rode Teufel the most was Darryl Strawberry, at least after the outfielder had taken a few drinks on a plane flight. Teufel let it go by until August, when he finally confronted Strawberry. Pearlman quoted Tim himself: "There's a breaking point to every person in their pride and character and who they are. No man is going to just sit there and be a marshmallow." Pitcher Bob Ojeda said, "From that day forward Teuf became a better ballplayer. He was just pushed and pushed and pushed, and he was tired of it. It woke something up in him."[14]

Pearlman's book also devotes as much space as anyone could possibly need to the club's most infamous off-the-field episode that year: the July 19 altercation at a Houston bar called Cooter's, and the subsequent arrest of four Mets, including Teufel. It started innocently enough, as a celebration of the birth of Tim's first child, a boy named Shawn. It was also ironic, since Teufel was a loyal husband and good Christian who only went out with the boys on occasion for a beer or two in the spirit of team solidarity.

That night, however, he went over his limit. According to Houston police, Teufel began to cause a disturbance inside the bar around 2 A.M. and was asked to leave. He tried to exit with a bottle of beer, which would have been illegal, and a scuffle ensued. Teufel and Ron Darling each wound up being charged with aggravated assault on a police officer. They, Bob Ojeda, and Rick Aguilera all spent 11 hours in jail before posting bond. According to Teufel, who was badly shaken by the episode, he was severely beaten.[15] Eventually, in January 1987, Teufel and Darling both got a year's probation and a $200 fine after a plea bargain reduced their third-degree felony charges to the misdemeanor of resisting arrest.[16]

Tim finished the regular season hitting just .247, with 4 homers and 31 RBIs. One of those round-trippers was a pinch-hit grand slam off Philadelphia's Tom Hume to end a game at Shea Stadium on June 10.

Teufel started twice in the National League Championship Series, both times against Astros lefty Bob Knepper, and went 1-for-6. He wasn't around for the end of either dramatic comeback victory. Len Dykstra won Game Three with a homer off Dave Smith in the ninth inning, and Game Six was the incredibly suspenseful 16-inning affair at the Astrodome.

Tim got three more starts in the World Series against the Boston Red Sox, each against lefty Bruce Hurst, going 4-for-9. The only run of Game One scored when the second baseman let Rich Gedman's grounder get through his legs in the seventh inning. Although Tim was not known for his defense, this related more to his range and turning the double play. Third baseman Ray Knight said, "He had the softest hands on our team."[17] Yet to his credit, Teufel stood up and faced the media's questions until they were all done.

Tim was 2-for-4 with a homer in Game Five as the Mets lost, 4-2. The Mets pulled off another exciting comeback in Game Seven, but again Teufel was not on the field as the game ended. Even just 10 years later, he told Mets beat writer John Harper of the *New York Daily News*, "It feels like a lifetime ago." Harper wrote, "They quickly became the team everybody loved to hate, and that, said Teufel, 'brought us even closer together. We would do anything for each other.' " Tim further observed, "In baseball, and especially in that clubhouse in '86, there was an old-school way. You needed to do things a certain way to be part of the team. ... As far as off the field, there were two or three different groups of guys on that team. But they all mixed well in the clubhouse, on the plane. That was the chemistry. You could go whichever direction you wanted."[18]

The 1987 season was Teufel's most productive. Despite getting just 351 plate appearances in 97 games, he exactly matched his career highs in homers with 14 and RBIs with 61. His batting average of .308 was easily his best. One standout performance came at Cincinnati's Riverfront Stadium on July 5, 1987. In a 7-5 loss to the Reds, Teufel homered twice against Tom Browning. He did better during his career against the lefty than any other mound opponent: 22-for-48 (.458) with five home runs. After that game Teufel said modestly, "I've got a hot bat right now. He threw me a good variety of pitches, but they were all over the plate. Next time it might not be the same story."[19]

The Backman-Teufel platoon remained in effect through 1988. Unfortunately for Tim, he reverted to 1986 levels with the bat; his home run and RBI totals were identical (4 and 31), while his average was even lower at .234. Teufel had gotten into Tom Browning's head, though. After singling twice in three at-bats on April 30, 1988, he annoyed the pitcher by stepping out of the batter's box as Browning started his windup. Browning stopped and plate umpire Eric Gregg called a balk; Teufel then got plunked in the back with the next pitch. Darryl Strawberry ran out of the dugout and charged the mound, sparking a bench-clearing fight.

When the Los Angeles Dodgers beat the Mets in the 1988 NLCS, they used just one left-handed starter: John Tudor in Game Four. Teufel went 0-for-3 before leaving in the ninth inning of what proved to be a deflating loss. That was the last time his team reached the postseason.

In September 1988 the Mets had brought up their most prized prospect of the time, infielder Gregg Jefferies. That December they traded away Backman and gave the second base job to Jefferies for 1989, disbanding the platoon. As a result, Teufel started just 30 games at second that year—plus 28 more at first base, a position he had played just seven times before in the majors. He hit a career-low two homers and drove in just 15 runs in 83 games and 254 plate appearances.

The most notable incident of Teufel's '89 season came on July 8 against Cincinnati at Shea Stadium. He went 4-for-4 that day, with the first three hits against (who else?) Reds starter Tom Browning. In the eighth inning, with the Mets up 8-0, hot-tempered Rob Dibble nailed Tim in the back with one of his 100-mph fastballs. "I looked up," Teufel recalled, "and there he was, spittin' and grinnin'."[20] Tim charged the mound, and a brawl erupted, in which he bloodied Dibble's lip. "Order was restored, but only briefly. After Dibble was ejected, he began yelling at Teufel and the whole mess erupted anew. 'He came out of the dugout and started pointing at me,' Teufel said. 'Am I going to start backing down then? That's not going to happen.'"[21]

Although Teufel still got into 80 games for the Mets in 1990, his plate appearances tailed off further to 192, with a batting line of .246-10-24. He saw even less action in the early going in 1991. On May 31, feeling the need for a backup shortstop, the Mets traded Tim to the San Diego Padres for Garry Templeton. He spent the rest of that year in San Diego—even turning down a trade to his former club, the Twins, who wanted him during the pennant race. Though it would have meant another World Series ring, what meant more to him was the gesture by Padres general manager Joe McIlvaine to let the decision be Tim's.[22]

Teufel could have signed with the Reds or the Giants that offseason, but he returned to San Diego, where he spent two more seasons. During his time with the Padres, he appeared in 294 games, starting 202, mainly at second base, but also a good few at third and a handful at first. He batted .232 with 24 homers and 98 RBIs. STATS Inc.'s 1994 *Scouting Report* nicely summed up Tim's contribution the previous year: "As usual, the solid veteran did a productive job. With so many young players on the roster and so much turmoil generated by the dumping of salaries, manager Jim Riggleman appreciated that Teufel set an example of how to conduct oneself as a professional."[23]

The Padres chose not to re-sign free agent Teufel heading into the 1994 season, and he did not get any other offers. After retiring, he worked as an investment banker in the San Diego area for the next several years.[24] He then got back into baseball, rejoining the Mets organization as a scout in November 1998. In 2001 and 2002, he was their minor-league infield coordinator. He also managed the Mets' Instructional League teams.[25]

Teufel became a regular-season manager for the first time in 2003. He started with the Brooklyn Cyclones in the short-season New York-Penn League. He then led the St. Lucie Mets (Florida State League, high Class A) in 2004 and 2005. Former Mets teammate Gary Carter took over at St. Lucie in 2006, and so Tim took a break from baseball for a year. He owned a tile establishment in Port St. Lucie, but he dissolved that partnership when he got a chance to manage a new Mets farm club, the Savannah Sand Gnats, in 2007. "I love coaching," he said. "I love being around the game. You get the itch. You love the game. It's easy to come back. It wasn't a hard decision."[26]

Teufel returned to St. Lucie for the 2008 and 2009 seasons. Perhaps the biggest news from this period came off the field, though. In February 2009, it was revealed that Tim and his wife, Valerie, were among those holding accounts with Ponzi schemer Bernard L. Madoff. Mets owner Fred Wilpon was among the most prominent figures—especially in terms of financial exposure—on the "Madoff List," but other famous names included Wilpon's friend Sandy Koufax and actor John Malkovich.

Teufel received a promotion to Double-A Binghamton in the Eastern League for the 2010 season. That fall there was talk that he might interview for the open position with the big club that eventually went to Terry Collins. The interview did not take place, and shortly thereafter more unpleasant news came on the Bernie Madoff front. On behalf of the investors who had been duped, in an effort to make good their losses, court-appointed trustee Irving Picard filed a "clawback" suit against Tim (among various other former Madoff clients) for $1.2 million. Things looked up in January 2011, though, as Teufel took over for Ken Oberkfell as manager of Triple-A Buffalo, while old platoon partner Wally Backman stepped into the job at Binghamton.

As a skipper, Teufel knew the value of hard work and perseverance from his own example as a player. He also drew from the approach of the '86 Mets, who were known for making comeback after comeback. "I think that's where I got some of my attitude," he said in 2010. "You always feel like you're in the game no matter what the score is. You're always fighting to claw your way back. That's part of the spirit of the game."[27]

Teufel returned to the majors for the 2012 season, becoming the Mets' third-base coach. He also worked with the team's infielders. After the 2014 season, there was some talk that he could become hitting coach in New York, but his role remained the same for the 2015 season.

Tim and Valerie Scheidt Teufel were married in 1981. After Shawn, they had three daughters, Kenley, Kelly, and Amber Grace. The Teufels settled in Jupiter, Florida, but Tim maintained strong ties to his native Connecticut. Among other good works, starting in 1991 he hosted the Tim Teufel Celebrity Golf Tournament at Tamarack Country Club in Greenwich, for the benefit of various charities. The 24th edition was held in 2014. "Greenwich will always be a special place for me," he said in 2006. "It was a great place to grow up and play baseball. Greenwich was the beginning of my baseball career. It was my foundation."[28]

SOURCES

In addition to the sources cited in the Notes, the author also consulted:

baseball-reference.com

retrosheet.org

thebaseballcube.com

kettleers.org

NOTES

1 Jeff Pearlman, *The Bad Guys Won* (New York: HarperCollins Publishers, 2004), 114. William Teufel Jr. obituary, *Press of*

Atlantic City, August 11, 2003. This obituary referred to only two sons, William and Tim, which implies that the other brother died at some point.

2 Bobby Ciafardini, "Amazin' Mets Memories: Teufel Looks Back on Spirit of '86," *Connecticut Post*, July 28, 2006.

3 Ibid.

4 John Kovach, "Mets' Teufel doesn't forget former coach," *The Hour* (Norwalk, Connecticut), January 23, 1990: 23.

5 Ciafardini.

6 Patricia Brooks, "Path to the Big Leagues Is Easier to Run," *New York Times,* June 23, 1991.

7 Ibid.

8 Ciafardini.

9 Patrick Reusse, "Castino Forecast: 'I'll be Moving On,'" *The Sporting News*, October 3, 1983: 21.

10 "Minnesota Deals Engle, Teufel," Associated Press, January 17, 1986.

11 Wire service reports, January 17, 1986.

12 Marty Noble, "Mets Swap for Teufel," *Newsday*, January 17, 1986.

13 Pearlman, 114-115.

14 Pearlman, 84.

15 Michael Martinez, "4 Mets Arrested in Fight," *New York Times*, July 20, 1986.

16 Joseph Durso, "Darling, Teufel Get Probation," *New York Times*, January 27, 1987.

17 Ibid., 218.

18 John Harper, "The Mighty Have Fallen," *New York Daily News*, March 31, 1996.

19 "Browning Sharp as Reds Beat Gooden," Associated Press, July 6, 1987.

20 Richard Scheinin, *Field of Screams* (New York: W.W. Norton, 1994), 384.

21 Helene Elliott, "A Kerplunk, a Jab, and a Brawl: Teufel Gets Hot, Then He Gets Even," *Newsday*, July 9, 1989.

22 Bob Nightengale, "Tim Teufel Has a Curious taste in Employers — the Padres," *Los Angeles Times*, February 28, 1992: C1.

23 John Dewan, ed., *The Scouting Report, 1994* (New York: HarperPerennial, 1994), 646.

24 George Albano, "Tim Teufel Discovers You Can Go Home Again," *Greenwich* (Connecticut) *Post*, August 30, 2007.

25 Patrick Mulrenin, "Teufel Takes On Manager Role," MLB.com, December 4, 2002.

26 Noell Barnidge, "Mets hire Teufel to Manage Sand Gnats," *Savannah Morning News*, January 10, 2007.

27 John Hartsock. "Lessons learned," *Altoona Mirror,* July 8, 2010.

28 Ciafardini.

MOOKIE WILSON

By Irv Goldfarb

MOOKIE WILSON STOOD AT THE PLATE IN the bottom of the 10th inning, arcing his bat, focusing intently on Red Sox pitcher Bob Stanley. He realized that he represented the potential winning run in the most important game of his life and he was determined not to make the final out. Wilson had come a long way in his relatively short major-league career: toiling for the New York Mets various farm teams; named the starting center fielder for the laughable big-league club; subsequently becoming the consensus face of their organization, all within six rapidly-moving seasons. He was 30 years old and he had already seen a lot…

William Hayward Wilson was born in Bamberg, South Carolina, on February 9, 1956, one of 12 children. Two of his brothers also played pro ball for a short time: John was drafted by the Mets and stole 56 bases for Columbia in the South Atlantic League in 1984; Phil played in the minors for the Minnesota and Montreal organizations, while a third brother, Richard, probably played the biggest role in his family life a number of years later.

Nicknamed Mookie as a child because of the way he asked for milk (or so the legend goes), Wilson pitched for Bamberg-Ehrhardt High School under coach Dave Horton, the local legend who became the first high-school baseball coach inducted into the South Carolina Athletic Hall of Fame. Wilson's years there included a state championship (one of 14 won by Horton.) After leaving Bamberg-Erhardt, Wilson signed a letter of intent with South Carolina State University, close to his hometown. But SCSU discontinued its baseball program literally days after his signing, spurring Wilson to attend Spartanburg Methodist College instead, playing there in 1974 and '75. It was while with the Pioneers that Wilson was drafted by the Los Angeles Dodgers in the fourth round of the 1976 amateur draft. Surprisingly, he decided not to sign with LA, transferring instead to the University of South Carolina, where he played the outfield and pitched, hoping to showcase his versatility to other major-league teams. His first coach there was former Yankees star Bobby Richardson. In 1977, now under the tutelage of June Raines, who had taken over the program after Richardson resigned at the start of that season, the Gamecocks played in the College World Series. They lost to Arizona State University, 2-1, but Wilson was named to the All-Tournament team outfield.[1]

The success of that South Carolina squad, along with Wilson's decision to turn down the earlier offer from the Dodgers, resulted in his being chosen again, this time in the second round of the 1977 draft by the New York Mets. He signed a contract and was assigned to Wausau, Wisconsin, a Mets affiliate in the Midwest League. Appearing in 68 games in the outfield for

Wausau, Wilson hit .290 in 245 at-bats; his power numbers (6 home runs, 32 RBIs) were not overly impressive, but that is not what had attracted pro scouts to him in the first place. It was his speed and defense that would keep him moving through the Mets' system and in that first half-season he stole 23 bases in 30 attempts. Promoted to Double-A Jackson, Mississippi, the next year, Wilson had 497 at-bats, hitting.292 with 15 triples and 38 steals.

It was during this season that Wilson's brother Richard affected his life. Richard had fathered a boy, now 4 years old, whom he would not or could not support, and on the night of June 22, 1978, Wilson married the boy's mother, Rosa Gilbert, at home plate at Jackson's Smith-Wills Stadium. The ceremony, held before a crowd of 1,200, included an archway of bats held up by team members. The reception took place on the field after the game, with everyone in attendance invited. Fans and teammates then chipped in for a bridal suite at a local hotel. (The marriage made Wilson, oddly enough, both the uncle and stepfather of Preston Wilson, who went on to have a career in the majors, crowning it with a World Series championship with the Cardinals in 2006.)

Called up to Triple-A Tidewater for 1979 and '80, the speedy outfielder (he had given up pitching by then) racked up a combined 99 stolen bases in 125 tries and scored 176 runs; along with his .295 average through August of 1980, the Mets had seen enough. It was time to bring Wilson up to the Big Apple. Wilson made his major-league debut on September 2, 1980, in Los Angeles against the Dodgers, the team that had originally drafted him four years earlier.

Batting leadoff, Wilson grounded out to short against Dodgers starter Dave Goltz, then did the same in the top of the third. He ended the game 0-for-4, but the night was not a total loss as he drove in second baseman Wally Backman with another groundball, this time off reliever Bobby Castillo, who had replaced Goltz during a Mets four-run rally in the top of the seventh. The Dodgers won, 7-5, and the Mets lost the next night as well, shut out 2-0 by LA's Burt Hooton, with Wilson going 0-for-3, with a walk.

It was not until his third game, a daytime contest at San Diego on September 4, that Wilson collected his first hit, a single to left field off Padres starter John Curtis in his second at-bat. The Mets lost that contest too as Curtis threw a complete game in the 3-2 win. In fact, the Mets lost 13 straight games during this stretch, not winning again until they beat the Cubs at home on September 13. The franchise struggled through another poor campaign in 1980, their fourth consecutive losing season, and the team was obviously hoping for a spark from its promising farm system (as a matter of fact, the September 4 loss to the Padres also marked the debut of the Mets' other projected star, third baseman Hubie Brooks). Wilson's call-up was not a cause for immediate celebration however: In just over 100 at-bats the rest of the 1980 season, he hit only .248 with eight extra-base hits (none of them homers) and just 12 walks versus 19 strikeouts. He stole seven bases and made only two errors in 229 innings, underscoring what the Mets knew were his greatest talents—above-average fielding and dazzling speed.

The following season showed a slight uptick in Wilson's offense as he batted .271 during the strike-shortened 1981 campaign. And though he drove in just 14 runs, he stole 24 bases and played all three outfield positions to the tune of a .983 fielding percentage. (Brooks on the other hand hit .307 in '81 with 38 RBIs; however, he also made 21 errors in 93 games. These early numbers were already foreshadowing the future careers of the two youngsters: one the superior hitter, the other the speedy defensive star.)

Wilson's next three seasons were eerily consistent as he hit .279 in 1982, then batted .276 in each of the next three years. He drove in between 51 and 55 runs each season and tied the team record with 9 triples in 1982, to go with 58 steals.[2] Though consistent, Wilson's offensive numbers were still not awe-inspiring. He led the league in at-bats in 1983, but struck out what would remain a career-high 103 times with only 18 unintentional walks. His on-base percentage in the modern SABRmetric world would probably have bought him a ticket back to Tidewater, averaging out to just .307 during this stretch. But his 10 home runs in 1984 would also be his career high, while his 10 triples that year set a new Mets record.

Despite his semi-anemic offensive numbers, Wilson became entrenched at the top of the Mets lineup as the team strengthened its personnel through the mid-1980s. The development of the franchise's next burgeoning star, Darryl Strawberry, along with the acquisition of recent MVP Keith Hernandez from the Cardinals, helped swing the team from the embarrassment of 94 losses in 1983 to a second-place, 90-72 finish in '84. The subsequent trade for All-Star Gary Carter from Montreal (in a deal that sent Hubie Brooks to the Expos) helped the Mets stay in the battle for the NL East crown late into 1985; they finally succumbed to the Cardinals, but enjoyed their best season since the Miracle Mets of 1969, racking up 98 wins and finishing three games behind St. Louis.

Unfortunately for Wilson, he missed much of the excitement. The center fielder had been experiencing discomfort in his right shoulder for more than a year and was finally forced to undergo surgery for torn cartilage on July 3, 1985. Surgeons reported the discovery of "fraying and tears of the labrum," along with other cartilage damage. Wilson did not return to the Mets until September 1 and did not see regular action until a week later. He ended the season with fewer than 400 plate appearances, once again hitting .276, with 26 RBIs and 24 stolen bases.

The next season, 1986, was the campaign that Met fans had been awaiting for 17 years. Wilson's year began as badly as the previous one had ended, however, as he was hit in the eye from 40 feet away by a ball thrown by shortstop Rafael Santana during a spring-training base running drill. The blow shattered the eyeglasses that Wilson had begun wearing the year before to cut down on outfield glare. He was carted off the field and took 21 stitches above the eye and four more on the side of his nose. "The glasses … took the full impact of the blow and probably prevented more damage," remarked the doctor attending the injury.[3] Wilson did not return to the lineup until May 9, but the team suddenly had some depth in the outfield with veterans George Foster and Danny Heep absorbing innings. When Wilson returned to the field, he found himself sharing center-field duties with young fireball Lenny Dykstra, who was playing his first full season. It was not until Foster was released in early August that Wilson was able to play regularly again, settling into left while Dykstra became the regular center fielder.

But the 1986 Mets could do no wrong: The team led the NL East practically wire-to-wire, winning 108 games. Their 13-3 record in April included a franchise-tying 11-game winning streak; they lost only 18 games between May and June, and by midsummer the division race was pretty much over. The team's stars and their exploits of that season are remembered not only by Mets fans but by fans of all teams; from Carter's 105 RBIs to Strawberry's 27 home runs, to pitching phenom Dwight Gooden's 17-6, 2.84 season. There was something special happening at Shea Stadium and at the top of the order every day sat the "Mookster." He was the team's sparkplug, still one of the most popular Mets among their fans, and his statistics were on the rise. His batting average jumped to .289, his on-base percentage to .345. He scored only 61 runs with just 25 stolen bases, but his 72 strikeouts were a new low for a full season. He also enjoyed his best season in the field, committing only five errors. But for this team the numbers were secondary as the Mets bulldozed their way through the National League, seemingly just waiting for their date with the postseason. It came in the form of the Houston Astros in the NLCS. Led by its ace, Mike Scott, Houston made the series uncomfortable for the Mets, dragging them through a nailbiting Game Six before the Mets finally prevailed in the 16th inning. Wilson dragged through the NLCS himself, collecting only three hits in 26 at-bats, striking out seven times and stealing just one base.

The Red Sox followed in the World Series and the two league champions fought through an all-time classic, the Mets battling back from a 2-0 hole to bring the Series back to Shea for Games Six and Seven. It all came to a crescendo on a cold Saturday night in October, with Wilson standing at the plate and 55,000 fans screaming in anticipation. Down 5-3 in the bottom of the 10th inning of Game Six, the first two batters flied out; then the gritty Mets bunched consecutive singles by Carter, rookie Kevin Mitchell, and third baseman Ray Knight to plate a run. Red Sox manager John McNamara called on veteran reliever Bob Stanley to replace Calvin Schiraldi and get the Series-clinching final out. Stanley had faced Wilson three times already in the Series and had retired him twice. After seven pitches, the count was 2-and-2, but on pitch number eight, the ball got away from catcher Rich Gedman, almost hitting Wilson, bouncing away and scoring Mitchell from third base. Two pitches later the most infamous groundball in World Series lore rolled down the first-base line and trickled into history. "I had a pitch I should've handled really well, middle in low, but kind of rolled over it," said Wilson when asked about the fateful pitch. "I knew the ball was hit slowly, so I gotta run, and the pitcher was slow getting there. I didn't see the ball go through (Bill) Buckner, I just saw it go behind him. . . ." Wilson maintained that he would have beaten the slow and injured Buckner to first, even had he made the play cleanly.[4] The Mets won Game Seven two nights later to capture the second world championship in their history. Wilson's numbers for the Series were a tad better than they had been for the NLCS: a .269 average, with a double and three stolen bases. He struck out six times.

As often happens with championship teams, the following year brings roster changes that ultimately affect team chemistry. In this case, the Mets decided they needed Kevin McReynolds, so they traded a package of young players (including one of '86's heroes, Kevin Mitchell) to the San Diego Padres. The acquisition did not sit well with Wilson or Dykstra, and Wilson even went so far as to request a trade, which was ignored; he and Dykstra ended up sharing time in center, with McReynolds playing left. It turned out to be one of Wilson's finest offensive seasons as he hit a career-high .299 in just under 400 at-bats, with 19 doubles, 34 RBIs, and 21 stolen bases. And despite 92 wins, the Mets found themselves looking up at St. Louis again, finishing three games behind the eventual NL champions.[5]

Wilson and Dykstra continued their tag-team act in 1988, but Wilson appeared to be on the downturn. Through the first hundred-plus games of the season, he was hitting only .234 with 19 RBIs and 31 runs scored. The team, however, was playing well. Ray Knight and Rafael Santana had been replaced by Howard Johnson and Kevin Elster respectively, but most of the roster from '86 was still intact and the Mets led the Pirates for most of the year. Beginning with a series in Pittsburgh on August 5, Wilson turned his season around, hitting .386 from that point on, driving in 22 runs and scoring 30 more.

On September 5 against the Pirates, he matched a career high with four RBIs, including a three-run homer in a 7-5 victory. The win gave the Mets a 10-game lead in the division and they cruised to their second postseason in three years. Wilson ended the '88 campaign at .296 with 41 RBIs. His strikeout-to-walk ratio was a respectable 63-27. But things did not go as well in 1988 as they had two years before and the Mets were upset in the NLCS by the Dodgers, a team they had beaten 10 out of 11 during the regular season. Wilson's performance did not help as he collected a measly two singles in 13 at-bats with two walks and a stolen base attempt that was unsuccessful.

The Mets showed their faith in Wilson when they picked up his option before the 1989 season. However, on June 18, he was the victim of another outfield glut as, with the Mets only two games behind the Cubs in the NL East, the team traded the popular Dykstra to Philadelphia for up-and-coming center fielder Juan Samuel. Understanding that the younger Samuel would get the bulk of playing time, Wilson once again requested a trade and this time the Mets accommodated him, sending him to the Toronto Blue Jays for reliever Jeff Musselman and minor-league pitcher Mike Brady at the July 31 trading deadline.[6]

Over all or parts of 10 seasons, Wilson ended his Mets career with a batting average of .276. He hit 60 home runs, drove in 342 runs, and scored 592 runs. He stole 281 bases, getting caught less than 100 times. His one outstanding blemish was an on-base percentage of just .318. During that decade, he could also lay claim to being one of the most popular Mets of all time.

But Wilson's career was not over. After hitting just .205 for New York in 80 appearances over the team's first 105 games (possibly another reason team management willingly accommodated his trade request), Wilson played in 54 games for Toronto, hitting .298. He also made his return to the postseason; the Blue Jays lost in the ALCS to Oakland.

Obviously, the Toronto organization liked what they saw and signed Wilson to a two-year contract in the offseason. A rejuvenated Wilson enjoyed a successful 1990. In 629 at-bats (the most he had since 1983), Wilson hit only .265 but drove in 51 runs (his most since '84) and stole 23 bases, scoring 81 times. Playing mostly center field, he made only five errors and posted a.992 fielding percentage, fifth among AL outfielders.

Wilson's playing time diminished greatly in 1991 when the Blue Jays acquired Devon White from the Angels. Playing in only 86 games, Wilson batted just .241. His OBP dipped below .300 and he scored just 26 runs. But the Jays made the playoffs once again, and Wilson snuck in eight more at-bats, collecting two singles and stealing a base. His last game in the major leagues was on October 13, 1991, when he started Game Five of the ALCS in left field against Minnesota, going 1-for-4 and scoring a run. The Jays lost 8-5, giving the Twins the AL pennant. The Blue Jays decided not to pick up Wilson's contract for 1992 and after some interest was expressed, ironically enough by the Red Sox, he got no more phone calls. Mookie Wilson's major-league career was over.[7]

Wilson went to college after he retired, receiving a bachelor's degree from Mercy College in New York in 1996, and obtained a commercial driver's license three years later. But his love was always baseball and he stayed involved.[8] He was the Mets first-base coach from 1997 through 2002, managed their rookie-league team in Kingsport, Tennessee, for two seasons, then moved on to skipper the Class-A Brooklyn Cyclones in 2005. He also served as the organization's baserunning coordinator, and returned to the major-league first-base coaching box in 2011.[9] After that season he was moved into a front-office "ambassador" position, and it was here that Wilson had his first whiff of controversy during his 30-plus years in baseball. "It's sad to say this, but I have basically become a hood ornament for the Mets, "Wilson wrote in his autobiography. "I would have liked an explanation as to why I was moved from first-base coach to the ambassadorship, but none was ever given. … I understand that jobs come and go in the baseball business, but sometimes management loses sight of how these moves play with people's lives. … They just dictated my career as a player and a coach and it wasn't right."[10] Nevertheless, Wilson did rejoin the Mets in 2012 in a job described as roving instructor and club ambassador.

As of 2015 Wilson was still married to Rosa and they have three children. They lived in Lakewood Township, New Jersey, and shortly after the 1986 World Series opened an educational center for girls called Mookie's Roses near their home. He also appeared at shows and on the field with the player he has become most associated with — Bill Buckner. Wilson said a day did not go by that he wasn't asked about the play, and that he approached it with mixed emotions. "Initially it did bother me that my career was defined by one play," he said. "I think I've done more for the game than just hit a groundball — not even a hard-hit groundball. But I came to understand … it's part of baseball history. It's part of the Mets history, and to deny being a part of it is wrong."[11]

There was not much wrong in William "Mookie" Wilson's career, least of all that little roller.

NOTES

1 imdb.com/name/nm1146525/bio. The All-Tourney second baseman was ASU's Bob Horner, who went on to star at first base with the Atlanta Braves.

2 Mookie Wilson profile, ultimatemets.com/profile.php?PlayerCode=0300.

3 Joseph Durso, "Right Eye Injured," *New York Times*, March 6, 1986.

4 David Itzkoff, "Mookie Wilson on Life After the Mets," *New York Times*, April 25, 2014.

5 "Question of the Week: Should Wilson and Dykstra Platoon?" *New York Times*, May 7, 1989; Craig Wolff, "Wilson Adapts to Platoon Job," *New York Times*, June 13, 1986.

6 Joseph Durso, "Wilson Sent to Jays in Musselman Deal," *New York Times*, August 2, 1989. Upon leaving the Mets, Wilson held the team record for stolen bases (281) and triples (62), but both records were surpassed by Jose Reyes.

7 "Blue Jays Drop Wilson," *New York Times*, October 29, 1991.

8 Ira Berkow, "Graduation Day for Wilson: Pomp and Studious Stance," *New York Times*, May 29, 1996.

9 Andrew Keh, "Mets Announce Coaching Changes," *New York Times*, October 5, 2011; George Willis, "Wilson to Take the Field as Mets' First Base Coach," *New York Times*, October 18, 1996.

10 Mike Puma, "Mookie Wilson: I Went From Mets Hero to 'Hood Ornament'," *New York Post*, April 25, 2014; Mookie Wilson with Eric Sherman, *Mookie: Life, Baseball and the '86 Mets* (New York: Berkeley Books, 2014).

11 Bill Price, "Mookie Wilson has come to understand his place in Mets history ahead of series with Red Sox," *New York Daily News* of Thursday, August 27, 2015.

DAVEY JOHNSON

By Mark Armour

AFTER A HIGHLY SUCCESSFUL PLAYING career as both a slick-fielding infielder and a slugger, Davey Johnson went on to an even more decorated career as a manager. His winning percentage of .562 is 10th all-time among managers with 1,000 victories, and is surpassed by only Earl Weaver among pilots who began their career after 1960. But it was while playing for Weaver in Baltimore that Johnson first became a prominent name in baseball, as the valuable second baseman for four pennant winners and the 1966 and 1970 champions. Four men share the record for starting 21 World Series games for the Orioles: Brooks Robinson, Frank Robinson, Boog Powell, and Dave Johnson.

David Allen Johnson was born in Orlando, Florida, on January 30, 1943. Johnson's father, Frederick, was a highly decorated World War II tank commander, who eventually rose to the rank of lieutenant colonel. Frederick left for the war just as Dave was born, and later spent time in an Italian prisoner-of-war camp, where he had his teeth pulled without an anesthetic. He later escaped, and lived with the Italian resistance. The stories of his wartime life were never discussed in the Johnson home—Dave did not learn of them until he was an adult himself. All he knew was that his father was deeply respected by other military men the family associated with. "Dad was very tough, a stubborn Swede on the outside but very caring down deep," recalled Johnson decades later. "I'm stubborn, too. Yet even if he was hard, you still knew he was always thinking about his family, his soldiers, that he'd try to move mountains for them."[1]

As the child of an Army officer, Johnson lived on Army bases in Germany, Georgia, Texas, and Wyoming. The family eventually settled in San Antonio, Texas, where Johnson first attracted baseball scouts at Alamo Heights High School. Johnson first went to Texas A&M, where he played shortstop for "the greatest coach in the world, Tom Chandler, a real classic who taught me real respect for the game, and gave me an opportunity to show what I could do."[2] After two years at College Station, where he also played guard for the varsity basketball team, Johnson entertained suitors from several major-league teams before signing with the Orioles. Scouts Dee Phillips and Jim Russo visited Johnson right after his last college game, and made a deal for a $25,000 bonus.[3]

After signing with the Orioles, Johnson joined the Stockton club in the California League. As a 19-year-old in 1962, he hit .309 as the club's shortstop, and became one of the best prospects in a system loaded with young talent. The next year he played under Earl Weaver at Elmira (Eastern League) and hit .326 before earning a promotion to Triple-A Rochester in July. The International League proved a bit tougher (.246 in 63 games) and the move also caused him to play regularly at second base, a position he took to

very well. He returned to Rochester in 1964 and hit .264 with 19 home runs, playing both middle infield positions, and developing as one of the more promising infielders in the minor leagues. Baltimore was a fine team, and Johnson's path was blocked by shortstop Luis Aparicio and second baseman Jerry Adair, both defensive stalwarts. Johnson made the club in 1965 and backed up at second, short, and third (manned by Brooks Robinson) for half a season before the Orioles decided to send him back to Rochester. He hit just .170 in 47 at bats in the big time, but .301 back in Triple-A.

In the spring of 1966 Orioles manager Hank Bauer turned the second-base job over to Johnson, bypassing incumbent Adair, who had held the job for five years. The promotion could have been temporary, but Adair complained enough to cause the Orioles to deal him to the White Sox in June. Johnson played in 131 games in 1966, and hit .257 with seven home runs. He drew raves for his defense and provided hope for his offense. "We feel," said general manager Harry Dalton, "that this boy is going to be a big hitter among big-league second basemen. He has done everything now that we have asked him to do. He has the intelligence to apply himself."[4] The Orioles also won the pennant in 1966, and Johnson's .286 average in the World Series contributed to the sweep of the Los Angeles Dodgers. Johnson earned the distinction of being the batter who got the final hit off Sandy Koufax, a single in Game Three.

Johnson built on his fine rookie year with fine defense and more power (ten home runs and 30 doubles) in 1967, though the Orioles fell to sixth place. After the season the Orioles traded Luis Aparicio to the Chicago White Sox, and the ascension of shortstop Mark Belanger completed the great infield (along with Johnson, third baseman Brooks Robinson, and first baseman Boog Powell) that helped define the great Orioles of the coming years. In the club's climb back to second place in 1968, Johnson hit .242 and made his first All-Star team, striking out against Ron Reed in his only plate appearance.

Johnson battled back woes in 1969, but still hit .280 with 34 doubles, his best offensive season to date. He was selected to another All-Star Game, though he did not play, and won his first Gold Glove for his defensive play. He did all this despite regular visits to the chiropractor and enough discomfort that he often could not sit down. He hit just .231 in the playoff series with the Twins, and was just 1-for-16 in the World Series loss to the Mets. "I'm still flabbergasted we lost," remembered Johnson decades later, "that destiny made all sorts of funky things happen. Gusts of wind blowing balls back to their outfielders, [Ron] Swoboda's diving catch, Al Weis hitting a home run; our winning just wasn't meant to be."[5]

Even early in his career Johnson's intellect was commented upon in the press. In 1969 he fed various batting orders into a computer at Trinity College, where he took classes, to see what the optimal Baltimore lineup would be. Pitcher Dave McNally, a longtime teammate, recalled a time Johnson visited him on the pitcher's mound, in order to explain to him about "unfavorable change deviation theory." McNally was wild that day, and Johnson was suggesting that he aim for the middle of the plate so that he would miss his spot and hit a corner.[6]

Johnson had another excellent year in 1970, hitting .281 with 38 extra-base hits. He started the All-Star Game (replacing the injured Rod Carew), going 1-for-5, and won his second Gold Glove award. He also starred in the postseason, hitting .364 with two home runs in the playoff series, then .313 in the Orioles' victorious World Series.

In early 1970 Johnson spoke out about his annual contract hassles, and announced that he had asked the club to trade him. "It's not the city," he said. "I like Baltimore. I like the players, the coaches, and the manager. I don't like management."[7] In the spring he even suggested he might retire and go sell real estate—he had recently earned his license. After his fine 1970 season, and the Orioles' championship, he signed for $50,000 early in the off-season and declared himself happy the following spring. He came through in 1971 with his best year yet, .282 with 18 home runs and 72 runs batted in and a third Gold Glove, helping the Orioles to a third straight league pennant. In the end, the club lost the World Series to the Pirates.

In 1972 Johnson battled shoulder and back woes and hit just .221 in 118 games, part of a season-long offensive malaise for the Orioles, who fell to third place. Johnson was also affected by the emergence of 23-year-old infielder Bobby Grich, who played 133 games mainly at shortstop and second base. Grich quickly became a star both at bat and in the field, making the 29-year-old Johnson expendable. On November 30, he was traded to the Atlanta Braves in a six-player deal. "I wanted to be traded to the National League," said Johnson, "and I'm happy to be coming to a good club."[8]

In 1973 Johnson made the most of his new league, belting 43 home runs and driving in 99 runs for the Braves. He joined with Darrell Evans (41) and Henry Aaron (40) to be the first set of three teammates to hit 40 home runs in a season. "It was the greatest thing that ever happened to me in baseball," Johnson said of the trade, "and the big reason was joining Aaron. He helped make me a better hitter." Aaron refused to take any credit, saying only, "Dave's a smart hitter. He knows what he's doing up there."[9] Aaron's chase of Babe Ruth's career record of 714 home runs captivated the baseball public, and he ultimately ended the season one short at 713.

Aside from the home-run barrage, Johnson's error total increased from six to a league-leading 30 in 1973. The next season he shifted between first base and second base in deference to Marty Perez. For the season Johnson started 70 games at first and 62 at second, and hit just .251 with 15 home runs. The next season he was tapped as a platoon first baseman, but after a single at-bat (a pinch-hit double) he signed with the Yomiuri Giants of the Japan Central League. He joined teammate Sadaharu Oh, who that same season hit his 715th home run, passing Babe Ruth's mark just as Henry Aaron had done the previous year.

The Giants were the most dominant and storied team in Japanese baseball, having won 15 Japan Series titles in the previous 24 seasons, featuring both Oh and Shigeo Nagashima. The immensely popular Nagashima had retired at the end of the 1974 season, and immediately was named manager. One of his first acts was to recruit Johnson as his replacement, making Johnson the first foreign-born player on the Giants in nearly 20 years and the first American star player to play in Japan. His 1975 season was a disaster—he hit just .197 with 13 home runs, he was heavily criticized by the press, the fans laughed at him, and he lost 25 pounds. "I swear," recalled Johnson, "I would go to bed sometimes and hear bells. I thought I was losing it there for a while."[10]

The next year he came back determined to make good. He reported for volunteer winter training in January and regained his starting job. He hit .268 with 26 home runs, was named the league's top fielding second baseman, made the postseason All-Star team, and helped lead the Giants to a league pennant. His tenure ended badly, however, as he clashed with Nagashima over a midseason arm injury and a late-season illness—in both cases his manager did not believe he was hurt, and publicly humiliated Johnson in front of the team. After his excellent season the Giants tried to get him to return, but Johnson would do so only if Nagashima apologized for his treatment. He would not, so Johnson returned to the United States.

Now 34 years old, Johnson signed with Philadelphia in February 1977. For the Phillies, he served as a reserve infielder, playing mostly first base. He hit well, batting .321 with eight home runs in 156 at bats. He also returned to the postseason, and played in the first game of the playoffs against the Dodgers at first base, going 1-for-4 at the plate. In 1977 Johnson returned in the same role, but as he was hitting only .191 in August, the Phillies traded him to the Cubs for relief pitcher Larry Anderson on August 6. He hit better in Chicago, .306 in 49 at-bats. Interestingly, Johnson's poor season with the Phillies included a historic accomplishment. Though he hit just two home runs for the club, he became the first major-league player to hit two pinch-hit grand slams in one year. After the season, Johnson decided to retire as a player.

Johnson had studied to be a veterinarian at Texas A&M, but continued his education in the off-season and earned a mathematics degree at Trinity College in San Antonio. Despite his success in baseball, he continued to learn new things. He became a licensed pilot, a scratch golfer, a talented fisherman, and a scuba instructor. He also became adroit at using a computer long before many people owned one, taking graduate classes at Johns Hopkins University while with the Orioles. With all of these hobbies and skills, Johnson knew what he wanted to do—stay in baseball as an instructor or manager.

Over the next five years Johnson managed three seasons in the minor leagues (taking one season off and working the other as an instructor) and won three league championships. His final minor-league season was in 1983 with Tidewater, the New York Mets' Triple-A affiliate, and it was a surprise to no one when in 1984 Johnson was promoted to manage the parent club, which had been floundering for many years. Johnson was 41 years old.

Johnson's boss in New York was general manager Frank Cashen, who had held the same position with the Orioles when Johnson played there. Johnson's first successful move was to persuade Cashen to promote 19-year-old pitch Dwight Gooden, whom Johnson had managed at the tail end of the 1983 season. Gooden won 17 games and the Rookie of the Year Award. This fit a pattern with Johnson, who favored several young players from the system over the mediocre veterans the Mets had been playing. The club won 90 games in 1984, the second best record the club had achieved in its 23-year existence.

The Mets won 98 games in 1985, then 108 and the World Series in 1986. The latter club was remarkably balanced, with league-leading pitching (Bobby Ojeda, Ron Darling, Gooden, Sid Fernandez, and Jesse Orosco) and hitting (Keith Hernandez, Gary Carter, Darryl Strawberry, Lenny Dykstra, and Mookie Wilson). The team was also very deep, and Johnson used his roster fully, as Earl Weaver had done with Johnson's Orioles clubs.

Although the Mets won 92 games in 1987, and 100 games and the division title in 1988, many observers considered the club a disappointment for reaching only a single World Series. Johnson had become the only manager in big-league history to win 90 games in each of his first five seasons, but his legacy in New York is marred by the team's reputation as a traveling frat party. Strawberry and Gooden both spent years battling cocaine addiction and other problems, Dykstra led a wild lifestyle, Hernandez battled drug issues—several books have been written about this club's off-field antics. Johnson was not directly involved, but he has been criticized for allowing it go on. After a second-place finish in 1989, a slow start in 1990 (20-22) led Cashen to fire Johnson in May.

Johnson spent the next three years out of baseball, managing some property in Florida when he wasn't fishing, flying, or golfing. Johnson had married Mary Nan in the early days of his baseball career, and the couple raised three children—David Jr., Dawn, and Andrea. The Johnsons' marriage ended in the late 1980s, and Johnson admitted that he developed a bit of a problem with alcohol in subsequent years.

Although his name often surfaced when there were job openings, his reputation as a strong and opinionated manager might have scared some teams off. Johnson had battled with Cashen constantly in New York. Finally, in May 1993 Johnson became manager of the Cincinnati Reds, working for their controversial owner Marge Schott. Johnson's hiring was not popular because the Reds had fired local favorite Tony Perez just 44 games into his first managerial season. The previous manager, Lou Piniella, had resigned in the off-season because of Schott's meddling.

The Reds finished just 53-65 under Johnson in 1993, but the next year they had the best record in the National League West (66-48) when the season was ended by the players strike in August. The 1995 season was delayed by the same strike, but once things got going Johnson brought the club home in first place in the new NL Central Division. The Reds swept the Dodgers in three straight in the first round of the playoffs, before falling to eventual champion Atlanta in the National League Championship Series.

Johnson began dating Susan Allen in the early 1990s, and it was their cohabitation that first earned him the wrath of Reds owner Schott. The couple married in 1994, but his relationship with Schott, who had her own off-field problems, did not improve. Despite two first-place finishes in his two full seasons, he was fired after the season.

Johnson was not unemployed for long, signing on to manage the Baltimore Orioles, the organization for whom he had played for 11 years. In Baltimore he worked for Pat Gillick, who had been his teammate in Elmira in 1963. As he had done everywhere, Johnson continued to win—88 games and a wild-card berth in 1996, then 98 and a division title in 1997. In each season the Orioles won a division series before falling short in the League Championship Series. His most challenging personnel decision was his move of Cal Ripken from shortstop to third base—briefly in 1996, then permanently to start the 1997 season. Ripken had not missed a game at shortstop in 14 years, but Johnson felt the 37-year-old would be more valuable and effective at a less demanding position. Ripken was cool to the idea, but adjusted and played every day at third base for two more seasons before ending his consecutive-game streak at 2,632 in September 1998.

Along with winning, Johnson's two years in Baltimore were marked by occasional public spats with owner Peter Angelos, who resented Johnson's "swagger."[11] After the 1997 season Johnson, who had not spoken to Angelos in six months, faxed a letter demanding either a contract extension or a buyout. Angelos considered the action yet another sign of insubordination. He accepted the resignation on November 5, 1997, the same day that Johnson was named Manager of the Year.

Johnson's final major-league assignment, with the Los Angeles Dodgers in 1999 and 2000, saw his team win 77 and 86 games. Johnson was let go with little fanfare after the latter season.

The ensuing years were a struggle for Johnson. In 2005 he suffered the tragic loss of his 32-year-old daughter, Andrea. She had once been a world-class surfer, but had suffered through years of depression and schizophrenia. Soon after her death Johnson developed stomach problems, eventually diagnosed at the Mayo Clinic as a ruptured appendix that cost him half his stomach and more than 50 pounds.

In 2003 he managed the Netherlands to a European championship, and in 2008 he skippered the United States team to a Bronze Medal in the Olympic Games in Beijing. He also led the American team in the 2009 World Baseball Classic. In 2006 he became an adviser for the Washington Nationals, and had spent two seasons coaching in the Florida Collegiate Summer League. "If you're a baseball person, and love it, it's what we do," he said.[12] In 2010 he was named to the New York Mets Hall of Fame, along with his former players Dwight Gooden and Darryl Strawberry, and his former boss, Frank Cashen.

After the surprising resignation of Jim Riggleman, in July 2011 the Nationals hired Johnson to replace him as manager. Helped by young phenoms Bryce Harper and Stephen Strasburg, the Nationals won 98 games in 2012, the most in the major leagues. Unfortunately, the club lost in the NL Division Series to the St. Louis Cardinals. The 70-year-old Johnson came back in 2013, and his club won 86 games but missed out on the playoffs by four games. In late September Johnson announced his retirement.

For his entire managerial career, Johnson managed 13 full seasons, and finished over .500 in 13 of them. He managed four different teams to the postseason. All this was on top of his long playing career as a four-time All-Star and two-time champion. A multi-talented player and a bright, innovative manager, Johnson accomplished much in his five decades on the scene.

NOTES

1. Edward Kiersch, "Davey's Destiny," *Cigar Aficionado*, September 1999.
2. Kiersch, "Davey's Destiny."
3. John Eisenberg, *From 33rd Street to Camden Yards* (New York: Contemporary Books, 2002), 134.
4. Furman Bisher, "An Oriole's Aim," *Sport*, April 1967.
5. Kiersch, "Davey's Destiny."

6 Mark Kram, "Mr. Hornsby, Meet, Uh, Mr. Johnson," *Sports Illustrated*, September 17, 1973.

7 Phil Jackman, "Orioles' Johnson Unhappy, Blasts Club Brass," *The Sporting News*, May 30, 1970.

8 Wayne Minshew, "Braves Sure They Landed Quality in 6-Player Swap," *The Sporting News*, December 16, 1972, 52.

9 Wayne Minshew, "Johnson credits HR Binge to Aaron," *The Sporting News*, November 10, 1973, 30.

10 Robert Whiting, *You Gotta Have Wa* (New York: Macmillan Inc., 1989), 163.

11 Tom Verducci, "Out in the Cold Again," *Sports Illustrated*, February 23, 1998.

12 Harvey Araton, "Former Mets Manager Johnson at Ease in Florida," *New York Times*, July 30, 2010.

FRANK CASHEN

By Mark Armour

FRANK CASHEN WAS ONE OF THE MOST SUC-cessful front-office executives of his time, taking part in the winning of five pennants and three World Series, and one of the more educated and erudite. "Frank is very bright man, a man for all seasons," remembered a former New York Mets vice president. "You hear about people who know a little bit about everything. Frank knows a lot about many things. I don't know many topics he can't discuss."[1] His knowledge was gathered through a love of books, and via his atypical path to baseball, a world he did not reach until age 40 but conquered quickly.

John Francis Cashen was born on September 13, 1925, in Baltimore, Maryland, the son of Cornelius Joseph "Connie" Cashen and the former Bridged Mary Ryan, both immigrants from County Tipperary in Ireland. Frank had two older sisters and a younger brother. Connie was the engineering supervisor for the Baltimore Public School System, while Bridged ran the strongly Irish-Catholic family. When his father came home from work, he would often take out his fiddle, or get out a book, and entertain the family for the evening. "I have always been incredibly proud of my parents," Frank recalled.[2] He attended St. Paul Parochial school and then Mount St. Joseph high school.

Cashen graduated at age 19 from Baltimore's Loyola University in 1945, with a double major in English and philosophy. In college he played a little basketball and baseball, though he claimed not to be particularly good at either.[3] While still in high school he got a job as a copy boy for the *Baltimore News-Post*. He worked with the paper for 17 years, the last 15 of them as a sportswriter. It was while in the newspaper business that Cashen picked up his lifelong habit of wearing bow ties—because they were less likely to get dragged through ink or get caught in printing presses. During his years as a writer he attended night classes at the University of Maryland Law School, specializing in labor law, earned his law degree, and passed the Maryland Bar.

With his new law degree in hand, in 1959 Cashen took a job as the director of publicity for the Baltimore Raceway, working for Jerrold Hoffberger, a prominent Baltimore businessman whose main concern was as president and chairman of the National Brewing Company. Although he loved the newspaper work, Cashen's growing family would eventually include seven children. "I'd reached a point where I could no longer say money didn't matter," he recalled.[4] Cashen loved horses and life at the track, and he eventually ran a few racetracks for Hoffberger.

After a few years, Cashen was transferred to the brewery, where he worked as Hoffberger's personal assistant and then as the advertising director, helping promote the brewery's brands, including National Bohemian ("Natty Boh") and Colt 45. In 1965 he was

turning 40 and had every reason to think he would play out his career at the brewery.

Hoffberger had long been the largest shareholder of the Baltimore Orioles (making "Natty Boh" the prime sponsor of the Orioles), and part of a group that had moved the team from St. Louis in 1953. In ensuing years he acquired more and more of the stock, finally acquiring controlling interest in 1965. Before his takeover, he had asked Cashen to spend a few months examining the business and preparing a report on the operation. A few months later, Hoffberger asked Cashen to run the Orioles, working alongside Lee MacPhail, the club's longtime vice president and general manager. MacPhail, sensing a decline in his authority, soon resigned to become the chief assistant to baseball's new commissioner, William Eckert. Cashen essentially became the CEO. He promoted farm director Harry Dalton to run baseball operations, and the two worked together on running the ballclub.

The Orioles had been a strong club for several years, winning 97 games in 1964 and 94 games in '65. Just before leaving the club, MacPhail had worked out a six-player trade with the Cincinnati Reds that would principally acquire Frank Robinson at the cost of starting pitcher Milt Pappas. Cashen and Dalton agreed to make the deal, one of the best in team history. Robinson won the Triple Crown in 1966, and the team waltzed to an easy pennant and a four-game World Series sweep over the Dodgers, the first championship in franchise history. Not a bad start for Frank Cashen.

After battling several injuries in 1967, over the next year the Orioles made a few key trades for the likes of Don Buford and Mike Cuellar, hired Earl Weaver as manager, and won three consecutive pennants from 1969 to 1971. These were extraordinary teams, led by Frank Robinson, Brooks Robinson, Boog Powell, Paul Blair, and three dominant starting pitchers—Jim Palmer, Dave McNally, and Mike Cuellar. The team averaged 106 wins, won the AL East by an average of 15 games, and swept all three playoff series. Although most historians consider this to be one of the best teams in baseball history, their fame is tarnished somewhat because they managed to win only one of the three World Series. After losing to the Miracle Mets in 1969, they dominated the Reds in five games in 1970, then lost a classic seven-game matchup with Roberto Clemente's Pirates in 1971.

After the 1971 World Series, Dalton resigned to assume a similar position, though with more authority, with the California Angels. For the next four years Cashen performed the general-manager duties for the Orioles himself, and the club continued to contend. His most famous deal came just a few weeks after Dalton left, when Cashen traded an aging Frank Robinson to the Dodgers. Cashen felt the team had sufficient replacements (especially Don Baylor), though the players later claimed to have missed Robinson's leadership. A teamwide batting slump dropped them to third place in 1972.

The Orioles bounced back with back-to-back division crowns in 1973 and 1974, both times losing in the ALCS to the Oakland Athletics, and then finished a strong second to the Red Sox in 1975. Much of the core from the Dalton teams—players like Brooks Robinson, Powell, and McNally—had slowed down considerably, but the team still had the great Jim Palmer, and was heavily fortified with players from the minors (Baylor, Bobby Grich, Al Bumbry) or acquired in Cashen deals (Ken Singleton, Tommy Davis, Mike Torrez, Lee May, Ross Grimsley). The mid-1970s Orioles were not the dynasty they had been, but they were still considered a top-notch organization.

By 1975 National Brewing was struggling, and Hoffberger merged the company with Carling. He asked Cashen to leave the Orioles and help manage the new organization. By 1979 Hoffberger no longer controlled the brewery, and had sold the Orioles. Cashen returned to baseball, working as an assistant to Commissioner Bowie Kuhn in New York. Kuhn delegated a lot of the office functions to Cashen, who helped set up the Jackie Robinson Scholarship Program in New York for minority students, and created a pension program for nonplaying personnel throughout the game.

He spent only about a year with Kuhn before answering the call to take over the New York Mets as chief operating officer and general manager in early 1980. The Mets were a terrible franchise at the time, with three straight 95-loss seasons, no talent on the farm, and dreadful attendance (fewer than 800,000 fans in 1979). "Talent-wise, we had nothing," recalled Cashen. "Fan support, there was nothing. In my estimation it was as ugly as you could get. Just terrible. We needed a complete overhaul of everything."[5]

Cashen told ownership that he needed at least four years to turn the organization around, and he began by revamping the scouting and minor-league systems. Although the team remained dreadful through 1983, the organization started to draft and develop talent, coming up with Darryl Strawberry, Dwight Gooden, Kevin Mitchell, Lenny Dykstra, Mookie Wilson, Rick Aguilera, and several others over the next few years. Unlike the more specialized front offices of today, Cashen ran everything in New York—marketing, TV and radio contracts, hiring announcers, public relations, and the baseball team.

Cashen made some early high-profile attempts to improve the big league team. He acquired sluggers Dave Kingman and Ellis Valentine in 1981, but neither helped much. Cashen dealt for George Foster in 1982, but the slugger's days of stardom proved to be over. Cashen first hit the jackpot in June 1983 when he traded pitcher Neil Allen to St. Louis for first baseman Keith Hernandez. Coupled with the debut of Strawberry a month earlier, the Mets now had arguably the two best position players they had ever fielded. "He was our general and we became winners," remembered Strawberry. "That's the bottom line, and Shea Stadium was packed. He came in and turned this franchise around."[6]

Cashen's biggest decision for 1984 was the hiring of a new manager—Davey Johnson, a bright mind whom Cashen knew from his Orioles days. (Johnson had been the club's star second baseman during their glory years.) Johnson had managed in the system, and like Cashen wanted to play the kids rather than continuing to lose with veterans. In 1984 the Mets finally broke through, winning 90 games after having won fewer than 70 for seven consecutive seasons. The biggest improvement on the club was the pitching, which featured three rookies: Ron Darling (acquired from Texas), Sid Fernandez (acquired from the Dodgers), and 19-year-old phenom Dwight Gooden.

In the following offseason Cashen landed third baseman Howard Johnson and catcher Gary Carter in separate deals, and suddenly the Mets had one of the game's best offenses to go with their great pitching. New York won 98 games in 1985 and took the Cardinals down to the season's final days before falling three games short. While Carter, Hernandez and Strawberry had good years, it was Gooden who had a season for the ages—a record of 24-4, with a stunning 1.53 ERA.

After the 1985 season Cashen made another great trade, dealing unneeded players to the Red Sox for pitcher Bob Ojeda. The resultant Mets made a mockery out of the league in 1986, winning 108 games and waltzing to the division title, then survived two brutal playoff series to win their first title since 1969. It was an extremely well-balanced team, with the best offense and pitching in the league, and only one player accumulating 5 WAR (Hernandez). The club was filled with young stars and seemed poised to win several more championships. "He was by far the smartest baseball man I've ever been in contact with," Ojeda said. "What the players loved about him was he cared more about you as a person than what you did on the baseball field."[7]

The Mets did not win more championships, even with Cashen making two more great trades that winter, landing Kevin McReynolds and David Cone. Gooden entered drug rehab in April 1987, and it was Gooden's problems more than any other that foretold the Mets' decline. They remained a competitive team for several years, and won 100 games and the NL East in 1988, but were never again able to put it together as they had in 1986. Gooden and Strawberry, their two bright young stars, had good years remaining, but both had long battles with drugs and crime, likely costing Hall of Fame induction for both. Hernandez and Carter declined for more conventional reasons—aging, and the team appeared rudderless by 1990.

Cashen let Davey Johnson go during another second-place finish in 1990, and resigned himself after the 1991 squad finished fifth. He remained an adviser to the Mets for several years. Cashen was inducted into the Baltimore Orioles Hall of Fame in 1999, and the New York Mets Hall of Fame in 2010.

Frank Cashen married Jean in 1951, and they raised five sons (Timothy, Brian, Sean, Gregory, and Terrance) and two daughters (Stacy and Blaise). In retirement, he and Jean lived in Easton, Maryland, where he followed the Orioles closely, and St. Lucie, Florida, where he spent time with the Mets every year in spring training. He died after a short illness on June 20, 2104, at Memorial Hospital in Easton. He was 88 years old, and he and Jean had been married for 64 years.

Cashen's front-office record is extraordinary. He directed a great organization in Baltimore, and after taking over as GM, he made some great trades to keep the Orioles in contention and won two division titles in four years. In New York he inherited a mess, and used the Oriole model to build the organization—scouting, player development, and excellent young pitching. Although it ended sooner than he would have liked, the seven-year run (1984-1990) averaged over 95 wins per season, finishing first or second every year, and captured a title. This was the most successful period ever for the club, on and off the field—coupled with a down period for the Yankees, the Mets were by far the most popular team in New York for several years, giving hope that they could be so once again with another great team.

"I've just had an incredible amount of luck," Cashen said late in life. "I was a writer by choice, a lawyer by education, a horseman by heritage, a brewery worker by necessity, and a baseball executive by good fortune."[8]

NOTES

1 Marty Noble, "Former GM Cashen dies at age 88," mlb.com, June 30, 2014.

2 Frank Cashen, *Winning in Both Leagues* (Lincoln: University of Nebraska, 2014), 14.

3 Cashen, *Winning in Both Leagues*, 59.

4 John Eisenberg, *From 33rd St. to Camden Yards* (New York: Contemporary Books, 2001), 156.

5 Jeff Pearlman, *The Bad Guys Won* (New York: Harper, 2004), 24.

6 Kevin Kernan, "Loss of a Legend—Frank Cashen dies at 88," *New York Post*, June 30, 2014.

7 Noble.

8 Kevin Willis, "Former Orioles and Mets GM Led Champions," *Loyola Magazine*, July 22, 2011.

ROLAND JOHNSON

By Alan Cohen

"I haven't worked a day since 1966!"—Roland Johnson, 2015.

IN 1967, HE BEGAN HIS FIRST BASEBALL-related job, and within 10 years he began his career as a scout. His more than 40 years in scouting have included more than 30 years with the New York Mets, for whom he served as Director of Scouting when the Mets won the World Series in 1986. Almost 30 years later he could be spied in his familiar post in the seats behind home plate, scouting Class-AA talent for the Mets as the 2015 minor-league season drew to a close in New Britain, Connecticut. Baseball scouts travel extensively and it is somewhat ironic that Johnson has spent his final years as a scout watching games a close distance from his lifelong home in Newington, Connecticut.

Roland T. Johnson was born in Newington on November 7, 1940. His father, Torsten Johnson, and mother, Anna Kindur Johnson, had come to the United States from their native Sweden when they were in their early 20s. Torsten was a machinist at Pratt and Whitney and Anna mostly stayed at home. Roland was the youngest of three siblings following two older sisters, Lily and Carol, into the world. Roland's mother Anna lived a rich full life, passing away in 1998 at the age of 94.

Roland had a lifelong interest in sports and played three sports while in high school. When he was not playing himself, he played board games and kept statistics. In addition to baseball, he played soccer and basketball. At Newington High School, he was a pitcher and third baseman. He went on to attend Trinity College in nearby Hartford, where he was converted to catcher in his junior year and captained the team in his senior year. At Trinity he played for coaches Dan Jessee and Robbie Schultz.

After graduating, Johnson had a shot to play professional ball with the Springfield (Massachusetts) Giants in the Class-A Eastern League. He tried out for the club and was given an offer. However, the team already had two catchers, Bob Barton and Denny Sommers. At the time, Barton, who had injured his leg on June 12, was on the disabled list, and would not return until July 5. Johnson was told by friends that he could be let go once Barton returned to the lineup. Hence, Johnson decided to turn down the offer and continue to play in the Hartford Twilight League while seeking employment outside of baseball.

Johnson married Judy Lauritzen on September 7, 1963. She had gone to Conard High School in nearby West Hartford, and was an x-ray technician at Hartford Hospital. They have two children, Jennifer

Roland Johnson. Photograph courtesy of Alan Cohen.

and Michael, born in 1969 and 1971, respectively. They also have six grandchildren.

In those days, Hartford was still the Insurance City and Johnson, who had majored in Economics at Trinity, took a position with Factory Insurance Association as an underwriter. He moved on to the Hartford insurance Group. But insurance was not for Johnson.

He commenced a letter writing project, hoping to get some kind of a job in baseball. In 1965, he saw an ad in *The Sporting News* saying "Wanted: Baseball Nut." He answered the ad, received a response and ultimately, in 1967, was hired as a researcher by a group that was producing a 2,500 page baseball encyclopedia. He worked with SABR's David Neft. Johnson, Neft, and two other researchers traveled the country, cross checking statistics and going through old newspapers. Johnson remembers one of his tasks was to compile RBIs prior to 1920. *The Baseball Encyclopedia* was published in 1969.

After the book was published, Johnson went back to Connecticut and took a position with the Travelers, but it was not long until he was back into baseball research.

The three men with whom he had worked on the *Baseball Encyclopedia* had gone on to work at *Sports Illustrated* in their games division, and invited Johnson to join them in Darien, Connecticut. They went on to form their own publishing company, Sports Products, Inc., putting out a number of books, including a smaller baseball encyclopedia entitled *The Sports Encyclopedia: Baseball.* They also produced a book entitled *Scrapbook History of Baseball.* Johnson opened up an office in his home town of Newington, allowing him to process mail orders and do further research. However, he had some extra time.

He was encouraged to check into part-time scouting and got a response from Dave Bartosch from the St. Louis Cardinals. Bartosch had a cup of coffee with St. Louis in 1945, and scouted for the Cardinals from 1969 through 1979. Johnson started working part-time from 1973 through 1976, earning $50 per month. He became a full-time area scout with the Cardinals in 1977, covering New York, New England and New Jersey, and sold out his interest in the publishing company. He was with the Cardinals through 1982. During that time, he became friendly with Joe McIlvane, the scouting director of the New York Mets, and he joined the Mets after the 1982 season, as a cross-checker, going around the country comparing high school and college prospects.

At the pre-draft meeting in 1983, Johnson, who had just come from the Cardinals to the Mets, was approached by Mets General Manager Frank Cashen. Keith Hernandez was available, and Cashen sought Johnson's opinion. Johnson applauded the idea and the Mets were able to obtain Hernandez in a trade for Neal Allen and Rick Ownbey.

Less than two years later, at the 1984 Winter Meetings, another name came up when GM Cashen was meeting with Murray Cook, his counterpart with the Montreal Expos. Although Johnson's focus, at the time, was on high school and college prospects, he was pleased to see the Mets obtain another piece of their 1986 mosaic, trading Hubie Brooks, Mike Fitzgerald, Herm Winningham, and Floyd Youmans to Montreal for Gary Carter.

There was one member of the 1986 Mets that Johnson scouted during his time with the Cardinals. This fellow pitched at Yale and Johnson still remembers the epic pitching duel between Frank Viola of St. John's and Ron Darling of Yale. It was the best college game that Johnson ever saw. In the 1981 draft, the White Sox were picking seventh and the Cardinals were picking eighth. The Cardinals had two players in mind. At the top of their list was Bobby Meecham. If he was not available, the Cardinals would have drafted Darling. The White Sox selected Daryl Boston, the Cardinals selected Meecham, and the Texas Rangers, picking ninth, selected Darling. By the time Johnson joined the Mets in 1983, Darling was in the New York organization. The Mets acquired Darling, along with Walter Terrell, in a trade for Lee Mazzilli prior to the 1982 season.

In talking about 1986, Johnson is quick to draw a comparison between the 21st century game and the game as played in 1986. The 1986 Mets team essentially had only nine pitchers on the roster, something never heard of in later years. Starting pitchers went deeper into games and the closer role had not yet fully developed. A reliever would come in when needed and would pitch as many as four innings. With five starters and four relievers, the Mets cruised to a 108-54 record and went on to win their League Championship Series and the World Series. Johnson remembers the leadership of Hernandez and Carter, and "dirt players" like Len Dykstra, Ray Knight, and Wally Backman.

Johnson and his wife Judy traveled with the team during the 1986 postseason. In Game Six of the World Series, they were back in New York at Shea Stadium. As the Mets fell behind, and the game entered its final innings, Judy couldn't bear to watch anymore and she went to Johnson's office to wait. The room was not near the field, and was eerily quiet. All of a sudden, through the walls, she could hear the loudest of noises. She turned on the television and the Mets had won the game. Meanwhile Rollie was upstairs in the stadium watching Haywood Sullivan and Lou Gorman of the Red Sox to see their reaction as, with two outs in the bottom of the ninth inning, victory was at hand. He expected to see an emotional victor. He wound up seeing the passive face of defeat. The Red Sox were all but dead with one game remaining.

Johnson is quick to share his stories of his years in scouting. One of his favorites dates back to 1979 when he was an area scout with the Cardinals. A player from New Hartford, New York appeared on the radar and Roland went up to take a closer look, and was convinced that he should be a first-round draft pick. This kid was such a fabulous athlete that he was offered a football scholarship at Penn State and a basketball scholarship at Syracuse. The cross-checkers came in and concurred with Johnson's appraisal. Time came for the final evaluation. It was a hot 85-degree day and Andy Van Slyke showed up for the tryout in just shorts and a t-shirt. Johnson also noticed that Van Slyke had welts on his forearms. His performance was not good. After the tryout, Johnson found out that Van Slyke had boxed four rounds the evening before, to take his mind off baseball, and those welts, which hindered his baseball swing, came from the boxing match.

The Cardinals, despite the one bad workout, elected to draft Van Slyke, making him their first pick (sixth overall) in the June 5, 1979 draft. The next day, Van Slyke played for his school in the State Championship game, and verified Johnson's faith in him—until he broke his wrist late in the game, tripping over first base when running out a base hit. The Cardinals brought him into St. Louis for an evaluation, signed Van Slyke, and he went on to a 13-year major-league career, winning five consecutive Gold Gloves with the Pirates.

Not all of Johnson's sightings became first-round draft picks. The Mets used their pick in the 44th round of the June 3, 1991 draft on an outfielder from Illinois. The local scouts saw something in the player's arm and thought he could make a good pitcher. Johnson, who was the Mets Director of Scouting at the time, dispatched one of his surrogates to check the kid out. Jason Isringhausen went on to pitch 16 major-league seasons, emerging as one of the top relief pitchers of the first decade of the 21st century.

During Johnson's tenure as Director of Scouting with the Mets, there were several notable draft picks including Todd Hundley in 1987. Johnson also remembers drafting Curtis Pride on the recommendation of an area scout. Pride was 95% deaf, but a great athlete, and a greater individual. He played in parts of 11 major-league seasons, and in recent years has led an exemplary life.

Johnson also remembers with a great degree of respect his boss Frank Cashen. Cashen would not interfere in scouting decisions. The scouts, in 1986, decided to use their first draft pick on Lee May, Jr., son of the of former Astro and Red first baseman. Unfortunately the draft pick did not work out for the best as May only made it as far as Class AAA in seven seasons in the Mets minor league system. Johnson also is grateful to Cashen for his role in extending the pension plan to non-uniform personnel including scouts, in 1979.

Johnson, after serving as Director of Scouting through 1992, went back to cross-checking in 1993 and moved on to a role as a professional scout in 1997. On July 22, 2015 following a Binghamton Mets visit to New Britain, Johnson filed his reports and, the next day, Michael Conforto, joined the parent club in its return to glory, 29 years after Johnson had served with the 1986 Mets as Director of Scouting.

SOURCE

The author conducted a formal interview with Roland Johnson on August 27, 2015.

The author also used the *Hartford Courant* and Baseball-Reference.com.

BUD HARRELSON

By Eric Aron

FOR A PLAYER WHO ENDURED NICKNAMES such as Twiggy, Mini-Hawk, and Mighty Mouse for his light weight and short stature, Bud Harrelson is perhaps best known to the casual baseball fan for getting into a fight. There's no doubt that Pete Rose got the better of him in their brawl at second base during Game Three of the 1973 National League Championship Series, but Harrelson's Mets got in the last punch: They won the pennant. And this came just four years after Bud had helped the Mets pull off the ultimate David vs. Goliath upset of the vaunted Baltimore Orioles in the 1969 World Series.

Bud was not known as much of a hitter—as his 16-year career average of .236 with only seven home runs attests—but his defense at shortstop was outstanding. His lifetime fielding percentage was .969 and he won a National League Gold Glove award in 1971. In addition to appearing in two All-Star Games, Harrelson set a since-broken major-league mark with 54 consecutive errorless games at shortstop in 1970. After his playing career ended, he was a coach, a scout, a special instructor, a broadcaster, and a manager in both the minor leagues and major leagues, all in the Mets organization. Said friend and teammate Tom Seaver, "We simply don't win two pennants without him."[1]

Derrel McKinley Harrelson was born on June 6, 1944 (the same day as the D-Day Invasion), in Niles, California, on the Oakland side of San Francisco Bay. After the second grade, his family moved to nearby Hayward. It was a working-class family. Bud's father, Glenn, was an auto mechanic and a foreman for a used-car agency. The Harrelsons were an athletic household; Glenn was a former football player who dropped out of high school to support his family. Bud's older brother, Dwayne was a running back in football and a shortstop and catcher in baseball. His mother, Rena, ran track in high school and supported her children's pursuit of athletics.

Dwayne unintentionally gave his kid brother the nickname Bud. Dwayne couldn't pronounce Derrel, so he called him Brother, which morphed into Bud. Dwayne was offered a professional contract by the Washington Senators after his senior year of high school, but he chose to go to college instead. An ankle injury dashed any hopes of a career in baseball.

Bud was a natural athlete. Despite his small size and weight, he made his high school football, basketball, and baseball teams. He weighed only 97 pounds when he played football. "I was all helmet and pads," he said, "but I played both ways—halfback and safety."[2] Through sheer toughness, he led his league in receptions and made all-star honors. In basketball, he was a great outside shooter, averaging 11 points per game, and an outstanding defender. He captained Sunset High in all three sports and was voted East Bay Athlete of the Year. His first love, of course, was baseball.

Bud played for his high school team in the spring, American Legion ball in the summer, and weekend semipro games in the fall. He had a great arm and played all positions in Little League. In Babe Ruth League he played mostly third base; he didn't move to shortstop until his sophomore year. He cited Coach Don Curley at Sunset High as the biggest mentor in his entire career. "With his help, I really worked at it," Harrelson said. "He taught me a lot and hit grounders to me for hours on end so I could practice. I worked and worked and worked, but I enjoyed it. I learned fast. Shortstop was always for me."

After high school graduation, no scouts would offer him much because of his size. He was turned down flat by his hometown team, the San Francisco Giants. Bud decided to go to college and improve his chances and mature as a ballplayer. Ironically, he won a basketball scholarship to San Francisco State, but played only baseball. He batted .430 in 30 games to help lead his team to a Far Western Conference Championship. "I was a physical-education major, but I had no intention of staying in school," Harrelson told a biographer. "I had already agreed to go to Alaska to play summer ball, which a lot of the college kids do, but when the scouts made serious pitches of bonuses at me I decided to sign."

Bud spoke to several scouts, notably from the Yankees, the Cubs, and the Cardinals. The Yankees offered him the most, but he didn't think he would get much playing time. The Mets, coming off their 40-120 inaugural season, offered a much better opportunity for advancement. Scout Roy Partee signed Harrelson on June 7, 1963, the day after the shortstop turned 19, for a little more than $10,000.

Harrelson's professional career began with the Salinas Mets of the Class-A California League. Playing not far from where he grew up, Harrelson was familiar with the area, but not with professional pitching. A right-handed hitter, Bud had no power and was taught how to just make contact and not be a free swinger. His season ended after only 136 at-bats when he was hit by a pitch that broke his left arm. He batted .221 with one homer, two triples, and knocked in nine. He made 18 errors in just 36 games.

That winter, Harrelson began a five-year hitch in the National Guard. In February 1964, he was invited to an early spring training session at St. Petersburg, Florida. He did his best to make the big league team that spring, with eating as big a part of it as hitting or fielding. Throughout his career he would lose weight off his meager frame as the season progressed. Even a dozen bananas a day didn't do much. In the end, he spent another summer in Salinas, where he showed he could stand up to the rigors of a full season. His fielding also improved; he made 34 errors in 596 chances to lead the league with a .943 fielding percentage. He batted .231 with three homers and 48 RBIs in 135 games.

In 1965, Harrelson moved up to Triple A with the Buffalo Bisons of the International League. He played in 131 games and batted .251 with 15 doubles, two home runs, and 36 RBIs. His fielding was erratic, as it would be early in his career. He led the league in errors with 31 and had a .950 fielding percentage. He was a September call-up for the Mets and made his major-league debut on September 2, 1965. He was inserted as a pinch runner in the eighth inning of a game against the Houston Astros at Shea Stadium, and played shortstop in the ninth.

Harrelson's first plate appearance came on September 5 in St. Louis. Taking over for Roy McMillan in the second game of a doubleheader, He grounded back to pitcher Ray Washburn. Harrelson's first hit was a single off Cubs pitcher Bob Hendley in the first inning of a game at Wrigley Field on September 19. He appeared in 19 games in all and had a meager 4-for-37 account (.108) in his first taste of the big leagues.

After the season, on December 17, Bud married his first wife, Yvonne. He started the 1966 season playing for the Jacksonville Suns, the franchise's new International League farm team. There he met future teammate Tom Seaver. The two Northern Californians—Seaver from Fresno and Harrelson from Hayward—became instant friends. They roomed together on the road with the Mets from 1968 until Seaver's departure from the club in 1977.

At Jacksonville, Harrelson taught himself to become a switch-hitter. One day he tried batting left-handed in the batting cage, and impressed manager Solly Hemus and the director of player development, Bob Scheffing. They suggested that he try it during an exhibition game. Harrelson played a game later that day and bunted left-handed against White Sox knuckleballer Hoyt Wilhelm.

Appearing in 117 games for Jacksonville, Harrelson hit .221 with five triples and 26 RBIs. He made 28 errors in 601 chances for a .953 fielding percentage. Called up to the Mets on August 12, 1966, he played in 33 games, hit .222, stole seven bases including home against the Giants, and made just one error in 144 chances (.993 fielding percentage).

Harrelson became the Mets starting shortstop in 1967, already the 18th in the team's brief history. That happened after his predecessor and mentor Roy McMillan felt a pop in his shoulder during spring training. McMillan's playing career was over. The Mets had acquired Sandy Alomar during that spring to help with the infield, but he contributed little offensively or defensively (Alomar went 0 for 22 as a Met). That left Harrelson, who did not start the season well. He committed 21 errors in his first month, but made only 11 the rest of the season. (In a career that lasted another decade in New York, his 144 starts at shortstop were more than every year except 1970.) McMillan helped Bud work on his fielding, while Coach Yogi Berra taught him how to make better contact and use a heavier bat. Skipper Wes Westrum was pleased with the results, even Harrelson's .254 batting average (only his 1973 average of .258 would surpass it in his Mets tenure). Harrelson's speed was also a tremendous asset, as he was successful in his first seven major-league steal attempts, though he was eventually caught 13 times in 25 tries).

Bud hit first major-league home run on August 17, 1967. It was an inside-the-park job in the eighth inning while batting right-handed at Pittsburgh's Forbes Field. "Juan Pizarro was the pitcher," he recalled. "I hit it right down the line in right field and Al Luplow tried to make a shoestring catch and missed. It rolled all the way to the wall and then it rolled away from him after it hit the wall. I kept running and I had an inside-the-parker. It won the game for us, too."

Harrelson's offense fell precipitously in 1968, but that wasn't uncommon in the Year of the Pitcher. The Mets now had Gil Hodges running the team—Westrum had resigned in the next-to last week of New York's 101-loss 1967 season—and Harrelson spent much of '68 fulfilling his military obligation, dealing with knee problems, and fighting to keep his batting average out of the low .200s. He finished with a .219 average and then had cartilage removed from his knee, which he had first injured with Jacksonville in 1966 during a takeout slide. With an expansion draft coming and each team required to make players available, Harrelson wasn't worried about being taken by either Montreal or San Diego. He joked that the Mets' owner, thoroughbred enthusiast Joan Payson, would not allow him to be left unprotected. He figured she could count on him to ride one of her horses if he could not play.

Harrelson arrived in St. Petersburg in 1969 having spent the winter lifting weights and quitting smoking. He came in weighing 165 pounds and ceded the lightest-Met prize to 157-pound Amos Otis. Gil Hodges favored platoons for his club at the corners in the outfield and infield, plus second base. Catcher, center field, and shortstop were too important to Hodges to tinker with, even though Jerry Grote was no great shakes with the bat and Tommie Agee in center had a lower 1968 batting average than Harrelson (.217).

Harrelson was sorely missed when he had to serve his military obligation starting in July. Al Weis filled in at shortstop and—true to form for the Mets that year—hit both of his home runs for the season in a huge series at Wrigley Field. Harrelson started just one game in a five-week span because of his obligation, and his batting average, which had surpassed .290 at the beginning of June, got over .250 only a couple of times the rest of the season; he finished at .248. His .341

on-base percentage was crucial since he usually batted second against right-handers and slid down to eighth against southpaws. But on a team with the pitching the '69 Mets had, his glove was more important than what he generated with his bat. Harrelson committed just 19 errors in 119 games at shortstop; his best remembered play of that season was grabbing Joe Torre's grounder and starting the double play that clinched the first Eastern Division title in National League history and set off a riot at Shea Stadium on September 24. Harrelson's game-winning single the night before against Bob Gibson had set the party in motion by assuring the Mets of at least a tie for the division title.

Harrelson was practically flawless in the field in the miraculous postseason. His only error in 44 chances came with one out and no one on in the seventh inning of New York's 11-6 win over the Braves in Game Two of the National League Championship Series. Though he was only 2 for 11 in the NLCS, he drove in three runs and both his hits went for extra bases—giving Harrelson, who would have a lifetime .288 slugging percentage, a stunning .455 slugging mark in the Mets' three-game sweep. He batted .176 in the World Series against the Orioles, but he had three singles and three walks to give him a .300 on-base percentage.

Harrelson played 157 games for the Mets in 1970 and appeared in his first All-Star Game. He went 2 for 3 and scored twice in the game that ended with Pete Rose barreling over Ray Fosse to win the game in the 12th inning. Bud started the All-Star Game the next year at Tiger Stadium as part of a National League lineup that included Hank Aaron, Willie Mays, Willie McCovey, Willie Stargell, and Johnny Bench—Roberto Clemente didn't even start! The game is best remembered for Reggie Jackson's home run off a light tower. Bud told a sportswriter he was intimidated. "I didn't even want to take batting practice with those guys. . . . They were hitting balls on the roof and beyond. I know the fans didn't want to see me hit. I think I took two swings and let the other guys get a few more cuts."

Harrelson at least had an out-of-the-park home run under his belt by that time. It came on April 17, 1970, off Phillies lefty Grant Jackson: "I was sort of stunned," Harrelson said of the moment. "As I saw it go out, I considered sliding into second, third, and home on my way around, but decided I better not...As I ran around the bases I got some looks from the Phils standing there. You know, the who-you-kidding kind of looks. If I smiled, I'd be agreeing with them that it was an accident. I wasn't going to give them the satisfaction, so I didn't smile. As I rounded third, coach Eddie Yost yelled, 'Smile,' but I didn't dare."[3]

The 1970 season was arguably Harrelson's best. To go along with his fence-clearing blast, he knocked in 42 runs and drew 95 walks, by far the most in either category in his career. He also had career highs in games (157), at-bats (564), runs (72), and doubles (18); he flexed as much power as he would ever conjure, with eight triples and eight sacrifice flies. He stole 23 bases in 27 tries after stealing just once successfully in '69. He had a good follow-up season in 1971, winning his only Gold Glove, batting .252, and collecting a career-best 138 hits and 28 steals, but after that season Harrelson's frail frame was seemingly banged up more often than not. He missed 300 games with injuries to his hands, sternum, back, and knee over the next four seasons.

In 1973, the Mets almost pulled off another miracle. They spent most of the year in last place in the National League East and ended the season near the bottom of the league in virtually all offensive categories: 11th in batting (.246), home runs (85), runs (608), and stolen bases (27). Yet they won the pennant.

The Mets were devastated by injuries as they staggered through much of the first five months of the '73 season. Harrelson himself went on the DL twice. He was out of commission with a fractured wrist from June 5 to July 8, and with a fractured sternum in August. When he returned August 18, the Mets were in last place, 13 games under .500, and were still in the cellar on August 30. But propelled by their pitching, the Mets went 19-8 in September to win the division at just three games over .500 (82-79). Harrelson started every game during the stretch run and batted .280 while scoring 12 times and drawing 13 walks in September.

The Mets clinched the NL East on October 1. It was the 161st game of the '73 campaign, played the day after the season ended because the Mets and Cubs had waited out two days of rain at Wrigley Field. The Cincinnati Reds, the West Division winners, were the odds-on favorites to win the best-of-five NLCS. The five games were slated to be played on successive days with the first two games in Cincinnati. The Mets managed a split at Riverfront Stadium, with Tom Seaver losing a 2-1 game and Jon Matlack following with a two-hit shutout.

Back at Shea, the Mets trounced Cincinnati, 9-2, backed by a complete-game, nine-strikeout performance by Jerry Koosman and two home runs by outfielder Rusty Staub. In the fifth inning, already leading by seven runs, the Mets turned a far-from-routine 3-6-3 double play.

The day before, asked by reporters about the way the Reds had hit in the game, Harrelson said, "They all look like me hitting."[4] During pregame warmups for Game Three, Reds second baseman Joe Morgan grabbed Bud by his uniform shirt and said, "If you ever say something like that about me again, I'll punch you out!" Morgan told Harrelson, "Pete (Rose) is going to use this to get the club fired up. If he has a chance, he is going to come and get you at second."[5]

The game was so far gone that Reds relief pitcher Roger Nelson batted for himself and fanned to start the fifth against Koosman. Batting second was Rose, who singled to center. The next hitter was Morgan, who hit a ground ball to Milner at first base. Milner scooped up the ball and threw to Harrelson at second, who fired back to Milner to complete the double play. In the process, Rose had slid hard into second, hitting Bud with his elbow. The 160-pound shortstop then said to the man 40 pounds heavier, "That was a cheap (bleeping) shot." Rose said, "What did you say?"[6] and Harrelson repeated the words, after which Rose grabbed Bud and pinned him to the ground. The first to come out to join the fracas was Mets third baseman Wayne Garrett. Next came the Reds coaches and then seconds later both benches cleared and the bullpens charged in.

Immediately after the dust had seemed to settle, there was another brief altercation between a Red and a Met. Mets reliever Buzz Capra was struck by Reds reliever Pedro Borbon. After that fight was broken up, players from both sides put on their caps. Borbon put on what another teammate told him was a Mets cap. Borbon, who earned the nickname Dracula after another incident in 1974, took off the cap and bit a hole in it with his teeth.

Harrelson was left with a bruise over his eye, which he said came from having his sunglasses broken. Neither Rose nor Harrelson was ejected … and that was a mistake. The game was nearly called after the Reds took the field in the bottom of the inning. Rose had taken left field when an array of objects were thrown his way, including a whiskey bottle. Manager Sparky Anderson took his team off the field as the game was delayed for 20 minutes. National League president Chub Feeney, who after conferring with the six umpires, the commissioner, and both teams, decided to send out players from the Mets dugout to restore order. It was only after Willie Mays, Seaver, Staub, Cleon Jones, and Yogi Berra came out to the field to try to calm the fans that play was resumed.

"Being a little guy, I always wore a Superman T-shirt under my jersey," Harrelson said. "When the reporters came over after the game, I taped (an X) over the Superman logo and said, 'It looks like Pete had a load of kryptonite today.'"[7]

With Game Three finally in the books, the Mets had an unlikely lead in the series. But not for long. Rose came back to homer in the 12th inning of Game Four and even the series. Game Five was a lot like Game Three, except the riot took place after the game. The Mets had a comfortable lead and after Tug McGraw squelched a Reds rally in the ninth, the Shea field was instantly filled with people and the players had to run for their lives.

The Mets nearly knocked off another Goliath in the Oakland A's. Harrelson batted .250 against the A's in the World Series, but his most memorable moment came while running the bases. With Game Two tied in the 10th inning, Harrelson tried to score from third on a short fly by Felix Millan. Joe Rudi's throw to the plate was gloved by catcher Ray Fosse, who "tagged" out Bud...according to umpire Augie Donatelli. Willie Mays, in the on-deck circle, got down on his hands and knees and questioned how Donatelli could make the call. Manager Yogi Berra and Harrelson were more demonstrative in their arguments. The call stood but Harrelson did come around to score the go-ahead run in the 12th inning when he led off with a double and Mays singled him home. The Mets scored three more times and won the game, thanks to two errors that inning by Mike Andrews.

The Mets dropped the World Series after heading to Oakland leading three games to two. It was a sour ending to a great run, but it had been so unexpected that it was hard to say it was heartbreaking. Yet the 13 years that would follow without a pennant would be heartbreaking indeed.

Though Harrelson was injured for much of the four seasons that followed, there was still a core group of the 10 Mets who'd appeared in the 1969 and 1973 World Series. Tug McGraw, Ken Boswell, and Duffy Dyer had been traded after the 1974 season, Cleon Jones was released after an ugly episode in 1975, and Garrett had been dealt during the 1976 season. These Mets had been together through Gil Hodges, Yogi Berra, interim skipper Roy McMillan, Joe Frazier, and now Joe Torre, who'd been elevated from the roster to become manager.

The night before the trade deadline of June 15, 1977, Harrelson, Jerry Grote, Jerry Koosman, and Tom Seaver all went out together. "We were in Atlanta and we went out to dinner, kind of like the Four Musketeers," Harrelson recalled. "Seaver said, 'Come on, we're going out tonight. I will be gone tomorrow.'"[8] Sure enough, a deal went down right before the deadline. The Franchise was dealt to the Cincinnati Reds for pitcher Pat Zachry, infielder Doug Flynn, outfielder Steve Henderson, and outfielder Dan Norman. The Miracle was a distant memory.

"You know you grow close to a guy after playing with him for 10 years," Harrelson told a reporter after the trade. "You're with him 172 days a year—having hundreds of dinners together, exchanging hundreds of bad jokes. We were perfect roommates. Tom did all the reading and I did all the talking."[9]

Harrelson finished out the year on the Seaver-less Mets. He played against his old friend when Seaver returned to Shea on August 21. Seaver struck out Harrelson the first two times the old roommates faced each other. Harrelson singled his third time up and scored the only run against Seaver that day on a sacrifice fly by Ed Kranepool, who was also a holdover from '69 and '73. Koosman had the tough assignment of starting against Seaver and—of course—taking the loss.

Infielder Tim Foli, a one-time Mets prospect sent to Montreal in the Rusty Staub deal in 1972, was purchased from San Francisco in the 1977 offseason. The Mets felt Harrelson was done and they handed the job to Foli, and in the words of *Daily News* beat man Jack Lang, "Harrelson just sat and twiddled his thumbs in spring training. The Mets weren't going to use him, and Bud was unhappy with a bench role."[10]

So at the end of spring training, the Mets sent Harrelson to the Phillies for cash and Fred Andrews, an infielder whose .174 average had been even lower than Harrelson's anemic .178 in 1977. Andrews didn't even make the lowly Mets club and spent a year playing at Triple-A Tidewater. Harrelson, reunited with old friend Tug McGraw, played second base for the first time in his career. He played all three games of Philadelphia's first trip to Shea Stadium. It was far from the packed homecoming Seaver received and though Harrelson had a hit and scored a run, the Mets came away with the win when they roughed up McGraw and won in the ninth. Harrelson had only one more hit the rest of the weekend, including an 0-fer against Koosman. Harrelson wound up hitting .125 at Shea and .214 overall as a Phillie in 1978. He did not appear in the postseason as the Phillies lost to the Los Angeles Dodgers.

In 1979, Harrelson was joined in Philadelphia by Pete Rose. The former combatants now played on the same side of the infield, though Rose was in the lineup far more frequently than Harrelson. They had patched up the ill feelings about their fabled fight years before. Harrelson told Met Lee Mazzilli about his first trip to Cincinnati after the fight on May 27, 1974. "After Pete was booed in New York, the Reds fans had to boo me," Mazzilli recalled Harrelson telling him. "In my first at-bat [actually his third] I hit a home run to left field over Pete Rose's head. Between innings Rose waited for me at shortstop and told me, 'You got to be (bleep) kidding me' shaking his head."

Harrelson wound up hitting .282 for the Phillies with a .395 on-base percentage. Those were the highest numbers of his career, though the 71 at-bats were his fewest since he debuted in 1965. He became a free agent after the season and had one more reunion, with ex-Mets Matlack and Staub in Texas. Harrelson returned to shortstop and started 77 games there for the Rangers. He hit his final career home run on June 18, giving him seven for his career—all of them coming batting right-handed, his natural side. In his final game, on October 5, 1980, Harrelson started at shortstop and spent the last five innings at second. He committed an error in the ninth inning, but handled the last ball hit to him cleanly. Seattle's Mike Parrott retired him on a grounder back to the mound to give him a .272 average for the year and a .236 career mark. He played in 1,533 games, 1,322 as a Met. That is still second in franchise history to Ed Kranepool; Harrelson also remains second in at-bats (4,390). He retired as one of just three Mets to have reached the four-digit mark in hits (1,029), and while he dropped a few places on the list, it seems ironic to see the diminutive shortstop's name a few hits ahead of Mike Piazza and Darryl Strawberry on the team rolls. Bud's 45 triples, 115 steals, and 573 walks were all tops in Mets history when he retired. He has since been surpassed in those categories, but Harrelson and Rusty Staub will always share the distinction of being the first Mets players inducted into the club's Hall of Fame, in 1986.

On November 2, 1981, Harrelson was named first base coach for the Mets under manager George Bamberger for the 1982 season. In 1983, he broadcast games for the SportsChannel cable network with Tim McCarver and Ralph Kiner. He became a manager of the first time in 1984, when he skippered the Class-A Little Falls Mets to a 44-31 record and a New York-Pennsylvania League championship. His other minor-league assignment came the following year, 1985, with the Columbia Mets of the Class-A South Atlantic League. He managed for 35 games, going 22-13, before being promoted to New York to take over for Bobby Valentine as third-base coach after Valentine left to manage the Texas Rangers.

Under manager Davey Johnson, the Mets were suddenly a formidable club again. Johnson, whose flyout to Cleon Jones as a member of the Orioles had clinched the 1969 world championship at Shea, managed the team to its second world championship. The 1986 team was the most dominant in Mets history. While the Mets had rallied past the Cubs to take the NL East in 1969, the 1986 Mets had the division wrapped up all summer. They won 108 games, winning the division by 21½ games, beat the Houston Astros in a thrilling six-game NLCS, and defeated the Boston Red Sox in a World Series that will forever be known for Bill Buckner's error at first base in the 10th inning of Game Six. Harrelson, coaching at third, had one of the happiest responsibilities in franchise history, waving Ray Knight home with the winning run and running with him across home plate and into the waiting arms of the entire team. "They've got pictures of me racing home with Ray Knight," Harrelson said. "I tell everybody, 'Yeah, actually, I was leading.' I got so excited I was running until I figured out he had to be the one to touch home plate."

Harrelson was the only Met to be in uniform for both the 1969 and 1986 world championships, but his old roommate was in uniform in the other dugout: Tom Seaver, who had been traded to the Red Sox during the season but was injured and unable to pitch (he would never pitch again in the majors, though he have an aborted comeback with the Mets in '87). When it seemed the Red Sox were going to win the Series in the bottom of the 10th, Seaver had caught Harrelson's eye, held his thumb to his ear, and his pinky to his mouth to indicate "I'll call you." When the Mets won Game Seven, Harrelson made the same gesture to his old friend in the Red Sox dugout.

Harrelson remained a coach for the Mets throughout Davey Johnson's tenure. He even had a very brief comeback as a player, appearing for the St. Lucie Legends of the short-lived Senior Professional Baseball Association. Harrelson played just one game and went into the books with a .333 average.

One of his dreams was to manage the Mets and on May 29, 1990, he got that chance when Johnson was fired. Under Harrelson, the Mets won 10 of 17 games before reeling off 11 straight victories to put them three percentage points ahead of the eventual division champion Pirates. The Mets slumped in September, but the club stayed in contention until the last week despite a slew of injuries and new players inserted into a ragtag lineup

But in 1991, with Darryl Strawberry gone to the Dodgers, the remnants of the contending clubs of the 1980s and the replacement parts the Mets had gotten when they'd sent those players away made for a poor mix. Harrelson's managing instincts were sometimes questioned by the media and players. Bench coach Doc Edwards was accused by players of running the team. During a game, Edwards called a pitchout for David Cone to throw while he was facing the Reds pitcher Kip Gross. The June 4, 1991, TV broadcast from Cincinnati captured a finger-pointing exchange between Cone and Harrelson over the call. One player commented, "Buddy has spent the whole season managing like he was everyone's pal, and that doesn't work."[11]

Although the Mets put together a 10-game winning streak to start July of 1991, when the streak was over, the team's season soon followed. The Mets were 2½ games behind the Pirates with a 49-34 record, but New York dropped 50 of its last 78 games. The Mets finished in fifth place, 20½ games out of first place; it was the team's worst finish since 1983, the year before Davey Johnson arrived.

Bud was replaced by as manager by Coach Mike Cubbage in the final week of the '91 season. After his firing, Bud said, "If the public wanted a manager with vast experience, I wasn't it. ... If they wanted somebody who would grow with the organization, I think that was me."

At the time of his dismissal, he held the second-best winning percentage among Mets managers (.529), behind Davey Johnson (.588) and even ahead of mentor Gil Hodges (.523).

In the late 1990s, Bud was instrumental in bringing minor-league baseball to Long Island. The Long Island Ducks began play in 2000 as part of the independent Atlantic League, with Harrelson as co-owner, first-base coach, and senior vice president for baseball operations. "It might sound crazy, but this is the best thing I've done in baseball," said Harrelson. He managed the Central Islip-based team during their inaugural season and led the Ducks to a tie for first place, at 82-58. In 2004, under manager Don McCormack, the Ducks won the Atlantic League championship.

Harrelson was one of the 43 former Mets on hand for the final game at Shea Stadium in 2008. When they cued up to touch home plate for the last time, Harrelson jumped on it to a big ovation.

Years after it happened, the 1973 playoff fight between Harrelson and Pete Rose became a marketing tool. They appeared together signing photos of the famous incident. "Pete and I got along fine when we played on the Phillies, and I still see him today," Bud said.

After his divorce from his first wife, Harrelson married Kim Battaglia in 1975. He became the father of five: Kimberly, Tim, Alexandra, Kassandra, and Troy Joseph. He moved permanently to Long Island on Opening Day 1969, and never left. "I'm not from New York," Bud said, "but I always say I grew up in New York."

SOURCES

"That Championship Season: 1973." Mets official Yearbook, 1983.

Associated Press. "Just a Melody Lingers for Harrelson." June 18, 1977. Clipping in Harrelson's player file, National Baseball Hall of Fame, Cooperstown, New York.

Blatt, Howard. *Amazin' Met Memories: Four Decades of Unforgettable Moments* (Atlanta: Albion Press, 2002).

Borgi, Augie. "Bud Impressed Braves, but Winning's the Thing," *New York Daily News.* May 13, 1976.

Centerfield Maz blog, June 5, 2008, http://centerfieldmaz.blogspot.com/2008/06/bud-harrelson-met-of-day-born-june-6th.html).

Daley, Arthur. "The Big Switch," *New York Times,* March 24, 1968.

Doyle, Al. "The Game I'll Never Forget: Former Mets shortstop recalls 1969 World Series When New York Upset the Baltimore Orioles," *Baseball Digest*, August 2005.

Elliot, Rich. . "Harrelson a Good Luck Charm for Mets," *Connecticut Post*, September 29, 2006. http://www.connpost.com/richelliott/ci_4415977

Gergen, Joe. "Managers Have Star-Studded Resumes," Newsday.com, July 11, 2002, http:www.newsday.com/sports/columnists/ny-gerg1127809oojul11.column

Herrmann, Mark. "Buddy: The Mets Long-Haul shortstop," Newsday.com.

Lang, Jack, and Peter Simon. *The New York Mets: Twenty-Five Years of Baseball Magic* (New York: Henry Holt, 1986).

Libby, Bill. *Bud Harrelson: Super Shortstop* (New York: G.P. Putnam's Sons, 1975).

Ryczek, William. *The Amazin' Mets 1962-1969* (Jefferson, North Carolina: McFarland & Company, Inc. 2008).

Sexton, Joe. "Two Out: Harrelson Joins Cashen," *New York Times*, September 30, 1991.

Young, Dick. *New York Daily News,* February 5, 1970.

NOTES

1 Tom Seaver, "Bud Harrelson has a Fan: It's Seaver," Bud Harrelson player file, National Baseball Hall of Fame, Cooperstown, New York.

2 *Baseball Digest*, 1970, player file.

3 Dick Young, "Young Ideas," player file.

4 https://www.youtube.com/watch?v=CDkRC520-iY.

5 http://www.foxsports.com/mlb/story/bud-harrelson-recalls-arguably-most-infamous-mlb-brawl-ever-with-pete-rose-100913.

6 "Bud Harrelson Remembers NLCS Brawl with Pete Rose," http://www.foxsports.com/mlb/story/pete-rose-bud-harrelson-40th-anniversary-of-bench-clearing-brawl-in-nlcs-100813, October 8, 2013.

7 Centerfield Maz blog, June 5, 2008, http://centerfieldmaz.blogspot.com/2008/06/bud-harrelson-met-of-day-born-june-6th.html)

8 Player file.

9 "Just a Melody Lingers for Harrelson," June 18, 1977, player file.

10 Jack Lang, "Harrelson Wants Trade," *New York Daily News*, March 4, 1978, player file.

11 Bob Klapisch, "Is the System Really Buddy's?" *New York Daily News*, May 30, 1991.

VERN HOSCHEIT

By Jimmy Keenan

VERN HOSCHEIT'S CAREER IN PROFESsional baseball spanned six decades. Signed as a catcher by the New York Yankees in 1941, he had little hope of making the major-league roster with Bill Dickey and later Yogi Berra ensconced behind the plate. The Yankees front office took notice of Hoscheit's leadership potential and made him a player-manager for its McAlester (Oklahoma) club at the age of 26. Although Hoscheit never was called up to the big leagues, he ended his minor-league career with a solid .283 batting average. Then he made his mark in the majors as the bullpen coach on four World Series winners. One of baseball's true unsung heroes, he taught the fundamentals of the game to hundreds of players in five different major-league organizations, as well as scores of youngsters in American Legion ball.

Whitey Herzog, who played for Hoscheit in the minors, told *The Sporting News*, "He was a good manager for young people, a good teacher. He drove the bus, handed out meal money, did the laundry. He'd catch and he'd pitch. He was really the only extra guy we had. I think we carried 16 guys, one for each position, plus the pitchers."[1]

Player and manager Davey Johnson wrote about Hoscheit in his book on the 1985 Mets, "Vern, whom all the players call 'Dad,' is the greatest coach of catchers I have ever known. We have been friends since I was in the Baltimore organization, where he trained Andy Etchebarren, Larry Haney, and Curt Blefary. He gave Curt an extra three or four years in the big leagues. When he was hired by the Oakland A's, he made Adrian Garrett into a catcher for manager Dick Williams and then his big coup was transforming outfielder Gene Tenace into a major-league catcher."[2]

Vernard Arthur "Bud" Hoscheit was born on April 1, 1922, in Brunswick, Nebraska. The first German families had settled in the rural farming community in 1879. By 1915 the town had a bank, a 30-room hotel, and a railroad depot supported by a population of 300. The 1930 US census shows Vernard and his younger sister, Delores, along with their parents, Walter and Elsie (Westerhoff) Hoscheit, living on the family farm in Brunswick.

Hoscheit played his first organized baseball with an American Legion team, the Neligh Antelopes. He graduated from Brunswick High School in 1939. The 5-foot-9, 190-pound Hoscheit was a natural catcher who also played both the infield and outfield. Known for his strong arm and defensive skills, he was also a good hitter with an instinctual knowledge of the game.

In 1940 Hoscheit was the star catcher for Concordia, Kansas, in the Ban Johnson League, and drew the attention of New York Yankees scout Lou Maguolo, who signed him to his first professional contract. Starting the 1941 campaign with the Norfolk Yankees in the

Class-D Western League, Hoscheit hit .284 while catching and playing the outfield. Norfolk won the pennant and Hoscheit was named to the All-Star team.

The next year, Hoscheit moved up a rung on the Yankees' minor-league ladder to the Joplin Miners of the Class-C Western League. On May 26, 1942, he married the former Helen Edwards in Joplin. That same night, the newlywed belted a grand slam in the bottom of the ninth to give the Miners a 9-8 victory.

In November 1942, he joined the Army Air Corps and was stationed at Lincoln Airfield. While serving at Lincoln, he caught for the base's baseball team. Discharged in January 1946. Hoscheit resumed his professional baseball career in 1947 with the Norfolk Tars in the Class-B Piedmont League. After hitting .354 in 19 games, he was promoted to Binghamton (New York) in the Eastern League, where he finished out the season.

The following year, Hoscheit split time between Binghamton, Norfolk, and Triple-A Kansas City (American Association). Named player-manager of the McAlester Rockets in the Class-D Sooner State League, Hoscheit batted .335 while guiding his team to the best record in the circuit. Grateful fans presented him with a new car at the end of the season. The Rockets were out of contention in 1949 but captured the playoffs in 1950-51. Hoscheit had the most productive year of his professional career in 1951, hitting .354 with 11 home runs and 109 RBIs. Future Yankee first baseman-outfielder Norm Siebern was a member of the 1951 McAlester club. The 17-year-old rookie credited Hoscheit with being a major influence on his baseball career.

Hoscheit was the first person, other than his immediate family, that Whitey Herzog thanked during his Hall of Fame induction speech in 2010. Herzog, who played for McAlester in 1949-50, wrote of his former minor-league manager in his autobiography, *White Rat: A Life in Baseball:* "Hoscheit was very good at his job. He could teach every phase of the game and he was just hard enough to make everyone a little scared of him. He really taught me what being a professional baseball player is all about."[3]

Vern and Helen liked McAlester so much that they lived in town full-time during his four-year run with the team. In 1952 Hoscheit took over as manager of the Joplin Miners in the Class-C Western Association. The Miners won the second-half title of a split season and then defeated Muskogee in the league playoffs.

Hoscheit's next managerial post was with the Quincy Gems in the Class-B Three-I League in 1953. He was named general manager in 1955, serving as manager and GM of the Gems through the 1956 season. His last year with Quincy was his final season as an active player. Hoscheit told the *New York Times,* "I hit a ball off the center-field fence and barely made it into second base. Lee MacPhail, who was in charge of the Yankee minor-league teams, told me it was time to retire."[4]

From there Hoscheit was assigned to Peoria, Durham, and finally Greensboro, where he held the dual roles of manager and general manager. In 1959 he left the Yankees organization and became a scout for the Baltimore Orioles. Soon after, he was notified that he had been elected president of the Three-I League. Although he neither sought nor applied for the post, he was voted in unanimously by all eight representatives of the clubs in the circuit. He resigned at the conclusion of the 1961 season after serving two terms as president.

In 1962 Hoscheit returned to the Orioles as a scout, covering Illinois, Iowa, and Wisconsin, while doing double duty as the club's minor-league coordinator. He managed Baltimore's rookie-league team for three years, winning the Florida Instructional League pennant in 1965. Vern also coached the Orioles in spring training during Hank Bauer's tenure as manager.

Late in the 1967 season, Orioles general manager Harry Dalton asked Rochester Red Wings manager Earl Weaver to recommend new coaches for the major-league club. Weaver said that Hoscheit would be his choice for bullpen coach because he was a no-nonsense kind of guy. On October 3, 1967, Hoscheit was hired, replacing Sherm Lollar, who had been released at the end of the season. Earl Weaver and George Bamberger were also brought on as coaches.

Orioles ace Dave McNally credited Hoscheit and pitching coach Bamberger with helping him battle through control problems. Hoscheit was responsible for the development of catchers Elrod Hendricks, Andy Etchebarren, and Larry Haney. He also tutored Curt Blefary on the finer points of catching when the Orioles decided to use the former Rookie of the Year behind the plate.

Hank Bauer was fired as Orioles manager in July 1968, and was replaced by Earl Weaver, who kept Hoscheit on as a coach. On September 29 Oakland A's owner Charlie Finley hired Bauer as manager, and Bauer chose Hoscheit as his bullpen coach. Hoscheit resigned from the Orioles coaching staff to take the job.

For the next few years in Oakland, Hoscheit worked under managers Bauer, John McNamara, Dick Williams, and Alvin Dark. Vern always backed up his players and that included bench-clearing brawls. On July 19, 1972, at County Stadium in Milwaukee, three Brewers batters hit catcher Dave Duncan with their backswings and finally Brewers pitcher Jim Colborn nailed him with a curve. Duncan charged the mound as both benches and bullpens emptied on to the field. The 50-year-old Hoscheit, attempting to join the fray, injured his arm while jumping over the high wall in front of the visitors bullpen. Although Hoscheit was unable to participate in the on-field scuffle, the A's players appreciated his game effort.

Oakland went on to defeat the Cincinnati Reds in the World Series. Hoscheit made sure that 64-year-old advance scout Al Hollingsworth received recognition for his spot-on assessment of the Reds players. "If this man does not get the credit he deserves, it is a real shame," Vern told the Associated Press.[5] Then, turning to Hollingsworth, Hoscheit said, "They did everything you told us they would."[6] Among many observations, the keen-eyed Hollingsworth noted that the Reds scored twice on a pair of two-out bunt singles during their playoff series with Pittsburgh. A's manager Dick Williams took Hollingsworth's advice and played third baseman Sal Bando up to take away the bunt, which he did successfully throughout the Series.

During spring training in 1973, the A's had a doubleheader scheduled in Mesa, Arizona, but there were no umpires available. Hoscheit, who had done everything at the ballpark during his minor-league days from concessionaire to groundskeeper, went behind the plate for both tilts, earning an extra $200 from owner Finley.

Hoscheit was instrumental in developing Rollie Fingers into one of the game's best relief pitchers. Dick Williams recounted how Fingers had difficulty as a starter: "The closer it got for him to start—and they went every fourth day not every fifth day—the more nervous and hyper he'd get. He'd last one inning or at the most two or three. Bill Posedel was our pitching coach at the time. We finally stuck (Fingers) in the bullpen. Vern Hoscheit was our bullpen coach and he made sure the reliever, whoever it was, knew who he was going to face. And he pumped that into Rollie. Then when Rollie got to the mound, I'd ask him, what did Vern say? He said, well, Vern said I was going to face so and so. I said how are you going to pitch him? He said Vern told me this way. Okay, as long as you know. He put him in some games that didn't mean anything, as the score indicated. He did well. Put him in a little tougher situation, he did well. Put him in a save situation—what they call a save situation now—and he did well. So that's how he became a relief pitcher. And he got better as he went along."[7]

Hoscheit tutored catchers Dave Duncan, Adrian Garrett, and Gene Tenace during his time with Oakland. He was able to take Tenace, an average outfielder, and turn him into an excellent defensive backstop.

After the 1973 World Series, Dick Williams shocked the baseball world when he resigned. He was replaced by Alvin Dark. On July 9, 1974, Charlie Finley gave Dark permission to fire Hoscheit and third base coach Irv Noren. Oakland was in first place at the time. Dark had previous issues with Noren over the signals he was giving the batters from third base. In Hoscheit's case, he and Dark had been at odds over the team's policy requiring players to sign up days in advance for extra batting practice. Dark said, "This is no reflection on their ability. I want my own people as coaches."[8] Hoscheit said, "When you have to work for people like that it is time to get out. Dark is a horse feathers manager and Finley is no good either. He promised us a raise and he never kept his word." [9]

Reggie Jackson, in his book *A Season With A Superstar,* wrote that when Alvin Dark took over as manager, he rarely spoke to Hoscheit. The A's slugger found it odd that although Hoscheit kept notes on how to pitch to every hitter in the league, Dark never consulted him on pitching strategy. Aside from Wes Stock, the team was purged of every coach who had an allegiance to former manager Williams.

In October 1975, Hoscheit was reunited with Dick Williams, now the manager of the California Angels, who hired him as a coach. Hoscheit initially was the first-base coach. In July, he moved to third base when Norm Sherry took over for the fired Williams as manager.

Hoscheit retired from baseball after the 1976 campaign. He went back home to Plainview, Nebraska, where he ran a liquor store and managed the local American Legion team. But in 1983 he accepted an offer from the New York Mets to become the team's minor-league catching instructor. That same year, he managed the Mets' Sarasota team in the Florida Gulf Coast League. After the 1983 season Davey Johnson was hired to manage the Mets and he named Hoscheit as his bullpen coach. Johnson had known Vern since his days in the Orioles organization.

For the next few years, Hoscheit handled the Mets' bullpen duties while tutoring the backstops on the finer points of catching. On July 22, 1986, the Mets got into a fight with the Cincinnati Reds. Sportswriters noted that every player and coach, including the 64-year-old Hoscheit, got into the action, while Mets outfielder George Foster never left the bench. The Mets went on to defeat Boston in the World Series, giving Hoscheit his fourth World Series title as a bullpen coach.

Hoscheit was popular with the players but he meant business when it came to following team rules. His quote in the *1987 Mets Yearbook* said it all: "The bus leaves in ten minutes, be on it or under it."

Hoscheit retired again in October 1987. But his absence from baseball was short-lived; a few months later he was again named the Mets' minor-league catching instructor. Among his many duties he was called into help recently-acquired catcher Phil Lombardi, who was having difficulty throwing the ball back to the pitcher. Hoscheit advised the young catcher not to look at the ball before tossing it back to the mound. He was able to help Lombardi with his throwing, but the highly touted prospect was unable to adjust to major-league pitching and was soon out of baseball.

Hoscheit retired from professional baseball for good in 1991, returning home to Plainview. He stayed involved with the game, coaching in the local American Legion team. Hoscheit enjoyed hunting and fishing. He also owned a kennel of hunting dogs. One of his business interests was a celebrity fishing camp in Ocala, Florida, that he co-owned with Whitey Herzog and Davey Johnson.

After a long illness, Hoscheit died at Pierce Manor Nursing Home in Creighton, Nebraska, on June 11, 2007. His wife, Helen, had died in August of 2001. He was survived by his son, Billy Ray Hoscheit; two daughters, Sherri Ann Huigens and Cathy Jean Brodhaugen; a sister; eight grandchildren; and one great grandchild. He was buried in Plainview Cemetery.

SOURCES

In addition to the sources cited in the notes, the author also consulted:

Baseball-Reference.com

Wooldridge, Clyde, Hoscheit Obituary, *McAlester News-Capitol*, June 16, 2007. Posted on Frank Russo's Deadball Era website.

Gary Bedingfield's baseballinwartime.com.

Jackson, Reggie, with Bill Libby, *A Season With a Superstar* (Oakland: Playboy Enterprises Inc.) (Quote excerpted from the *Palm Beach Post* August 27, 1975, 30).

Markusen, Bruce, *Baseball's Last Dynasty: Charlie Finley's Oakland A's* (Indianapolis: Masters Press, 1998), 116, 211, 305-06.

Hummel, Rick, "Herzog Retraces his Steps to Cooperstown," *St Louis Post-Dispatch*, July 26, 2010.

Bergman, Ron, "A's Chopping Block Claims Noren, Hoscheit," *The Sporting News,* July 27, 1974, 27.

BR Bullpen, Sooner State League.

Telephone interview on August 10, 2013, with Lois Olson (Plainview Historical Society).

Vern Hoscheit obituary and tribute page, Brockhausfuneralhome.com.

Vern Hoscheit, Ultimate Mets Website, Ultimatemets.com

Eugene (Oregon) *Register Guard*

Gadsden (Alabama) *Times*

Lewiston (Idaho) *Evening Journal*

Milwaukee Sentinel

Palm Beach Post

St. Joseph (Missouri) *Gazette*

Dubuque (Iowa) *Telegraph-Herald*

*The Hour (*Connecticut)

(Ontario, Canada*) Windsor Star*

Youngstown (Ohio) *Vindicator*

I would like to thank the following people who assisted me with this biography:

Lois Olson, historian at the Plainview Historical Society.

Lyle Spatz and Rod Nelson for providing the name of the Yankees scout, Lou Maguolo, who signed Hoscheit.

NOTES

1 Joe Gergen, "No Fish Tale: Herzog and Johnson in Same Boat," *The Sporting News*, July 13, 1987: 8.

2 Davey Johnson and Peter Golenbock, *Bats* (New York: G.P. Putnam's Sons 1986), 56.

3 Whitey Herzog with Bill Horrigan, *White Rat: A Life in Baseball* (New York: Harper and Row, 1987), 39-40.

4 Murray Chass and Thomas Rogers, *New York Times*, November 12, 1983.

5 "Super Scout Helped Beat Reds," *Observer-Reporter* (Washington, Pennsylvania), October 24, 1972: 16.

6 Ibid.

7 Fay Vincent, *It's What's Inside the Lines That Counts*: *Baseball Stars of the 1970s and 1980s* (New York: Simon & Schuster 2010), 69.

8 Associated Press, "Dark Fires A's Coaches After Oakland Tops Tribe," *Toledo Blade,* July 10, 1974: 17.

9 United Press International, "Dark Takes Charge, Fires Two Coaches," *Milwaukee Journal*, July 10, 1974: 20.

GREG PAVLICK

By Leslie Heaphy

WHILE HE MAY NOT HAVE HAD MAJOR-league success as a player himself, Greg Pavlick has certainly had a long baseball career. Pavlick has been involved in professional baseball since 1971 and helped nurture the careers of countless young players within the Mets and Yankees organizations.

Gregory Michael Pavlick was born on March 10, 1950, in Washington, D.C. Growing up he loved sports and excelled at baseball for Thomas A. Edison High School in Alexandria, Virginia. His accomplishments earned him the chance to play for the University of North Carolina Blue Devils in 1970-71, earning a varsity letter as part of the baseball team and a degree in political science. Pavlick pitched and played third base for the Blue Devils. A 6-foot-3 right-hander, Pavlick had good-enough stuff in high school to be drafted by the Houston Astros in 1968 in the seventh round of the amateur draft (135th overall; he did not sign with the Astros). Pavlick was in good company that year as some of the top picks included Thurman Munson, Bobby Valentine, and Greg Luzinski.[1] In 1971 he was drafted out of North Carolina by the New York Mets in the second round (47th overall). Scout Bill Herring saw something in the young right-hander that gave Pavlick his chance at a professional baseball career.

Pavlick began his journey through the Mets farms system starting with the Marion Mets in 1971. He made steady progress through the organization, from Pompano Beach to Visalia to Memphis before finally making it to the Triple-A Tidewater Tides in 1977. But Triple-A as a 27-year-old was as high as Pavlick would go in his playing career. He pitched in four games for Tidewater, a total of nine innings, with no decisions. Pavlick's best year came in 1973 with the Class-A Visalia Mets. He pitched in 141 innings and was 7-7 with a 3.45 ERA. Apparently Pavlick had control issues he never seemed to conquer. In 1972 with Visalia, he walked 75 batters in 117 innings. With Tidewater in 1977 he walked 10 in 9 innings.[2]

While Pavlick never made it to the majors as a player, his career continued from 1977 as a coach for the Mets and later the Yankees organizations. Pavlick's high point as a coach came in 1986 as part of the World Series champion Mets. Still working as of 2015, he said he was proud of the contributions he made to that team and its pitching staff.

Pavlick started his coaching career in the same way he did his playing career, in the minor leagues and moving up the ranks. Until 1982 he worked as a roving pitching instructor in the lower minor leagues. In 1983 Pavlick was the bullpen coach for Columbia in the South Atlantic League, and then in 1984 for Double-A Jackson. Pavlick got his first major-league chance with the Mets beginning in 1985-86 as bullpen coach, replacing Frank Howard, who left to join the

Milwaukee Brewers. Reflecting on this first call to the majors, Pavlick remarked, "Sure there were times when I felt I might never make it, but I enjoyed what I was doing and I was just hoping that sooner or later a spot would open up for me."[3] Commenting on Pavlick's importance to the team, manager Davey Johnson said, "Perhaps Greg's main duty was to assist Mel Stottlemyre with our pitchers. He really made a contribution too. I think his biggest asset was his familiarity with the staff because he had seen so many of them throw in our system."[4]

In 1987 Pavlick returned to the Mets minor leagues as a roving pitching instructor. Part of his responsibility was to supervise Doc Gooden's return to pitching form after his release from drug rehab. Johnson praised Pavlick's work with Gooden: "Greg did a super job with Dwight. He got him ready to go for us under very difficult circumstances. Greg Pavlick deserves a great deal of the credit for the fine season Dwight had on his return"[5]

Pavlick returned to the Mets again from 1988-1991, working under Buddy Harrelson as a bullpen coach and then first-base coach when Mike Cubbage moved over to be the third-base coach. From 1992 through 1993 Pavlick resumed his roving minor-league instruction before getting the call again in 1994; this time becoming the Mets pitching coach in 1994-1996 after Mel Stottlemyre left. Pavlick served under manager Davey Johnson before his final stint under Dallas Green. GM Joe McIlvaine said of selecting Pavlick to replace Stottlemyre, "There's continuity, a good working knowledge of what we have on the major league and minor league levels."[6] Gooden was also happy with the change, having worked with Pavlick during his rehab assignment. After the 1996 campaign Green and Pavlick, along with bench coach Bobby Wine, were let go by the Mets. Pavlick was replaced by former Mets pitcher Bob Apodaca, who was brought up from Tidewater where he had previously been Bobby Valentine's pitching coach.[7]

While working under Davey Johnson, Pavlick and the other coaches often played golf together in their off-time. They usually played at Piping Rock Golf Course on Long Island. The coaches all stayed at an old estate kept by the Mets for them and Pavlick served as the group's dishwasher along with Johnson. Their cook was Vern Hoscheit and Bill Robinson did their grocery shopping.[8]

Pavlick left the Mets organization with 26 years of service to join the coaching staff of the Tampa Yankees in 1997. With some changes in Yankees management, Pavlick was promoted to be pitching coordinator in 1999.[9] He moved up to the Columbus Clippers in 2000-2001. He was the pitching coach for the Clippers for two seasons and then worked on the staff of the Class-A Tampa Yankees from 2002 until 2015. One of Pavlick's best seasons as a pitching coach came in 2009 when the young Tampa staff finished fourth in ERA at 3.45 and also fourth in saves with 39. His pitchers threw 10 shutouts that season and two complete games. Eleven members of that staff went on to pitch in the majors. Lance Pendleton, who pitched 18 innings in the majors, led the 2009 squad with an 11-5 record.[10] Under Pavlick's direction, the Tampa pitchers helped their team finish first in their division in both 2007 and 2010. They also won the league championship in 2009 and 2010.

At the end of the 2013 season Pavlick received consideration for the Yankees bullpen job after Mike Harkey left to become the pitching coach for the Arizona Diamondbacks. The Yankees had a number of internal candidates to consider but chose Gary Tuck from outside the organization to be the new bullpen coach. Tuck had been with the Yankees previously as well as the Red Sox and Marlins.[11]

Though he never played in the majors, Pavlick made a long and successful career for himself as a bullpen coach and pitching coach. He worked with some great pitchers, including Dwight Gooden, Jerry Koosman, and Jon Matlack of the 1986 Mets staff, while also nurturing the careers of hopefuls like the Yankees' Michael Pineda when he found himself on a rehab stint in Tampa in 2013.

SOURCES

Besides the sources cited in the Notes, the author also consulted baseball-reference.com and Pavlick's file at the Baseball Hall of Fame library. All statistics come from baseball-reference.com.

NOTES

1 baseball-almanac.com/draft/baseball-draft.php?yr=1968.

2 ultimatemets.com/profile.php?PlayerCode=5296; player contract in Hall of Fame file, Cooperstown, New York.

3 1985 Mets Media Guide.

4 1985 Mets Media Guide, 22.

5 Murray Chass, "Gooden Leaves Center," *New York Times*, April 30, 1987; 1988 Mets Media Guide, 15.

6 "Howard Joins Mets as Coach," *New York Times,* October 27, 1993.

7 "Pavlick Named as Coach," *New York Times*, March 21, 1985.

8 Joseph Durso, "Johnson Cool in Command," *New York Times*, September 15, 1985.

9 "Cashman to Receive Contract Extension," *New York Times*, February 3 1999, D7.

10 tampa.yankees.milb.com/documents/2010/01/05/7877952/1/Tampa_Yankees_Press_Release_-_2010_Staff2.pdf.

11 George A. King III, "Yankees Need 'Pen Coach after Harkey's Departure," *New York Post,* November 29, 2013; Mike Axisa, "Yankees Name Gary Tuck Bullpen Coach, Announce Three other Hires," riveraveblues.com/tag/matthew-krause/.

BILL ROBINSON

By Alan Cohen

IT WAS ONE WEEK INTO THE 1977 SEASON. JIM Kaplan of *Sports Illustrated* alluded to 34-year-old Bill Robinson's frustrations in his 10th major-league season:

"No matter where he is playing—be it Cincinnati or New York or Los Angeles—he is sure to hear it. 'Weaser,' someone will call to him from the stands. 'Hey, Weaser.' And Bill Robinson of the Pirates will know someone from his hometown of Elizabeth, Pa., just outside Pittsburgh, is on hand. Why was he given the name? Robinson doesn't know. What does Weaser mean? That's also a mystery. The nickname is downright befuddling, which makes it especially appropriate for Robinson, a .300 hitter with power and a good glove who, confoundingly enough, cannot get a regular job. 'I am the No. 1 utility man in baseball,' he says joylessly."[1]

"But in the Panglossian (excessively optimistic) world of Pittsburgh's new manager, Chuck Tanner, Robinson occupies the best of all possible positions. " 'People call him a super-sub,' says Tanner. 'I call him a super-regular. He's more valuable than most regulars, because he can play so many positions."[2]

"Robinson's pre-batting ritual includes a quick Lord's Prayer while he crosses himself several times. Then he rubs his forehead from eyebrows to hairline with the middle and index fingers of his right hand, a relaxation technique he picked up from a kinesiologist. Finally Robinson assumes an upright stance made all the more menacing by his 6' 3", 200-pound frame[3] and lashes downward at the ball with a whippy 33-ounce bat. 'I try to make the top of the ball mine,' he says. 'I swing for grounders and line drives. After all, how often does a guy drop a fly? But the big thing is, I've learned to relax and meet the ball instead of trying to overpower it. I've eliminated the word "pressure" from my vocabulary.'"[4]

" 'His attitude has changed completely,' says Del Unser of the Expos, a close friend and former teammate of Robinson's in Philadelphia. 'He was very high-strung with the Yankees [1967-69] and at times with the Phillies [1972-74]. Now he can wait out a pitcher and hit breaking stuff. I think if he hadn't had to break in as a Yankee, he'd have been where he is now five years ago.'"[5]

William Henry Robinson Jr., the first-base coach and hitting instructor for the 1986 New York Mets, was born on June 26, 1943, in McKeesport, Pennsylvania. His father, Bill Sr., was a steelworker. His mother, Millie Mae, was a cook in a restaurant, and when the scouts visited during Bill's senior year of high school, she made sure they were well fed.

Robinson starred in baseball (as a pitcher/outfielder) and basketball at Elizabeth-Forward High School in McKeesport and had a basketball scholarship offer from Bradley University. He chose baseball and was

signed in June 1961, when he graduated from high school, by John O'Neil of the Braves for a figure between $12,000 and $16,000.

Robinson's career got off to a less than resounding start. His travels began in 1961 at Wellsville in the Class-D New York-Penn League. Although he batted only .239, he had 15 doubles in 67 games and was off to Dublin in the Georgia-Florida League for the 1962 season. While there, he experienced the racial segregation that was inherent in the South in those years, but did not let it affect his play on the field. From there, Robinson headed up the ladder. He batted .304 at Dublin and followed that up with a .316 at Waycross in the Class-A Georgia-Florida League the following season. At Waycross he had 10 home runs, a league-leading 132 hits and 10 triples, 62 RBIs, and 29 stolen bases. He topped the league with a .478 slugging percentage. The 1964 season found him at Yakima in the Class-A Northwest League, where he had his best season so far, banging 24 doubles and 18 homers with 81 RBIs en route to a .348 batting average in 104 games.

Robinson had married his childhood sweetheart, Mary Alice Moore, in December 1963. Bill III came along in 1964 and Kelly was born in 1969. The Robinsons eventually settled in Washington Township, New Jersey. Bill was active in his community and received the George Washington Carver Award for community service in 1978.[6]

Despite his achievements, Robinson gained the reputation as a worrier, as noted in a small piece in *The Sporting News* in 1965.[7] Robinson spent all of the 1965 season with the Atlanta Crackers, the Braves' Triple-A farm team. He got off to a great start with three hits in his first game and went 7-for-16 in his first four games. The accolades were flowing and Toledo's manager, Frank Verdi, considered him to be "the best looking rookie I have seen in the league this year."[8] For the season, he batted .268. In 1966 the Milwaukee Braves moved to Atlanta, and the Braves moved their Triple-A team to Richmond. Robinson responded to the move with a .312 batting average and career highs of 20 home runs and 79 RBIs. He was named to the International League All-Star team.

Robinson, then 23, was called up to the Braves at the end of the 1966 season and saw his first action on September 20. He ran for Henry Aaron and finished the game in right field. His first hit came on September 25. Starting the game in left field, he singled in the eighth inning off Pittsburgh's Al McBean, driving in a run. He was given another start in the season finale against Cincinnati and went 2-for-4, including his first major-league extra-base hit, an RBI triple. In his six games with the Braves, he went 3-for-11.

But the Braves were fully stocked with outfielders and traded Robinson to the New York Yankees for Clete Boyer. The aging Yankees had fallen on hard times, falling to sixth in 1965 and 10th in 1966. Roger Maris had been traded to St. Louis, and it was expected that Robinson would take over in right field.

Robinson was counted on to save the franchise, and things started off fairly well. As Robinson remembered it, "(W)e opened in Washington (on April 10), and I hit a home run my first time up in an 8-1 win. They said 'God's here.'"[9] The score was actually 8-0, with the win going to Mel Stottlemyre, who limited the Senators to two hits.

As Marty Appel notes in *Pinstripe Empire*, "Robinson was a personal favorite of (team president Mike) Burke's. He wanted him to succeed badly. He was tall and rangy, he was black, and he seemed like a good statement for a team 'moving in new directions.'"[10] Burke was alluding to the fact that since Jackie Robinson entered baseball in 1947, the Yankees had been very slow to integrate, with only one black player of note, Elston Howard, playing for the club during the first 20 years of integration.

But the rest of the 1967 season for Bill Robinson was a disappointment. He suffered a shoulder injury, which he tried to hide. The fans were tough on him. "The boos really tore me up when I was with the Yankees," he said in 1974. "All ballplayers hear them and I couldn't take it. I'd be across the George Washington Bridge and heading home (to New Jersey) before the people even got to the clubhouse. I just couldn't face it anymore."[11] He batted only .196 with seven homers and 29 RBIs in 116 games, as the Yankees placed ninth for their third consecutive lower division finish.

Looking back on his season, Robinson said, "I was pressing too hard. Every time I came up, I wanted to hit a home run to impress people. Finally it got to the point where I was holding the bat so tightly I couldn't even hit the ball."[12]

Postseason shoulder surgery repaired the injury, but Robinson continued to struggle. He batted .240 in 1968 and .171 in 1969. In 1970 he was sent down to Triple-A Syracuse and batted .258. In December the Yankees traded Robinson to the Chicago White Sox for pitcher Barry Moore.

Appel noted, "It would forever be a mystery as to what went wrong with Bill Robinson in New York, and why that promise was never fulfilled"[13] (until he shined for Philadelphia and Pittsburgh).

The White Sox sent Robinson to Triple-A Tucson (Pacific Coast League), where he batted .275 with 14 homers and 81 RBIs in 1971. Frustration set in when he was not called up to the White Sox, and he even thought about quitting. His hopes were renewed when Chicago dealt him to the Philadelphia Phillies for minor-league catcher Jerry Rodriguez.

In 1972 Robinson was still in the PCL, this time with Eugene, and batted .304 with 20 homers and 66 RBIs in 66 games. That earned him a call-up to Philadelphia in June, and he saw his first action with the Phillies on June 24, doubling against the Expos in a pinch-hitting role. During his days in the minor leagues, he learned of what he came to call the Willie Davis theory, which goes as follows: "It's not my life, and it's not my wife, so why worry about it." Basically, he learned not to dwell over everything and only worry about items of the utmost personal importance. The theory stood him well as he embarked on the most productive years of his career. There would be bumps along the way, but, for the most part, Robinson took things in stride and learned to relax.

Robinson got into 82 games with the Phillies in 1972, batting .239, but was in the majors to stay.[14] Actually, when he came to spring training in 1973, he was still 52 days short of qualifying for the major-league pension plan. Job number one was just to make the team. He exceeded all expectations. New manager Danny Ozark inserted Bill into the lineup more regularly and he batted .288 with 25 home runs and 65 RBIs in 124 games. It appeared as though Robinson had it made. Manager Ozark remarked, "He gave it his all and produced. I understood the problems he had in New York. He wasn't sure of himself. Now he'd got the confidence. If he could go back 10 years, he would be another Aaron or Mays."[15]

No sooner was Robinson a regular than his bad luck returned. He had offseason surgery for bone chips in his left elbow and found that, despite his fine performance, he came to spring training in 1974 without a regular job. A somewhat overblown dispute with Ozark would ultimately result in his leaving the Phillies.

"I saw the lineup card without my name on it and took a swipe at it, not meaning to touch it," Robinson recalled. "But it came off, and Ozark was watching. He called me into his office, which he had a perfect right to do, and we both let off a lot of steam. When I was leaving, I tried to close the door gently, but there was a breeze and it slammed."[16]

Robinson got into only 100 games with Philadelphia in 1974 and his average dropped to .236 with only 5 home runs and 21 RBIs. After the season, he was traded to Pittsburgh for pitcher Wayne Simpson, and with the Pirates he blossomed.

Robinson joined the Pirates in 1975 at the none-too-tender age of 32 and was the fourth outfielder behind Richie Zisk, Al Oliver, and Dave Parker. He batted .280 with 6 homers and 33 RBIs. He started 41 games for the Pirates and had 16 multiple-hit games. The Pirates won the National League East title before being swept by Cincinnati in the League Championship Series. Robinson went hitless in two at-bats in the LCS.

The following season, Robinson saw more action, with 416 at-bats in 121 games. His batting average soared to .303, his first time above 300. He was the Pirates' leading right-handed slugger and the team's most valuable player. He received the Roberto Clemente Memorial Award from the Pittsburgh sportswriters. He performed at five different positions and pinch-hit .455.[17] His power numbers were solid (21 homers, 64 RBIs) and the best was yet to come.

Off this showing, Robinson was slated for third base in 1977, but once again he would be denied. The Pirates traded for Phil Garner. Instead of blowing up as he had in Philadelphia, he calmly talked out his disappointment with two friends from his minor-league days and his father. "They all told me the same things," Robinson said, "that I still had a job and that things could be worse. So I didn't do anything rash, and I'm glad. We got a heck of a third baseman in the deal, and because I had thought I would start, I had gotten into the best shape of my life mentally and physically."[18]

"It's true we led Bill to believe he'd be starting at third this season," said General Manager Pete Peterson, "but we couldn't resist picking up Phil Garner from the A's. He (Garner) plays third, and Willie Stargell plays first. We want to stick with Al Oliver in left and Dave Parker in right, and we feel Omar Moreno in center gives us the kind of outfield defense we haven't had since Roberto Clemente. Not that Bill isn't good defensively. He is, and he's our top sub at all five positions. He may not get 400 at bats, but he'll get plenty with his versatility."[19]

It wasn't long before Robinson saw action, filling in for injured Pirates in the outfield and at first base. It was early on that the Pirate injury list started to grow, and Robinson was a disgruntled bench warmer for just the first four innings of the season. When Al Oliver was sidelined because the pain from a mouth ulcer became too acute, Robinson moved into the outfield. Two games later, Stargell began suffering, first from a strained right knee, then from dizzy spells, and Robinson was moved to first base. Through the first seven games of the season, he was hitting .348 and leading the Bucs with eight runs batted in. There was even talk in Pittsburgh that the Pirates would trade one of their regulars so that Robinson can have a spot to call his own in the lineup.[20]

Despite this early activity, he was hampered by muscle pulls in his legs and started only 19 games during the first two months of the season. Everyone seemed to have suggestions to get him going and, at the suggestion of teammate Rich Gossage, he took to wearing pantyhose beneath his uniform pants.[21] He took more than his share of kidding, but went onto start 32 consecutive games between May 31 and July 2, batting .339 over that stretch.

It got better. From July 21 through August 2, Robinson had a power surge. He had five homers, including grand slams on July 28 and July 30, and batted in 21 runs. His batting average during the 13 games was .390 and his slugging percentage was a hefty .712. But he did not forget that it had not always been so easy. He could relate to "the guys sitting on the bench, because I have been in their spot for a long, long time. The toughest part of coming off the bench is that you know eventually you're going back to the bench. That's tough for any athlete to take."[22]

On August 15 of that season, the Pirates issued a press release which highlighted his exploits from June 24 through August 2, a period during which he had eight game winning hits. It was also noted that through August 14, he had come to the plate 24 times with a runner on third with less than two out, and driven in the runner on 22 of those occasions.[23]

For the record, Bill Robinson in 1977, despite not being a "regular," played in 137 games, 127 as a starter. The versatile Robinson started 79 games at first base, 11 games at third base, 36 games in left field, and 1 game in center field. He came to the plate 544 times. He set career highs, batting .304 with 26 homers and 104 RBIs.

During the offseason, Al Oliver was traded and Bill Robinson, at age 35, became the everyday left fielder in 1978. However, his numbers dropped off significantly. He batted only .246 with 14 home runs and 80 RBIs. A thumb injury early in the season set him back and as he continued to fail to produce, he began to press.

Manager Chuck Tanner and his teammates were in his corner. Tanner said, "You don't give up on his type. He's giving it all he has and one day he'll get it all back and he'll win plenty of games for us."[24]

Robinson didn't let his off year at the plate affect his fielding as he led National League left fielders with a .989 fielding percentage. He stole a career high 14 bases. He did have his moments during the season, with a pair of two-home-run games against the Cubs at Wrigley Field.

And then came 1979. Robinson got his home-run swing back and slammed 24 along with 75 RBIs as the "We Are Family" Pirates won their division for the sixth time in 10 years, and the first time since 1975. Robinson appeared in a career record 148 games for Pittsburgh, again without a regular position or place in the lineup. He was platooned with John Milner, and when Willie Stargell needed a rest, the Pirates would play both Robinson and Milner, and they were up to the task.

Actually, the Pirates got off to a slow start in 1979. They were six games under .500 on May 16 before taking 16 of 21 games to move into third place, three games out of first. During that stretch, Robinson batted .322 with seven homers and 19 RBIs, including two homers in a win on June 6. As the Pirates righted their ship, Robinson said "It was just a case of putting it together. We know we have the talent here. We know we can win. We have all the ingredients of a winner and many of us are tired of finishing in second place."[25] But then, the team treaded water.

As late as July 8, they were in fourth place, seven games behind the league leaders. Then they took off. They won 16 of 21 to move into first place for the first time on July 28. It became a two-team race between the Pirates and the surprising Montreal Expos the rest of the season.

On the decisive last day of the campaign, the Pirates hosted the Chicago Cubs. Robinson came off the bench in the top of the sixth inning to replace Milner in left field. His first, and only, plate appearance was in the bottom of the seventh inning. He came to the plate with the bases loaded and two outs. He delivered a single, driving in two runs to give the Bucs a 5-2 lead. The final score was 5-3, and the victorious Pirates advanced to the postseason. They defeated the Reds in the NLCS to advance to the World Series against Baltimore. After going 0-for-3 in the LCS, Robinson went 5-for-19 in the World Series as the Pirates defeated the Orioles in seven games. Robinson had his first World Series ring, and a full World Series share worth $28,236.87.

During the offseason, the Pirates, looking to shore up their pitching, offered Robinson as trade bait, but there were no nibbles.[26] Injuries plagued Robinson in 1980, and he played in only 100 games, 74 as a starter. He batted .287 with 12 home runs and 36 RBIs. The following season, he saw even less action, batting .216 and playing in only 39 games. The Pirates finished third in 1980 with an 83-79 record and, in the strike-shortened 1981 season were 46-56.

By 1982 the Pirates were showing their age. Although they finished with a winning record of 84-78, some of their players, most notably Robinson (39) and Willie Stargell (42) were getting old. On June 15, 1982, Robinson and his .239 batting average were traded to the Phillies for Wayne Nordhagen. As Robinson parted with the Pirates, Stargell said, "Bill Robinson is one helluva man, nothing but a plus in anybody's life. He is a caring, concerned man.[27]

In the remaining months of 1982, Robinson played in 35 games for the Phillies, batting .261 (18-for-69). He saw his last action in 1983, getting into only 10 games, and was released on May 23. Teammate Mike Schmidt remembered back to 1972 when he was at Eugene, Oregon, his last stop in the minors, and was teamed with Robinson. Schmidt remembered that Robinson "respected me as a player, and knowing that made me feel good. He kind of took me under his wing. … (J) ust a good friend, a guy that had been there before. … Robbie is a credit to the game of baseball. I don't know how to put it any other way."[28] Robinson finished his 16-year major-league playing career with a .258 batting average, 166 home runs and 641 RBIs.

In his last weeks with the Phillies, Robinson took the time to counsel rookie pitcher Charles Hudson on the importance of relaxing, and learning to "alleviate pressure."[29] He would spend the better part of his remaining years instilling that lesson on a new generation of players.

In 1984 Robinson joined the New York Mets as hitting instructor and first-base coach, and "Uncle Bill" was with the Mets for six years during which time the team never finished lower than second place. Robinson got his second World Series ring in 1986, and was a valued instructor working with the likes of Darryl Strawberry, who became his special project.

Ron Darling was in his first full season with the Mets in 1984, and on August 7 pitched against the Cubs at Wrigley Field. By day's end, he would know first-hand the value of Bill Robinson to the New York Mets. Darling was pulled from the game not long after hitting Dave Owen of Chicago in the fifth inning. An irate Cubs fan threw a cup of beer at Darling as he left the field. Darling was about to go back on the field and pursue his attacker when Robinson grabbed hold of him and set him down. Robinson, of course, could display his temper, and was about to pursue the fan. He backed off when the fan was escorted from the premises by security guards. When Robinson returned to the dugout, he shot a knowing glance in Darling's direction, which the young pitcher took as a much needed sign of encouragement.[30]

Robinson looked for every edge for his players, and was quick to accuse Pirates pitcher Rich Rhoden of doctoring the ball in a game against the Mets on July 6, 1986, in Pittsburgh. He confronted Rhoden after the pitcher struck out Gary Carter to end the fifth inning. A shoving match ensued and, before long, the benches cleared. Robinson was fined $500, but his players knew where he stood.

During the stretch drive in 1986, Robinson made it a point to put a picture in Strawberry's locker of Darryl hitting a line drive, just to remind his star pupil how he looked when swinging well.[31] During the last 11 games of the regular season, Strawberry batted .306 with 6 home runs and 15 RBIs. During his six years working with Robinson, Strawberry averaged over 30 home runs per season.

During the 1986 World Series, Robinson spoke of the challenges he faced with the Mets and the approach he had taken. "I think that with these young kids, you've got to be more than a hitting instructor. I'm not their father but you've got to give them fatherly street advice. It certainly helps me, not only being black, but talking to all the guys it helps a lot that I have a son who is the same age as most of these guys. I respect them all and think they respect me. They're trying to get where I've been."[32] Bill's son at the time became very close with Strawberry and Gooden. Every time Gooden had an issue, he was able to come to Robinson, who was much more than a hitting instructor.

And on that magical (for the Mets) evening in October, Bill Robinson was standing in the first-base coaching box when, in that fateful bottom of the 10th inning of Game Six of the World Series, every player got the low two when he arrived at first base. The rallying cry was "Don't make the last out!"[33] And then, Mookie Wilson hit a groundball in the direction of first base. "It made three nice bounces. Bounce ... bounce ... bounce. And then it hit something and didn't come up again. That fourth bounce. It was just our year."[34] Wilson remembered that during that fateful bottom of the 10th inning, each of the Mets involved in the rally told Robinson that they were not determined to make the last out.[35]

The Mets were unable to build on the success of 1986, and in 1989 after finishing in second place, six games behind the division-winning Cubs, Robinson was fired. After spending two years with ESPN, in 1992 he took a managing job at Shreveport in the Double-A Texas League and led the Giants affiliate to the championship with a 77-59 record. He was frustrated at not being given an opportunity to rise higher, as he aspired to eventually get a major-league managing position. He did feel that race had something to do with his not moving higher, stating: "If (becoming a big league manager) doesn't happen, it won't surprise me. Whether it's prejudice, whether it's timing, or whatever, it's always excuses."[36]

Robinson's next stop was back with the Phillies, as a minor league hitting instructor in 1994, and as manager at Reading in the Eastern League in 1996. The following season he moved up to Triple-A Scranton-Wilkes-Barre as hitting instructor, and was inducted into the Pennsylvania Baseball Sports Hall of Fame.

Robinson was doing what he loved. In 1998 he said, "It's been fun, gratifying to help young kids. I had delusions of being a major-league manager, but I know that's not going to happen. Baseball doesn't owe me a thing. As long as I have a uniform on, I'm grateful. I've been successful. Maybe not in a material way, but I have the Lord on my side and my family. What more could a man ask?"[37]

In 1999 Robinson was back in the Yankees organization, working with the hitters at Triple-A Columbus. He was rewarded for his efforts with a World Series ring when the Yankees won the championship that year. He stayed with Columbus for three years before returning to the majors as the hitting instructor for the Montreal Expos in 2001.

Robinson was ecstatic about returning to the big leagues as a coach. "I had waited 12 years to get back to the major leagues. After I accepted (the offer from Expos manager Jeff Torborg), I walked out on Madison Avenue (in New York), raised my hands to the sky, and said, 'Thank God.'"[38]

In 2003 Robinson was with the Florida Marlins and returned to the World Series, facing the Yankees and winning his fourth World Series ring as the Marlins defeated the Yankees. George Vecsey of the *New York Times* perhaps summed things up the best: "Whether (the Marlins) know it or not, their paternal hitting coach is an inspiration for athletes — or anybody else who has a bad day or a bad couple of years. You can come back. You can go from failure to the World Series."[39]

Robinson died suddenly on July 29, 2007, in Las Vegas while working as a minor-league hitting coordinator for the Los Angeles Dodgers. He was survived by his wife, Mary Alice, and their two children. William III played three years of minor-league baseball before moving into broadcasting, and Kelley worked in the fashion industry.

SOURCES

In addition to the sources cited in the notes, the author also consulted:

Vecsey, George. "And Here's To You Mr. Robinson, My Friend," *New York Times*, August 2, 2007: D-1.

Baseball-Reference.com.

Robinson's file at the Baseball Hall of Fame library.

NOTES

1. Jim Kaplan, "He's an Irregular Regular," *Sports Illustrated*, April 25, 1977
2. Kaplan.
3. Baseball-reference.com lists Robinson at 6-feet-2 and 189 pounds.
4. Kaplan.
5. Kaplan.
6. Jack Chevalier, *Philadelphia Tribune*, September 19, 2003.
7. *The Sporting News*, May 1, 1965: 42.
8. Furman Bisher, "Robby Came for Cup of Coffee, Stayed to Feast with Crackers," *The Sporting News*, July 24, 1965: 37.
9. Sam Smith, "Bill Robinson, In Search of Confidence," *Black Sports*, September, 1974: 23.
10. Marty Appel, *Pinstripe Empire: The New York Yankees from Before the Babe to After the Boss* (New York: Bloomsbury, 2012), 368.
11. Smith, 31.
12. Neil Amdur, "Robinson of Yanks Is Relaxed for His Second Time Around," *New York Times*, April 8, 1968: 67.
13. Appel, 378.
14. Ed Rumill, "Phillies Robinson Glad He Didn't Quit," *Christian Science Monitor*, June 27, 1973.
15. Smith, 47.
16. Kaplan.
17. Kaplan.
18. Kaplan.
19. Kaplan
20. Kaplan

21 Charlie Feeney, "Robinson Snubbed as All-Star, Glistens as Buc," *The Sporting News*, June 25, 1977: 15

22 Charlie Feeney, "Lucky Bucs Find Robinson Can Do Job on Daily Basis, *The Sporting News*, August 13, 1977: 8.

23 23 Pittsburgh Pirates Press Release, August 15, 1977, in Robinson file at the Baseball Hall of Fame.

24 Charlie Feeney, "Bucs Waiting For Robinson to End Slump," *The Sporting News*, July 8, 1978: 28.

25 25 Feeney, "Bucs Cash in on Robinson's Waiting Game," *The Sporting News*, June 23, 1979: 17.

26 Charlie Feeney, "Bucs Get No Nibbles With Robinson as Bait," *The Sporting News*, December 22, 1979: 61.

27 Frank Dolson, "Baseball Can't Lose People Like Robinson," *Philadelphia Inquirer*, June 6, 1983: 7-C.

28 Dolson.

29 Dolson.

30 Ron Darling with Danie Paisner, *The Complete Game* (New York: Random House, 2009), 133-34.

31 Jim Naughton, *New York Daily News*, October 5, 1986.

32 Malcolm Moran, "Robinson and His Gifted Student," *New York Times*, October 23, 1986: B16.

33 Interview with Bill Robinson III, June 2015.

34 Vic Ziegel, "Robby Back Where He Belongs," *New York Daily News*, March 27, 1998.

35 Mookie Wilson (with Erik Sherman), *Mookie: Life, Baseball, and the '86 Mets*, (New York: Berkley Books, 2014), 6.

36 Taylor Batten, Associated Press, "Is There Racism in Baseball?" *Mobile* (Alabama) *Register*, July 22, 1992: 26.

37 Ziegel.

38 Jack Chevalier, *Philadelphia Tribune*, November 13, 2011: 2C

39 George Vecsey, "Ex-Yankee Robinson Returns as a Winner, *New York Times*, October 20, 2003: D-4.

MEL STOTTLEMYRE

By Gregory H. Wolf

A BASEBALL LIFER, MEL STOTTLEMYRE burst on the scene as a midseason call-up for the New York Yankees in 1964, helping the club win its fifth consecutive pennant and starting three games in the World Series. One of the most underrated and overlooked pitchers of his generation, Stottlemyre won 149 games and averaged 272 innings per season over a nine-year stretch (1965-1973) that corresponded with the nadir of Yankees history. Only Bob Gibson (166 victories), Gaylord Perry (161), Mickey Lolich (156), and Juan Marichal (155) won more during that period; only Perry tossed more innings, and only Gibson fired more shutouts (43) than Stottlemyre's 38. Stottlemyre was the "epitome of Yankee class and dignity," wrote longtime New York sportswriter Phil Pepe. "[He was] a throwback to a winning tradition in those years of mediocrity."[1] After a torn rotator cuff ended his playing career at the age of 32 in 1974, Stottlemyre embarked on a storied career as a big-league pitching coach, most notably for the New York Mets (1984-1993) and Yankees (1996-2005). Denied a championship as a player he won five as a coach (1986, 1996, 1998-2000).

Melvin Leon Stottlemyre was born on November 13, 1941, in Hazleton, Missouri, the third of five children born to Vernon and Lorene Ellen (Miles) Stottlemyre. Vernon was a pipefitter and moved the family from south-central Missouri to Oregon and South Carolina before settling in the early 1950s in Mabton, a small farming town in Washington's Yakima Valley, where he was employed at the Hanford Atomic Energy plant. The elder Stottlemyre, a former sandlot player, introduced Mel and his younger brother, Keith, to baseball and took them to local semipro games. According to his autobiography with John Harper, *Pride and Pinstripes*, Mel spent countless hours as a teenager in his backyard with his brother replaying the New York Yankees and Brooklyn Dodgers games they read about.[2] Growing up in a blue-collar family in a rural area, Mel's experience with baseball in organized leagues was limited until high school. The tall, bashful right-hander with sandy blond hair pitched and occasionally played shortstop for Mabton High School, which had just 10 players when he graduated in 1959.

On the strength of a 13-0 record as a senior, Mel accepted a scholarship to attend Yakima Valley Junior College, but got off to a rough start both in school and on the diamond. Declared academically ineligible because of poor grades in 1960, he played in a local summer league. He returned to the junior college in 1961 and went 7-2 for legendary coach Chuck "Bobo" Brayton.[3] Stottlemyre worked out for the Milwaukee Braves at their minor-league affiliate in Yakima, but was rejected because he didn't throw hard enough. While toiling on a farm and resigned that his baseball days were probably over, he was surprised by a visit

from Yankees scout Eddie Taylor. With no negotiations and no bonus but unequivocal support from his folks, Stottlemyre signed a minor-league contract with his favorite team. "He had the effortless way of throwing the ball," recalled Taylor.[4]

Just 19 years old, the unheralded Stottlemyre began his professional baseball career splitting his time with the Class-D Harlan (Kentucky) Smokies in the Appalachian League and the Auburn (New York) Yankees in the New York-Penn League in 1961. A combined 9-4 record and 3.27 ERA in 99 innings earned him a promotion to Class-B Greensboro in 1962. Described by sportswriter Moses Crutchfield as the "hottest prospect" in the Carolina League, Stottlemyre relied on a fastball, slider, and sinker to post a 17-9 record with a stellar 2.50 ERA in a league-leading 241 innings, including a stretch of 28⅔ scoreless frames early in the season.[5] "His biggest asset," wrote Crutchfield, "is his ability to keep the ball low."[6] That quality turned out to be Stottlemyre's calling card to the big leagues.

The Yankees brass was impressed with Stottlemyre's unexpectedly quick progress. He was invited to participate in spring training in 1963 as a nonroster player and was subsequently assigned to the Triple-A Richmond Virginians (International League). The youngest player on the club, Stottlemyre struggled against seasoned competition, posting a 7-7 record and splitting his time between starts (16) and relief appearances (23). The Yankees, fresh off a 104-win season that ended in a drubbing by the Los Angeles Dodgers in the World Series, did not invite the 22-year-old to spring training in 1964. Stottlemyre began the season in the bullpen for Richmond, but the lanky righty scuttled those plans by tossing a shutout in a spot start on Memorial Day. He worked his way into the rotation and won 10 consecutive decisions, earning a berth on the league's All-Star team.

While Stottlemyre was leading the IL in wins (13), ERA (1.42), and shutouts (6), the Yankees were in a tense, three-way battle with the Baltimore Orioles and the Chicago White Sox for the 1964 pennant. When longtime ace Whitey Ford went down with a hip injury in late July, New York called up Stottlemyre, who arrived on August 11.

Stottlemyre's debut on August 12 was "movie script stuff," wrote New York sportswriter Til Ferdenzi.[7] The rookie tossed a complete-game seven-hitter to defeat Chicago, 7-3. In what developed into a refrain heard over the next decade, hitters pummeled Stottlemyre's sinker into the ground all afternoon. "He sure knows how to serve up those grounders," said batterymate John Blanchard as the Yankees recorded 19 groundouts.[8] Stottlemyre's fairy tale continued throughout the regular season. On September 17 he recorded his seventh victory in nine starts to give the Yankees a psychological boost by pushing them into first place, tied with the Orioles and White Sox, for the first time in almost six weeks. Nine days later, he blanked the Washington Senators at Griffith Stadium on two hits (his first of seven career two-hitters) and tied a big-league record for pitchers by collecting five hits (four singles and a double). The Yankees' most effective hurler, Stottlemyre finished the campaign with a 9-3 record and a team-best 2.06 ERA in 96 innings. Most importantly, Stottlemyre stabilized a shaky staff and helped the club win 34 of its final 52 games and capture its fifth consecutive AL pennant.

After the Yankees' loss in Game One of the World Series against the St. Louis Cardinals, Stottlemyre tossed a seven-hit complete game, defeating hard-throwing Bob Gibson, 8-3, at Sportsman's Park. "The kid's got the best sinker and curve I've seen," said Cardinals third baseman and NL MVP Ken Boyer. "There isn't a pitcher in the National League with this kind of stuff."[9] Facing Gibson again, in Game Five at Yankee Stadium, Stottlemyre held the Redbirds to six hits and two runs (one earned), but was lifted for a pinch-hitter with New York trailing 2-0 in the bottom of the seventh in an eventual 5-2 defeat in 10 innings.

Then first-year skipper Yogi Berra sent the 22-year-old Stottlemyre on two days' rest to face "Gibby" for the third time with the championship on the line. In the fourth inning, with two on and no outs, Stottlemyre induced Tim McCarver to ground into what appeared to be an easy double play. While covering first, Stottlemyre hurt his shoulder diving for a poor throw by Phil Linz, filling in for Tony Kubek at shortstop. Boyer scored on the play, and the floodgates were open. Stottlemyre surrendered two more singles and two runs (one on McCarver's steal of home on the front end of a double steal), and was lifted for a pinch-hitter the next inning. "The fielders sabotaged [him]," wrote Yankees beat reporter Leonard Koppett of Stottlemyre's performance in Game Five and Seven. "His hitters didn't make a run while he was in the game. With a little support, Stottlemyre could have been the hero."[10]

The Yankees' 7-5 loss in Game Seven marked the end of an era. After winning 29 AL pennants and 20 World Series from 1921 to 1964, the team embarked on what historian Robert W. Cohen called the "lean years" over the next decade.[11] A new era had indeed dawned. The Yankees were an aging club that had failed to sign top African American prospects, unlike other teams around baseball, including their opponents in the 1964 World Series. Although New York led the AL in attendance in 1964, its average of 15,922 per game was the club's lowest since 1945 and suggested Americans' general lack of interest in major-league baseball. At the end of the season, CBS purchased 80 percent of the team from owners Dan Topping and Del Webb. Stottlemyre's emergence as a bona-fide big-league ace corresponded with the Yankees' plunge to depths not witnessed since before the acquisition of Babe Ruth for the 1920 season. For the remainder of Stottlemyre's career, a discussion of his accomplishments was often accompanied by the nostalgic remark that he arrived on the team 10 years too late.

In 1965 the Yankees experienced their first losing season since 1925 and fell to the second division for the first time since 1917, but Stottlemyre emerged as one of baseball's best hurlers. He set the tenor by shutting out the California Angels in his season debut. Remarkably consistent, Stottlemyre paced the AL with 18 complete games in 37 starts, led the league with 291 innings (including consecutive 10-inning affairs), won his 20th game in his final start of the season, and posted an impressive 2.63 ERA. He was named for the first of five times to the AL All-Star squad (he did not pitch) and to *The Sporting News* All-Star team.

Stottlemyre's success is often attributed to his sinker, which Yankees coach Jim Hegan compared to that of his former batterymate with the Cleveland Indians, Hall of Famer Bob Lemon. They both threw the sinker overhand, whereas most throw it side-arm or three-quarters because of how difficult a pitch it is to control.[12] Said Stottlemyre, "When [the wind] blows in, I may be a bit faster, but my ball straightens out. When the ball blows out, my ball sinks."[13] Cerebral and reflective, Stottlemyre also succeeded because of his ability to adjust over time. Around 1962 he took pitching coach Johnny Sain's advice and began gripping the ball with the seams instead of across them in order to get a bigger break.[14] This change made his fastball as effective as his sinker. "I created some movement with my delivery and the way I held the ball, but mostly it was just natural."[15] Often touted for his good control (2.7 walks per nine innings in his career), Stottlemyre himself admitted, "I couldn't throw the ball straight if I wanted to."[16]

Described as "strangely inconsistent" in 1966, Stottlemyre's season was a study in contrasts for a team in turmoil.[17] The Yankees' experiment with Johnny Keane, the former Cardinals skipper hired after he beat the Bronx Bombers in the '64 Series, ended 20 games into the season with the club in last place. He was replaced by Ralph Houk, who could do little to keep the Yankees from finishing in the cellar for the first time since 1912, when the club was known as the Highlanders. One of the team's few early season standouts, Stottlemyre carved out a sturdy 2.71 ERA through the end of June (despite a 7-8 record) before the bottom the fell out. Excluding a two-inning outing in the All-Star Game in which he yielded one hit and one walk, Stottlemyre's ERA almost doubled (5.02) for the remainder of the season, and he concluded a frustrating campaign by becoming the first Yankee hurler to lose 20 games (12-20) since Sad Sam Jones in 1925. "I was giving in (to the hitters)," Stottlemyre told Phil Pepe. "Instead of walking them, I came in with a fat pitch and they hit it."[18] His ERA jumped to 3.80 overall and he completed just nine of 35 starts. "I learned a lot through adversity. I got to the point where I almost hated to walk out to the mound," recalled Stottlemyre later in his career.[19]

Recognizing that he needed to make adjustments, Stottlemyre dumped his slow curve, which had affected his sinker, in 1967, and honed his rising fastball. The sailing heater "makes batters hesitate about leaning out to hit my slider," said Stottlemyre.[20] The changes paid immediate dividends as Stottlemyre blanked the Washington Senators on two hits on Opening Day and the Boston Red Sox on four hits in his second start. In late April he developed tendinitis in his right shoulder, which required X-ray treatment and caused him to miss two starts. For the rest of his career, Stottlemyre contended with shoulder soreness. In a workmanlike season, the right-hander re-established himself as the Yankees ace, going 15-15 and posting a 2.96 ERA in 255 innings. Even in a pitchers' era, the Yankees were an especially atrocious offensive team, batting just .225 and scoring an AL-low 522 runs as they finished in ninth place. In 14 of Stottlemyre's losses, New York scored two runs or fewer (16 total runs).

Stottlemyre reported to camp in 1968 in good spirits following surgery to correct lingering problems with his right foot, which had affected his stamina the previous two seasons, limiting him to just 19 complete games.[21] His mood soon turned sour when tendinitis resurfaced in his shoulder and caused him to miss two weeks. Thus, a pattern was established.[22] Plagued annually by bouts of shoulder tendinitis, Stottlemyre was eased into spring training for the remainder of his career.

After walking a career-high 3.1 batters per nine innings in 1967, Stottlemyre made yet another adjustment. "I've always thrown across my body, but I was throwing more and more across my body and it was affecting my control," he explained. "I tried to widen my stance at the end of my follow-through and this cut down a lot on my body crossing."[23] Stottlemyre's walk ratio fell to a career-low 2.1 per nine innings. He fired shutouts in three of his first seven starts, including a three-hitter against the Detroit Tigers at Yankee Stadium on April 26 when Mickey Mantle blasted home run number 521 to tie Ted Williams for fourth place on the all-time list. Named to the All-Star Game for the third time, he faced only one batter, Hank Aaron, whom he struck out in the ninth. The 26-year-old set career career bests in wins (21) and ERA (2.45), finished tied for second in the league in complete games (19) and shutouts (6), and placed third in innings (278⅔) while the Yankees enjoyed their first winning season since 1964. "There is no question that Mel rates with the top five pitchers in baseball," said skipper Houk.[24]

People regularly praised Stottlemyre for his character, sportsmanship, and unassuming leadership. "He doesn't moan when you don't get him runs," said Houk, "[or] when they kick ones behind him."[25] Quiet and self-effacing, Stottlemyre rarely sought the spotlight or chewed out his teammates. He was seen as "old school" before the term was common, an embodiment of Yankees style more reflective of the 1940s and 1950s than the mid- to late 1960s and early 1970s. "In the second-division days around the stadium," wrote beat reporter Jim Ogle, "Stottlemyre is one Yankee who retains the old championship aura and class."[26] Stottlemyre's outwardly quiet demeanor belied a passion and desire to succeed. Said one-time Yankees backup catcher Bob Schmidt, "He works like a machine, never showing his feelings. Inside he's thinking and fighting and planning to win."[27]

Often described as a country boy, Stottlemyre shunned the media capital and returned to his beloved Washington state to spend the offseasons hunting and fishing, and above all to be with his wife, Jean (Mitchell), whom he married in November 1962. The "big city hasn't spoiled him," opined Ogle.[28] A consummate teammate, Stottlemyre also had a humorous side and enjoyed joking with his teammates. "I was a quiet prankster," he once said. "I could get away with a lot of things [because] no one ever suspected."[29]

An excellent and agile fielder, the 6-foot-1, 180-pound Stottlemyre might have been considered the best at his position in the AL had Jim Kaat (who won 16 consecutive Gold Gloves from 1962-1977) not been in the league. Stottlemyre led AL pitchers in fielding and assists twice and in putouts three times. Not an automatic out at the plate, Stottlemyre batted .160 (120-for-749), homered seven times, and knocked in 57 runs. Four of those came in a victory over the Red Sox at Yankee Stadium on July 20, 1965, when he became the first hurler since 1910 to hit an inside-the-park grand slam. Said Jim Turner, a baseball lifer and longtime Yankees pitching coach, "[He] would be an outstanding pitcher in any era. He is intelligent, a fine fielder, has three or four big-league pitches, a perfect temperament, and is a great competitor."[30]

In 1969 the Yankees had a losing record (80-81) for the fourth time in Stottlemyre's five full seasons, but the righty was not to blame. In the wake of Mantle's retirement on March 1, Stottlemyre inherited the Commerce Comet's mantle of leadership. "There's no more respected player with the Yankees than Stottlemyre," wrote Ogle.[31] He made a seamless transition to the lowered pitching mound mandated by Major League Baseball to generate more offense following the "Year of the Pitcher." In his last start of the season, Stottlemyre won his 20th game and finished with 303 innings, the first Yankee to break the 300-inning barrier since Carl Mays in 1921. He set numerous career highs, including starts (39), innings, and complete games (24, to lead the AL). His 2.82 ERA trailed only lefty Fritz Peterson (2.55) among Yankees starters. Tabbed to start the All-Star Game, Stottlemyre was rocked for four hits and three runs (two earned) to get tagged with the loss in one of the few blemishes in an otherwise stellar campaign.

The Yankees made Stottlemyre the highest-paid pitcher in team history in 1970 when they signed the 28-year-old for $70,000.[32] He put up typical numbers (37 starts and 271 innings), but was bothered all year by chronic shoulder pain that limited him to a 15-13 record and just 14 complete games. "I was afraid to cut loose because my arm was tight," he said.[33] In his final All-Star appearance, he tossed 1⅔ hitless innings of relief. Led by rookie catcher Thurman Munson and outfielder Bobby Murcer, the Yankees won 93 games but finished well behind the Baltimore Orioles, winners of 108 games.

"We couldn't sustain our success," said Stottlemyre in his biography. "CBS owned the ballclub … and the feeling among the players, based on what we knew, was that there was no strong baseball presence in the front office. It was a true corporate ownership."[34] In 1971 the club regressed to 82-80 as offense around the majors plummeted despite the lowered mound. After arguably his worst outing as a big leaguer (seven hits and six runs in one-third of an inning against the Minnesota Twins), Stottlemyre surged, completing six of his final 10 starts of the season. Included were three shutouts (two of them three-hitters), and he forged a stellar 2.05 ERA in 79 innings. "He doesn't embarrass you," said teammate Roy White. "He doesn't overwhelm you. He's an annoying kind of pitcher. He just gets you out."[35] Stottlemyre led the corps with 16 wins, a 2.87 ERA, 19 complete games, and seven shutouts to anchor a staff that boasted four hurlers (Stottlemyre 269⅔ innings; Peterson 15-13, 274; Stan Bahnsen 14-12, 242; and Steve Kline 12-13, 222⅓) with at least 200 innings, the most since five turned the trick in 1922.[36]

"The best word to explain the year for me is frustrating," Stottlemyre told Jim Ogle as the 1972 season, which was marred by the first players' strike in history, came to a conclusion.[37] While the Yankees finished in fourth place in the AL East, Stottlemyre enjoyed stretches when he was either very good or very bad. In May he tossed three shutouts in four starts; fired two more shutouts and tossed 10 scoreless innings for another victory during a two-week period in July; and was on fire in September, posting a 1.67 ERA over 54 innings, but won just twice, both shutouts. However, he struggled in June (4.28 ERA), and in seven starts in August he yielded 33 runs in 40⅔ innings. "That stretch was the worst I ever had," he said.[38] He finished with 14 wins and seven shutouts, but completed only nine games while his ERA (3.22) was higher than the league average. His 18 losses tied for the AL lead in that dubious category, but the Yankees didn't help him much, scoring two runs or fewer in 16 of those defeats.

In 1973 Stottlemyre split 32 decisions, completed half of his 38 starts and logged 273 innings for the Yankees, who finished in fourth place for the third consecutive year. Newsworthy at the time, Stottlemyre also broke Red Ruffing's team record by starting his 243rd consecutive game without a relief appearance (and set a then big-league record by starting his 274th game without a start, in 1974) Arguably the season's most memorable moment came when pitchers Fritz Peterson and Mike Kekich announced during spring training that they were trading lives, including wives, kids, and houses. George Steinbrenner had purchased a majority stake in the Yankees prior to the 1973 season and vowed to make substantial changes to return the team to glory. After a failed and litigious attempt to sign former Oakland A's manager Dick Williams for the 1974 season, "The Boss" signed Bill Virdon. Under Virdon, the Yankees were one of the surprise teams in baseball in 1974, winning 89 games and occupying first place as late as September 22 in their first pennant race since Stottlemyre's rookie season, before finishing in second place.

As fate would have it, the stoic pitcher was relegated to a fan for much of the pennant race. After enduring years of regular cortisone shots in his shoulder to numb the pain and make pitching possible, Stottlemyre was diagnosed with a torn rotator cuff after 15 starts in 1974, effectively ending his career at the age of 32. Years before corrective surgery was devised, Stottlemyre rested his shoulder, but continued to pitch on the side, probably damaging his shoulder even more. Not ready to give up, Stottlemyre reported to spring training in 1975, but pain limited him to pitching only batting practice. In late March the Yankees stunned baseball by releasing him. "It seems like a heartless move to cut loose so coldly such a loyal and devoted servant," decried Phil Pepe.[39] "I am not surprised," said Stottlemyre, "but I am disappointed."[40] In nine full seasons and parts of two others, Stottlemyre compiled a 164-139 record with a 2.97 ERA in 2,661⅓ innings, 40 shutouts, and 152 complete games.

With "bitter memories" about his release, Stottlemyre returned to Washington state and his wife, Jean.[41] They had three children—Todd, Mel, and Jason. He operated a sporting-goods store and coached his sons' youth baseball teams, but recognized that he missed the big leagues. He inaugurated the second phase of his career in baseball when he accepted the expansion Seattle Mariners' offer to serve as a roving pitching instructor. He resigned in 1981 when his youngest son, Jason, succumbed at the age of 11 to a five-year battle with leukemia. In an ironic twist, Todd was chosen by the Yankees, with whom Stottlemyre had lost all connections, in the 1983 amateur draft. Though he never donned the pinstripes, Todd fashioned a 14-year career, winning 138 games. Mel Jr. was a first-round draft pick by the Houston Astros in 1985, and enjoyed a cup of coffee in the majors with the Kansas City Royals in 1990.

After a three-year hiatus, Stottlemyre returned to the big leagues in 1984 as the pitching coach for the New York Mets. From 1984 to 1990, the Mets averaged more than 95 wins per season, but finished in first place just twice, in 1986 and 1988. These teams were led by catcher Gary Carter, third baseman Howard Johnson, and volatile slugger Darryl Strawberry; however, the face of the franchise was the pitching staff and especially Dwight "Doc" Gooden. Widely considered one of the best teams in baseball history, the 1986 squad won 108 games and defeated the Boston Red Sox in seven games in the World Series. The starting rotation was led by Gooden (17-6, 2.84 ERA), Ron Darling (15-6, 2.81), Bob Ojeda (18-5, 2.57), and Sid Fernandez (16-6, 3.52), and each logged in excess of 200 innings. Those successful years stand in stark contrast to the period from 1991-1996 when injuries, age, free agency, and rumors of widespread drug use among players led to six consecutive losing seasons that reached their nadir in 1993 (103 losses and Stottlemyre's dismissal).

After a two-year stint as the pitching coach for the Houston Astros, Stottlemyre reconciled with Steinbrenner and accepted his offer to become the club's pitching coach for new manager Joe Torre. For the next 10 seasons (1996-2005), Stottlemyre enjoyed the fruits of unimaginable success, including nine first-place finishes, 10 playoff appearances, six pennants, and four World Series championships. In 1999 Stottlemyre was diagnosed with multiple myeloma, a cancer of plasma cells, and ultimately recovered after intensive chemotherapy. In the wake of the Yankees' collapse in the 2001 World Series, Stottlemyre's relationship with Steinbrenner became strained as the owner privately and publicly second-guessed his pitching coach. "Baseball was my life," said Stottlemyre, trying to explain why he didn't walk away.[42] That changed in 2005, when the stress of the situation had finally begun to take a toll on Stottlemyre's health, and he retired at the end of the season.

Retirement didn't last long. After a one-year break, he served as a special-assignment instructor for the Arizona Diamondbacks in 2007. The next season he was back in a big-league dugout when he joined the Seattle Mariners' coaching staff. Approaching his 69th birthday, Stottlemyre retired after the 2008 season.

A quiet, unassuming player and a dedicated, well respected coach, Stottlemyre spent almost 50 years in Organized Baseball. As of 2015 he still resided in Washington state.

SOURCES

In addition to the sources listed in the notes, the author consulted:

Baseball-Reference.com.

Retrosheet.org.

SABR.org.

Mel Stottlemyre's player file, National Baseball Hall of Fame, Cooperstown, New York.

NOTES

1 Phil Pepe, "Stottlemyre's Courage Showed In His Son," *New York Daily News*, March 16, 1981.

2 Mel Stottlemyre with John Harper, *Pride and Pinstripes* (New York: Harper, 2007), 16.

3 A member of the NCAA Hall of Fame, Brayton coached at Yakima State Junior College from 1951 to 1961, compiling a 251-68 record, including 10 championships in 11 seasons; he piloted the Washington State Cougars for 33 years (1962-1994) and compiled a 1162-523-8 record.

4 *The Sporting News*, October 24, 1964: 9.

5 *The Sporting News*, May 9, 1962: 41; and August 11, 1962: 42.

6 *The Sporting News*, August 11, 1962: 42.

7 *The Sporting News*, October 24, 1964: 9.

8 *The Sporting News*, August 29, 1964: 21.

9 Sy Berwick, "Stottlemyre Had No Choice, Only the Yanks Offered a Contract." *Dayton* (Ohio) *Daily News*, October 9, 1964: 9.

10 *The Sporting News*, October 31, 1964: 21.

11 Robert W. Cohen, *The Lean Years of the Yankees*, 1965-1974 (Jefferson, North Carolina: McFarland, 2004).

12 *The Sporting News*, August 29, 1964: 21.

13 *The Sporting News*, July 24, 1965: 9.

14 *The Sporting News*, May 1, 1965: 10.

15 Stottlemyre, 24.

16 Ibid.

17 *The Sporting News*, August 6, 1966: 15.

18 *The Sporting News*, September 18, 1971: 5.

19 Ibid.

20 *The Sporting News*, April 29, 1967: 19.

21 *The Sporting News*, June 15, 1968: 18.

22 *The Sporting News*, April 13, 1968: 37.

23 *The Sporting News*, April 27, 1968: 20.

24 *The Sporting News*, August 24, 1968: 17.

25 Larry Fox, "Houk Rates Stottlemyre in Top Five," *Daily News* (New York), July 26, 1968.

26 *The Sporting News*, June 15, 1968: 18.

27 *The Sporting News*, December 5, 1964: 5.

28 *The Sporting News*, May 3, 1969: 3.

29 Ross Forman, "Mel Stottlemyre: From pitching star to pitching coach," *Sports Collectors Digest*, August 7, 1992: 181.

30 *The Sporting News*, May 3, 1969: 3.

31 Ibid.

32 *The Sporting News*, February 21, 1970: 21.

33 *The Sporting News*, June 19, 1971: 19.

34 Stottlemyre, 48.

35 Neil Offen, "... Then Along Came Stottlemyre," *New York Post*, May 13, 1971: 6C.

36 In 1922 five Yankees pitchers hurlers hurled 1,320⅔ of the team's 1,393⅔ innings: Bon Shawkey (20-12, 299⅔; Waite Hoyt (19-12, 265), Sad Sam Jones (13-13, 260), Bullet Joe Bush (26-7, 255⅓), and Carl Mays (13-14, 240).

37 *The Sporting News*, October 7, 1972: 8.

38 Ibid.

39 *The Sporting News*.

40 United Press International, "Stottlemyre Not Surprised," *Beckley* (West Virginia) *Post-Herald and Register*, March 31, 1975: 31.

41 Forman: 190.

42 Stottlemyre, 23.

RALPH KINER

By Warren Corbett

RALPH KINER WAS BASEBALL'S LEADING home-run hitter for a few years after World War II. As a broadcaster for the New York Mets, he became famous for his verbal strikeouts. Although best remembered for his long career behind the mike, he still ranks as one of the premier sluggers in baseball history.

Ralph McPherran Kiner was born in Santa Rita, New Mexico, on October 27, 1922. His mother, Beatrice Grayson, came from Oregon and had served as a nurse in France during World War I. His father, Ralph Macklin Kiner, was a baker. He died when Ralph was 4. The widowed Mrs. Kiner took a job in Alhambra, California, near Los Angeles.

Ralph said he developed his baseball skills by playing year-round in the sunny climate and was encouraged by a neighbor who befriended the fatherless boy. He played shortstop for a youth team sponsored by the Yankees, but Pittsburgh scout Hollis Thurston convinced Kiner that the Pirates offered him a better opportunity than the talent-rich Yanks. He signed with Pittsburgh as soon as he graduated from Alhambra High.

Kiner began his professional career in 1941 as an outfielder with Albany in the Class-A Eastern League, two steps below the majors. In two seasons there he batted .279 and .257. In 1942 his 14 homers led the pitcher-friendly league.

He joined Toronto in 1943, but within a few weeks he was inducted into the Navy Air Corps. He spent World War II as a Navy pilot flying antisubmarine missions in the Pacific, and said he "barely touched a bat."[1]

When he joined the Pirates for spring training in 1946, Kiner had added 20 pounds; at age 23, he had grown from a boy to a man, 6-feet-2 and 195 pounds. He was a springtime sensation. Pittsburgh sportswriter Charles J. Doyle gushed, "Kiner can run like a deer, he can throw like a DiMaggio and when his bat clicks nothing but the fences will stop his line drives."[2] This was spring-phenom hype; according to most later accounts, Kiner had a weak arm and was a slow runner, although he played center field for the Pirates in his rookie year.

Manager Frankie Frisch, who was notoriously hard on young players, declared, "Kiner looks like he's going to be the best [outfielder] we've ever had."[3]

Kiner lived up to the hype to some extent. He batted just .247 in his rookie year and struck out 109 times (the only time he exceeded 100), but he led the National League in homers with 23. He admitted this was a fluke; the Giants' Johnny Mize, who finished just one behind him, missed several weeks with a broken wrist.

The 23 homers tied the Pirates' club record, set by Johnny Rizzo in 1938. Pittsburgh's Forbes Field was a mammoth ballpark that produced more triples than

any other park, but yielded few home runs. The right-handed-batting Kiner hit only eight at home.

Baseball gave no official rookie of the year award in 1946, but *The Sporting News* named Philadelphia outfielder Del Ennis the National League's top rookie. The "Bible of Baseball" reported that Ennis had led all NL rookies in home runs (wrong—he hit 17) and RBIs (wrong—he had 73 to Kiner's 81). The bizarre travesty of journalism carried the byline of editor J.G. Taylor Spink, but was probably written by one of his ghosts.

In fact, Ennis was the more productive hitter; he outdid Kiner .849 to .775 in on-base plus slugging percentage (OPS), a statistic that was then unknown but is now regarded as an accurate shorthand measure of a hitter's value. Ennis's .313 batting average was likely the deciding factor, because most baseball authorities then considered that stat to be the measure of a batter's worth. They were not likely to honor a .247 hitter.

In 1947 the Pirates acquired 36-year-old Hank Greenberg from Detroit. Greenberg had once hit 58 home runs and had led the American League in 1946 with 44. In spring training Kiner met the man he would call "the single biggest influence of my adult life."[4] On the first day, Greenberg suggested they take extra batting practice. That was Kiner's first lesson: Hard work is the way to succeed. The young slugger and the old one became friends and roommates on road trips. Kiner said Greenberg made him a pull hitter and built up his confidence. Greenberg also gave him a wardrobe makeover after he spotted Kiner wearing brown shoes with a tuxedo.

Greenberg's arrival made a more tangible contribution to Kiner's development as a home-run hitter: To make Forbes Field friendlier for the veteran, the club built a bullpen in left field, cutting the 365-foot foul line to 335. The left-center power alley shrank from a formidable 406 feet to 376. The new bullpen—actually about average home-run distance for a big-league park—was dubbed "Greenberg Gardens."

When Kiner started slowly in 1947, manager Billy Herman wanted to send him back to the minors. Greenberg persuaded owner Frank McKinney to veto that idea. By the All-Star break in July, Kiner had 20 homers. He got hot in August, belting homers in four consecutive at-bats over two games and ringing up seven in four games. On August 16 he became the first Pirate to homer three times in a game. But *The Sporting News* harrumphed that, if he broke Babe Ruth's record of 60, it would be tainted because of Greenberg Gardens.

Kiner hit four homers in a doubleheader in August and eight in four games—a record. On September 18 he became the fifth player to hit 50 home runs in a season. The Giants' Mize joined the club two days later. They finished tied for the league lead with 51.

By then sportswriters had renamed Greenberg Gardens "Kiner's Korner." (Greenberg, in his last season, hit 25 homers.) Kiner hit 28 of his home runs in Forbes Field, 23 on the road. The left-handed-batting Mize, playing his home games in the Polo Grounds with its short right-field fence, hit 29 at home, 22 on the road.

The Pirates' home attendance spiked by 71 percent over 1946. Kiner was the main attraction on a club that finished tied for last place. The owners tripled his salary to $30,000 for 1948. His teammate, pitcher Fritz Ostermueller, commented, "Home run hitters drive Cadillacs. Singles hitters drive Fords."[5] (There are several versions of this quote, but they all agree on the essential elements.) Kiner did buy a Cadillac; Ostermueller's choice of transportation is not recorded.

Kiner fell off to 40 home runs in 1948, again tying Mize for the league lead. (Stan Musial of St. Louis also hit 40, but one of them was erased in a rainout, preventing Musial from winning the Triple Crown as the leader in homers, RBIs, and batting average.) The Pirates rose to fourth place, posting their only winning record during Kiner's years in Pittsburgh.

Pittsburgh attendance grew 18 percent to another record, 1.5 million. The 1948 season was the peak of the postwar baseball boom; major-league teams drew nearly 21 million fans, the most until 1962, when both leagues had expanded to 10 teams.

Kiner was convinced that the absence of Greenberg or a similar feared hitter behind him in the lineup enabled pitchers to pitch around him. He drew 112 walks, 14 more than the previous year, and was walked at least 100 times in each of his next five seasons.

The club bumped Kiner's 1949 salary to $40,000. He started strong and had 23 home runs at the season's midpoint, but was six games behind Ruth's 1927 pace. On September 11 and 13 he hit homers in four consecutive at-bats, becoming the first man to do that twice. The next day he stroked number 49. He had hit 12 homers in 14 games, but with only 16 left to play, he had given up on catching Ruth.

Kiner put his byline on a ghostwritten article in *The Saturday Evening Post* magazine titled "The Home Run I Would Hate to Hit." He said he didn't want to break the Babe's sacred record. More than 50 years later, he wrote, "That was a big fat lie."[6]

Kiner did have a shot at Hack Wilson's National League mark of 56 homers. He hit his 54th on the next-to-last day of the season. (He had lost one in a rainout.) Forty thousand fans came to Forbes Field for a season-ending doubleheader, but Kiner fell short of Hack Wilson. He was the first National Leaguer to hit 50 homers twice; only Babe Ruth and Jimmie Foxx had done it in the American League. No one would equal that accomplishment until the schedule expanded to 162 games.

Kiner also led the league with 127 RBIs. He placed fourth in the Most Valuable Player voting by baseball writers, his highest finish ever; Jackie Robinson, the batting champion for pennant-winning Brooklyn, won the award.

The Pirates signed Kiner to a two-year contract, unusual at the time, at $65,000 a season. He was the highest-paid player in the National League; American Leaguers Joe DiMaggio, Ted Williams, and Bob Feller made more. Kiner said club owner John Galbreath also cut him in on some real-estate investments.

But that was far less than Kiner was worth, as big-league players would find out when free agency arrived a quarter-century later. A Pittsburgh theatrical booking agent remarked, "If Kiner were as big a figure in show business as he is in baseball, he would draw down a stipend of $30,000 a week."[7]

At that time Kiner was still living with his mother in Alhambra. The singer Bing Crosby, a minority owner of the Pirates, drew the young, single star into his Hollywood circle, even arranging for Kiner to escort 17-year-old actress Elizabeth Taylor to a movie premiere. He built a house in Palm Springs, California, then just emerging as a golf and tennis resort for the Hollywood set; Kiner was an avid golfer. Friends and neighbors included Frank Sinatra and Lucille Ball and her husband and co-star, Desi Arnaz.

Kiner dated other Hollywood starlets, but on October 13, 1951, he married 22-year-old tennis star Nancy Chaffee, the sixth-ranked American player. Greenberg served as best man at the wedding. Kiner proudly recounted that, after two years of lessons, he was able to beat Nancy at tennis—two weeks before she gave birth to their first child.

In 1950 Branch Rickey, the baseball legend who had built dynasties with the St. Louis Cardinals and Brooklyn Dodgers, became the Pirates' general manager, but the club fell to last place. Kiner clubbed 47 home runs in 1950 (*The Sporting News* named him Player of the Year), then 42, then 37 in 1952. He led the league each year. His seven consecutive home-run titles are a record; not even Ruth did that.

The Pirates' owners signed Kiner to a $90,000 contract for 1952. The price tag outraged Rickey, of whom Kiner would say later, "He was cheap."[8] Many others shared that opinion. Baseball historian Bill James wrote, "Rickey, in one of the oddest moves of his career, [was provoked] to begin systematically destroying Kiner's reputation as a player, so that he could trade him; it's nuts, but that's what he was doing."[9]

In Rickey's papers at the Library of Congress, his biographer, Murray Polner, found a "confidential" letter to owner John Galbreath. Kiner, Rickey wrote, "would not throw or run and could not field and was a self-appraised star and could have no part ever in a pennant-winning club." He complained that Kiner was given special privileges by the manager, demanded "highly expensive" air-conditioning in the clubhouse, and insisted that his contract include a clause guaranteeing that the shorter fences in Kiner's Korner would stay. Kiner denied all this in his 2004 memoir. Polner concluded, "Kiner became the scapegoat for [Rickey's] failure to improve the club."[10]

The 1952 Pirates lost 112 games, the worst record of any major-league team since 1935. Home attendance dropped by about one-third and Kiner's batting average fell to .244. Despite his league-leading home-run performance, Rickey cut his salary to $75,000. When Kiner objected, Rickey told him, "Son, we can finish last without you."[11]

Kiner's fellow players had elected him their National League player representative. He and Yankees pitcher Allie Reynolds, representing the American League, renegotiated the pension plan during the offseason. Piling on, Rickey told owner Galbreath that Kiner's leadership role was bad for the team

In June 1953 Rickey traded Kiner and three others, including future broadcaster Joe Garagiola, to the Chicago Cubs for six players and a cash payment reported to be as much as $150,000. Pittsburgh fans hanged Rickey in effigy and some prominent citizens proposed a boycott of Forbes Field until Rickey was fired. But Rickey was right about one thing: The Pirates did finish last without Kiner in 1953 and for the next two years.

Rickey was right in another way: Kiner was only 30 years old, but he was suffering from back problems. Other home-run kings—Ruth, Aaron, and Bonds—were still clearing the fences as they approached or passed their 40th birthdays, but Kiner was just about done.

In Chicago Kiner joined Hank Sauer, who had tied him for the 1952 home-run championship and had won the MVP award. Both were slow outfielders with poor throwing arms. Manager Phil Cavaretta moved Sauer to right field so Kiner could play left. Sauer protested that his arm was not strong enough to play right. Cavaretta replied, "But it's still better than Kiner's."[12]

The two leadfoots in the outfield corners were the butt of jokes. Whenever a fly ball was hit, it was said, Kiner and Sauer shouted to center fielder Frank Baumholtz, "Plenty of room, Frankie."[13] Years later center fielder Sauer denied that he ever ran into foul territory to catch a fly.

Kiner had another strong season in 1953, racking up 35 homers and 116 RBIs with Pittsburgh and Chicago combined. But the following year he fell off to 22 home runs, playing 147 games despite continuing back pain.

The Cubs sold him to the Cleveland Indians after the season for a sum variously reported as $60,000 to $150,000. The deal involved several other players. The acquisition of Kiner was front-page news in Cleveland, even in the midst of the notorious Sam Sheppard murder trial. His friend Greenberg was the Indians general manager; the field manager, Al Lopez, had been another of his mentors during his rookie year in Pittsburgh.

Cleveland had won the 1954 AL pennant with a league-record 111 victories, ending the Yankees' five-year championship run, but the New York Giants swept them in a four-game World Series. Greenberg said Kiner would add the power the club needed.

Kiner was able to play only 113 games in 1955, with 18 home runs and a .243 average. He said doctors gave 50-50 odds that surgery would fix his back. Instead he retired at age 32 to become general manager of the Pacific Coast League San Diego Padres, a Cleveland farm club.

In San Diego Kiner got his first taste of play-by-play broadcasting because, he said, he couldn't afford to hire an announcer. When his old Pittsburgh club played in the 1960 World Series, he did a postgame show on local radio. He was hired to broadcast Chicago White Sox games in 1961 when Greenberg was the team's general manager.

In 1962 Kiner joined the broadcast team of the expansion New York Mets. He said the Mets hired him "because I had a lot of experience with losing."[14] The Mets lost 120 games in their first season, even more than the 1952 Pirates.

His TV post-game show was called *Kiner's Korner*. In an early broadcast, he interviewed the Mets' catcher, Choo Choo Coleman, who was not a talkative man.

Kiner asked, "What's your wife's name and what's she like?"

Coleman replied, "Mrs. Coleman, and she likes me, Bub."[15]

Kiner, Lindsey Nelson, and Bob Murphy broadcast Mets games for the team's first 17 seasons. Nelson left in 1979; Murphy retired in 2003. Kiner, after a stroke, worked part-time until 2013.

As a broadcaster, his thoughts seemed to detour between his brain and his mouth. Among the famous Kinerisms:

"On Father's Day, we again wish you all Happy Birthday." "Solo homers usually come with no one on base." "All of his saves have come in relief appearances." "If Casey Stengel were alive today, he'd be spinning in his grave." "We'll be back after this word from Manufacturers Hangover."

Occasionally Kiner produced a gem. Describing a wide-ranging center fielder, he said, "Two-thirds of the Earth is covered by water. The other third is covered by Garry Maddox."[16]

Kiner and Nancy Chaffee divorced in 1968. They had three children: sons Michael, who played briefly in the Mets' farm system, and Scott and daughter Kathryn, known as K.C. Nancy Chaffee later married sportscaster Jack Whitaker and died in 2002. Kiner married again in 1969 to Barbara George. When they divorced, he claimed, many items of baseball memorabilia disappeared with her. In 1982 he married DiAnn Shugart, a businesswoman in the Palm Springs area. She died of cancer in 2004 at age 70. In his 80s Kiner married, then divorced, Ann Benisch.

Baseball writers elected Ralph Kiner to the Hall of Fame in 1975, his 15th and final year on the ballot. He squeaked in with just one vote more than the 75 percent required for election.

Many fans and analysts have questioned whether Kiner deserves the honor, since he hit "only" 369 home runs and played just 10 seasons. When Kiner retired in 1955, however, he ranked sixth on the career home-run list, just ahead of Joe DiMaggio and Johnny Mize. Sixty seasons and many sluggers later, he was 78th in 2016. He was still fifth in home run frequency, with 1 in every 14.1 at bats, behind only Mark McGwire, Babe Ruth, Barry Bonds, and Jim Thome. He stood 23rd on the all-time list with a .946 on-base plus slugging percentage. There is no doubt how Kiner ranked when he was active: *The Sporting News* chose him for its major-league all-star team four times in five years from 1947 through 1951. Bill James noted, "Musial, Williams, DiMaggio and Kiner—those were the greatest outfielders of this period."[17]

Ralph Kiner died at age 91 on February 6, 2014, at his home in Rancho Mirage, California.

NOTES

1 Ralph Kiner with Joe Gergen, *Kiner's Korner* (New York: Arbor House, 1987), 64.

2 Charles J. Doyle, "California Sun, Buc Pitching Turn Back Clock for Frisch," *The Sporting News* (hereafter *TSN*), February 28, 1946, 8.

3 Milt Woodard, "Bucs Come Up With Corker in Kiner," *TSN*, March 28, 1946, 7.

4 Ralph Kiner with Danny Peary, *Baseball Forever* (Chicago: Triumph Books, 2004), 11.

5 Kiner, *Kiner's Korner*, 22.

6 Kiner, *Baseball Forever*, 145.

7 Les Biederman, "Kiner Mourns Six 'Lost Homers' of '49," *TSN*, October 12, 1949, 16.

8 William R. Marshall, *Baseball's Pivotal Era* (Lexington: The University Press of Kentucky, 1999), 350.

9 Bill James, *The New Bill James Historical Baseball Abstract* (New York: Free Press, 2001), 663.

10 Murray Polner, *Branch Rickey* (New York: New American Library, 1982), 229-230.

11 Kiner, *Kiner's Korner*, 24.

12 James, *New Bill James*, 663.

13 Peter Golenbock, *Wrigleyville* (New York: St. Martin's Press, 1996), 321.

14 Bruce Weber, "Ralph Kiner, Hall of Fame Slugger and Longtime Mets Voice, Dies at 91," *New York Times*, February 7, 2014, A1.

15 Kiner, *Baseball Forever*, 197.

16 Weber, "Ralph Kiner."

17 Bill James, *The Bill James Historical Baseball Abstract* (New York: Villard Books, 1986), 377.

TIM MCCARVER

By Dave Williams

FOR THOSE WHO SAW TIM MCCARVER BREAK in with the St. Louis Cardinals more than 40 years ago, it is probably a surprise that he became better known for his broadcasting career than for his days as a catcher. Not that he wasn't always articulate and glib, and that his finding a home in the broadcast booth is a shock; it's just that he was a pretty good ballplayer who was a major contributor on championship teams.

James Timothy McCarver was born on October 16, 1941, in Memphis, Tennessee. A police officer's son, he had three brothers and one sister. Surprisingly, it was his sister, Marilyn, that he gave much of the credit to for his early development. She turned him into a left-handed hitter and worked with young Tim on his fielding. By the time he graduated from Christian Brothers High School in 1959, he was a three-sport athlete, shining in football and baseball. He was all-state in both sports as well as captain of both squads. His football team was a powerhouse that won 20 straight games. Tim was a standout at linebacker and was recruited by both Tennessee and Notre Dame. He played American Legion baseball for Tony Gagliano, uncle of Phil Gagliano, who also later played with Tim in St. Louis.

McCarver was signed in 1959 by Cardinals scout Buddy Lewis for $75,000. The New York Yankees were also interested in him. His first assignment was at Keokuk of the Midwest League, where Brent Musburger, later a broadcaster, served as home-plate umpire in his first professional game. One can only imagine the in-game chatter between those two future broadcast legends. McCarver hit .360 in 275 at-bats and was promoted to Rochester of the International League, where he hit .357 in 70 at-bats. This earned McCarver a late-season promotion to the Cardinals and his first look at big-league pitching; he had four hits in 24 at-bats (.167).

In 1960 McCarver had a big year at Memphis of the Southern Association. He batted .347, good for second in the league. This earned him another late-season call-up to the big leagues. He played in 10 games for the Cards and batted .200 (2-for-10). The year 1961 would not be so kind, however. McCarver stumbled to a .229 average while playing for San Juan/Charleston of the International League. Another promotion to the Cardinals saw him get his first significant playing time in the majors, 20 games and 67 at-bats. The results weren't overwhelming, as McCarver batted just .239, but he did hit his first home run on July 13, a solo shot to right field off Tony Cloninger of the Milwaukee Braves.

In 1962 McCarver had his last stint in the minor leagues. He played for Atlanta of the International League and had a solid season with a .275 average, 11 homers, and 57 RBIs. Because Atlanta was in the

playoffs, McCarver played in the minors into early October; he had to wait until the next spring to see the majors again. When he did, he was there to stay and impressed from the start. Despite his youth, McCarver exhibited leadership skills, and St. Louis liked him enough to trade starting catcher Gene Oliver, who had clubbed 14 homers in '63, in a trading deadline deal for Lew Burdette of the Braves. The trade officially anointed McCarver as the starting catcher and he responded with a .289 average, 4 homers, and 51 RBIs. He also had seven triples. In 1966 his 13 triples tied him with Johnny Kling (1903) for the post-1900 record for triples by a catcher.

Showing rare speed for a man of his position, McCarver displayed some in a June 1963 game against the Mets when he hit his first career grand slam, a rare inside-the-park grand slam. McCarver hit a shot at the Polo Grounds that Mets center fielder Rod Kanehl slipped going after, and McCarver raced around the bases before Kanehl could recover. McCarver was also a popular player in the clubhouse. Not surprisingly, he was viewed as a cerebral player who liked to pick at the nuances of the game, but he also had a very keen sense of humor. He was noted for his dead-on impersonation of Frank Fontaine, the rubber-faced funnyman Crazy Guggenheim on the *Jackie Gleason Show*.

A July 22, 1967, article in *The Sporting News* recapped some pretty heady praise McCarver inspired in his rookie season. Wally Schang, known both for his days as a catcher with Connie Mack's Philadelphia Athletics and for the first three Yankees pennant-winning teams, said, "The kid reminds me of Mickey Cochrane. I don't know if McCarver will hit with Cochrane, but he's got Mickey's same aggressiveness and speed. And as a kid, McCarver's a pretty good hitter right now."[1] Branch Rickey was quoted in the same article as comparing McCarver to Bill DeLancey, a catcher with the 1934 Cardinals' Gas House Gang: "DeLancey had the stronger throwing arm, but Tim's arm is strong enough. McCarver's a solid .280 hitter. He could hit .300 and he can run faster than DeLancey could. He has the same aggressiveness and baseball intelligence."[2]

Success did not go to his head, and 1964 proved to be a big year for McCarver and the Cardinals. He followed his strong rookie campaign with another good season as he batted .288 with nine homers and 52 RBIs. He hit three triples, a falloff from seven the year before. The Cards found themselves in a tight pennant race in September 1964, a season that is known for the collapse of the Philadelphia Phillies. On September 21, with a 6½-game lead and World Series tickets already printed, the Phillies dropped 10 consecutive games and found themselves in a four-way race along with St. Louis, San Francisco, and Cincinnati. Despite losing two straight games to the lowly Mets on the final weekend of the season, the Cards pulled out the pennant when they finally beat the Mets in the last game while the Reds, with manager Fred Hutchinson dying of cancer, lost to the Phillies.

St. Louis headed off to the World Series to play the Yankees. McCarver was a standout. In the critical Game Five, with the Series squared at two games apiece, Bob Gibson had the Yankees shut out until Tom Tresh hit a two-run homer in the bottom of the ninth inning to knot the score, 2-2. McCarver then hit a three-run homer in the top of the 10th inning and the Cards held on for a 5-2 victory and the Series lead. St. Louis won the Series in the seventh game and had its first world championship since 1946. McCarver batted .478 with 11 hits in 23 at-bats, knocking in five runs and scoring four. He also tied a Series record by hitting safely in all seven games. It was quite a year for a young man who turned 23 the day after the Series ended. He capped the year by marrying his high-school sweetheart, Anne McDaniel, on December 29, 1964. The McCarvers would eventually have two daughters, Kelly and Kathy.

The year 1965 began inauspiciously for McCarver; he broke a finger in spring training and missed the first week of the regular season. Battling injuries all season that limited him to 113 games, he was still productive at the plate, finishing with 11 homers, 48 RBIs, and a .276 batting average. The Cardinals slumped to a seventh-place finish as several key players—most notably Ken Boyer, Ray Sadecki, and Curt Simmons—had significant dropoffs in performance. The club improved only slightly to a sixth-place finish in 1966, but McCarver had another fine season at the plate. He improved to 12 home runs, 68 RBIs, and a .274 average, and set a record for catchers with a league-leading 13 triples. He stayed injury-free and was a workhorse behind the plate, catching in 148 games.

The 1966 All-Star Game was held in St. Louis, and McCarver was selected for the first time to represent the National League. On a very hot day, McCarver began a game-winning rally in the bottom of the 10th with a single. He was sacrificed to second by Ron Hunt and scored on a single by Maury Wills, beating Tony Oliva's throw to the plate.

An interesting incident in April 1966 that shed some light on the relationship between players and management pre-Marvin Miller. McCarver and veteran pitcher Bob Purkey represented the players in a meeting with management in a dispute over compensation for appearances for pregame and postgame shows. The players were not being paid and they wanted $25 for radio and $50 for television appearances. Management pointed to small print in the player's contract stipulating that they agree to "cooperate with the club and participate in any and all promotional activities of the club and league." That was the end of that.

The year 1967 was big for McCarver and the Cardinals. Buoyed by a near-MVP season from first baseman Orlando Cepeda, St. Louis won the pennant by a comfortable 10½-game margin over the San Francisco Giants. McCarver was batting .348 at the All-Star break and earned a second and final trip to the mid-season classic. His average tailed off to .295, but he still finished with career highs in home runs (14) and RBIs (69). The Cardinals went into the 1967 World Series to face the "Impossible Dream" Boston Red Sox. Boston, which had finished ninth the season before, was led by Triple Crown winner Carl Yastrzemski and pitcher Jim Lonborg, who won 22 games. The Series was hard-fought, and finally the Cardinals rode the strong arm of pitcher Bob Gibson to a seven-game victory. McCarver did not have the same outstanding performance as he did in the 1964 Series, batting only .125 with three hits in 24 at-bats.

The last year in the great run for the Cardinals was 1968. They captured their third pennant in five years, again finishing comfortably ahead of the Giants. The 1968 season was known as the Year of the Pitcher, and St. Louis was carried by Bob Gibson's historic 1.12 ERA and 22 victories. McCarver saw his average dip to .253, but he atoned for his poor performance in the 1967 World Series against Detroit with a very good 1968 Series. He batted .333, and among his nine hits was a three-run home run in the fifth inning of Game Three off Pat Dobson that put the Cards ahead and spurred them on to a 7-3 victory. Alas, things did not turn out as well for St. Louis as they had in 1964 and 1967. The Cardinals stormed out to a three-games-to-one lead before the Tigers mounted a comeback and took three games in a row to win the world championship.

McCarver ended his first tour of duty with the Cardinals in 1969 with another solid season: 7 home runs, 51 RBIs, and a .260 average. The club slumped to fourth place, 13 games behind the first-place "Miracle Mets." In a historic trade, McCarver was sent off to the Philadelphia Phillies along with Curt Flood in a seven-player trade that also saw the enigmatic Dick Allen go to St. Louis. Flood refused to report to the Phillies and took his case all the way to the U. S. Supreme Court. This was the precursor to all the player-management labor issues in the '70s that changed the baseball landscape forever.

This also began the vagabond part of McCarver's career. He began the 1970 season as the Phillies' starting catcher, but in a microcosm of all the troubles that befell the Phillies in those days, McCarver broke his finger on a foul ball off the bat of Willie Mays in early May. In the same inning, backup catcher Mike Ryan suffered a similar injury and both were shelved for a good part of the season. McCarver already possessed a less-than-powerful arm, and the broken finger did not heal straight. The effect was that his throws moved like a cut fastball.

McCarver returned to form with the Phillies in 1971. He played in 134 games and again produced solid offensive numbers, with a .278 average to go along with eight round-trippers and 46 RBIs. An interesting incident with his former Cardinal teammates took place in September. It began when McCarver dropped a popup near the St. Louis dugout. Cardinal players began riding him and really got under his skin when they began yelling from the dugout, "There he goes!" with the slow-footed Joe Torre on first base—the implication being that his throwing problems would not even allow him to catch a pedestrian Torre on a stolen-base attempt. When Lou Brock was at the plate, he was brushed back by pitcher Manny Muniz on two consecutive pitches. Brock made a comment and the two former teammates and current friends began to scuffle. Umpire Al Barlick ejected McCarver.

The two teams met again the following week. Brock was on third when Torre lifted a shallow fly ball to right field. Brock tried to score and Willie Montanez's throw easily beat him to the plate, leaving him no choice but to bowl over McCarver. There was a brief moment when it appeared that the previous week's fight would resume, but Brock picked up McCarver's cap and handed it to him, which put an end to the hostility.

McCarver's first stint with the Phillies ended in 1972 with a deadline trade to the Montreal Expos. Of the trade, McCarver said, "Being traded is something I'm acclimated to, but it would be easier to accept if the people being traded and their families were treated with respect."[3] Two things bothered him: that he never heard from general manager Paul Owens, who traded him; and that he had just put $1,100 down on an apartment in Philadelphia.

McCarver's time in Montreal was brief, but for the first time in his big-league career he played other positions besides catcher. He appeared in six games as a third baseman and 14 as an outfielder. Traded after the season, McCarver returned to his baseball roots in St. Louis in 1973. He appeared in 130 games—77 of them at first base—and hit a respectable .266. The 1974 season saw another move: McCarver was sold to the Boston Red Sox in a stretch-drive move aimed at strengthening the bench for their pennant battle with the Baltimore Orioles. He was not much help as he batted only .250 with one run batted in, and the Red Sox fell short in their bid to unseat Baltimore as American League Eastern Division champions.

It was expected that the Red Sox would release McCarver after the season, but they held on to him. A spring-training talk with manager Darrell Johnson convinced him that his chances of making the team were good and he would be counted on to contribute. At some point in early 1975, he reportedly said, "I'm not here to be a fill in. ... I have a little pride with the good years I have had behind me." But things did not work out so well for McCarver. He played in four games in May but didn't start until June; he was released soon after despite a .381 batting average when Carlton Fisk was reactivated.

Thinking his playing days were over, McCarver did some audition tapes for Philadelphia TV stations. Before anything came of it, the Phillies signed him to a contract and his career continued. There would prove to be some productive times ahead. In 1975, with Phillies ace Steve Carlton struggling, manager Danny Ozark began having McCarver catch Carlton on his turn through the rotation, with good results. In 1976, with Carlton off to a slow start, Ozark paired the two again, and Lefty won four starts in a row with McCarver behind the dish. He became Carlton's personal catcher and the Phillies won the Eastern Division, making the postseason for the first time since 1950. McCarver showed he could still hit as he batted .277. Philadelphia lost the NLCS to the eventual World Series champion Cincinnati Reds.

An unfortunate McCarver incident occurred on July 4 as the nation celebrated its bicentennial. He hit a grand slam into the right-field seats in Pittsburgh's Three Rivers Stadium, and on his way around the bases he inadvertently passed teammate Garry Maddox. He was called out for passing the base runner and received credit for a single and three RBIs.

Another good year for the McCarver-Carlton tandem and the Phillies was 1977. Carlton went 23-10 en route to his second Cy Young Award while McCarver batted .320. The Phillies won their second consecutive division title, but again lost in the NLCS, this time to the Los Angeles Dodgers.

McCarver's playing days wound down in 1978 and 1979. He still caught Carlton regularly, but some of his starts were handled by regular catcher Bob Boone. He retired at the end of the 1979 season and was hired into the broadcast booth by the Phillies. He immediately took to the job, and a second career was born. His playing days were not quite finished, as he returned to the playing field in September of 1980 to become one of the few players, and the first twentieth-century catcher, to play in four decades. He moved over to the New York Mets broadcast booth in 1983 and would soon receive national recognition as an insightful analyst.

Just days before the 1985 World Series, ABC fired Howard Cosell, and McCarver was invited to share the booth with Al Michaels and Jim Palmer. He was an instant success on the national stage. In October 2003, McCarver was said to reflect, "I was nervous, very nervous. Broadcasting a World Series was not even close to playing in one. As a player, you have a chance to do something about the outcome... From a player's standpoint you think you know about 85 percent of the game. Then you go upstairs and find out you're wrong about that."

If that is the case, then McCarver has certainly proved that he has learned about the game. Opinionated, studious, and witty, McCarver has survived in the booth for longer than he was a player. He broadcast the Mets from 1983-98, the Yankees from 1999-2001, and the Giants in 2002, and hosted a weekly syndicated television interview.

Blues Stadium in Memphis was renamed Tim McCarver Stadium for the 1978-99 seasons, before it was replaced. McCarver won four Telly Awards and six national Emmys as Best Sportscaster/Analyst, and he has authored six books on baseball. In 2012 he was honored by the National Baseball Hall of Fame with its Ford C. Frick Award, granted annually for broadcasting excellence.

From 1996 to 2013 McCarver worked as a color commentator for the World Series on the Fox network. In 2014 and 2015 he was a part-time analyst on Cardinals games for Fox Sports Midwest.

SOURCES

Besides the sources cited in the Notes, the author consulted the following:

The Baseball Encyclopedia, 10th ed.

St. Louis Post-Dispatch.

Tim McCarver player file, National Baseball Hall of Fame Library, Cooperstown, New York.

NOTES

1 Neal Russo, "Cards Tickled With Terrific Tim," *The Sporting News*, July 22, 1967: 3.

2 Ibid.

3 Sam Goldaper, "Phillies Trade McCarver to Montreal for Bateman," *New York Times*, June 15, 1972: 34.

FRAN HEALY

By Alan Cohen

"**I REALIZED THAT THIS WAS A SHORT-LIVED** career, and I did something to prepare myself for what was to come later. I never spent a winter without doing something constructive. I never played winter ball. I went to school or I took courses in advertising, radio and TV production. I even took books on the road."[1] That foresight paid off for Fran Healy.

In 1986 Healy, who in 1978 went straight from the playing field to the broadcast booth, was one of the Mets play-by-play announcers as they put together their best season in many years and won the World Series.

Healy had a good baseball pedigree: His uncle Francis had played with the New York Giants and St. Louis Cardinals, and was a member of the Gas House Gang that won the World Series in 1934. His father, Bernard, had played minor-league ball in the Cardinals organization.

Francis Xavier Healy was born on September 6, 1946, in Holyoke, Massachusetts, one of five children. His mother, Marina, worked in the purchasing department at Providence Hospital.

Fran attended Holyoke High School, batting .408 in his sophomore year and starring on the basketball team, before transferring to the private Tabor Academy in January of his junior year. He starred in American Legion ball for Holyoke Post 351, and was selected to represent the Boston area in the Hearst Sandlot Classic in 1963. He returned to Holyoke High School in 1964, and after graduation was signed by Cleveland Indians scout Hoot Evers for a $40,000 bonus. He was in the Cleveland farm system from 1965 through 1968.

Healy's minor-league travels began in Dubuque, Iowa of the Class-A Midwest League. After batting only .168 in 49 games in 1965, he was batting .258 in 48 games in 1966 when he was called up to Pawtucket of the Double-A Eastern League. He was in the Eastern League through 1968. In 1966 and 1967, he batted .267 and .269, respectively, at Pawtucket, making the league's All-Star team in 1967. When the Indians switched their Double-A affiliation to Waterbury in 1968, he batted .238 and was in the pool of players for the American League's postseason expansion draft.

Healy was selected by the new Kansas City Royals, and the fact that he was their 28th choice did not bode well for his future. Nevertheless, he persevered, and spent the better part of two years at Omaha in the American Association. In 1969 he batted .282, and was called up to the Royals at the end of the season. In his first major-league game, on September 3, 1969, he had two singles against the Detroit Tigers' Denny McLain.

On January 31, 1970, Healy married Gloria Turcotte. They had two daughters, Deborah Michele and Kara.

During spring training in 1970, Healy developed a case of baseball's yips and was having trouble making routine throws back to the pitcher. "I started spring training right after being in military service and I had a hurt muscle in my left shoulder," he said several years later. "I never had thrown the ball back real hard. Maybe (Charlie) Metro mentioned it the year before." Metro had served as director of player procurement for the Royals before taking over as manager in 1970, and saw Healy's slow throws to the mound as a weakness. "He got on me and told everybody I couldn't throw. I guess I sort of got a mental block about the whole thing."[2]

The decision was made to send Healy back to Omaha for another season. He was embittered, but under the tutelage of manager Jack McKeon he improved on his 1969 performance, batting .294 with 5 home runs and 36 RBIs in 82 games. Healy gave all the credit to McKeon, saying, "I'm just glad I got to go to the guy who could recycle me. I had a lot of maturing to do."[3] In his last game of the regular season, on August 31, 1970, Healy was ejected from a game for the first time, after arguing that he had beaten out a groundball to shortstop.

The Royals were out of options on Healy, and rather than expose him to the postseason draft and risk getting little back on their investment in him, they traded Healy to the San Francisco Giants for pitcher Bob Garibaldi. Healy then played in the major leagues continuously from 1971 through the beginning of 1978. He was with the Giants in 1971 and 1972, serving as a backup to Dick Dietz in 1971 and Dave Rader in 1972.

In 1971 Healy batted .280 as the Giants finished first in the NL West. In his first at-bat of the season, on April 15, he hit a walk-off pinch-hit homer in the 10th inning as the Giants defeated Houston. Two days later, he got his first start of the season in the second game of a doubleheader against the Chicago Cubs. He went 4-for-4 with a two-run homer and four RBIs as the Giants won their eighth straight, 8-1, and led the division by three games. Those two homers were all the backup would get in 1971. But by the end of June he was batting .422 (19-for-45). He finished the season batting .280 in 47 games, but did not see action in the postseason.

In 1972 Healy had a great spring and was the Giants' Opening Day catcher. He started 11 of the team's 14 games in April, but was batting just.100 at the end of the month. For the rest of the season, he watched as Dave Rader took over behind the plate. Healy's highlights for the season came in May. In a 2-0 loss to Cincinnati on May 16, he singled in the third inning to break a 0-for-30 drought, and in the first inning he gunned down Joe Morgan and Bobby Tolan in consecutive theft attempts. Later in the game, he threw out Don Chaney. Two days earlier, against the Mets, he had gunned down the Mets' first baseman, who had previously played for the Giants and had stolen 336 bases for them in 21 seasons. Willie Mays had just been traded to the Mets and was in his first game with his new team.

It was usually a long time between starts for Healy. He got the call on July 6, after Rader had 18 straight starts, and responded with a 2-for-4 performance as the Giants beat the Phillies 6-4 in Philadelphia. For the season, he batted only .152 in 45 games as the Giants finished fifth in the NL West.

As the 1973 season was getting under way, Healy returned to Kansas City, in a trade for pitcher Greg Minton. He had his best years with the Royals.

In his first year back with the Royals, Healy was reunited with Jack McKeon, then in his first year as a big-league manager. McKeon had urged the Royals to reacquire Healy. On April 27 Healy caught Steve Busby's no-hitter against Detroit. But Healy was not hitting well. He played in only 24 of the Royals' first 56 games, batting .197. The other catcher, Carl Taylor, was also batting under .200. On June 9 McKeon made Healy the regular catcher. For the balance of the season, he justified McKeon's choice, batting .300 with 6 home runs and 30 RBIs in 71 games, during which the Royals went 40-31. He fashioned hitting streaks of 8 and 11 games. On July 9 Jerry Bell of Milwaukee threw three successive brushback pitches at Healy, who charged the mound. A brawl ensued and Bell and Healy were ejected.

In late August Associated Press sportswriter Robert Moore proclaimed, "Fran Healy has finally made the grade as a major league catcher."[4] But after injuring his wrist on August 31, Healy played only six games in September, The Royals played .500 ball in September and finished six games behind the eventual World Series champion Oakland A's. Over the course of the season, Healy threw out 31 of 69 runners trying to steal, finishing fifth in the league with a 44.9 caught-stealing percentage. For the season Healy played in 95 games and batted .276.

In 1974 Healy played in a career-high 139 games, and his 138 games behind the plate were more than any other big-league catcher that season. He set career highs in home runs (9) and RBIs (53). Early in the season, he had four multiple-hit games in a five-game stretch, batted .409 and had three home runs. He was named American League Player of the Week on May 5. The Royals were in second place, within four games of the lead on August 27, but fell out of contention by losing 25 of their last 33 games and finished fifth in the AL West. Healy batted.252 with a career-high 9 homes runs and 53 RBIs.

In 1975, Healy was injured often and played in only 56 games. The injuries started early on. In the second game of the season, Tommy Harper collided with Healy at home plate and Healy suffered a severe Achilles tendon strain. He missed 32 games. Shortly after returning in mid-May he hit an upper-deck job at Yankee Stadium off Doc Medich in the 10th inning that gave the Royals a 4-1 win. A few days later, back home against the Yankees, he tied the game in the ninth inning with a single, then singled again in the 11th inning to set up a walk-off suicide squeeze by Frank White.

Healy credited Harmon Killebrew, who was winding down his career with the Royals, for his improvement at the plate that began in May and extended into early June. Healy noted, "I've always had the problem of lunging at pitches. … Harmon worked with me during spring training. Now if I lunge, he lets me know in his quiet way."[5]

Healy's batting average went over.300 and on June 9, after a 2-for-5 performance against Milwaukee, it stood at .309. Then he slumped badly and a 17-for-81 stretch took his average down to .250 by the end of June. On July 9 Healy was again involved in a collision, when Gorman Thomas of the Milwaukee Brewers bowled him over while scoring. Back problems resulting from the collision caused Healy to miss all but 11 of his team's last 78 games. For the season he batted .255 with 2 home runs and 18 RBIs.

Going into the 1976 season, question marks surrounded Healy's status with the Royals. He regained his starting job during spring training, but was batting .071 after four games and found himself on the bench, with Buck Martinez taking over behind the plate. Not playing regularly, Healy requested a trade to an East Coast team, to be closer to his New England roots. On May 16, after playing in only eight games with the Royals, Healy was traded to the Yankees for pitcher Larry Gura. The departing Healy said, "I've been here for years and I have a lot of memories. I'll treasure most of them. I've met some great people and there are some great people in the Royals' organization. I was disappointed I didn't get to catch more, but baseball has its ups and downs."[6] With the Yankees, he became Thurman Munson's backup. He played in 46 games the rest of the season, batting .267. He started behind the plate in 23 games and threw out 10 of 17 (59 percent) of would-be stealers. The Yankees won their division and defeated Healy's old team, the Royals, to advance to the World Series, which they lost to Cincinnati. Healy did not play during the postseason.

In 1977 the Yankees acquired Reggie Jackson and the tempestuous Jackson and Healy became fast friends. Indeed, when Jackson was enshrined in Cooperstown in 1993, he mentioned in his induction speech that "I never got the support from any player like I got from Fran."[7] Healy saw little action but was pressed into service in early June when Munson was badly cut on the right hand in a home-plate collision. Healy played six straight games, contributing five RBIs as the

Yankees won four of the six. For the season, he played in only 27 games, batting .224. Healy's chief value to the Yankees was neither behind the plate nor at the bat. It was in the clubhouse, where his friendship with Jackson paid big dividends for Reggie and the Yankees.

That may have been exemplified by the notorious flareup between Jackson and Yankees manager Billy Martin in front of a national TV audience in a game at Fenway Park in Boston. Martin had pulled Jackson from the game and Reggie erupted. Three decades later, Jackson said, "Finally, Fran Healy came into the clubhouse from the outfield (bullpen) and said 'Reggie, get dressed, and change and go home. Because no matter what you do, whether he (Martin) hits you first or you grab him, you're gonna be wrong. So get dressed and go home.' [It was the] smartest thing I was ever told to do and luckily one of the smarter things I did."[8]

An instance of how close the relationship between Healy and Jackson was occurred prior to Game Five of the 1977 American League championship series. The Yankees were playing the Royals, and Billy Martin, in spite, elected to bench Jackson in the deciding game of the five-game series. It fell to Healy to break the news to Jackson. As Mike Lupica said, "It is a good thing Healy was around, because there is no telling what might have happened between Reggie and Martin."[9] Eventually, Martin called upon Jackson to pinch-hit in the eighth inning, and Reggie's hit propelled the Yankees to within a run of the Royals. One inning later, the Yankees rallied to win the game and were on to the World Series.

Healy finished his playing career with the Yankees in 1978, playing only once, on April 21. Suffering from recurring neck problems, he asked the Yankees to release him. He debuted in the Yankees announcing booth shortly after. Although he had made only a cameo appearance on the field in 1978, Healy was voted a $500 share of the World Series money when the Yankees repeated as world champions.

Healy was aware of his situation. As he noted shortly after switching from the playing field to the broadcast booth, "If you're 22 and you're screaming about not playing, they'll listen to you. If you're 32, they'll tell you to take a walk."[10] For Healy, the walk was fortuitous.

During his early years in baseball, Healy had continued his studies at American International College in Springfield, Massachusetts. In 1973 he received his degree, with a major in history, from American International College. He worked as a broadcaster for the Yankees from 1978 to 1983, first with Mel Allen and Phil Rizzuto, and later with Frank Messer and Bill White. It is his time with Rizzuto for which he is best remembered. Healy and Rizzuto were, as *New York Times* sportswriter Ira Berkow wrote, "a comedy team, one that also interspersed solid bits of baseball information that were a treat for Yankee fans. Healy was Abbott to Rizzuto's Costello. The straight man and the laugh-getter. They insulted each other, they goaded each other, and they did so with warmth and, to a fair degree, good taste."[11]

Healy joined the Mets in 1984, working with Tim McCarver and Ralph Kiner on SportsChannel telecasts, and producing the "Halls of Fame" television series. He did Mets broadcasts through 2005.

In 1986 Healy was part of the announcing team as the Mets won it all. In remembering that team, he said, "Every position on the team you could associate a strong adjective to the position. The pitching staff was unbelievable. They had one of the best catchers in the game (in Gary Carter). Certain teams win, but they're not glamorous. That was a glamour team. Nobody used the term 'swagger' back then, but that team had swagger, and I mean a lot of it."[12]

In 1992, in a ceremony in his hometown of Holyoke, Healy received the Massachusetts American Legion Graduate of the Year Award.

After the terrorist attacks of September 11, 2001, baseball entered a brief hiatus. In the first game back at Shea Stadium, on September 21, emotion filled the air as Healy and his broadcast partner, Howie Rose, took to the airwaves. For 7½ innings, they were able to follow the commissioner's dictum to keep the event solemn. But when Mike Piazza hit a home run that put the Mets ahead in the bottom of the eighth, there was an uproar from the more than 40,000 spectators, and the announcers displayed emotion. Healy said, "This place exploded! It's been waiting to explode all night." And there was a sense of normality.[13]

Healy, who was under contract to the Madison Square Garden Network, left the booth after the 2005 season when the SportsNet New York got the contract to broadcast the Mets games. He remained with MSG, among other things hosting the Game 365 series.

SOURCES

In addition to the sources cited in the notes, the author consulted the Fran Healy file maintained at the Giamatti Research Center, National Baseball Hall of Fame and Museum, Cooperstown, New York; the *Omaha World-Herald*, and the newspaper articles cited below. Statistics have been taken from Baseball-Reference and Retrosheet.

Bordman, Sid. "Healy Quick Cure for Royal Mitt Aches," *The Sporting News*, August 18, 1973: 16.

Brown, Garry. "Fran Healy and Reggie Jackson: Baseball's Version of Odd Couple," *Union-News* (Springfield, Massachusetts), January 7, 1993: 27.

Frizzell, Pat. "Big League Heritage Behind Giants' Backstop Healy," *The Sporting News*, May 6, 1972: 10.

McGuff, Joe. "Healthy Healy Royals Chief Concern," *The Sporting News*, January 17, 1976: 41.

NOTES

1 Phil Pepe, "Healy's First Death," *New York Daily News*, May 12, 1978.

2 Joe McGuff, "Gritty Healy Repays Royals With First-Rate Mitt Work," *The Sporting News*, June 8, 1974: 20.

3 Ibid.

4 Robert Moore, "Healy Helping Royals Toward Pennant," *Daily Herald* (Biloxi-Gulfport, Mississippi), August 24, 1973: 21.

5 Sid Bordman, "Healy Gets Healthy and So Does Royals' Catching," *The Sporting News*, June 14, 1975: 14.

6 Joe McGuff, "Royals Find Bullpen Help in the 'Hall-Way,'" *The Sporting News*, June 5, 1976: 3.

7 John Rawlings, *The Sporting News*, August 9, 1993: 6.

8 *New York Post*, October 28, 2011.

9 Mike Lupica, *New York Daily News*, October 18, 2012.

10 Tony Kornheiser, "They've Done It All, But Not Too Often," *Washington Post*, August 3, 1980.

11 Ira Berkow, "Healy's Gone, So Who's on First, Now," *New York Times*, February 6, 1982: 17.

12 Tim Smith, *New York Daily News*, February 9, 2011.

13 Justin Tasch, "A Time to Heal," *New York Daily News*, September 21, 2014.

RUSTY STAUB

By Norm King

DANIEL STAUB? WHO THE HELL IS DANIEL Staub?

Nobody has ever heard of a ballplayer named Daniel Staub. But everyone has heard of Rusty Staub, and for the French and English fans of a brand-new ball club in Montreal, Quebec, Canada, he was known—and loved—as Le Grand Orange.

Daniel Joseph "Rusty" Staub was born on April 1, 1944, in New Orleans, one of two boys born to Ray Staub, a schoolteacher, and his wife, Alma Morton Staub. As his mother told it, Daniel became Rusty even before he left the hospital.

"I wanted to name him Daniel so I could call him Danny for short, "Alma recalled. "But one of the nurses nicknamed him Rusty for the red fuzz he had all over his head and it stuck."[1]

Ray Staub was a catcher with the Gainesville G-Men of the Class-D Florida State League in 1937-38. When Rusty was only 3, Ray give him a bat and told him to start swinging at anything round, such as fruit, rocks, softballs—you name it. Rusty took to the bat the way Canadian kids take to hockey skates, and as he got older, he became a good hitter.

Staub and his older brother, Chuck, played at Jesuit High School in New Orleans. With Rusty at first and Chuck in center field, Jesuit won the 1960 American Legion national championship and the 1961 Louisiana State AAA championship. As a result, major-league teams scouted Staub heavily, this being the days before the amateur draft. The Boston Red Sox even sent Ted Williams to talk to him. Scouts from 16 teams beat a path to Staub's door, but ultimately he accepted an offer with a $100,000 bonus from the spanking new Houston Colt .45s, an expansion team about to play its inaugural season in 1962. Staub's signing was literally a whirlwind event, as general manager Paul Richards arrived in New Orleans at the height of Hurricane Carla to get his signature on a contract.

After batting .299 in the Arizona Fall League in 1961, the 18-year-old Staub dominated the Class-B Carolina League in 1962 while playing for the Durham Bulls. He led the league in hits with 149, and batted .293 with 23 home runs and 93 RBIs. Not surprisingly, he won league rookie of the year honors, and a trip to the big club for 1963.

Staub wowed team management during spring training in 1963. "Staub right now is the best hitter on our ballclub," said Richards. "I realize that may not sound so good at the end of the first 30 days if we decide he'd be better off playing in San Antonio. But I repeat, right now he's the best hitter we have."[2]

As well as he hit in spring training, Staub was not going to take the first-base job away from Pete Runnels, who

came to Houston after winning the 1962 American League batting title with Boston. Manager Harry Craft had Staub in right field and batting cleanup on Opening Day against the defending National League champion San Francisco Giants. He made an impressive debut, going 1-for-3 with a walk and an RBI, even though the Colt .45s lost 9-2. However, a solid debut does not a season make, and it was clear that Staub was overmatched, despite the best cheerleading efforts of the press.

"It was a big joke to everyone but the Houston Colts when they started a rosy-cheeked 19-year-old kid as a cleanup hitter on Opening Day, a little more than a month ago," wrote Kenneth Carr on May 17. Daniel Rusty Staub *[sic]*, two summers out of a New Orleans high school, still bats cleanup for the Colts, but nobody laughs anymore."[3]

Maybe not, but some were probably snickering, because at that point of the season, Staub had zero home runs and 15 RBIs and was batting .248. He finally hit his first big-league home run on June 3—a game-winner off future Hall of Famer Don Drysdale, no less—one of only six he hit all year, along with 45 RBIs and a .224 batting average.

As Staub prepared for the 1964 season in spring training, a newspaper story showed that he had a good perspective being hyped as a future star at such a young age. "Everybody asks if being overpublicized hurt me," he said. "Not that much. It was a great year for me. ... I made a lot of lousy, stupid plays but the mistakes stick with you. When you make a mistake up here, you remember it and don't do it again if you can help it."[4]

Staub did not hit well enough as a rookie to have a sophomore jinx, but he had one anyway. While playing first base against St. Louis on June 23, he dropped two throws on batted balls in the seventh inning that led to the winning run for St. Louis. By July 3 he was hitting only .202 with 4 homers and 27 RBIs, so the club decided to send him down to their Triple-A affiliate, Oklahoma City of the Pacific Coast League. Staub was devastated.

"Sometimes it seems like the world comes to an end, but maybe it just starts over," he said. "I hope so. But it's tearing me up now."[5]

Staub tore up Pacific Coast League pitching during his time there; in 71 games he hit 20 home runs, drove in 45 runs, and hit .314. If nothing else, the demotion restored his confidence. He was called up in mid-September, and in his final 16 games, he doubled his home run total for the year, to eight, and batted .271.

Baseball entered a new era in 1965 with the opening of the Houston Astrodome, baseball's first indoor facility. Staub became the first person to hit a ball into the stands at the ballpark during a preseason batting practice session in February, where singer Anita Bryant had a gay old time throwing out the first pitch to stadium architect Bob Michew.

Staub began his rise to becoming an All-Star-caliber player with the newly christened Astros from the start of the 1965 season. He got off to a rough start early in the season, but by July the alarm clock in his head finally went off. His batting average rose from .216 on June 28 to .256 at the end of the season. He reached double figures in home runs, with 14, and had 63 RBIs.

In 1966 Staub improved even more with a .280 batting average, 13 home runs, and 81 RBIs, and won the team's most valuable player award as selected by the Houston baseball writers. By 1967 any doubts about his star potential disappeared as he started hitting early and never let up. He was batting .346 by the All-Star break, with 7 home runs and 39 RBIs, and was named to his first All-Star Game by National League manager Walter Alston. Staub pinch-hit and singled in the 11th inning of a classic game in Anaheim that the National League won 2-1 in 15 innings on a Tony Perez home run.

Staub's consistency at the plate continued in the second half. He finished the year with a .333 average, 10 home runs, and 74 RBIs, which was good enough for fifth in the National League batting race.[6] He also hit a league-leading 44 doubles. The baseball writers chose him as the team's MVP again, this time by one vote over Jimmy Wynn.

"I stopped trying to go for the long ball," Staub explained. "I thought I was a home run hitter when I signed, but now I don't go for the pump (the long ball), especially since we play 81 games in the Astrodome."[7]

The 1968 season began with Staub holding out for eight days before finally signing a contract reportedly for $45,000. The Astros moved him back to first base because he had injured his groin several times the previous season.

Staub lost approximately $300 of that salary when he and teammate Bob Aspromonte were each docked one day's pay for refusing to play against the Pirates on June 9. President Lyndon Johnson had designated that date as a day of national mourning after the assassination of Senator Robert Kennedy.[8] Aspromonte lost approximately $200.

"After talking with the players Monday, I am convinced that these two fine young men had very strong convictions and deep feeling for the late Senator Kennedy," said Astros general manager H.B. Richardson. "Therefore the penalty was not as great as it might have been."[9]

The Astros had an off day on June 10, but on the following day, both Staub and Aspromonte received telegrams from Kennedy's press secretary, Frank Mankiewicz, thanking them for their stand. Staub then went out and drove in two runs as the Astros defeated Philadelphia 5-1. One week later, on June 17, the Astros fired Grady Hatton as their manager and replaced him with their batting coach, Harry "The Hat" Walker. This move would have a profound effect on Staub's career, and his life.

Staub was batting .317 by the All-Star break. He was the lone Astro selected for the National League All-Star team and popped to third as a pinch-hitter as the National League defeated the American League 1-0 at the Astrodome. He slumped in the second half, as his average fell to .291, which tied him with Roberto Clemente for ninth place among National League batters in the Year of the Pitcher. He hit six home runs and had 72 RBIs.

The truth was, Walker and Staub did not get along. As a batting coach, Walker did not like the fact that Staub often experimented with batting stances and grips on his own. In addition, Astros management felt that the bonus-baby power hitter they paid all that money was not giving them a good return on their investment—never mind the fact that Staub played half his games in the Astrodome, which was not a good home-run park.

Major League Baseball expanded to four new cities for the 1969 season, one of which was Montreal. "Seizing on an opportunity to bail on a player he didn't like, Walker huddled with Richardson on trade possibilities that could whisk Staub out of town, preferably for proven talent," wrote Jonah Keri in his history of the Expos. "The Expos, by their own design, would prove to be the perfect fit. . . . They'd collected multiple flappable veterans to dangle in trade for just such an opportunity."[10]

Anyway, Houston traded the 24-year-old Staub to Montreal for 33-year-old Donn Clendenon and 26-year-old Jesus Alou. That is when the fun began. Clendenon, an African-American, had the Mississippi-born Walker as a manager in Pittsburgh and felt that Walker was racist. He refused to report to Houston and retired instead to work for the Scripto Pen Company in Atlanta. The issue got complicated—even Commissioner Bowie Kuhn got involved—and eventually the Expos sent Jack Billingham, Skip Guinn, and $100,000 to the Astros.[11]

To put it bluntly, the Astros got taken. Rarely have a player and a city—make that an entire country—been such a perfect fit. Being from Louisiana, Staub was no stranger to French culture. Even so, the love affair between Montreal and Staub was something to behold. Sportswriter Ted Blackman of the *Montreal Gazette* soon bestowed the nickname *Le Grand Orange* on him, after Staub hit a two-run homer and caught the final out against the right-field fence to preserve a win that broke a 20-game losing streak. To this day, people who do not speak any French refer to him by that moniker.

It did not hurt that Staub hit .302 with 29 home runs and 79 RBIs, but what really endeared him to Montreal's French population was his sincere effort to learn *la langue francais*.

"I took about 25 French classes after the first season and the next year I took longer classes," recalled Staub. "There's not a question that my making that effort is part of the reason that whatever *Le Grand Orange* represented to all those fans, they knew I cared and I tried."[12]

Staub also braved Montreal winters, living there year-round and traveling across the country to promote baseball and the Expos. He developed many business interests, including an association with the Bank of Montreal that led to the Young Expos Club that drew members from across Canada. "The first year we had 25,000 children. The second year it was 75,000 and then the third year we had over 150,000 children in the program across the country," Staub recalled. "To be able to do that and have a real part in it was very fulfilling, like I was doing something above being a player."[13]

During his time in Montreal, Staub developed—how often do you write this about a ballplayer?—a taste for fine wine. Charles Bronfman, chairman of Seagram's Distillery, owned the Expos when Staub played there. Bronfman and his friends gave Staub books on wine and took him to tastings. He eventually became quite the connoisseur. He also enjoyed cooking. He began to cook when he was in the Arizona Fall League and his mother would send him recipes by mail, and he dated a restaurant manager in Montreal who taught him about the business side of running a restaurant. His celebrity status also gave him easy access to chefs in their kitchens. Staub would use the knowledge he gained in Montreal and New York after he retired.

It did not hurt Staub's reputation any that he fulfilled with the Expos the promise that he showed with the Astros. In 1970 he hit 30 home runs and drove in 94 runs while batting .274, and followed that up with 19 home runs, 97 RBIs, and a .311 average in 1971. He was the Expos' lone representative at the All-Star Game both seasons; he pinch-hit in the 1970 game and didn't play in 1971.

Despite all the fine statistics and mutual love between player and city, there was still one problem—the Expos were not winning. After a 52-110 inaugural season, they improved to 73-89 in 1970 and declined slightly to 71-90 in 1971. The team's brain trust decided that a significant move was necessary to improve the team, so on April 5, 1972, the Expos traded Staub to the New York Mets for Tim Foli, Mike Jorgensen, and Ken Singleton. As happy as Staub was to leave Houston, he was just as devastated when he left Montreal. He even cried when he heard the news.

The 1972 season introduced Staub to two unfamiliar elements—winning and injury. He arrived in New York at a tumultuous time. The players were on strike, and the Mets' beloved manager Gil Hodges had died of a heart attack on April 2. Yogi Berra took over and led the team to an 83-73 record. It was the first time in his career that Staub was with a team that finished over.500. He was not around much to enjoy the winning because he played in only 66 games that season after Cincinnati's Ross Grimsley broke his hand with a pitch on June 18. He sat out a month, played on July 18, and then had surgery to repair the hand. He returned on September 18 after missing 82 games and finished the year with 9 home runs and 38 RBIs—which was good enough to tie for third among the team's RBI leaders despite his missing more than half the season (Cleon Jones led the team with 52 RBIs.)

The term "Least Division" may have been invented for the National League East division in 1973. On August 5, the Mets were in last place with a 48-60 record, 11½ games off the pace, then went on a 34-19 run to win the division with an 82-79 mark. Staub had his weakest season in several years, not counting injury, batting .279 with 15 home runs and a team-leading 76 RBIs.

The Mets faced the mighty Cincinnati Reds in the National League Championship Series and won the best-of-five affair in part due to Staub's three home runs, including two in Game Three, as well as five RBIs. Staub also made a terrific defensive play in Game Four. With the score tied 1-1 in the 11th inning and two runners on, Staub ran back and caught a deep fly ball by Dan Driessen, saving one, if not two, runs. The play proved costly, as Staub bruised his shoulder running into the fence after the grab. He did not play in the NLCS clincher, and could not put anything on his throws during the World Series, which the Mets lost in seven games to the Oakland A's. Staub got 11 hits in the Series, including one home run, as well as six RBIs.

Staub turned 30 in 1974 and it seemed as if age was catching up to him, as he hit only .258, his lowest batting average since 1965, with 19 home runs, and a team-leading 78 RBIs. Then in 1975 Staub went where no Met had gone before; he became the first Amazin' to drive in more than 100 runs in a season, when he drove in 105, to go along with 19 home runs and an improved .282 batting average. It was the first time in his career that Staub passed the century mark.

General managers sometimes make bizarre trades for reasons beyond their control. The Mets were planning on trading Staub to Baltimore for Doug DeCinces, who had 31 games of major-league experience. Team president Donald Grant approved the deal, but he wanted to hold off announcing it until he explained the transaction to the team owner, Lorinda de Roulet. She did not like the trade because she did not want to exchange Staub for a rookie. The Mets instead traded Staub, coming off one of his most productive years, to the Detroit Tigers for 34-year-old Mickey Lolich, who had lost 39 games in the previous two seasons. There were also business reasons for the trade; Staub had the second-highest salary on the team ($120,000) behind Tom Seaver, and 1976 would have been his fifth with the Mets, after which he would have been a 10-5 man, and would have had the right to veto any trade.[14]

Anyway, the Mets got a pitcher who went 8-13 with a 3.22 ERA in his only season with the team. The Tigers got a player who hit .299, swatted 15 home runs, drove in 96 runs, and started the All-Star Game.

Staub played 126 games in right field with the Tigers in 1976, but he was used exclusively as a designated hitter over the following two seasons. For whatever reason, being the DH improved Staub's home-run stroke, as he cracked 22 in 1977 to go along with 101 RBIs and a .278 batting average. He followed that up in 1978 with 24 home runs and, with Ron Leflore and Lou Whitaker hitting in front of him much of the season, a career-high 121 RBIs. He also hit .273.

The 1979 season got off to a poor start for Staub. In fact, it almost did not start at all. He had signed a three-year contract in 1978 at $200,000 annually. When spring training rolled around in 1979, Staub decided he wanted more security, and held out for a contract extension at the same salary. In fact, he threatened to quit baseball and devote all his energies to the restaurant he had opened up in New York. Spring training came and went, then the season started, and still no Staub. He looked into the eye of the Tigers, and they looked back at him with a growl. He finally backed down, reported to the team, and played his first game on May 3.

By this time Staub was 35, and missing spring training prevented him from finding his batting stroke. By mid-July, he was hitting only .236 with 9 home runs and 40 RBIs, so on July 20 the Tigers did something almost as momentous as the landing on the moon that occurred 10 years before to the day—they traded him back to the Expos for a player to be named later and cash.[15]

The franchise Staub joined was not the same nascent operation he left in 1972. This team played in the huge Olympic Stadium, not tiny little Jarry Park. More importantly, they were winning; the fans were attending Expos games in droves, so getting Staub was not a gimmick to sell tickets; Montreal needed a pinch-hitter.

The Expos' first home date after Staub's return was a July 27 doubleheader against the Pirates, who were two games behind Montreal before play began. The Expos were behind 5-4 in the eighth inning when Pittsburgh brought Grant Jackson in to replace Kent Tekulve. While Jackson warmed up, a familiar face came out of the Expos dugout to pinch-hit for pitcher Elias Sosa. More than 59,000 fans rose up and gave him a five-minute standing ovation. Unfortunately for the Expos, he popped out.

"That first at-bat when they pinch-hit me against the Pirates ... the ovation they gave me, it was overwhelming," recalled Staub. "I tried to contain it but I didn't do a real good job."[16]

The Expos came in second in the NL East in 1979, two games behind the Pirates. They traded Staub again during spring training in 1980, this time to the Texas Rangers for minor leaguers Chris Smith and LaRue Washington. He played in 109 games for Texas, primarily as a DH, with some time in both left and right field. By this time, Staub's numbers were clearly declining. He had a .300 batting average, but hit only nine home runs and drove in 55 runs. The Mets signed him as a free agent in 1981, and he spent the remainder of his career in New York, mainly as a pinch-hitter, but with the occasional foray into the outfield or first base. He retired after the 1985 season, having hit 13 home runs and driven in 102 in those five seasons, with a cumulative batting average of .276. One of his last career highlights came on September 25, 1984, when he hit a home run against the Phillies, becoming only the second player (after Ty Cobb) to hit a home run in the majors both as a teenager and after turning 40.[17] Staub retired as the only major leaguer ever to have at least 500 hits with each of four different teams.

The lifelong bachelor stayed in New York after his career ended. He had opened up his first restaurant, Rusty's, in 1977 and followed that up with a second, Rusty Staub's on Fifth, in 1989. (Both closed in the 1990s.) He was a radio and television broadcaster for Mets home games from 1986 to1995, providing color commentary with Ralph Kiner and Tim McCarver. He received a World Series ring from Mets general manager Frank Cashen after New York won it all in 1986.

The honors accumulated for Staub after he retired. The Mets had Rusty Staub Day on July 13, 1986, to acknowledge his contributions to the team and he was inducted into the Mets Hall of Fame. He also became the first Expo to have his number retired, in 1993. He has been enshrined in the Louisiana Sports Hall of Fame (1989), the Texas Baseball Hall of Fame (2006), and the Canadian Baseball Hall of Fame (2012). Staub also received an honorary doctor of humane letters degree in 2004 from Niagara University.

Staub also gives back to the community through two foundations he started while still playing. In 1984 he created the New York Police and Fire Widows and Children Benefit Fund to raise money for the families of first responders killed in the line of duty. The following year he started the Rusty Staub Foundation, which provides food pantries for underprivileged children in New York.

On October 2, 2015, Staub suffered a heart attack on a flight from Ireland to New York. He recovered well enough to throw out the ceremonial first pitch at the third game of the National League Division Series at Citi Field between the Mets and the Los Angeles Dodgers on October 12.

SOURCES

In addition to the sources cited in the Notes, the author also consulted:

Berkshire Eagle (Pittsfield, Massachusetts)

Bonham (Texas) *Daily Favorite*

Cashen, J. Frank. *Winning in Both Leagues: Reflections From Baseball's Front Office* (Lincoln: University of Nebraska Press, 2014).

CBS New York.

Daytona Beach Morning Journal.

Kingston (New York) *Daily Freeman.*

Knowla.org.

New Orleans Times-Picayune.

New York Post.

New York Times.

Ottawa Journal.

Palm Beach Post.

Sportsnola.com.

Statesville (North Carolina) *Record and Landmark.*

Wellsville (New York) *Daily Reporter.*

NOTES

1 Gary Ronberg, "Houston's Boy Is Now a Man," *Sports Illustrated*, August 14, 1967.

2 "Houston Colts To Give Youths A real Chance," *Valley Morning Star* (Harlingen, Texas), April 7, 1963.

3 Kenneth Carr, "Today's Sportrait," *McKinney* (Texas) *Daily Courier-Gazette,* May 17, 1963.

4 Jack Hand, "Rusty Staub Relates Adventures of 19-Year-Old Baseball Rookie," *Corsicana* (Texas) *Daily Sun,* March 30, 1964.

5 "Colts Send Rusty Staub to Oklahoma," *Denton* (Texas) *Record-Chronicle*, July 7, 1964.

6 Roberto Clemente won the batting title with a .357 mark.

7 "Can Staub Be Astro Super-Star," *Galveston Daily News*, March 30, 1968.

8 Kennedy was assassinated by Sirhan Sirhan on June 5, 1968, in Los Angeles. Maury Wills of the Pirates also refused to play, as did Milt Pappas of the Braves.

9 "Staub, Aspro Lose Day's Pay," *Abilene* (Texas) *Reporter News*, June 11, 1968.

10 Jonah Keri, *Up, Up, & Away: The Kid, The Hawk, Rock, Vladi, Pedro, Le Grand Orange, Youppi, The Crazy Business of Baseball, & the Ill-fated but Unforgettable Montreal Expos* (Toronto: Random House Canada, 2014).

11 Clendenon unretired when he knew he wasn't going to Houston, and when the Expos added $14,000 to his salary. They traded him to the Mets later in the season, and he led them to a World Series victory, earning MVP honors in the process.

12 Stu Cowan, "Staub Found a Way Into Our Hearts," *Montreal Gazette*, March 31, 2012.

13 Richard Griffin, "Griffin: Expos' Rusty Staub Deserves His Place in Canadian Baseball Hall of Fame, *Toronto Star*, February 7, 2012.

14 The 10-5 rule allows any player with 10 years of major league service, including five with one team, to veto any trade.

15 The Expos sent minor leaguer Randall Schafer, who never made it beyond Double-A to the Tigers in December 1979.

16 Video, *Les Expos Nos Amours*, produced by TV Labatt, 1989.

17 Since then, as of 2015, Gary Sheffield and Alex Rodriguez have accomplished the feat.

STEVE ZABRISKIE

By Alan Raylesberg

"THE INEVITABLE HAS BECOME REALITY." WITH those words, on WOR Channel 9's telecast, Steve Zabriskie announced that the Mets had clinched the 1986 National League Eastern Division title. Nearly 40 years later, those words still echoed as part of a video and audio montage of Mets highlights included in television ads for 2016 Mets season tickets.

Zabriskie broadcast for the Mets on WOR from 1983 through 1989, along with Ralph Kiner, Tim McCarver, and Rusty Staub. As a member of the Mets broadcast team, Zabriskie won three Emmy awards. His broadcasting career covered more than 30 years. In addition to announcing Mets games, Zabriskie was an announcer for ABC, ESPN, CBS, and the Boston Red Sox before retiring as an announcer in 1997, at the age of 50.

Steven Kenneth Zabriskie was born on May 13, 1947, in Palo Alto, California, the oldest of four siblings. His father was a manager for Woolworth's before embarking on a career in sales.[1] His father's jobs resulted in Steve and his family moving several times to new locations in California and then, soon after Zabriskie started high school, to Edmonds, Washington, a suburb northwest of Seattle.[2] At Edmonds High School, Zabriskie was a multi-talented athlete, lettering in football, baseball, track, and wrestling. At 6-feet-2 and 215 pounds, he was a powerful running back and received Honorable Mention High School All American honors. In baseball he played the outfield and some first base.

After graduating in 1965, Zabriskie received an offer from the California Angels, but turned it down to attend the University of Houston on a football scholarship. A knee injury ended his football career and, after a short attempt at playing professional baseball, Zabriskie began a career in broadcasting.

In 1968, through a family friend, Zabriskie met the program director of KTRH, the CBS radio news station in Houston. The program director thought Zabriskie "had a nice voice" and gave him a job broadcasting sports news.[3] From Houston Zabriskie landed his first TV broadcast position, at KHFI in Austin, Texas, reporting sports news. He also did play-by-play for the first time, announcing University of Texas football, baseball, and basketball games.[4]

Starting in 1971, Zabriskie refined his play-by-play skills at KTUL-TV, the ABC affiliate in Tulsa, broadcasting Oklahoma football and local college basketball games.[5] In 1975 he moved to WATE-TV, the ABC affiliate in Pittsburgh, where he worked as a local sportscaster with some gigs for ABC Sports, first as a freelancer, then full time from 1979 to 1982, and part

Courtesy of Steve Zabriskie

time thereafter until he retired in 1997.[6] For ABC Zabriskie announced college football and major-league baseball and did features for *Wide World of Sports*. In 1988 and 1989, he did NFL play-by-play for CBS.

After his stint with the Mets from 1983 to 1989, Zabriskie broadcast major-league baseball and college basketball for ESPN from 1990 to 1993. ESPN promoted him in their ads, noting that he was part of an "all-star lineup of commentators" and that Friday night doubleheaders would feature Zabriskie in the first game together with Hall of Famer Jim Palmer.[7] In 1993 Zabriskie played himself in the movie *The Program* (about the pressures of playing college football), starring James Caan and Halle Berry.[8] In 1994 and 1995 he was an announcer for The Baseball Network, a short-lived joint venture between ABC, NBC and Major League Baseball. In 1996 he was a play-by-play announcer on some Boston Red Sox games. In 1997, tired of all the travel that went with a 30-year career in sports broadcasting and wanting to spend more time with his family, Zabriskie ended his broadcast career.[9]

Zabriskie's career as a Mets announcer began in 1983, the same year that Tim McCarver began his 16-year announcing career with the Mets.[10] The two events were not entirely coincidental. With his contract for full-time work at ABC coming to an end, Zabriskie was actively seeking an opportunity to do play- by-play for a major-league team.[11] The Mets job was one of two opportunities that arose. Learning that McCarver had joined the Mets as a broadcaster, Zabriskie relished an opportunity to work with the former catcher, whom he knew from his days at ABC, and he accepted the Mets' job offer.[12] As the 1983 season began, Zabriskie replaced Lorne Brown on the WOR-TV team.[13] In the booth Zabriskie and McCarver joined Hall of Famer Ralph Kiner, who had been broadcasting Mets games since the franchise's inception in 1962. Zabriskie, with his deep baritone voice and professional manner, was the "straight man" to the more colorful Kiner and McCarver. And although he was not a former big leaguer as they were, Zabriskie's athletic prowess did not go unnoticed. When he joined the Mets broadcast crew, the 36-year-old Zabriskie worked out with the Mets every day, "taking infield practice and batting the ball with such vigor that there was some suspicion that he might be a secret weapon for the Mets."[14] Manager George Bamberger told Zabriskie (perhaps tongue-in-cheek, perhaps not), "I like the way you throw, and if we get in a jam or have any injuries, we'll use you in the spring."[15] While Zabriskie never got into a game, he did pitch batting practice on occasion to the Mets pitchers.[16]

Zabriskie announced for the Mets on WOR-TV for seven seasons. Some Mets games were also broadcast on cable television during those years. Zabriskie was not part of the cable-TV team, making way for Fran Healy. After the 1989 season, Zabriskie wanted to cut back from calling about 110 games a year and constantly being away from his family in Orlando, Florida.[17] ESPN had just signed to do major-league baseball and Zabriskie joined the cable channel, on which he would generally work one game a week.[18] *The Sporting News* described his departure from the Mets as "an amicable split," and noted that Zabriskie would continue to run the Mets winter fantasy camp.[19] (The paper wrote that the Mets "were unable to find a replacement" for Zabriskie and would go with the two-man team of Kiner and McCarver in 1990.)[20]

Zabriskie's 1986 season was not without a tinge of controversy. On September 17, in what turned out to be the division-clinching game, Zabriskie was doing the play-by-play. (Rusty Staub was doing the commentary.) With two outs in the ninth inning and the Mets leading, Zabriskie said, "These Mets fans have waited for this, really, for the better part of three seasons, ever since the '84 campaign when the Mets became a contender, and they are ready to bust loose in more ways than one." Then came the final play of the game, a groundout to second base. After excitedly announcing "a ground ball to second, Backman to Hernandez," Zabriskie said the word "The," followed by an awkward pause and then "unbelievable season is not over but the championship is here in New York," before uttering his memorable phrase: "The inevitable has finally become a reality."[21]

Some fans were critical of Zabriskie's pause and for not immediately coming up with a stronger "call" at the moment that the Mets had clinched the NL East title.[22] Zabriskie later apologized on the air, indicating that he was sorry if he had disappointed anyone with the way he made the final call of the historic game.[23] Zabriskie had at least one influential advocate: the *New York Times.* Commenting that having five broadcasters (Kiner, McCarver, Zabriskie, Staub, and Healy) is "too many," the *Times* praised the skills of Kiner and McCarver, and wrote that "[t]he best of the rest is Steve Zabriskie . . .. He has a strong voice, a laugh that rumbles like a freight train in the night, which is to say, pleasantly, and a quick wit, often aimed at himself. (His hair and weight seem to give him trouble, as well as a source of humor.) Each year, he exhibits a little more certainty about his role"[24]

Speaking to the author, Zabriskie said he had "so many memories" that it was hard to single out one in particular as the most memorable. But he said his most "overriding" memory was of games he did not broadcast—the League Championship Series between the Mets and the Houston Astros, with its intensity and "unrelenting pressure." In his 30 years in baseball, he said, the 1986 LCS stood out as one of his "greatest experiences." He was not on the broadcast team for the national network telecast, but did do pregame and postgame shows on WOR. Zabriskie vividly recalled Mike Scott's dominance of the Mets and the "multiple games going into extra innings," including Game Six, which the Mets won in 16 innings, tying the game with three runs in the ninth inning and then, after going ahead with three runs in the top of the 16th, holding on as the Astros' two-run rally in the bottom of the inning fell short.

Besides the leaders of the 1986 team –Keith Hernandez, Gary Carter, Dwight Gooden, and Darryl Strawberry—Zabriskie credited Ray Knight and Kevin Mitchell with making a "huge difference" in the Mets' success, especially their "tremendous contributions in the clubhouse," their "professionalism," their "quiet leadership," and their "intangible qualities."[25]

After ending his broadcasting career in 1997, Zabriskie retired to Orlando, where he lived for nearly 25 years, from 1984 until 2008, before moving to Santa Rosa, California where he resided as of 2015. He and his first wife, Lynne, raised three daughters. Lynne died of cancer in 2009 after a 4½-year battle with the disease. In 2014 Zabriskie remarried, he and his wife, Linda, combining (as of 2015) to have seven children and nine grandchildren.[26]

Zabriskie launched a second career focused on a desire to help others. He became an ordained minister in the Church of Jesus Christ and became actively engaged in volunteer work on behalf of the church.[27] In 1998 he wrote a book, *Be a Hitter... A Young Player's Guide to the Winning Art of Hitting.*[28] While still working as a broadcaster, Zabriskie ventured into several business interests. He was the president of Separation Technology Inc., a medical products business based in Florida, from 1988 until he sold the business in 1995.[29] In the early 1990s Zabriskie owned a New York Mets fantasy camp near his home in Orlando.[30] Beginning in 1995, and until his wife took ill in 2005, he ran his own management consulting firm, Business & Financial Consultants LLC, also based in Florida.[31] In 2011 Zabriskie joined the New York Life insurance company and as of 2015 was a partner in New York Life's office, in Santa Rosa, California.[32]

Zabriskie briefly returned to his broadcasting career in 2008. Although he had not worked in radio since 1971, his ailing wife wanted "to hear his voice again [on the radio]." Zabriskie became the morning news announcer for KZST-FM radio in Santa Rosa and kept the job until 2010.[33]

When Mets fans think of the team's announcers over the years, names like Lindsey Nelson, Bob Murphy, Ralph Kiner, Gary Cohen, Keith Hernandez and Ron Darling come to mind before one thinks of Steve Zabriskie. But in the memorable 1986 season, it was Steve Zabriskie who called the Mets games on their flagship TV station and who, as such, will always be part of the history of the New York Mets.

SOURCES

In addition to the sources cited in the notes, the author also consulted:

Mets.com, the Official Site of the New York Mets. nymets.mlb.com/nym/history/broadcasters.jsp.

"Questions for Steve Zabriskie," The Crane Pool Forum, archives. cranepoolforum.net/1600fl_tl642.shtml.

NOTES

1 Steve Zabriskie, telephone interview, October 16, 2015 (hereafter Zabriskie interview).

2 Zabriskie interview.

3 Zabriskie interview.

4 Zabriskie interview.

5 Zabriskie interview.

6 Zabriskie interview.

7 ESPN Advertisement, *The Sporting New,* July 2, 1980.

8 *Internet Movie Database*, imdb.com.

9 Zabriskie interview.

10 "I70 Baseball," i70baseball.com/2011/p2102/mccarver-shannon-vie-for-frick-award.

11 Zabriskie interview.

12 Zabriskie interview.

13 Ira Berkow, "Scouting: On-Job Training," *New York Times,* March 23, 1983.

14 Berkow.

15 Berkow.

16 Zabriskie interview.

17 Zabriskie interview.

18 Zabriskie interview.

19 *The Sporting News,* October 23, 1989.

20 *The Sporting News,* March 19, 1990.

21 "Twenty Five Years Ago Mets Clinch NL East", video of last play of clinching game available on StudiousMetsimus, studiousmetsimus.blog.spot.com/2011/09/25-years-ago-mets-clinch-nl-east.html.

22 "Share Your Memories of Steve Zabriskie," The Ultimate Mets Database, ultimatemets.com, ultimatemets.com/profile.php?PlayerCode=6592.

23 "Share Your Memories of Steve Zabriskie"; Zabriskie interview.

24 Michael Goodwin, "Fine Year in Mets' Broadcast Booth, Too," *New York Times*, October 2, 1986.

25 Zabriskie interview.

26 Zabriskie interview.

27 Zabriskie interview.

28 *Be a Hitter ...* A *Young Player's Guide to the Winning Art of Hitting,* listed on Amazon.com.

29 Zabriskie interview; Profile of Steve Zabriskie on *LinkedIn* Separation Technology Inc. website, separationtechnology.com.

30 Jill Cousins, "Mets Fantasy Camp Turns Back the Clock," *Orlando Sentinel,* January 27, 1991.

31 Zabriskie interview; Profile of Steve Zabriskie on *LinkedIn.*

32 Zabriskie interview; Profile of Steve Zabriskie on *LinkedIn*; New York Life Northern California Office website, northerncalifornia.nyloffices.com/Management-Team.3.htm.

33 Zabriskie interview.

APRIL 30, 1986

NEW YORK METS 8, ATLANTA BRAVES 1, AT ATLANTA-FULTON COUNTY STADIUM

By Irv Goldfarb

DWIGHT GOODEN CALLED IT HIS "WORST game in a long time. 'I embarrassed myself,' said Doc. 'I couldn't pitch, I couldn't hit, I couldn't field.'"[1] He also had trouble controlling his curve. But none of that mattered. When the New York Mets walked off the field at Atlanta-Fulton County Stadium after their game on April 30 1986, they were the owners of an 11-game winning streak, the longest in the National League since the Philadelphia Phillies had done the same during their pennant-winning season of 1983. It also matched the streak the Mets posted during their world championship season of 1969 and accomplished again three seasons later. Their 13-3 record for the month of April was the hottest start in Mets history.

With the 11 straight wins, the swagger the '86 Mets became known for began to show as well: Back in spring training, "(A) couple of our guys said, 'Wouldn't it be something if we got off like the Tigers did?'" recalled backup third baseman Howard Johnson, a member of that iconic Detroit team that rocketed to a 35-5 start in 1984 and coasted to the AL pennant and the World Series championship.[2]

This was a memorable week in professional sports: Just the night before, Roger Clemens had struck out 20 Seattle Mariners at a raucous Fenway Park; and on the night of this game, rookie defenseman Steve Smith of the NHL's Edmonton Oilers had knocked the puck off goaltender Grant Fuhr's skate and into his own goal to give the Calgary Flames a Game Seven division-final victory, temporarily stalling the Edmonton Stanley Cup dynasty at two. But in New York, it was the NL East standings that dominated the back pages.

When their streak began on April 18 against Philadelphia, the Mets, five games into the new season, had been 2½ games behind St. Louis and only a game ahead of the last-place Cubs. But a three-game sweep at home of the Phillies, then two straight over the Pirates at Shea Stadium were followed by a rare four-game road sweep of the Cardinals. A 10-5 victory over the Braves the night before had made it 10 in a row.

The 8-1 victory over Atlanta for number 11 began the way many Mets games did that season, with New York jumping on right-hander Joe Johnson in the first inning. Leadoff hitter Lenny Dykstra bunted his way on, stole second and third and, after Wally Backman walked, scored on a single by first baseman Keith Hernandez.

When right fielder Darryl Strawberry singled in Backman, the Mets had a 2-0 lead they would not give up. The game ended with the box score showing Strawberry enjoying a 5-for-5 night, including a two-run homer and three RBIs; catcher Gary Carter adding another two-run blast that ended a personal 0-for-12 streak; and, despite his harsh self-criticism, Gooden's first career win over the Braves. He now had a winning record against every team in the league (albeit just 2-1 versus Atlanta) and a win in every ballpark in the league, though it was the start of only his third big-league season. The game was also the ninth in a row in which the team homered, one short of the team's record set in 1970 and repeated in '75.

The other dugout was not without its own story: star center fielder Dale Murphy had sliced the palm of his right hand the night before, running into the outfield wall while chasing a ball hit by Hernandez. The cut required nine stiches and the fear was that Murphy's

NEW YORK METS TICKET ORDER FORM
NUMBER OF TICKETS

GAME DATE	BOX $9.50	RESERVED $8.00	TOTAL AMOUNT
Add $1.00 Postage and Handling			$ 1.00
TOTAL AMOUNT ENCLOSED			$

Name
Organization
Address
City
State Zip
Phone
Credit Card #
Expiration Date
Signature

MAKE CHECK OR MONEY ORDER PAYABLE TO NEW YORK METS AND MAIL TO:
METS TICKET DEPT.
SHEA STADIUM
FLUSHING NY 11368

EASY WAYS TO BUY METS TICKETS IN ADVANCE

ADVANCED TICKET WINDOW AT SHEA STADIUM
126 St. and Roosevelt Ave., near Gate D
Hours: Mon.-Fri. 8-6, Sat., Sun. & Holidays 9-5

ALL TICKETRON outlets 212-399-4444

TELETRON TELEPHONE CREDIT CARD RESERVATIONS
(212) 947-5850 (201) 343-4200 MC, V, AMEX
(914) 681-0365 (516) 794-2560 (203) 777-7920

BY MAIL WITH ATTACHED ORDER FORM
Be sure to specify game date(s) and number of tickets desired. Enclose check or money order payable to New York Mets or indicate credit card number (MC, V or AMEX)

We Make Your Singles Double And Triple.
MANUFACTURERS HANOVER
The Financial Source™ Worldwide.
Member FDIC

*1986 PROMOTION DATES

Opening Day (All)	Monday, April 14
Opening Day II (All)	Wednesday, April 16
Snapper Calendar Weekend (All)	Saturday & Sunday April 19 & 20
Starter Wrist Band Day (14 & under)	Saturday, May 10
SiDARi Mother's Day Tote Bag (16 & Older)	Sunday, May 11
Kool Aid Baseball Glove Night (14 & under)	Saturday, May 31
BabyRuth & Butterfinger Cap Day (All)	Sunday, June 1
Sports Bag Day (All)	Saturday, June 14
Emerson Banner Day	Sunday, June 15
Kahn's Meats Kids Jersey Day (14 & under)	Sunday, June 22
Kool Aid Fireworks Night (All)	Thursday, July 3
MHT 25th Anniversary Cap Night (All)	Saturday, July 5
Equitable 25th Anniversary Oldtimers' Day (All)	Saturday, July 12
Back to School Day (14 & Under)	Monday, September 1
Snapper Umbrella Day (15 & Older)	Saturday, September 6
Purolator Fan Appreciation Ski Cap Day (All)	Sunday, September 21

For Ticket Information – Call (718) 507-TIXX

1962 Mets 1986
25th ANNIVERSARY
'86 OFFICIAL SCHEDULE

Courtesy of Bob Brady.

676-game streak, which had begun on September 25, 1981, would be broken.

But Murphy refused to stay off the field ("It wasn't like it was amputated," he declared[3]) and pinch-hit for Johnson in the fifth, hammering a home run off Gooden. It was the first earned run off the right-hander in 16 innings and was the first hit Murphy had collected off Gooden in eight plate appearances. "He wanted it, I guess," conceded Gooden, who ended the night with a 4-0 record and a neat 1.26 ERA.

Strawberry ended up batting .372 during the stretch, belting three homers and driving in 13 runs. The 11-game winning streak during the last two weeks of April catapulted the Mets into first place in the National League East, five games ahead of the Montreal Expos. It was a lead they would not relinquish for the rest of the season.

"It's not something you think about when you're playing," said Howard Johnson while comparing the Mets' hot start to that of his former team, the 1984 Tigers. "But when you see the standings, you might think about it."[4]

The streak ended the next night when the Braves hit four home runs off Mets pitcher Rick Aguilera in a 7-2 victory. Then the Mets proceeded to win another seven in a row.

SOURCES

In addition to the sources cited in the notes, the author also consulted:

Noble, Marty. "Murphy's Injury Will End Streak," *Newsday*, April 30, 1986.

"Gooden Now 2-1 Against Atlanta," *New York Times*, May 1, 1986.

NOTES

1 Marty Noble, "11 and Counting," *Newsday*, May 1, 1986.

2 Marty Noble, "Hojo Knows What It Takes," *Newsday*, May 1, 1986.

3 "11 and Counting."

4 "Hojo Knows What It Takes."

A FIGHTING MATTER: DARLING WHIFFS 12 IN COMPLETE-GAME VICTORY MARRED BY BRAWL

MAY 27, 1986: NEW YORK METS 8, LOS ANGELES DODGERS 1, AT SHEA STADIUM

By Gregory H. Wolf

THE NEW YORK METS WERE IN A BAD MOOD. After bolting out of the gate and looking seemingly invincible with a 20-4 record to start the 1986 season, they had appeared all too human, posting just a 6-5 record on their recently concluded 11-game road trip. Manager Davey Johnson, in his third season as the club's pilot, hoped the nine-game homestand would cure whatever ills had befallen his club, which occupied first place in the NL East with a major-league best 27-11 record. The homestand began with a three-game set against the Los Angeles Dodgers on Tuesday, May 27. The Dodgers were playing their best ball of the young season. Victorious in 8 of their last 11 games, skipper Tom Lasorda's team had evened its record (22-22), which was good enough for only fifth place in the competitive NL West.

Toeing the rubber for the Mets was 25-year-old right-hander Ron Darling, whom Craig Wolff of the *New York Times* described as "present[ing] perhaps the Mets biggest melodrama."[1] The good-looking hurler from Hawaii had a career record of 34-18 in parts of four seasons, including a 5-0 start in 1986; however, the New York media had reported on his supposedly contentious relationship with his oftimes prickly manager. "I don't have a feud with Ronnie," said Johnson. "Maybe I expect too much out of him."[2] Even little squabbles could be blown up in Gotham, where Mets fans starved for their first division crown since the "you gotta believe" club in 1973. "I don't pay any attention to what Davey says about me," said Darling somewhat nonchalantly. "It's not like a new thing. He does it because I can do better."[3]

For decades the Dodgers had cultivated a feel-good, all-American reputation, but they were on edge, too. Prior to their game against the Mets, a clubhouse fight broke out between All-Star second baseman Steve Sax and his double-play partner, first sacker Greg Brock. Tom Niedenfuer, a stout 6-foot-5 relief pitcher, who was officially listed at 225 pounds, but might have been 25 pounds heavier, stepped in to break up the brouhaha. Sax and Brock downplayed the altercation and assumed the role of church choirboys to the national media. "We grew up together, came up through the system together," said Brock. "We go a long way back."[4]

Los Angeles threw the proverbial first punch of the game when Ken Landreaux parked a one-out offering by Darling in the stands for his third round-tripper of the season, giving the Dodgers a 1-0 lead and hushing the partisan crowd of 35,643. The Dodgers' starting pitcher, 29-year-old right-hander Bob Welch, with a 96-67 career record, including 3-3 in '86, mowed down the first nine batters he faced. The Mets tied the game in the fourth when Gary Carter hit a sacrifice fly to right field to drive in Wally Backman.

Darling and Welch did their best Seaver and Koufax impressions by recording all six outs via strikeouts in the fifth inning. Darling had whiffed the side in the third, as well, and with eight punchouts through five innings had already exceeded his previous season high of five.

Depending on one's perspective, the sixth inning was either memorable or forgetful. The first five Mets collected hits off Welch. Backman doubled down the right-field line to drive in Lenny Dykstra and Carter singled to short right-center to plate Backman and increase the Mets' lead to 3-1. Danny Heep, starting in right field in place of slugger Darryl Strawberry (sidelined with sprained ligaments in his left thumb), singled to load the bases and send Welch to the showers.

Tom Niedenfuer, fresh off his pregame domestic peace-keeping mission, replaced Welch to face 37-year-old George Foster. In his 18th and final big-league season, the five-time All-Star with his trademark sideburns was no longer the home-run threat that he had been with the Big Red Machine, for whom he belted 52 and 40 round-trippers to lead the NL respectively, in 1977 and 1978; however, he was in the right situation at the most opportune time. Niedenfuer, making his 21st appearance of the season, had been struggling with the long ball, and had yielded five homers in just 27 innings. "It took just one quick turn on a fast-ball thrown across the letters," wrote Craig Wolff, to change the tenor of the game.[5] On an 0-and-1 count, Foster clouted one over the 388-foot sign in left field for the 13th and final grand slam of his career, and gave the Mets a seemingly insurmountable 7-1 lead. The strikeout-prone, right-handed hitting Foster was originally not scheduled to start against the righty Welch, but Johnson had made a lineup change at the last minute. "I guess it was good I played," said Foster after the game.[6]

Foster's hit, wrote Craig Wolff, "turned a cool quiet evening at Shea Stadium into a rollicking, explosive affair."[7] With his next pitch, Niedenfuer hit Ray Knight on the left forearm. Knight, whose wife, professional golfer Nancy Lopez, had given birth to a child the previous day, was a former Golden Gloves boxer with a chiseled 185 pounds on a 6-foot-1 frame.[8] "I charged the mound," said Knight. "He [Niedenfuer] tried to tackle me. Then I hit the ground—people were scratching at my face, so I started swinging again."[9] A benches-clearing brawl ensued with players coming together in one large rugby-like scrum. When order was finally restored, neither Knight nor Niedenfuer was ejected, drawing the wrath of Lasorda. "I felt he threw at me," explained Knight after the game. "I've always had the philosophy that I would never charge the mound unless I knew for sure."[10] Niedenfuer, who had hit only one batter in 106⅓ innings of work in '85, denied throwing at Knight. The pitch to Foster was "not where I wanted it to be, and neither was the one to Knight," he said.[11] After Foster's smash, Niedenfuer yielded a single to Rafael Santana and misplayed Darling's bunt to load the bases, and his night was over. Reliever Ed Vande Berg got out of the jam by retiring Dykstra on a short fly to center, and then induced Backman to hit into an inning-ending double play.

Through all of the chaos, Darling kept his cool on the mound, but was not surprised by the brawl. "Whenever someone hits a grand slam to more or less put the game out of reach, you can anticipate something like this happening," he said. "Being a pitcher, I can understand what's going through Niedenfuer's mind. I know I was the first one off the bench."[12] Darling quashed a mini-rally by the Dodgers in the seventh (runners on first and second with one out) by fanning Franklin Stubbs and dispatching Mariano Duncan on a grounder to short. Darling benefited from yet another run of support when Keith Hernandez led off the seventh with his third home run of the season to give the Mets an 8-1 lead. Typically regarded as a finesse pitcher, unlike his hard-throwing teammates Dwight Gooden and Sid Fernandez, Darling recorded his 11th and 12th punch outs in the final frame sandwiched around a one-out double by Steve Nicosia. He induced Stubbs to ground out to second for the last out of the game and tied a team record with his sixth consecutive victory to start a season.

"I think I've had just as good stuff in other games, but today I got ahead of hitters," said Darling, whose curveball and split-finger fastballs mesmerized Dodger hitters, eight of whom were rung up looking.[13] His 12 strikeouts tied a career high, and it was the third of eight times in his 13-year career (364 starts) that he whiffed at least 10 batters. Darling often struggled with control, leading the NL with 114 walks in '85, but issued only two free passes while recording his first complete game of the season.

With the victory the Mets moved to 28-11, and two games later completed the three-game sweep against the Dodgers behind Gooden's complete-game five-hitter with 10 strikeouts and Fernandez's four-hitter over eight strong frames.

NOTES

1 Craig Wolff, "Slam by Foster Powers Mets," *New York Times*, May 28, 1986: A19.

2 Ibid.

3 Ibid.

4 Sun News Services, "Dodgers do some swinging in New York. Brawls mars L.A.'s 8-1 loss to Mets," *San Bernardino County* (California) *Sun*, May 28, 1986: C1.

5 Wolff.

6 Ibid.

7 Ibid.

8 Lou Rabito, UPI, "Game marred by Melee: Mets Clip LA, 8-1," *Daily Herald* (Tyrone, Pennsylvania), May 29, 1986: 5.

9 Ben Walker, AP, "Mets Explosion Wins Fight Fight-Marred Game," *Daily Sitka* (Alaska) *Sentinel*, May 28, 1986: 8.

10 Sun News Services, "Dodgers do some swinging."

11 Ibid.

12 Ibid.

13 Ibid.

METS BRAWL AND BASH BRAVES AS FERNANDEZ TOSSES TWO-HITTER AND CARTER CRANKS TWO HOMERS

JULY 11, 1986: NEW YORK METS 11, ATLANTA BRAVES 0, AT SHEA STADIUM

By Gregory H. Wolf

THE 1986 METS LED THE NL IN SCORING, but pitching was the club's backbone. The staff was anchored by four legitimate All-Stars, right-handers Dwight Gooden and Ron Darling, and southpaws Sid Fernandez and Bob Ojeda, each of whom won at least 15 games, logged in excess of 200 innings pitched, and had a winning percentage of .714. Though Gooden, coming off a phenomenal season in 1985 with 24 wins and a 1.53 ERA, garnered most of the media's attention, Fernandez, the stocky Hawaiian affectionately known as "El Sid," tossed the team's best game of the season as the Mets pulled out all of the punches.

Skipper Davey Johnson's Mets were in a bad mood as they prepared to play a four-game set with the Atlanta Braves heading into the All-Star break. They had just been swept by player-manager Pete Rose's Cincinnati Reds in a three-game set at Shea Stadium, and had lost four of five games. Ojeda ended the team's hitherto longest losing streak of the season by tossing a seven-hitter to beat Atlanta in the first game, but the club was out to prove that its hot start was no fluke. The Mets (56-25) led the NL East by 10½ games. Chuck Tanner, in his first season as Atlanta's pilot, had his club playing inspired ball. Coming off a 96-loss season in '85, the Braves had been four games above .500 on July 3 before losses in six of seven games dropped them to 42-43, in fourth place in the NL West.

Enjoying a breakout season, Sid Fernandez entered the game tied with the Dodgers' Fernando Valenzuela and the Phillies' Shane Rawley for the NL lead in victories with 11. The Mets had high expectations for the 23-year-old hurler, acquired in a trade with Los Angeles in December 1983. After an early season call-up in 1985, Fernandez won six of his final nine decisions and led the NL in fewest hits allowed (5.7) and most strikeouts (9.7) per nine innings. "I don't think we're as surprised as Joe Fan is [about Fernandez's success]," said Mets pitching coach Mel Stottlemyre. "After last year, several people thought he had a chance to win 20. Maybe we're surprised with the consistency of the stuff he's had, but we're not surprised he's won 11."[1]

Like many left-handers, Fernandez sometimes struggled with his control despite a robust 2.89 ERA in 109 innings. He had issued at least five walks in six of his 16 starts thus far in '86. Ken Griffey (not yet known as Senior), drew a two-out walk in the first and stole second, but the hard-throwing Fernandez whiffed sluggers Dale Murphy and Bob Horner to end the inning.

The Mets wasted no time attacking David Palmer, a 28-year-old right-hander who entered the game with a 5-7 record (3.17 ERA) and a 43-33 record in parts of seven big-league seasons. After Lenny Dykstra drew a leadoff walk, Wally Backman beat out a drag bunt by evading first baseman Horner's diving tag. Both runners moved up on Keith Hernandez's groundout. Gary Carter, the Mets' inspirational team leader and Palmer's former teammate with the Montreal Expos, clouted a home run to deep left field, sending the partisan crowd of 39,924 into a loud, raucous standing ovation. A fan favorite, Carter came out of the dugout for a customary curtain call. According to *New York Times* sportswriter Joseph Durso, he "raised his fist" triumphantly to the crowd.[2]

Some fans in the vibrating stadium probably knew what was coming. With his next pitch, Palmer plunked Darryl Strawberry in the back. "Without hesitating," wrote Durso, "[Strawberry] ran straight to the mound," while Palmer flung his glove at the charging batter as the benches emptied.[3] The Braves catcher, Ozzie Virgil, tackled Strawberry while several players subdued Palmer. No punches were landed, and after a few minutes order was restored. Neither Strawberry nor Palmer was ejected. "They act as though they won the seventh game of the World Series," said Palmer after the game. I told Keith Hernandez when we were scuffling around: I don't care if you hit 15 home runs, but don't show me up."[4] On a team with a tough-guy attitude that never shied away from a brawl, Strawberry had no apologies. "You have to protect yourself," he said. "When a guy hits you, then stares at you, what are you supposed to do?"[5] Palmer didn't find any support from his former batterymate either. "I was his catcher for six years in Montreal," said Carter. "He was frustrated and he took it out on Strawberry."[6]

Palmer regained his composure to retire the next two batters, but his evening only got worse. The Braves failed to take advantage of Terry Harper's leadoff single in the second when Fernandez sandwiched two more punchouts around an infield popup. In the bottom of the second, with Fernandez on first via an infield single, Backman lined a two-out, seeing-eye single to move the stout, 6-foot-1, 225-pound hurler to third. Backman took second on Palmer's wild pitch and the bases were loaded after Hernandez walked. Up stepped Carter. "The Kid" sent an 0-and-2 pitch over the left-field fence for his 10th of 11 career grand slams to give the Mets a 7-0 lead. And just as he did an inning earlier, Carter made another curtain call, doffing his cap as the Mets faithful stood and cheered. His seven RBIs were a career high, and one off the Mets' record, set by Dave Kingman in 1976.

The Mets waited an inning to slug reliever Craig McMurtry, who struck out Strawberry to end the second. In the bottom of the third with Ray Knight on third via a triple and Kevin Mitchell occupying first on a walk, it was Fernandez's turn to take a swing. He belted a double down the left-field line, driving in Knight and making it 8-0. Dykstra followed with another double, driving in two more. After Hernandez walked, Carter blasted what looked like his third straight home run, to deep center field, but Dale Murphy ran it down for the last out of the frame. McMurtry was there to take one for the team and eat some innings. In the fourth Knight knocked in the Mets' 11th and final run on a single, driving in Strawberry, who had reached first on an error by shortstop Andres Thomas.

Staked to an insurmountable lead, Fernandez baffled the Braves with his assortment of fastballs, hard and slow curves, and changeups. He had a peculiar, deceptive delivery in which he hid the ball behind his back and drove to the mound in a long stride. After yielding his second hit, in the third inning (a double by Thomas), Fernandez hurled 6⅔ hitless innings. He had a hiccup in the eighth when he issued a leadoff walk to Ken Oberkfell and hit Ted Simmons with two outs. Perhaps Fernandez was still a little winded after legging out a double down the left-field line to lead off the seventh. He tossed a 1-2-3 ninth to complete the game in 2 hours and 39 minutes.

New York "brutalized" the Braves, opined Durso, as El Sid fanned nine and walked three in his first of nine career shutouts and five career two-hitters in 300 starts, and also collected a career-best three hits.[7] (He never threw a one-hitter or no-hitter). Described as the "ace of the brilliant Met staff," Fernandez was arguably the hottest pitcher in the league.[8] He won his career-best seventh consecutive start in a dominating stretch during which he crafted a 1.76 ERA and held opponents to a .182 batting average. Earlier in the week Fernandez became the first Hawaiian-born athlete in any US sports league to be named an All-Star when Whitey Herzog selected him to his first of two straight NL All-Star squads, joining teammates and starters Carter, Hernandez, and Strawberry, as well as Gooden. It was widely believed that Fernandez would get the starting nod, but that honor went to Gooden, whose 10-4 record and 2.77 ERA was impressive in its own right.

The Mets took the next two games from the Braves (10-1 and 2-0) to sweep the series and conclude a weekend of festivities, which included an old-timers' reunion prior to the game on Saturday, and a celebration for Rusty Staub on Sunday, to commemorate their 25th season. As of 2015, the Mets' 59-25 record at the All-Star break was the best in club history.

NOTES

1 Malcolm Moran, "Fernandez Works on 'Longevity,'" *New York Times*, July 8, 1986: B9.

2 Joseph Durso, "Mets Win on Fernandez's 2-Hitter," *New York Times*, July 12, 1986: 45.

3 Ibid.

4 Ibid.

5 Don Hafner, "National League Roundup. Carter Hits 2 Homers, including Grand Slam," *Los Angeles Times*, July 12, 1986.

6 Durso.

7 Ibid.

8 Hafner.

METS WIN EXTRA-INNING SLUGFEST VIA BRAWL AND HOME RUN

JULY 22, 1986: NEW YORK METS 6, CINCINNATI REDS 3 AT RIVERFRONT STADIUM

by Michael Huber

RODNEY DANGERFIELD IS CREDITED WITH saying, "I went to a fight the other night, and a hockey game broke out."[1] If we replace *hockey* with *baseball*, we could get an idea of what happened in Cincinnati on July 22, 1986. In what he termed "the strangest game I've ever been in,"[2] New York Mets manager Davey Johnson piloted his team to a 6-3 victory over the Cincinnati Reds before 23,707 fans, in a game that included a bench-clearing brawl, several ejections, and two Mets pitchers playing musical chairs. Johnson juggled his players on a carousel trying to cover positions and pitch to Reds batters. The slugfest actually had a few long fly balls, including a Howard Johnson home run with two aboard in the top of the 14th for the win.

Bob Ojeda took to the mound for the visiting Mets, with Scott Terry as the Reds' starting pitcher. Each team had two hits but no runs through the first two innings. In the bottom of the third, Terry helped his own cause and singled to left. He moved to second on a sacrifice. With two outs, Dave Parker crushed his 21st home run of the season, giving Cincinnati a 2-0 lead. Rafael Santana led off New York's half of the fifth inning with a walk. Ojeda tried to sacrifice him to second, but first baseman Tony Perez fielded the bunt and gunned down Santana at second, putting the Mets pitcher on at first. Lenny Dykstra tripled to the gap in right-center and Ojeda scored. Wally Backman hit a grounder to second and Cincinnati's Ron Oester threw home, nailing Dykstra at the plate and preserving the 2-1 lead. In the bottom half of the fifth, Kal Daniels pinch-hit for Terry and singled up the middle, but he was picked off at first by Ojeda. That proved to be a crucial lapse by Daniels because one out later, Buddy Bell connected for his sixth home run of the season, restoring the Reds' two-run cushion.

In the sixth inning New York's Darryl Strawberry led off and argued a called third strike with umpire Gerry Davis, who sent the Mets outfielder to the showers. Kevin Mitchell replaced him in right field. Tim Teufel hit for Backman in the seventh, using yet another position player for New York. From the sixth through the ninth, New York used three relievers (Rick Anderson, Randy Myers, and Doug Sisk).

In the top of the ninth, still trailing by two runs, Davey Johnson brought in Howard Johnson as a pinch-hitter for Santana. Johnson struck out, but the ball bounced off the glove of catcher Bo Diaz, and Johnson ran for first base, kicking the ball in the process. Reds pitcher Ron Robinson scooped up the ball and fired to first, but Johnson appeared to be running out of the baseline and the ball hit him in the back. Safe at first. Reds coach Billy DeMars raced out to argue and after some heated exchanges he was ejected by home-plate umpire Davis. Mookie Wilson, who had entered the game as a defensive replacement in the eighth inning, then grounded into a 4-3 double play. New York was down to its final out trailing 3-1. Dykstra worked Robinson for a walk. Teufel doubled to deep center, and Dykstra pulled up at third, playing it safe because his run would not decide anything. Reds skipper Pete Rose then walked to the mound and called for a double switch: He brought in closer John Franco from the bullpen and signaled for Sal Butera to catch for Diaz (the pitcher's position would be up third in the bottom of the ninth). Franco faced Keith Hernandez, who lifted a fly ball to the warning track in right field. Dave Parker waited under the ball, only to have it pop out of his glove for a two-run error (both runs unearned). The game was suddenly tied, and both teams had to consider extra innings. Five more extra innings.

The Mets had two walks and a single in the top of the 10th, but Franco scattered three strikeouts, the last with the bases loaded, to get out of the jam. In the bottom of the inning, Rose pinch-hit himself for Franco, setting up "the main event."[3] He singled off the Mets' fifth pitcher of the game, Jesse Orosco, and then pulled himself from the game for pinch-runner Eric Davis. Davis stole second, his 46th swipe of the season. On the next pitch, he took off for third and easily beat the throw from catcher Gary Carter for steal number 47. As Davis popped up from his slide, a pushing match began between him and third baseman Ray Knight. Said Knight: "When he elbowed me, I said to him, 'What's your problem?' He said, 'You pushed me.' We had hit each other solidly, but I knew he had the base. I'm at peace with myself about it. I don't like to fight with anybody, but I felt threatened."[4] Words and punches were exchanged and both benches cleared. The brawl delay lasted for 16 minutes.[5] Dave Parker told reporters after the game that the fight "was triggered by Knight. He pushed Davis off the base. That's the second time in this series that it's happened, and both times it was at third base with him. He was aggressive, and Eric just reacted."[6] Davey Johnson said, "I want to say we show a lot of fight, but that's not what I mean. We're hard competitors, but we're not malicious. We don't like people to cuss us, and that's what Davis did. That's what caused tempers to flare."[7]

After the game, instead of "laughing over the lunacy of the game,"[8] Mets players resented the fact that George Foster had not left the bench to participate in the brawl. Manager Johnson decided to not use Foster as part of his left-field platoon, and within weeks Foster was no longer with the team. When the dust settled and all the gloves and caps were picked up, four players had been ejected (Knight and Mitchell of the Mets and Davis and Mario Soto of the Reds). Cincinnati pitcher Tom Browning came on to run for Davis at third (remember, Davis was safe). Davey Johnson put catcher Gary Carter in at third replacing Knight,[9] and Ed Hearn went in to catch. Johnson also moved Orosco to right field to replace Mitchell, and summoned Roger McDowell to pitch. At this point, there was no one else to play for the Mets. The Mets manager noted, "I'm out of pitchers, and I'm out of extra players."[10] The only players left in the dugout were starting pitchers Dwight Gooden, Ron Darling, and Sid Fernandez. McDowell retired Wade Rowdon on a groundout to second to end the inning and extend the game into the 11th.

In the 11th, Cincinnati's Tony Perez singled and moved to second on a sacrifice. With two outs, Orosco and McDowell switched positions — Orosco returned to the mound and McDowell replaced him in right field. The strategy succeeded when Orosco struck out the Reds' Max Venable. In the 12th, after the Reds' Buddy Bell reached on an infield hit with nobody out, McDowell and Mookie Wilson changed positions; Wilson moving to center field and McDowell to right. After the switch, Orosco gave up another hit, but got out of the inning on a bunt that turned into a double play, and a fly ball.

In the bottom of the 13th McDowell returned to the mound and Orosco went to right field. With one out, Cincinnati's Perez hit a line drive to right field. Center fielder Dykstra couldn't reach the ball, so Orosco had to make the play. "I squeezed it so hard, the stuffing could have come out," he said after the game.[11]

In the top of the 14th inning, Hearn led off with a double to right center. Right fielder Orosco walked and reliever Ted Power struck out pitcher McDowell, bringing up Howard Johnson, who sent a pitch from Power over the right-field wall for a three-run home run. McDowell then retired the Reds on three groundouts to preserve the win.

Both Orosco and McDowell had entered the game in the bottom of the 10th inning as pitchers. McDowell then played right field, moved to left field, and returned to the mound for the last two innings. Orosco also pitched in the 10th, went to right field, pitched again, and returned to right field. In the 12th and 14th innings the Mets had pitchers Orosco and McDowell batting back-to-back. In the 12th, Orosco was the guy on the mound and McDowell was in right field, and in the 14th, Orosco was in right and McDowell was on the hill. Orosco had pitched two innings and McDowell three after the regulation nine innings.

In the losing cause, the Reds had left 11 men on base; the Mets had stranded 16 runners. The Mets' victory increased their lead in the National League East to 14 games, their largest margin of the season to that date.

SOURCES

In addition to the sources mentioned in the notes, the author consulted baseball-reference.com and retrosheet.org.

NOTES

1 brainyquote.com/quotes/quotes/r/rodneydang100124.html.

2 "Mets Win on Clout in 14; Four Ejected After Brawl," *New York Times*, July 23, 1986.

3 Shane Tourtellotte, "Baseball's craziest game?" hardballtimes.com/baseballs-craziest-game/.

4 *New York Times.*

5 You can watch the action on a YouTube video (youtube.com/watch?v=jQLZaVIXFJM).

6 *New York Times.*

7 Ibid.

8 Tourtellotte.

9 Carter had brief experience, having played third base in one inning in a 1975 game for the Montreal Expos.

10 *New York Times.*

11 Tourtellotte.

SEPTEMBER 4, 1986: NEW YORK METS 7, BOSTON RED SOX 3, AT FENWAY PARK

PRELUDE TO A CLASSIC (CHARITY GAME FOR JIMMY FUND OF DANA-FARBER CANCER INSTITUTE)

By Saul Wisnia

LOOKING BACK ON IT NOW, IT WAS SOMEthing akin to a 1972 moviegoer watching the final scene of *The Godfather* and immediately thinking, "I hope they make another one." Sequels were not commonplace then, but it seemed everyone wanted to see more of Michael Corleone and his trigger-happy family.

So it was with the September 4 exhibition game played between the first-place Mets of the National League East and the first-place Red Sox of the American League East. Billed as a possible World Series preview, the game captured the public's attention and drew a near-sellout crowd of 33,057 to Fenway Park despite having no bearing on the standings. In the days before interleague play, it was a chance for players and fans of both clubs to see each other up close, savor the moment, and dream of a Boston-vs.-New York showdown in October.[1]

This was a contest 19 months in the waiting. The Red Sox and Mets announced in February 1985 that they would play a pair of charity exhibition games the next two seasons, first at Fenway and then at Shea Stadium. The Boston game in '86 would benefit the Jimmy Fund of Dana-Farber Cancer Institute, which had been the Red Sox' official charity for more than 30 years; the Flushing Meadows contest in '87 would support amateur baseball in New York.

When the announcement was made, the Mets were a team on the rise and the Red Sox one in a rebuilding mode. By the time the 1986 game came to fruition, however, both clubs were genuine championship contenders.

New York was well on its way to a 100-win season, with a 20-game lead in its division and a star-studded lineup that included five-tool outfielder Darryl Strawberry, slick-fielding, clutch-hitting first-baseman Keith Hernandez, future Hall of Fame catcher Gary Carter, and 20-year-old pitching ace and reigning Cy Young Award winner Dwight Gooden. Boston had two future Hall of Famers in third baseman Wade Boggs (en route to his third batting title) and left fielder Jim Rice (homing in on his eighth 20-homer, 100-RBI campaign), as well as an ace pitcher in Roger Clemens (20-4 on the day of the game) who would win his first of seven Cy Young Awards that year. Complementing them were top veterans like Gold Glove right fielder Dwight Evans, gritty first baseman Bill Buckner, and DH Don Baylor (like Rice, a former AL MVP).[2]

Before the game the entire roster of players on both clubs were introduced to the crowd, as if it were a postseason game. Even the travel accommodations for the visitors had a playoff feel. The Mets had flown their entire team into Boston on a chartered plane that day, along with assorted wives, club executives, and staff members—nearly 100 people in all. Red Sox fans likely got a chuckle when they heard that the Mets players' bus broke down between Logan Airport and the Sumner Tunnel, and that 10 taxicabs and additional private cars were needed to get the New York squad to Fenway. In fact, the day's MVP might have been Mets equipment manager Charlie Samuels, who flagged down an airport limousine to transport the club's 70 bags of bats and other gear to the ballpark.

Once they finally got there, New York players expressed excitement at seeing the ballpark and taking a crack at the Green Monster left-field wall. "It's awesome," said Mets reliever Roger McDowell. He spent much of the pregame snapping photos of the Monster, and said later of the 37-foot-high fence, "It's the ninth wonder of the world. I stood out there and threw balls against the wall, as though I were Carl Yastrzemski waiting for the rebound."[3]

Red Sox rookie reliever Calvin Schiraldi, a former hotshot Mets prospect who failed to live up to his promise in New York and was traded to Boston the previous November, took the high road when asked his feelings about the game. "This is good for me," said Schiraldi, who had shined as Boston's closer since a midseason call-up. "I didn't perform to my ability with the Mets. I stunk it up with them. That's why I'm glad the Red Sox gave me a chance."[4]

Some Mets were also more than willing to state for the record that they hoped to be back at Fenway again soon in contests that counted. "I'm pulling for the Red Sox," said New York third baseman Ray Knight. "I'd love to be playing the big games here. In this atmosphere."[5] Mets manager Davey Johnson, one of the few on his team with a history against the Red Sox—having spent eight seasons battling them as an Orioles second baseman from 1965 to 1972—hoped New York might have a psychological edge in the exhibition contest because its own regular-season race was all but over.

"There's been less griping about this game than any exhibition I can remember," Johnson told reporters. "First, it's against the Red Sox, the team with the best record in the American League. Second, we have a 20-game lead. A 20-game lead makes a lot of things easier. I'm sure we feel a lot better about this game than the Red Sox do."[6]

During batting practice the centers of attention had been Gooden and Clemens, as the two premier young pitchers in the game posed for cameramen behind the cage. Mets utilityman Howard Johnson fondly recalled hitting a home run off Clemens a couple years earlier while with the Tigers, but he wouldn't get a chance for a return act on this night. The starters were rookie Jeff Sellers for the Red Sox—just up from minor-league Pawtucket—and swingman Rick Aguilera for New York. The home club took a 2-0 lead in the third on singles by Tony Armas and Boggs, a walk to Marty Barrett, and a two-run hit by Buckner. This was nothing new, as the first baseman was one of Boston's top run producers all year and in the midst of a hot spell that would result in 8 homers and 22 RBIs during his last 26 regular-season games.

In the top of the fourth inning Buckner was involved in another play that while insignificant in an exhibition contest would prove an eerie foreshadowing of future events. After Wally Backman walked for New York, Lee Mazzilli hit a groundball that "Billy Buck" booted for an error.[7] Carter, serving as DH on this night, made Boston pay for the gaffe with a sacrifice fly to center that cut the lead to 2-1. The Red Sox went back up by two in the home half of the fourth on a walk to Evans and singles by Armas and Spike Owen.

The lead held until the eighth, when the Mets jumped on Boston reliever Joe Sambito. Tim Teufel and Mazzilli started it off with singles, Ray Knight had a pinch-hit double to make it 3-2, and then, after two outs, New York scored five more runs on an error by third baseman Ed Romero, an RBI single by John Gibbons, a walk to Kevin Elster, and a two-run hit by Kevin Mitchell. That was it for the scoring, as the Mets won 7-3.[8]

Afterward, as before the first pitch, nobody really wanted to dwell much on this game; the focus was on whether there would be four to seven *more* games between Boston and New York in October. *Boston Globe* columnist Leigh Montville called the night, coming near the end of a fantastic regular season by the Red Sox, "a chance to dream . . . a sneak preview of the dessert that possibly could follow this satisfying best of all possible main courses that is almost finished."[9]

And while Davey Johnson may have hoped that the one-game diversion would stall Boston's momentum, this wasn't the case. The Red Sox, whose AL East lead at the time was 4½ games over second-place Toronto entering the night, came into the exhibition with a five-game winning streak; after it, they won six more in a row to stretch their division advantage to 8½ games. As expected, the Red Sox and Mets each clinched their respective divisions by September's end.[10]

The stage was indeed being set for a return engagement.

SOURCES

In addition to the sources in the notes, the author also consulted:

Associated Press. "Red Sox and Mets Plan Charity Series," *New York Times,* February 17, 1985.

"In '86 Mets-Red Sox Exhibition, a Sign of Things to Come," *New York Times,* May 21, 2009.

NOTES

1 The Mets were the first National League team to play at Fenway Park since the Montreal Expos appeared in an exhibition game there in 1981. The Jimmy Fund charity aided by the Boston game was one with strong ties to the city's baseball history, as it was started with large help from the NL's Boston Braves in 1948, five years before they left the city for Milwaukee. Tommy Holmes, director of amateur baseball relations for the '86 Mets, had been a star outfielder on the '48 Braves and an early celebrity fund-raiser for the Jimmy Fund.

Although the Red Sox and Boston Braves battled from 1901 to 1952 for the city's mythical baseball supremacy, they were partners in their support of the Jimmy Fund of Boston's renowned Dana-Farber Cancer Institute. Braves owner Louis Perini had made the Jimmy Fund his team's primary charity, and he, his staff, and players including Holmes helped raise more than $1 million in five years of appeals—an astronomical amount for the period. Then, when Perini moved his club west in the spring of 1953, he appealed to Red Sox owner Tom Yawkey to take over stewardship of the Jimmy Fund. Yawkey complied, and for many years the Braves returned to Boston for Jimmy Fund benefit games at Fenway. Today, more than 60 years later, the Red Sox-Jimmy Fund union is recognized as the longest-standing and most extensive team-charity relationship in all of professional sports, and is responsible for millions raised for pediatric and adult patient care and cancer research at Dana-Farber. (A detailed look at this unique partnership can be found at jimmyfund.org/about-us/boston-red-sox/ and in *The Jimmy Fund of Dana-Farber Cancer Institute,* by Saul Wisnia.)

2 Nobody knew the makeup of both clubs better than Boston general manager Lou Gorman. A Rhode Island native and lifelong Red Sox fan, he had been director of baseball operations for the Mets in the early 1980s when the team was developing great young players like Strawberry, Gooden, left-handed pitcher Ron Darling, and outfielder Mookie Wilson. Then in 1984 he got his dream job in Boston and helped transform a last-place team into a pennant-winner in three years.

3 Joseph Durso, "Mets Beat Red Sox, 7-3, Just for the Fun of It All," *New York Times,* September 5, 1986.

4 Dan Shaughnessy, "This Time It's All in Fun; Sox Face Mets—For Charity, Not a World Series Championship," *Boston Globe,* September 5, 1986.

5 Leigh Montville, "Still Rolling Along," *Boston Globe,* September 5, 1986.

6 Ibid.

7 This was not the only eerie prologue to Buckner's infamous error in Game Six of the 1986 World Series. On October 6, after the Red Sox had entered the AL playoffs, Buckner was interviewed by reporter Don Shane of WBZ-TV in Boston and was quoted on air as saying, "The dreams are that you're gonna have a great series and win. The nightmares are that you're gonna let the winning run score on a groundball through your legs. Those things happen, you know. I think a lot of it is just fate." "Bill Buckner Talks Before 1986 World Series," WBZ-TV Boston interview, YouTube (youtube.com/watch?v=gb9ziUKRU3I), October 6, 1986. See also "What Bill Buckner Said 19 Days Before Game Six of the '86 World Series," mentalfloss.com, October 25, 2011.

8 Sambito's shellacking in the eighth may have resulted from his being such a familiar face. He had pitched against the Mets often during eight years as a reliever with the Houston Astros, and had even briefly been a Met himself in 1985 after coming back from Tommy John surgery. Released by New York that August, he had signed on with the Red Sox as a free agent in January of '86 and contributed a 2-0 record and 12 saves out of the Boston bullpen that year.

9 Montville, "Still Rolling Along."

10 The 1986 World Series was nearly a match-up of 100-win teams. The Mets finished 108-54; the Red Sox were 90-57 after beating Milwaukee on September 18, but went just 5-9 the rest of the season—including a four-game sweep at the hands of the Yankees to close out the campaign. Although Boston no doubt took its foot off the gas after clinching the AL East on September 28 with seven games to play, history would likely look back on the '86 fall classic as less of a David-vs.-Goliath duel had Boston been 100-62 instead of 95-65 in the regular season.

Even after their disastrous collapse at Shea Stadium in Games Six and Seven of the World Series, the Red Sox kept their commitment to play the second charity exhibition game against the Mets at this House of Horrors on May 7, 1987. The Mets won yet again, 2-0, before 32,347 fans, and the much-maligned Bill Buckner showed great humility and humor when he called out to Mookie Wilson—who had hit the grounder that skidded through his legs in Game Six, "Mookie, what do you say you hit me some groundballs?" See "A Hint of October on a Spring Night," *New York Times,* May 8, 1987.

BEHIND GOODEN'S COMPLETE GAME AND MAGADAN'S CLUTCH HITTING, METS WRAP UP FIRST DIVISION TITLE SINCE '73

SEPTEMBER 17, 1986: NEW YORK METS 4, CHICAGO CUBS 2, AT SHEA STADIUM

By Gregory H. Wolf

I CAN'T SAY ENOUGH ABOUT IT, OR SAVOR IT enough," said inspirational team leader Gary Carter after his New York Mets clinched the NL East crown by defeating the Chicago Cubs.[1] While hard-throwing Dwight Gooden buoyed the team with a sparkling six-hitter, September call-up Dave Magadan, making his first big-league start, supplied the offensive fireworks by collecting three hits and knocking in two runs. The Mets "ended their six-month pursuit of a title in high style," wrote Joseph Durso of the *New York Times*;[2] however, "Shea Stadium was transformed into a house of mayhem," wrote the *Chicago Tribune's* Fred Mitchell, when hundreds of fans poured onto the field causing massive damage in a riot-like environment.[3]

There was never any doubt that the Mets would eventually capture their first NL East title in 13 years; the only question was when it would take place. With a record of 94-50, New York enjoyed a commanding 18-game lead over the second-place Philadelphia Phillies as the club headed to Shea Stadium on September 17. The Mets had been in sole possession of first place since April 23 and had enjoyed a double-digit lead in the standings for all but about a week since June 14. They were led by the NL's highest-scoring offense and best pitching staff featuring a quartet of starters (Gooden, Ron Darling, Sid Fernandez, and Bob Ojeda), who each won at least 15 games and logged in excess of 200 innings in 1986. But after winning 16 of 19 games to increase their lead to 21 games on September 7, manager Davey Johnson's squad had hit a rough patch, losing six of seven games, before beating the St. Louis Cardinals at Busch Stadium the previous night behind Carter's three hits. The fifth-place Chicago Cubs (61-83), whose title aspirations 17 years earlier were derailed by the Amazin' Mets' first NL East title, hoped to play spoiler, at least for a game or two.

The Mets and their fans felt confident with 21-year-old right-hander Doc Gooden on the mound. Arguably the NL's most exciting pitcher, Gooden had won the Cy Young Award the previous season with a league-leading 24 wins, a 1.53 ERA and 268 strikeouts. Not quite as dominant in '86, Gooden had won 14 of 20 decisions, giving him a career record of 55-16 with a 3.04 ERA. Toeing the rubber for the North Siders was 31-year-old Dennis Eckersley (6-9, 4.63), in his 12th and final season as a regular starter before his transformation into one of baseball's best relievers following his trade to the Oakland A's in 1987.

Under a brightly lit full moon, a sellout crowd of 47,823 packed Shea Stadium, the Mets' home since 1964. Security was tight, with a visible police presence along the first- and third-base lines to maintain order and ensure safety. The raucous fans vented their collective displeasure by booing rookie Dave Magadan when he was announced as the starting first baseman instead of fan favorite Keith Hernandez, who was suffering from a bad cold.

On a team filled with offensive threats, Magadan proved to be the catalyst in this game. "I found out I was going to play tonight on the plane last night from St. Louis," he said after the Mets' victory. "I was just glad I was able to put all the fans out of my mind when I was at the plate."[4] He silenced his naysayers in the first inning when he sliced a two-out single and moved to third on Carter's double. The Mets' first scoring threat ended when Darryl Strawberry flied out to center. With Lenny Dykstra and Wally Backman on first and second in the third inning, Magadan hit a one-out single to knock in the game's first run (and the first in his career) as the partisan crowd cheered its new hero. Two batters later, Strawberry collected the Mets' fourth single of the inning and drove in Backman for a 2-0 Mets lead.

While Gooden mowed down the Cubs, yielding just three hits in the first five frames, the Mets appeared on the verge of breaking the game open in the fifth. Following Dykstra's leadoff double, Eckersley bobbled Backman's sacrifice bunt and threw late to first. In a fairy-tale night, Magadan collected his third single, driving in Dykstra. Strawberry drew a one-out walk to load the bases, but Mookie Wilson hit into a 6-4-3 double play to end the inning. As Shea Stadium vibrated with championship-hungry fans, Mets GM Frank Cashen appeared on the video scoreboard prior to the beginning of the sixth inning imploring fans to celebrate responsibly and spare the field.[5]

Magadan led off the seventh by reaching base for the fourth consecutive time when first baseman Leon Durham booted his grounder. The cousin and godson of then New York Yankees manager Lou Piniella, Magadan received a thunderous ovation when he was replaced by pinch-runner Stan Jefferson, who subsequently scored on Strawberry's single to give the Mets an apparently comfortable lead, 4-0.

The backslapping and smiling morphed into nervous anticipation just minutes later when Cubs rookie Raphael Palmeiro belted a one-out, two-run homer over the 400-foot sign in right-center field. But it was Gooden's game to win or lose, and he retired the next two batters. The Cubs had the go-ahead runner at the plate with one out in the ninth inning via a walk and a pinch-hit single by Chris Speier, but Davey Johnson's confidence in Gooden didn't waver. Doc fanned pinch-hitter Jerry Mumphrey and got Chico Walker to ground weakly to second base to end the game in 2 hours and 32 minutes.

Hundreds of fans streamed onto the field even before Backman completed his throw to first baseman Keith Hernandez, whom Johnson had inserted to begin the eighth inning so the 13-year veteran could be on the field for the victory celebration. "I could see the wave coming, but I ran into the pile," said Hernandez. "I'm not going to run for my life. Somebody stole my cap, my gamer, and they tried to take my glove right off my hand, but they didn't realize how strong my hand is."[6] Backman took a different approach: "I just started jumping over people to get off the ground."[7]

Fans "starting chewing up the Shea Stadium grounds like so many locusts," wrote Windy City sportswriter Fred Mitchell.[8] When order was finally restored, the field looked like a "cratered landscape," observed Joseph Durso, with large chunks of grass missing and even the bases stolen.[9] "There's heavy damage, everywhere," said Pete Flynn, the head groundskeeper, who dispatched a crew of 20 to resod the infield overnight in preparation for the next day's game. "The infield is a mess."[10] Not all of the fans were pleased with the riotous behavior. "It's a sin the way they're ripping the field apart," said one spectator from Long Island.[11]

"It's safe to look now, faint hearts," wrote George Vecsey of the *New York Times* somewhat sarcastically." The Mets have survived the desperate hours."[12] In the dugout after the game, Mets players expressed both relief and exhilaration. "It's been a long time and I don't think I ever believed there would be a day like this," said Backman, batting a team-best .334.[13] "It's a great, great thrill," cried Gooden, who finished with a six-hitter and eight strikeouts, but also walked five.[14] Even New York City Mayor Ed Koch, who had not been to a Mets game since Opening Day, chimed in:."Sonny, it's not just how you play the game," he recalled a saying from his grandmother. "You've also got to win."[15] With 17 regular-season games remaining, the Mets were peaking at the right time.

NOTES

1 Fred Mitchell, "Mets Take NL East: Gooden Stops the Cubs," *Chicago Tribune*, September 18, 1986, D1.

2 Joseph Durso, "Finally, the Mets Achieve the Inevitable Title; Mets 4, Cubs 2," *New York Times*, September 18, 1986, A1.

3 Mitchell.

4 Ibid.

5 Alex Yannis, "Fans Rip Up the Field: Game Today Will Go On," *New York Times*, September 18, 1986, B17.

6 George Vecsey, "The Danger's Over," *New York Times*, September 18, 1986, B17.

7 Mitchell.

8 Ibid.

9 Durso.

10 Ibid.

11 Yannis.

12 Vecsey.

13 Mitchell.

14 Durso.

15 Ibid.

STRAWBERRY DELIVERS

SEPTEMBER 28, 1986: NEW YORK METS 4, PITTSBURGH PIRATES 1, AT THREE RIVERS STADIUM

By Jack Zerby

THE MISERY THAT WAS THE 1986 NATIONAL League East pennant race for every team except the New York Mets was just about over. There was just a week left in the season; the Mets had already won 102 games. They led the second-place Phillies by 20 games and were in Pittsburgh on Sunday, September 28, to face the last-place Pirates, 40 games back. The proverbial fat lady had indeed sung.

Manager Jim Leyland's Pirates had had no success at all against the Mets in 1986. The teams had opened at Pittsburgh's Three Rivers Stadium on April 8; the Mets won, 4-2. They had also prevailed in 12 of the next 13 meetings, losing only the first game of a June 6 doubleheader in Pittsburgh.[1] In this series, they had already won twice, 3-1 on Friday and 4-2 on Saturday. The Saturday win was by way of a two-run Pittsburgh error in the top of the 11th inning.

Only 13,210 had come out on Saturday to watch their cellar-dwelling Bucs, but the Sunday game was the last home date of the season, one traditionally observed as Fan Appreciation Day in Pittsburgh. The Pirates did not disappoint, rolling out over a thousand prizes including a new Cadillac, chicken dinner for everybody, and a promised postgame concert featuring the Four Tops and Chuck Berry. The festivities brought out 30,606, the third largest crowd of the season, and one that moved the Pirates over a million in attendance for the first time in three years.[2]

The throng settled in for a pitching matchup that augured more Mets success. Manager Davey Johnson sent out 17-game winner Bob Ojeda, a left-hander, against Pittsburgh's Bob Patterson. Patterson, a fellow lefty, was at 27 years old just a year younger than Ojeda but far less experienced; he had made the Opening Day roster, but spent the summer with the Pirates' Pacific Coast League affiliate in Hawaii. He'd earned a September recall, but had pitched only 28⅓ major-league innings, including four the prior year with San Diego. His prospects were shaky as he faced the formidable Mets.[3]

With the divisional title long since clinched, the Mets rested first baseman Keith Hernandez. Gary Carter moved to first from behind the plate, Ed Hearn took over there, and Tim Teufel, part of a platoon with Wally Backman all season, manned second against left-handed pitching. The Pirates had few names recognizable outside the western Pennsylvania/northern West Virginia/eastern Ohio fan-base area; one who would be much recognizable later, Barry Bonds, was a rookie in 1986 but not in the day's lineup.[4]

Patterson impressed through the first three innings, yielding only a two-out single to Ray Knight in the second and striking out five, including Carter and Darryl Strawberry in succession before Knight's single. The Mets broke through in the fourth, though, as Teufel hit a leadoff double, reached third with two outs, and scored on Strawberry's infield single. Although Patterson then balked Strawberry to second and Knight singled, Pittsburgh center fielder Bobby Bonilla cut down Strawberry at the plate to save a run and end the half-inning.

Ojeda, meanwhile, didn't allow a Pittsburgh baserunner until Tony Pena singled with two outs in the fifth inning, but he was quickly erased on a force play. Light-hitting Pirates shortstop Sammy Khalifa singled to lead off the sixth. Patterson sacrificed him to second and he went to third on a groundout by

Rafael Belliard. The threat ended, though, when Ojeda struck out Bonilla.

Still hanging tough into the New York eighth, Patterson ran through some raindrops at that point as Hearn and Rafael Santana singled to open the inning. Ojeda laid down a bunt, but the Pirates were able to nip Hearn at third. They got another crucial outfield assist when the next batter, Mookie Wilson, lined to Mike Brown in right and Brown's throw to first baseman Sid Bream caught a straying Ojeda for a double play.

Pena led off the Pittsburgh eighth with a single and after Brown fouled out, Leyland sent out three straight pinch-hitters. Johnny Ray walked, but Junior Ortiz, hitting for Patterson, and U.L. Washington failed to move the runners. It was still Mets 1, Pirates 0.

Leyland's new pitcher, Don Robinson, made quick work of Teufel, Kevin Mitchell, and Carter in the Mets' ninth. Likewise, Ojeda efficiently disposed of Bonilla and Mike Diaz in the bottom of the inning to bring cleanup hitter Jim Morrison to the plate as the Bucs' last hope.

Morrison hadn't gotten the ball out of the infield in three tries against Ojeda. But this time, he launched his 22nd home run of the season to center field, forging a 1-1 tie. After Sid Bream flied out, there was free baseball in Pittsburgh to go with the waiting chicken and concert.

Robinson pitched around an error and a hit batsman to escape the New York 10th. Howard Johnson, one of three pinch-hitters in the inning, had struck out for Ojeda, who was now finished for the day with a frustrating four-hit, one-walk effort and no chance to be the winning pitcher. His replacement, Rick Aguilera, yielded a walk and a single in the bottom half, but, aided by his own skill in turning a would-be sacrifice into a 1-6-3 double play, never allowed a runner past first base.

Leyland had hit for Robinson in the 10th; righty Bob Walk came on as the third Pittsburgh pitcher in the 11th inning. He struck out Wilson and Teufel, but Lenny Dykstra[5] singled to right and Carter followed with a single to center.

Strawberry, who had been booed in New York,[6] especially during a late-July-through-mid-August swoon,[7] and had been occasionally benched against left-handed pitching,[8] batted next. Walk, after a visit from Leyland, worked a 2-and-2 count before Strawberry "stepped out and told myself to try something new. I choked up on the bat about half an inch," something he said teammate Keith Hernandez had recently suggested to provide a quick, short swing.[9]

It worked, and Strawberry later reported "it felt pretty good,"[10] as he drove Walk's next pitch into the center-field seats for a three-run homer. It was his 24th of the season. His four RBIs accounted for all the New York scoring in the game.

Knight fanned to end the half-inning, but the snake-bitten Pirates rolled three harmless groundballs in their half off Aguilera, who got the 4-1 win.

Davey Johnson lamented for Ojeda: "It's a shame Bobby couldn't have won it, because he deserved to the way he pitched. If there's anybody on my staff who qualifies for the Cy Young Award, he's right there."[11]

Jim Leyland lamented the weekend of close losses for his club, now 32 games under .500: "If we had been able to execute just one more thing in each game, we could have swept this series. We gave them a battle, but that's still no consolation when you get swept."[12]

And the crowd lamented that it took extra innings to sink their Bucs. Chuck Berry's contract stipulated that he would start before 5 P.M. When the game ran past that, he refused to perform. Fortunately, the fans, bolstered by 60,000 pieces of chicken, 4,400 pounds of cole slaw, 40,000 dinner rolls, and freely-flowing Coca-Cola all around, got to see an extra half-hour of the obliging Four Tops.[13]

SOURCES

In addition to the sources cited in the Notes, the author utilized the Baseball-Reference.com and Retrosheet.org websites for box scores, player, team, and season pages, pitching and batting logs, and other data pertinent to this article.

NOTES

1 The Mets finished 17-1 against the Pirates in 1986, including a three-game season-ending sweep in New York October 4-5.

2 Murray Chass, "Mets Win On Homer In 11th," *New York Times,* September 29, 1986: C5, accessed June 5, 2015, at nytimes.com. Chass also noted this "mark[ed] the first time all [then-] 26 major league teams have reached that plateau in the same season."

3 Patterson's ERA in four innings with San Diego in 1985 was 24.75. He was at 5.55 in nine major-league appearances in 1986 when he started on September 28.

4 Bonds, hitting .226 on September 28, had gone 2-for-5 against the Mets the day before with a double and stolen base. He finished sixth in the 1986 NL Rookie of the Year voting.

5 Dykstra had entered the game in the ninth inning as a defensive replacement for Kevin Mitchell. Mitchell had been in left field, but Dykstra went to center field and Mookie Wilson, who had started the game in center, went to left.

6 Chass.

7 Strawberry hit .130 (9-for 69) from July 22 through August 17. His batting average dropped from .289 to .257; he finished the season at .259. "Reporters have criticized [Strawberry] for failing to reach the level expected of him, 40 home runs and 100 runs batted in, for example." Chass, "Mets Win On Homer In 11th." Strawberry finished with 27 home runs and 93 RBIs, nine of which came in the last four games of the season.

8 *The Sporting News,* August 11, 1986: 28.

9 Chass.

10 Ibid.

11 "Bucs Fall To Mets, Go Over Million Mark," Associated Press, *Titusville* (Pennsylvania) *Herald*, September 29, 1986: 6. Ojeda finished fourth in the 1986 Cy Young voting, behind Mike Scott (Astros), Fernando Valenzuela (Dodgers), and Mike Krukow (Giants). Ron Darling, Ojeda's teammate, was fifth.

12 Ibid.

13 Stephen Mulligan, *Were You There? Over 300 Wonderful, Weird, and Wacky Moments* (Pittsburgh: Rose Dog Books, 2011), 153. The 1986 Fan Appreciation Day also featured a pregame wedding with a party of 16. Jim Leyland kissed the bride and several players autographed the marriage certificate. Ibid.

THE NATIONAL LEAGUE CHAMPIONSHIP SERIES

By Rory Costello

THE 1986 NLCS – LIKE ITS AMERICAN LEAGUE counterpart—piled on the dramatic tension. When baseball is at its best, the suspense builds slowly and inexorably. Over the course of this series, there were ebbs and flows and undercurrents. It built to a nerve-wracking crescendo.

The Mets and their opponent, the Houston Astros, both came into the series hot. Houston had won five games in a row and eight out of 10. New York was also on a five-game winning streak but had won nine of 10. They were both deep and well-balanced teams; in fact, Detroit Tigers manager Sparky Anderson called them carbon copies of each other. Anderson pointed to the greatest strength of each. "It all comes down to one thing, pitching. And the two clubs look even. I'd hate to have to bet any money on either of them."[1]

Astros first baseman Glenn Davis talked about the matchup: "The way our staff has been going the last few weeks, it has to be a question mark in (the Mets') minds. Our guys have been firing blanks at everybody. But they have great pitchers too. This series is going to be a pitchers' duel all the way."[2]

GAME ONE

October 8, 1986: Houston 1, New York 0, at the Astrodome

Davis was right. Setting the tone was Game One, a purists' delight: just one run scored. On the mound for the home team, Houston, was Mike Scott—a Mets draft pick back in 1976. From 1979 through 1982, the righty posted a mediocre record in the majors of 14-27 with a 4.64 ERA (though the Mets were dreadful in those years). In December 1982 New York traded Scott to Houston for outfielder Danny Heep. Scott pitched fairly well in 1983 but had a poor year in 1984. Then in the offseason he consulted with pitching coach Roger Craig, who was in temporary retirement at the time. Craig, guru of the split-finger fastball, taught Scott the potent out pitch—and at 30 years old, Scott emerged as an ace. He had a fine year in 1985 but was even better in '86; after the season ended, he was named the NL's Cy Young Award winner.

In mid-August, Scott Ostler of the *Los Angeles Times* stated, "Mike Scott is the best pitcher in baseball right now. ... This season, he is a monster."[3] Just how dominant was Scott at that time? His won-lost record in the regular season was not spectacular at 18-10, though he did lead the league in ERA at 2.22. After the All-Star break, he was 9-4, 2.13 in 15 starts. He struck out 139 in 114 innings, while allowing just 68 hits and 29 walks for a WHIP of 0.85. On September 25 he threw a no-hitter against San Francisco to clinch the NL West division title.

Facing Scott was the NL's reigning Cy Young Award winner, Dwight Gooden. "Doctor K" had come down from his unearthly year in 1985, but was still impressive, posting a 17-6 record with a 2.84 ERA. After a brilliant start, Gooden struggled at times in 1986. Pitching coach Mel Stottlemyre admitted that he had told the power pitcher to change his approach, not to try for as many strikeouts and to go for more groundballs (which was how Stottlemyre himself had pitched).[4] Of course, it later emerged that Gooden had developed substance-abuse problems, which impaired his performance.

Nonetheless, Mets manager Davey Johnson still expressed confidence in his 21-year-old star, saying "Doc ... tried to do a little too much a few times this year and didn't stay within himself. But he's right there at his peak now."[5] Johnson's opposite number, Hal Lanier, said, "It will be like Sandy Koufax pitching against Juan Marichal a few years back. One of the best pitching matchups in baseball in a long time."[6]

The Mets and others thought, however, that there was something else to Scott's success besides the splitter. "I was his catcher in the [1985] All-Star Game," said Gary Carter. "There's no doubt in my mind that Mike scuffs the ball with sandpaper. He won't admit to it; no pitcher will. But it's pretty obvious. When I caught him in the All-Star Game, a couple of his pitches that were supposed to be fastballs really took off, in a manner that they wouldn't have otherwise. One pitch to Jesse Barfield, I'm telling you, must have broken by 2½ feet. It was just unbelievable. And one day Leon Durham (of the Cubs) found a little piece of sandpaper behind the mound. They said the grounds crew had been sanding the pitching rubber clean. I mean, really ..."[7]

The Durham episode came after a game at Wrigley Field the year before (May 26, 1985). Cubs manager Jim Frey had umpire John Kibler check Scott on the mound, and the players saw something drop from Scott's glove. Frey later sent an advisory letter to Chub Feeney, president of the National League.[8]

The Mets' anti-scuffing campaign against Scott became a prominent running theme in the series. It started in the first inning of Game One, when Carter asked home-plate umpire Doug Harvey to inspect the ball after swinging and missing at strike two. Harvey looked at the ball and tossed it back to Scott, who promptly struck Carter out on the next pitch. Harvey—known as "The Lord" for his authority—later said, "(The ball) was as clean as this desk, gentlemen. And the man had just exploded two tremendous pitches."[9]

The game lived up to Lanier's expectations—though his team missed several scoring chances. Davis, Houston's leading slugger with 31 homers during the regular season, led off the bottom of the second by clearing the center-field fence. The Astros loaded the bases after that with just one out, but Gooden got out of the inning. The third inning could have been trouble, but first baseman Keith Hernandez and third baseman Ray Knight both made great plays on smoking grounders to save extra-base hits. The Doctor also escaped a bases-loaded, one-out jam in the fourth when Scott grounded into a 6-4-3 double play. In the fifth, with the infield in, Billy Hatcher was thrown out at the plate trying to score on a groundball. In the sixth, Bass got to third. That was as close as the Astros came to scoring the rest of the way off Gooden (who went seven innings) and Jesse Orosco.

Meanwhile, the Mets could do little with Scott, who struck out 14, walked just one, and scattered five singles. New York got a baserunner to second three times, but that was the extent of their offense. Their frustration was clearly visible. As Bruce Keidan of the *Pittsburgh Post-Gazette* wrote, "The Mets spent most of the night bickering with Doug Harvey. ... First they complained that Scott was scuffing the ball. Later, they argued that Harvey was giving Scott more of the outside corner than the pitcher deserved." Davey Johnson said, however, "The umpiring didn't beat us. Mike Scott did."[10]

GAME TWO

October 9, 1986: New York 5, Houston 1, at Astrodome

Of the six games in the 1986 NLCS, four were decided by one run and another by two runs. Game Two was the only one that had any margin of comfort. After Scott dominated the Mets in Game One, New York turned to Bob Ojeda. Heading into the playoffs, Davey Johnson reaffirmed, "There is no question that he is my most consistent pitcher. He's been great, outstanding. He's ready."[11]

Ojeda justified Johnson's faith, throwing a complete game. It wasn't easy—he allowed 10 hits and two walks, and the leadoff batter reached base in five different innings. Even so, the Astros couldn't break through. "We had enough hits," said Hal Lanier. "But we didn't get them at the right time. You also have to give credit to Ojeda." Johnson said, "I thought Bobby Ojeda pitched a very gutty game."[12]

The finesse pitcher defeated 39-year-old fireballer Nolan Ryan, who pitched five innings and gave up all five runs the Mets scored. Early on, though, Ryan continued Scott's mastery. He retired the first nine men he faced, five of them with his trademark strikeout.

"The first time I came up I just got a brief glance at his fastball," said Ray Knight. "He threw it right by me—and not many pitchers can get it by me."[13]

In the fourth, however, New York finally got on the scoreboard. With one out, both Wally Backman and Keith Hernandez singled. Then Gary Carter doubled off the right-field wall and Darryl Strawberry hit a sacrifice fly. "We were a little nervous," said Ojeda. "But when we broke the ice, you could feel a sigh of relief."[14]

The next inning, the Mets again got something going with one out. Knight popped out to lead off, but he later observed, "(Ryan) either had lost a little off his fastball or he didn't get the location he wanted."[15] Light-hitting shortstop Rafael Santana singled, and after Ojeda forced him at second, Len Dykstra singled and so did Backman. Ojeda scored, and then Hernandez tripled in New York's final two runs of the night. "When Nolan threw the ball up over Dykstra's head, I sensed some emotion in our dugout," Johnson noted. "That inspired us to go out and score more runs."[16]

"I thought that I had pretty good stuff," said Ryan, "But I let it get away from me."[17] Lanier echoed Knight, saying, "(Ryan) threw the ball well velocity-wise. He didn't get the ball where he wanted to."[18]

Houston had missed an excellent opportunity to go ahead in the bottom of the second inning. Kevin Bass doubled with one out and advanced to third on an infield single by José Cruz off Ojeda's glove. Alan Ashby then hit a checked-swing bouncer back to Ojeda, and Bass was out as he tried to score. Dickie Thon then struck out looking.

The Astros got their leadoff man on first base in the fourth, fifth, sixth, seventh, and ninth innings. A study published on the baseball research website Fangraphs.com, covering the 1952-2009 period, showed that such runners scored 38 percent of the time.[19] Thus, one could reasonably have expected Houston to get two runs in those innings. With well-timed hits, it could have been more. Yet, just one run came out of those situations, thanks to a two-out single by Phil Garner in the seventh.

By contrast, even though the Mets had only one leadoff batter reach base, they strung their hits together and maximized their opportunities. Therefore they came out of the Astrodome with a split. "If you say we have the edge now, I disagree," said Hernandez. "Obviously, we were glad to split in Houston. But this is one of the best playoff matchups in a long time, and we have the two best pitching staffs in the league. Now, we bring the playoffs home in front of our fans."[20] They flew back to New York and prepared to host Games Three through Five at Shea Stadium.

GAME THREE

October 11, 1986: New York 6, Houston 5, at Shea Stadium

"This is a great feeling," said Len Dykstra after the game. "The last time I hit a home run in the bottom of the ninth to win a game, I was playing my Strat-O-Matic baseball game, rolling dice against my brother Kevin."[21]

During the 1986 regular season, Dykstra was the most frequent leadoff hitter for the Mets. Wally Backman was the team's most frequent number-two batter. They were often known as the "little pests"—a label they wore with pride. They were tobacco-chewing dirty-uniform guys who set the table well for the big bats in the lineup. Yet that Saturday afternoon, with lefty Bob Knepper starting, both were on the bench as the game began. And it was Backman who sparked the ninth-inning rally with a drag bunt to lead off. One out later, Dykstra—who had just eight regular-season homers—took Houston closer Dave Smith deep to end the game.

Smith (who died at age 53 in 2008) was a good closer, if not a great one. He had a career-high 33 saves in 1986, and although blown saves weren't tabulated back then, a retroactive calculation shows just six for him in the regular season that year. He relied on a sinker and forkball, and he was not prone to giving up the long ball: five in 56 innings in 1986, and just 34 in 809⅓ regular-season innings lifetime.

He had not been effective against the Mets in '86, though—especially in back-to-back games on July 19 and 20 in Houston. The Astros eventually won both of those, but Smith blew the save in the first game by giving up a ninth-inning homer to Darryl Strawberry. The next afternoon he was largely responsible for losing a three-run lead in the ninth, though technically the blown save was Frank DiPino's.

Like all closers, though, Smith tried not to dwell on the past. After Game Three of the NLCS, he was forthcoming with the media. "You approach a hitter like (Dykstra) differently," he said. "He's not a slugger. You try to make him hit it on the ground. I was trying to throw him a forkball, low and away. It stayed out over the plate and it was up a bit." Even though a stiff wind was blowing from right field at Shea Stadium, Smith knew it was gone as soon as Dykstra hit it.[22]

"Dykstra does like to swing for the fences," said Davey Johnson. "I tell him all the time: 'If you hit line drives, you'd hit .330 every year.' But I forgive him today."[23] Johnson was more critical in the spring of 1988, when "Nails" reported to camp after packing on more than 20 pounds of muscle.[24] Ever after that, the cloud of performance-enhancing drugs would hang over Dykstra.

Hal Lanier's postgame comments were curt. Setup man Charlie Kerfeld, the goofy chowhound from Knob Noster, Missouri, had breezed through a 1-2-3 eighth inning. "I didn't see any reason not to bring in my number-one man," Lanier said. "If you get beat with your number-two guy, you leave yourself open to a lot of second guesses. What would you guys write if Dykstra hit that off Kerfeld and Smith was still in the bullpen?" He also dismissed the idea of bringing in Smith to start the eighth.[25]

Early on, it didn't seem that a save situation would arise. Mets starter Ron Darling allowed two runs in the first inning and another pair in the second, on a two-run homer by Bill Doran. Davey Johnson said, "Darling was a little tentative and not very aggressive, like he was during the season. But we battled back, and that's the big thing."[26] Indeed, that was the hallmark of the Mets' entire season.

Knepper shut out New York through five innings, but the Mets tied it in the sixth. The big blow was a three-run homer by Strawberry. The Astros promptly went ahead again, though, scoring an unearned run. Third baseman Ray Knight stood to be the goat because of his throwing error.

In the bottom of the seventh, even though Knepper was still pitching, Johnson decided to send Dykstra up as a pinch-hitter for Rick Aguilera. "I was taking a gamble putting Dykstra in the game," the manager later said.[27] "I called upstairs and found out that Knepper had thrown about 100 pitches. I thought Hal Lanier would probably hook Knepper after that inning and then I'd have Lenny in the game against their right-handed relief pitchers. And when I saw Hal shake Knepper's hand in the dugout after the seventh, I knew I was all right."[28]

Johnson was also looking ahead when he replaced Tim Teufel at second base with Backman in the top of the ninth. As Mookie Wilson later wrote, "Wally ... could always be counted on to get on base in a big spot. I wanted Wally to bunt, walk, slash, dive into first, whatever it would take to get on base."[29] After laying down his drag bunt, Backman wriggled around the tag of first baseman Glenn Davis. "I felt Wally went two to three feet out of the baseline," said Lanier, "and Glenn couldn't touch him." Dave Smith said, "I was surprised that they didn't call him out of the baseline because I saw him run on the grass."[30]

First-base umpire Dutch Rennert told Lanier, however, that Backman was already by Davis. "I was conscious of the three feet at all times," Rennert said, referring to the limed line three feet to the right of the first-base foul line. "And the home-plate umpire, Frank Pulli, could also call him out, but there was no doubt in my mind."[31]

Backman agreed with Rennert. "The first baseman was out of my vision behind me," he said. "The key for me on that bunt is to make the first baseman field it. And after I got past him, I was just trying to slide head-first into the bag and grab it with my left hand. He added, "I didn't think they'd have had me even if I went in straight up. I slid right on top of the line and kicked up all the chalk. I didn't think there was much of an argument there."[32]

Danny Heep, pinch-hitting for Rafael Santana, was ordered to bunt. After Heep fouled one off, an inside pitch got by catcher Alan Ashby for a passed ball. "That's when I thought the momentum changed," Davey Johnson said later. "I don't like to bunt and now I didn't have to."[33]

Heep worked the count full but then flied out to short center field. That brought up Dykstra, batting ninth because he'd entered in a double switch.

When Dykstra came to the plate, he remembered another Astros game at Shea from that Fourth of July, when he had doubled home the winning run against Smith with the score tied 1-1. "He threw me a fastball that time. This time, I didn't think he would. He threw me a fastball on the first pitch, and I fouled it off. Then I knew I wouldn't get a fastball, and sure enough the next pitch was a forkball."[34]

"He's got pop in his bat," said Smith. "And anybody in a big-league lineup can hit the ball out of the park if he guesses right on a pitch."[35]

Had Smith been able to nail down the save, Lanier had previously stated that he would turn to his number-four starter, rookie Jim Deshaies, in Game Four. His alternate decision was already made too. Seeking the equalizer—and looking ahead to a possible Game Seven as well—the call went to Mike Scott.[36]

GAME FOUR

October 12, 1986: Houston 3, New York 1, at Shea Stadium

"I think we put a little bit of pressure on [Houston]," said Len Dykstra after his game-ending homer put the Mets up two games to one in the 1986 NLCS. "Now they have to come back with Mike Scott, and I know he would like to have another day off."[37] The Astros' ace, working on three days' rest, responded with his second complete-game victory of the series. He allowed just three hits while walking none. Afterward, Scott—the second of just three Most Valuable Players from the losing team in an LCS—said, "I don't know if I've ever thrown better than in the last four or five games."[38]

Scott had started 13 times during the regular season on three days' rest, the last on August 2. He was 5-3 with five no-decisions in those games, posting a 2.60 ERA, somewhat higher than his league-leading 2.22 mark over the course of the full year. But Hal Lanier had already decided before Game Three: If the Astros lost, he'd go with Scott. "I think that's the only way to do it," he said."[39]

Scott agreed. "Not too many guys go on three days' rest anymore," he said after winning Game Four. "A lot of pitchers don't want to do it. I believe in this situation: If you can throw, you should go out there and throw."[40]

On the mound for New York was lefty Sid Fernandez. The hefty Hawaiian was celebrating his 24th birthday. He had won 16 games in 1986, which proved to be a career high, against six losses. "El Sid" had been a member of the National League All-Star team that summer, winning seven starts in a row from June 8 through July 11. He cooled off in the second half, but in those 15 appearances, he still struck out well over a batter an inning with his deceptive slinging motion.

Fernandez pitched fairly well that evening, but he gave up a two-run homer in the bottom of the second inning to Alan Ashby, who'd gone deep only seven times that whole season. Glenn Davis had led off with a single, but Kevin Bass and José Cruz struck out. Fernandez looked to be out of the inning when Ashby hit a high foul pop, but Rafael Santana didn't make the play. The shortstop had called off third baseman Ray Knight—wrongly, in Knight's view.[41] Santana thought he had a better angle, but was disoriented.[42] The Mets had placed two extra rows of folding chairs behind makeshift walls down each baseline. (Ironically, plenty of season-ticket holders were not in attendance because it was Yom Kippur.) Santana could not backhand the ball over a kneeling Knight, and it dropped into the first row of the temporary VIP seats.

After fouling off one more pitch, Ashby got a fat one on a full count and drove it. "I got a break," he said. "The fact that they sold the extra seats helped me out." Davey Johnson said, "We don't make a lot of mistakes like that. But that one cost us." He added, "The key was (Fernandez) took a little off his fastball to Ashby."[43]

Houston's only other hit off Fernandez, who pitched six innings, was also a homer. The batter was the eighth man in the order, shortstop Dickie Thon, who'd hit just three long balls in the regular season. Thon had shown power in the past, with 20 homers in 1983—but in April 1984, in a game against the Mets at the Astrodome, his career had nearly ended when a high and tight Mike Torrez fastball hit him in the face.

Three runs were more than enough for Scott. He held the Mets hitless until Knight's two-out single in the fifth. He had allowed just one other baserunner before that, when he was charged with an error for obstructing Wally Backman on a slow roller down the first-base line. The Astros argued long with first-base umpire Joe West, but to no avail. However, even though Backman followed by stealing second, Keith Hernandez grounded out and Gary Carter struck out.

Although Scott struck out only five Mets, down from 14 in Game One, his command was superb. "'He didn't have the really good fastball this time," said Davey Johnson, "but he threw some outstanding split-fingers."[44] "I've never seen anything like it in my life," said Dykstra. "It's like a Wiffleball moving in the wind."[45]

Hernandez said, "I came to the bench in the sixth inning and said he's lost his good fastball. After that, he threw 95 percent split-fingers. He painted us with it. I pride myself in having a good eye at the plate, but I swung at good pitches and missed."[46] Knight said, "Once he gets two strikes on you, he's probably the toughest guy in the league to get the fat part of the bat on."[47]

Scott's remarks tallied exactly with Johnson and Hernandez's. "I didn't have the good fastball," he admitted, "so I knew I had to go to the split-finger more. I wanted to keep the ball down. I knew I had to keep it down, away, and in the ballpark. I had a little arm fatigue in about the sixth inning. That's when I decided to continue to go more with the split-finger fastball. There are times when every pitcher doesn't feel that he is 100 percent, but they still have to go out and do what they can."[48]

The Mets scratched out their only run in the eighth inning when Mookie Wilson led off with a single. Knight then hit a sharp grounder on which opposing third baseman Phil Garner made a diving stop. Wilson, always a speedy and daring baserunner, took third—"barely hesitating as he rounded second"—as Garner threw Knight out.[49] Danny Heep then hit a sacrifice fly.

Roger McDowell retired the Astros in order in both the seventh and eighth innings, and Doug Sisk threw a shaky but scoreless ninth. The Mets' table-setters, Dykstra and Backman, then threatened to ignite a rally. Dykstra singled to lead off, and Backman—again bunting for a base hit, as he had done in the ninth inning of Game Three—nearly made it work. Scott lunged and gloved the ball before it got by him, though, and threw Backman out. He then again retired Hernandez and Carter to end it.

The question that still loomed large in the Mets' minds was whether Scott was doctoring the ball. Before Game Three, Backman—a minor-league teammate of Scott's—said, "I don't believe Scott would do anything illegal. I know him. Other people have come up with new pitches. Why can't people admit Scott has and leave it at that?"[50]

After Game Four, Backman changed his tune. "Every single ball was scuffed. Every one of them. You know there are people in the game who cheat. I never knew until late in the game, but when you have 15 or 20 balls that have been scuffed, you know it's not done by fouling them off. I don't know how he was doing it. I assume it's something in his glove hand."[51]

"None of this is evidence," conceded Howard Johnson. "You have to catch him doing it. But he does it."[52] The home-plate umpire for Game Four, Dutch Rennert, said that the Mets had not asked him to examine any balls and that he had not seen any scuffed balls. "Maybe they were scuffed from guys hitting them," said Rennert. Backman grumbled, "It's meaningless to argue. You complain, and nothing happens."[53]

Crew chief Doug Harvey emphasized (as he had after Game One), "I have never found any evidence that Scott has been doing anything wrong."[54] A quarter-century later, Scott remained cagey. "They can believe whatever they want to believe. Every ball that hits the ground has something on it. ... I've thrown balls that were scuffed but I haven't scuffed every ball that I've thrown."[55]

After Game Four, Bob Harig of the *St. Petersburg Evening Independent* wrote, "Scott, continuing the psychological wars that have developed over the issue, said what the Mets do to balls in their locker room isn't his concern."[56] The pitcher had tapped into what made Gaylord Perry so effective on the mound: mind games. The very idea of a defaced ball was another potent weapon against batters. Scott said, "I think the hitters lose some of their concentration when they worry about other things besides hitting."[57]

Looking ahead to another potential date with Scott in Game Seven, the Mets expressed outward confidence—yet clearly Scott was in their heads. Carter said, "I don't think we should let it build in our minds that he's unbeatable. He lost 10 games this year. Somebody beat him."[58] Knight said, "We're too good an offensive club not to make adjustments."[59] Davey Johnson said, "If it goes that far, I believe in percentages and the percentages are in our favor to beat him one game." Yet Johnson added, "Hopefully it will not go that far."[60]

GAME FIVE

October 14, 1986: New York 2, Houston 1 (12 innings), at Shea Stadium

Before the 1986 NLCS started, many observers pointed to the greatest mutual strength of the teams: pitching. Games One through Four surpassed those expectations. "I didn't think it would be *that* great a pitching series," said Mets batting coach Bill Robinson.[61]

In Game Five, it got even better. Nolan Ryan pitched nine innings for the Astros, allowing just one run on two hits while striking out 12. Houston scored just once off Dwight Gooden in 10 innings. Finally, in the 12th, Mets cleanup hitter Gary Carter singled up the middle to bring in the game's only other run.

Carter entered Game Five with just one hit in 17 at-bats, and he was 0-for-4 before coming through with his game-winner. Before the game, teammate Ray Knight said, "Gary's pressing, there's no question. He wants to do well. He drives himself very hard, and he's his own worst critic. Anytime you take the game to heart the way Gary [does], it's hard. Every time he makes an out, it wears on him. I told him, 'You'll get hot. He's capable of exploding at any time."[62] After the game, Keith Hernandez said, "Strong men rise to the occasion."[63]

The game was scheduled for Monday, October 13, but rain postponed it. Therefore, Hal Lanier again passed over rookie left-hander Jim Deshaies and gave the start to Ryan, who returned on a normal four days' rest after losing Game Two. Exactly 17 years before, Ryan—then a Met—had made the only World Series appearance of his long career, and it was also at Shea Stadium. "Was it the same date?" asked Mets third-base coach Bud Harrelson, the team's shortstop in 1969. "No wonder I felt a strange twitch today."[64]

Ryan was remarkably durable, but he had spent two stretches on the disabled list in 1986 with elbow problems. The Astros were counting his pitches, something that was anathema to him. "I was available," he had said on Monday. "I'm not surprised [by Lanier's original plan to use Deshaies] but I'm a little disappointed. After being put on the disabled list, I guess there are no surprises." He admitted that a rain delay could give him problems, though, and agreed that it would have been nice to pitch Game Six—potentially a clincher—at home in Texas.[65]

It was still rainy in New York City on Tuesday afternoon—Game Five finally started after a 22-minute delay. The sun broke through in the middle innings, though, and the field was fairly dry by the end of the game.[66]

A pivotal moment came in the second inning, when a dubious call deprived Houston of a run. Kevin Bass led off with a single and went to third on a looping base hit to shallow center by the next batter, José Cruz. Alan Ashby struck out. Then Craig Reynolds grounded to second base. Wally Backman got the force at second, but the relay throw from Rafael Santana appeared to arrive late. Nonetheless, first-base umpire Fred Brocklander called Reynolds out, so Bass did not score.

The crafty Hernandez may have swayed Brocklander. "I cheated a little bit because I felt it was going to be a close play," the first baseman said. "I yelled 'Out' when I caught the ball because I saw the umpire a little bit in question and I just wanted to put the out in his head."[67]

Reynolds exploded. He charged Brocklander and appeared to bump the ump in the chest. Someone remarked to Reynolds, "Some of your teammates say they've never seen you that mad." The shortstop responded, "I haven't been." He also said, "If I bumped (him) it was accidental, and I'm glad Fred didn't throw me out of the game."[68]

Lanier ran out right behind Reynolds to argue. He later said, "When my first-base coach Matt Galante argues, I have to figure (Brocklander) missed the call. I thought Reynolds beat the ball by half a step."[69] He added, "It's not going to do me any good to rant and rave or tear the clubhouse apart. We had some other opportunities to win, and we didn't."[70]

Brocklander stood by his call even after viewing replays. He said, "It was just a question that his foot was this far off the bag. It was a bang-bang play. … There was just a little daylight." He also claimed that "depth perception" was why the TV cameras made it appear that Reynolds was safe.[71] If today's expanded replay review rule had been in effect then, Lanier would have been able to issue a challenge.

Houston got on the scoreboard in the top of the fifth. Ashby doubled to lead off and Reynolds singled him to third. Ryan tried to move Reynolds up with a bunt, but Gooden got a force out. Bill Doran then grounded sharply to second; it looked like a perfect double-play ball, but it got stuck in Backman's glove long enough for the speedy Doran to beat Santana's relay to first. This time there was no question about Brocklander's call.

Doran stole second, and Billy Hatcher walked, but Denny Walling flied out to end the inning. Houston's best scoring chance after that came in the eighth, and it featured the same three batters. Doran bunted his way on to lead off and Hatcher sacrificed him to second. "Hernandez let Hatcher's bunt roll and roll and roll, hoping it would go foul, and picked it up just in time to tag Hatcher. Walling then lined hard toward left. Off the bat it sounded like a single, and Doran was running full speed."[72] Instead, Mookie Wilson came in, picked off the liner, and turned it into an easy double play.

Meanwhile, Ryan had retired the first 13 batters he faced, striking out eight. But then, on a full count, Darryl Strawberry homered off a low fastball. Many of Strawberry's homers were majestic moon shots. This one was a tracer that he ripped down the right-field line, just over the wall.

Ryan and Gooden were both renowned for their fastballs, but that day, they relied on other parts of their repertoire. "I didn't have a very good curveball," said Ryan, "but I went to the changeup in the middle of the game."[73] Gooden, who struck out just four, said, "I went into the game wanting to establish my off-speed pitches early in the count. I was able to do that, and that prevented the Astros from sitting on the fastball."[74]

Houston threatened again in the 10th. With two out, Terry Puhl, pinch-hitting for Ryan, singled. Ryan, who had thrown 134 pitches, called it "the right decision," adding, "I was tiring. I would have given them one more inning, but it made sense to hit for me."[75] Puhl stole second and Doran then walked. Gooden escaped by getting Hatcher to fly out.

"I let everything I had go in the ninth inning because I had never pitched 10 innings before," said Doctor K. "I figured that was my last inning. Then, when I came back to the dugout after the ninth, nobody said anything. It was like getting ready for the game all over again." He also said, "I was surprised when they told me to go back in there. I was worried that I wouldn't have anything left. But I felt fine. I think I could have gone longer."[76]

Charlie Kerfeld replaced Ryan and retired the side in order in both the 10th and 11th. That brought his string of consecutive outs in the series to 10. Jesse Orosco also set down all six men he faced in the 11th and 12th.

The Mets finally reached Kerfeld in the bottom of the 12th. Backman led off with a hard one-hopper that bounced high off the glove of third baseman Walling for a single. He took second base on Kerfeld's wild pickoff throw. The Astros then walked Hernandez intentionally to bring up Carter—"I had the matchup I wanted," said Lanier.[77] Kerfeld fell behind 2-and-0, but got back to a full count. Carter fouled off two pitches. He then lashed a grounder behind Kerfeld and into center field.

"I'd be less than honest to say I wasn't frustrated at that point," said Carter. "But I didn't bring one negative thought to the plate with me. I believed something good was going to happen—and it did."[78] The Mets mobbed and embraced The Kid, whose reaction was typically ebullient. The image of Carter with two fists in the air, leading the crowd's postgame cheers, wound up on the cover of his 1987 book, *A Dream Season*.

At least one headline said that the Mets were in the driver's seat as the series shifted back to Houston. Veteran New York sportswriter Dick Young put it differently: "The Mets were supposed to be in what Red Barber called 'the catbird seat.' ... And yet, I didn't feel that way, and I don't think the Mets did either."[79] If New York didn't win Game Six, the specter of Mike Scott loomed.

GAME SIX

October 15, 1986: New York 7, Houston 6 (16 innings), at the Astrodome

Time and again during their run to the world championship in 1986, the Mets clawed back in desperate situations. Later this October, they were all but eliminated in Game Six of the World Series, when the Red Sox were one strike away from winning it all for the first time since 1918. Yet in Game Six of the NLCS that year—an excruciating 16-inning battle—the Mets also climbed out of a deep hole. The incredibly suspenseful game had sportswriters from around the nation at their best. Mike Downey of the *Los Angeles Times* wrote, "(The Astros) made the Mets sweat and suffer, made them charge from behind and gasp to stay in front. ... They were enervated, drained, battle-fatigued."[80] In his chronicle of the '86 Mets, *The Bad Guys Won*, author Jeff Pearlman also vividly portrayed the mental and physical exhaustion that the players felt. *Newark Star-Ledger* columnist Jerry Izenberg devoted an entire book to this single contest entitled *The Greatest Game Ever Played*.

Unlike Game Six of the '86 World Series, New York's season would not have ended with a loss to Houston. The Mets had won three of the first five games, including a 12-inning 2-1 victory the day before at Shea Stadium. Had the Astros won Game Six, though, they would have sent Mike Scott to the mound the next day. Scott had thrown a five-hit shutout in Game One, making a single second-inning run stand up. He went all the way again to win Game Four, 3-1. He was on a lethal roll with his split-finger fastball.

The Mets continued to believe that something else was helping Scott's splitter to "drop off the table." Davey Johnson showed a group of reporters eight balls that were scuffed in exactly the same spot—a mark about the size of a 50-cent piece. Johnson said, "It [sandpaper] is in his palm. He doesn't rotate the ball, he just makes a grinding motion. It's blatant to me." However, NL President Chub Feeney called Scott "innocent until proven guilty"—though he added, "We will be watching closely the next time he pitches."[81]

Had the series gone to Game Seven, Scott would have faced Ron Darling. Darling had pitched well during the regular season (15-6, 2.81) but had given up four runs in five innings in Game Three, which the Mets came back to win on Len Dykstra's two-run homer in the bottom of the ninth. In 2006 Darling said, "I felt I couldn't give up any runs because Mike Scott wasn't going to."[82]

The adverb "desperately" has often been used to depict how much the Mets wanted to win Game Six. In their own words, this supremely confident team—viewed as arrogant in many quarters—didn't evince desperation. It is fair to say, however, that the lingering threat of Scott was a strong psychological undercurrent as the series shifted back to the Astrodome. Plus, the Mets' poor long-term record there led Hal Bock of Associated Press to dub it "their personal house of horrors" after Game Five.[83]

Another aside on that venue is in order, too. The Astrodome—once known as the Eighth Wonder of the World—hosted its last big-league game in 1999. It then fell into disuse and disrepair. In 1986, however, the Dome was also home to the Houston Oilers of the NFL. The Oilers had hosted the Chicago Bears just three days before Game Six—yard lines were still visible on the Astroturf.

The starters in Game Six were both lefties: Bob Knepper for Houston and Bob Ojeda for the Mets. The reliable Ojeda had gone the route as the Mets won Game Two, 5-1. But the Astros got to him for three runs in the first inning, and it might have been more except that Kevin Bass was tagged at home on a missed suicide squeeze attempt. Ojeda settled down after that and did not allow another run before coming out for Rick Aguilera in the sixth inning. Aguilera pitched three shutout innings, giving up just one hit.

Meanwhile, Knepper—17-12, 3.14 in the regular season, with a no-decision in Game Three—was cruising. He'd given up just two hits and a walk as he took a shutout into the ninth inning. Yet the Mets broke through for the tying runs; pinch-hitter Dykstra ignited the rally. As he had in Game Three, Johnson again made the unorthodox choice to send the lefty swinger up to lead off against Knepper. Bass in right field and José Cruz in left were playing deep, but center fielder Billy Hatcher remained shallow. He could not get back to make the play on Dykstra's fly ball, which became a triple.

Mookie Wilson singled off the tip of Bill Doran's glove to score Dykstra. One out later, Keith Hernandez doubled, Wilson scored, and Houston closer Dave Smith entered. Smith, who'd given up Dykstra's homer in Game Three, was ineffective again. He walked the first two men he faced. With the count 1-and-2 to Ray Knight, home plate umpire Fred Brocklander—whose controversial call at first base took a vital run away from Houston in Game Five—had the Astros screaming again when he called a ball. Two pitches later, Knight brought in the tying run with a sacrifice fly.

Roger McDowell entered in the bottom of the ninth for the Mets and went on to pitch five superb innings. He faced the minimum 15 batters; the only baserunner he allowed, Bass, was caught stealing second base. It was McDowell's longest relief stint ever in the majors; his only longer outing came in one of his two big-league starts as a rookie in 1985. Smith pitched a scoreless 10th for Houston, and Larry Andersen blanked the Mets from the 11th through the 13th.

In the 14th the Mets got a run against veteran reliever Aurelio López. The portly Mexican was no longer "Señor Smoke" at this stage of his career, allowing a single and a walk to lead off before Wally Backman's one-out RBI single. However, López contained the damage with runners on second and third. Jesse Orosco came on to try to get the save for the Mets, but with one out Hatcher pulled a drive high and deep. Would it stay fair? It hit the screen on the left-field foul pole, and the game was tied again.

After a scoreless 15th, New York put up three runs in the top of the 16th. López gave up one on a double and a single, then gave way to Jeff Calhoun, who fueled the rally with two wild pitches. One question about this game is why Hal Lanier chose not to use lefty Jim Deshaies—twice passed over for starting assignments and thus well rested—at any point. Lanier said that Deshaies had not faced that kind of pressure before. But bullpen coach Gene Tenace apparently told Lanier that Deshaies didn't have good stuff while warming up.[84]

Yet the tension was far from over—the Astros chipped away for two. They had the tying run on second base and the winning run on first with two out and Bass at the plate. Hernandez warned the weary Orosco (accounts vary as to the choice of words) not to throw a single fastball. The count ran full, and Mets announcer Bob Murphy said, "Pulsating baseball.... Nobody has sat down for the last four or five innings.... Incredible." Finally—on the sixth straight breaking ball—Bass fanned.[85] The Mets had won the NL pennant, and Orosco leaped in exultation. It had been the longest game in terms of innings in postseason history.[86]

Even if Houston had extended the series, at least some of the combative Mets still liked their chances against Scott. After Game Four, Ray Knight said, "You have to get that [the talk of scuffing] out of your mind and start thinking, 'What approach is best suited to hit this pitch?' and then you have to make adjustments at the plate."[87] The scrappy Backman said, "We're ticked and we're not going to take this lying down. I don't care if he scuffs 400 balls. I don't care if they're scuffed before the game. I don't think any pitcher can beat us three times in a row."[88]

On the flip side, however, Backman admitted, "If we had lost and had to face Scott tomorrow, I wouldn't have slept at all." Gary Carter said, "Mike Scott was our incentive to win."[89] Davey Johnson added, "Amen. I feel like I'm on parole, like I've just been given a pardon."[90] Perhaps a better choice of words would have been "reprieve"—the 1986 Mets just went from one grueling drama to the next.

NOTES

1 John Nelson, "Astros, Mets deemed 'carbon copy teams,'" Associated Press, October 5, 1986.

2 John Nelson, "Mets, Astros out to keep winning," Associated Press, October 8, 1986.

3 Scott Ostler, "Great Scott, He Throws a 'Splitter'," *Los Angeles Times*, August 14, 1986.

4 "Mets now admit Dwight Gooden's problems may lie in his mechanics," Associated Press, July 22, 1986.

5 "NL set for dream matchup," *New York Times*, Associated Press, October 8, 1986.

6 Ibid.

7 Brian Kappler, "Carter says Scott scuffs up ball," *Montreal Gazette*, October 8, 1986, C-1.

8 Joe Mooshil, "Scott 'Roughed Up' by Frey," Associated Press, June 5, 1985.

9 "Mets can't hit Scott," Associated Press, October 10, 1986.

10 Bruce Keidan, "Scott holds angry Mets at bay," *Pittsburgh Post-Gazette*, October 9, 1986.

11 "Mets sweep Pirates in playoff tuneup," Associated Press, October 5, 1986.

12 "Mets topple Astros behind Ojeda," United Press International, October 10, 1986.

13 "Mets regain the spark," Associated Press, October 10, 1986.

14 "Mets topple Astros behind Ojeda."

15 "Mets regain the spark."

16 Ibid.

17 Ibid.

18 "Mets topple Astros behind Ojeda."

19 "The Leadoff Walk," Fangraphs.com, September 15, 2010 (fangraphs.com/community/the-leadoff-walk/)

20 "Mets pick up split-finger advantage," Associated Press, October 11, 1986.

21 John Nelson, "Dykstra's homer gives Mets comeback victory," Associated Press, October 12, 1986. Dave Anderson, "Sports of the Times: Dykstra 'Nails' Astros," *New York Times*, October 12, 1986.

22 Nelson, "Dykstra's homer gives Mets comeback victory." Hal Bock, "Wrong Time for Smith," Associated Press, October 12 1986.

23 Joseph Durso, "Homer Gives Mets 6-5 Win," *New York Times*, October 12, 1986.

24 Joseph Durso, "Dykstra Displays New Look," *New York Times*, February 25, 1988.

25 "Wrong Time for Smith."

26 Nelson, "Dykstra's homer gives Mets comeback victory."

27 Durso, "Homer Gives Mets 6-5 Win."

28 Anderson, "Sports of the Times: Dykstra 'Nails' Astros."

29 Mookie Wilson with Erik Sherman, *Mookie Deluxe: Life, Baseball, and the '86 Mets* (New York: Berkeley Publishing Group, 2014). The irony is that Wilson was referring to Game Six of the World Series, when Backman failed to get on base to start the fateful bottom of the 10th inning.

30 Ira Berkow, "Smith speaks of 'terrible pitch' to Dykstra in 9th," *New York Times*, October 12, 1986.

31 Anderson, "Sports of the Times: Dykstra 'Nails' Astros."

32 Nelson, "Dykstra's homer gives Mets comeback victory."

33 Anderson, "Sports of the Times: Dykstra 'Nails' Astros."

34 Nelson, "Dykstra's homer gives Mets comeback victory."

35 "Smith speaks of 'terrible pitch' to Dykstra in 9th."

36 "Homer Gives Mets 6-5 Win." "Lanier Names Pitchers," wire service reports, October 11, 1986.

37 "Dykstra's homer gives Mets comeback victory," Associated Press, October 12, 1986.

38 Joseph Durso, "Scott Stymies Mets; Series Tied, 2-2," *New York Times*, October 13, 1986. The other League Championship Series MVPs from losing teams, as of 2014, were Fred Lynn (1982, California Angels) and Jeffrey Leonard (1987, San Francisco Giants).

39 "Lanier names pitchers."

40 Joe Illuzzi, "Houston evens series at two games apiece," United Press International, October 13, 1986.

41 "Extra seats leads to Mets' defeat," United Press International, October 13, 1986.

42 Hal Bock, "Knight, Santana cost Mets in second inning," Associated Press, October 13, 1986.

43 Tim Rosaforte, "Scott Deceives Mets Once Again With Three-hitter," *Palm Beach Sun-Sentinel*, October 13, 1986.

44 "Houston evens series at two games apiece."

45 "Scott Stymies Mets; Series Tied, 2-2."

46 "Scott Stymies Mets; Series Tied, 2-2."

47 "Houston evens series at two games apiece."

48 Harry Atkins, "Great Scott hunts down Mets," Associated Press, October 13, 1986.

49 "Scott, Ashby help Astros stop Mets," Associated Press, October 13, 1986.

50 Bob Elliott, "Pencil Scott in for Game Four," *Ottawa Citizen*, October 11, 1986, E3.

51 "Great Scott hunts down Mets."

52 "Scott Stymies Mets; Series Tied, 2-2."

53 Bock, "Knight, Santana cost Mets in second inning"

54 Charley Feeney, "Umps: Scott doesn't scuff," *Pittsburgh Post-Gazette*, October 14, 1986, 32.

55 "Network recalls 1986 postseason," Major League Baseball press release, November 4, 2011 (m.mlb.com/news/article/25882718/). Quote from in an interview Scott gave for Major League Baseball's documentary *A Postseason to Remember: 1986.*

56 Bob Harig, "Mets accuse Houston's Mike Scott of scuffing baseball," *St. Petersburg Evening Independent*, October 14, 1986, C1.

57 "Umps: Scott doesn't scuff."

58 "Scott Stymies Mets; Series Tied, 2-2."

59 "Great Scott hunts down Mets."

60 "Houston evens series at two games apiece."

61 "Mets accuse Houston's Mike Scott of scuffing baseball."

62 Ibid.

63 Hal Bock, "New York uses hits wisely to escape grip of Ryan," Associated Press, October 15, 1986.

64 George Vecsey, "Ryan returns to New York," *New York Times*, October 16, 1986.

65 "Ryan returns to New York."

66 "Mets outduel Astros, 2-1, in 12 innings," Associated Press, October 15, 1986.

67 "Ump says runner out at 1st base," Associated Press, October 15, 1986.

68 Mark Whicker, "On Replay after Replay, Reynolds Is Safe," *Philadelphia Inquirer*, October 15, 1986.

69 "Ump says runner out at 1st base."

70 Gene Guidi, "Mets back in driver's seat," Knight-Ridder Newspapers, October 15, 1986.

71 Harry Atkins, "Ump Stands by Critical Out Call on DP," Associated Press, October 15, 1986.

72 John Nelson, "Carter's Hit Gives NY Series Lead," Associated Press, October 15, 1986.

73 "Mets take Series lead as Carter gets winning hit," Associated Press, October 15, 1986.

74 Robbie Andreu, "Bang-Bang Play Shot Down Astros' Early Scoring Threat," *Palm Beach Sun-Sentinel*, October 15, 1986.

75 "Ryan returns to New York."

76 "Carter's Hit Gives NY Series Lead"; "Bang-Bang Play Shot Down Astros' Early Scoring Threat".

77 Bruce Keidan, "A mad twist," *Pittsburgh Post-Gazette*, October 15, 1986, 13.

78 "Mets back in driver's seat"

79 Dick Young, "Scottphobia," *New York Post*, October 16, 1986.

80 Mike Downey, "All That Houston Has Ahead of It Now Is a Winter of Wondering," *Los Angeles Times*, October 16, 1986.

81 "Mets accuse Houston's Mike Scott of scuffing baseball"; "Feeney clears Scott—for now," Associated Press, October 15, 1986.

82 Richard Sandomir, "Mets' Announcers Slide into New Roles," *New York Times*, October 14, 2006.

83 "New York uses hits wisely to escape grip of Ryan." In the 22 seasons from 1965, when the Astrodome opened, through 1986, the Mets had a regular-season record there of 54-90 (.375). Over that period, their overall winning percentage was .472 and their winning percentage in road games was .450. They had a winning record at the Astrodome in just three seasons, though two of them were in 1984 and 1985.

84 Gordon Edes, "Mets Admit They're Glad to Get Off Scott-Free," *Los Angeles Times*, October 16, 1986.

85 Mike Downey described Bass as "overanxious" and Bass later confirmed this in a December 2010 meeting with SABR's Larry Dierker (Houston) chapter. See Bill McCurdy, "1986 NLCS Game 6: A Sacher Masoch Revisitation" (bill37mccurdy.wordpress.com/2010/12/15/1986-nlcs-game-6-a-sacher-masoch-revisitation/).

86 On October 9, 2005, the Astros and Atlanta Braves played 18 innings in Game Four of the National League Division Series.

87 "Mets accuse Houston's Mike Scott of scuffing baseball."

88 Terry Taylor, "Mets complain Mike Scott is 'scuffing' their attack," Associated Press, October 14, 1986.

89 Wire service reports, October 17, 1986.

90 Associated Press, October 16, 1986.

THE 1986 WORLD SERIES

By Matthew Silverman

IT HAD BEEN A HALF-GENERATION SINCE EITHER franchise had seen the World Series. And each team was somewhat haunted by failures late in its seven-game losses, resulting in grueling "what if?" scenarios due to obscure left-handers. For the New York Mets it was George Stone, having a career year in 1973 but bypassed for the Game Six start in Oakland with the Mets needing to win just one game. Mets manager Yogi Berra opted for ace Tom Seaver and his ailing shoulder on short rest. New York's seven-game loss to the Swingin' A's, though bitter, paled in comparison to Boston's Game Seven loss in 1975. Coming one night after the epic Game Six win on Carlton Fisk's 12th-inning home run, the '75 Red Sox let a 3-0 lead get away in Game Seven, but they were still tied with the Reds when manager Darrell Johnson brought in left-handed Jim Burton to pitch the ninth. Burton was victimized by a bloop single by Joe Morgan that gave the Reds the game and the world championship, 4-3.

No Met remained in 1986 from the 1973 pennant winner, though '73 shortstop Bud Harrelson had become the third-base coach and ace Tom Seaver was in a Red Sox uniform, but unable to pitch because of a bad knee. Two-thirds of the Red Sox outfield had been on the team in 1975: Dwight Evans and Jim Rice. Though Evans put his talents on display in 1975 with a game-tying home run in the ninth inning of Game Three and a tremendous game-saving catch (and throw) in the 11th inning of Game Six, Rice—who placed second in Rookie of the Year voting and third in MVP balloting to teammate Fred Lynn—sat out the 1975 postseason after a pitch broke his left hand. Now, 11 Octobers later, the future Hall of Famer finally got his first taste of the World Series.

It would be a momentous World Series, the first Series meeting between New York and Boston since the 1912 World Series, and the first meeting since 1960 by two Northeastern teams (taking into account teams from New England to Pennsylvania). It was not Yankees-Red Sox, one of baseball's fiercest rivalries, but it was a new and exciting twist coming after both the Mets and Red Sox endured palpitating League Championship Series: The Red Sox claimed the pennant by rallying from being down three games to one and trailing by three runs in the ninth inning of Game Five, while the Mets beat the Astros three times in their last at-bat, culminating in a 16-inning epic Game Six at the Astrodome that was the longest postseason game played to that time.

It was riveting television, even if it took a while for the Series to go from ho-hum to humdinger. The 28.6 rating for the 1986 World Series was almost as high as Boston's epic seven-game 1975 World Series loss. The 1986 Series was watched by more people than Mets World Series in 1969 and 1973, in a pre-cable era with

Ed Sherman's press pass, courtesy of Bob Brady.

a lot less competition on TV. The 1986 World Series was seen by an average of 36.37 million viewers per night. A 46 ratings share for the '86 Series remains untouched as of 2015.[1]

No matter which side you rooted for, the 1986 World Series was something you couldn't look away from. While it represented a bitter chapter in the annals of Boston, which has enjoyed multiple world championships since then, it has remained a touchstone for Mets fans. Their dominant team that won more than any major-league club from 1984 to 1990 did not reach another World Series during that span, and in the intervening years went to the Series just twice more, falling in five games to the Yankees in 2000 and the Royals in 2015. Losing to the Yankees in the World Series is something the Red Sox can't even claim. But the Red Sox would endure one of their bitterest moments in the final week of October 1986. For the Mets, as announcer Bob Murphy said moments after the final, "The dream has come true."[2]

NOTES

1 "World Series Television Ratings." baseball-almanac.com/ws/wstv.shtml.

2 "Murphy's Classic Calls." MLB.com, August 4, 2004. newyork.mets.mlb.com/content/printer_friendly/nym/y2004/m08/d04/c818742.jsp.

OCTOBER 18, 1986: BOSTON RED SOX 1, NEW YORK METS 0, AT SHEA STADIUM

GAME ONE / 1986 WORLD SERIES

By Matthew Silverman

IF THE LAST WORD ON THE 1986 WORLD SERIES was "unforgettable," the first word was "freezing." The heaters were on full blast in both dugouts at Shea Stadium, pitchers were allowed to blow on their hands, and bats were wrapped in towels. The fall classic felt like winter, but both teams would rather be in frigid New York than warm at home in front of the television.

"If you ever wondered what happened to Johnny Unitas's old cleats, Bill Buckner is wearing them," Vin Scully told the NBC audience early in the Series opener.[1] The announcers and many in the press treated Buckner playing on his painful ankles as heroic, or at least admirable. "When your requirement for a hotel room, the most important thing is to be near the ice machine to ice down your leg, that tells you the determination of that fellow," Scully's partner, Joe Garagiola, chimed in about Buckner.[2]

But from his first at-bat, when he bounced into a double play in the first inning, it was clear that Buckner's mobility was severely compromised, even though he said his new high-top shoes made a difference. Sitting and watching from the dugout was perfectly healthy Don Baylor, who had started at first base 13 times in '86 while committing just one error. But without the designated hitter in the National League park, Baylor was stapled to the Boston bench at Shea Stadium. The DH had been used in both the AL and NL park in the World Series in even years from 1976 through 1985, until the rule was changed by Commissioner Peter Ueberroth late in the 1986 season to follow the rule of the home park starting with the '86 World Series.[3] So Baylor, a former MVP with 31 home runs in 1986, who had waited 15 years as an everyday player—plus four losing American League Championship Series—to finally reach the World Series, would have to wait a couple of days longer.

A future manager, Baylor had plenty of time on the bench to think about how the recent rule change could affect the Series. "The advantage will probably be to the Mets because they can get a hitter four or five swings," Baylor said. "But if I have to sit and watch, that takes away a regular from us."[4] He was forced to watch Bruce Hurst bat for the first time in the majors, striking out all three times. But no one was talking about Hurst's hitting.

With the wind off Flushing Bay pushing the temperature down into the 40s, Hurst handcuffed the Mets from the outset. He struck out the first two Mets, Mookie Wilson and Lenny Dykstra, and fanned four his first time through the lineup. The second time through, however, Wilson and Dykstra each reached base and Hurst had to navigate Keith Hernandez and Gary Carter to get out of the third inning. It was the last time the Mets had multiple runners on base all night.

Ron Darling wasn't bad, either. After a single by Marty Barrett in the first, he retired the next nine batters before Buckner singled with two outs in the fourth. Darling wild-pitched him to second and then walked Jim Rice, but Dwight Evans, whom Darling had watched from the Fenway Park bleachers growing up in Worcester, Massachusetts, flied out to end the inning. Someone Darling had played against in high school in Worcester in the 1970s would hit the ball that proved the difference in the 1986 World Series opener.

"We went to different schools, rival schools," Gedman recalled three decades later as hitting coach for the Red Sox Double-A affiliate in Portland, Maine. "He's a couple of years younger than I am. But still it's nice to see somebody from the area make it to the major leagues — not only make it to the major leagues, but have an opportunity to win a world championship. It's a shame that both can't win, but I was happy for him."[5]

Gedman's routine grounder in the seventh inning went through Mets second baseman Tim Teufel's legs and brought home Jim Rice with the game's only run.

Seeing that the Red Sox had a chance to take the opener on the road from the brash 108-win Mets, the overwhelming World Series favorites among Las Vegas oddsmakers at 2½ to 1, Boston manager John McNamara pulled out all the stops. And he pulled his starting pitcher — not to mention his first baseman.

Calvin Schiraldi, the key player the Red Sox got from the Mets the previous offseason in the eight-player deal that sent Bob Ojeda to New York, came on to pitch the ninth inning after Hurst had limited the Mets to four hits and four walks. (Ron Darling, on the short side for the Mets, allowed just three hits and three walks in seven innings.) McNamara sent up Mike Greenwell to bat for Hurst with two outs in the top of the ninth after left fielder Kevin Mitchell threw out Dwight Evans at the plate on Dave Henderson's single. Boston never got that insurance run, but the Red Sox did have defensive insurance. As McNamara had done in all four wins in the ALCS, Dave Stapleton came on to play first base for the hobbled Buckner with Boston leading.

After Schiraldi walked Strawberry to open the bottom of the ninth, Stapleton fielded Ray Knight's bunt and got the lead runner at second. Schiraldi retired former teammates Wally Backman and Danny Heep and the Red Sox had Game One. The Mets, who hit just .189 in the NLCS in Houston but hit the jackpot three times in their last at-bat, looked more anemic than unlucky against Boston in the Series opener. The Mets had not been shut out at Shea Stadium since September 1985, but the second postseason series in as many weeks began with a 1-0 Mets loss. For the Red Sox, facing Dwight Gooden the next evening

Shortstop Rafael Santana (#3) being introduced and greeting his teammates before one of the games.

with their own ace, Roger Clemens, on the mound, winning Game One was just what the doctor ordered. Well, maybe not Doc Gooden.

NOTES

1 New York Mets 1986 World Series Collector's Edition, Game One. MLB Official DVD, A&E Home Video, 2006.

2 Ibid.

3 G. Richard McKelvey, *All Bat No Glove: A History of the Designated Hitter* (Jefferson, North Carolina: McFarland & Co., 2003), 86, 92.

4 George Vecsey, "The Designated Hitter Rule Is Unfair to Don Baylor," *New York Times*, October 19, 1986.

5 Author interview with Rich Gedman, August 14, 2014.

OCTOBER 19, 1986: BOSTON RED SOX 9, NEW YORK METS 3, AT SHEA STADIUM

GAME TWO / 1986 WORLD SERIES

By Matthew Silverman

FOR EVERY GREAT WORLD SERIES PITCHER'S duel, there are a dozen duds that don't live up to the hype. Game Two certainly fell into the latter category; the hype belonged in a class by itself. The game's starting pitchers had each put together 24-4 seasons by age 24—Dwight Gooden pulled off the feat in 1985 at age 20 and the elder Roger Clemens did it in 1986, starting the year by winning his first 14 decisions and setting a major-league record by fanning 20 in an April game. Game Two of the World Series also featured the same starters from that year's All-Star Game. The only other time it happened was in 1939 between Red Ruffing of the Yankees and Cincinnati's Paul Derringer.1 That World Series game had been a pitcher's duel pulled out by New York in its final at-bat. This time ... not so much.

Gooden's 1986 had not been a 24-4, Triple Crown season like his 1985, but his 17-6 mark, 2.84 ERA, and 200 strikeouts all stood in the top five in the NL—along with his 250 innings, .739 winning percentage, 12 complete games, and 1.108 WHIP. Toss in 17 innings with just two runs allowed in the NLCS against Houston. But New York writers had spent much of the year postulating after almost every bad inning, "What's wrong with Doc?" That thinking was on the mark in Game Two.

Gooden got through the first two innings allowing only one baserunner but four hard-hit outs. His luck ran out in the third. After Gooden walked Spike Owen to lead off—despite being ahead 1-2—Roger Clemens came up for his first major-league at-bat. It was a tough assignment, with Keith Hernandez charging in full tilt as he'd done for years against National Leaguers, collecting every Gold Glove since 1978 (and winning 11 straight Gold Gloves eventually). Hernandez got to the bunt quickly enough, but he hurried unnecessarily and bounced the throw to second. Everybody was safe. The next three hitters each drove in runs with hits, including what would be Bill Buckner's only RBI of the World Series. Boston held a 3-0 lead on the night of the full harvest moon. "So far at least it's been the Red Sox doing the harvesting," offered Vin Scully on NBC.[2]

The Mets finally scored in their 12th inning at the plate in the World Series, and even then they were frustrated by two superb plays by Wade Boggs to rob the Mets of hits—and runs. With Boston up 4-2 and two Mets aboard and two outs in the fourth, Davey Johnson let Gooden bat. Bill Buckner made a nice play on Gooden's grounder and threw to Clemens covering to end the threat. Letting a Cy Young winner hit in the fourth inning of a two-run game didn't seem too controversial a decision ... until the top of the fifth. Then, after Jim Rice singled, Dwight Evans launched a ball on the roof of the tent over the picnic area in left field. Gooden trudged off the mound, struggling through the fifth, his night clearly done. Who would have thought he'd outlast Clemens?

Having a four-run lead and needing two outs to qualify for the win, Clemens was removed at the end of a long talk with John McNamara with two Mets on base. The eventual Cy Young winner and AL MVP gave way to middle reliever Steve Crawford. He allowed a single to his first batter, Gary Carter, to make it a 6-3 game, and then Crawford retired both Darryl Strawberry and Danny Heep. Heep in left field and Howard Johnson at third base were shake-up-the-lineup moves by Davey

Johnson that didn't work. At least on this night. That pair replaced Ray Knight and Mookie Wilson, who'd had big hits late in the marathon NLCS Game Six in Houston, and would have some magic left in them yet in October. But Heep and HoJo could have gone 6-for-6 between them in Game Two and the Mets would still have been far off the Boston hit parade. The Red Sox outhit the Mets, 18-8, including five straight singles in the eighth.

The Red Sox were looking to turn back the clock many decades. The year 1918, the season Boston won its last world championship, was brought up repeatedly in the press and on the air. Boston's odds-defying five-game winning streak since they'd stared defeat in the face in Anaheim seemed to be gaining momentum, especially as the Series shifted to Fenway Park. The Red Sox had beaten both Darling and Gooden and now they had to face a pitcher they knew so well they'd shipped him out of town the previous winter.

NOTES

1 Associated Press, "Scherzer Outduels Harvey in Battle of All-Stars." Yes Network. web.yesnetwork.com/news/article.jsp?ymd=20130824&content_id=58228382&oid=0&print=true.

2 *New York Mets 1986 World Series Collector's Edition*, Game Two. MLB Official DVD, A&E Home Video, 2006.

OCTOBER 21, 1986: NEW YORK METS 7, BOSTON RED SOX 1, AT FENWAY PARK

GAME THREE / 1986 WORD SERIES

By Matthew Silverman

BOB OJEDA HAD NO LOVE LOST FOR THE Red Sox, and the feeling was mutual. The free-thinking and independent southpaw had not always fit in when Fenway was his home park, and his hard-line pro-union stance leading up to the previous year's two-day strike had not endeared him to all of the team's veterans. He got a fresh start in New York. Lou Gorman, Frank Cashen's assistant in New York, had returned to his native New England to take over as Boston's GM in 1985, and his big move in terms of pitching was to send Ojeda to New York in an eight-man deal that netted Calvin Schiraldi, who eventually became Boston's closer. Ojeda had to work his way into New York's rotation from the bullpen. That probably cost him 20 wins, but his 18-5 mark produced the best winning percentage (.783) of any pitcher in the National League—in fact, the top four pitchers in winning percentage were all Mets, including the Mets' other lefty starter, Sid Fernandez. After the beating the Mets took in Game Two, Davey Johnson reworked his rotation on the fly and moved Fernandez, an All-Star with 16 wins and 200 strikeouts, to the bullpen. And then he gave the Mets all of Monday off, telling his players to stay at the Sheraton while he went to Fenway Park and took the heat. The Mets had played at Fenway in a charity exhibition game six weeks earlier. They'd already *ooh-ed* and *ah-ed* at the fabled Green Monster and taken their practice swings at the big wall. Now it was for real.

Lefty-swinging Lenny Dykstra wasn't aiming at the left-field wall, but he was thinking home run. And the Mets leadoff hitter, with just eight homers all year—plus a game-winning blast in the NLCS—pulled Oil Can Boyd's third pitch inside the foul pole in right. The mood on the Mets bench changed completely and the next three batters all hit the ball hard and reached base. Gary Carter's double made it 2-0 and put runners on second and third. Yet when Darryl Strawberry fanned for the 17th time in 29 postseason at-bats, it looked as if Boston might avoid a big inning when Ray Knight hit a grounder to third.

Keith Hernandez should have been out dead to rights, but he stopped and headed back to third. Catcher Rich Gedman threw to Boggs in the baseline instead of Spike Owen at the base and the runner was safe. But Carter was just a few steps from third and now he was in a rundown. When Hernandez faked home, Marty Barrett shifted his full attention as if the Mets first baseman had transformed into Rickey Henderson, but Barrett's fleeting glance back was all it took and Carter dove back into second. The bases were loaded.

While Red Sox fans still had their hands on their head wondering what happened, Danny Heep—the first designated hitter in Mets history—lined a single to score both Hernandez and Carter. The slow-footed but quick-minded baserunners had helped the Mets score as many runs in one inning as they had in the first two games.

The Mets had just one baserunner over the next six innings against Oil Can Boyd, but it all came apart for the Can in the seventh. Rafael Santana and Dykstra singled—his third of four hits in the game –and with two outs Boyd walked Keith Hernandez on four pitches to bring up Gary Carter. Boyd got ahead 0-and-2. Carter pulled a single into left and tried to take second on the throw but was caught in a rundown. This time the Red Sox tagged him out. Too late to do any good.

Dennis "Oil Can" Boyd pitching for Boston in Game Three of the World Series.

Bob Ojeda, who stood between his old team taking complete control of the World Series and his new team getting back into it, did not look like the pitcher who came into the night with a lifetime 4.39 ERA at Fenway Park. A free spirit who spoke his mind, he was not quite Bill Lee rebelling against Red Sox management a few years earlier, but Ojeda was motivated to beat his old team. He played it more diplomatically, though far from dully, in an interview NBC broadcast during the game: He told NBC, "Part of me is still here, beyond a doubt because I left some blood here and some tears here, as dramatic as that sounds, and I grew up here. But I belong somewhere else now, but I enjoyed my time here."[1]

Ojeda buzzed through Boston with his assortment of off-speed pitches and his well-placed fastball. "The left-hander changed speeds like an Indy 500 driver," *New York Daily News* columnist Phil Pepe wrote of Ojeda's Game Three start.[2]

The Red Sox reached base eight times against Ojeda, just two times fewerthan the Mets did against Boyd, but the Mets got the big hits with men on base. The Red Sox went 1-for-7. When three Red Sox reached base in the third inning and scored their lone run—on a Marty Barrett single—Ojeda was visited by manager Davey Johnson, as opposed to pitching coach Mel Stottlemyre. Ojeda responded by fanning Bill Buckner on four pitches and getting Jim Rice, representing the tying run, to ground out on the first pitch. On his 114th and final pitch of the night, in the seventh, he retired another future Hall of Famer, Wade Boggs. This time the game wasn't on the line, it was in his back pocket.

Roger McDowell retired all six batters he faced to finish the 7-1 victory. Davey Johnson's decision to give the Mets Monday off and not make them come to Fenway and be prodded by the hungry media looked brilliant. After the game Johnson said, "It's my job to sense things on the ballclub and to do things that will stimulate them. I felt they needed their rest."[3] Three decades later, Johnson was more pragmatic. "I couldn't get away with that today," he said. "If I did that today I'd probably be fined $250,000, I don't know. But I just felt like we needed a break, you know?"[4]

NOTES

1 *New York Mets 1986 World Series Collector's Edition*, Game Three. MLB Official DVD, A&E Home Video, 2006.

2 Phil Pepe, "Wall Falls to Ojeda," *New York Daily News*, October 22, 1986.

3 Ibid.

4 Author interview with Davey Johnson, March 31, 2015.

OCTOBER 22, 1986: NEW YORK METS 6, BOSTON RED SOX 2, AT FENWAY PARK

GAME FOUR / 1986 WORLD SERIES

By Matthew Silverman

IF BOBBY OJEDA TANTALIZED THE TEAM HE ONCE played for in Game Three of the 1986 World Series, Ron Darling tortured the team he grew up rooting for in Game Four. A night after Ojeda got the Mets on the board for the first win of the Series by holding Boston to 1-for-7 with runners in scoring position, Darling allowed 10 Red Sox to reach base. None of them scored.

Darling was just 7 years old when the 1967 Red Sox won the Impossible Dream pennant and took the Cardinals to Game Seven of the World Series. At 15, he was in the bleachers for fabled Game Six of the 1975 World Series at Fenway Park as a high-school student. He attended Yale and performed well enough to be a first-round pick by Texas before winding up with the Mets system in a trade a year later.

Hawaiian-born, Ivy-educated, a *GQ* cover boy, and second in the Mets rotation only to phenom Dwight Gooden, Darling had something for everybody. George Vecsey of the *New York Times* described Darling that week as "a walking display for the polyglot beauty of Hawaii: the looks of his French father and Chinese mother making him strikingly handsome even among his healthy young colleagues. Yale University certainly claims him, even if he doesn't have his degree yet. And in the crush of the 1-0 loss on Saturday night, which included a painful collision with Dave Henderson near home plate, Darling found time to be extra gracious to a reporter from Worcester, Mass., his home town since the age of 7."[1]

But all that experience and awareness didn't mean he wasn't nervous heading into his first-ever game at the ballpark he thought of as home. His pregame warmup had not been good and ended early, but his nervousness began to pass after he spotted Ron Darling Sr. on the field in uniform for the National Anthem with the Air Force Reserve. Ron Jr. went and stood by his dad during the anthem at Fenway. "In my head, at least, I was transformed," Darling later wrote. "I went from someone who couldn't throw a strike to someone would not be denied, all in the space of a pregame ritual."[2]

The Red Sox loaded the bases in the bottom of the first, with Darling issuing back-to-back two-out walks to Jim Rice and Don Baylor to face Dwight Evans, who had made a spectacular, game-saving catch in front of Darling in the Fenway bleachers in Game Six of the 1975 World Series. Now Darling saved himself, inducing Evans to ground out and stranding three. He allowed a leadoff double in the second to another familiar face, Worcester high-school rival turned Red Sox catcher Rich Gedman. Gedman went to third on a grounder but stayed there when Darling retired Wade Boggs to end the threat.

When the Red Sox took a two-games-to-none lead in the World Series, John McNamara opted to stay with the four-man rotation, while his counterpart, Davey Johnson, felt compelled to cut down to a three-man rotation. And while Darling—pitching on short rest—labored the first time through the Boston order, Al Nipper, who had last appeared in a game 17 days earlier, pitched to just one Met over the minimum with eight groundouts and a strikeout to go with one measly single. Then Wally Backman led off the fourth with a single through the middle. McNamara called for a pitchout, but Keith Hernandez threw his bat at the ball and hit a grounder to shortstop. Though Hernandez was out, Backman moved up a base. And

Excited Fenway Park crowd before one of their home games in the World Series.

Nipper soon wished he had been more careful against Gary Carter with a base open.

Carter crushed Nipper's first-pitch fastball into the net over the Green Monster. Suddenly Nipper looked rusty. Darryl Strawberry doubled and Ray Knight singled him home to make it 3-0 Mets.

Darling retired 10 straight until he walked Spike Owen in the fifth. Owen failed to take second when Carter could not locate a pitch in the dirt, and that cost Boston when Marty Barrett's single moved Owen two bases. As he did all night, Darling was unhittable with runners in scoring position and he got Bill Buckner to pop up to end the threat.

The Mets failed to add top their lead when Gary Carter was thrown out by Jim Rice trying to tag up to end the top of the sixth, but an even more crucial—and unexpected—outfield assist ended the bottom of the sixth. With Dwight Evans on first, Rich Gedman hit a wall ball against Darling. But the Mets had an ace up their sleeve: the former manager of the Red Sox. Darrell Johnson, who managed the 1975 Red Sox to the pennant, was now a scout for the Mets and gave a detailed report on Boston's tendencies. Keith Hernandez recalled years later how the Mets prepared for one bit of intel. "They hit flyballs off the Monster and Darrell Johnson and Davey [Johnson] told them how when you get a ball off the Monster, you think it's a double, but you've got a chance to throw the runner out," Hernandez said. "The runner on first is not going to score on that double, but you have a chance to throw that runner out at second base if you field the ball off the wall cleanly because it's so close … and Mookie fielded it cleanly and threw it in to second base. Right to second base."[3] Gedman was out and the inning was over. Both the crowd and the Boston bench remained frustrated.

The Mets roughed up Nipper's replacement, Steve Crawford. Lenny Dykstra's drive in the seventh inning glanced off Dwight Evans's eight-time Gold Glove and landed in the visiting bullpen for a home run. Gary Carter hit a no-doubter in the eighth, his second homer of the night clearing the Green Monster as well as the screen and disappearing under a van across Lansdowne Street.

As a final bit of torment, Darling walked two batters in his final inning, but his 115th pitch was popped up by Bill Buckner. Roger McDowell ran into trouble in relief in the eighth, allowing two runs on three hits and a walk, but Jesse Orosco came in and got Wade Boggs to ground out and strand two more baserunners. The Red Sox left 11 men on base. They left their World Series lead behind as well.

NOTES

1 George Vecsey, "Ron Darling in the Fourth," *New York Times*, October 20, 1986.

2 Ron Darling, and Daniel Paisner, *The Complete Game: Reflections on Baseball, Pitching, and Life on the Mound* (New York: Alfred A. Knopf, 2009), 72.

3 Author interview with Keith Hernandez, December 22, 2014.

OCTOBER 23, 1986: BOSTON RED SOX 4, NEW YORK METS 2, AT FENWAY PARK

GAME FIVE / 1986 WORLD SERIES

By Matthew Silverman

AFTER GAME FOUR, REPORTERS ASKED Red Sox manager John McNamara about his slumping hitters, notably former batting champion Bill Buckner and reigning batting champ Wade Boggs, who against the Mets were hitting a combined .171 (6-for-35), effectively neutering the advantage provided by their hottest hitter, Marty Barrett, who batted between the lefties in the lineup and was hitting .412 (7-for-17). "Sure I'm concerned," the manager replied, "but what am I going to do about it."[1] Starting Bruce Hurst would help a great deal.

Buckner and Boggs were not the heroes in Game Five, but they each hit safely against Dwight Gooden. The Red Sox hammered Dr. K again, waiting him out as he tried to beat them with his curveball. On a night when his fastball did not have its usual movement, half of his 82 pitches were curves. *Boston Globe* reporter Dan Shaughnessy likened that idea to "a *Playboy* centerfold trying to impress her date in the kitchen."[2] Gooden's strategy cooked up trouble. He reached two strikes a dozen times, but fanned just three while allowing seven singles and two triples. Boston also coaxed two walks from Gooden and took advantage of a key infield error.

With Boston leading 1-0 on a Spike Owen sacrifice fly, Bill Buckner hit a grounder that shortstop Rafael Santana mishandled. Jim Rice walked and Don Baylor struck out, bringing up Dwight Evans with two outs. Two days in a row Evans had been retired with the bases loaded to end the first inning; now up with two men on in the third, he lined a Gooden fastball into right-center field with Buckner hobbling home and bellyflopping across the plate as the throw sailed wide. "He's got the Red Badge of Courage on his chest," NBC's Vin Scully said as Buckner scraped his battered body off the ground for congratulations in the Boston dugout.[3]

Bruce Hurst, pitching on four days' rest, was not as sharp as he'd been in Game One, but he was just as effective. He stranded two Mets in both the third and fifth, striking out Lenny Dykstra and retiring Tim Teufel after the Mets put runners on second and third with one out. Boston doubled its lead in the home fifth as the first three Red Sox hit safely to start the inning. Davey Johnson handed the ball to Sid Fernandez.

Fernandez, an All-Star, 16-game winner, and 200-strikeout pitcher in 1986, had been banished to the pen when the Mets manager cut his four-man rotation to three after his team's Shea debacle to start the World Series. Asked to stem the tide in Game Five, Fernandez allowed a run-scoring double to Dave Henderson to make it 4-0, which was no crime given that Hendu's average stood at .471 as he stood on second base. But Fernandez got out of the jam and allowed just two other hits, walked none, and fanned five while pitching the final four innings. It may have been too late to save the game, but just giving a night's rest to weary Mets relievers Roger McDowell and Jesse Orosco was a positive.

Hurst didn't need any relievers, though John McNamara had the bullpen warming up as the game neared its conclusion. The Mets finally scored on Hurst after 15⅓ innings of frustration when Tim Teufel hit an opposite-field home run on an 0-and-2 pitch in the eighth. McNamara had batted for Hurst in the ninth inning of Game One with a one-run lead, but at Fenway Park, with the designated hitter preclud-

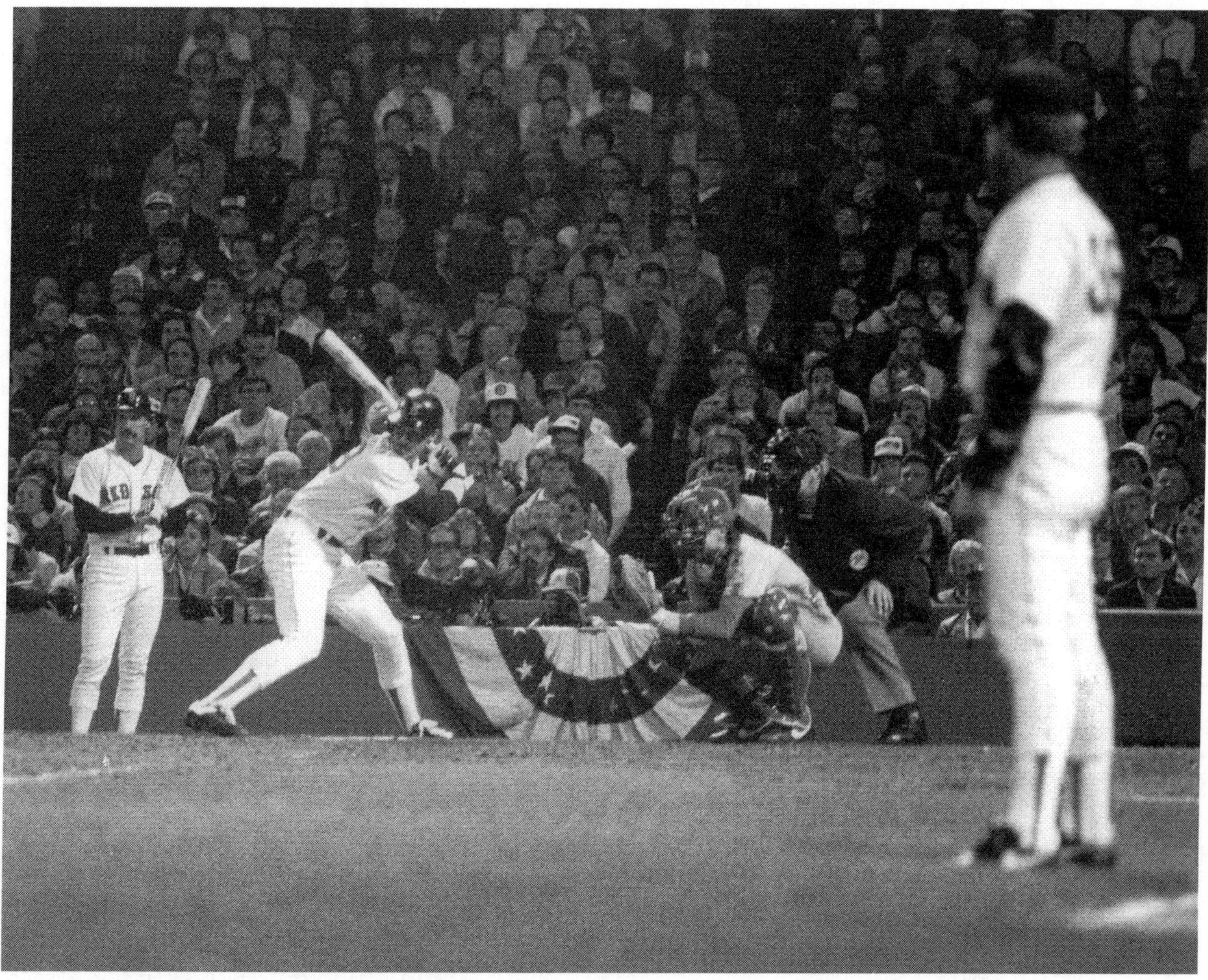

Boston Red Sox left fielder Mike Greenwell batting; Wade Boggs on deck. Gary Carter is catching.

ing Hurst from batting, McNamara stayed with the southpaw. He did send in a new first baseman, however. As he'd done in Boston's six previous postseason wins in October 1986, Dave Stapleton came in for defense. He made the first two putouts of the ninth. The third out did not come as easily.

Mookie Wilson doubled to left and Rafael Santana singled to score Wilson and bring the tying run to the plate. Up came Lenny Dykstra, who'd homered the past two nights and won a game in New York with a homer in the ninth inning in the NLCS. This time he chased a high fastball for strike three and Boston led the Series once more, breaking the visiting team's mojo to boot. Finally, a home team won a game in the 1986 World Series. It would not be the last time.

NOTES

1 *New York Daily News Scrapbook History of the N.Y. Mets 1986 Season* (New York: New York News, 1987), 235.

2 Dan Shaughnessy, *One Pitch Away* (New York: Beaufort Books Publishers, 1987), 247.

3 *New York Mets 1986 World Series Collector's Edition*, Game Five. MLB Official DVD, A&E Home Video, 2006.

OCTOBER 25, 1986: NEW YORK METS 6, BOSTON RED SOX 5 (10 INNINGS), AT SHEA STADIUM

GAME SIX / 1986 WORLD SERIES

By Matthew Silverman

RIGHT FROM THE FIRST INNING IT WAS obvious this was not going to be a typical game. Even by World Series Game Six standards, this one was out of this world. And that is where Mike Sergio came from, drifting down onto the Shea Stadium infield in a parachute with a modest "Go Mets" sign hanging off it. A veteran skydiver and a middling actor, he made the jump because he was incensed by a balloon-festooned banner at Fenway Park that he had seen on TV. He would serve jail time the following summer for his breach of airspace and flouting of an untold number of laws. But he was quickly hustled off the field in Game Six and the first pitch by Bob Ojeda was thrown less than a minute after he landed. The game was what mattered. And what a game.

After being so rudely interrupted from above, the Red Sox scored in the first on a double by Dwight Evans and added another in the second on Marty Barrett's RBI single. That seemed as though it could go a long way with Roger Clemens on full rest pitching full bore and no-hitting the Mets through four innings, but the Mets were making Clemens work. He threw 72 pitches (49 strikes) to get that far and the crowd was working him, too. Chants of "Ro-ger! Ro-ger" were payback for the derisive catcalls by the Fenway faithful of "Dar-ryl! Dar-ryl!" Strawberry started the home fifth with his second walk of the night and—just as he'd done in the second inning—he stole second. On the next pitch Ray Knight singled through the middle and Strawberry crossed the plate to cut Boston's lead in half. Mookie Wilson singled to right field and Knight took third with no one out when Evans bobbled the ball. That proved key since Danny Heep, batting for Rafael Santana, bounced into a double play that tied the game. It marked the first time, other than 0-0, that a 1986 World Series game was tied.

Given a reprieve, Bobby Ojeda batted for himself (he grounded out) and threw another inning. Going six innings was quite a feat for Ojeda since Boston had runners on base in all but one inning yet left eight on base against Ojeda. The Red Sox took advantage of shoddy defense by the Mets in the seventh against Roger McDowell, with Knight's errant throw pulling Keith Hernandez off first to put runners on the corners. Boston, without a steal attempt in the Series, tried the hit-and-run several times and usually sent runners on 3-and-2, as the Red Sox did Jim Rice in the seventh. His jump enabled him to beat a throw to second on what looked like a double-play ball. The Mets got Dwight Evans at first, but because Rice was safe at second, Marty Barrett crossed home plate for a 3-2 Boston lead. When Rich Gedman followed with a single it looked as if Boston would double its lead, but for the second time in the Series, Mookie Wilson, who had a notoriously weak arm and had undergone shoulder surgery the previous winter, threw to Gary Carter on the fly and the catcher rode Rice away from the plate for the third out. Rice's speed, or lack thereof, had kept him from scoring on Evans's rattling ball in the gap in the first inning, and it haunted Boston again, but not nearly as much as much as a decision by John McNamara that would stay with Red Sox fans for years to come.

A blister on Roger Clemens' pitching hand kept him from being effective with his breaking pitches and he logged 134 pitches through seven innings, but it was a time when the number of pitches was often ignored and Clemens had thrown 10 complete games during the season while logging 155⅔ more innings than the previous year (not even counting his five postseason starts covering an additional 34 innings). But with a runner on first and no one out in the eighth inning against McDowell, McNamara had Spike Owen bunt, and then he batted for Clemens with Mike Greenwell—highlight on "green" for the 23-year-old outfielder who had yet to even play enough to qualify as a rookie. He fanned on three pitches.

With Clemens done, ex-Met Calvin Schiraldi came in in the Mets eighth to try to finish off the first Red Sox title in 68 years. He gave up a hit to the first batter he faced, Lee Mazzilli, batting for Jesse Orosco, who had thrown one pitch to finish the Red Sox eighth. Lenny Dykstra followed with a bunt and Schiraldi bounced the throw to second. The Mets wound up tying the game on Gary Carter's sacrifice fly. The tension trebled.

The bottom of the ninth seemed like a carbon copy of the eighth, with the Red Sox messing up the force play on a bunt. This time it was Rich Gedman who made a bad throw. The difference was that Davey Johnson, never a fan of the sacrifice, bunted twice in a row in the eighth and the Mets scored; in the ninth, pinch-hitter Howard Johnson looked bad trying to bunt the first pitch, swung away on the next, and fanned on the third pitch. The Mets did not score and the game moved to the 10th.

The second-guessers took a front-row seat when Dave Henderson homered just above the "a" in the *Newsday* sign. Many scribes started moving toward the visiting clubhouse, where champagne—loaned to the Red Sox by the Mets—was now being iced. The championship indeed looked for all the world to be on ice when Boston scored a second run off Rick Aguilera on Marty Barrett's single.

With two outs in the bottom of the 10th, with the baseball world wondering how the Mets hadn't bunted a second time in the ninth, with writers—depending on where they hailed from—either spouting lyrically about the end of an epic New England baseball drought or New York's failure to get down a bunt, and with frustrated Keith Hernandez sitting in his manager's office drinking a beer, the game changed. Gary Carter singled. Pinch-hitter Kevin Mitchell singled. Ray Knight, down 0-and-2, singled to center to score Carter and send Mitchell to third. John McNamara came out, took the ball, and handed it to Bob Stanley.

Mets catcher Gary Carter being interviewed.

Stanley, who led Boston with 16 saves—Schiraldi, not called up from the minors until late July, was third on the club with nine—faced Mookie Wilson, whom he'd faced three times, retired twice, and struck out once in the Series. With the count 2-and-2, Wilson jackknifed out of the way of a slider that, in the words of the man who called it, Rich Gedman, "ran inside a little bit and I didn't get it."[1] The ball went to the backstop, Kevin Mitchell scored, and the game was tied. With Shea Stadium shaking, the Mets dugout ecstatic, Keith Hernandez superstitiously refusing to leave the manager's office during the rally, and Mookie Wilson still at the plate, the game hurtled toward its implausible climax.

On the 10th pitch from Stanley, Wilson hit a "little roller up along first," as Vin Scully said of almost every such groundball in the Series, but this was no routine grounder. The ball skipped through Bill Buckner's legs and Ray Knight scored. "Behind the bag! It gets through Buckner! Here comes Knight and the Mets win it!"[2]

No words were spoken on NBC for three minutes as announcer and network let the reactions on camera and the screaming by the fans say it all. Sometimes words just can't adequately capture a moment. When Marv Albert put microphones in front of Wilson and Knight, they didn't have much luck, either. There wasn't much left to say, or give. "I'm just exhausted right now," Knight admitted. "I'm happy, but I've never been more tired than I am right now."[3] Boston was sick and tired, especially given that Dave Stapleton had replaced the ailing Buckner at first base for defense every time Boston held the lead in the final inning during the postseason. With one unforgettable exception.

NOTES

1 Author interview with Rich Gedman, August 14, 2014.

2 *New York Mets 1986 World Series Collector's Edition*, Game Six. MLB Official DVD, A&E Home Video, 2006.

3 Ibid.

OCTOBER 27, 1986: NEW YORK METS 8, BOSTON RED SOX 5, AT SHEA STADIUM

GAME SEVEN / 1986 WORLD SERIES

By Matthew Silverman

IN THE YEARS THAT FOLLOWED, IT WAS SIMPLE to say that victory in Game Seven was preordained after their miraculous escape from Game Six, but triumph in the deciding game was far from assured. As in the 1975 World Series, the Red Sox—after their own legendary '75 Game Six win on Carlton Fisk's home run—took a 3-0 lead in Game Seven. Both 1975 and 1986 ended with Game Sevens Boston wished it could it forget but could not; those with longer memories recalled Game Sevens from 1946 and 1967.

First, all parties had to wait an extra day in 1986. After the Mets' dramatic Saturday-night victory, Sunday was a washout and the teams convened again on Monday night. The two baseball teams did not only have to contest each other, but the game also went up against Giants-Redskins from the Meadowlands on *Monday Night Football.* The competition was a total rout in terms of ratings, with baseball on NBC garnering a 38.9 rating and 34 million viewers, the largest audience ever for a World Series contest, while the football game had just an 8.8 rating, ABC's lowest since *MNF* debuted in 1970. In addition, the reactions from the crowd at Giants Stadium were such that they confused the football players on the field who were not following the goings-on at Shea Stadium.[1] What a game they missed.

Dwight Evans and Rich Gedman hit back-to-back home runs for the Red Sox in the second inning, with Gedman's ball bouncing off irate Darryl Strawberry's glove on its way over the fence. Then Wade Boggs singled home Dave Henderson and it was 3-0. Two innings later, with a man on second and two outs, Mets starter Ron Darling was replaced by Sid Fernandez, an All-Star who had been bounced from the rotation when the Mets fell behind two games to none. Now he played as important a role as any Met in 1986. Standing between the Mets and oblivion, El Sid walked his first batter, batting champion Wade Boggs, to bring up Marty Barrett, who had already tied a World Series record with 13 hits. Fernandez got him to fly to right to end the inning and start a stretch of seven straight batters retired to take the Mets through the top of the sixth.

Like Ron Darling, Boston's Bruce Hurst was making his third start of the World Series. The rainout bumped Oil Can Boyd from the rotation, and Hurst, pitching on three days' rest, was brilliant. He retired 16 of the first 17 batters with Rafael Santana grounding out to start the home sixth. And just like that, everything changed.

Lee Mazzilli, batting for Fernandez, singled to left. Another switch-hitter, Mookie Wilson, followed with a single. The tying run came to the plate for the first time in the game, yet Hurst could have gotten out of the jam by getting Tim Teufel to hit into a double play. He pitched carefully to Teufel, who had hit him better than any other Met in the Series, going 4-for-9 and breaking up Hurst's string of 15⅓ innings of shutout ball in the Series with a home run in Game Five. In Game Seven, Teufel walked on five pitches to load the bases.

That brought up a left-handed batter against the southpaw, but lefty vs. lefty was secondary as Keith Hernandez stepped to the plate. He was as qualified for the job as any player in Mets history. To that point he had the franchise's highest career average by 22 points (Hernandez at .309 topped Steve Henderson's

Darryl Strawberry hit a solo home run in the eighth inning of Game Seven to help the Mets beat Boston.

.287 for best average in at least 1,000 at-bats by a Met through 1986) and he had led the juggernaut '86 Mets in batting average, runs, hits, and doubles.[2] And Hernandez as a St. Louis Cardinal had come through in almost this exact same spot in the 1982 World Series against the Milwaukee Brewers, following a walk by a lefty (Bob McClure) to a right-handed batter (Gene Tenace). Back then Hernandez cracked a game-tying two-run single off McClure and the Cards went on to beat the Brewers.

"I was like, 'You've got to be kidding me,'" Hernandez said of the similarities between his sixth-inning World Series at-bats in Game Seven in '82 and '86. "It was the same situation basically, which I thought was kind of ironic."[3]

And he came through again. Hernandez's two-run single got the Mets on the board. And while Hernandez didn't tie the game as he had in the 1982 World Series, Gary Carter followed by knocking in the tying run. Hurst got through the inning, but when Tony Armas pinch-hit for him the following inning, it became a battle of bullpens—and that played to the Mets' strength. Roger McDowell, who had won 14 games and saved 22 during the season, fanned Armas while setting down the Red Sox in order in the seventh. In the bottom of the inning Calvin Schiraldi returned to the scene of New England's nightmare two nights earlier. Ray Knight, who scored the winning run on Bill Buckner's fateful error in Game Six, scored the tiebreaking run again, this time under his own power. He drilled Schiraldi's fastball over the wall in left-center as the Mets took a 4-3 lead. Schiraldi allowed a hit to Lenny Dykstra, a wild pitch, and an RBI single to Rafael Santana. After McDowell's sacrifice, John McNamara replaced Schiraldi with Joe Sambito, who walked two batters (one intentionally) and permitted an insurance run when Hernandez drove home another run home against a lefty. Bob Stanley ended the rally by retiring Gary Carter.

Boston came ever so close to tying the score in the eighth inning. In his 82nd appearance and 142nd inning of relief (postseason included), McDowell was done. The first three Red Sox got hits off him, with Dwight Evans' two-run double making it a 6-5 game. Jesse Orosco, who had saved 21 games during the year, plus three wins and a save in October, came in with the tying run on second and no one out. Rich Gedman hit a bullet that was snagged by Wally Backman, brought in for defense. Orosco fanned Dave Henderson, and Don Baylor, in his only at-bat of the Series in the NL park, grounded out to end the threat.

The Mets opened up the lead when Darryl Strawberry homered and Jesse Orosco—in the old "butcher boy play"—pulled back a bunt attempt and singled through the vacated hole to take an 8-5 lead into the ninth. With two down, nobody on, and New York preparing to explode, Marty Barrett swung through the fastball. Orosco's glove went airborne, and the Mets were world champions.

What had been a rather ho-hum World Series for five games turned into an all-time classic thanks to the comebacks in the final two games. Parachutists dropping in, balls going through infielders' legs, balls bouncing off gloves into the stands for home runs, teams skipping workouts, botched bunt plays, muffed rundowns, designated hitters, pitching changes that were made, pitching changes that weren't, and curses unleashed by long-dead sluggers—it wasn't a work of art, but the images produced in the 1986 World Series were indelible marks on the baseball landscape. The pain stayed with Red Sox fans for 18 years, until they finally won their next World Series, and the memory of '86 glory would have to last as Mets fans endured decades without a title and their own brand of demons.

NOTES

1 Michael Goodwin, "NBC Scored in Game 7, Too," *New York Times*, October 29, 1986.

2 *1987 Mets Information Guide*: 216.

3 Author interview with Keith Hernandez, December 22, 2014.

MIKE SERGIO: DROPPING IN TO GAME SIX

By Bill Nowlin

GAME SIX OF THE 1986 WORLD SERIES featured one of the most discussed endings of any baseball game in history. Bill Buckner ended up being embarrassed. So did Bob Stanley and Rich Gedman. Mike Sergio ended up in jail.

In the Sixties, Sergio's mother worked for concessionaire Harry M. Stevens at Shea Stadium. He himself has become an Emmy Award-winning director. In the top of the first inning of Game Six, Sergio entered the game in spectacular fashion. He even got Vin Scully to describe his arrival. Larry David was told it was going to happen, but he didn't believe it. Sergio may have been fortunate that the Mets won the game. The hammer might have come down harder on him had they not.

It was a World Series in which the Red Sox won both Games One and Two, at Shea. The Mets won Games Three and Game Four, at Fenway. Early in Game Four, during the bottom of the second inning, a cluster of balloons drifted out over the park and then onto the field at Fenway, only to be retrieved by Mets shortstop Rafael Santana. Attached to the balloons was a sign reading, "Go Red Sox!" In New York, Mike Sergio says, "I remember the sportswriters up there going, 'Oh, look at our fans, how they love our team. This and that, blah blah blah.' And in my head, I was like, 'Oh, yeah? Watch THIS!'"[1]

The TV show *Seinfeld* started in 1989. In 1986, Larry David was living in the building next to Sergio on 43rd Street. The next day, after Game Four, Sergio ran into Larry David on the street. "I said, 'Larry, I got to go buy a sheet.' I didn't even know where to buy a sheet. I'm a guy. What do I know about where to buy a sheet? He goes, 'What do you want to buy a sheet for?' I go, 'I'm going to jump into Shea Stadium on Saturday.' He said, 'Fuck you, Sergio. Why are you always fucking with me. What the hell's the matter with you?'"

Who is Mike Sergio? "I'm a real New York guy, born in a New York City hospital. Manhattan. 1949. In 1986, I was 36. I'm a New Yorker, 100%. I don't think I even left the City until I was like 19." The *Sports Illustrated* article reported that "Sergio was born on East 122nd Street in Harlem, around the corner from where his father still runs the family waterproofing business."[2]

He was 13 when the Mets first played. "My mother worked for Harry M. Stevens. I was in Shea Stadium, when Stevens hired the first crew of people who were going to work at the stadium. I was in there running around. The original design—when the Jets were in there—the ground-level bleachers rotated. We used to play as a kid under those bleachers. She was working at one of the concessions stands.

"From the time I could do anything, I was singing and playing. I was in rock bands and all that stuff. I don't think I had a New Year's Eve that I wasn't in a bar until I was like 24. From the time I was like 13, the band was always playing somewhere. I went from that into acting.

"I was one of the house singers at the New York Improvisation Club on 44th Street and 9th Avenue for 17 years, from when I got out of college to when it closed in 1992, I believe. I opened shows and sang for just about every comic you can imagine. They used to put me on after Andy Kaufman all the time. Andy, unlike us thinking how great he was today, Andy was... the audiences didn't get him. He would actually get up on stage and start doing '99 Bottles of Beer on the Wall' and start counting down. By bottle 87, they were ready to kill him. He'd destroy the room and Bud Friedman, the Improv owner, would say, 'Mike, get up there' and I'd grab my acoustic guitar and play and sing and bring the room back."

Jumping into major-league ballparks had been done before. And Mike Sergio had a lot of experience jumping. He'd just never parachuted into a stadium before. Five years earlier, George Steinbrenner had invited the jump team he was on to jump into Yankee Stadium, but weather prevented that jump. By October 1986, Sergio had 2,300 jumps to his credit. He was far from a novice.

"That summer alone I made over 200 jumps," he recalled. "I was an accelerated freefall instructor." He started skydiving at age 19. "There was a TV show called *Ripcord.* Look at it now, it's extremely corny. Then my friend Pete the Greek in Astoria, he asks me, "Hey, you want to jump out of an airplane?" I said, "Oh, that's a good idea." We went down to a place called Ripcord, in Jersey. My first jumpmaster was a croupier, at a casino. Everybody you meet in this sport, they were just characters.

"Let me tell you something about that sport. When you actually get into it, it becomes such a Zen experience. For 20 years of my life, I followed the skydiving stuff. From dropzone to dropzone…after 2,300 jumps, I was like, OK, I could really keep doing this and get to 10,000 jumps. I almost had to tear myself away. The sport so had me. It was so in my veins. There was so much in me, though. So much creativity, so many other things that I just needed to do. I knew that if I kept jumping out of airplanes until I was 60, I'd say, 'There was something else that you should have also been doing.'

"In the summer of 1975, my skydiving instructor Owen Quinn calls me up and he goes, 'I'm going to jump off the World Trade Center tomorrow.' I said, 'Yeah, that's a good idea.' He said, 'You want to help me?' I said, 'Sure, I'll help you out. What's the deal?' So we went down to Astoria Park and we packed his parachute and stuff and then the next day we snuck up on top of the World Trade Center. If you Google search my name and a photo called Point of No Return, you'll see the photo I took of him going off the northwest corner of the North Tower of the World Trade Center."

Interested readers can visit this link:

http://www.basejumper.com/photos/Building/Owen_Quinn_Twin_Tower_1_2123.html

"Now, with that thing, we went to court 13 times and then they just dismissed it. Some guy climbed the side of the building, and they charged him a penny a floor. There was never anything serious that came out of this kind of stuff. It was always, 'It's New York. It's a fun place. Good seeing you. Blah blah blah.'

"I've been to competitions where you jump and aim at a 10-centimeter target, which is the size of a cigarette in a circle on the ground. I've done that in Europe, at ski resorts where they put it on the side of a mountain. When somebody says, Jump into Shea Stadium, that's like saying, Jump into the Atlantic Ocean. Not a lot of challenge, technically, to make the jump itself. There's really nothing to it. When you know what you're doing, there's nothing to it. If it gets where it's too windy, you just don't do it. On a normal day, like the Shea jump, it's a piece of cake.

"The only thing novel about it when I did it was that it was the biggest bandit jump ever done. But there was nothing difficult about it."

Mike will still not talk about how the jump was executed. It's something he prefers to keep to himself. Even though any statute of limitations has long since passed, he would rather not implicate anyone else.

He bought the sheet at Woolworth's and spray-painted the "GO METS" slogan on it. The article in *SI* says that a pilot who owed Quinn a favor found a conveniently unlocked airplane waiting at Kobelt Airport (Wallkill, New York).

Suffice it to say, Sergio was transported from somewhere to some number of feet above Shea Stadium and then a couple of minutes later he landed on the field.[3]

One can see Mike Sergio's landing online on a number of websites. The YouTube clip is at:

https://www.youtube.com/watch?v=NObcKmgW5fA

He'd intended to land during the National Anthem, with a friend carrying an American flag who backed out at the last moment. By the time the Cessna got to the field, they were running a little late.

It was the top of the first inning and Bill Buckner was at the plate, the third batter. Wade Boggs had singled and was on first base. There was nobody out. Bobby Ojeda threw ball one to Buckner. Then the TV camera picked up the image of a man parachuting in with the large "GO METS" sheet, as Vin Scully says, "An unexpected guest at Shea Stadium." Sergio landed, on his feet, almost directly on the first-base line about midway between first and home, where he was immediately greeted by a policeman who took him by the arm and through the Mets dugout (one sees Ron Darling hold out his palm in greeting and Sergio slap him on it). Scully said, "Well, he took the expression 'Why don't you drop by literally and figuratively.' Dwight Evans is seen smiling in the Red Sox dugout. He said it was just about the only way to beat traffic in the town Scully added, "Everybody got a kick out of it." Then he said that Mets second baseman "Wally Backman almost jumped out of his uniform when that fan came down in front of him." Various Mets are seen laughing on the bench.

"In that moment when I was landing, I knew that I had to make it look easy. If I even went to my knees…it could look bad. Any landing you can walk away from's a good one, but if I didn't make it look like a walk in the park, it would look like it was…something else than it was. I still remember when my toes skimmed in, the grass was surprisingly deeper than I thought it would be."

What happened next? That, Mike Sergio is willing to talk about.

"To me, it was just an incredibly great performance. You couldn't imagine having more fun than that. They took me to a little room that had like a cage—not a bar cage but like a screen cage. I remember there were two people already in that cage. They must have done something. I don't know what they did, but they were holding them in that thing. I'm 6'2" and with the parachute in my arms when they put me in the cage, the two guys backed up against the wall (laughs) looking like, 'You're not going to put this guy in with us.' It was just hysterical.

"At the time, my brother David was a police officer—he passed away a year later. All the cops in the Queens precinct started coming down. It just turned into this party. It was unbelievable. So they took me out of the cage and I started packing the parachute and already the autographs start. Then they take me over to the local precinct, at 110th Street and Roosevelt. The second I got there, every cop in Queens came by. My brother was there. He was there at the station. He knew it was going to go down. He waited outside the stadium until the game started and said, 'Oh, I guess he didn't make it'—and left. And then like two minutes later, I did the jump. It was one of those things.

"But every cop in Queens went down there. It was just phenomenal. It was phenomenal. I sat around with all the guys and it was just like a party. It turned into a party. I actually watched the last couple of innings there at the station. That was just a total party.

"I remember I'd been thinking to myself, when the game started going south, 'Oh man, if this thing goes bad, they're going to blame me for this. I'm going to have to move out of New York.' But then when it turned around, it was just like a fairy-tale ending."

Then things got a little more serious.

"At some point after the game, the sergeant or somebody said, 'The federal guy's here to talk to you. We gotta put you in.' So they put me in a room and this gentleman walks in, and it was just like somebody out of *The X Files*. He actually looked like the cigarette man from *The X Files*. Central Casting couldn't have sent a better guy in. Central Casting's version of a 1940s Fed. He's got like a London Fog coat on, with a hat. He comes in and takes the hat off, takes the coat off, folds the coat very neatly, takes out a book and he opens the book. He's ready to write in the book, and he says, 'Who's the pilot?' Nothing else. That's what he says to me.

"I said, 'I'm not going to be rude or anything, but I'm just not going to talk about it.' He goes, 'What's the tail number on the plane?' I said, 'I'm actually not going to speak about this.' He looks at me. He closes the book, stands up, puts his coat on, puts his hat on, puts the book under his arm, and walks out. And I thought to myself, 'I might be in trouble.'

"Basically, I stayed overnight in the local jail and I was in custody until they took me to the Queens Courthouse, which is very close to where Shea Stadium was. And they brought me in front of a judge. He was the first guy I came across as an official who had a good sense of humor. Even the court guards were just laughing. Everybody was laughing. The judge himself said, 'You know, I was at the game last night and I was more worried about the airplanes going overhead than I was about Mr. Sergio. I thought that was kind of interesting.' I don't think he actually used the word 'interesting,' but to paraphrase what he said, it was 'No, I'm not putting him in jail. Come back on November 4 [or whatever it was] and we'll figure it out then.' Basically, he said he kind of enjoyed the whole thing. He was there with a date.

"Then there was a woman judge at the very end who wrote me a poem. That was terrific.

"Game Seven was even better; they actually won it. On a personal note, if they'd lost Game Six, I would have been in trouble, but they won Six so I wasn't hearing any 'You made them lose the game.' Game Seven was just an absolutely ecstatic cherry on top of the cream pie there.

"Some of the players contacted me and they put me in touch with an attorney. They were very instrumental in helping me out at the beginning. They recommended a guy to me and he did it pro bono. The city thing came down to 100 hours of working in the Children's Zoo in Central Park. I don't think I'd ever been around a sheep in my life. They're actually really adorable little creatures. I worked the hundred hours and I was done and never heard anything gain.

"But the Feds were a whole different ballgame. The Feds wanted to know who the pilot was. I started getting pulled into all sorts of different stuff. I said in front of the Federal judge in the courthouse, 'Listen, I can't tell you. I'm a New York guy, but I might have to move to Canada or live on a farm, but I can't tell you.' The second I said that, they went nuts. Just went nuts, that I wouldn't tell them. They put me in on contempt of court. There is no definitive time for contempt of court. It's not like you robbed a bank and get 7-10 years. Contempt of court doesn't have that. It's a coercive measure. But the government can't keep you forever. It can only keep you up to 18 months. If you haven't told them after 18 months, they have to let you go. So I figured, 'Hey, I'm 36. When am I going to have 18 months to myself? I'm going to prison. I'll just work out. I'll get strong and healthy. When am I going to get 18 months on my own? I'll do the time.'

"So he said, 'All right. You're in.' The D.A. was just hardcore. Meanwhile, this is starting to piss me off. What's the big deal?

"It all got so blown out of proportion that it actually pissed me off. I was always courteous about it, but inside....I'm from New York. I've got to wait for that subway every day. I get my chops busted. I know what's a good thing and what's a bad thing in this city. This ain't a bad thing. If you come to me and act like it's a bad thing, No, I'm not giving you nothing.

"I wasn't going to give him up anyway [the pilot] but I could have not given him up in a more pleasant way.

"So now they're holding me at MCC, the maximum Federal holding facility in downtown New York. It was really, really interesting. There was an Irish guy who had been in there like 12 years or something. I was in with him. There was also this pizza connection thing going on with the Italians at the time. When I walked in, I was so freaking scared. No doubt about it. They give you some blankets as you walk in—it was just like you see in an old-time police movie about prison. When I walked in, they put you on a training floor to teach you how to be a prisoner. The routine. When I walked in, there were two lines, a line on the left... All the guys had lined in when I walked in. Because I didn't rat, because I was in there because I didn't rat, as I walked in down this line, they were applauding.

They were clapping. 'Good for you, man. Good for you.' To them, it was like, here's a guy who didn't rat out. 'Look at him, he didn't do anything wrong *and* he didn't rat out.' Compared to anyone who was in there, I didn't do anything wrong. I had such a terrific experience in there. Really terrific.

"There were a lot of Spanish guys in there and the Spanish guys were all right. It was a very cool situation. I also think if you can handle yourself as a guy...if you go into jail and you can't handle yourself on the street, you're going to be in trouble. You've just got to know how to be savvy and if you go inside, you use a different part of your brain, but you just have to handle yourself. You're not going to put up with any nonsense, you're not going to make any trouble, but you're not going to take any, either. It's just one of those attitudes. That's kind of a natural thing for a kid from New York anyway.

"So now I'm in there. OK, they got me in the belly of the beast. How am I going to get out of this? I was in the entertainment business. I thought, OK, you know how I'm going to get out? They swallowed me. I'm going to make it really hard for them to keep me down. That was actually my plan. I said, Well, there's pay phones here. Let me just call every radio station that I can, every day I can, as much as I can. Every day, I started talking to Howard Stern. I was talking to Bob Grant. I was talking to everyone and they started to expect my phone call during their show. Howard Stern started saying, 'Hey, man. Did Bubba get you yet? Are you somebody's bitch? What's going on?' Barry Gray was great: 'We've got Mike Sergio in now, while we've got all this crime on the street....' I just hammered the system. Every day.

"There was always a line for the phones. They had like payphones in there. Every time I would go to the phone, all the guys in the line would just let me get on the phone and they'd go to the radio and listen to me talking on the radio. Then I brought a couple of them on. 'C'mon, you want to talk to Howard?' And Howard would talk to them. I just thought the only way I'm going to get out of this, is I've got to make them throw me up, throw me out of their belly. And it worked!

"My agent at the time, her sister—who was in D.C.—knew [Secretary of Transportation] Elizabeth Dole. Her sister was at a dinner with Elizabeth Dole and said, 'Do you know what they're doing to Mike Sergio up in New York?' Apparently, there were Federal judges at the table, and they said, 'Yeah, New York is making us look bad, the federal judge in New York.' And she just says, between the broccoli and the cauliflower, 'Let him go.' That was it. Now it takes three days for that to filter back up to New York. It really was not a bad experience at all.

"The professionals running Corrections and the guys in there, everyone felt there was this kind of injustice. 'Why is this guy sitting in jail over this? That doesn't make sense.' It became that there was something wrong with the system. And now people were laughing at the system. I was turning them into a joke. That's why they let me out, and at that point I think they were happy to see me go.

"I was there 21 days. They were going to put me upstate. The first night I was in, you really gotta deep-breathe the first night. It's not like the jails in the movies with bars where you can look out. It's like a metal door with a little slit. I sat on the bottom bunk.

"My brother had cancer through this whole thing. He was a police officer. He was getting weaker and weaker. One of the great joys for me is that at the end of his life he had such a great time with the fact of the jump, that it was his brother who did it. He was just so happy—being a New York City cop and your brother jumped into Shea Stadium...it was just good for him. You know who ended up best understanding it? All the cops. How great they were to me. They know the difference between crime and....

"A few months after I got out of jail, my brother David passed away. But it really brought a lot of pleasure to him. Anything I went through with that was actually worth it for the pleasure it brought him."

Today, in 2016, Mike Sergio is still just as much of a New York character as ever. He's still signing in clubs all around the city...and he has a new jazz album about to come out. CAVU Pictures, his film production & distribution company that he started with producing partner Isil Bagdadi in 2001, continues to release award-winning indie films into theaters nationwide. It has been said that CAVU Pictures has become the go-to film distribution company for young filmmakers. Mike's also still writing screenplays and he's working on launching a new TV show about comedy clubs.

And if you see Mike on the street or in a club and you go up to him and ask, "Hey, aren't you the guy....?" His eyes will still light up and he'll answer almost all your questions. Except if you ask him who the pilot was. Then he'll just shrug and not say a thing. And if you ask him why not, he'll smile and just say, "Hey, if I tell you, I'd have to move out of New York."

NOTES

1 All quotations attributed to Mike Sergio come from an interview with the author on November 5, 2014.

2 Stephen Kiesling, "Dropping in on the Series," *Sports Illustrated*, October 9, 1989.

3 *Sports Illustrated* reported the plane as a 1964 Cessna 182, flying out of the Ranch Skydiving Club in Gardiner, New York (about 80 miles north of New York City.)

BY THE NUMBERS

By Dan Fields

1986 BOSTON RED SOX

1st

Major-league pitcher to strike out 20 batters in a nine-inning game: Roger Clemens, on April 29 against the Seattle Mariners. He had eight consecutive strikeouts (fourth inning to sixth inning) to tie the AL record. He didn't walk a batter and gave up only three hits. The Red Sox won 3-1.

1st

Starting pitcher since 1971 to win an MVP Award: Roger Clemens. He was the unanimous selection for the AL Cy Young Award. Clemens led the majors in wins (24, the most by a Red Sox pitcher since 1949) and winning percentage (.857) and led the AL in ERA (2.48), WHIP (0.969, the lowest by a Red Sox pitcher since 1914), and hits per nine innings pitched (6.3). He finished second in the AL in strikeouts (238). Clemens was also the MVP of the 1986 All-Star Game on July 15 in Houston; he was the AL's starting pitcher and threw three perfect innings.

1.89

Walks per nine innings pitched by Oil Can Boyd, second best in the AL.

2

Grand slams by Jim Rice in a three-game series against the Minnesota Twins on September 5 through 7. During the series, he had seven hits in 12 at-bats and drove in 10 runs.

2.18

Ratio of strikeouts to walks by Boston pitchers, best in the AL.

2.99

ERA of Bruce Hurst, fourth lowest in the AL.

4

Shutouts by Bruce Hurst, tied for second in the AL.

8.62

Strikeouts per nine innings pitched by Bruce Hurst, second best in the AL. Roger Clemens was third in the league, with 8.43 strikeouts.

11

Consecutive games won by the Red Sox from August 30 to September 10.

14

Consecutive wins by Roger Clemens to start the season. His first loss was on July 2 against the Toronto Blue Jays.

18

Sacrifice hits by Marty Barrett, most in the AL and tied (with Robby Thompson of the San Francisco Giants) for most in the majors.

20

Consecutive games in which Wade Boggs had a base hit, from August 29 to September 18. During the streak, he hit nine doubles and batted .405.

20th

Consecutive year in which Tom Seaver started at least 20 games. In his final season, Seaver started 12 games for the Chicago White Sox and 16 games for the Red Sox. He finished his career with a record of 311-205, an ERA of 2.86, and 3,640 strikeouts.

21-7

Record of the Red Sox during May.

24-5

Score by which the Red Sox beat the Cleveland Indians on August 21. Spike Owen (batting ninth) scored six runs to tie a twentieth-century major-league record, Tony Armas hit two home runs (including a grand slam) and drove in six runs, Bill Buckner had five hits (all singles), and Marty Barrett and Dwight Evans each drove in four runs.

24-10

Record of the Red Sox in one-run games. The .706 winning percentage was best in the majors.

25

Double plays grounded into by Bill Buckner, second most in the majors.

25.2

At-bats per strikeout by Bill Buckner, the highest ratio in the majors. Marty Barrett had 20.2 at-bats per strikeout and finished second in the majors.

31

Home runs by Don Baylor, tied for sixth in the AL. He hit 22 homers on the road, second most in the majors.

35

Times that Don Baylor was hit by a pitch, an AL record (through 2014). He was hit by two pitches in three games (on May 1, May 17, and June 30).

36

Complete games by Boston pitchers, second most in the majors. The Twins had 39 complete games.

41

Stolen bases by the Red Sox, fewest in the majors. The team with next fewest steals, the Baltimore Orioles, had 64.

47

Doubles by Wade Boggs, second in the majors. This was the most by a Red Sox player since 1938, when Joe Cronin hit 51. Marty Barrett, Bill Buckner, and Jim Rice each had 39 doubles in 1986 and tied for third in the AL.

54

Base runners caught stealing as catcher by Rich Gedman, most in the AL.

66

Games played by Bob Stanley, tied for fifth in the AL.

95

Wins by the 1986 Red Sox, against 66 losses. The Sox won the AL East by 5 1/2 games over the New York Yankees.

105

Walks drawn by Wade Boggs, most in the majors. He had at least 200 hits and 100 walks in four consecutive seasons (1986 through 1989). Dwight Evans drew 97 walks in 1986, second in the majors. In a 12-inning game against the California Angels on July 10, Evans drew four walks.

107

Runs scored by Wade Boggs, tied for fifth in the majors.

110

RBIs by Jim Rice, fourth in the AL. He had two five-RBI games, on May 28 and September 5. Bill Bucker had 102 RBIs and finished 10th in the AL.

207

Hits by Wade Boggs, fourth in the AL. He had two five-hit games in a 12-day span (May 20 and May 31). Jim Rice had 200 hits, tied for fifth in the league.

.298, .345, and .542

Batting average, on-base percentage, and slugging average of Rich Gedman on the road. His numbers at Fenway Park were .214, .284, and .299. He hit 14 home runs on the road, two at home.

312

Times on base by Wade Boggs, most in the majors. Jim Rice got on base 266 times and finished third in the AL.

320

Doubles by the Red Sox, most in the majors and a franchise record at the time.

334

Putouts as a left fielder by Jim Rice, most in the majors.

.346

On-base percentage of the Red Sox, second highest in the majors. The Yankees had an OBP of .347.

.357

Batting average of Wade Boggs, highest in the majors. He was consistent, hitting .357 at home and .356 on the road and going .359 against right-handed pitchers and .352 against left-handed pitchers. Jim Rice had a .324 average in 1986 and finished fifth in the AL.

.367

Batting average of Marty Barrett (11 for 30) in the AL Championship Series against the Angels. He had four multi-hit games, with three hits each in Game Two and Game Six. The Red Sox eliminated the Angels in seven games, and Barrett was chosen the MVP.

.453

On-base percentage of Wade Boggs, highest in the majors.

474

Walks allowed by the Red Sox, fewest in the majors.

707

Strikeouts by Boston batters, fewest in the majors. The team with the next fewest strikeouts, the Blue Jays, had 848.

713

Plate appearances by Marty Barrett, fourth in the majors.

.939

OPS of Wade Boggs, second best in the majors.

1986 NEW YORK METS

1-2-3-4

Rank in winning percentage in the NL by Bob Ojeda (.783), Dwight Gooden (.739), Sid Fernandez (.727), and Ron Darling (.714).

1.090 and 1.108

WHIP of Bob Ojeda and Dwight Gooden, who finished third and fourth in the NL.

2.57, 2.81, and 2.84

ERA of Bob Ojeda, Ron Darling, and Dwight Gooden, who finished second, third, and fifth in the NL.

3.11

ERA of the Mets, lowest in the majors.

4

Mets players who started at the 1986 All-Star Game. At the age of 21 years, 7 months, and 30 days, Dwight Gooden was the youngest pitcher to start an All-Star Game. Batting third, fourth, and fifth for the NL were first baseman Keith Hernandez, catcher Gary Carter, and right fielder Darryl Strawberry. Gooden gave up two runs in three innings and took the loss.

5

Hits by Darryl Strawberry on April 30 and Mookie Wilson on May 23.

7

RBIs by Gary Carter on July 11 against the Atlanta Braves. He hit a three-run homer in the first inning and a grand slam in the second inning, both off David Palmer.

8.8

Strikeouts per nine innings pitched by Sid Fernandez, third in the NL.

9th

Consecutive Gold Glove Award at first base won by Keith Hernandez. He also won in 1987 and 1988 to run the streak to 11.

12

Complete games by Dwight Gooden, tied for second in the NL.

14

Strikeouts by Sid Fernandez in seven innings on September 1 against the Giants.

14

Games won in relief by Roger McDowell, including his first seven decisions of the year.

15

Sacrifice flies by Gary Carter, most in the majors.

17.6

At-bats per home run by Darryl Strawberry, third in the NL. Gary Carter had 20.4 at-bats per home run and finished seventh.

18, 17, 16, and 15

Wins by starting pitchers Bob Ojeda, Dwight Gooden, Sid Fernandez, and Ron Darling, respectively. All finished in the top 10 in the NL.

20-4

Record of the Mets through May 10. The team won 11 consecutive games from April 18 through April 30.

After losing to the Braves on May 1, the Mets won seven straight.

21

Double plays grounded into by Gary Carter, tied (with Tony Pena and Johnny Ray, both of the Pittsburgh Pirates) for most in the NL.

21 1/2

Games by which the Mets won the NL East over the Philadelphia Phillies.

22 and 21

Saves by Roger McDowell and Jesse Orosco. The 1986 Mets were the third team in major-league history with two pitchers who had at least 20 saves in a season.

27

Home runs by Darryl Strawberry, tied for fifth in the NL. Gary Carter had 24 home runs and finished ninth.

75

Games played by Roger McDowell, second among NL pitchers.

94

Walks drawn by Keith Hernandez, most in the NL.

94

Runs scored by Keith Hernandez, tied for fifth in the NL.

103

Home runs allowed by the Mets, fewest in the majors.

105

RBIs by Gary Carter, third in the NL. Darryl Strawberry had 93 RBIs and finished seventh.

108

Wins by the 1986 Mets, the most in the majors since the Cincinnati Reds won as many in 1975.

141

Strikeouts by Darryl Strawberry, tied for second in the NL.

.189

Batting average of the Mets in the NL Championship Series against the Houston Astros, who batted .218. The Mets won the series in six games, and the final game (16 innings) was the longest in postseason history until 2005. Jesse Orosco had three wins, all in relief. Mike Scott of the Astros, who threw a shutout in Game One and allowed one run in a complete-game win in Game Four, was named the MVP.

200

Strikeouts thrown each by Sid Fernandez and Dwight Gooden, tied for fourth in the NL.

250

Innings pitched by Dwight Gooden, fifth in the NL.

.263

Batting average of the Mets, highest in the NL.

269

Times on base by Keith Hernandez, third in the NL.

.310

Batting average of Keith Hernandez, fifth in the NL.

.339, .401, .and .740

On-base percentage, slugging average, and OPS of the Mets, all best in the NL.

.379

Batting average of Ray Knight against left-handed pitchers, best in the majors. He hit .243 against right-handed pitchers.

.4126

On-base percentage of Keith Hernandez, second in the NL. He was edged by Tim Raines, who had an OBP of .4133.

.507

Slugging percentage of Darryl Strawberry, second in the NL.

631

Walks drawn by the Mets, most in the NL.

783

Runs scored by the Mets, most in the NL.

.865

OPS of Darryl Strawberry, fourth in the NL. Keith Hernandez had an OPS of .859 and finished seventh in the league.

.9963

Fielding percentage as first baseman by Keith Hernandez, best in the majors. He edged Don Mattingly of Yankees, who had a .9960 fielding percentage.

1,083

Strikeouts by New York pitchers, second most in the majors.

2,767,601

Attendance of the 1986 Mets at Shea Stadium, a franchise record at the time.

1986 WORLD SERIES

0

Stolen bases by the Red Sox during the Series. The Mets had seven steals, including three each by Darrly Strawberry and Mookie Wilson and one by Wally Backman.

0-2

Record of Boston reliever Calvin Schiraldi, who took the loss in both Game Six and Game Seven, and New York starter Dwight Gooden, who lost Game Two and Game Five.

2-0

Record of Bruce Hurst, who won Game One and Game Five. He also started Game Seven. Hurst had an ERA of 1.96 in 23 innings during the Series.

6

Runs scored each by Dave Henderson and Jim Rice during the Series.

9

RBIs each by Gary Carter and Dwight Evans during the Series.

.391

Batting average of Ray Knight (9 for 23). With two outs in the bottom of the 10th inning of Game Six and the Mets trailing by two runs, Knight singled to drove in Gary Carter and advance Kevin Mitchell to third. Mitchell then scored on Bob Stanley's wild pitch, and Knight advanced to second. Knight scored the winning run after Mookie Wilson's grounder went through the legs of Bill Buckner. Knight also hit the tie-breaking home run in the seventh inning of Game Seven. He was voted MVP of the World Series.

.433

Batting average of Marty Barrett (13 for 30). Dave Henderson hit .400 (10 for 35). Barrett's total of 24 hits in the ALCS and World Series were a single-season postseason record at the time.

AROUND THE MAJORS IN 1986

1

Hit allowed by Jimmy Jones of the San Diego Padres in his first major-league game, a 5-0 shutout of the Astros on September 21. He threw only two more shutouts in his eight-year career.

1st

Game at shortstop by Barry Larkin of the Reds, on August 17 against the Padres. He would play 2,075 games at short, winning nine Silver Slugger Awards and three Gold Glove Awards.

1st

Pitcher to clinch a playoff spot with a no-hitter: Mike Scott. He struck out 13 and walked two while no-hitting the Giants on September 25 to clinch the NL West title for the Astros. Scott led the majors in ERA (2.22), strikeouts (306), innings pitched (275⅓), WHIP (0.923), hits per nine innings pitched (5.95), strikeouts per nine innings pitched (10.0), and ratio of strikeouts to walks (4.25), and he tied with teammate Bob Knepper for most shutouts in the NL (five). He was the winner of the NL Cy Young Award.

1st

Year in which every major-league team had a home attendance of at least 1 million. The Pirates topped the mark in its last home game (September 28), finishing with 1,000,917.

1st

Major-league pitch faced by Jay Bell of the Indians, which he hit a home run off Bert Blyleven of the Twins on September 29. In 1986, two other players hit a home run in their first major-league at-bat: Will Clark of the Giants (April 8, off Nolan Ryan of the Astros) and Terry Steinbach of the Oakland A's (September 12, off Gregg Swindell of the Indians).

2

Grand slams by Larry Sheets and Jim Dwyer of the Orioles in the fourth inning on August 6 against the Rangers. Toby Harrah of the Texas Rangers hit a grand slam in the second inning. It was the first game in major-league history with three grand slams. The Rangers won 13-11.

2

Inside-the-park home runs by Greg Gagne of the Twins on October 4, both off Floyd Bannister of the White Sox. He also hit a triple in the game.

2

Players who hit for the cycle in 1986: Tony Phillips of the A's on May 16 and Kirby Puckett of the Twins on August 1.

2

Players with at least 25 home runs and 80 stolen bases: Eric Davis of the Reds (27 home runs and 80 stolen bases) and Rickey Henderson of the Yankees (28 home runs and 87 stolen bases). They are the only players in major-league history to achieve this feat in a season (through 2014).

2

Players with at least 200 hits, 20 home runs, and 20 stolen bases: Joe Carter of the Indians (200 hits, 29 home runs, and 29 stolen bases) and Kirby Puckett (223 hits, 31 home runs, and 20 stolen bases). They were the first players in AL history to accomplish the feat.

3

Home runs by designated hitter Juan Beniquez of the Orioles, on June 12 against the Yankees. In 112 other games in 1986, Beniquez hit a total of three home runs.

3

Home runs by Reggie Jackson of the Angels, on September 18 against the Kansas City Royals. He joined Stan Musial and Babe Ruth as the only players aged 40 or older to hit three home runs in a game.

3

Batters hit by Mitch Williams of the Rangers in 1⅓ innings on July 30 against the Orioles.

3

Hits by Russ Morman of the White Sox in his first three at-bats in the major leagues, on August 3 against the Detroit Tigers. In the second inning, he hit a single off Randy O'Neal. In the fourth inning, he hit a solo home run off O'Neal and a run-scoring single off Jim Slaton,

3

Wild pitches thrown by Mark Clear of the Milwaukee Brewers in ⅓ of an inning on September 16 in the second game of a doubleheader against the Red Sox.

3

Players with 500+ home runs who hit their first in 1986: Barry Bonds of the Pirates (June 4), Mark McGwire of the A's (August 25), and Rafael Palmeiro of the Chicago Cubs (September 9). All later faced allegations of using performance-enhancing drugs.

3rd

NL MVP Award won by Mike Schmidt. He joined Roy Campanella and Stan Musial as the only three-time winners in the senior circuit. Schmidt led the NL in home runs (37), RBIs (119), slugging average (.547), OPS (.937), and at-bats per home run (14.9), and he tied with teammate Von Hayes for most extra-base hits (67). He also led the majors in intentional bases on balls (25), and he won his 10th and last Gold Glove Award at third base.

4

Home runs allowed by Mario Soto of the Reds in the fourth inning on April 29 against the Montreal Expos.

4

Doubles by Rafael Ramirez of the Braves on May 21 (13 innings) and Damaso Garcia of the Blue Jays on June 27.

4

Times that Robby Thompson of the Giants was caught stealing (in four attempts to steal second base) on June 27 against the Reds. He was thrown out by Bo Diaz in the fourth, sixth, ninth, and 11th innings.

4

Home runs by Bob Horner of the Braves on July 6 against the Expos. He hit three solo homers and a three-run homer. Despite Horner's efforts, the Braves lost 11-8.

4

Errors by third baseman Bob Brenly of the Giants during the fourth inning on September 14 against the Braves. He did better at the plate, hitting a solo home run in the fifth, a two-run single in the seventh, and a walk-off solo homer in the bottom of the ninth as the Giants won 7-6.

4:16

Duration of a nine-inning game between the Orioles and Yankees on June 8, setting an AL record. The Orioles won 18-9.

5

Consecutive batters struck out by Fernando Valenzuela of the Los Angeles Dodgers at the 1986 All-Star Game, equaling Carl Hubbell's 1934 feat. Valenzuela struck out Don Mattingly, Cal Ripken, and Jesse Barfield in the fourth and Lou Whitaker and Teddy Higuera in the fifth.

5

Triples hit by the Phillies on August 2 against the Cubs. They also had seven doubles. Gary Redus hit two triples and a double, and Juan Samuel hit two doubles and a triple.

5

Stolen bases by Tony Gwynn of the Padres on September 20 against the Astros. He stole both second base and third base in the first and sixth innings and stole third base in the eighth inning.

6

Shutouts by Jack Morris of the Tigers, most in the majors.

7

Walks thrown by Joe Cowley of the White Sox in a no-hit game on September 19 against the Angels. He allowed one earned run. Cowley never won another major-league game, losing his last two decisions in 1986 and going 0-4 with the Phillies in 1987.

8

RBIs by Alvin Davis of the Mariners on May 9 against the Blue Jays. He hit a three-run home run in the first inning, a run-scoring single in the second inning, and a grand slam in the seventh inning.

8

Consecutive batters struck out by Jim Deshaies of the Astros to start the game on September 23 against the Dodgers — a twentieth-century record.

9

Leadoff home runs by Rickey Henderson, a single-season record at the time.

10th

Career game with five hits by Pete Rose of the Reds, on August 11 against the Giants. In his 24th and final season as a player, the player/manager batted .219 in 72 games. Rose retired with 4,256 hits in 3,562 games, both major-league records (through 2014).

11

Players on the Angels in 1986 who were at least 35 years old: catcher Bob Boone, second-baseman Bobby Grich, third-baseman Doug DeCinces, left-fielder Brian Downing, right-fielder George Hendrick, designated hitter Reggie Jackson, utility infielder Rick Burleson, and pitchers Ken Forsch, Vern Ruhle, Jim Slaton, and Don Sutton.

12

Losses in relief by Ken Howell of the Dodgers.

13

Consecutive games played by pitcher Dale Mohorcic of the Rangers between August 6 and August 20. During the streak, he had two saves, two blown saves, and one loss.

14

Triples by Brett Butler of the Indians, most in the majors. Mitch Webster of the Expos led the NL with 13 triples.

14.1

At-bats per home run by Rob Deer of the Brewers, best in the majors.

15

Consecutive road losses by the A's from May 24 to June 23.

17

Years as teammates by Tony Perez and Pete Rose (1964 to 1976 with the Reds, 1983 with the Phillies, and 1984 to 1986 with the Reds).

18

Innings played by the Astros and the Cubs in a September 2 game at Wrigley Field that was suspended for darkness in the 15th inning and completed on September 3. A total of 53 players appeared in the game, including Greg Maddux of the Cubs in his major-league debut (as a pinch-runner in the 17th inning). The Astros won 8-7.

18

Losses by Rick Mahler of the Braves, most in the majors. Richard Dotson of the White Sox and Mike Morgan of the Mariners led the AL with 17 losses.

19.0

At-bats per strikeout by Ozzie Smith of the St. Louis Cardinals, best in the NL.

20

Complete games by Fernando Valenzuela, most in the majors. Tom Candiotti of the Indians led the AL with 17 complete games.

21

Wins by Fernando Valenzuela, most in the NL.

22

Wild pitches by Bobby Witt of the Rangers, most in the majors. In his second major-league game, he threw four wild pitches and eight walks in five no-hit innings on April 17 against the Brewers. Nolan Ryan led the NL with 15 wild pitches.

23

Age in years of Jamie Moyer of the Cubs made his major-league debut, on June 16. He faced off against 41-year-old Steve Carlton of the Phillies and got the win. Moyer was 49 years old when he played in his final game on May 27, 2012.

25

Consecutive games with a base hit by Steve Sax of the Dodgers, from September 1 to September 27. During the streak, he hit 10 doubles and batted .406.

28

Double plays grounded into by Julio Franco of the Indians, most in the majors.

30

Strikeouts in a nine-inning game between the Mariners (18 strikeouts) and A's (12 strikeouts) on April 19 to set a modern-day record.

30 ⅔

Consecutive innings in which the Blue Jays did not score a run, from July 25 to July 28.

31 ⅔

Consecutive innings in which the White Sox did not allow a run, from August 31 to September 3.

32

Consecutive innings in which Jack Morris did not allow a run, from July 4 to July 23.

35

Home runs by Dave Kingman of the A's, setting a record for most homers by a player in his final season.

36

Saves by Todd Worrell of the Cardinals, most in the NL. He was named the league's Rookie of the Year.

39

Games started by Tom Browning of the Reds and Rick Mahler of the Braves, most in the majors. Mike Moore of the Mariners and Frank Viola of the Twins led the AL with 37 starts.

40

Home runs by Jesse Barfield of the Blue Jays, most in the majors.

43 and 41

Age in years of Tommy John and Niekro, starting pitchers for the Yankees in a doubleheader on August 30 against the Mariners. They were the first pair of 40-plus teammates to start a doubleheader since 1933.

46

Saves by Dave Righetti of the Yankees, a major-league record at the time. He broke the former record of 45 by saving both games of a doubleheader against the Red Sox on the last day of the season.

50

Home runs allowed by Bert Blyleven, a major-league record (through 2014). He allowed five home runs in 5⅓ innings on September 13 against the Rangers. Kevin Gross of the Phillies led the NL with 28 home runs allowed.

53

Doubles by Don Mattingly of the Yankees, most in the majors. He also hit 31 home runs, becoming the first AL player since Hank Greenberg in 1940 to have at least 50 doubles and 30 home runs in a season. Von Hayes led the NL with 46 doubles.

83

Games played by Craig Lefferts of the Padres, the most by any pitcher in the majors. Mitch Williams led the AL with 80 games, a league record by a rookie pitcher at the time.

86

Extra-base hits by Don Mattingly, most in the majors.

107

Stolen bases by Vince Coleman of the Cardinals, most in the majors. It was the second of three consecutive years in which he stole at least 100 bases. Rickey Henderson led the AL with 87 steals.

117

RBIs by AL Rookie of the Year Jose Canseco of the A's, the most by a rookie since Walt Dropo had 144 in 1950. Canseco became the first player in major-league history to drive in at least 110 runs with a batting average of .240 or lower.

121

RBIs by Joe Carter, most in the majors.

130

Runs scored by Rickey Henderson, most in the majors. Tony Gwynn and Von Hayes led the NL with 107 runs.

143

Walks allowed by Bobby Witt, most in the majors, in only 157⅔ innings. Floyd Youmans of the Expos led the NL with 118 walks.

163

Games played by Tony Fernandez of the Blue Jays, most in the majors.

185

Strikeouts by Pete Incaviglia of the Rangers, most in the majors and an AL record at the time. Juan Samuel led the NL with 142 strikeouts.

238

Hits by Don Mattingly, most in the majors and a new Yankees record. Tony Gwynn led the NL with 211 hits.

241

Wins by Steve Carlton with the Phillies between 1972 and 1986.

245

Strikeouts thrown by Mark Langston of the Mariners, most in the AL. He also led the league in strikeouts per nine innings pitched, with 9.2.

.256

Batting average of Willie McGee of the Cardinals, down almost 100 points from his league-leading average of .353 in 1985.

271 ⅔

Innings pitched by Bert Blyleven, most in the AL.

300th

Career win by Don Sutton of the Angels, on June 18 against the Rangers. He became the 19th pitcher to reach the mark. On June 28, he and 47-year-old Phil Niekro of the Indians became the first 300-win pitchers to face each other since 1892. On July 27, Sutton and Tom Seaver faced off as 300-game winners.

.334

Batting average of Tim Raines of the Expos, best in the NL.

388

Total bases by Don Mattingly, most in the majors. Dave Parker of the Reds led the NL with 304.

.433

Batting average of Randy Bush of the Twins as a pinch-hitter (13 for 30). Candy Maldonado of the Giants had a .425 average as pinch-hitter (17 for 40, including four home runs).

475

Estimated length in feet of the first major-league homer by Bo Jackson of the Royals, on September 14 off Mike Moore of the Mariners. Jackson was the 1985 Heisman Trophy winner and the first overall pick in the 1986 NFL draft, but he chose to play with the defending World Series champions instead. Jackson played in the majors until 1994 and also played with the Los Angeles Raiders from 1987 to 1990.

.573

Slugging average of Don Mattingly, best in the majors.

600

At-bats without a home run by Vince Coleman.

687

At-bats by Tony Fernandez, most in the majors. Tony Gwynn led the NL with 642 at-bats.

742

Plate appearances of Don Mattingly, most in the majors. Steve Sax led the NL with 704.

.967

OPS of Don Mattingly, best in the majors.

1,015

RBIs by Eddie Murray in his first 10 seasons (1977 to 1986), all with the Orioles.

1,148

Strikeouts by Seattle batters, an AL record at the time.

1,480

Games won by Earl Weaver in 17 years as Baltimore's manager (1968 to 1982 plus 1985 and 1986).

2,181

Games played during 18 seasons with the Dodgers by Bill Russell, who retired after the 1986 season.

2,000th

Career hit by Robin Yount of the Brewers, on September 6. He was 10 days shy of his 31st birthday. Only six other players had reached the mark at a younger age.

3,000th

Career strikeout by Bert Blyleven, on August 1 against Mike Davis of the A's. He became the 10th pitcher to achieve the milestone.

4,000th

Career strikeout by Steve Carlton of the Giants, on August 5 against Eric Davis of the Reds. He became the second pitcher (after Nolan Ryan) to accomplish the feat.

SOURCES

Nemec, David, ed. The Baseball Chronicle: Year-by-Year History of Major League Baseball (Lincolnwood, Illinois: Publications International, 2003).

Society for American Baseball Research. The SABR Baseball List and Record Book (New York: Scribner, 2007).

Solomon, Burt. The Baseball Timeline (New York: DK Publishing, 2001).

Sugar, Burt Randolph, ed. The Baseball Maniac's Almanac (third edition) (New York: Skyhorse Publishing, 2012).

baseball-almanac.com

baseballlibrary.com/chronology

baseball-reference.com

retrosheet.org

thisgreatgame.com/1986-baseball-history.html

HOW THE 1986 METS WERE BUILT

By Rod Nelson

Name	Salary	Acquired	POS	SCOUTING DIR	SCOUT1	SCOUT2	ORG	SIGN YR	SIGN DATE	Type	Rnd	Num
Rick Aguilera	$130,000	Amateur Draft	P	McIlvaine, Joe	Partee, Roy		NYM N	1983	09/09/1983	Reg	3	58
Wally Backman#	$325,000	Amateur Draft	2B	Gebrian, Pete	Scott, Marvin		NYM N	1977		Reg	1	16
Lenny Dykstra*	$92,500	Amateur Draft	OF	McIlvaine, Joe	Pines, Myron	Jongewaard, Roger	NYM N	1981	07/03/1981	Reg	13	315
Kevin Elster	$60,000	Amateur Draft	SS	McIlvaine, Joe	Jongewaard, Dean		NYM N	1984	05/21/1984	Reg	2	28
John Gibbons	$65,000	Amateur Draft	C	Gebrian, Pete	Hughes, Jim		NYM N	1980		Reg	1	24
Dwight Gooden	$1,320,000	Amateur Draft	P	McIlvaine, Joe	Pascual, Carlos		NYM N	1982	06/10/1982	Reg	1	5
Stan Jefferson#		Amateur Draft	OF	McIlvaine, Joe	Monzon, Dan	Morgan, Julian	NYM N	1983		Reg	1	20
Barry Lyons		Amateur Draft	C	McIlvaine, Joe	Mason, Joe		NYM N	1982		Reg	15	370
Dave Magadan*		Amateur Draft	3B	McIlvaine, Joe	Terrell, Jim	Mason, Joe	NYM N	1983	06/23/1983	Reg	2	32
Roger McDowell	$185,000	Amateur Draft	P	McIlvaine, Joe	Wellman, Bob		NYM N	1982	06/10/1982	Reg	3	59
Randy Myers*		Amateur Draft	P	McIlvaine, Joe	Scott, Marvin		NYM N	1982	06/08/1982	Sec	1	9
Darryl Strawberry*	$945,000	Amateur Draft	OF	Gebrian, Pete	Jongewaard, Roger		NYM N	1980	07/11/1980	Reg	1	1
Mookie Wilson#	$700,000	Amateur Draft	OF	Gebrian, Pete	Britton, Wayne		NYM N	1977		Reg	2	42
Kevin Mitchell	$60,000	Amateur Free Agent	OF	Gebrian, Pete	Jongewaard, Dean		NYM N	1980	11/16/1980	FA	ND	-
Doug Sisk	$275,000	Amateur Free Agent	P	Gebrian, Pete	Scott, Marvin		NYM N	1980	06/10/1980	FA	ND	-
Rick Anderson		Free Agency	P	Gebrian, Pete	Scott, Marvin		NYM N	1978		Reg	24	580
Tim Corcoran*	$220,000	Free Agency	1B	Lajoie, Bill	Deutsch, Jack		DET A	1974	06/10/1974	FA	ND	-
Ed Hearn	$60,000	Free Agency	C	Green, Dallas	Seminick, Andy		PHI N	1978	06/06/1978	Reg	4	101
Terry Leach		Free Agency	P	Lucas, Bill*	Martin, Dickey		ATL N	1976	05/28/1977	Fo	ND	-
Lee Mazzilli#	$60,000	Free Agency	OF	Burbrink, Nelson	Harper, Al		NYM N	1973		Reg	1	14
Rafael Santana	$235,000	Free Agency	SS	Gillick, Pat	Guerrero, Epifano (Epy)		NYY A	1976	08/31/1976	Fa	x	
Bruce Berenyi		Traded	P	Bowen, Joseph	Clark, Bill		CIN N	1976		Sec	1	3
Gary Carter	$2,160,714	Traded	C	Didier, Mel	Zuk, Bob		MON N	1972		Reg	3	53
Ron Darling	$440,000	Traded	P	Klein, Joe	Robinson, Eddie	Lewis Sr., Joe W.	TEX A	1981		Reg	1	9
Sid Fernandez*	$200,000	Traded	P	Wade, Ben	Maehara, Iron	Henley, Gail	LA N	1981	06/21/1981	Reg	3	73
George Foster	$2,800,000	Traded	OF	Hubbell, Carl	Genovese, George		SF N	1968		Reg	3	55
Danny Heep*	$350,000	Traded	OF	Stallings, Lynwood	Hollmig, Stanley		HOU N	1978		Reg	2	37
Keith Hernandez*	$1,650,000	Traded	1B	Silvey, George	Sayles, Bill	Johnston, James J. "Jim"	STL N	1972		Reg	42	785
Howard Johnson#	$227,500	Traded	3B	Katalinas, Ed	Reasonover, Bob		DET A	1979	01/09/1979	Sec	1	12

Name	Salary	Acquired	POS	SCOUTING DIR	SCOUT1	SCOUT2	ORG	SIGN YR	SIGN DATE	Type	Rnd	Num
Ray Knight	$645,000	Traded	3B	Bowen, Joseph	Zuraw, George		CIN N	1970		Reg	10	231
Ed Lynch	$530,000	Traded	P	Keller, Hal	Klein, Joe		TEX A	1977		Reg	22	547
John Mitchell		Traded	P	Kasko, Eddie	Digby, George		BOS A	1983		Reg	7	177
Randy Niemann*	$83,000	Traded	P	Gillick, Pat	Morgan, Wayne		NYY A	1975		Sec	2	30
Bob Ojeda*	$550,000	Traded	P	Kasko, Eddie	Flynn, Larry		BOS A	1978	05/20/1978	FA	ND	-
Jesse Orosco	$825,000	Traded	P	Brophy, George	Flores Sr., Jesse		MIN A	1978		Reg	2	41
Tim Teufel	$200,000	Traded	2B	Brophy, George	Robbins, Spencer (Red)		MIN A	1980		Reg	2	38

Note: Darryl Strawberry received a $200,000 bonus. Gary Carter received a $48,500 bonus.

CONTRIBUTORS

NIALL ADLER has been paid to watch sports (and sometimes theatre) since 1998. Everything from diving to swimming, water polo, Aussie Rules, horse racing, hockey, futbol and gridiron, and... baseball on four continents and at two of the top collegiate programs, Long Beach State and Stanford. He's even judged a demolition derby. Educated at the University of San Francisco and farther South in Melbourne, Australia, he's worked some larger events like BCS Bowl Games, the Australian Open, Pan American Games and the Melbourne Cup.

MALCOLM ALLEN, a loyal Baltimore-born Orioles fan and former Memorial Stadium usher, worked distributing vintage Jamaican music all over the world for much of his adult life. Raising two daughters, Ruth and Martina, he is also working on a full-length biography of Joaquin Andjuar.

WILL ANDERSON, who died in March 2015, wrote nine books on beer but is noted in baseball circles as a 2002 inductee into the Maine Baseball Hall of Fame and member of the committee to bring the Portland Seadogs to Maine. He also wrote about roadside architecture, baseball, and 1950s Rock and roll, and was honored with the Maine Historic Preservation Award for his "diligent and dedicated service in support of Maine's historic and cultural heritage." He authored the 1992 book which was a precursor of SABR's "team books"— *Was Baseball Really Invented in Maine?* He followed that work with *The Lost New England Nine (2003)*, by which time the Tom Simon-edited *Green Mountain Boys of Summer* (2000) had also been published.

AUDREY LEVI APFEL is a leading research analyst for Gartner, Inc., advising organizations worldwide and publishing research on technology trends and projects. Her contribution to this book represents the first time she has written about her lifelong passion and interest in all things baseball—particularly New York baseball. She was raised in Queens, in the shadow of Shea Stadium. Audrey resides in the strong baseball outpost of Stamford, Connecticut - where Bobby Valentine and Brian Cashman have been known to rappel off of a 22-story building together at Christmastime dressed as elves.

MARK ARMOUR, the director of the Baseball Biography Project and the co-author of the 2015 book *In Pursuit of Pennants* (Nebraska) writes baseball from his home in Corvallis, Oregon. Some say that the recent Red Sox championships have wiped out the pain of 1986. They are wrong.

ERIC ARON has been a SABR member since 2002. In addition to his writing for SABR, he has contributed to other websites and magazines, including Throughthefencebaseball.com, NewEnglandFilm.com, and *Imagine Magazine*. He lives in Boston and holds a Master's degree in Public History & Museum Studies. He enjoys documentaries, playing hoops, and laughter Yoga. When he was 13 growing up in Rye, New York, he watched Game Six on television with his father. After the Mets won, his father, a lifelong Brooklyn Dodgers fan, kept shaking his head over and over, repeating "I don't believe it...I don't believe it!"

TYLER ASH graduated Elon University ('15) with a Bachelor of Arts Degree in Communication, concentrating in print journalism and minoring in business administration. He wrote for rantsports.com, covering the New England Patriots. He interned at the *Revere Journal* in the sports department and was a contributor to the *Pendulum*, Elon University's news outlet. Tyler is a member of SABR who has written SABR BioProject biographies, and maintains a personal blog—tylerashsportsblog.com. He was a featured radio personality on *One on One Sports* for WSOE 89.3, Elon's student radio home for weekly sports talk.

A lifelong Blue Jays fan who was born and raised in Toronto, Thomas Ayers has earned degrees from the University of Toronto, the London School of Economics and Queen's University. Currently practicing labour and employment law, he has contributed several other biographies to the SABR Baseball Biography Project. He attended Game Five of the 2015 ALDS between the Texas Rangers and Toronto Blue Jays, which was certainly the most memorable game he's ever seen.

RICHARD BOGOVICH is the author of *Kid Nichols: A Biography of the Hall of Fame Pitcher* and *The Who: A Who's Who,* both published by McFarland & Co. Most recently he wrote a chapter on Jorge Comellas of the Cubs for *Who's on First: Replacement Players in World War II*, after having contributed to *Inventing Baseball: The 100 Greatest Games of the Nineteenth Century*. He resides in Rochester, Minnesota.

BOB BRADY joined SABR in 1991 and is the current president of the Boston Braves Historical Association. As the editor of the Association's quarterly newsletter since 1992, he's had the privilege of memorializing the passings of the "Greatest Generation" members of the Braves Family. He owns a small piece of the Norwich, Connecticut-based Connecticut Tigers of the New York-Penn League, a Class-A short-season affiliate of the Detroit Tigers. Bob has contributed biographies and supporting pieces to a number of SABR publications as well as occasionally lending a hand in the editing process.

FREDERICK C. (RICK) BUSH, his wife Michelle, and their three sons Michael, Andrew, and Daniel live in northwest Houston. He has taught both English and German and is currently an English professor at Wharton County Junior College in Sugar Land. Though he is an avid fan of the hometown Astros, his youth has left him with an abiding affinity for the Texas Rangers and Pittsburgh Pirates as well. He has contributed articles to SABR's BioProject and Games Project sites and, in addition to his contribution to this volume, he has written articles for SABR books about the 1979 Pittsburgh Pirates, 1972 Texas Rangers, Milwaukee's County Stadium, the Montreal Expos, and baseball's winter meetings. Currently he is also serving as an associate editor, photo editor, and contributing author for a SABR book about the Houston Astrodome.

AUGUSTO CÁRDENAS lives in Maracaibo, Venezuela, and is the author of *My Story: Luis Aparicio*, the authorized biography of the only Venezuelan inducted into the Hall of Fame, and also the baseball beat writer of *Diario Panorama*, a local newspaper with 100 years of experience. He has covered the Venezuelan Winter League since 2000, and has been the special correspondent for his newspaper to cover Major League Baseball games, MLB Spring Trainings, All-Star Games, the World Baseball Classic, the Nippon Professional Baseball and the Caribbean Series. Cárdenas is a SABR member who loves to write about the Venezuelan players who saw playing when he was a just a kid.

RALPH CARHART is a theatrical production manager and director by trade. He is also an amateur baseball historian with a particular interest in the origins of the game. He received the 2015 Chairman's Award from the SABR 19th Century Committee and is a member of the 19th Century Baseball Grave Marker Project, spearheading the effort to place stones at the unmarked graves of forgotten pioneers. For the last five years he has been working on a project he calls "The Hall Ball," in which he is attempting to take a photograph of a single baseball with every member of the Hall of Fame, living and deceased. The ball is pictured in either the hands of the living baseball great, or at the grave of those who are no longer alive. As of this writing he has photographed 264 of the 310 members. To see the photos he's taken so far, visit www.thehallball.sportspalooza.com.

ALAN COHEN has been a member of SABR since 2011, and is vice president/treasurer of the Connecticut Smoky Joe Wood Chapter. He has written more than 25 biographies for SABR's BioProject, and has contributed to several SABR books. His first game story about Baseball's Longest Day—May 31, 1964 (Mets vs. Giants) has been followed by several other game stories.

His research into the *Hearst Sandlot Classic (1946-1965)*, an annual youth All-Star game which launched the careers of 88 major-league players, including 1986 Mets manager Davey Johnson and 1986 Mets announcer Fran Healy, first appeared in the Fall, 2013 edition of the *Baseball Research Journal*, and has been followed with a poster presentation at the SABR Convention in Chicago. He is currently expanding his research and is looking forward to having a book published. He serves as the datacaster (stringer) for the Hartford Yard Goats, the Colorado Rockies affiliate in the Class-AA Eastern League. Born in the shadow of Shea Stadium, he grew up on Long Island and graduated from Franklin and Marshall College in Lancaster, PA with a degree in history. He has four grown children and six grandchildren and now resides in West Hartford, Connecticut with his wife Frances, two cats and two dogs.

WARREN CORBETT is the author of *The Wizard of Waxahachie: Paul Richards and the End of Baseball as We Knew It*, and a contributor to SABR's Baseball Biography Project. He lives in Bethesda, Maryland.

RORY COSTELLO, a lifelong Mets fan, was at Shea Stadium for Games Three and Four of the 1986 NL Championship Series. The first World Series game he attended was none other than Game Six in 1986. He remembers seeing the premature congratulations to the Red Sox flashing on the Diamond Vision screen and feeling Shea rock on its foundation with the energy of the crowd. Rory lives in Brooklyn, New York with his wife Noriko and son Kai.

JOHN DIFONZO grew up in Somerville, Massachusetts where he was the Sports Editor for his high school newspaper. He is a lifelong Red Sox fan and season-ticket holder since 2004 currently living in Beacon Hill with his wife, Gabriella. John is a graduate of Tufts University and holds a Master of Science in Finance from Bentley University and is a CFA charterholder.

ALEX EDELMAN is a 2012 graduate of New York University, where he majored in English literature and wrote a thesis on the concept of landlessness in *Moby Dick*. This is the seventh BioProject collection he has appeared in. His second effort, on 1967 Red Sox pitcher Billy Rohr, received a Jack R. Kavanaugh Award. A native of Boston who spent several years working in PR departments at the Red Sox, Dodgers, and Brewers, Edelman is also an acclaimed professional stand-up comedian. In 2014, he won the Foster's Edinburgh Comedy Award for Best Newcomer, the first American to do so since 1997. He enjoys Italian food and the work of David Foster Wallace.

JEFF ENGLISH is a graduate of Florida State University and resides in Tallahassee, Florida with his wife Allison and twin sons, Elliott and Oscar. He is a lifelong Cubs fan and serves as secretary of the North Florida/Buck O'Neil SABR chapter. He has contributed to multiple SABR projects.

GREG ERION is retired from the railroad industry and currently teaches history part-time at Skyline Community College in San Bruno, California. He has written several biographies for SABR's BioProject and is currently working on a book about the 1959 season. Greg is one of the leaders of SABR's Baseball Games Project. He and his wife Barbara live in South San Francisco, California.

DAN FIELDS is a manuscript editor at the *New England Journal of Medicine.* He loves baseball trivia, and he attends Boston Red Sox and Pawtucket (Rhode Island) Red Sox games with this teenage son whenever he can. Dan lives in Framingham, Massachusetts, and can be reached at dfields820@gmail.com.

T.S. FLYNN is an educator and writer in Minneapolis who has published short fiction, essays, reviews, and articles. His blog, *It's a long season*, is a hobby and habit, and he is currently working on his first book-length project, an excavation of the 65-year baseball career of Tom Sheehan.

JAMES FORR is a past winner of the McFarland-SABR Baseball Research Award, and co-author (with David Proctor) of *Pie Traynor: A Baseball Biography*. He lives in Columbia, Missouri and is one of the leaders of SABR's Games Project.

DAVID FORRESTER recalls his brother breaking an antique piece of furniture during the seventh game of the 1986 ALCS. Or it might have been himself. David is a nonprofit executive and lifelong Red Sox fan now living in exile with the Seattle Mariners. He joined SABR over a decade ago when his historical research uncovered Allie Moulton, the first person of African American ancestry known to have played in the segregated major leagues.

IRV GOLDFARB has been a member of SABR since 1999 and has written numerous bios and articles for various SABR publications. He is a member of the Black Sox, Deadball, Origins, and Negro League committees. Irv works at the ABC Television network and lives in Union City, New Jersey with his wife Mercedes and their cat, Consuelo. They are all New York Met fans and would rather not talk anymore about the 2015 World Series.

JOHN GREGORY is a retired software developer. He has been a SABR member since 1984, and was one of the founders of the SABR-L mailing list in 1995. John currently lives in the Boston area, but maintains an abiding love for the Minnesota Twins.

GENE GUMBS worked in higher education for 25 years as a director of athletic communications. He also had stints as a sports editor for newspapers, a college and high school assistant basketball coach, and six years as a television color commentator for minor-league hockey and college football, basketball, and ice hockey. He currently works as a manuscript editor for a publishing company, and does stat work and broadcasting for local colleges and universities. He also maintains a personal blog and podcast — thesportsmicroscope.com. A lifelong Red Sox fan, Gene holds a degree in English from Franklin Pierce University in New Hampshire. He contributed a chapter to *Spahn, Sain, and Teddy Ballgame: Boston's (almost) Perfect Baseball Summer of 1948,* a SABR publication (Rounder Books, 2009).

DONNA L. HALPER is an Associate Professor of Communication at Lesley University, Cambridge Massachusetts. A media historian who specializes in the history of broadcasting, Dr. Halper is the author of six books and many articles. She is also a former broadcaster and print journalist.

LESLIE HEAPHY, a lifelong Mets fan, is a history professor at Kent State University at Stark. She is a member of the SABR Board of Directors and is the editor of the national journal, *Black Ball.* She has published numerous articles and books on the Negro Leagues and women's baseball.

PAUL HENSLER is a longtime Angels fan who witnessed Dave Henderson's derring-do in Game Five of the 1986 ALCS. The author of *The American League in Transition, 1965-1975: How Competition Thrived When the Yankees Didn't,* Paul has contributed to SABR's *Baseball Research Journal* and *NINE: A Journal of Baseball History and Culture.* He also has presented at the Cooperstown Symposium on Baseball and American Culture.

SABR member **MICHAEL HUBER** is Dean of Academic Life and Professor of Mathematics at Muhlenberg College in Allentown, Pennsylvania, where he teaches an undergraduate course titled "Reasoning with Sabermetrics." He has published his sabermetrics research in several books and journals, including *The Baseball Research Journal, Chance, Base Ball, Annals of Applied Statistics,* and *The Journal of Statistics Education,* and he frequently contributes to SABR's Baseball Games Project.

JOANNE HULBERT, co-chair of the Boston Chapter and the SABR Arts Committee, cherishes the art and poetry of baseball, must still avert her eyes when watching the 1986 film clip of the ball skittering through Buckner's legs, yet has found a modicum of relief from anguish while researching her portion of the Red Sox - Mets World Series history and is able now to at least watch until the ball approaches that pivotal moment and may soon be able to visually endure the ball passing through that inverted "V" that portended a lost victory.

DAVID KAISER, a historian, is the author of *Epic Season: the 1948 American League Pennant Race*, as well as six other books on diplomacy and international politics. He is a frequent contributor to the SABR-L list and has given two presentations at national SABR conventions. A former faculty member at Harvard University, Carnegie Mellon, the Naval War College, and Williams College, he lives in Watertown, Massachusetts.

MARK KANTER grew up in Bristol, Pennsylvania, where he became a life-long Philadelphia Phillies fan. He got the itch while watching the last few outs of Jim Bunning's perfect game on Father's Day in 1964. He graduated from the Pennsylvania State University attaining a bachelor's degree in Psychology with a minor in Middle Eastern History. He attended the University of Maryland studying Sports Studies. He received a master's degree in Industrial Engineering from the University of Massachusetts. He has written several articles for SABR's *Baseball Research Journal* and was the editor for Boston SABR 2002 convention publication. He has been a member of 10 SABR Team Trivia Championships since 1997, inclusive. He decided to take on the challenge of writing the Marty Barrett biography because one of his best friends is a friend of Marty's cousin. He and his wife, Lynne, who is also a great baseball fan in her own right, live in the idyllic seaside community of Portsmouth, Rhode Island.

MAXWELL KATES is a chartered accountant who lives and works in Toronto. He recently stepped down after 12 years as Director of Marketing for the Hanlan's Point Chapter. His feature article on Tom Seaver has previously appeared in *The Miracle Has Landed*, along with biographies of Tom Terrific's 1969 Mets teammates Ron Taylor and Rod Gaspar. Years before, he worked in sports radio for News Talk 610 CKTB in St. Catharines, Ontario. Years before that, in true New York Mets fashion, he submitted a banner for a summer camp ecology project which read "Save Water - Don't Send Mets Pitchers to the Showers!" The banner was rejected; the camp director was a Mets fan.

JIMMY KEENAN has been a SABR member since 2001. His grandfather, Jimmy Lyston, and four other family members were all professional baseball players. A frequent contributor to SABR publications, Keenan is the author of *The Lystons: A Story of One Baltimore Family* and *Our National Pastime*. He is a 2010 inductee into the Oldtimers Baseball Association of Maryland's Hall of Fame and a 2012 inductee into Baltimore's Boys of Summer Hall of Fame.

NORM KING lives in Ottawa, Ontario, and has been a SABR member since 2010. He has contributed to a number of SABR books, including, *"Thar's Joy in Braveland": The 1957 Milwaukee Braves* (2014), *Winning on the North Side. The 1929 Chicago Cubs* (2015), and *A Pennant for the Twins Cities: The 1965 Minnesota Twins* (2015). He thought he was crazy to miss his beloved Expos after all these years until he met people from Brooklyn.

LEE KLUCK of Stevens Point, Wisconsin worked as a processor in Transportation Operations Support for Sentry Insurance. A Sentry transportation motto circa 1988 is: "The Speed of the Leader Determines the Rate of the Pack."

RUSS LAKE lives in Champaign, Illinois, and is a retired Professor Emeritus. He was born in Belleville, Illinois, on the "other side of the river" from downtown St. Louis. The 1964 Cardinals remain his favorite team, and he was grateful to go to 28 games at Sportsman's Park (aka Busch Stadium I) before it was demolished in late 1966. His wife, Carol, deserves an MVP award for watching all of a 14-inning ballgame in Cincinnati with Russ in 1971—during their honeymoon. He joined SABR in 1994 and, later in that same year, was an editor for David Halberstam's *October 1964*.

BOB LEMOINE grew up in South Portland, Maine, and watched the 1986 World Series on a black-and-white TV with rabbit ears. His mom didn't sleep very well during the series with all the yelling coming from downstairs. While Bob's own high school years were scarred with the Red Sox losing the World Series, he recovered and now works as a high school librarian in New Hampshire, surrounded by students who have never heard of rabbit ears. Bob joined SABR in 2013 and has contributed to several publications. He is a co-editor with Bill Nowlin on an upcoming

SABR book, *Boston's First Nine: the 1871–75 Boston Red Stockings*. He's glad to have seen the Red Sox win three world titles in color.

LEN LEVIN attended Game Three of the 1986 World Series. The Red Sox lost, but happily, he has seen the Olde Towne Team win many other games. A retired editor at the *Providence Journal* and the *Quincy Patriot Ledger*, Len copyedits many of SABR's publications, including this one, and also edits the written decisions of the Rhode Island Supreme Court.

DAN LEVITT is the author (with Mark Armour) of *In Pursuit of Pennants: Baseball Operations from Deadball to Moneyball*, published in 2015 by the University of Nebraska Press. He is also the author of several other notable baseball books including *The Battle that Forged Modern Baseball: The Federal League Challenge and Its Legacy* and *Ed Barrow: The Bulldog Who Built the Yankees' First Dynasty*. In 2015, Dan received the Bob Davids Award.

MICHAEL MARTELL is currently a student at Kent State University, majoring in business management. Michael is a diehard Cleveland sports fan. He attended his first Cleveland Indians baseball game at two months of age, and his love of baseball continues to this day. He can often be found at Progressive Field, located on the corner of Carnegie Avenue and Ontario Street. That location is where he eagerly awaits to see the Indians first World Series championship in over 60 years.

SHAWN MORRIS is a newer member to SABR. As a doctoral candidate in the history program at Kent State University, he aims to focus his dissertation upon how sports has, and continues to, successfully break down social and cultural barriers. He has also authored articles regarding the historiography of Negro League Baseball in Cleveland, and the city's first professional black baseball team, the Tate Stars.

ROD NELSON (SABRscouts@gmail.com) is the former Research Services Manager for the Society for American Baseball Research. He is Chairman of the SABR Scouts Committee and project leader for the Who-Signed-Whom database and Scouts Register which has been integrated into the *Diamond Mines* exhibit at the National Baseball Museum in Cooperstown, accessible at http://scouts.baseballhall.org. Nelson launched the Baseball Necrology online forum which has stimulated activity in this important area of baseball research.

SKIP NIPPER is the author of *Baseball in Nashville* (Arcadia Publishing, 2007) and shares his love of Nashville's famous ballpark, Sulphur Dell, through www.sulphurdell.com. A 1972 graduate of Memphis State University, Nipper is a retired sporting goods sales representative. He was a co-founder of the Grantland Rice-Fred Russell Nashville chapter of SABR, and currently serves as secretary for the Old Timers Baseball Association of Nashville. He also has contributed to *Sweet 60: The 1960 Pittsburgh Pirates*, and *The Team That Time Won't Forget: The 1951 New York Giants*. His wife Sheila calls baseball his "other woman," which allows him to research and write about his favorite subject without trepidation. The Nippers reside in Mt. Juliet, Tennessee.

BILL NOWLIN, for better or worse, still vividly remembers the elation of Hendu's homer that spared the Sox from losing the ALCS and the deflation that followed the ball skittering through Buckner's legs, and all that fell apart from that point forward. There was, after all, Game Seven, when the Red Sox led 3-0 through five innings. Like most Red Sox fans, he wallowed in loserdom until 2004. Then things got better. A veteran of more than 45 years in the record business, Bill spends most of his time writing or editing books about baseball.

ARMAND PETERSON is a retired engineer and manager, living in Maple Grove, Minnesota. He's been hooked on baseball since he saw some cousins play a town team game on a hardscrabble field in eastern South Dakota when he was nine years old. He was Yankees and Mickey Mantle fan in his youth—thanks to indoctrination by his baseball-playing older cousins—but switched his allegiance to the Minnesota Twins when the Senators moved to Minnesota in 1961. Since retirement he has co-authored Town Ball: The Glory Days of Minnesota Amateur Baseball, and has contributed to several other SABR biographies.

RICHARD J. PUERZER is an associate professor and chairperson of the Department of Engineering at Hofstra University in Hempstead, New York. His previous research and writings on baseball have appeared in *Nine: A Journal of Baseball History and Culture*, *Black Ball*, *The National Pastime*, *The Cooperstown Symposium on Baseball and American Culture* proceedings, and *Spitball*. He was co-director of The 50th Anniversary of the New York Mets Conference, held at Hofstra University in April, 2012.

DAVID RAGLIN has been a member of SABR for 30 years, and serves as the Vice President of the Bob Davids (Mid Atlantic) Chapter of SABR. He is the co-author of three books on the Detroit Tigers, has served as an editor, fact-checker, and writer for two SABR BioProject books (*Go Get 'Em Tigers* on the 1968 Tigers, and *What a Start! What a Finish* on the 1984 Tigers). He also wrote a biography for the BioProject book on the 1934 Tigers. Dave and Barb met at a SABR event in 2001 and have been married for 13 years.

ALAN RAYLESBERG is an attorney in New York City. He is a lifelong baseball fan who enjoys baseball history and roots for the Yankees and the Mets. Alan also has a strong interest in baseball analytics and is a devotee of baseball simulation games, participating both in draft leagues and historical replays.

MIKE RICHARD is a lifelong Red Sox fan who still counts the Impossible Dream season as his greatest all-time baseball thrill. However, 1986 rates high in his memory because that was the year he took his son Casey (then three) to his first Red Sox game. He retired as a guidance counselor from Gardner (Massachusetts) High School and is a sports columnist for the *Worcester Telegram & Gazette*. A Massachusetts high school sports historian, he has authored two high school football books: *Glory to Gardner: 100 Years of Football in the Chair City*, and *Super Saturdays: The Complete History of the Massachusetts High School Super Bowl*. He has also documented the playoff history (sectional and state championships) of all high school sports in Massachusetts. He lives in Gardner and also owns a home in Sandwich on Cape Cod with his wife Peggy. They are the parents of a son Casey, a daughter Lindsey, and have a grandson Theo.

CARL RIECHERS retired from United Parcel Service in 2012 after 35 years of service. With more free time, he became a SABR member that same year. Born and raised in the suburbs of St. Louis, he became a big fan of the Cardinals. He and his wife Janet have three children and he is the proud grandpa of two.

JOEL RIPPEL is the author or co-author of nine books on Minnesota sports history. He has contributed to several SABR publications including *The National Pastime*, *The Emerald Guide to Baseball* and *A Pennant for the Twin Cities: The 1965 Minnesota Twins*.

MATTHEW SILVERMAN has written numerous books on baseball, including the recently released book from Lyons Press on the 1986 Mets, *One-Year Dynasty*. He also authored *Swinging '73*, and *100 Things Mets Fans Should Know and Do Before They Die*. An alum of Ted Williams Baseball Camp, he has written on the Olde Towne team many times, including *Red Sox by the Numbers* with Bill Nowlin, which has recently been updated and released, along with uniform number books he co-authored on the Mets and Cubs. He flew from college in Virginia to New York to attend Games One and Two of the 1986 World Series, but those aren't exactly the games at Shea that everyone remembers.

MARK SIMON works for ESPN Stats and Information, editing their blog and helping run the @ESPNStatsInfo Twitter feed. He also writes regularly about baseball for ESPN.com. In his spare time he has written a book on Yankees history (published by Triumph Books in June 2016) and obsessively studied every aspect of Game Six of the 1986 World Series.

DAVID E. SKELTON developed a passion for baseball as a child when the lights from Philadelphia's Connie Mack Stadium shone through his bedroom window. Long since removed from Philly, he graduated from the

University of Texas at Tyler with a Bachelor in Business Administration. He now resides with his family in central Texas but remains passionate about the sport that evokes many childhood memories. Employed for over 30 years in the oil and gas industry, he became a SABR member in early 2012 after a chance holiday encounter with a Rogers Hornsby Chapter member.

DOUG SKIPPER has contributed to a number of SABR publications, presented research at national and regional conventions, and profiled more than a dozen players, managers, and game profiles for the SABR Baseball Biographical Project. A SABR member since 1982, he served as president of the Halsey Hall (Minneapolis) Chapter in 2014-2015, and a member of the Deadball Era Committee and the Lawrence Ritter Award Committee, and is interested in the history of Connie Mack's Philadelphia Athletics, the Boston Red Sox, the Minnesota Twins, and old ballparks. A market research consultant residing in Apple Valley, Minnesota, Doug is also a veteran of father-daughter dancing. Doug and his wife have two daughters, MacKenzie and Shannon.

CURT SMITH shows that "writing can be art," said *USA Today*, which calls him "the voice of authority on baseball broadcasting." His 16 books include the classic *Voices of The Game*, *Pull Up a Chair: The Vin Scully Story*, *A Talk in the Park: Nine Decades of Baseball Tales from the Broadcast Booth*, and his newest, *George H. W. Bush: Character at the Core*. In 1989-93, Smith wrote more speeches than anyone else for President George H.W. Bush, *The New York Times* terming his work "the high point of Bush familial eloquence." Smith is a GateHouse Media columnist, Associated Press award-winning radio commentator, and senior lecturer of English at the University of Rochester. He has hosted or keynoted the Great Fenway Park Writers series, numerous Smithsonian Institution series, and the Cooperstown Symposium on Baseball and American Culture. The former Gannett reporter and *The Saturday Evening Post* senior editor has written ESPN TV's *Voices of The Game* documentary, created the Franklin Roosevelt Award in Political Communication at the National Radio Hall of Fame, and been named to the prestigious Judson Welliver Society of former Presidential speechwriters.

While laid up with a ruptured Achilles tendon in 1998, **JON SPRINGER** began a research project to chronicle every uniform number in Mets history. That project became the acclaimed Mets By The Numbers website (mbtn.net), and book of the same name. A graduate of the University of Delaware, Jon is an editor at a business publication in New York and a former daily newspaper sports writer. He lives in Brooklyn with his family.

MARK S. STERNMAN serves as Director of Marketing and Communications for MassDevelopment, the quasi-governmental economic-development authority of Massachusetts. In October 1986, he had just started his freshman year at Dartmouth College. Returning from a frat party in the late stages of Game Six, he saw the fateful final frame in the company of a fellow freshman from Boston's Chinatown who cried silently as the game ended. A fan of the Expos and the Yankees, Sternman liked and likes neither the Mets nor the Sox, but did root for Mike Stenhouse thanks to his Montreal ties.

ANDY STURGILL lives in suburban Philadelphia where he grew up rooting for Lenny Dykstra and the Macho Row Phillies. He enjoys reading and visiting ballparks with his wife, Carrie.

CECILIA TAN has been writing about baseball since her fourth grade book reports on the biographies of Willie Mays and Reggie Jackson. She is the author of *The 50 Greatest Yankees Games*, and her work has appeared in *Yankees Magazine*, *Gotham Baseball*, *Baseball Ink*, and *Baseball Prospectus*. She has served as SABR's Publications Director since 2011.

JOAN M. THOMAS is a freelance writer and long-time SABR member. Her published books on baseball include *St. Louis' Big League Ballparks* and *Baseball's First Lady*. She has also written a dozen biographies for SABR's BioProject web site. Following the St. Louis Cardinals while living in that city for decades, she moved back to her native Iowa in 2014. She is now engrossed in the research of baseball in that state.

CINDY THOMSON is a freelance writer and co-author of *Three Finger, The Mordecai Brown Story*, the biography of a Cubs Hall of Fame pitcher. She is also the author of a historical fiction series. The final novel, *Sofia's Tune*, released in 2015. She has written for SABR's BioProject, and contributed to several SABR publications including *Deadball Stars of the American League*, *Detroit Tigers 1984*, *New Century, New Team: The 1901 Boston Americans*, and *The Great Eight: The 1975 Cincinnati Reds.* A life-long Reds fan, she writes full time from her home in Central Ohio where she and her husband Tom raised three sons to root for Cincinnati. She also mentors writers and is a member of the American Christian Fiction Writers and the Historical Novel Society. Visit her online at: http://www.cindyswriting.com.

CLAYTON TRUTOR is a PhD candidate in US History at Boston College. His dissertation examines the politics and the cultural response to the arrival of professional sports in Atlanta. He teaches US History at Northeastern University in the College of Professional Studies. He has contributed to several SABR biographical projects and writes about college football for several blogs on SB Nation. You can follow him on twitter @ClaytonTrutor.

ALFONSO TUSA is a writer who was born in Cumaná, Venezuela and now writes a lot about baseball from Los Teques, Venezuela. He's the author *Una Temporada Mágica* (A magical season), *El Látigo del Beisbol. Una biografía de Isaías Látigo Chávez.* (The Whip of Baseball. An Isaías Látigo Chávez biography), *Pensando en ti Venezuela. Una biografía de Dámaso Blanco.* (Thinking about you Venezuela. A Dámaso Blanco biography) and *Voces de Beisbol y Ecología* (Voices of Baseball and Ecology). He contributes in some websites, books and newspapers. He shares many moments with his boy Miguelin.

NICK WADDELL is a graduate of Wayne State University and DePaul University College of Law. He's a lifelong Tigers fan, and previously wrote the biography on Al Kaline for *Sock It To 'Em Tigers.* He thinks a good baseball game involves peanuts, keeping score, and trying to decode the other team's signs.

JOSEPH WANCHO lives in Westlake, Ohio, and is a lifelong Cleveland Indians fan. He has been a SABR member since 2005. He serves as the chair of SABR's Minor Leagues Research Committee. He was the editor of the book *Pitching to the Pennant: The 1954 Cleveland Indians* (University of Nebraska Press, 2014).

STEVE WEST is a math nerd, a history nerd, and a wannabe writer. Combine these with his love of baseball and the SABR BioProject is right in his wheelhouse. Steve works as a data analyst in the energy industry, messing around with computers and numbers all day long, and comes home and does the same with baseball stats while watching Rangers games at night. Steve (a SABR member since 2006), his wife Marian and son Joshua are die-hard Rangers fans, which is one reason why Steve is now editor of a BioProject book on the 1972 Texas Rangers.

DAVE WILLIAMS is a lifelong Mets fan. He is currently a Territory Manager with Wilson Sporting Goods in Glastonbury, Connecticut where he resides with his wife and daughter. They do not understand how he can agonize over the Mets' lack of offense year after year.

SAUL WISNIA still recalls being chased to his Syracuse dorm room by taunting Mets fans after Game Seven of the 1986 World Series, and then waking up to a door plastered with jubilant *Daily News* headlines. He recovered to write numerous books on Boston baseball, including *Fenway Park: The Centennial, Miracle at Fenway*, and *For the Love of the Boston Red Sox.* He's also been a sports and news correspondent at the *Washington Post,* a feature writer for the *Boston Herald,* and a contributor to numerous SABR publications, the *Boston Globe,* and *Sports Illustrated.* Since 1999, he has chronicled the Red Sox-Jimmy Fund relationship as senior publications editor-writer at Dana-Farber Cancer Institute, where his office sits 300 yards from Fenway Park.

A lifelong Pirates fan, **GREGORY H. WOLF** was born in Pittsburgh, but now resides in the Chicagoland area with his wife, Margaret, and daughter, Gabriela. A Professor of German Studies and holder of the Dennis and Jean Bauman Endowed Chair in the Humanities at North Central College in Naperville, Illinois, he edited the SABR books *"Thar's Joy in Braveland." The 1957 Milwaukee Braves* (2014), *Winning on the North Side. The 1929 Chicago Cubs* (2015), and *A Pennant for the Twins Cities: The 1965 Minnesota Twins* (2015). He is currently working on a project about the Houston Astrodome and co-editing a book with Bill Nowlin on the 1979 Pittsburgh Pirates.

ALLAN WOOD has written about sports, music, and politics for numerous magazines and newspapers for 35 years. He is the author of *Babe Ruth and the 1918 Red Sox* and the co-author of *Don't Let Us Win Tonight: An Oral History of the 2004 Boston Red Sox's Impossible Playoff Run.* He has also written The Joy of Sox blog since 2003, and has contributed—as a writer or editor—to five books published by SABR. He lives in Mississauga, Ontario, Canada.

JACK ZERBY grew up following the Pirates. Writing about the Mets' late-season visit to Three Rivers Stadium in 1986 brought back memories of Fan Appreciation Day at old Forbes Field. Jack joined SABR in 1994 and co-founded the Seymour-Mills Chapter in southwest Florida. Now retired from law practice and work as a trusts/estates administrator, he lives in Brevard, North Carolina, with his wife Diana, a professional violinist.

The SABR Digital Library

The Society for American Baseball Research, the top baseball research organization in the world, disseminates some of the best in baseball history, analysis, and biography through our publishing programs. The SABR Digital Library contains a mix of books old and new, and focuses on a tandem program of paperback and ebook publication, making these materials widely available for both on digital devices and as traditional printed books.

Greatest Games Books

BRAVES FIELD:
Memorable Moments at Boston's Lost Diamond
From its opening on August 18, 1915, to the sudden departure of the Boston Braves to Milwaukee before the 1953 baseball season, Braves Field was home to Boston's National League baseball club and also hosted many other events: from NFL football to championship boxing. The most memorable moments to occur in Braves Field history are portrayed here.
Edited by Bill Nowlin and Bob Brady
$19.95 paperback (ISBN 978-1-933599-93-9)
$9.99 ebook (ISBN 978-1-933599-92-2)
8.5"X11", 282 pages, 182 photos

INVENTING BASEBALL: The 100 Greatest Games of the Nineteenth Century
SABR's Nineteenth Century Committee brings to life the greatest games from the game's early years. From the "prisoner of war" game that took place among captive Union soldiers during the Civil War (immortalized in a famous lithograph), to the first intercollegiate game (Amherst versus Williams), to the first professional no-hitter, the games in this volume span 1833–1900 and detail the athletic exploits of such players as Cap Anson, Moses "Fleetwood" Walker, Charlie Comiskey, and Mike "King" Kelly.
Edited by Bill Felber
$19.95 paperback (ISBN 978-1-933599-42-7)
$9.99 ebook (ISBN 978-1-933599-43-4)
8"x10", 302 pages, 200 photos

BioProject Books

WHO'S ON FIRST:
Replacement Players in World War II
During World War II, 533 players made the major league debuts. More than 60% of the players in the 1941 Opening Day lineups departed for the service and were replaced by first-times and oldsters. Hod Lisenbee was 46. POW Bert Shepard had an artificial leg, and Pete Gray had only one arm. The 1944 St. Louis Browns had 13 players classified 4-F. These are their stories.
Edited by Marc Z Aaron and Bill Nowlin
$19.95 paperback (ISBN 978-1-933599-91-5)
$9.99 ebook (ISBN 978-1-933599-90-8)
8.5"X11", 422 pages, 67 photos

VAN LINGLE MUNGO:
The Man, The Song, The Players
Although the Red Sox spent most of the 1950s far out of contention, the team was filled with fascinating players who captured the heart of their fans. In *Red Sox Baseball*, members of SABR present 46 biographies on players such as Ted Williams and Pumpsie Green as well as season-by-season recaps.
Edited by Bill Nowlin
$19.95 paperback (ISBN 978-1-933599-76-2)
$9.99 ebook (ISBN 978-1-933599-77-9)
8.5"X11", 278 pages, 46 photos

Original SABR Research

CALLING THE GAME:
Baseball Broadcasting from 1920 to the Present
An exhaustive, meticulously researched history of bringing the national pastime out of the ballparks and into living rooms via the airwaves. Every play-by-play announcer, color commentator, and ex-ballplayer, every broadcast deal, radio station, and TV network. Plus a foreword by "Voice of the Chicago Cubs" Pat Hughes, and an afterword by Jacques Doucet, the "Voice of the Montreal Expos" 1972-2004.
by Stuart Shea
$24.95 paperback (ISBN 978-1-933599-40-3)
$9.99 ebook (ISBN 978-1-933599-41-0)
7"X10", 712 pages, 40 photos

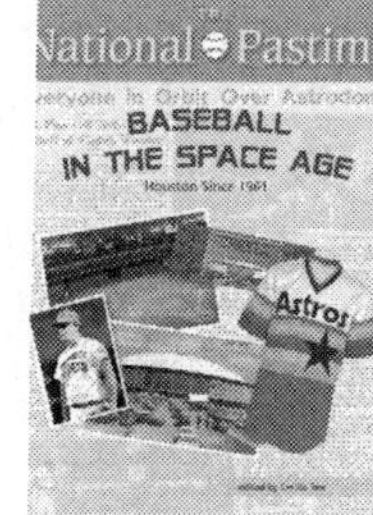

BASEBALL IN THE SPACE AGE:
Houston Since 1961
Here we have a special issue of *The National Pastime* centered almost entirely on the Houston Astros (né Colt .45s) and their two influential and iconic homes, short-lived Colt Stadium and the Astrodome. If you weren't able to attend the SABR convention in Houston, please enjoy this virtual trip tour of baseball in "Space City" through 18 articles.
Edited by Cecilia M. Tan
$14.95 paperback (ISBN 978-1-933599-65-6)
$9.99 ebook (ISBN 978-1-933599-66-3)
8.5"x11", 96 pages, 49 photos

NORTH SIDE, SOUTH SIDE, ALL AROUND THE TOWN: Baseball in Chicago
The National Pastime provides in-depth articles focused on the geographic region where the national SABR convention is taking place annually. The SABR 45 convention took place in Chicago, and here are 45 articles on baseball in and around the bat-and-ball crazed Windy City: 25 that appeared in the souvenir book of the convention plus another 20 articles available in ebook only.
Edited by Stuart Shea
$14.95 paperback (ISBN 978-1-933599-87-8)
$9.99 ebook (ISBN 978-1-933599-86-1)
8.5"X11", 282 pages, 47 photos

THE EMERALD GUIDE TO BASEBALL: 2015
The Emerald Guide to Baseball fills the gap in the historical record created by the demise of *The Sporting News Baseball Guide*. First published in 1942, *The Sporting News* Guide was truly the annual book of record for our National Pastime. The 2015 edition of the *Emerald Guide* runs more than 600 pages and covers the 2014 season; it also includes a 2015 directory of every franchise, rosters, minor league affiliates, and career leaders for all teams.
Edited by Gary Gillette and Pete Palmer
$24.95 paperback (ISBN 978-0-9817929-8-9)
8.5"X11", 610 pages

SABR Members can purchase each book at a significant discount (often 50% off) and receive the ebook editions free as a member benefit. Each book is available in a trade paperback edition as well as ebooks suitable for reading on a home computer or Nook, Kindle, or iPad/tablet.
To learn more about becoming a member of SABR, visit the website: sabr.org/join

Society for American Baseball Research

Cronkite School at ASU
555 N. Central Ave. #416, Phoenix, AZ 85004
602.496.1460 (phone)
SABR.org

Made in the USA
Middletown, DE
14 March 2021